Defenders of the Faith

Studies in Nineteenth-
and Twentieth-Century
Orthodoxy and Reform

Touro University Press Books

Series Editor
MICHAEL A. SHMIDMAN, PhD (Touro College, New York)
SIMCHA FISHBANE, PhD (Touro College, New York)

Defenders of the faith

Studies in Nineteenth- and Twentieth-Century Orthodoxy and Reform

JUDITH BLEICH

New York
2020

Library of Congress Cataloging-in-Publication Data

Names: Bleich, Judith, 1938- author.

Title: Defenders of the faith: studies in nineteenth- and twentieth-century Orthodoxy and Reform / Judith Bleich.

Description: New York: Touro University Press, 2020. | Includes index.

Identifiers: LCCN 2019029144 (print) | LCCN 2019029145 (ebook) | ISBN 9781644691441 (hardcover) | ISBN 9781644691458 (adobe pdf)

Subjects: LCSH: Orthodox Judaism—Relations—Nontraditional Jews. | Orthodox Judaism. | Reform Judaism. | Judaism—19th century. | Judaism—20th century.

Classification: LCC BM197.6 .B54 2020 (print) | LCC BM197.6 (ebook) | DDC 296.8/3209034—dc23

LC record available at https://lccn.loc.gov/2019029144
LC ebook record available at https://lccn.loc.gov/2019029145

Copyright © Touro University Press, 2020
Published by Touro University Press and Academic Studies Press.
Typeset, printed and distributed by Academic Studies Press.
ISBN 9781644691441 (hardcover) ISBN 9781644692639 (paperback)
ISBN 9781644691458 (electronic)

Touro University Press
Michael A. Shmidman and Simcha Fishbane, Editors
320 West 31st Street, Fourth Floor,
New York, NY 10001, USA
tcpress@touro.edu

Academic Studies Press
1577 Beacon Street
Brookline, MA 02446, USA
press@academicstudiespress.com
www.academicstudiespress.com

Book design by Kryon Publishing Services, Inc.
kryonpublishing.com
On the cover: Six-page pamphlet. Shelomei Emunei Yisra'el/Treue Glaubige in Israel, c1845. (Rabbinic Manifesto in response to the first Reform Conference, Brunswick, 1844). Courtesy of the Leo Baeck Institute, New York.

Table of Contents

Preface

The present volume is a collection of essays on Orthodoxy and Reform that appeared over a span of years, presented here with relatively minor additions and revisions. I wish to express my gratitude to the publishers of the journals and books in which these papers were originally featured. The following is a list of these essays and the publications in which they appeared: "The Emergence of an Orthodox Press in Nineteenth-Century Germany," *Jewish Social Studies* 13, nos. 3–4 (Summer/Fall 1980), 323–344; "The Testament of a Halakhist," *Tradition* 20, no. 3 (Fall 1982), 235–248; "Rabbinic Responses to Nonobservance in the Modern Era," in *Jewish Tradition and the Nontraditional Jew*, ed. Jacob J. Schacter, vol. 2 of the *Orthodox Forum Series* (Northvale, NJ: Jason Aronson, Inc., 1992), 37–115; "Between East and West: Modernity and Traditionalism in the Writings of Rabbi Yehi'el Ya'akov Weinberg," in *Engaging Modernity: Rabbinic Leaders and the Challenge of the Twentieth Century*, ed. Moshe Z. Sokol, vol. 6 of the *Orthodox Forum Series* (Northvale, NJ: Jason Aronson, Inc., 1997), 169–273; "Liturgical Innovation and Spirituality: Trends and Trendiness," in *Jewish Spirituality and Divine Law*, ed. Adam Mintz and Lawrence Schiffman, vol. 10 of the *Orthodox Forum Series* (New York: Yeshiva University Press, 2005), 315–405; "Military Service: Ambivalence and Contradiction," in *War and Peace in the Jewish Tradition*, ed. Lawrence Schiffman and Joel B. Wolowelsky, vol. 15 of the *Orthodox Forum Series* (New York: Yeshiva University Press, 2007), 415–476; "The Circumcision Controversy in Classical Reform in Historical Context," in *Turim: Studies in Jewish History and Literature Presented to Dr. Bernard Lander*, vol. 1, ed. Michael A. Shmidman (New York: Touro College Press, 2007), 1–28; "Intermarriage in the Early Modern Period," in *Conversion, Intermarriage and Jewish Identity*, ed. Robert S. Hirt, Adam Mintz and Marc Stein, vol. 23 of the *Orthodox Forum Series* (New York: Yeshiva University Press, 2015), 3–46; and "Clerical Robes: Distinction or Dishonor?" in *Dynamics of Continuity and Change in Jewish*

Religious Life, ed. Simcha Fishbane and Eric Levine (New York: Touro College Press, 2018), 198–225.

As is evident from the foregoing, many of the essays included in this work were delivered as papers at symposia sponsored by the Orthodox Forum and were published in volumes of the *Orthodox Forum Series.* I am indebted to the Forum for serving as a stimulus to my research and wish to voice my appreciation and gratitude to the participants in the Forum, to the editors of the various volumes and to the general editor of the series, Rabbi Robert S. Hirt.

I wish to express my appreciation to Ekaterina Yanduganova of Academic Studies Press for her painstaking efforts in preparing the manuscript for publication; to Max Lindenfeld for his meticulous proofreading of the galleys; to Karen Rubin, Administrative Manager, Touro College Graduate School of Jewish Studies, for her constant helpfulness; and to Carol Schapiro and Toby Krausz of the Touro College Graduate School Library for their gracious assistance.

It has been my singular privilege and pleasure to be a member of the faculty of Touro College for well over four decades, surrounded by dedicated scholars in a rare atmosphere of intellectual rigor, idealism and warmth. I am indebted in particular to the unforgettable visionary and indefatigable pioneer, Dr. Bernard Lander, of blessed memory, founder and first president of Touro College; to his worthy successor, Dr. Alan Kadish; to the beloved Dean of the Graduate School of Jewish Studies, Dr. Michael A. Shmidman; to Dr. Marian Stoltz-Loike and Dr. David Luchins, devoted Deans of Lander College for Women; to the distinguished former Chairman of the Judaic Studies Department at Lander College for Women, Dr. Samuel N. Hoenig; to my esteemed colleagues; and especially to the generations of students with whom I have had the honor and privilege of studying Torah.

Above all, I thank the Almighty for my cherished collaborators, the members of my family. Our prayer to the Almighty is that we merit to continue to witness children and children's children immersed in Torah and mitzvot.

Introduction
Nineteenth to Twenty-First Centuries: From Pessimism to Optimism

Jewish history has been marked by recurrent periods of spiritual deprivation and religious apathy. Despite those vicissitudes, Rabbenu Bahya, *Ḥovot ha-Levavot, Sha'ar ha-Teshuvah*, chapter 6, offers optimistic assurance that at no time will the people of Israel be bereft of leadership: "Thus has it been in all periods and all countries. There has never been lacking a *"kor'e el ha-Elokim ve-el avodato u-moreh et Torato*—a person who calls [his coreligionists] to God and to His service and teaches His Law."

The crumbling of the walls of the ghetto in the years following the Emancipation created welcome economic, social, and political opportunities but at the same time brought in its wake novel and unprecedented problems. Tides of assimilation eroded the religious spirit that had successfully withstood centuries of persecution and direct onslaught. It was generally accepted, almost axiomatically, that the social transformations that characterized the times spelled the inevitable demise of a traditional lifestyle that was incompatible with the regnant modernity. Protests and remonstrations expressed in shrill tones by old-time patriarchal figures were deemed to be nothing more than the death throes of an outmoded and anachronistic clerical establishment.

To the radical Reform ideologue, Samuel Holdheim, adherence to rabbinic Judaism necessarily entailed removing oneself from the contemporary stage. There was, he claimed, a clear-cut choice: "Either to be a rabbinic Jew and live outside the times or live within the times and cease to be a rabbinic Jew...."

Rabbinic Judaism is the diametric opposite of our time."[1] No wonder that the masterful bibliographer Moritz Steinschneider, to whom "*Wissenschaft des Judentums* was an end in itself,"[2] described his meticulous recording of rabbinic texts as an honorable burial for a moribund culture.[3]

The prominent nineteenth-century American Reform spokesman, Isaac Mayer Wise, mistakenly predicted that in the twentieth century the majority of Americans of all faiths would become Jews, but he also foretold that there would be no future for adherents of what he termed the "half-civilized orthodoxy" and those who "gnawed the dead bones of past centuries."[4] He was fully conscious of the sharp divide between Reform congregations and other elements of the Jewish populace and was even desirous of formalizing a schism.

---

1 Samuel Holdheim, *Das Cermonialgesetz im Messiasreich* (Schwerin, 1845), 122–123, cited in translation by Michael A. Meyer, "Should and Can an Antiquated Belief Become Modern? The Jewish Reform Movement in Germany as Seen by Jews and Christians," in *The Jews in European History: Seven Lectures*, ed. Wolfgang Beck (Cincinnati: Hebrew Union College Press, 1994), 65.

2 Michael A. Meyer, *Response to Modernity: A History of the Reform Movement in Judaism* (New York and Oxford: Oxford University Press, 1988), 76.

3 Steinschneider's statement to this effect has been widely cited and disparaged. See, for example, Milton Himmelfarb, *The Jews of Modernity* (New York: Basic Books, 1973), 8 and Arthur Hertzberg and Aron Hirt-Manheimer, *Jews: The Essence and Character of a People* (San Francisco: Harper Collins, 1998), 240–241. However, the accuracy of the attribution of this comment has also been the subject of dispute. The remark, "*Wir haben nur noch die Aufgabe die Überreste des Judenthums ehrenvoll zu bestatten*" ("We now only have to give a decent burial to the remains of Judaism"), famously attributed to Steinschneider, is not found in his published writings but was posthumously attributed to him by Gotthold Weil, *Jüdische Rundschau*, February 8, 1907, 54. See the intriguing account by Charlies H. Manekin, "Steinschneider's 'Decent Burial.' A Reappraisal," in *Study and Knowledge in Jewish Thought*, ed. Howard Kreisel (Beer Sheva: Ben Gurion University Press, 1996), 239–251. For Gershom Scholem's trenchant criticism of Steinschneider see Gershom Scholem, "Mitokh Hirhurim al Ḥokhmat Yisra'el," in *Devarim be-Go* (Tel Aviv: Am Oved, 1975), 385–405. Compare, however, the strong reaction of Avriel Bar-Levav, "A Living Citizen in a World of Dead Letters: Steinschneider Remembered," *Studies on Steinschneider: Moritz Steinschneider and the Emergence of the Science of Judaism in Nineteenth-Century Germany* (Leiden: Brill, 2012), 339–348. See the more recent carefully reasoned and measured assessment of Michael A. Meyer and Ismar Schorsch, "'Zunz and Steinschneider Would be Astonished— and Reassured': Two Senior Scholars of *Wissenschaft* Reflect on Its 200th Anniversary," *Pardes, Journal of the German Association for Jewish Studies* 24 (2018), 19–23. Whether or not the comments attributed to Steinschneider are indeed his exact words and accurately reflect his sentiments, they certainly typify the views espoused by many of the exponents of *Wissenschaft des Judentums* and are emblematic of the attitude so forcefully attacked by the Orthodox critics of the *Wissenschaft* agenda. See, for example, Samson Raphael Hirsch, *The Collected Writings*, vol. VII (Jerusalem and New York: Feldheim Publishers, 1997), 42.

4 *The American Israelite* 33, no. 31 (Jan. 28, 1887), 4.

Quite bluntly, he stated: "It is next to an impossibility to associate or identify ourselves" with the Orthodox because "We are Americans and they are not. ... Besides the name we have little in common; we let them be Jews and we are American Israelites."[5]

What, one wonders, would be the reaction of those individuals were they magically transported to the twenty-first century and shown the wall-to-wall bookshelves within synagogues and houses of study from New York to Los Angeles, from Sydney to Perth, from Hong Kong to London, from Berlin to Moscow, from Boston to Buenos Aires, from Safed to Beersheba, all filled from floor to ceiling with rabbinic works, old and new, revised editions, annotated, critical editions of classical texts and innumerable current halakhic writings in Hebrew, French, English, Spanish and, of late, even in Russian, as well as, once more, in German?[6]

The majority of the essays included in this work describe the tensions between the opposing Jewish denominations during the nineteenth and the early twentieth centuries. Some focus upon the yeoman efforts of the stalwart individuals who refused to be silenced by derision and ridicule or swayed by despondency and dire predictions. The dwindling numbers of loyal coreligionists and their unpopularity succeeded neither in quenching their ardor nor in lessening their adherence to Jewish tradition and their fealty to Torah and mitzvot.

Activists such as Rabbis Azriel Hildesheimer and Samson Raphael Hirsch succeeded in effecting a dramatic reversal. Rabbi Hildesheimer sought to counter the pessimistic attitudes of his colleagues by focusing on multifaceted educational reforms, urging the religious leadership in both Germany and the Holy Land to establish institutions whose curricula included secular as well as Jewish studies and by establishing a rabbinical seminary which he hoped would mold an Orthodox intelligentsia.

Rabbi Samson Raphael Hirsch was a towering personality, the first rabbi to respond to the challenge of modernity by embarking on an imaginative and all-encompassing edifying program of communal activities while at the same time formulating a philosophical system that rendered those programs meaningful. Rabbi Hirsch sought to elucidate Torah teachings in a manner

5 Ibid.
6 Would Steinschneider yet object, as he once did, to having his own works translated into Hebrew and would he recoil, as he did in his own lifetime, when he encountered Hebrew and Zionist texts? See Himmelfarb, *The Jews of Modernity*, 8 and compare the comments of Marcus Ehrenpreis, cited in Avriel Bar-Levav, "A Living Citizen," 342.

that would find receptivity among members of a community whose cultural frame of reference was that of the modern world. Utilizing both the spoken and the written word, he sought to infuse religious practices with new levels of understanding and to interpret the underlying principles of the law in an original manner designed to make its concepts inspiring and relevant. In doing so, Rabbi Hirsch wrought a cultural and intellectual revolution in the Jewish community and halted the landslide that had previously swept countless numbers to Reform Judaism.

In responding to the social transformations that characterized his times, Rabbi Hirsch's method was unique in its espousal of what appeared to be an astounding contradiction: fidelity to the old and embrace of the new. In point of fact, the path that he blazed involved a subtle intertwining of tradition and innovation, restatement of truths in nomenclature that couched age-old ideas in a modern intellectual idiom without compromising the integrity of either Jewish thought or law. At first, that approach evoked annoyance and displeasure among adherents of all camps, innovators and conservatives alike, until it proved itself in the crucible of life to be not merely tenable, but also highly effective in countering the erosion of the values and practices of traditional Judaism.

Those endeavors were further advanced with varying degrees of success in twentieth-century Germany by a number of scholars, the most prominent of whom were Rabbis David Zevi Hoffmann and Yehi'el Ya'akov Weinberg.

In Germany, despite the lapses in observance on the part of large numbers, radical Reform failed to establish its hegemony with the result that, by and large, the complexion of the communal institutions remained traditional. However, in the United States the situation was quite different. While yet a young man, Kaufmann Kohler—who later achieved preeminence in the Reform movement—expressed disillusion engendered by the stagnation of the German Reform establishment: "A common solidarity of liberal forces, of which I dreamed in my Berlin idealizing dream-life, has no existence in the religious province. There is no sympathy for anyone who, following the insistent urge of his heart, desires to break through the obstacles which surround a great and free Judaism and hinder its development."[7] Consequently, he set his heart upon immigration to America because only in the New World did he believe that creative Reform had a future.

---

7 Cited by Addreas Gotzmann, *Jüdisches Recht im kulturellen Prozess: Die Wahrnehmung der Halacha im Deutschland des 19. Jahrhunderts* (Tübingen: Mohr Siebeck, 1997), 390 n. 77.

As Kohler envisioned, it was in the United States that the Reform movement rapidly achieved a dominant position in the religious life of American Jews. Nevertheless, when the masses of Eastern European Jews arrived on these shores, they did not find themselves at home in Reform institutions, but neither did they succeed in integrating within a firm traditional framework.

Then came the cataclysm. European Jewry was never to be the same again; nor was America to remain unaffected. Devastating losses and wondrous revival are the hallmarks of our age. My own earliest childhood memories are of the refugee communities in England during the closing years of World War II and of my family's subsequent arrival in North America. Those memories are intertwined with a flow of *niggunim* (melodies) that seem almost paradoxically to have emerged from the horrors and atrocities of the war. It was as if, despite everything, our people could and would yet sing. Their songs expressed two central themes: gratitude for survival and an unextinguished and inextinguishable love for Torah.

The melodies resonated with the words of "*Ḥasdei Ha-Shem ki lo tamnu ...*" (Lamentations 3:22); "*Zot neḥamati be-onyi ... zeidim helitzuni ad me'od, mi-Toratekha lo natiti ...*" (Psalms 119:50–51); and "*Lulei Toratekha sha'ashu'ai az avadeti be-onyi*" (Psalms 119:92). In retrospect, I now realize that the words of these songs were an expression of the absolute commitment and boundless love that was to become the driving, energizing force for the regeneration of a Torah community that was to rise phoenix-like from the ashes of the crematoria.

In a proclamation heralding the yeshiva he sought to establish, R. Hayyim of Volozhin called for public support, not so much for the benefit of the yeshiva, but because of a compelling need for Jews to cleave to Torah as to a life-saving raft.[8] In his *Nefesh ha-Ḥayyim*, R. Hayyim of Volozhin renders the phrase "It is a tree of life to those who seize it" (Proverbs 3:18) quite literally, declaring that the verse teaches a simple truism: a swimmer who finds himself in turbulent waters will hang on to a floating plank for his very life. So also does a Jew cast adrift amidst the perils of a turbulent world hang on for dear life to the Torah as a veritable life-preserver.[9]

Orthodox Judaism certainly existed in the United States before World War II, but it was an embattled Orthodoxy. Standards of observance had become eroded and ignorance of things Jewish was ubiquitous.

8 Open Letter, dated Fast of Gedalia, 5563 (1802), published in Moshe Shmuel Shapiro-Shmukler, *Toledot Rabbenu Ḥayyim mi-Volozhin* (Bnei Brak, 1957), 167.
9 *Nefesh ha-Ḥayyim* (New York, 1944), *sha'ar* 4, chap. 3, 124.

There was an old comedy routine that went something like this: Question: What is the difference between ignorance and indifference? Answer: I don't know and I don't care. During the early decades of the twentieth century American Jewry was characterized by profound ignorance and pervasive indifference. Ignorance and indifference were intertwined in a symbiotic relationship in which each nourished and nurtured the other. What passed for Jewish education was an embarrassment. There were few religious functionaries whose credentials inspired confidence and rabbinic erudition was conspicuous in its absence. Endemic ignorance permeated every facet of Jewish law and ritual, history, lore, custom and practice. There was precious little engagement with, or feel for, the texture of the cultural and religious life of Jews of earlier times and climes. Ludwig Lewisohn once described the lack of knowledge of all matters Jewish among the vast majority of fellow American Jews he had encountered as "an ignorance that was world-wide and many-sided."

Ignorance was at one and the same time the cause and the result of lack of both interest and concern; in turn, ignorance and lack of concern spawned apathy and negligence in matters religious. Boredom further quenched any residual desire for knowledge and served to hasten the move away from tradition. "Making it" socially, financially, and even academically, in the secular American environment was the overarching goal. Jewish religious life came to be viewed as an unwelcome encumbrance meriting, at the very most, perfunctory lip-service.

The tide was finally turned by a small group of loyal and committed individuals whose pioneering efforts led to the establishment of day schools and yeshivot. With sacrificial devotion and selfless determination, a small coterie of communal activists joined by an influx of post-war immigrants made Jewish education a matter of highest priority. In an era in which federations and major Jewish communal organizations set themselves a thoroughly secular philanthropic agenda, Orthodox Jews concentrated their energies and resources upon Torah education.

Among the immigrants who arrived in the wake of World War II were remarkable individuals who devoted their talents to furtherance of the goal of Torah study as an end in itself. Rabbi Aaron Kotler, of blessed memory, and the *kollel* he founded in Lakewood—a phenomenon looked upon in its time as a preposterous endeavor in an American milieu—the transplantation of the Mirrer Yeshiva together with reestablishment of other yeshivot as well as the endeavors of individual scholars who found their way to faculties of existing Torah institutions all combined to create a new intellectual climate. No longer were yeshivot regarded simply as institutions for the training of religious professionals. Torah study came into its own not only as an intrinsic value but as the paramount value in the lives of members of a rapidly expanding Torah community. A concomitant of the new reality was the establishment of *yeshivot ketanot,* or elementary day schools, throughout the length and breadth of the country. Products of the newly established or freshly invigorated Torah institutions had a burning desire to devote their lives to further study and teaching. Their love of Torah was infectious. The result was a renaissance of Jewish education and scholarship on every level.

The late Rabbi Pinchas Teitz once remarked that, during the early decades of his rabbinate in Elizabeth, New Jersey, on the rare occasions that he entered a congregant's home and found a *shas* (a complete set of folio volumes of the Talmud), he could be quite certain that the volumes belonged to an aged grandfather. In later years when he entered a congregant's home and beheld a *shas,* he could be quite certain that the owner of the volumes was a young grandson. Today, those grandsons have grown to maturity and their children possess, and assiduously use, even more enhanced libraries of their own.

A prominent educator has commented:

> The domestic Jewish miracle of the 20th century was the recreation of Jewish life and learning in the United States after the destruction of the Holocaust. In 1944, there were two dozen Jewish schools in New York, with no more than 5,000 students. Today, there are 165,000 students enrolled in more than 400 Jewish elementary and high schools in New York State, and an equal number elsewhere across the United States. Those students and schools are not a result of the growth of the Jewish community, they are the cause of it.[10]

Whatever the failures and flaws of our times—and they are manifold— the criticism that the Gemara, *Bava Metzi'a* 85b, levels at the Jews of the Second Temple era "who did not bless the Torah first," that is, neglected Torah study by not placing it at the forefront of their concerns, does not apply to the post-war generation of the Torah community. Nor has our youth flocked to Torah as an intellectual escape or as salvation from the threats posed by an alien culture. Rather, they have responded to Torah study as a sheer delight. Intoxicated with its majesty, they are passionate in their love of learning.

---

10 Rabbi Yaakov Bender, "State Rules Ignore Parochial Schools' Special Mission," *Times Union of Albany,* January 20, 2019, D2.

In some circles the passion for learning and fervent religiosity has bred a certain narrowness of focus. Often, however, that narrowness has been a result, not of a conscious negation of secularity, but of an intensive concentration upon Torah learning to the exclusion of all else. This absorption has led to a single-minded dedication to Torah study in the spirit of the Psalmist's yearning, "One thing have I asked of the Lord, that shall I seek ... that I dwell in the House of the Lord all the days of my life" (Psalms 27:4).

Unlike those of previous generations who often stood in exaggerated awe of the grandeur of the university, our own youth reflect an attitude resonating with the view expressed by *Maharal* of Prague. With all due regard for worldly wisdom and science, *Maharal* asserted that "the wisdom of all the wise men of the gentiles is considered as naught and nothingness in contrast to the least of their [the Torah Sages'] words."[11] Certainly, in the early days of the nascent *kollel* movement, the turn toward more intensive engagement in Torah study and the concomitant neglect of secular studies represented a choice freely made only after thoughtful examination of alternative options.[12]

It must also be recognized that the *kollel* enterprise in this country succeeded because of another phenomenon, namely, the unprecedented emphasis on formal Torah education of women. As a result, many young women exhibited remarkable dedication in fostering Torah study. In the final analysis, it was Jewishly educated women as mothers, wives and teachers whose influence was crucial in transforming the texture of the Orthodox community.

The role of Rabbi Joseph B. Soloveitchik, of blessed memory, should also be appreciated. As an extraordinarily eloquent exponent of the analytic methodology of the Lithuanian school of talmudic scholarship, he demonstrated the intellectual rigor of rabbinic scholarship in a manner that could not fail to make a profound impression upon university-trained audiences. The

---

11 See *Maharal, Be'er ha-Golah, be'er ha-ḥamishi,* and *Ḥiddushei Aggadot, Yevamot* 62b.

12 It is noteworthy that, as a pedagogue, R. Samson Raphael Hirsch counseled that religious schools not overly delay exposure of youngsters to secular studies lest those students feel resentment and "robbed of their youth." In a positive vein, he maintained that general knowledge should be acquired in order to understand and evaluate social phenomena and the human condition under which men live. He regarded such education as crucial in learning how to appreciate the values of Judaism from the perspective of the outside world and, conversely, how to test the values of the world from the perspective of Judaism. See, for example, Hirsch, *The Collected Writings,* vol. VII, 22–23, 169, 415, and 457. In the United States the ready availability of secular studies assured that the election of exclusive *kollel* study by those young men who were so inclined was a free and willing choice. The extent to which, in face of cultural pressures prevalent in some circles, that situation still pertains and will continue to pertain in the next generation of students is another matter.

net result is that Torah scholarship has acquired not only respect but also a certain cachet. Today, we see the fruits throughout the spectrum of the Jewish community. Thirst for Jewish learning is pervasive and has brought with it a corresponding enhancement in the observance of mitzvot. The newly evolved dedication to Torah study for its own sake has had a profound effect beyond the confines of the recently developed Orthodox enclaves. The mere presence of this community with its norms and values served to establish a new model and demonstrated quite dramatically that Old World Judaism could transplant itself, survive and thrive, even in America.

The transformation of Orthodoxy that has accompanied the phenomenal growth of Torah study on these shores is wondrous. In the Orthodox community, Jewish literacy is the rule, not the exception, meaningful Jewish education is virtually universal, and great numbers achieve a high degree of proficiency in textual study. And, at least equally important, with knowledge has come passionate involvement and deeply-rooted pride.[13] Defying prophets of doom, twenty-first-century American Orthodoxy exhibits an unanticipated dynamism and boasts of variegated flourishing communities.[14]

---

13 In the opening sentence of his *Judaism as a Civilization* (New York: Macmillan, 1934), Mordecai M. Kaplan observed, "Before the beginning of the nineteenth century all Jews regarded Judaism as a privilege; since then most Jews have come to regard it as a burden." In point of fact, it was well before the nineteenth century, at the dawn of the Enlightenment, that Rabbi Jacob Emden, in the introduction to his comments on the Prayerbook (*Siddur Bet Ya'akov, Sullam Bet El* [Lemberg, 1904], 9b-10a) insightfully attributed the religious deficiencies of his age to a lack of Jewish pride: "I am wont to say that I presume that the general deterioration among the children of our nation [stems] from a lack of the trait of pride, among our many sins." Absence of pride leads to a loss of distinctive Jewish identity and, admonishes Rabbi Emden, although abandonment of Jewish consciousness may be accompanied by short-term gain in the form of ostensive welcome and acceptance of Jews by society at large, ultimately Jews will be reviled and ostracized precisely because of their lack of religious and ethnic pride.

The positive and beneficial effects of pride were known in much earlier times as well. Tempering his extolment of the virtues of humility, the great medieval religious thinker Rabbenu Bahya ben Pekuda, *Ḥovot ha-Levavot, Sha'ar ha-Kniyah*, chap. 9, asserts that there is one form of pride that is entirely salutary: pride in spiritual attainment. Rabbenu Bahya finds approbation for such pride in the verse "*Va-yigba libbo be-darkei Ha-Shem*" ("And he held his heart high in the ways of the Lord", II Chronicles 11:6).

14 The changes in the Orthodox community in the United States between the 1930s and the present have been so dramatic and momentous that no historian of American Jewry can fail to take note of those phenomena. Arthur Hertzberg, in his insightful study *The Jews in America: Four Centuries of an Uneasy Encounter* (New York: Simon and Schuster, 1989), and later Jonathan D. Sarna, in his comprehensive *American Judaism: A History* (New Haven and London: Yale University Press, 2004), have written of the growth and development

However, the stark reality is that the Orthodox are but a relatively small fraction of the Jewish people. The major problem confronting contemporary Jewry is not tension between traditionalists and innovators; it is the absence of any form of religious identification on the part of vast numbers of Jews. In an increasingly thoroughly secular world, allegiance to religion among twenty-first-century youth is waning. The dramatically soaring rate of intermarriage is certainly incontrovertible testimony to the loss of religious commitment on the part of contemporary Jews. As Alan Dershowitz's son incisively noted regarding his own intermarriage, one should not refer to intermarriage as interfaith marriage, but, more accurately, as interfaithless marriage.[15] Indeed, usually, neither party to an intermarriage has a meaningful connection to any religious faith. Questioned regarding the religious group with whom they identified, the response of far too many millennials was "None."[16] The challenge of denominationalism pales before that of disinterest and apathy.

Daunting as such disinvolvement may be, we are nonetheless assured— and confident—that from the ranks of the cohorts who today engage in dedicated study of Torah there will emerge passionate spirited leaders who, for this generation, as Rabbenu Bahya foretold, will be "*kor'im el ha-Elokim ve-el*

---

of a newly vibrant and self-confident Orthodoxy and have sought to analyze the impact of the influx of the post-war immigration of European Jews upon the more acculturated, if embattled, indigenous Orthodox community. However, academic historians have failed properly to acknowledge the contributions of visionary educators such as Reb Shraga Feivel Mendlowitz, Rabbi Baruch Kaplan and Rebbetzin Vichna Kaplan. Nor have they adequately assessed the resilience of the hasidic communities and the trailblazing and ongoing outreach activities of Habad carried out by a global network of idealistic emissaries. The subtle nuances of the interactions of these groups, and the manner in which the newcomers and the already established observant population have together fashioned the current Orthodox community have yet to find their chronicler. It is a tableau that at times is illuminated more clearly between the lines of personal accounts of individuals in the Orthodox community who lived through that period. As Bertrand Russell would say, knowledge by description can never match knowledge by acquaintance or experience. See Bertrand Russell, "Knowledge by Acquaintance and Knowledge by Description," *Proceedings of the Aristotelian Society* 11 (1910), 108–128.

15 See Alan M. Dershowitz, *The Vanishing American Jew: In Search of Jewish Identity for the Next Century* (Boston and New York: Little, Brown and Company, 1997), 34.

16 Pew Research Center, "'Nones' on the Rise: One in Five Adults have no Affiliation," *Pew Forum on Religion and Public Life*, October 9, 2012, http://www.pewforum.org/2012/10/09/nones-on-the-rise/, accessed January 25, 2019. Cf. also Pew Research Center, "A Portrait of Jewish Americans Finding from a Pew Research Center Survey of U.S. Jews," *Pew Research Center's Religion and Public Life Project*, October 1, 2013, 43–64, http://www.pewresearch.org/wp-content/uploads/sites/7/2013/10/jewish-american-full-report-for-web.pdf, accessed January 25, 2019.

avodato u-morim et Torato—calling [their coreligionists] to God and to His service and teaching His Law," who will engage even the currently distant and disaffected, and with patience and forbearance—"precept by precept, precept by precept, line by line, line by line, here a little, there a little,"[17]—with enthusiasm and zeal, will convey to them the "Torah commanded to us by Moses" and restore it to its luster as "the heritage of the congregation of Jacob."[18]

---

17 Isaiah 28:13.
18 Deuteronomy 33:4.

CHAPTER 1

Rabbinic Responses to Nonobservance in the Modern Era

"But if the watchman see the sword come and blow not the trumpet, and the people be not warned: if the sword come and take any person from among them, he is taken away in his iniquity, but his blood will I require at the watchman's hand. So you, O son of man, I have set you a watchman unto the House of Israel: therefore you shall hear the word at my mouth, and warn them from me" (Ezekiel 33:6–7). It was with these prophetic words that the Orthodox rabbis who appended their signatures to the manifesto *Shelomei Emunei Yisra'el* (*The Faithful Believers of Israel*) opened their official document of protest in the wake of the Reform Rabbinical Conference that had taken place in Brunswick, Germany, in 1844. Similarly, when these same individuals resolved to publish a Hebrew-language journal "to raise the honor of Torah and to remove stumbling blocks from the path of faith," they gave the journal the title *Shomer Tziyyon ha-Ne'eman* (*Faithful Guardian of Zion*) and inscribed on the masthead of each issue the words: "founded by an association of rabbis and scholars standing in the breach and guarding the holy charge."

In seeking to analyze the various forms of response toward the nonobservant as gleaned from nineteenth- and twentieth-century rabbinic writings one must understand that, for the most part, the authors were responding, under pressure of events, to what they regarded as an organized, concerted attack upon the foundations of Judaism. Their responses, whether overly restrictive or (on rare occasions) surprisingly mild, were prompted by a conviction that, as the watchmen unto whom had been entrusted the preservation of the embattled fortress, they must safeguard against the breaches that might bring down even the outer walls and turrets and thereby leave the inner precincts exposed.

Nonobservant individuals were always to be found within the Jewish community. At times their numbers were few; at other times, many. Toward the end of the eighteenth century one finds increasingly frequent references to transgressors and a change in the tone of rabbinic homilies and admonitions in reaction to the rising incidence of nonobservance and the increasing severity of infractions. In the course of time, remonstrations concerning lack of meticulousness in observance, self-indulgence, pursuit of luxury, and even undue attention to changing fashions in attire gave way to rebuke of those who concern themselves with secular education rather than Torah study and of those who transgress Jewish law publicly and defiantly.[1]

These admonitions were usually addressed to anonymous individuals and apparently generated little, if any, opposing response. With the growing laxity of observance there came a new disregard for rabbinic authority. The issue was first joined in 1782 in the clash between traditional rabbinic leaders and Naphtali Hertz Wessely over the projected educational program advocated in the latter's *Divrei Shalom ve-Emet*.[2] But it was with the advent of an organized movement for religious reform in the early nineteenth century that the issue of nonobservance assumed an entirely new guise. From that point on, rabbinic reaction focused upon the fact that the nonobservant were no longer religiously weak or even recalcitrant individuals but were adherents of a movement that sought to supplant traditional Judaism. The Reform movement was regarded as posing such a threat because of four factors: (1) the public and communal nature of the transgressions of its adherents, (2) recognition of deviationist rabbinic authorities as mentors, (3) the open and avowed agenda for innovation, and (4) renunciation of fundamentals of faith. With the emergence of institutionalized Reform as a separate and distinct religious denomination, rabbinic responses differed radically from those of an earlier age.[3]

---

1 See, for example, the admonitions of R. Jacob Emden, *Siddur Bet Ya'akov* (Lemberg, 1904), *Mussar Na'eh, Ḥalon ha-Shevi'i*: 314–15; R. Jonathan Eibeschutz, *Ya'arot Devash* (Lemberg, 1863), 1: 11 a-12a; 2:23a, 65a-66b; and R. Ezekiel Landau, *Derushei ha-Tzelaḥ*, 47–38, 103–04. See also Azriel Shohet, *Im Ḥilufei Tekufot: Reshit ha-Haskalah be-Yahadut Germanyah* (Jerusalem: Bialik Institute, 1960), 35–42, 89–122, 139–73.

2 See the very pertinent discussion in Jacob Katz, *Out of the Ghetto: The Social Background of Jewish Emancipation 1770–1870* (New York: Schocken Books, 1978), 145–50.

3 Much of the historical and bibliographical literature regarding this period of history has been written from a partisan point of view and reflects a pronounced bias, if not outright distortion of facts. Recent work in this field is far more objective and has done much to redress the balance. Significantly, the standard history of the Reform movement, David Philipson, *The Reform Movement in Judaism* (New York: Ktav, 1967) has been superseded

The responses to this challenge were manifold and diverse and each merits separate examination and analysis.

THE INITIAL RESPONSE: ELEH DIVREI HA-BERIT

The innovations of the Hamburg Temple prompted the first major response of the Orthodox in the form of a classic work of responsa, *Eleh Divrei ha-Berit* (Altona, Germany, 1819), a collection of twenty-two responsa signed by forty rabbis from Germany, Poland, France, Italy, Bohemia, Moravia and Hungary. Appended to the Hebrew text are German excerpts in both Hebrew and Gothic characters. The material published in *Eleh Divrei ha-Berit* contains virtually all the substantive arguments offered in objection to Reform innovations. In subsequent polemics the sources and arguments set forth in that volume were cited over and over again.

Needless to say, publication of this work evoked a shrill response. The respondents in *Eleh Divrei ha-Berit* were berated by defenders of Reform on account of their excessive legalism, despite the fact that they were merely rebutting the purportedly halakhic arguments of Reform innovators. In much of the secondary literature, writers who have focused attention upon the liturgical controversies have found fault with this collection of responsa[4] while only a few have recognized that the rabbinic writers did forthrightly confront the

---

by an excellent work, Michael Meyer's *Response to Modernity: A History of the Reform Movement in Judaism* (New York: Oxford University Press, 1988), which strives for the objectivity and evenhandedness that is notably absent in Philipson's writing. Nevertheless, even this outstanding work, at times, misses the mark in understanding and analyzing the reaction of the Orthodox and certainly does not even lay claim to detailing their response.

4   From Graetz (Heinrich Graetz, *Geschichte der Juden*, 2nd ed., rev. by M. Brann [Leipzig: O. Leiner, 1900], 12:396–97) to Plaut (W. Gunther Plaut, *The Rise of Reform Judaism* [New York: World Union for Progressive Judaism, 1963], 34–37) and Petuchowski (Jacob J. Petuchowski, *Prayerbook Reform in Europe: The Liturgy of European Liberal and Reform Judaism* [New York: World Union for Progressive Judaism, 1968], 90–97), writers who have focused on these liturgical controversies have maligned *Eleh Divrei ha-Berit* and its propositions as mostly not valid and some of them "downright childish" (Graetz, 396). Israel Bettan, writing in 1925 ("Early Reform in Contemporaneous Responsa," in *Hebrew Union College Jubilee Volume*, ed. David Philipson [Cincinnati: Hebrew Union College Press, 1925], 425–43), in a somewhat patronizing and condescending tone, did recognize that some of these responsa reflected a different intellectual tradition as depicted by "the best products and truest exponents of a Jewish culture which though not wholly past is fast receding from the horizon of Jewish life" (423). But, even in 1990, when Bettan's predictions have proved false, few have conceded that *Eleh Divrei ha-Berit* reveals an eerie perspicacity and, sadly, a sound prophetic sense.

wide spectrum of issues involved and that *Eleh Divrei ha-Berit* reveals an almost uncanny prescience. The respondents had realized that what appeared to be minor ritual innovations heralded a revolutionary approach to Jewish law. As they predicted, in the following decades Reform spokesmen abandoned all allegiance to halakhah and instituted full-fledged reforms in all areas of Jewish religious life.

Yet, at the outset, one of the striking features of the encounter between Orthodoxy and Reform was the focus on questions of Jewish law and the attempt of writers who favored Reform to prove that the new norms of conduct could be justified on the basis of halakhic sources. In the first decade the language of the debate was Hebrew and the style and content that of classic responsa literature.[5]

Menahem Mendel Steinhardt of Hildesheim served as one of the three rabbis who were appointed to head the Jewish Consistory of Westphalia. While in that office, Steinhardt's erudition was enlisted in the attempt to give

---

5 Writing of this extended "battle of the proof texts," Petuchowski (*Prayerbook Reform*, 98) notes that it is of abiding interest that the early Reform writers sought to justify their actions in the arena of halakhah, for this underscores the fact that they assuredly had no intention of founding a new religion but wished to base their liturgical reform on a Judaism rooted in the Bible, Talmud, and Codes. His assessment is predicated upon the assumption of intellectual honesty on the part of these early writers, i.e., the assumption that they actually believed that the proof-texts and precedents cited served to support the conclusions they set forth.

In contradistinction, one of Rabbi Tzevi Hirsch Chajes's gravest accusations in refuting Reform halakhic arguments was the charge of intellectual dishonesty. See *Minḥat Kena'ot*, published in *Kol Sifrei Maharatz Ḥayes*, vol. 2 (Jerusalem: Divrei Hakhamim, 1958), 973–1036. Chajes claimed that many of the halakhic rulings of Reform writers were based on their finding a precedent in some totally obscure source, giving such precedent undue weight and, moreover, frequently, even citing the obscure leniency out of context in a manner that served to distort its original intention. Such distortion and citation out of context could lead the reader to the most bizarre conclusions:

The rabbis at their forefront justify their actions, saying the law is on their side and they are acting in accordance with Torah ... based on some isolated dicta that are found in the Talmud or Midrash with regard to other matters and they endow them with alien connotations ... in order to lead the masses of the people astray. They base themselves on esoteric nonnormative opinions, which can, at times, be found in the writings of decisors or on an unclear expression that may be found in some verse that, at first glance, seems tangentially to have some relationship to the matter at hand, even if, after study of the source, one recognizes that they have not penetrated to the depth of its meaning. ... And even if it were so ... in any event there is not sufficient basis in isolated words and the statements of individuals to supersede all the other words of the Sages that are clear and explicit ... [ibid., 986–988]. They search as for treasures and precious jewels for these obscure sources that have not been found by any previous great Torah scholars. [ibid., 988, n.].

legitimacy to Israel Jacobson's earliest religious reforms. While Steinhardt's *Divrei Iggeret*, published in Rödelheim in 1812 with the addition of comments and notes by Wolf Heidenheim, certainly falls within the ambit of mainstream halakhic literature, in many significant respects it prefigures the style, motifs, and even insinuations, of later defenders of Reform practice.[6]

Continued opposition to the ritual innovations in Berlin prompted the Reform partisans to commission another halakhic defense of their innovations. In 1818, in Dessau, Germany, Eliezer Liebermann, a Hungarian Jew regarding whose credentials there is only uncertain information,[7] published a treatise of his own, *Or Nogah*, together with a collection of responsa of others, *Nogah ha-Tzedek*. The latter responsa were authored by Sephardic rabbis in Italy, Shem Tov Samum of Leghorn and Jacob Recanati of Verona, and two Hungarian rabbis, Aaron Chorin of Arad and Moses Kunitz of Ofen. These responsa dealt with the earliest ritual innovations, in particular, use of the organ in the synagogue and prayer in the vernacular. Interestingly, while he maintained that daily prayer with a *minyan* is not an obligation, nor even a mitzvah, Aaron Chorin urged the Reform congregation to arrange for public prayer on weekdays. Chorin cited an opinion of Maharil that advises individuals to pray at home with proper devotion. For while the Talmud (*Berakhot* 6b) states that God is angry if He comes to the synagogue and does not find ten men there, this is not the case when the holiness of the synagogue is desecrated by individuals whose behavior is indecorous. However, noted Chorin, the criticism and conclusion of Maharil apply to the Orthodox whose communal prayers lack reverence and solemnity. Since Reform congregants do conduct themselves with decorum, they, then, might indeed arouse God's ire if they fail to pray with a *minyan*.[8] Ironic was Liebermann's suggestion in *Or Nogah* that German Jews should pray in their vernacular but that Polish Jews should pray in Hebrew, not simply because their knowledge of the holy tongue was superior to that of their German coreligionists, but because they should not be encouraged to pray in "the corrupt German in which they are fluent as a patois."[9]

---

6   See my "Menahem Mendel Steinhardt's *Divrei Iggeret*: Harbinger of Reform," in *Proceedings of the Tenth World Congress of Jewish Studies*, division B: *History of the Jewish People*, vol. 2 (Jerusalem: World Union of Jewish Studies, 1990), 207–14.

7   Regarding the somewhat mysterious Eliezer Liebermann, see Yekutiel Greenwald, *Korot ha-Torah va-ha-Emunah be-Hungaryah* (Budapest: Katsburg, 1921), 41–43; idem, *Li-Flagot Yisra'el be-Hungaryah* (Deva: Markovitch and Friedman, 1929), 8–9; Meyer, *Response to Modernity*, 50, 407 n. 151.

8   Eliezer Liebermann, "Kin'at ha-Emet," in *Nogah ha-Tzedek*, 25.

9   Eliezer Liebermann, *Or Nogah*, pt.1, 8–9.

Much of the technical legal argumentation presented in *Eleh Divrei ha-Berit* represented an attempt on the part of the Orthodox to discredit *Or Nogah* and *Nogah ha-Tzedek*, both their content and the reliability and authoritativeness of the respondents.

In their introductory comments to *Eleh Divrei ha-Berit* the members of the Hamburg *Bet Din* emphasized that these responsa were not the product of a predisposition to negativism or of a zeal to condemn.[10] They underscored the salient distinguishing characteristics of the social and religious problem posed by the innovations introduced by the members of the Hamburg Temple Society: The changes constituted the actions of a group that had separated itself from the traditional community for the express purpose of instituting changes in both custom and law. They represented a carefully designed agenda and were the product of a concerted, organized plan to establish alternative ecclesiastic authorities to rule on matters of religious ritual. Moreover, the innovations did not represent the private acts of individuals but were public in nature and involved an entire community. Sinners and backsliders were always to be found, and, sadly, more so in recent times, the rabbis averred, but "they did not separate themselves entirely from the community to constitute separate councils and to motivate the children of Israel publicly to change the customs of Israel and the laws of our holy Torah."[11] There was always reason to hope for repentance and spiritual improvement of transgressors. In such individual cases, benign neglect might, in the long run, constitute a wiser policy than denunciation or punitive measures. But the public, communal, and divisive nature of the actions of the Hamburg Temple Society necessitated a reasoned and forceful response that might have been avoidable under other circumstances:

> [For] now, on account of our great sins, the disease has spread in the Jewish community, for some persons have begun to gather together to legislate laws of iniquity, to change the customs of Israel in contradiction of the words of our holy Sages. ... The page is too short to include all their deleterious practices and customs in which they have chosen arrogantly to oppose the holy words of our Sages, the *Bet Din* of their city and the vast majority of our congregation who are faithful and observant of the divine laws.[12]

---

10 *Eleh Divrei ha-Berit*, introduction, ii.
11 Ibid., iii.
12 Ibid., iii–iv.

Moreover, the official community could not allow itself the option of silence in the face of such organized rebellion lest silence be mistaken for agreement: "Then we said that now is not the time to be silent or to place a hand over the mouth. If we are silent we will be found guilty for people will say, 'The rabbis have been silent, and silence is acquiescence.'"[13]

The substantive portions of most of these responsa deal with technical, halakhic questions regarding changes in the liturgy, recitation of prayer in the vernacular, and use of the organ in the synagogue both on the Sabbath and on weekdays. Some respondents simply cited general dicta opposing abrogation of time-hallowed practice (*minhagan shel Yisra'el Torah hu*),[14] while others cited a host of halakhic sources and precedents to bolster their restrictive pronouncements.[15]

Apart from their particular arguments against abrogation of established practices, the writers protested the hubris of the innovators in relying upon little-known individuals whose scholarship and authority were, at best, dubious. A number of respondents explicitly cast aspersions upon the character and qualifications of the champions of Reform, Eliezer Liebermann and Aaron Chorin.[16] The recantation of Aaron Chorin and his renunciation of the innovations he had earlier espoused are of particular interest. Chorin's recantation is appended by *Ḥatam Sofer* to the latter's third letter in *Eleh Divrei ha-Berit*. Even more remarkable is the fact that Chorin later retracted his recantation.[17]

Vituperation and invective were not wholly absent. The Reform clergy were characterized as evil and wicked men. It was imperative to combat such individuals for "the hands of the wicked" must be weakened and "the house of the wicked" must be eradicated.[18] Some respondents urged representations

---

13 Ibid., v.

14 See, for example, ibid., 1–3, 70.

15 See, for example, the discussion regarding the use of an organ, ibid., 30–32, 67, 74–79, 85–86.

16 See, in particular, ibid., 21–22, 30ff., 77, 89.

17 Ibid., 97–98. On Chorin and the recantation see Meyer, *Response to Modernity*, 158, 432 nn. 41, 42; Philipson, *The Reform Movement*, 442 n. 112.

18 See, for example, *Eleh Divrei ha-Berit*, 24, 26, 53, 59, 64, 84. For the often-employed play on words *moreh hora'ah—moreh ha-ra'ah*, see Solomon Schreiber, *Iggerot Soferim* (Vienna: Joseph Schlesinger, 1933), sec. 1, 51. With respect to the language employed, one should be mindful of the style and idiom of rabbinic pronouncements in general and their penchant for hyperbole. Much of the polemical literature on both sides was couched in derogatory and derisive language. See Alexander Guttmann, *The Struggle over Reform in Rabbinic Literature During the Last Century and a Half* (New York: World Union for Progressive Judaism, 1977), 139–46. In *Eleh Divrei ha-Berit*, 21, 24, *Or Nogah* was referred to as *Divrei Aven*, Words of Iniquity (the term *Aven* was formed as an acrostic derived from the first two letters of the

to civil authorities in order to gain their assistance in the repression of this dangerous movement.[19]

A variety of other motifs may also be found in *Eleh Divrei ha-Berit*. A staunch championship of the privileged position of Hebrew as the language of prayer and spiritual contemplation is found in the responsa of R. Mordecai Benet,[20] R. Jacob of Lissa,[21] R. Moses Sofer,[22] and R. Akiva Eger.[23]

---

word *Or* and the initial letter of *Nogah*) and those who followed the prescriptions of the "Shining Light" (in Hebrew, *Or Nogah*) were described as "walking in darkness, not light." The Reform writers employed a similar style. Eliezer Liebermann, *Or Nogah*, pt. 2, 4, wrote of the Orthodox that their eyes were blinded and therefore they could not see the truth. The Orthodox were branded as *stillständler* (inert) and mocked as backward and unenlightened. See Plaut, *The Rise of Reform Judaism*, xxiii. In the protracted debate concerning the question of delayed burial one finds, at times, particularly tasteless comments of Reform partisans regarding efforts on the part of the Orthodox to secure timely burial. A sensitive reader would certainly find sarcastic remarks concerning the bereaved and their sincere attempts to honor the dead to be offensive. See, for example, "Die Beerdigung der jüdischen Leichen in Altona," *Der Israelit des Neunzehnten Jahrhunderts* (*IdNJ*) 6 (1845), 214–15.

19 *Eleh Divrei ha-Berit*, 23, 26.
20 Ibid., 15.
21 Ibid., 79–81.
22 Ibid., 10–11, 38. Cf., also, *Teshuvot Ḥatam Sofer, Ḥoshen Mishpat*, no. 192 and *Likkutim*, vol. 6, nos. 84, 86. On the use of Hebrew, see also *Eleh Divrei ha-Berit*, 49–50, 65–66, 73, 89. Cf., also, R. Jacob Emden, *Siddur Bet Ya'akov*, 314; and R. Jonathan Eibeschutz, *Ya'arot Devash*, pt. 2, 18a, 78a.
23 *Eleh Divrei ha-Berit*, 27–28. As early as September 5, 1815, R. Akiva Eger authored a brief responsum in which he explicitly opposed proposals that prayer services be conducted in the vernacular. This responsum is published in L. Wreschner, "Rabbi Akiba Egers Leben und Wirken," in *Jahrbuch der Jüdisch-Literarischen Gesellschaft* (*JJLG*) 3 (1905), 75–77 and in *Likkut Teshuvot ve-Ḥiddushim mi-Rabbi Akiva Eger* (Bnei Brak, 1968), 11–13. R. Akiva Eger's opinion on this matter was, in all likelihood, solicited by Rabbi Meir Weyl, then Associate Chief Rabbi of Berlin, who sought to stymie the religious reforms introduced into private synagogues in Berlin that very year by Israel Jacobson and advocated before the Prussian authorities by David Friedlander. As one of his most extensive correspondents, Weyl, at times, consulted Eger on matters of policy concerning negotiations with government officials and Reform partisans. See Wreschner's articles in *JJLG* 2 (1904), 41, 60–62, and 3 (1905), 35. Cf. Ludwig Geiger, *Geschichte der Juden in Berlin*, vol. 2 (Berlin: J. Guttentag, 1871), 210–30. For the scholarly correspondence of Eger and Weyl, see *Teshuvot Rabbi Akiva Eger*, vol. 1 (Warsaw, 1834), nos. 23, 40, 64, 107, 112, 154, and *Teshuvot Rabbi Akiva Eger*, vol. 2 (Vienna, 1859), nos. 75, 82, 83, 85, 94, 118, 119; *Teshuvot Rabbi Akiva Eger mi-Ketav Yad* (Jerusalem, 1965), nos. 37, 39, 43, 71, 84; *Teshuvot Ḥadashot le-Rabbenu Akiva Eger* (Jerusalem, 1978), *Yoreh De'ah*, no. 2, and *Ḥoshen Mishpat*, nos. 2, 9. In his responsum, Eger expressed opposition to the use of the vernacular in the liturgy for reasons that were based entirely upon technical application of halakhic requirements. However, his negativism toward this innovation clearly extended beyond halakhic technicalities. More significant than the legal argumentation is his analysis of the motivation underlying this

R. Akiva Eger associated a sense of fierce national pride with advocacy of the use of Hebrew. R. Mordecai Benet voiced concern for the education of future generations in predicting that if the passages regarding the ingathering of exiles and the rebuilding of Jerusalem were to be eliminated from the prayers, future generations would lack an appreciation for these fundamentals of faith.[24]

In bemoaning the motives of the Reform leaders, many of the respondents underscored the desire of the innovators to ingratiate themselves with non-Jews and to assimilate. "Truthfully," wrote R. Eleazar Flekeles, "they are lacking in faith and all their intent is but to acquire a name among the nations ... but in truth they are neither Jews nor Christians."[25] As R. Moses Sofer put it in his letter, "The intent of these individuals is to curry favor in the eyes of the nations and the officials."[26]

Turning aside from the intricacies of the halakhic disputations regarding the question of whether an organ might be used in the synagogue or whether the formulae of certain prayers might be changed at will, the respondents emphasized the significant theological and philosophical issues raised in the particular liturgical changes adopted in the Hamburg Temple Prayerbook. The innovators had tampered with the text of prayers concerning the Messiah, the rebuilding of Jerusalem, the ingathering of the exiles, and resurrection of the dead. The alterations introduced in the text of these prayers reflected a rejection of fundamental principles of faith. R. Mordecai Benet declared that one who questions these beliefs is, if not a heretic, at the very minimum, spiritually misguided. Eliminating such passages from the prayerbook would result,

---

specific reform and the tenor of his concluding comments which constitute a call for self-pride and self-awareness: "He whose intent is for the sake of Heaven and whose desire is not specifically to preen himself in the eyes of the nations and to be similar unto them and to lower the language of splendor, the holy tongue, from its honor, will concede the truth" (Wreschner 3:37).

It is instructive to compare this responsum with what is perhaps the very earliest responsum regarding prayer in the vernacular. That responsum, dated March 20, 1809, and authored by Samuel Eger of Brunswick, a cousin and colleague of Akiva Eger, addressed itself to the introduction of prayer in the German language by Israel Jacobson in his school in Cassel. Unlike Akiva Eger, Samuel Eger readily concedes the halakhic argument but similarly focuses on the motivation of the innovators. Use of the vernacular, he asserts, will only give support to those who seek to undermine tradition and will eliminate all incentive for the study of Hebrew. Moreover, retention of Hebrew in prayer serves as a necessary link uniting Jews throughout the world. The responsum is published in B. H. Auerbach, *Geschichte der israelitischen Gemeinde Halberstadt* (Halberstadt: H. Meyer, 1866), 219–21.

24 *Eleh Divrei ha-Berit*, 13.

25 Ibid., 17.

26 Ibid., 33. Cf. the language of R. Akiva Eger, in his 1815 responsum (cited in n. 23 above).

heaven forfend, in future generations being cut off from the historic traditions of *kelal Yisra'el* and becoming "totally separated from the body of the entire congregation of Israel."[27]

The respondents certainly had a clear understanding of the theological chasm that existed between the exponents of Reform and the traditionalists. The Orthodox rabbis did not believe in the slightest that the controversy revolved upon merely minor cosmetic changes in the ritual. R. Akiva Eger wrote bluntly, "Is not this, heaven forfend, the overthrow and uprooting of religion?" Changing minor details, he argued, would ultimately cause the unraveling of the entire fabric of religious life.[28]

In a succinct statement decrying any form of ritual innovation, Eger presented the ideological substratum upon which this viewpoint was based. He underscored the interrelationship and interdependence of the Oral and Written Law in declaring, "They are united and bound together and are inseparable," and asserted that without rabbinic interpretation as expressed in the Oral Law, biblical commandments are incomprehensible. For example, absent rabbinic exegesis, biblical terms describing *tefillin* are entirely unintelligible. The characteristics of acts labeled as "labor" and proscribed on the Sabbath are not delineated in Scripture.[29] Therefore, as he argued elsewhere, "without total faith in the words of the Talmud according to tradition the entire Torah would fall."[30]

The strongest criticism of the innovators was the charge that they had sundered the unity of the community. In sharpest language, R. Eliezer of Triesch in Moravia (present-day Třešť), in his second letter, criticized the motives and actions of the Hamburg Temple leaders and accused them of destroying the solidarity of the Jewish people:

> And now let us judge together. ... Why have you separated yourselves from the community? And why were you not concerned regarding [the prohibition of] "And you shall not make groups and groups" that our Sages have interpreted as "you shall not create separate groups?" ... Why are you relying ... on the decision of one rabbi printed in the work called *Nogah Tzedek* [*sic*] ... and why did you not consult the scholars of your city, the great

---

27 *Eleh Divrei ha-Berit*, 13. Cf. ibid., 22, 67.

28 Ibid., 27.

29 Ibid., 27.

30 *Iggerot Soferim*, sec. 1, 50. Cf. also *Drush ve-Ḥiddush mi-Ketav Yad*, 176.

rabbis of your *Bet Din Tzedek* from whom goes forth Torah to the residents of your esteemed community? ... What benefit will accrue to you if you separate from the community and from the entire body politic of the people? ... It will be devastating for generations to come ... if you be separated from Jews and not reckoned among the nations. ... What will you answer on the Day of Judgment? What will you say on the Day of Reckoning? ...

People of the Lord of Abraham! Look to the Rock whence you are hewn. Are we not all sons of one man? Do we not all have one Father? ... Who knows if you will not, heaven forfend, cause lamentation for generations and all the children of Israel shall weep for you?[31]

R. Jacob of Lissa pleaded, "We, too, call out to you with an entreaty of love.... What is the benefit of creating a split and separation of hearts in Israel?"[32]

Its many harsh comments notwithstanding, *Eleh Divrei ha-Berit* was not entirely strident in nature. A conciliatory note is sounded by R. Eliezer of Triesch in the same letter in which he berates adherents of Reform for sowing dissension in the Jewish community. He goes so far as to apologize in case he has inadvertently been too negative or stinging in expressing his opposition to the innovators:

If my pen has slipped ... do not count it to me as a sin, for from my great pain and distress I have spoken thus and for the zeal of the Lord of Hosts ... and what shall I do, my Father in Heaven has decreed ... in an explicit commandment of the Torah, "You shall surely reprove your fellow and not bear sin on his account." I have shown you the good and correct way and far be it from me that I should cease to pray on your behalf.

I shall raise my hands to the Lord and pray to the God of heaven and earth and their hosts, forgive the transgressions of your servants for the entire people are unwitting and give them a new heart, and a correct spirit renew in them, and let them all form together one association to serve you with a perfect heart.[33]

Most striking is the self-critical note struck by R. Eliezer of Triesch and his positive suggestions for self-improvement in the practices of the Orthodox

---

31 *Eleh Divrei ha-Berit*, 92.
32 Ibid., 82.
33 Ibid., 93.

community. He draws attention to the rabbinic teaching that transgression breeds further transgression and that punishment is often encountered in the very area in which one has sinned. Surely the religious community must examine its own actions and practices with a critical eye. If contention and controversy have erupted in matters of synagogue ritual perhaps it is a reflection of negligence and contentiousness among the observant in precisely that area of divine service. It is for the leaders and rabbis of the community to seek, in the spirit of authentic Jewish tradition, to make synagogue services more edifying. It is for them to eradicate all manner of social inequity and to concentrate on enhancement of brotherly love and neighborliness in the community. Their own leadership must be free of moral flaws. Above all, they must strive to promote the ideals of harmony and love for fellow Jews, for no Jews—by implication, not even backsliders—are without redeeming qualities.[34] The dissidents must be approached with love and gentleness, "with a soft expression and intelligent ethical reproof," and brought back "to be one people with us as they were until now, all together in one accord to serve the great and awesome God."[35]

The issues raised by the writers in *Eleh Divrei ha-Berit* were amplified by rabbinic writers in the years that followed and, as we shall note, were the subject of ongoing rabbinic discussion.[36]

---

34 Ibid., 94–96.

35 Ibid., 96.

36 Publication of *Eleh Divrei ha-Berit* engendered several replies, among which was a satire, *Ḥerev Nokemet Nekom Berit*, published anonymously by Meyer Israel Bresselau in 1819. That work has been praised excessively for its unusual Hebrew satirical style. See Meyer, *Response to Modernity*, 60, 409 nn. 183, 184; Plaut, *Rise of Reform Judaism*, 37; and Petuchowski, *Prayerbook Reform*, 97. It is indeed a not too remarkable satire of the style typically associated with Purim parodies. Notable are two sharp ripostes to comments in *Eleh Divrei ha-Berit*. Rabbi Moses Sofer had commented, *inter alia*, that a further reason for recitation of prayer in Hebrew is the fact that the holy tongue is the language of the King of kings. In appearances before royalty, subjects speak the language of the sovereign they address, even if he understands other tongues. Similarly, in addressing the King of kings it is seemly to use His language (*Eleh Divrei ha-Berit*, 10–11). Bresselau responded by asking, "What has happened to the man Moses (i.e., Moses Sofer)? Is God to be likened to a human being? 'And to whom shall you liken Me?' (Isaiah 40:25)" (*Ḥerev Nokemet*, 15). Turning to the responsum of R. Jacob of Lissa, Bresselau is more stinging. R. Jacob had cited Isaiah 6:9, "Hear you, but understand not," and argued that we must follow tradition even if we comprehend it not. We may not rely solely on the perceptions of our own intelligence for our intelligence is all too limited (*Eleh Divrei ha-Berit*, 79). Indeed, countered Bresselau, we may not follow "our own intelligence" for it is all too limited. R. Jacob has written well regarding himself! And, by implication, Bresselau hints, regarding all the Orthodox who are categorized by know-nothingism, following and understanding not (*Ḥerev Nokemet*, 15).

The satiric style was continued in some of the pamphlets published on both sides of the debate, all too often in a form more puerile than witty. A curious example of this genre which

POSSIBLE SCHISM OR BAN?

As the Reform movement grew and established itself as a separate denomination, the policy to be adopted with regard to those who identified publicly with the movement became a major issue. Were they to be treated simply as transgressors or were stronger communal sanctions to be imposed?

As one of the staunchest advocates of Orthodoxy who countered fiercely any encroachment of Reform, Ḥatam Sofer coined the aphorism ḥadash asur min ha-Torah (that which is new is forbidden by the Torah) as a battle slogan in opposing all manner of Reform innovation.[37] As a champion of Orthodoxy, he inveighed against exponents of Reform "who have distanced themselves from God and His Torah, due to our many sins," and cautioned against any association with them: "Do not dwell in their vicinity and do not associate with them at all … and do not say, the times have changed. For we have an old Father, may his name be blessed, and He has not changed and will not change … ."[38] Nevertheless, even Ḥatam Sofer stopped short of issuing an outright interdict or ban. In one of his responsa Ḥatam Sofer comes close to endorsement of a ban, but even in that statement he takes note of possible repercussions at the hands of civil authorities and limits himself to the hypothetical declaration that "if their judgment were in our hands" he would rule that the status of adherents of Reform is identical to that of sectarians and heretics and would demand total separation from them. Those comments, published in his responsa collection, are quite emphatic:

> If their judgment were in our hands, it would be my opinion to separate
> them from our domain; our daughters not to be given to their sons, nor
> their sons [to be taken] for our daughters, so that we should not come to

---

surfaced in the United States is the brief pamphlet *Emek Refa'im* by M. E. Holzman, published in New York in 1865 and addressed to the "Doctors" (*Refa'im* a pun on the Hebrew *rof'im*, doctors) of the Reform clergy and, in particular, to one "Doctor Lavan" (German *weiss*, white), Dr. Isaac Mayer Wise. Following dissemination of Wise's prayerbook, *Minhag America* (Cincinnati, 1857), the author undertook to warn Wise in a satiric manner that America is a "free country," but not free from divine retribution.

The satiric style continued to characterize the Reform-Orthodox debate at a much later time. In a letter regarding a pamphlet entitled *Kuntres le-Ma'an Aḥai ve-Re'ai*, which attacks Reform, Rabbi A. I. Kook criticizes the use of satire in the course of polemic: "Satire is a medium that it is fitting to employ with caution and in a precise measure, both from the vantage point of propriety and, more so, from the vantage point of the law . . . ." See *Iggerot ha-Reiyah*, vol. 2 (Jerusalem: Mossad ha-Rav Kook, 1968), 144.

37 See, for example, *Teshuvot Ḥatam Sofer, Oraḥ Ḥayyim*, no. 28.

38 See Ḥatam Sofer's last will and testament printed in S. Schreiber, *Ḥut ha-Meshulash* (Tel Aviv: Mesorah Press, 1963), 152–53.

be drawn after them and that their congregation be like the congregation of Zadok and Boethus, Anan and Saul, they for themselves and we for ourselves. All this appears to me as halakhah, but not to be implemented in practice in the absence of permission and authorization of the government; in the absence of this [permission] my words should be void and considered as naught.[39]

Twenty-odd years later, following the Reform rabbinical conferences, the possibility of ban (*ḥerem*) or schism again loomed large on the horizon. It is instructive to examine several responses to these conferences in order to appreciate the tension in the Orthodox camp and the reluctance to take so final a step.

In Altona, Rabbi Jacob Ettlinger and his colleagues published a formal protest in the form of a written manifesto entitled *Shelomei Emunei Yisra'el*, encompassing both a Hebrew and German text and bearing the signatures of seventy-seven Orthodox rabbis. This manifesto came to be regarded as the official statement of the Orthodox and received much wider endorsement. In the years that followed, the number of signatories rose to over three hundred.[40]

It must be noted that references to the manifesto as a ban or anathema are simply misstatements of fact.[41] The document contains no anathema or imprecation, nor does it single out any individual for attack. Even its critics admitted that the manifesto was restrained in expression and did not strike the strident note they associated with many other Orthodox pronouncements.[42] The relative moderation of tone reflected in the manifesto was the product of the influence of R. Jacob Ettlinger.[43]

Although Ettlinger's influence was decisive with regard to the manifesto, his moderation was not always accepted with equanimity by the more extreme among his colleagues. Probably the best example of those disparate modes of

---

39 *Teshuvot Ḥatam Sofer*, vol. 6, no. 89.

40 The manifesto is dated 1845 but the pamphlet does not indicate the city of publication. The German text was republished in *Der Israelit* 10 (1869), 177–80. An English translation was published in the British *Voice of Jacob* 4 (1845), 136–37, 142–43 and in the American *Occident* 3 (1845–46), 146–49, 198–201. *Der Israelit* 10 (1869), 177, refers to 300 signatories. Cf. *Iggerot Soferim*, sec. 1, 85. On the reaction evoked by the protest, see Philipson, *The Reform Movement*, 159–62.

41 "Die Beerdigung," *IdNJ* 6 (1845), 213.

42 Ibid., 100.

43 On R. Ettlinger's role in organizing and publicizing this protest see Chajes, *Minhat Kena'ot* 2:1019, note; *Iggerot Soferim*, sec. 3, 6–7; *IdNJ* 6 (1845), 213; *Der Israelit* 10 (1869), 569; 12 (1871), 941; and *Die jüdische Presse* 3 (1812), 343.

reaction is to be found in an encounter that took place between Ettlinger and Rabbi Solomon Eger. Following the conferences in Brunswick and Frankfurt, R. Solomon Eger, son and successor of R. Akiva Eger and a renowned authority in his own right, resolved to issue a ban against Reform Jews declaring them to be outside the pale of the community of Israel. Eger informed Ettlinger of his intention whereupon the latter summoned Eger to Altona to discuss the matter in person. Eger undertook the journey and was received with great cordiality and honor by Ettlinger as well as by the rabbis and *Klaus* scholars of Hamburg and Altona. Eger anticipated Ettlinger's unreserved endorsement and cooperation in circulating the text of the proposal but was soon disenchanted. Ettlinger conceded that, in theory, Eger was justified in wishing to pronounce a ban; however, in practice, he refused to sanction such a course of action. This policy of restraint had other prominent advocates as well. R. Solomon Eger also describes a meeting with R. Nathan Adler of London who was visiting in Hanover at the time.[44] Eger wished to obtain the support of Adler, but his entreaties were deflected.

In a private communication in which he discussed the incident and described his keen disappointment, Rabbi Solomon Eger interpreted the attitude of Ettlinger and his colleagues as the product of fear of untoward repercussions:

> Although they were forced to admit that the matter was halakhically correct, they were unwilling to act upon it. For the sage, the Chief Rabbi of Altona, despite all his piety and despite all that has been done through him to denigrate the deeds of these rebels in the pages of the *Guardian of Zion* through Dr. Enoch,[45] is yet afraid to do such a thing against the wicked who rule over him. For so do they honor and elevate him in accordance with the custom of the people of Germany ... that he conducts his rabbinate in such a manner as [was customary] in the past and no small or big matter is changed in the synagogues of Altona and Hamburg without permission of the rabbinate. I was greatly impressed with their ancient customs. ... The rabbis of Germany are afraid to quarrel publicly with the wealthy and to publicize a ruling such as this against the heretics

---

44 *Iggerot Soferim*, sec. 1, 83. Adler had returned to Hanover from London for the celebration of his mother's eightieth birthday. The visit is described in the Orthodox weekly *Der treue Zionswächter* (*TZW*) 3 (1847), 230–31, 238–39, and in *Voice of Jacob* 6 (1847), 192.

45 Rabbi Samuel Enoch, principal of the Jewish secondary school in Altona, served as editor of *TZW* until he became rabbi of Fulda in 1855.

lest these turn to evil ways in public and they [the rabbis] lose the good status they yet enjoy.[46]

Eger later observed that it would have been wiser to have approached the rabbis of Hungary for assistance in his campaign against Reform.[47] This assessment of the difference in approach on the part of the rabbis of the Hungarian school and that of Jacob Ettlinger and Nathan Adler is well founded. It is, however, incorrect to attribute the reaction of Ettlinger and Adler to cowardice or self-serving motives. Their refusal to be party to a formal ban or interdiction was a reasoned decision consistent with a carefully formulated policy eschewing methods judged to be counter-productive.[48]

Even more restrained was the position of R. Eliyahu Ragoler of Kalisch, who not only cautioned against issuing a ban but even questioned the wisdom of publishing public protests lest such action fan the flames of controversy and only exacerbate the problem: "It is necessary to be very careful ... in determining how to publish against them," wrote Ragoler, "for even from a controversy between great Sages of the land, both of whose intentions were for the sake of Heaven, there sprang many evils."[49]

In 1849 the prominent Galician rabbinic scholar, R. Tzevi Hirsch Chajes, published a Hebrew monograph entitled *Minhat Kena'ot* written in response to the Brunswick and Frankfurt Reform Rabbinical Conferences of 1844 and 1845.[50] *Minhat Kena'ot* presents one of the most comprehensive halakhic discussions of Reform innovations, ranging from details of synagogue ritual to

---

46 *Iggerot Soferim*, sec. 1, 84.

47 Ibid., 85.

48 Cf. Yonah Emanuel, "Perakim be-Toldot ha-Rav Ya'akov Ettlinger z'l," *Ha-Ma'ayan* 12 (1971–1972), 32, on the opposition of R. Samson Raphael Hirsch and R. Azriel Hildesheimer to the issuance of bans.

49 *Teshuvot Yad Eliyahu, Pesakim*, pt. 1, no. 25.

50 The thrust of many of Chajes's previous scholarly writings, *Torat Nevi'im* (1836), *Darkei Hora'ah* (1842–43), and *Mevo ha-Talmud* (1845), had been directed to a defense of tradition and an attempt to discredit the work of innovators and critical scholars. The Reform Rabbinical Conferences gave further impetus to this apologetic and polemical bent. In the introduction to *Minhat Kena'ot*, Chajes writes that he had prepared that monograph in response to the Frankfurt Rabbinical Conference and wished to publish it as a *davar be-itto*, a timely response in the proper time and place, while the influence of the conference was yet palpable, but his efforts had been stymied by official censors who prevented publication of the work at that time. See Chajes, *Minhat Kena'ot*, 975, and Mayer Herskovics, *Maharatz Hayes: Toldot Rabbi Tzevi Hirsch Hayes u-Mishnatto* (Jerusalem: Mossad ha-Rav Kook, 1972), 196–97, 490–91.

questions of Sabbath observance, circumcision, and intermarriage. In *Minḥat Kena'ot* Chajes presents a historical and theological elucidation of sectarianism and of sects prevalent during the talmudic period. Chajes traces sectarianism from its earliest manifestations reflected, in his opinion, in the biblical account of the golden calf and of the adherents of Korach (following *Tanḥuma* and *Midrash Yalkut*) and later in the worship of the devotees of the Shrine of Micah and of the shrines in Beth-el and Dan as well as the heresies of the Sadducees, the Essenes, the early Christians, and the Karaites.[51] His historical survey concludes with a discussion of the innovators of his own time whom he regards as having set themselves apart as a separate sect and as having utterly rejected the binding force of Torah as one discards old fashions in favor of new. Chajes endeavors to place the Reform movement in a historical perspective and to compare and contrast it to earlier deviations from normative Judaism. He concludes in no uncertain terms that, halakhically, the status of exponents of the Reform movement is in no way different from that of members of the sects of antiquity:

> There is no doubt whatsoever that all the rulings that our Sages of blessed memory decreed for the Sadducees and Karaites apply to them ... i.e., to those who comport themselves according to the Rabbinical Conferences and separate from their brethren and join to choose for themselves innovations of which our forefathers could not conceive. ... I frankly do not know whether they continue to have any relationship whatsoever with us ... save for the fact that the majority of them yet circumcise their children. ... Except for that, they have already separated from us in all matters of faith and practice.[52]

Despite the strong and unequivocal nature of this statement, as well as of other statements couched in similar language elsewhere in *Minḥat Kena'ot* and his other writings, Chajes was ambivalent about implementing in practice what he deemed valid in theory:

> Behold I will not hide the truth. Greatly is my heart pained to pronounce my verdict against them in this manner, to estrange from us a large populace,

---

51 Chajes, *Minḥat Kena'ot*, 981–85. See the lengthier discussion in *Darkei Mosheh*, in *Kol Sifrei*, vol. 1, 442–53.

52 Chajes, *Minḥat Kena'ot*, 1012.

particularly our brethren of German descent, who are accomplished in wisdom and knowledge, far superior to other members of our nation in other countries.[53]

Quite apart from his hesitation to alienate and estrange a large number of his coreligionists, Chajes was also wary lest internal dissension and rift within the Jewish community serve as ammunition for anti-Semites at the very time that Jews were under keen scrutiny as they fought to gain rights and privileges from European governments. He was extremely wary of adding fuel to possible anti-Semitic allegations at such a sensitive time. Above all, he sought to avoid an irreparable schism.

Drawing on a biblical precedent, Chajes cites the reaction of the Jewish people following the outrage at Gibeah (Judges 21:3). After taking an oath not to marry members of the tribe of Benjamin, all Israel lifted up their voices and wept sorely and they said, "Oh, Lord, God of Israel, why has this come to pass that there should be today one tribe lacking in Israel?" How can it have come to pass, writes Chajes, that we should ourselves cut off our own flesh and blood in our own day? What has become of the imperative to seek peace in one's own locale and pursue it elsewhere? As the Sages teach, he adds, even if Israel worships idols, if there be peace among them, punishment is mitigated.[54]

Accordingly, Chajes equivocated and put aside his theoretical ruling, noting that the Reform movement was losing some of its initial impetus. In Galicia, it had not secured a foothold. Even in Germany the conferences did not engender overwhelming popular support. Certainly, the Breslau Conference had not been a raging success. The initial glamor and attraction of change had already begun to pale. Hence, concludes Chajes, "since the danger is not so terrifying for us now, perhaps it is no longer so urgent on our part for us to battle to separate a great multitude from our community."[55]

But that was not Chajes's final word on the subject. He again vacillates and notes the various provisions of Jewish law applicable to those who lead the community astray. He further cites the talmudic judgment that an act of mercy toward those who seduce the innocent ultimately results in malevolence toward the rest of the world. Finally, Chajes concludes that the negative rulings pronounced against the Reform movement should be regarded

---

53 Ibid., 1012–13.
54 Ibid., 1013.
55 Ibid., 1013.

as applying only to its leaders, not to their followers. He contends that the masses had been led astray by their leaders and that, accordingly, their seduction by skilled demagogues must be deemed a mitigating circumstance constituting quasi-duress.[56]

During the following decades other rabbinic decisors appear to have followed the same pattern. They held up the specter of schism but threatened it as a last resort to be implemented only in the event that the Reform movement proceed to adopt drastic innovations in areas of marital law. Thus R. Hayyim Ozer Grodzinski, who maintained that secession from a unified community was a question of policy dependent on local conditions rather than a clear-cut matter of halakhah, wrote explicitly that should Reform leaders institute certain further innovations with regard to marriage and divorce it would become necessary for the entire community to separate itself totally from adherents of Reform. But at no time was this threat carried out in practice.[57]

ENLISTMENT OF CIVIL AUTHORITIES

Yet another form of response to the activities of the nascent Reform movement involved complaints to civil authorities and efforts to secure governmental intervention in the internal religious affairs of the Jewish community. Involvement of civil authorities became an extremely sensitive matter and an area of strife in the Reform-Orthodox struggle. Attempts to involve the civil authorities were possible because not only was there no separation of Church and State in nineteenth-century Germany but also because the *kehillah* was a

---

56 Ibid., 1014. The ambivalence inherent in this position did not pass without notice by Chajes's detractors. They did not understand, or wish to understand, his inner torment. One of the most virulent of these, the Galician scholar and satirist, Joshua Heschel Schorr of Brody, who criticized Chajes's stringencies mercilessly, cites *inter alia* contradictory statements in *Minḥat Kenaʾot*: "The generation is evil and licentious" and "The danger is great" as opposed to "Praise the Lord, in Galicia they have no foothold" and "The danger is not so pressing." In a biting satire and play on the well-known *piyyut* of the evening service of the Day of Atonement "As clay in the hands of the potter," he writes of Chajes: "Behold, as the curtain in the hands of the embroiderer, at will he makes it even; at will he makes it uneven. So is the truth in the hands of this sophist. At will he makes his tongue smooth, and at will jagged." And he concludes bitingly: "A hypocrite and a chameleon is this rabbi!" See Herskovics, *Maharatz Ḥayes*, 325–26.

57 *Aḥiʿezer: Kovetz Iggerot*, ed. Aaron Suraski, vol. 1 (Bnei Brak: Netzach Press, 1970), 244–45. This "Letter Regarding the *Kehillot* in Germany" was also published in *Sefer ha-Zikaron le-Rav Weinberg*, ed. E. Hildesheimer and K. Kahana (Jerusalem: Philipp Feldheim, 1969), 9–12.

quasi-governmental body subject to regulation by the State. Moreover, the civil authorities had reason to fear every liberal movement as a potential challenge to the authoritarian nature of the State and were also motivated by a desire to preserve the religious status quo on the assumption that State-supported established religious denominations would continue to promote loyalty and submissiveness to the authority of the State.[58]

There is no gainsaying the fact that the Orthodox were prepared to enlist the cooperation of government officials in their attempt to stymie the advances of Reform. The Orthodox authorities in Berlin had no compunctions in encouraging the suspicions of Prussian government officials who, for reasons of their own, found Reform innovations unwelcome.[59] Similarly, in Breslau, R. Solomon Tiktin and his supporters did not hesitate to encourage the Prussian authorities in their investigations into Geiger's purportedly radical political activities.[60] In responsa included in *Eleh Divrei ha-Berit* one finds the suggestion of R. Eliezer of Triesch that requests be addressed to civil authorities to assist in suppression of these dangerous Reform tendencies[61] and the even more aggressive advice of R. Abraham Eliezer ha-Levi of Trieste urging that Jews in positions of influence press the authorities to harass leaders of the Reform movement relentlessly.[62] Years later, in the manifesto *Shelomei Emunei Yisra'el*, the same tactics were again advocated: "Embrace all means in your power, every legally permitted method, to defeat their counsels and to frustrate their designs." Accompanying that exhortation was the observation that the beneficent and liberal governments under whose rule Jews found themselves favored a society firmly based upon sound and well-established religious principles rather than upon the untested innovations of exponents of Reform.[63] A contemporaneous communication of the Jerusalem rabbinate was even

---

58 Cf. Robert Liberles, *Religious Conflict in Social Context: The Resurgence of Orthodox Judaism in Frankfurt am Main, 1838–1877* (Westport, CT: Greenwood Press, 1985), 12, 15, 235 n. 23, on government support of Reform in the 1830s and 1840s. See also Guttmann, *Struggle over Reform*, 97–104.

59 Michael Meyer, *Response to Modernity*, 46; and idem, "The Religious Reform Controversy in the Berlin Jewish Community, 1814–1823," *Leo Baeck Institute Year Book* 24 (1979), 139–55.

60 Max Wiener, *Abraham Geiger and Liberal Judaism: The Challenge of the Nineteenth Century*, trans. from the German by Ernst J. Schlochauer (Cincinnati: Hebrew Union College Press, 1981), 18–19.

61 *Eleh Divrei ha-Berit*, 22–24.

62 Ibid., 26.

63 Page 1 of the Hebrew text. *Voice of Jacob* 4 (1845), 136, contains an inaccurate translation.

more explicit: "Whoever has influence with the government, turn your attention to the capital in order to strengthen the breaches of the perfect Torah."[64]

Reform writers have objected that "once religion became the object of the struggle for power, those involved persuaded themselves that the end justified the means."[65] However, in point of fact, partisans of the Reform movement, when capable of doing so, sought to involve government authorities in such controversies no less so than did the Orthodox. This was the case in the election of Rabbi Akiva Eger to the chief rabbinate of Posen which was fraught with tension and conflict. Despite his unquestioned position as the preeminent talmudist of the era—or, arguably, precisely because of that status—his candidacy was vigorously contested by a group of young intellectuals who did not hesitate to make representations to government officials charging that Eger was known to be a "fanatic ... not in a position to teach pure religion and true morality" and that he "diametrically opposes the spirit of the times [and] promotes only bigotry and prejudice. ..."[66] In a deposition dated August 28, 1815, bearing the signatures of twenty-two opponents, it was contended that not only would Eger be unable to fulfil the functions of a preacher and teacher of morality as demanded by the times, but that his very presence in Posen would serve to stifle intellectual progress. Revealing their deep-seated animosity, opponents of his candidacy declared, "He will deaden any disposition toward enlightenment and culture, while the number of [Talmud] students, augmented on account of him, will contribute to the unsettling of all intelligence, will muddle the senses of the youth and thwart the true development of their spiritual potential."[67]

Even more significant is the fact that the very earliest religious reforms instituted in Westphalia were imposed upon the populace without their consent by the Consistory headed by Israel Jacobson who employed the coercive force of the secular authorities for that purpose. It is ironic that, although the Consistory specifically proscribed private services under penalty of fine and a threat that if obedience were not forthcoming "unpleasant measures of force would be necessary,"[68] Jacobson was outraged when, after the dissolution

---

64 *Shomer Tziyyon ha-Ne'eman* (*STN*), no. 10.
65 Wiener, *Abraham Geiger*, 19–20. Cf. Philipson, *The Reform Movement*, 24, 35.
66 Wreschner, "Leben and Wirken," 9–10. See also Philipp Bloch, "Die ersten Culturbestrebungen der jüdischen Gemeinde Posen unter preussischer Herrschaft," *Jubelschrift zum 70. Geburtstage von H. Graetz* (Breslau: S. Schottlaender, 1877), 200–01.
67 Wreschner, "Leben Und Wirken," 9–10.
68 *Sulamith* 4, no. 1 (1811), 366–80 (see especially sec. 43). The royal edict of July 5, 1811 imposed financial penalties on those who worshiped other than at the official synagogues. *Sulamith* 3, no. 2 (1810), 211–13. These efforts to promote standardized services evoked

of the Consistory, his own private services in Berlin were banned.[69] Later, in Hamburg, both sides vied for government support to such an extent that Gabriel Riesser was prompted to comment wryly: "The great majority of the members of our Congregation would much rather endure the displeasure of Almighty God than that of the Senate ... in which noble sentiment the Orthodox party is fully their equal."[70]

COMMUNAL STRINGENCY

Because of the relatively rapid growth of the Reform movement, many rabbinic authorities—particularly Hungarian rabbis of the school of *Hatam Sofer*— were moved to adopt an even more stringent policy with regard to any ritual change than they might have advocated under other circumstances. The phenomenon of communities in which relatively minor aesthetic innovations were swiftly followed by the adoption of full scale programs of liturgical and ritual reform reinforced the opinion of these rabbinic leaders that the wisest policy was a stance of absolute conservatism. Resistance even to insignificant changes in synagogue practice that might have been sanctioned from the vantage point of halakhah was perceived as the prudent course of action. Accordingly, a form of siege mentality prevailed under which any accommodation in matters of synagogue and ritual affairs was eschewed; Specific issues—such as location of the *bimah* in the center of the synagogue, wearing of clerical robes, performance of weddings in the synagogue, and preaching in the vernacular—regarding which there might have been legitimate differences of opinion and with regard to which permissive as well as restrictive opinions were forthcoming in other times and other places, were all decided in a restrictive manner by the vast majority of these Hungarian rabbis in order to present a united Orthodox front against innovation.

---

much resentment and the authorities were deluged with petitions for private services at least for the High Holy Days. Following repeated remonstrations, Jews in Hanover obtained the right for one private synagogue to continue to function. See Ludwig Horwitz, *Die Israeliten unter dem Königreich Westfalen* (Cassel: Calvary, 1900), 66–70. Cf. Auerbach, *Geschichte*, 140, 145–46.

69 Jacob Rader Marcus, "Israel Jacobson," *Central Conference of American Rabbis Yearbook* 38 (1928), 456, notes that "the tolerance which he refused to accord, he demanded of others. Like all men passionately engrossed in a great idea he was blind to the other man's point of view. I suspect that Jacobson, although a very witty and genial man, completely lacked a sense of humor."

70 Cited in Moshe Rinott, "Gabriel Riesser," *Leo Baeck Institute Year Book* 7 (1962), 22.

These authorities were entirely candid in enunciating the considerations underlying this policy. In a discussion of the changes instituted in the *Chorshulen* (choral synagogues),[71] R. Judah Aszod conceded that many of his interlocutors had noble intentions but warned that they erred nonetheless "as experience has taught" because the new modes of behavior "that are known as Reform" frequently began with minor matters, only for the true agenda to be revealed later. The result was the eradication of the unique characteristics of Jewish worship and the erosion of Jewish law. Therefore, concluded Rabbi Aszod, "Anyone who changes is at a disadvantage ... and this has been our uniqueness ... not to change a thing in any matter of new practice."[72] *Maharam Shik* similarly wrote, "Experience testifies unto us that as long as Israel preserved their customs there was Torah and fear [of God] among Israel and from the time that they have begun to make changes in their customs, religion has been constantly deteriorating."[73] R. Abraham Samuel Benjamin Sofer (known as *Ketav Sofer*) also wrote that instigators of Reform initially introduced relatively innocuous changes: "Not with big things did they begin, but with minor customs and enactments." It is that experience, he asserted, that evoked rabbinic resistance since the experiences of "these communities are always before our eyes."[74]

Ḥatam Sofer, asked to rule on the permissibility of moving the *bimah* from its central position, issued an unequivocal negative ruling, voicing his oft-quoted aphorism: "Innovation is forbidden by the Torah."[75] Thereafter, the issue of the location of the *bimah* was elevated by the Orthodox in Hungary to a position of a fundamental principle and became symbolic of the entire struggle

---

71 The *Chorshulen* were Orthodox synagogues that boasted male choirs with no instrumental accompaniment. The choir was derided by some as a modern innovation inconsistent with traditional practice. Advocates of the *Chorshulen* favored adaptations designed to promote decorum and aesthetically pleasing services.

72 *Teshuvot Yehudah Ya'aleh, Yoreh De'ah*, no. 39.

73 *Teshuvot Maharam Shik, Even ha-Ezer*, no. 87.

74 *Iggerot Soferim*, sec. 3, 10. See also R. Solomon Schreiber, *Ohel Leah*; published as the introduction to Rabbi Abraham Samuel Benjamin Sofer, *Sefer Ketav Sofer al ha-Torah* (Tel Aviv: Sinai Press, 1980), 27–28. R. Solomon Schreiber relates that his father, *Ketav Sofer*, declined to join forces with R. Meir Eisenstadt, author of *Teshuvot Imrei Esh*, in an organized protest against a group of radical Reform partisans. *Ketav Sofer* stated that he was not concerned with opposing radical innovators since their views would, in any event, not influence the broad masses of Hungarian Jews. He was, however, far more distressed when the innovators accepted basic halakhic premises but "were permissive with regard to rabbinic enactments and customs of Israel."

75 *Teshuvot Ḥatam Sofer, Oraḥ Ḥayyim*, no. 28.

for and against Reform. Moving the *bimah* from the center of the synagogue came to be regarded by the Orthodox as the thin edge of the wedge of Reform. Some followers of Hatam Sofer went so far as to rule that it is preferable to pray privately than to pray in a synagogue without a central *bimah*.[76] In a responsum dealing with that very question, R. Azriel Hildesheimer emphasized that it was an issue that many rabbis had raised to the level of "an obligatory battle" and hence had come to represent the much broader issue of rabbinic authority. Moreover, he noted that he had never seen this innovation instituted in a community unless they had a "spark" of Reform and, as a result, he deemed it to be a matter with regard to which rabbis should not turn a blind eye.[77] Nevertheless, others did not view this ruling as absolute: At a much later date, Rabbi Moses Feinstein wrote that the stringent attitude of Hungarian rabbis who forbade prayer in an edifice in which the *bimah* was not located in the center of the synagogue was a *hora'at sha'ah*—an ad hoc ruling promulgated as a means of stemming the tide of Reform and applicable only in that locale and at that time.[78]

Another area in which rabbis tended to extreme stringency because of these considerations was the issue of change in the nature of the *mehitzah*, or partition, between the men's and the women's sections of the synagogue. Asked whether it would be permissible to accede to a request to change a partition fashioned of wide boards for one of narrow slats "permitting people to see and be seen," *Maharam Shik*, in a strongly worded negative reply, remarked that the matter is one of gravity "especially in our generation when it might be likened to the Jewish custom regarding the shoelace, for which one is obligated to sacrifice one's life if need be" (*Sanhedrin* 74b).[79] Responding to a similar query, Rabbi Hillel Lichtenstein extended the ruling in declaring that even if there is not a single woman present in the synagogue, one may not pray there since "on account of this willful violation it has become desecrated."[80] In a discussion of laws pertaining to synagogue construction, Rabbi Hayyim of Sanz stressed that with regard to the determination of this question local custom plays a decisive role and it is therefore forbidden "to vary and build a synagogue

---

76 See the discussion in R. Zalman Sorotzkin, "Be-Iyan ha-Amadat ha-Bimah be-Emtza Bet ha-Knesset," *No'am* 5 (1961), 55–57.

77 *She'elot u-Teshuvot Rabbi Ezri'el, Yoreh De'ah*, no. 20.

78 *Iggerot Mosheh, Orah Hayyim*, vol. 2, nos. 41, 42. Elisha S. Ancselovits, in his unpublished paper "The Boundaries within which Traditional Judaism Faced Modernity: Part I, Opposition to the Relocation of the Bimah and Wedding Ceremony," examines several other sources relating to this topic.

79 *Teshuvot Maharam Shik, Orah Hayyim*, no. 77.

80 *Teshuvot Bet Hillel*, no. 104.

in a fashion other than in accordance with the custom that we have always followed in this country." R. Hayyim of Sanz also added the comment that this is a matter regarding which the talmudic ruling requiring martyrdom for violation of even the most minor of Jewish customs is applicable.[81]

In other countries and at a later date other halakhic issues became the rallying point in the struggle again sectarian practices. In the United States a major issue in the early part of the twentieth century was that of mixed pews. That, however, was an issue involving an unequivocal breach of halakhah. In his written comments on this matter—one of the rare occasions on which he expressed his views in writing—Rabbi Joseph B. Soloveitchik declared that a synagogue that adopts mixed seating forfeits its sanctity and that one should forego *tefillah be-tzibbur* even on the High Holy Days rather than pray in such a synagogue. He, too, ruled that organized hostility toward religious practices requires a "heroic stand" even in matters involving a minor custom:

> I know beforehand the reaction to my letter on the part of our apostles of religious "modernism" and "utilitarianism." They will certainly say that since a great majority of the recently constructed synagogues have abandoned separated seating, we must not be out of step with the masses. This type of reasoning could well be employed with regard to other religious precepts, such as the observance of Sabbath, or the dietary laws. However, we must remember that an ethical or Halachic principle decreed by God is not rendered void by the fact that the people refuse to abide by it. ... The greater the difficulty, the more biting the ridicule and sarcasm, and the more numerous the opponent then the holier is the principle, and the more sacred is our duty to defend it. In my opinion, the Halachic dictum, *bishe'ath gezerath ha-malchuth afillu mitzvah kallah kegon le-shinuye arketha de-mesana, yehareg ve-al ya'abor* [at a time of religious persecution through governmental decree, even for a minor custom, such as involving changing a shoelace, let one suffer death sooner than transgress it] (Sanhedrin 74b), requiring of us a heroic stand in times of adversity, applies not only to political or religious persecution originated from some pagan ruler, but also to situations in which a small number of God-fearing and Torah-loyal people is confronted with a hostile attitude on the part of the majority dominated by a false philosophy.[82]

---

81 *Teshuvot Divrei Ḥayyim, Oraḥ Ḥayyim*, no. 18.
82 "Message to a Rabbinic Convention," *The Sanctity of the Synagogue*, ed. Baruch Litvin (New York: The Spero Foundation, 1959), 110–11.

It is important to note that even those authorities who ruled permissively with regard to some of these matters were aware of the need for extreme caution because of the nature of the controversy with Reform. Thus, in his discussion of the relatively moderate innovations introduced in the *Chorshulen*, R. Tzevi Hirsch Chajes was careful to state that, in themselves, those changes did not, strictly speaking, constitute halakhic violations. Chajes clearly expressed his approval of sermons in the vernacular and the elimination of *piyyutim* as modifications that serve to enhance decorum during the services. He, however, cautioned against excessive expenditure for synagogue edifices and added the halakhic ruling that architectural designs that consciously simulate church architecture are forbidden by Jewish law. He included in that category the bells placed on several synagogues in Germany for the purpose of summoning worshippers to services—an innovation first instituted in the Temple of Jacob inaugurated by Israel Jacobson in Seesen in 1810.[83] However, elsewhere Chajes was careful to point out the manner in which even permissible innovations should be introduced, and cautioned that sensationalism and publicity must be avoided in order to prevent confusion on the part of the untutored masses. Enumerating customs that can and should be modified in synagogue practices—for example, sale of Torah honors and recitation of some of the *piyyutim*, which are essentially impermissible interpolations in the blessings of the *Shema*—he noted that such practices were abrogated by individual rabbis in certain areas of Poland and Russia and that quarrels or divisiveness had not ensued. Chajes attributed this to the fact that these changes were instituted without publicity, formal gatherings, or public announcements. He stated that with reference to innovations or changes in ritual, it is of paramount importance to recognize that gatherings and fanfare are generally harmful for a number of reasons but primarily because the untutored masses are unable to distinguish between customs that have the force of law and mere folkways. If folkways are abrogated, the ignorant may mistakenly conclude that the law can also be altered arbitrarily. For this reason, explained Chajes, the Sages counsel conservatism and caution with regard to changing any aspect of synagogue practice. He also contended that customs and practices pertaining to the synagogue and communal life have a certain spiritual power and serve to strengthen bonds of solidarity and feelings of national pride among the scattered Jewish people.[84] For that reason one must exercise exceeding caution with respect to

---

83 Chajes, *Minḥat Kena'ot*, 990–91. Cf. also *infra*, chapter 9, n. 142.
84 Tzevi Hirsch Chajes, *Darkei Hora'ah*, chaps. 6 and 7 in *Kol Sifrei*, vol. 1, 238–42.

their observance; vigilance is necessary lest divisiveness be created and "the people thereby become sundered in half."[85]

THE NONOBSERVANT AS INDIVIDUALS

Changing sociological realities prompted rabbinic authorities to undertake a fundamental reassessment of certain time-hallowed distinctions. Although rabbinic authorities reacted with stringency to ritual innovations even remotely akin to those advocated by exponents of Reform, their response to lapses in observance on the part of individuals was far more tolerant. There was even an underlying feeling of sympathy for the plight of those whose deficiencies in observance were motivated by economic hardship. Increasingly large numbers of individuals no longer conformed to Orthodox standards of religious and ritual observance.[86] Confronted with this fact, many authorities drew a crucial distinction between individuals whose deviation from religious practice was prompted by economic considerations, or was born of ignorance, and those whose nonobservance was the result of an ideological metamorphosis.

This distinction was enunciated and justified in halakhic categories in a seminal responsum authored by Rabbi Jacob Ettlinger.[87] In talmudic sources the status of a "*mumar* with regard to the entire Torah," a person who rejects the commandments of the Torah in their entirety, is tantamount to that of an apostate. The Gemara (*Ḥullin* 5a) declares that one who desecrates the Sabbath in public is to be regarded as a "*mumar* with regard to the entire Torah." Rashi, *ad locum*, elucidates this categorization by noting that public desecration of the Sabbath, *ipso facto*, constitutes denial of the divine role in creation of the universe. In publicly rejecting his obligation with regard to Sabbath observance the transgressor denies both God as Creator and the veracity of the biblical account of creation. Hence the Sabbath-desecrator is a "*mumar* with regard to the entire Torah."

The novel socio-religious phenomenon of otherwise devout and believing Sabbath-desecrators prompted Ettlinger to a reassessment of the implications of such desecration. Although he appended a caveat declaring that his

---

85 Ibid., 242.
86 See Salo W. Baron, "The Modern Age," in *Great Ages and Ideas of the Jewish People*, ed. Leo W. Schwartz (New York: Random House, 1956), 363–64. Baron notes that as early as 1770 an anonymous writer (Mordecai van Aron de Pinto) urged abolition of the Sabbath and holidays for economic considerations.
87 *Binyan Tziyyon he-Ḥadashot*, no. 23.

discussion was only theoretical in nature and not intended as a normative ruling, Ettlinger noted that the Sabbath-desecrators of his day could hardly be categorized as heretics:

> However, as to Jewish sinners of our time I do not know how to consider them. ... For because of the multitude of our sins the sore has spread greatly, to such an extent that for most of them the desecration of the Sabbath has become like a permissible act. ... There are those among them who offer Sabbath prayers and recite the *kiddush* and then violate the Sabbath. ... The Sabbath desecrator is considered a *mumar* only because, by denying the Sabbath, he denies the creation and the Creator. But this man acknowledges them by his prayer and *kiddush*. And certainly their sons who arise in their places, who neither know nor have heard of Sabbath ordinances, are like ... children taken captive. ...

Ettlinger believed that the motives prompting many of his contemporaries to become lax in religious observance were economic rather than ideological in nature. Yet, although he was not prepared to regard the masses as heretics, he nevertheless emphasized that this liberal stance could not be extended to encompass those individuals who flagrantly rejected fundamental dogmas of Judaism. Accordingly, he declared that his ruling could not be regarded as applicable in instances in which "it is clear to us that [the individual] is aware of the Sabbath laws and yet audaciously desecrates the Sabbath in the presence of ten assembled Jews, for such a person is comparable to an absolute mumar. ..."[88]

The practical consequences of the ruling were significant. Although Ettlinger presented this decision only as a theoretical hypothesis (*she-lo le-halakhah le-ma'aseh*), it soon became standard practice to count Sabbath-desecrators as members of the quorum for public prayer and to accord them the privilege of being called to the Reading of the Law. Neither practice could have been permitted other than on the basis of a rationale similar to that advanced by Ettlinger. To this day, when pressed for a defense of such practices, rabbinic authorities invariably reply with a citation to this responsum. Of particular

---

88 In the United States, R. Abraham Rice affirmed the position that Sabbath desecrators should not be called to the Torah and when his opinion could no longer prevail he ruled that one should not answer "Amen" to the blessings recited by a Sabbath desecrator. This unpopular stance aroused much dissension. See Israel Tabak, "Rabbi Abraham Rice of Baltimore," *Tradition* 7, no. 2 (Summer 1965), 107–108.

interest arc the permissive rulings of R. David Zevi Hoffmann[89] and, more recently, of the late R. Moses Feinstein,[90] both of which cite Ettlinger as precedent.

The reasoning underlying this pivotal halakhic decision is also reflected in a basic theological distinction formulated by Ettlinger. In several passages in his homiletical-exegetical work, *Minḥat Ani*, he draws a sharp distinction between individuals who have abandoned observance for pragmatic and financial reasons and those whose rejection of mitzvot is predicated upon ideological considerations. In his commentary on *Be-Ha'alotekha* Ettlinger states:

> For there are two categories of transgressors, [there are] transgressors by virtue of [human] nature, those who do not overcome their passions but in their hearts believe in the Torah and the commandments and there are sinners … who sin not on account of desire, but because they do not believe in the Torah and deny its commandments. The distinction between these two [categories], in which there may be discerned the origin of their transgression, is if they only sin to transgress a negative commandment so that they do not put a rein on their passions to guard against forbidden pleasures, but they observe the positive commandments which are not contrary to their passions. In this it may be recognized that they believe in the Torah. However, if not only do they sin in transgressing negative commandments, but also do not observe the positive commandments of the Torah, this indicates that they deny the Torah.[91]

Individuals who desecrated the Sabbath for material gain, but nevertheless participated in rituals associated with Sabbath observance (e.g., the recitation of *kiddush*) were, according to Ettlinger's analysis, to be regarded as "transgressors by virtue of [human] nature," but not as heretics. It is to the status of such individuals that Ettlinger's halakhic ruling was addressed.

It was Ettlinger's contention that a considerable number of those who were attracted to the Reform movement were individuals whose motivation was primarily economic or social in nature. Accordingly, they sought to

---

89 *Melamed le-Ho'il, Oraḥ Ḥayyim*, no. 29

90 *Iggerot Mosheh, Even ha-Ezer*, vol. 2, no. 20. Rabbi Feinstein disagrees with Ettlinger's line of reasoning but reaches the same conclusion on different grounds. See also ibid., *Oraḥ Ḥayyim*, vol. l, no. 33. Cf. the discussion of these responsa in Samuel Morrell, "The Halachic Status of non-Halachic Jews," *Judaism* 18 (June 1969), 455–57.

91 Rabbi Jacob Ettlinger, *Minḥat Ani* (Jerusalem, 1963), 91a.

disregard those commandments which might lead to financial hardship or create embarrassment in association with non-Jews. Ettlinger underscored the need to differentiate between individuals whose intent was merely "to ease the yoke of Torah according to the needs of the times" and individuals who denied the divinity of the Torah and rejected its basic doctrines.[92] Those whose transgression was motivated by passion could more readily be guided back to the path of Torah.[93]

While many who assimilated were indeed motivated by social or economic considerations and the desire for material success that appeared to them to be contingent upon acculturation and loss of ethnic distinctiveness, there were a growing number of individuals whose nonobservance was founded upon an intellectual rejection of the fundamentals of faith. It was this latter group to whom rabbinic figures found it much more difficult to relate. Although Ettlinger presumed that the vast majority of the nonobservant were motivated by materialistic concerns, he nevertheless cautioned that even those individuals who were motivated by heretical views and who must be deemed to be "total transgressors" were not to be written off as hopelessly lost to Judaism.[94] But, as will be shown, it was his disciples who were to turn their energies to that segment of the nonobservant population.

NONOBSERVANT CLERGY

The celebrated Geiger-Tiktin controversy constituted one of the earliest clashes between proponents of the nascent Reform movement and the traditional establishment. With the election of Abraham Geiger in 1838 as a rabbinic colleague of the aged Solomon Tiktin, the Breslau *kehillah* became embroiled in a protracted and acrimonious dispute over rabbinic leadership. Although the conflict eventually culminated in an uneasy truce, by no means were its reverberations stilled. Over one hundred and eighty years later, the issues raised in that controversy still divide the Jewish community and are the basis of dissension and discord among the various factions and segments of our people in the Diaspora as well as in the State of Israel.

While champions of Geiger have portrayed the struggle as a battle on behalf of the principle of freedom of thought,[95] the crucial issue at stake was

---

92 Ibid., 39b.

93 Ibid., 130b-131a. Cf. ibid., 110a-111a.

94 Ibid., 91b.

95 Philipson, *The Reform Movement*, 60.

the question "Who is a rabbi?" Under dispute was not Geiger's scholarship, talents, or abilities, but whether or not he could properly claim the right to exercise rabbinic authority or, more accurately, whether the incumbent rabbi, Solomon Tiktin, was acting correctly in refusing to serve with Geiger lest he thereby legitimate Geiger's position as a "rabbi and teacher in Israel."

At the time, writing in defense of Geiger, David Einhorn declared that departure from observance of ceremonial laws when prompted by sincere conviction does not render an individual unfit to hold rabbinic office.[96] Not surprisingly, a diametrically opposite view had been enunciated earlier by Rabbi Akiva Eger in a letter to residents of Eisenach in which he declared categorically that the mantle of rabbinic authority may not be donned by any and all. There are clear limitations upon who may be recognized as a rabbinic decisor. Responding to a detailed query, Rabbi Akiva Eger stated unequivocally that the halakhic decisions of an individual who does not himself abide by the strictures of both biblical and rabbinic law have no binding force whatsoever. Quite simply, Rabbi Akiva Eger argues, such an individual's conduct is governed by one of two motives; in either event he is unfit for rabbinic office. Either he lacks the requisite knowledge or he is knowledgeable but does not accept talmudic law as normative. If he is ignorant, how can he presume to issue legal rulings? If he is knowledgeable but knowingly repudiates talmudic law, how can he be regarded as a rabbinic decisor?[97] The view articulated by Rabbi Eger reflects the attitude of the Orthodox vis-à-vis sectarian clergy[98] that prevails to this very day.

CONCERN FOR UNITY

Contemporary attacks on the Orthodox community focus on Orthodox intransigence with regard to questions of personal status and call the Orthodox community to task for a lack of concern for the unity of kelal Yisra'el. Ironically, in Eleh Divrei ha-Berit the strongest and most penetrating criticism of the

---

96 Ibid., 70.

97 Iggerot Soferim, sec. 1, 51.

98 On clergy who differ in their theological views or who, even if observant, identify with non-Orthodox denominations see R. Moses Feinstein, Iggerot Mosheh, Even ha-Ezer, vol. l, no. 135; Even ha-Ezer, vol. 2, no. 17; Even ha-Ezer, vol 3, no. 3; Even ha-Ezer, vol. 4, no. 13, sec. 3, and no. 78; Yoreh De'ah, vol 1, no. 160; Yoreh De'ah, vol. 2, nos. 125, 128; Yoreh De'ah, vol. 3, no. 77; Rabbi Aaron Soloveichik, "Teshuvah be-Inyan Mikveh," Ha-Darom 55 (Elul 1986), 15–30; and idem, "Be-Inyan Kiddushei Shomranim," Ha-Pardes 61, no. 2 (November 1986), 8–19.

Hamburg Reform leadership is couched in identical terms. They were taken to task for instituting innovations that effectively shattered the cohesiveness and unity of the Jewish community:

> Why have you separated yourselves from the community? ... What benefit will accrue to you if you separate from the community and from the entire body politic of the people? ... It will be devastating for generations to come. ...[99]

A similar argument was formulated by an Orthodox rabbinic writer in the United States. Writing in *The Occident* in 1845, Rabbi Abraham Rice penned an eloquent plea for unity:

> The only and legitimate pride which the Jew bears in his heart is, that with us there are no sects, that the Jew in the East is like the one who lives in the West—that the religion in the South must be as it is in the North. This unity may be lost through a single ill-advised alteration; every ignorant man would daringly attempt to modify the religion according to the notions of his feeble intellect; and there would arise a multitude of sects without any parallel. But no! O God, Thy name is one and thy people Israel will remain one.[100]

The late Eugene Borowitz, a prominent contemporary Reform writer, candidly conceded that classical exponents of Reform did not regard unity as a paramount value:

> Had *Kelal Yisrael* been our most significant concern we could never have brought Progressive Judaism into being, for its creation seriously divided the Jewish community by defying the accepted community leadership and the established traditions of our people.[101]

Yet, more often rabbinic writers were placed on the defensive and accused of being those responsible for rendering Jewish unity a nullity since they would not compromise with regard to issues of Jewish law that threatened

---

99 *Eleh Divrei ha-Berit*, 92.
100 Rabbi Abraham Rice, "Erroneous Doctrines," *The Occident* 2 (1844–45), 471.
101 Eugene Borowitz, "Co-existing with Orthodox Jews," *Journal of Reform Judaism* 34, no. 3 (Summer 1981), 57.

to split the Jewish people asunder. An incisive response to these frequently voiced accusations may be found in *Minḥat Ani*, in comments on the scriptural portion of *Pinḥas*. Ettlinger asserted that although unity is a fundamental value and a prerequisite for divine redemption, it is but one value among many:

> If you see that there are rebellious individuals who wish to destroy your Torah, then it is the time to act for the Lord, to wage the war of the Lord against them.... And he who wages the war of the Lord against the heretics should not restrain himself on account of a false argument that peace is great and it is better to grasp in friendship anyone who may be termed a Jew than to create a separation of hearts ... and the reason for this is that although peace between man and man is great, nevertheless, even better is peace between Israel and their Father in Heaven. Therefore, he who avenges the vengeance of the Lord to strengthen the Torah, he is the one who desires peace and seeks it diligently.[102]

This principle is evidenced in the narrative of Phineas. In avenging the Lord, Phineas killed a prince of the tribe of Simeon and was nevertheless rewarded with the covenant of peace. Scripture states, "Behold, I give unto him my covenant of peace" (Numbers 25:12), and the Midrash adds, "it is indeed just (*be-din hu*) that he receive his reward ... My covenant of peace."[103] Although Phineas's action seemingly fostered dissension and aroused the antagonism of an entire tribe, ultimately this very action brought peace between the Almighty and Israel. Therefore, *Minḥat Ani* concludes, the Midrash uses the expression "it is indeed just (*be-din hu*)" with reference to Phineas's reward.[104]

Similarly, in his essay "Phineas–Eliyahu," Samson Raphael Hirsch emphasized that the covenant of everlasting priesthood was granted to Phineas for demonstrating by means of his zeal that there are values that supersede unity and peace:

> God has promised His true peace not to weakness, the weak acquiescence which allows events to take their course, which is bold only where there is no resistance and will advocate the good cause only when it meets with general approval and needs no defenders; He has not promised the

---

102 Ettlinger, *Minḥat Ani*, 106a.
103 *Bamidbar Rabbah* 21:1.
104 Ettlinger, *Minḥat Ani*, 104b–105a.

covenant of His rule to those who proclaim "peace, peace at any price."
He has promised it to those whose highest and ultimate aim is true peace
in Heaven and on earth. He has promised it to the zeal of Phineas, to the
very man who is assailed by all the zealous adherents of a false peace as if
he were a disturber of the peace; to him who in the name of God opposes
every mocking departure from the law of God, the only power before
which everyone has to bow; to him whose aim is to assert for the Law of
God the sole rule over the acts and consciences of men.[105]

The compromise of other values is too high a price to pay for unity and
there do exist overriding concerns in the face of which the ideal of unity must
be swept aside.

SECESSION

In the last decades of the nineteenth century, German Orthodoxy became
embroiled in an internal dispute which, in essence, involved a judgment of the
extent to which communal unity could be preserved when it came into conflict with ideological principle. The most radical response to the emergence of
Reform institutions was the policy of secession adopted and vigorously advocated by Samson Raphael Hirsch.[106] The Jewish community in each city was
organized as a *kehillah* recognized by the government and supported primarily by a tax earmarked for religious purposes, which was levied upon Jew and
Christian alike. The governing board of the *kehillah* was responsible for the
administration of religious, educational, social, and philanthropic institutions
and organizations. The establishment of Reform institutions under the aegis
of the *kehillah* evoked a reaction from Hirsch demanding that the Orthodox
withdraw from the *kehillah* and establish their own independent institutions.

---

105 Samson Raphael Hirsch, *Judaism Eternal*, trans. I. Grunfeld (London: Soncino Press,
1959), 2:293.
106 See the valuable discussion in Liberles, *Religious Conflict*, 165–226. It is commonly assumed
that separation as a policy of the Orthodox community began in the 1870s with Hirsch. In
fact, the idea of autonomous religious communities each practicing Judaism in accordance
with its own dictates dates from an earlier period and was viewed as a desideratum by exponents of Reform. Thus in the 1830s Abraham Geiger maintained that the only manner in
which the Reform movement could move forward at a suitable pace was by obtaining
permission to form autonomous religious organizations apart from the general community.
See Abraham Geiger, *Nachgelassene Schriften*, vol. 5 (Berlin, 1878), 54–55; and Wiener,
Abraham Geiger, 99–100.

Hirsch contended that membership in the communal organization constituted a form of endorsement or, *de minimis*, conferred legitimacy upon the ideological positions espoused by the institutions sponsored by the *kehillah*. Accordingly, Hirsch asserted that halakhah forbids such endorsement or conferral of legitimacy and hence ruled that formal association with any organization that denies the fundamental principles of Judaism is forbidden. It must be noted that in formulating this position Hirsch emphasized that his policy demanded, not disassociation from individuals, but secession from a communal system that he viewed as an institutionalized expression of heresy.[107]

However, as a practical matter, Hirsch was unable to act on his convictions immediately. Under German law, registration and membership in the local *kehillah* was automatic and a Jew could renounce membership only upon conversion to Christianity or upon a declaration that he was *konfessionslos* (without religion), a declaration that was widely regarded as tantamount to a renunciation of Judaism. Hirsch correctly considered this law to be an interference with the fundamental principle of freedom of religious conscience. As long as the law remained in effect the members of Hirsch's community had no choice but to retain their compulsory membership in the umbrella *kehillah* even after forming the autonomous *Israelitische Religionsgesellschaft*.

In 1873 the Prussian Parliament promulgated a law that enabled Christians of different denominations to disassociate themselves from the established church and to form their own religious communities. For Hirsch, passage of this law was the harbinger of a new era and signaled the possibility of establishing an independent and proud community that would be able to tap additional sources of revenue to be utilized in achieving enhanced spiritual and communal accomplishments.[108] To Hirsch, secession was a logical step

---

107 *Offener Brief an Sr. Ehrwürden Herrn Distrikts-Rabbiner S. B. Bamberger in Würzburg* (Frankfurt am Main: L. Kaufmann, 1877), 6ff. This letter was included in *Gesammelte Schriften von Rabb. Samson Raphael Hirsch* (Frankfurt am Main: I. Kaufmann, 1908), 4: 316–43. An English translation of this document as well as of Bamberger's response and Hirsch's counterreply may be found in Samson Raphael Hirsch, *The Collected Writings*, vol. 6: *Jewish Communal Life and Independent Orthodoxy* (New York and Jerusalem: Philipp Feldheim, 1990), 198–317.

108 In the implementation of a policy such as secession, the sociological realities are often more dispositive than the theoretical or philosophical arguments. Liberles (*Religious Conflict*) quite correctly underscores the fact that secession was not "the cause of the strengthening of Orthodoxy in Germany.... Rather it was an expression of that strength." He concludes: All Orthodox leaders including Bamberger welcomed the law of separation, but only Hirsch approached it from a perspective of strength. For the others it was a guarantee of minority rights; for Hirsch it represented the right to be fully independent; ... for Hirsch,

since he was sincerely convinced that "within none of the Christian churches is there a deeper cleavage than between Reform Judaism ... and Orthodox traditional Judaism."[109] Hirsch immediately began to lobby for a similar right to be granted to Jewish citizens. With the assistance of an influential statesman, Eduard Lasker, Hirsch finally succeeded in this endeavor. On July 28, 1876, the Prussian Parliament passed the Law of Secession granting Jews the right to withdraw from the organized community without renouncing Judaism and the concomitant right to form independent Jewish communities.

Following promulgation of the Law of Secession, Hirsch urged his congregants to secede from the established Jewish community of Frankfurt since it was now legally permissible for them to belong to the Orthodox community exclusively. Some congregants followed Hirsch's directive; however, a large number elected to remain within the general *kehillah* as well. To a large extent it was the relative newcomers to Frankfurt who followed Hirsch unconditionally while members of many of the older Frankfurt families who had a deep attachment to the historic *kehillah* and its institutions chose to maintain dual membership. Many of the latter were particularly loath to surrender their burial rights in the communal cemetery in which their forebears were interred.[110]

A very tense situation developed within the Frankfurt community, a situation that became exacerbated when the renowned Rabbi S. B. Bamberger of Würzburg issued a ruling supporting the decision of those who chose to remain

---

emancipation was an opportunity. In that he was unique, as early as 1836 and as late as 1877. [pp. 225ff.]

109 *Denkschrift über die Judenfrage in dem Gesetz betreffend den Austritt aus der Kirche* (Berlin, 1873), 6. The essay was published anonymously but later included in Hirsch's *Gesammelte Schriften*, vol. 4 (Frankfurt am Main: I. Kaufmann, 1908), 250–65.

110 See Liberles, *Religious Conflict*, 215–17. Of interest are analyses and reminiscences of the events in Frankfurt contained in *Historia Judaica* 10, no. 2 (October 1948). In three articles—[Saemy Japhet], "The Secession of the Frankfurt Community under Samson Raphael Hirsch" (100–22); Isaac Heinemann, "Supplementary Remarks on the Secession from the Frankfurt Community under Samson Raphael Hirsch" (123–34); and Jacob Rosenheim, "Historical Significance of the Struggle for Secession from the Frankfurt Jewish Community" (135–46)—the developments in Frankfurt are discussed by natives of the city who were intimately involved in its communal affairs. All three accounts provide intriguing background data but are highly subjective. An insight into Hirsch's thinking on secession and into the distinctions in approach between Hirsch and Hildesheimer may be obtained from the exchange of correspondence in Ezriel Hildesheimer, "Mi-toch Ḥiluf ha-Mikhtavim beyn Maran R. Ezri'el Hildesheimer Zatzal u-beyn Maran R. Shimshon Raphael Hirsch Zatzal u-Mekoravav," in *Yad Sha'ul: Sefer Zikaron al Shem ha-Rav Dr. Sha'ul Weingort*, ed. J. J. Weinberg and P. Biberfeld (Tel Aviv, 1952), 233–5.

within the general *kehillah*.[111] Much of the material contained in Bamberger's rebuttal of Hirsch's position, although intriguing and of weighty halakhic import, is a *non sequitur*. The only salient point is a fundamental and empirical disagreement with regard to whether continued participation in the *kehillah* did, or did not, constitute endorsement and legitimization of the views and policies espoused by institutions supported by the *kehillah*. Bamberger contended that the nature of the association with the Frankfurt *kehillah* was such that continued membership could not be construed as legitimization of heresy.

However, Bamberger was prepared to endorse retention of membership in the *kehillah* only in circumstances in which the Orthodox would be granted total autonomy in conducting the affairs of their own synagogues and religious organizations. As late as February 1877 he endorsed Hirsch's call for secession in Frankfurt[112] and reversed his position only when such autonomy was guaranteed by the *kehillah*. With regard to other communities in which the fundamental demands of the Orthodox were not granted, Bamberger ruled unequivocally that secession was not merely permissible but mandatory. In a responsum concerning the question of secession, Bamberger's son Simchah notes explicitly that only when the specified conditions were met did his father "agree that there is no obligation to separate from the Reform congregation in accordance with his reasoning. However, when these considerations are absent, his opinion has been recorded three and four times, namely, in the

---

111 Rabbi S. B. Bamberger, *Offene Antwort auf den an ihn gerichteten offenen Brief des Herrn S. R. Hirsch* (Würzburg: J. Frankschen Buchhandlung, 1877). The sole rabbinic personality of stature to oppose Hirsch was Bamberger. Citation of Ettlinger's view by R. Zevi Yehudah Kook as recorded in *Hatzofeh*, December 29, 1972, is an obvious error of fact since at the time of the dispute between Hirsch and Bamberger over secession, Ettlinger was no longer alive. The rejoinder of David Henshke, "Maḥloket le-Shem Shamayim," *Ha-Ma'ayan* 13, no. 4 (1973), 41–51, is very much to the point. Henshke also cites a similar error in Judah Leib Maimon, *Ha-Ra'iyah* (Jerusalem, Mossad ha-Rav Kook, 1965), 123.

In a communication to Bamberger urging the latter to reverse his ruling regarding the Frankfurt community, *Maharam Shik* (*Teshuvot Maharam Shik, Oraḥ Ḥayyim*, no. 306) conceded that Hirsch had overstated the case in condemning as sinners those who did not join the secessionists since there were many devout individuals who hesitated to take that step for reasons that were entirely sociological in nature. *Maharam Shik* expressed his personal view, confirmed by his own experience, that, quite apart from the halakhic considerations involved in the question of secession, continued association with the nonobservant in a common *kehillah* structure would, in the course of time, prove deleterious. Furthermore, he stated that he was the recipient of a "tradition" handed down by *Ḥatam Sofer* that one should "distance oneself as much as possible from them and their cohorts and not be in one association with them."

112 Bamberger, *Offene Antwort*, 14.

matter of Karlsruhe, Vienna, Wiesbaden and Frankfurt, that it is incumbent upon the law-abiding to separate themselves from the Reform congregation."[113]

Later, after concessions had been granted to the Orthodox community in Frankfurt assuring them of autonomy in matters of religious practice, Bamberger ruled that *Austritt* (secession) was not mandatory in that community under the then prevailing circumstances. However, he did not view *Austritt* to be either forbidden or repugnant. He simply recognized the cogency of the familial, social, and emotional motives for remaining within the *kehillah*. While he fully recognized that remaining in the *kehillah* would minimize divisiveness within the community and provide opportunities for positive influence over others, he did not raise continued association to the level of an ideological imperative. Not so the leaders of the Frankfurt *kehillah*. For them secession was a breach of the unity of the community and unity was not only a cardinal principle but one with regard to which there could be no disagreement. Although tolerant of diverse theological positions with regard to all fundamentals of Jewish faith and practice, they regarded unity as the one dogma to which all must subscribe: "There will be no end to sectarianism if every tiny faction which does not agree with the forms recognized by the majority has the right, on that account, to withdraw from the whole."[114] Later, they wrote, "The religion of the majority alone, according to the principles of Judaism, is the true and legitimate religion."[115]

From that point on, the German Orthodox community was sharply divided. Following Hirsch's policy of *Trennungsorthodoxie* (separatist Orthodoxy) Jewish communities in several cities, notably those of Berlin, Wiesbaden, Darmstadt, and Mainz, established separatist Orthodox congregations. On the other hand, a large segment of Orthodoxy, whose position was considerably strengthened by Bamberger's sanction, chose to administer their own Orthodox institutions under the auspices of the overall community. Proponents of the latter policy, which came to be known as *Gemeindeorthodoxie* (communal Orthodoxy), established such communal arrangements in many towns, notably in Berlin, Cologne, Frankfurt,

---

113 *Teshuvot Zekher Simḥah*, 230. Republished in Rabbi S. Bamberger, *Teshuvot Yad ha-Levi*, vol. 2 (Jerusalem, 1972). For a fuller analysis of Bamberger's position as well as of other considerations reflected in both sides of the dispute, see my "The Frankfurt Secession Controversy," *Jewish Action* 52, no. 1 (Winter 1991–92), 22–27, 51–52.

114 From a memorandum of the Frankfurt *kehillah* board to the city Senate in 1854, cited by Liberles, *Religious Conflict*, 179.

115 From a memorandum of the Frankfurt *kehillah* board to the city Senate in 1858, ibid.

Hamburg, and Breslau.[116] Frequently, the very threat of secession appears to have had a significant effect in prompting the *kehillah* to accommodate the concerns of the Orthodox.[117] Certainly this was the case in Frankfurt itself where the various concessions granted the Orthodox within the *kehillah* were surely the result of the desire to limit the number who seceded. This rift within Orthodoxy did not heal with time and the two camps remained separate and distinct until the Holocaust decimated German Jewry.

Much has been written regarding the respective merits and failings of both approaches. The separatists have been taken to task for engendering a tragic waste of resources and for promoting divisiveness and disharmony. Hirsch's defenders, on the other hand, have maintained that were it not for the Law of Secession and the viable option of establishing autonomous Orthodox communities even *Gemeindeorthodoxie* would have been unable to wrest any concession from the general communities which were dominated by Reform elements. Very much to the point are the remarks of the Lithuanian rabbinic authority Rabbi Hayyim Ozer Grodzinski. R. Grodzinski hesitated to offer a

---

116 Despite the wealth of analytic comment in Noah Rosenbloom's *Tradition in an Age of Reform: The Religious Philosophy of Samson Raphael Hirsch* (Philadelphia: Jewish Publication Society, 1976), that work is marred by a partisanship that moves the author to interpret objective data in a manner that is not compelling. In particular, Rosenbloom's account of the controversy over secession is flawed. Rosenbloom is certainly entitled to regard secession as having been an unwise policy. But labeling Hirsch's action as "heedlessness" (p. 117) is hardly an appropriate designation if Hirsch believed he was "heeding" a higher imperative. The portrayal of those in other communities who followed Hirsch's secessionist policy as "malcontents" is also entirely unsupported and without basis in fact. Rosenbloom writes, "As expected, Hirsch's action was emulated by malcontents in other communities in Germany, such as Baden, Karlsruhe, Darmstadt, Wiesbaden, Giessen, Cologne, Bingen and Strassburg" (p. 119). The implication that those who—correctly or misguidedly— followed this policy were misanthropic, dyspeptic individuals, unhappy because of petty concerns or jealousies, can only reflect an unscholarly bias.

117 Although, as noted above (n. 108), Liberles maintains that the Law of Secession was a manifestation of the strength of the Orthodox, its enactment certainly served to enhance that strength (cf. Liberles, *Religious Conflict*, 211). While the situation in Austria was not identical to that in Germany, the threat of *Austritt* served to curb radical Reform tendencies in that country as well. The Austrian government rejected a petition presented by the Orthodox members of the *Schiffschul* in 1872 for permission to secede and form a separate community. Nevertheless, the possibility that the Orthodox might eventually obtain such permission and act upon it influenced Vienna's Jewish communal leaders to desist from introducing ideological reforms in the communal synagogues. See Marsha L Rozenblit, "The Struggle Over Religious Reform in Nineteenth-Century Vienna," *AJS Review* 14, no. 2 (Fall 1989), 209–21. Significantly, Rozenblit demonstrates that the fear of loss of tax revenue was an important factor in the ultimate decision (219).

definitive opinion with regard to what he viewed as a dispute whose resolution was contingent upon familiarity with the details of the local situation and subsequent determination of the wisest course of action under the circumstances, but nevertheless declared that in his opinion Hirsch's action was necessary for the preservation of Orthodoxy:

> There is no doubt that the sage and saint Rabbi S. R. Hirsch, of blessed memory ... did a great thing in founding the admirable and outstanding *Religionsgesellschaft* which became an exemplary Jewish community. Had the God-fearing not separated themselves by means of a separate *kehillah*, due to their minority status they would have become submerged within the general community—[a development] which did not occur when they separated and developed on their own. Then even the general community was forced to improve itself and to conduct the general institutions in a sacred manner.[118]

Whatever arguments may be presented in favor, or in criticism, of the wisdom and value of Hirsch's policy, several important points must be emphasized in the interests of historical accuracy. Hirsch's argument against enforced membership in, and taxation on behalf of, an overall religious superstructure was based upon considerations of freedom of conscience and infringement of basic civil liberties. Freedom of religion, argued Hirsch, entails not only freedom to desist from a form of worship which runs counter to an individual's convictions, but also freedom to refrain from actively supporting such forms of worship and the propagation of theological tenets offensive to a person's convictions. Thus, Hirsch claimed that the legal right of secession was based upon the fundamental principle of freedom of religious conscience which includes an individual's right to form his own independent community.

It is a distortion of fact to contend that Hirsch's practical policy of separation from the larger Jewish community was indicative of a lack of concern for individuals who did not accept the teachings of traditional Judaism.[119] Hirsch's *Nineteen Letters*, published in 1836, and a significant portion of his subsequent writings were addressed precisely to the questing and the nonobservant. Ultimately, the policy of separatism did in fact lead to an attitude of introversion and to an unfortunate erosion of interest in the well-being and welfare of the wider community.

---

118 *Aḥi'ezer: Kovetz Iggerot*, 1:243.
119 See the discussion in David Henshke, "Maḥloket le-Shem Shamayim," 44–47.

However, Hirsch himself cannot be faulted on that account. Quite to the contrary, Hirsch castigated those whose concern was limited solely to the religiously observant. Most revealing is Hirsch's discussion of the scriptural narrative of Abraham's quest for ten righteous men within the city of Sodom. He notes:

> The idea of a righteous man in the midst of Sodomite depravity which Abraham visualizes, for whose sake the city might be saved, is not one who keeps to his own four walls, in haughty pride of his superiority gives up the masses and just looks on at their ruinous moral lapses, who thinks he has done quite enough if he saves himself and at most his own household. Yea, such a one Abraham would not class as righteous. He would not consider that he had at all fulfilled the duty which lies on every good man in bad surroundings. The ruin of the masses whom he had long given up would leave such a man cold. He might even possibly feel a certain smug satisfaction in it. That is not Abraham's "righteous man" out of consideration for whom the salvation of the city should be affected. His righteous man is to be found "in the midst of the city" and in lively connection with everything and everybody. He never leaves off admonishing, teaching, warning, bettering wherever and however he can. He takes everybody and everything to heart; he never despairs, he is never tired of trying, however distant the hopes of success may be. These are the righteous ones whom he presumes must be "in the midst of the city" who would feel grief and pain at the death of each individual of these thousands. ... [120]

Moreover, in formulating his position, Hirsch emphasized that his policy demanded, not disassociation from individuals, but secession from a communal system that he viewed as an institutionalized expression of heresy. In effect, Hirsch argued that the admonition "Do not associate with the wicked, even for purposes of Torah" (*Avot de-Rabbi Natan* 9:4) is not applicable to the heretics of the modern era and ruled that heretics and *apikorsim* such as those with whom the Sages forbade all form of social contact no longer exist in our time. The religious views of the nonobservant of modern times have been shaped by parents, educational institutions, and a climate of opinion over which they have no control. They are the products of their culture and are not to be held responsible for what they are. [121] From a halakhic perspective they are to be

---

120 Commentary on Genesis 18:24, English translation by I. Levi (London, 1959), 325–26.
121 Cited by Hirsch, *Collected Works*, 6:207.

considered in a category identical to those *apikorsim* and Karaites of whom Maimonides declared in *Hilkhot Mamrim*:

> However, the children and grandchildren of these errants, whose parents have misled them, those who have been born among the Karaites who have reared them in their views, are like a child who has been taken captive among them, has been reared by them, and is not alacritous in seizing the paths of the commandments, whose status is comparable to that of an individual who is coerced; and even though he later learns that he is a Jew and becomes acquainted with Jews and their religion, he is nevertheless to be regarded as a person who is coerced for he was reared in their erroneous ways. Thus it is those of whom we have spoken who adhere to the practices of their Karaite parents who have erred. Therefore it is proper to cause them to return in repentance and to draw them nigh with words of peace until they return to the strength-giving Torah. [3:3]

Perhaps the best exposition of the arguments both for and against secession may be found in the previously cited letter of R. Hayyim Ozer Grodzinski. R. Grodzinski recognized the cogency of both positions as well as the sincere positive intentions of the protagonists. He wrote:

> Regarding the question of association with sinners, in the opinion of the separatists they see in this a great danger to Judaism that [people] will learn from their actions and by their proximity they may influence the future generation in a negative manner. It is axiomatic that a matter that concerns the foundations of Judaism involves a grave proscription. However, in the opinion of the accommodationists, they see in this matter a great mitzvah, not to estrange a large portion of the Jewish people and bring them merit, and they see no loss in this for the faithful who are separated with regard to religious needs. And, thus, this does not involve a question regarding which one says, and do you tell an individual, sin in order that you bring merit to your friend? For, in the opinion of the accommodationists, this does not entail any sin or transgression, rather, to the contrary, it is a mitzvah to bring merit to the many. Accordingly, what the separationists see as a great transgression in uniting, in this, the accommodationists see a mitzvah. The doubt, according to this, is in the very act itself, whether it is a mitzvah or a transgression.[122]

---

122 *Aḥiʿezer: Kovetz Iggerot* 1:243–44.

What was apparent to R. Hayyim Ozer Grodzinski, writing in the early part of the twentieth century, has become even more evident as the events of recent history have vindicated the arguments of both proponents and opponents of secession.[123]

Nevertheless, since as R. Hayyim Ozer Grodzinski noted, the decision to secede from the wider community is to be reached on the basis of a variety of considerations that depend on the needs and problems of the particular locale, the philosophy and rhetoric of secession of the 1870s may be sorely out of place at a later time. Of interest in this regard is a statement of a number of rabbis of the London Orthodox community issued in 1979 in opposition to joint communal programs to be undertaken under the auspices of Orthodox Jews in association with Jews in Liberal-Reform congregations. Noteworthy is not so much the decision itself, which may or may not be compelled by halakhic and/or socio-religious considerations, but the language in which it is couched. In a publication addressed to the broader general community, the Orthodox rabbis state: "Anyone who imagines that these dissenters can be brought back into the fold by consorting with them is deluding himself and misleading others. Indeed, such conduct will repel the Orthodox and those awaiting proper spiritual guidance."[124]

---

123 Hirsch was not moved to formulate the policy of *Austritt* in the 1870s because of disinterest in the welfare of the nonobservant. His teachings and writings were addressed to that constituency and his concern for them was very real. However, if there is a shortcoming to be ascribed to the remarkable *kehillah* in New York City that has inherited the traditions of Frankfurt am Main, it is an insularity and isolationism, which is not the cause, but the product, of *Austritt*. Lack of contact over a period of years is bound to decrease a sense of concern and ongoing interest. With the passage of decades the *kehillah* has increasingly focused in an inward direction and has had little contact with individuals of different religious outlook and orientation. The result has been a sad loss for the wider Orthodox community. The standards, integrity, cohesiveness, and faith of the *kehillah* have produced outstanding educational and communal institutions greatly benefiting both residents of its environs and the entire city. But the general Orthodox community in the United States, not to speak of those beyond the pale of Orthodoxy, has not had the benefit of its guidance or leadership.

On the other hand, the ability of the *kehillah* to recreate itself on these shores after dislocation and war, despite relatively meager financial resources during its early years, and to develop into a community that is a model *kehillah*, stands as a tribute to the staunch advocates of *Torah im derekh eretz* among its adherents and to their total commitment to its religious ideals. It is a singular community in which the word of the *Rav* remains unquestioned law, *kevod ha-rabbanut* is a meaningful phrase, and the label of the community, K'hal Adath Jeshurun, stands for a level of religious probity and reliability that is acknowledged by the entire spectrum of Orthodox Jewry.

124 *The Jewish Chronicle* (London), April 20, 1979, 21.

This is not a halakhic pronouncement, but a descriptive statement of fact. Is this a statement that had validity in the 1980s? Does it have continuing validity?

SELF-CRITICISM

Rare, but not entirely absent, in rabbinical writings of this period is the expression of a sense of responsibility bordering on guilt on the part of the rabbinic leaders themselves for the failings of the generation. In the earliest responsa focusing on Reform collected and published in *Eleh Divrei ha-Berit*, R. Eliezer of Triesch turned to his colleagues and admonished that the movement for reform in religious worship served as a sign that the Orthodox were indeed found wanting in precisely that aspect of religious life. If there were inadequacies in ritual and communal life it was rabbinic leaders who bore the brunt of the responsibility for improvement. Moreover, only individuals who were themselves of exemplary moral stature could hope to exert influence on the wayward.[125]

Of the various writings that focused on halakhic problems relating to the nonobservant, R. Tzevi Hirsch Chajes's *Minḥat Kena'ot* was unique in its scathing self-critique and indictment of the Orthodox rabbinate and its failure to respond to the needs of the time. In the opinion of Chajes, the early successes of the Reform movement were directly attributable to this deficiency.

It is on account of this self-critique that *Minḥat Kena'ot* occupied a position of unique importance in the polemical literature of the time and that it may have had a salutary impact. Most polemics fail to persuade since the argument is addressed to, read by, and accepted by, only an already committed audience. In Reform-Orthodox polemics, the Orthodox preached to the Orthodox concerning the failings of the Reform rabbinate and the Orthodox agreed; the Reform preached to the Reform concerning Orthodox shortcomings and adherents of Reform agreed. In *Minḥat Kena'ot*, in an unusual volte-face, an Orthodox writer castigated his Orthodox colleagues, in Hebrew, regarding their own failings.

Whatever hesitation and ambivalence Chajes may have experienced in pronouncing judgment upon exponents of Reform, he hesitated not a whit in his

---

125 *Eleh Divrei ha-Berit*, 94–96. Cf., also, comments in *Minḥat Ani*, regarding the responsibilities of religious leaders, 5b, 87a–88a, 99a, 129b–130a.

sharp critique and condemnation of his Orthodox colleagues. In *Minḥat Kena'ot*, he declared unequivocally: "I know the responsibility for the religious warping of the generation rests solely upon our contemporary rabbis. Theirs was the obligation to stand on the look-out."[126] Again and again, he calls the rabbis to task in the words of the prophet Ezekiel, "But if the watchman sees the sword come and blows not the horn, and the people be not warned and the sword do come and take any person from among them … but his blood will I require at the watchman's hand" (33:6). In his analysis of the paralysis in Orthodox leadership Chajes differentiated between various categories of rabbinic leaders, all of whom he regarded as having fallen short of the mark. He divided those rabbis into four groups: to three of these groups he directed counterarguments and words of inspiration and encouragement; with regard to the fourth group he simply bemoaned the fact that he could find no common ground for discourse.

There are a significant number of rabbis among the Orthodox, wrote Chajes, who simply are unaware of the cataclysmic events taking place all around them. They have no knowledge of Reform circles in Germany; they have not followed the proceedings of the Reform Rabbinical Conferences as reported in the press and they are ignorant of the extent of the changes that have been instituted in various synagogues. In strongest tones, Chajes expressed disdain for such leadership:

> With such rabbis I can have no relationship whatsoever, since I know with certainty that they do not fulfill the obligations that devolve upon them by virtue of their standing in the community. Their standing demands of them not to be silent, bovine-like, concerned only with their immediate surroundings, unaware of what transpires among their people. Rather, an obligation devolves upon them to be informed.[127]

Complaints regarding know-nothingism among rabbis are a recurrent theme in Chajes's private correspondence. He repeatedly assailed defects in the religious education of the age. At an earlier date Chajes had authored a memorandum to the government containing practical suggestions regarding the training of rabbis and the responsibilities of their office in the community.

---

126 Chajes, *Minḥat Kena'ot*, 1019. See Chajes's almost identical language in the introduction to *Darkei Hora'ah*, 209.

127 Chajes, *Minḥat Kena'ot*, 1016.

In a private communication in which he described candidates for rabbinic office in Galicia, Chajes candidly wrote:

> Even that segment of the youth who prepare to devote themselves to a rabbinical career have not the vaguest notion of the scope of that office....
> Of the vast corpus of the laws, of *Oraḥ Ḥayyim* they study only the laws of Passover, and even that section not in its entirety ... and then of *Yoreh De'ah*, the laws of ritual slaughter, *terefot*, milk and meat, and forbidden mixtures. This constitutes their entire course of study. If one of them has a smattering of proficiency in these areas, even if he does not know that David reigned after Saul, he will be recommended by the Rabbis as the most qualified rabbinical candidate for even the most prestigious cities.[128]

In another communication Chajes bemoaned in particular the lack of appreciation of the importance of the study of history among members of the Polish rabbinate: "In particular, among our coreligionists in the provinces of Poland, knowledge of the events of history is regarded as a useless matter and they have no desire to pursue it, deeming such study a waste of time and effort."[129]

However, the vast majority of Orthodox rabbis, Chajes claimed, were indeed aware of the dangers of the innovators but, nevertheless, had been unable to respond adequately. Chajes divides those rabbis into three subgroups:

1. Those who were afraid to be vocal in opposition to Reform lest their own response focus even more attention upon Reform deviation and inadvertently enhance its success. Eastern European masses who had hitherto followed tradition unquestioningly might learn of innovations introduced by adherents of Reform and find them to be appealing. Accordingly, those rabbis regarded silence as the better part of valor.
2. A second group consisted of rabbis who were well aware of their own failings and lack of skill in the art of debate. They feared public confrontation lest their lack of expertise bring dishonor to their cause.
3. Finally, a third segment of the rabbinate consisted of talented and learned individuals who enjoyed positions of prestige in the

---

128 The full text is cited in Herskovics, *Maharatz Ḥayes*, 367–68. See also N. M. Gelber, *Toldot Yehudei Brody* (Jerusalem: Mossad ha-Rav Kook, 1955), 288.

129 Herskovics, *Maharatz Ḥayes*, 215. Cf. Chajes, *Darkei Hora'ah*, 209–10, where Chajes observes that Maimonides did not utilize historical research. For Chajes's own positive sentiments regarding this discipline, see *She'elot u-Teshuvot Maharatz Ḥayes*, no. 12, 647–49; Herskovics, *Maharatz Ḥayes*, 215, 280.

community but considered themselves to be above the fray and believed it to be beneath their dignity to engage in debate with individuals who were not their equals in rabbinic scholarship.

Turning to the first two groups, Chajes stated simply that fear of publicity was vain. Regardless of what would or would not be done on the part of the Orthodox, the masses could not long remain in ignorance of the activities of Reform innovators. Chajes recognized adoption of an ostrich-like mentality to be ridiculous and candidly remarked, "Whether or not the innovators are knowledgeable or pious, they are assuredly most adept in the art of communication in public and they know how to present their programs in an attractive format."[130] Whoever would not hear about those matters from the periodicals and newspapers would not be likely to learn about them from learned scholarly debates. To the second group, Chajes offered advice and encouragement. He cautioned that fear of dishonor is but a defense mechanism and added that perhaps these individuals merely seek noble excuses to avoid challenge.

However, upon the third group, Chajes vented his spleen in language bespeaking pain and bitterness. He felt that they had abdicated their role as rabbis since they placed their personal honor and glory above the welfare of their communities. In the sharpest of tones he catalogued the shortcomings of the Orthodox rabbinate: their poor communication skills; their lack of pastoral technique; their failure to promote the welfare of their constituents; and their abysmal failure to understand the spirit that animates contemporary society and the very real social, ideological, and intellectual problems with which their coreligionists were confronted. In their self-absorption they had even failed to address the single most important need of the hour: establishment of appropriate educational institutions. Unfortunately, conceded Chajes, they were, and deserved to be, a target for the criticism of Reform adversaries: "Because of the behavior of the rabbis of our country, our adversaries have found a place to make claims against rabbis of the old school saying that those who follow talmudic Judaism are as sheep who have no shepherd or guide."[131] On the other hand, wrote Chajes, the leaders of the Reform movement had excelled in the very areas in which the Orthodox had failed so abjectly.

In a remarkable departure from the recriminatory style of Orthodox polemicists, Chajes candidly conceded the ability of Reform leaders to address the concerns of their followers and bemoaned the inability of most traditional

---

130 Chajes, *Minḥat Kena'ot*, 1017.
131 Ibid., 1018.

rabbis to understand the very real ideological problems with which their constituents were confronted. In all honesty, one must admit, wrote Chajes, that whether or not the innovators are knowledgeable and while they may not be pious, "they certainly do have manners and culture and an ability to speak." No wonder, he added, that even formerly traditional congregations in large cities in Eastern Europe availed themselves of the services of these preachers.[132] Chajes's devastating critique of the Orthodox leadership and his intriguing analysis serve as a harbinger of what was to become the agenda for counter-Reform in the 1850s and 1860s.

One of the major rabbinic figures at the helm of the movement for counter-Reform and a creative leader in the revitalization of Orthodox educational institutions in Germany and Hungary was Azriel Hildesheimer. In many of these endeavors he was motivated by a visionary zeal shared by few of his contemporaries. He, too, turned a keenly critical eye upon the rabbinate and, in numerous letters and writings, sought to arouse his colleagues from their lethargy and to spur them to positive endeavors:

> The greatest enemies in our midst are fear, confusion and dread ... our side is silent and continues to be silent. ...[133] Indeed, I am assured that only with regard to what should not be done is there ever agreement among *Gedolei Yisra'el*, but not with regard to what may be done; ... always in our midst there is only "No" and "No." But ... the main thing is to build.[134]

POSITIVE RESPONSES

Responses to Reform were by no means entirely negative in nature. In a limited sense the Reform movement occasioned salient introspection and self-criticism of the type called for by R. Tzevi Hirsch Chajes and improvements in such relatively minor matters as synagogue decorum. That reaction was prompted, in part, by recognition of the fact that these matters did indeed require correction

---

132 Ibid., 1019. R. Meir Schapiro would later poke fun at modern rabbis and their penchant for sermonizing. In a play on the biblical verse Exodus 32:7 and the Yiddish *reden*, "preach", which in Hebrew means "go down"—he commented, "*Lekh red*, When does one need to keep preaching? '*Ki shihes amkha*,' 'when your community is on a low level.'" *Zikhron Meir*, ed. A. Schapiro (New York, 1954), 63. Chajes had no such compunctions. He readily conceded that the strength of Reform leaders lay in their homiletical skills.

133 Mordecai Eliav, ed., *Iggerot Rabbi Ezri'el Hildesheimer* (Jerusalem: Rubin Mass, 1963) (Hebrew section), 30, 31.

134 Ibid., 35.

but, primarily, by a desire for containment, that is, eliminating the factors that might prompt further alienation and defection.

The prospect of the alienation of additional Jews, the aggregate number of whom could not be foretold, was certainly a matter of concern. But no less significant was the challenge of winning back the hearts and minds of those already attracted to the Reform movement. Many of the methods employed in that endeavor would also serve to stem the ongoing loss of those who, with the enticing availability of Reform as an option, were becoming disaffected with Orthodoxy. Although not all Orthodox leaders recognized that a positive program was imperative, some realized quite clearly that, ultimately, the only effective response to Reform and nonobservance was to be found in a positive approach, and that an effective agenda must include the founding of appropriate educational institutions, publication of journals and books for a popular audience, as well as the reopening of channels of communication and instruction.

One of the earliest rabbinic figures to express the need for such a positive approach was R. Jacob Ettlinger. His awareness of this need is articulated in a number of highly significant passages in *Minḥat Ani*. In those comments Ettlinger called upon rabbinic leaders to concentrate their efforts upon a program of instruction and careful explanation geared to those whose faith had faltered. He stated emphatically that criticism and didacticism alone would continue to be ineffective; emphasis must be placed upon teaching and clarification of the practices and traditions of Judaism. Commenting on the double Hebrew expression for reproof (*hokheiaḥ tokhiaḥ*) employed in the biblical admonition "You shall surely reprove your friend" (Leviticus 19:17) and upon the dual connotations of the Hebrew term *hokhaḥah*, as meaning proof as well as reproof, Ettlinger notes:

> The repetition of [the word] *hokheiaḥ* denotes that it is of the essence
> of reproof that when one says to one's friend, "Do not do that" if he has
> committed a transgression or, "Do so and so" if he has ceased to observe
> a commandment, one should not do so without explaining the reason to
> him. ... Rather, one should explain the matter to him so that he himself will
> understand the purpose of that which he admonishes him to do or to cease
> doing. ... And that is what is meant by "You shall surely reprove" (*hokheiaḥ
> tokhiaḥ*), with evidence and with logic you shall reprove him. ...[135]

---

135 Ettlinger, *Minḥat Ani*, 63a. See also ibid., 5b, 87a–88b, 99a–100a, 129b–130a.

Ettlinger's positive approach undoubtedly molded the thinking of his disciples Samson Raphael Hirsch and Azriel Hildesheimer. Assuredly, the greatest accomplishments of these two leading ideologues of modern Orthodoxy in Germany were their innovative programs designed to satisfy the intellectual needs of their age.

Hirsch's first major literary works were the *Nineteen Letters*, published in 1836 under the pseudonym of Ben Uziel, and *Horeb*, subtitled *Essays on Israel's Duties in the Dispersion*, a compendium of halakhot and their underlying rationale and interpretive meaning, published in 1837.[136] In the case of the *Nineteen Letters*, in a sense, the medium was the message; the format was as significant as the content. The letters were presented in the form of a dialogue via correspondence. In the first letter, a questioning and questing individual addresses a young rabbi and the rabbi replies in the following eighteen epistles. The salient feature is that there is a dialogue between two different individuals with two differing perspectives. The one doubts, hesitates, queries, questions. The other discusses, explains, argues, rhapsodizes, and interprets. At no time, however, does the respondent castigate or berate. The message of the format is clear and unequivocal: The author recognizes that there are different perspectives and, more significantly, that these differing perspectives are cogent and sincere. Hirsch is saying to the questioner: I realize that you have questions; I know that there are ample reasons to question;

---

136 Almost two hundred years after their publication, the written works of Hirsch remain a treasured resource for the Orthodox student and scholar. If these works do not have the same magnetic effect upon some contemporary readers that they had in earlier decades, it is simply because of their particular potency in striking resonant chords that were uniquely nineteenth century in nature. The effectiveness of Hirsch's writings at the time of their publication is to be attributed, in part, precisely to the manner in which they captured the idiom, the mind-set, and the sensibilities of nineteenth-century Germany. Although to today's reader sections of these works may seem too forced, too heavy, or too didactic in tone, it is those very qualities that contributed to their popularity at a different stage in time.

The value of Hirsch's written works was fully appreciated by leading Torah scholars both of his own generation and of the generation that followed. Rabbi Israel Salanter sought to promote the translation of the *Nineteen Letters* into Russian. See Dov Katz, *Tenu'at ha-Mussar*, 3rd ed. (Tel Aviv: A. Zioni, 1958), 1:223. R. Hayyim Ozer Grodzinski, *Aḥi'ezer: Kovetz Iggerot*, vol. 2, also commended translations of Hirsch's writings and wrote in superlative terms of "the Gaon and scholar, of blessed memory, who knew the ailments of the children of his generation and endeavored to cure them and was successful in drawing pure, living waters, waters of healing and refreshment for those who suffer maladies of the soul" (589–90). Cf. the encomium of Rav Kook, *Iggerot ha-Re'iyah* 1:182: "The giant in knowledge, noble prince of God, the Gaon, R. Shimshon Hirsch, who with the saving might of his right hand preserved the remnant of Western Jewry."

I wish to teach, to explain, and to provide answers. Your questions are well founded; I understand your doubts and hesitations. I even recognize that, in part, the shortcomings of our own community have caused your doubts to become even stronger. In the broad Orthodox community the neglect of spirituality has fostered a type of arid observance that is unattractive and hollow. No wonder that such rote observance has failed to inspire your confidence. But do not permit the failings of contemporary coreligionists to quench your own thirst for spirituality and do not permit the failings of our coreligionists to becloud the beauty of the traditions of our people.

Although the dialogue is not continued and the doubter is not afforded an opportunity to challenge the answers provided in the form of the literary device of further letters, the message of the format is nevertheless not lost: The message is one of respect, of concern, of cordiality, and of availability. Moreover, although the questioner is afforded but one letter.[137] Hirsch, in his replies, frequently presents the opposing arguments and gives credence to many of the well-taken criticisms of exponents of Reform.[138] Indeed, perhaps the most powerful of Hirsch's methods is his utilization of the skilled debater's technique of stealing the opponent's thunder by conceding the opponent's best arguments in presenting them oneself.

Also noteworthy in terms of format is another stylistic characteristic which might easily be overlooked by a twenty-first-century reader. Accustomed as we are to "equal opportunity" language, we may not notice the sensitivity to, and awareness of, the role of women and the conscious effort to address the concerns of "sons and daughters."[139] Such awareness and sensitivity is highly unusual in a nineteenth-century Orthodox writer.

Horeb presents a response to the challenge of Reform on an entirely different level. The basic thrust of Reform was radically antihalakhic, if not completely antinomian. Rather than debating fundamental questions of the

---

137 Indeed, this was Geiger's criticism of the *Nineteen Letters* and it is well-taken. See Geiger's review, "Rezensionen, *Iggerot Tzafon: Neunzehn Briefe über Judenthum*, Erster Artikel," *Wissenschaftliche Zeitschrift für jüdische Theologie* 2 (1836), 355; and Liberles, *Religious Conflict*, 122.

138 For example, Samson Raphael Hirsch, *The Nineteen Letters of Ben Uziel*, trans. Bernard Drachman (New York: Bloch, 1942), 98–100, 147–148, 173, 185–87, 190–93, 195–96, 202–05. Cf. the letter from Hirsch to his friend Z. H. May in Hamburg included in *Horeb*, trans. I. Grunfeld (New York: Soncino, 1962), cxlii-cxliii.

139 Hirsch, *Nineteen Letters*, 199, 201, 203, 220. The title page of the first edition of *Horeb* bore the dedication, "To Israel's thinking young men and women"; and in the Foreword, the author writes, "I ventured to lay my essays before my brothers and sisters because the time seemed to demand something of the kind" (clxi).

theological or philosophical basis for the continuing binding force of halakhic rules or responding technically with involved arguments regarding the parameters of particular laws, Hirsch, in this work, adopted a quite different tactic. In *Horeb*, Hirsch undertook to delineate the laws, to teach their details, and to offer interpretations of their significance and symbolic or spiritual meaning. Rather than debate the case, Hirsch presented the law as a given. However, the detailed, precise, loving exposition of the law in its minutiae was, in itself, the answer to Reform. In effect, Hirsch was saying: This, the law, the 613 mitzvot, presented herewith in six divisions, is Judaism. This is the heart and soul of our religion. Reject the law and you are rejecting the heart and soul of Judaism.

Apart from his literary efforts, Hirsch played a major role in the modernization of Jewish education. In Frankfurt, Hirsch made establishment of a school that would offer a dual curriculum of religious and secular studies a matter of highest priority. Schools established by the Orthodox in Altona and Halberstadt had introduced the combined study of religious and secular subjects and use of current educational methodology.[140] Hirsch deemed such educational enterprises to be fundamental for the survival of Orthodoxy. Indeed, his earliest literary endeavors had been spurred by his concern to provide textbooks for teachers.[141] The school he founded in Frankfurt in 1853, the *Unterrichtsanstalt der Israelitischen Religionsgesellschaft*, attracted a significant enrollment and became an important institution for the training of Orthodox laymen.[142]

The second major ideologue of the time, R. Azriel Hildesheimer, recognized that it was not sufficient to create institutions for elementary education. The need of the hour was for the training of rabbis who would be equipped to respond to the unique demands of the time. Writing to a group

---

140 Mordecai Eliav, *Ha-Ḥinnukh ha-Yehudi be-Germaniyah be-Yemei ha-Haskalah ve-ha-Emantzipatziyah* (Jerusalem: The Jewish Agency, 1960), 159–61, 232–35.

141 In his letter to Z. H. May dated April 13, 1835, Hirsch writes, "I am in charge of a few hundred young souls; I have to provide teachers for them, of whom I have to ask that they introduce our youth into Judaism. But I cannot ask that of the teachers, because they themselves do not know what Judaism really means, and one cannot even really blame them for their ignorance. Moreover, there is no text-book available which I could give them for guidance" (*Horeb*, cxliv). Similarly, in the *Nineteen Letters*, Hirsch asserts, "I rejoice that the impulse to these essays was derived from the necessity of supplying the teachers of the schools under my supervision with a book in which they could read themselves into Jews before they began to rear young souls for Judaism" (p. 219).

142 Eliav, *Ha-Ḥinnukh*, 227–32. See also Liberles, *Religious Conflict*, 152–55; and Rosenbloom, *Tradition*, 104.

of lay leaders in May 1872, Hildesheimer, then in Berlin, extolled the positive achievements of a reinvigorated, restructured Orthodoxy and the establishment of independent congregations and journals. Yet, in a *cri de coeur*, he expressed his anxiety that, these developments notwithstanding,

> Where can we find ... in our camp an institution that, in some measure, can respond to the destructive tendencies of our time and answer the needs of the hour? ... Have we at all begun such an undertaking, even partially? ... He who does not wish to deceive himself must see that in our stance there is a narrowness that may quiet matters momentarily but will not provide a substantive solution. ... Whence shall we take rabbis? Whence shall we take teachers?[143]

Hildesheimer was not the first to perceive the need for a new type of institution for the training of rabbis. During the early years of the nineteenth century, the growth of *Haskalah* and impoverishment in some parts of Europe caused many of the yeshivot in Western Europe to close and the number of students in the ones remaining to dwindle.[144] Until that time, the yeshiva, with a curriculum of study consisting solely of Talmud and Codes, had served as the major source for the training of rabbis. The traditional yeshiva was an academic institution of higher learning concerned solely with rabbinic scholarship and made no effort to provide practical or professional training for rabbis. In response to cataclysmic change in the orientation of the Jewish community a demand arose for the establishment of a radically new type of educational instruction that was to differ from the yeshiva in three basic respects: (1) There was to be a pronounced professional orientation with courses in homiletics and practical rabbinics. (2) The curriculum was to include secular studies as well. (3) The religious studies program was to be broadened to include Jewish philosophy and history and a somewhat positive attitude to modern Jewish scholarship and *Wissenschaft*.[145]

Throughout the course of the nineteenth century the question of professional training for the rabbinate was the focus of heated controversy within

---

143 Published in Meir Hildensheimer, "Ketavim be-Dvar Yesod Bet ha-Midrash le-Rabbanim be-Berlin," *Ha-Ma'ayan* 14 (1974), 14–15.

144 Ibid., 18–19, Eliav, *Ha-Ḥinnukh*, 237–38.

145 Cf. the interesting comments and analysis of Mordecai Breuer, "Three Orthodox Approaches to Wissenschaft," *Jubilee Volume in Honor of Rabbi Joseph B. Soloveichik*, ed. S. Israeli, N. Lamm, and Y. Rafael (Jerusalem: Mossad ha-Rav Kook, 1984), 2:856–65.

the Orthodox community. A number of innovative proposals were vigorously endorsed by some authorities only to be violently contested by others. The earliest suggestion for the establishment of a rabbinical seminary is found in a little known work entitled *Mosdot Tevel*, authored by Rabbi David Friesenhausen and published in Vienna in 1820. Friesenhausen claims to have submitted his novel proposal to government authorities as early as 1806, but he surmised quite correctly that "the majority of rabbis will oppose this matter."[146] The rabbinic leaders who originally endorsed the plan were prevailed upon publicly to withdraw their support.[147] More realistic proposals for the establishment of a rabbinical seminary were advanced by Rabbi Jacob Ettlinger as early as 1829[148] and again, in greater detail, in 1846.[149] For a variety of reasons those projects were abandoned[150] but many aspects of the proposed curriculum were later adopted by the Orthodox seminary established by Hildesheimer.

What for others was but a dream became a reality as the result of the creative leadership of Hildesheimer. *Die Rabbinerseminar für das Orthodoxische Judentum* established by Hildesheimer in Berlin in 1873 became a potent force in the Orthodox community. Decades later, Joseph Wohlgemuth made the extravagant claim that the *Rabbinerseminar* had saved Orthodox Judaism in Western Europe and "only fools or zealots would not recognize this."[151] Apparently there are many whom Wohlgemuth would have considered to be fools and zealots since, despite its many successes, the *Rabbinerseminar* did not meet with universal approval in rabbinic circles.

Hildesheimer himself suggested that much of the opposition was based on previous negative experience with graduates of government-sponsored assimilationist seminaries and would dissipate when it became evident that his institution, staffed with an observant and dedicated faculty, was of a different genre.[152] But that was an oversimplification. Several of Hildesheimer's prominent colleagues in Germany remained notably cool toward the undertaking.

---

146 R. David Friesenhausen, *Mosdot Tevel* 91a.

147 Ibid., 92a. See also R. Solomon Schuck, *She'elot u-Teshevot Rashban al Even ha-Ezer* (Satmar, 1905), no. 157; and R. Moses Schick, *She'elot u-Teshuvot Maharam Shik, Oraḥ Ḥayyim*, nos. 306, 307.

148 Jaap Meijer, *Moeder in Israel: Een Geschiedenis van het Amsterdamse Asjkenazische Jodendom* (Haarlem: Bakenes, 1964), 80–81.

149 *TZW* 2 (1846), 241–45.

150 *Die jüdische Presse* 3 (1872), 343–44.

151 Cited in Moshe A. Shulvass, "Bet ha-Midrash le-Rabbanim be-Berlin," in *Mosdot Torah be-Europah be-Binyanam u-be-Ḥurbanam*, ed. Samuel K. Mirsky (New York, 1956), 697.

152 *Iggerot Rabbi Ezri'el* (Hebrew section), 34.

Rabbi Samson Raphael Hirsch was unenthusiastic. Although the relationship between Hirsch and Hildesheimer may not have been free of tension, Hirsch's distrust of the seminary was based upon ideological considerations.[153] The venerable Rabbi Seligmann Baer Bamberger of Würzburg, as Hildesheimer himself conceded, was opposed as a matter of "pure ideological conviction with no personal animus whatsoever" simply because he did not favor the mingling of secular and sacred studies in a rabbinical academy.[154]

Many rabbinic authorities regarded the *Rabbinerseminar* as highly effective in preserving Orthodoxy in Germany but considered it to be unacceptable as an ideal.[155] In particular, R. Isaac Elhanan Spektor and Rabbi Israel Salanter praised Hildesheimer's achievements in Berlin.[156] Yet, repeatedly, reservations were expressed regarding the suitability of such a program of study in Eastern Europe where Torah learning had not been diluted.[157] In a lengthy responsum

---

153 Shulvass, "Bet ha-Midrash," 694; Eliav, "Mekomo shel ha-Rav Ezri'el Hildesheimer be-Ma'avak al Demuttah shel Yahadut Hungariyah," *Zion* 27 (1962), 85–86.

154 *Iggerot Rabbi Ezri'el* (Hebrew section), 50. See also Yitzhak Adler, "*Minhagei ha-Rav Yitzhak Dov ha-Levi Bamberger Zatzal ve-Hanhagotav*," *HaMa'ayan* 19 (1979), 35, 35 n. 2.

155 Hungarian rabbis who had vociferously opposed Hildesheimer's earlier educational activities in Eisenstadt were muted in criticism of the Berlin seminary. See Eliav, "Mekomo," 66–67. Characteristic is an alleged comment of *Ketav Sofer* favoring Hildesheimer's Berlin endeavor because while "here he spoiled, there he will correct" (*Iggerot Soferim*, sec. 3, 41, n.).

156 See Hildesheimer, "Ketavim," 34–37; R. Yitzhak Ya'akov Reines, *Shnei ha-Me'orot*, pt. 2 (Pietrkov, 1913), *Ma'amar Zikaron ba-Sefer*, sec. 1, 46. Cf. D. Hoffmann, "*Festrede*," in *Zum hundertjährigen Geburtstage des Rabbiners und Seminardirektors Dr. Israel Hildesheimer* (Berlin: Jeschurun, 1920), 5–12.

157 On Rabbi Israel Salanter's reservations regarding professional schools for the rabbinate see Katz, *Tenu'at ha-Mussar* 1:226–27; and Rabbi Yehi'el Ya'akov Weinberg, *Seridei Esh*, vol. 4 (Jerusalem: Mossad ha-Rav Kook, 1969), 234–35. Although R. Israel Salanter was opposed in principle to the establishment of rabbinical seminaries in Eastern Europe, he was a proponent of a vigorous educational program directed toward both the broad masses and the intelligentsia. He attempted to foster translations of the Talmud into a European vernacular as well as into Hebrew in order to popularize its study and mounted a campaign for the inclusion of talmudic studies in the curricula of European universities. See Katz, *Tenu'at haMussar*, 221–22 and Hillel Goldberg, *Between Belin and Slabodka: Jewish Transition Figures from Eastern Europe* (Hoboken, NJ: Ktav, 1989), 30. Rabbi Israel Salanter believed that, apart from other benefits that might accrue, acceptance of Talmud in the academic curriculum of the university would lend it prestige in the eyes of assimilated Jews and might stimulate their own renewed interest in their heritage. He understood full well that they were enamored of secular and non-Jewish culture. Subjects held in esteem by non-Jews might arouse their own curiosity. If valued by non-Jews, then the Talmud might be seen as having enduring value by Jews as well. (It is related that when, on one occasion, a nonobservant *maskil* was called to the reading of the Torah in Brisk and recited the

in which, *inter alia*, he discussed the conditions under which secular studies might be included in the curriculum of communal schools, the head of the famed yeshiva of Volozhin, R. Naftali Zevi Yehudah Berlin, cautioned that one should not expect such schools to produce rabbis and arbiters of the law for "it is the way of Torah to endure ... and the goal of Torah study to be achieved, only in someone who devotes himself to it totally and exclusively."[158]

Decades later, some prominent Orthodox scholars continued to view rabbinical seminaries as, at best, an accommodation necessary to meet the needs of the Jewish communities of Western. Europe. In the early 1930s, during the early years of the Hitler regime, a plan was formulated to relocate the Hildesheimer seminary—then in the sixth decade of its existence—to Palestine. Meir Hildesheimer, the administrator, traveled to the Holy Land on an investigatory mission. However, upon his return to Berlin, the Board of Directors and teaching faculty vetoed the proposal.[159] In all likelihood a principal reason for abandonment of this plan was the avowed opposition to transfer of the seminary expressed by leading Orthodox rabbinical authorities in Jerusalem and in Eastern Europe. An explicit record of this opposition is to be found in a series of letters discussing the projected move written by R. Hayyim Ozer Grodzinski of Vilna to the heads of the Berlin seminary as well as to his rabbinic colleagues in Palestine, including Rabbi Joseph Tzevi Duschinsky in Jerusalem and Rabbi Abraham Isaiah Karelitz, the *Ḥazon Ish*, in Bnei Brak.[160]

Rabbi Grodzinski enumerated his reasons for opposing establishment of a rabbinical seminary in Palestine, succinctly stating that: (1) While the Hildesheimer seminary fulfilled "the need of the hour, the time and the place," and was essential in an age and a locale that required Orthodox communities to appoint rabbis who had also received a university education, such a need was limited to the acculturated German community of the late nineteenth and early twentieth centuries. (2) Palestine in the twentieth century had no need, wrote Rabbi Grodzinski, for such a "factory for the production of rabbis." Palestine

---

blessings, R. Joseph Ber Soloveitchik, the *Bet ha-Levi*, commented pithily, "He certainly should recite the blessing 'who has given us the Torah' for had God given the Torah to the non-Jews, he would feel bound to observe its tenets." See Aaron Suraski, *Marbitzei Torah u-Mussar* [New York, 1977], 1:83.)

158 *She'elot u-Teshuvot Meshiv Davar*, no. 44.

159 Shulvass, "*Bet ha-Midrash*," 712–13.

160 *Aḥi'ezer: Kovetz Iggerot* 2:443–47. Some of these letters are also to be found in Abraham L Karelitz, *Kovetz Iggerot* (Bnei Brak, 1956), 2:170–74. See also *Pe'er-ha-Dor, Ḥayyei ha-Ḥazon Ish* (Bnei Brak: Nenach Press, 1966), 1:315–16; and *Seridei Esh*, vol. 1 (Jerusalem: Mossad ha-Rav Kook, 1961), 307–08.

had great yeshivot of its own and did not require spiritual leaders to whom secular studies were primary and Torah studies secondary.[161] (3) Furthermore, in Rabbi Grodzinski's opinion, neither could graduates of such a seminary properly serve the Sephardic community in Palestine. Its graduates would not appeal to the traditional element among them. As for nontraditional Sephardic Jews, it was not likely that their needs would be met by "rabbis of the Berlin type." (4) Implementation of the project could only lead to a lowering of the standards of Torah in Palestine. Clearly, the opposition expressed echoed the twofold negative view with which the idea of a rabbinical seminary had been received since the days of R. David Friesenhausen: (1) Rabbinical seminaries are merely professional schools for which there is now no real need. (2) Protestations to the contrary notwithstanding, graduates of these seminaries achieve proficiency in secular subjects but are sorely lacking in rabbinic scholarship.

In his description of the aspirations of Hildesheimer, Rabbi Yehi'el Ya'akov Weinberg, who served for decades as a member of the *Rabbinerseminar* faculty, noted that Hildesheimer had envisioned the growth of an Orthodox rabbinate that would assert itself in every aspect of public life and one that would publicize

---

161   *Aḥiʿezer: Kovetz Iggerot* 2:444. In 1950 Rabbi Herzog expressed a similarly negative opinion regarding the establishment of rabbinical seminaries in Israel. While he favored the establishment of a university under Orthodox auspices, he emphasized that he viewed the establishment of an Orthodox rabbinical seminary to be detrimental and wrote bluntly: "The seminaries have not as yet provided us with a single great scholar (*gadol*). When great scholars entered them, some emerged as pygmies, while some emerged as great scholars. But it was not the seminaries that made them into great scholars." See Rabbi Isaac ha-Levi Herzog, *Teḥukah le-Yisra'el al pi ha-Torah*, vol. 3, *Ḥazakah, Ḥukkim ve-Takkanot ha-Rabbanut ha-Rashit*, ed. Itamar Wahrhaftig (Jerusalem: Mossad ha-Rav Kook and Yad Harav Herzog, 1989), 240. Cf., however, the assessment of Rabbi Weinberg, *Seridei Esh*, vol. 2 (Jerusalem: Mossad ha-Rav Kook, 1962), no. 30, who writes movingly, "It is proper to record that among the rabbis of Germany there were righteous, pious and holy men, who in other countries would have been pursued by tens of thousands of people seeking to benefit from their Torah and fear of God," and attests that, for these individuals, secular academic pursuits and attainments were secondary in nature and that they made use of their academic titles only in dealings with civil authorities or the assimilated.

Whatever may have been their attitude toward establishment of rabbinical seminaries, Torah scholars of every orientation exhibited an attitude of deep respect and fulsome appreciation for the contributions of both Hirsch and Hildesheimer. This attitude was based on the firm conviction that the synthesis of Torah and secular studies advocated by both Hirsch and Hildesheimer was predicated upon absolute and uncompromising faith and fear of Heaven and an unshakeable sincerity of commitment to Torah and mitzvot. As Rav Kook wrote (*Iggerot ha-Reʿiyah* 2:27) of both Hirsch and Hildesheimer, they manifested "the ability to unite knowledge of the world and of life with a stalwart fear of God and love of Torah and mitzvot, with faith and a perfect heart."

and explicate the Torah perspective with regard to the widest range of ethical and social questions. Hildesheimer had felt strongly that it was not sufficient for Orthodox rabbis to issue pronouncements on matters of ritual law alone. Rather, they must be thoroughly conversant with, and responsive to, the manifold sociological and philosophical issues that engage the attention of society.

Rabbi Weinberg stressed that, despite the name of the institution, Hildesheimer's goal had not been so much to establish a professional school as "to create an institution that would develop a religious intelligentsia."[162] The deterioration in the status of Orthodoxy in his generation was the result of the lack of precisely such a religious elite. The intelligentsia of the time consisted solely of the nonobservant who looked down on the Orthodox as lacking in culture and education. Torah scholars, for the most part, concentrated all their energies within the four ells of halakhah, and, as a result, had lost contact with the broad masses. They did not number among themselves Torah scholars such as Saadiah Gaon, Maimonides, Nachmanides, and Ibn Ezra of previous ages, scholars who had mastered the secular wisdom of the day and responded to its challenges. It was Hildesheimer's hope that among the graduates of his institution there would be individuals suited to such a mission, persons capable of communicating with modern intellectuals and trained to transmit Jewish values in the modern idiom.[163] Whether or not Hildesheimer succeeded in that goal is a different question.

With the passage of time the need for rapprochement with the nonobservant became ever more compelling.. It became increasingly evident to rabbinic leaders that positive approaches must be found in opening channels of communication. In a letter dated 25 Iyar 5672 addressed to those who were planning the first *Knessiah Gedolah* of the Agudath Israel movement, Rabbi Abraham I. Kook wrote that one finds "two spiritual strands ... two opposites that cannot be united, holy zealotry and patient tolerance (*ha-kinah ha-kedoshah ve-ha-savlanut ha-metunah*)." But these two opposing vector forces of zealotry and calm patience must be reconciled if efforts for the greater good of *kelal Yisra'el* are to be crowned with success. Only by fostering deep spiritual love for each member of the Jewish people can the tolerance and patience so sorely needed be acquired.[164]

---

162 Weinberg, *Seridei Esh* 1:2.

163 Ibid., 1:2.

164 Rabbi Abraham I. Kook, letter, 25 Iyar 5672 (May 12, 1912), in *Sefer Hayovel: Jubilee Book: On the Occasion of the Thirtieth Anniversary of the Agudas Israel World Organisation* (London: Agudas Israel Organisation, 1942), 57.

In even stronger words than those used by Bamberger and Hirsch in the 1870s, Rabbi Kook argued that deviationists of modern times must be approached in a conciliatory manner. He vigorously opposed the view that had been adopted by "the great majority of [Torah] scholars that in our times it is fitting to abandon those children who have been turned from Torah ways and the faith by the raging current of the time. I say emphatically, that this is not God's way!"[165] Such individuals must be regarded in every respect as acting under *force majeure*. "They are coerced in every sense of the word," wrote Rabbi Kook, "and heaven forbid us from judging the compelled as we do the self-willed."[166]

More than a hundred years later, the prophetic quality of the words penned by Rabbi Kook in 1908 becomes ever more evident. To the extent that rabbinic leaders erred in their assessment of, and response to, Reform, it was in the failure to develop avenues of communication with those whose deviation was intellectually motivated. The watchmen on guard on the watchtower, the *Shomrei Tziyyon*, had absorbed a siege mentality. But the watchmen referred to in Ezekiel are enjoined to be *tzofim*, those who stand on the lookout, those who look ahead to the future. Ultimately, as Rabbi Kook predicted,

> the transgressors and the rebels who are not prisoners of fashion but of misdirected reason will return at a highly exalted degree. For this reason, there is great hope for the vast majority of our children, so we must [hold] them and not forsake them "and it shall come to pass that, instead of that which was said to them, you are not my people, it shall be said of them, you are the sons of a living God." [Hosea 2:1][167]

---

165 Rabbi Abraham I. Kook, letter, May 20, 1908, *Iggerot ha-Re'iyah* 1:170–71. An English translation of this letter may be found in *Rav A. Y. Kook: Selected Letters*, trans. and annot. Tzvi Feldman (Maaleh Adumim: Maaliyot Publications, 1986), 51–54.

166 Rabbi Abraham I. Kook, *Iggerot ha-Re'iyah* 1:171.

167 Ibid., 171–172.

CHAPTER 2

The Emergence of an Orthodox Press in Nineteenth-Century Germany

Hyper-connected as we are today to multimedia sources of information, with global news instantaneously available at our fingertips, it takes a leap of imagination to appreciate what newspapers and journals meant to people in generations long gone by. The periodical that arrived in the post or that was purchased from the newsagent brought tidings and vital information to the thirsty homebound reader eager to hear of the welfare of kith and kin, to discover what was transpiring in faraway lands or to be emotionally transported by tales and stories of the great wide world.

The nineteenth century—particularly from the 1830s onward—saw an efflorescence of Jewish newspapers and journals throughout Europe and extending to the Caribbean and North America. During a period of intellectual, political, social and religious ferment, it was in the pages of the printed journals, the *Zeitschriften*, that passionate debates and arguments, visions and counter-visions were presented, scrutinized, contested and subjected to seemingly endless analysis.

In the mid-nineteenth century R. Jacob Ettlinger, chief rabbi of Altona, pioneered the development of a periodical literature which had a marked effect upon the dissemination of Orthodox ideology. He founded and edited a noted Hebrew journal, *Shomer Tziyyon ha-Ne'eman* (*The Faithful Guardian of Zion*), which injected a new measure of vitality into the field of rabbinic scholarship and also founded a German periodical, *Der treue Zionswächter*. The latter represents the earliest journalistic venture of German Orthodoxy in the vernacular. The first issue of the *Zionswächter* appeared on July 3, 1845 and predates the Hebrew language *Shomer Tziyyon ha-Ne'eman* which made its initial appearance approximately one year later in an issue dated 13 Tammuz 5606 (July 7, 1846). These periodicals serve as an invaluable source for the internal history of the Orthodox community about which a paucity of objective material exists.

Neither *Shomer Tziyyon ha-Ne'eman* nor the *Zionswächter* have received adequate treatment in histories of the Jewish press in Germany. Many scholars are unaware of the relative longevity of these journals. Indeed, several standard reference works err in reporting the appearance of only a few issues of these publications.[1] A number of writers note that they were unable personally to examine a copy of the *Zionswächter*.[2] While the neglect of *Shomer Tziyyon haNe'eman* in general studies of Jewish periodical literature has been partially alleviated by an evaluation authored by Yitzhak Rafael,[3] the *Zionswächter* has been relegated to almost total oblivion. There has been only one brief article in which this journal is discussed, a cursory study in Hebrew by Moshe Zinovitz,[4] which pinpoints the unique role of the *Zionswächter* and discusses the contents of but a few issues of the journal.

---

1 Cf. Yitzhak Rafael, *Rishonim ve-Aḥaronim* (Tel Aviv, 1957), 328. Margaret T. Edelheim-Muehsam, "The Jewish Press in Germany," *Leo Baeck Institute Year Book* 1 (1965), 165, erroneously reports that *Der treue Zionswächter* (hereafter *TZW*) appeared only for two years, 1854–1855. Even Mordecai Eliav, who has written extensively on the history of German Orthodoxy, lists *TZW* as having appeared from 1845–1848. See Mordecai Eliav, *Ha-Ḥinnukh ha-Yehudi be-Germaniah bi-Yemei ha-Haskalah ve-ha-Emantzipatziyah* (Jerusalem: The Jewish Agency, 1960), 349 and Mordecai Eliav, ed., *Iggerot Rabbi Ezri'el Hildesheimer* (Jerusalem: Rubin Mass, 1965), 63 n. 3 (German section).

2 See, for example, Baruch Mevorah, "Effects of the Damascus Affair upon the Development of the Jewish Press 1840–1846" (Hebrew), *Zion*, nos. 23–24 (1958–1959), 50 n. 20. Copies of *TZW* are difficult to obtain. A complete set including all editions of the periodical may be found in the library of Hebrew Union College in Cincinnati. Volumes 1 and 2 are available in the library of the Leo Baeck Institute, New York, volumes 2 and 5 in the Royal Library in Copenhagen and volumes 1–3 and parts of volumes 5 and 8 in the Jewish National and University Library, Jerusalem. Now, fortunately, *TZW* is available on Compact Memory. Compact Memory is a virtual archive of German-Jewish periodicals. This archive can be accessed at http://sammlungen.ub.uni-frankfurt.de/cm/nav/index/title/. As early as 1874, Ben Zion Ettlinger, *Binyan Tziyyon he-Ḥadashot* (Vilna, 1874), Introduction, remarked that copies of *Shomer Tziyyon ha-Ne'eman* (hereafter *STN*) were difficult to obtain and often damaged and incomplete. *STN* has now been republished in a bound offset edition (New York, 1963).

3 Rafael, *Rishonim ve-Aḥaronim*, 327–35.

4 "The First Traditional Newspaper" [Hebrew], *Ba-Mishor* 1, no. 7 (1940), 8–10; no. 8: 9–10; and no. 10: 10–11. This article was reprinted in *Hamsiloh* 7, no. 1 (1942), 5–7; and no. 2: 6–9.

The emergence of a thriving periodical literature was a phenomenon of singular significance in the development of the nineteenth-century German Jewish community. Periodical publications had appeared, to be sure, during earlier periods of European Jewish history. Generally regarded as the first Jewish magazine is *Peri Etz Ḥayyim*,[5] a Hebrew periodical incorporating rabbinic decisions of members of *Etz Ḥayyim*, the Sephardic *bet midrash* (House of Study) in Amsterdam. Although the first edition of *Peri Etz Ḥayyim* appeared in 1691, and further issues were published intermittently over the span of more than a century until 1807, this journal appeared only sporadically. Better known is the publication *Kohelet Mussar*, published in Germany by Moses Mendelssohn and Tobias Back. Again, however, only two issues of this publication were published, both in the year 1750. These limited endeavors aside, the true emergence of a Hebrew press dates from the appearance of *Ha-Me'assef*, a successful monthly organ which was founded at Mendelssohn's initiative by a group of his disciples in Berlin in 1784 and which appeared for a period of twenty-seven years. *Sulamith*, a monthly printed and written in the German language and with a pronounced Reform tendency, was founded in July 1806 by David Fraenkel and Joseph Wolf. These pioneering enterprises were soon followed by a proliferation of Jewish periodicals.

Whereas *Kohelet Mussar* was written and printed in Hebrew, and *Ha-Me'assef* was written in the Hebrew language but at times included German supplements, with the German articles on occasion printed in Hebrew characters, the later journals were primarily written in languages other than Hebrew. The majority of the new publications were German-language journals. The fourth decade of the nineteenth century was marked by an intensification of journalistic activity and the fifth decade was characterized by even greater journalistic productivity. During the latter ten years, five new Hebrew-language periodicals appeared in Germany and a total of twenty-five new German-language periodicals commenced publication. Seven of these were published outside of Germany.[6]

---

5 This honor has also been claimed for *Reshit Bikkurei Katzir*, which was published in Ferrara in 1715. See Rafael, *Rishonim ve-Aharonim*, 323 n. 3. Rafael draws attention to common errors with regard to the dates of publication of *Peri Etz Ḥayyim* which have crept into the literature on this periodical.

6 Richard Gottheil and William Popper, "Periodicals," *Jewish Encyclopedia* (New York, 1906), vol. IX, 602–604. Edelheim-Muehsam, "Jewish Press," 163, notes that from emancipation until 1938 well over two hundred Jewish publications appeared in Germany.

Periodical literature played an important role in the cultural life of nineteenth-century Jewry. The Hebrew-language periodicals had an enormous impact upon the development of Hebrew literature and upon the revival of Hebrew and its transformation into a modern language.[7] The influence of the German-language periodicals may be observed in a variety of areas. Initially, they served to educate the masses in preparation for emancipation and participation in modern society. Subsequently, many periodicals of a scholarly character served as a forum of expression for exponents of the *Wissenschaft des Judentums* and made a momentous contribution to the advancement of Jewish scholarship. Following the Damascus Affair, the Jewish press played an increasingly significant role in reporting news of political developments on the international scene and in fostering feelings of solidarity and reciprocal responsibility among Jews throughout the world.[8] The most striking feature of Jewish periodical literature of the mid-nineteenth century, however, was the manner in which it reflected the religious ferment of the times. With the growth of the Reform movement in the nineteenth century, factionalism had become a hallmark of Jewish life. By the second decade of the century the ideological cleavage within the ranks of Judaism had become pronounced and the Orthodox and Reform movements had emerged as clearly defined denominations pitted against one another in a struggle for supremacy. The majority of the early journals were published by exponents of Reform Judaism; only gradually did a press of a more moderate and, later, traditional orientation emerge.

In the early 1840s several successful Reform periodicals appeared in Germany. Included in this genre were *Sulamith*,[9] Geiger's *Wissenschaftliche Zeitschrift für Jüdische Theologie* (founded 1835), the *Allgemeines Archiv des Judenthums* (founded 1842), Jost's *Israelitische Annalen* (first edition January 4, 1839), *Der Israelit des Neunzehnten Jahrhunderts* (first edition June 15, 1839), *Sinai* (first edition January 5, 1846), Fürst's *Der Orient* (first edition January 4, 1840), with its literary supplement the notable *Literaturblatt*. The most influential Reform journal of the time, *Die Allgemeine Zeitung des Judentums*, was founded on May 2, 1837 by Ludwig Philippson.

The *Allgemeine Zeitung* was edited by Philippson for fifty-three years until his death in 1889 and did not cease publication until 1922. Of these

---

7 Meyer Waxman, *A History of Jewish Literature* (New York: Thomas Yoseloff, 1960), vol. III, 333–34.
8 Mevorah, "Effects of the Damascus Affair," 46–65.
9 Discontinued in 1848. See Edelheim-Muehsam, "Jewish Press," 165.

periodicals, the *Allgemeine Zeitung* came closest to being a newspaper in the modern sense of the term. Appearing with regularity at first three times a week and later on a weekly basis, it served as a steady source of news and information. Under the editorship of Philippson, the *Allgemeine Zeitung* developed into a powerful vehicle for advancing the Reform agenda. Publications such as the *Orient* and the *Sabbathblatt* (founded 1842) were far more conservative in orientation than journals such as the *Israelit des Neunzehnten Jahrhunderts* or the *Allgemeine Zeitung*. In 1844 Zacharias Frankel founded the *Zeitschrift für die Religiösen Interessen des Judenthums*, an important journal representing the emerging historical school. Common to all these periodicals was the fact that they represented viewpoints sharply at variance with the interests and ideology of the Orthodox.

This, then, was the state of the periodical literature at the time when R. Jacob Ettlinger founded *Der treue Zionswächter* in 1845.[10] A noted talmudic scholar and one of the foremost rabbinic authorities of his day, R. Ettlinger was one of the earliest Orthodox rabbis to receive a university education and to preach in the vernacular. He served as chief rabbi of Altona from 1836 to 1871 and in this post played a unique role as an architect of modern Orthodoxy.[11] R. Ettlinger's voluminous talmudic novellae, most of which appeared under the title *Arukh la-Ner*, established his reputation as one of Germany's foremost

---

10 Gottheil and Popper, "Periodicals," 604 and 638, note the brief appearance in 1845 of another Orthodox publication, a Hebrew-language periodical, *Ha-Yareah*. I have been unable to locate either the periodical or further reference to this publication. Other periodicals bearing the same name appeared in Königsberg, Prussia, in 1871–1872 and in 1896. See Getzel Kressler, "Hebrew Periodicals and Newspapers," *Encyclopedia Judaica* (Jerusalem, 1972), vol. I (index), 205.

11 Biographical sketches of R. Jacob Ettlinger are to be found in Eduard Duckesz, *Iwoh Lemoshaw* (Krakow, 1903), 114–24; Akiba Posner and Ernest Freimann, "Rabbi Jacob Ettlinger," in *Guardians of our Heritage*, ed. Leo Jung (New York: Bloch Publishing Co., 1958), 231 and 243; and Yonah Emanuel, "Perakim be-Toldot ha-Rav Ya'akov Ettlinger z'l," *Ha-Ma'ayan* 12 (1971–1972), 25–35. The biographical information is synopsized in brief encyclopedia articles by Gotthard Deutsch, "Jacob Ettlinger," *Jewish Encyclopedia* (New York, 1906), vol. V, 264–65; Samuel A. Horodetzky, "Jacob ben Aaron Ettlinger," *Encyclopedia Judaica* (Berlin, 1930), vol. VI, 826–27; and Shlomo Eidelberg, "Jacob Ettlinger," *Encyclopedia Judaica* (Jerusalem, 1971), vol. VI, 595–96. Unfortunately, these biographies take little account of the material on Ettlinger in the periodical literature of the time. In particular, *TZW* (vols. 1–10, 1845–1854), contains a wealth of material concerning Ettlinger's activities in Altona and constitutes a hitherto untapped source. See also this wrriter's unpublished doctoral dissertation, "Jacob Ettlinger, His Life and Works: The Emergence of Modern Orthodoxy in Germany" (New York University, 1974).

talmudists.[12] Universal recognition of R. Ettlinger as a talmudic authority enhanced his effectiveness as an arbiter of halakhah[13] and as a spokesman for all sectors of the Orthodox community.

The *Zionswächter* was published as a weekly from July 3, 1845 until June 28, 1850.[14] After a hiatus of a year, the journal resumed publication and appeared again, as a bi-weekly, from July 4, 1851 until March 28, 1856.[15] The Hebrew supplement, *Shomer Tziyyon ha-Ne'eman,* was published fortnightly

---

12 Ettlinger's published novellae include: *Arukh la-Ner* on *Makkot* and *Keritot* (Altona, 1855); *Arukh la-Ner* on *Rosh ha-Shanah* and *Sanhedrin* (Warsaw, 1873); *Arukh la-Ner* on *Sukkah,* also known as *Ittur Bikkurim* (Altona, 1858); *Arukh la-Ner* on *Yevamot* (Altona, 1850); *Bikkurei Ya'akov* (Altona, 1836), and *Tosefot Bikkurim* (Altona, 1858).

13 His collected responsa appeared in *Binyan Tziyyon* (Altona, 1868), and in the posthumously published *Binyan Tziyyon he-Ḥadashot.* A number of additional responsa appear in works of his contemporaries.

14 The immediate reason for suspension of publication appears to have been the editor's earnest request to be relieved of the burdens of editorial responsibility. In a closing statement, *TZW* 6 (1850), 208, the editorial committee observed that they viewed their primary objective as having been accomplished:

> Die Interessen des orthodoxen Judenthums, deren Wahrung diese Blätter einzig und allein ihre Begrundung verdankten, erscheinen gegenwartig der Art gesichert, dass eine Gefährdung derselben, seitens der Reform oder Umsturzpartei in Judenthums nicht zu befürchten. ... Unsere Aufgabe indess kann für's Erste ihre Endschaft erreicht haben. ... Freunden und Feinden aber die Versicherung, dass der Tag, der im Interesse des orthodoxen Judenthums sein Wiedererscheinen erheischte, den Wächter kampfgerüstet und muthig wie je, auf dem Kampfplatz bereit finden wird.

Many attributed the cessation of publication to the aftermath of the uprisings and strife in Germany. Cf. *STN*, no. 105, editorial note: "It is now a full year that we have rested on our guard post and, behold, a voice calls to us from far and near, 'Wherefore have you withheld your kindness from lovers of the Torah? If you have rested on account of the clamor of warfare which was then heard in your land, behold, at present, the land has respite and has quietened. Why are you yet silent?'"

15 The final issue included in the Compact Memory Collection is dated December 29, 1854. Richard Gotthard and William Popper, "Periodicals," in *Jewish Encyclopedia* (New York, 1906), vol. IX, 604, give 1855 as the final date. However, Rabbi Yehudah Aharon Horowitz, "Mi-Toldot ha-Meḥaber," in *She'elot u-Teshuvot Arukh la-Ner* (Jerusalem, 1989), vol. I, 35, relates that the final issue in the possession of his family, direct descendants of Rabbi Ettlinger, is dated March 28, 1856.

Editions of *TZW* and *STN* now appeared on alternate Fridays. In the second phase of its publication issues of *TZW* numbered only four pages in contrast to the original eight-page edition. The later issues of the magazine contain less original material; many articles that had appeared in the first volumes were also reprinted. Apparently, in response to popular demand, Enoch resumed the editorship; however, other commitments curtailed the time he was able to devote to editorial duties and, hence, the reduced frequency of appearance and curtailment of size and scope.

from July 1, 1846 until March 28, 1856, with an interruption of one year (July 5, 1850 to July 11, 1851). In all, two hundred and twenty-two issues of the Hebrew supplement were published.

R. Ettlinger engaged the services of Rabbi Dr. Samuel J. Enoch as editor of these periodicals.[16] At the time, Enoch was director of the Talmud Torah (Hebrew school) in Altona, and played a prominent role in communal and charitable activities. In 1856 Enoch was called to the rabbinate of Fulda. Apparently, the cessation of publication of the Hebrew periodical, *Shomer Tziyyon ha-Ne'eman,* that year was the result of Enoch's departure for Fulda.

The prospectus heralding the forthcoming *Zionswächter,* signed by Enoch, illustrates clearly that the journal was born of the Reform-Orthodox conflict and that its founders viewed its primary purpose as being an instrument through which the Reform movement might be contained. Enoch observes that the Orthodox voice could not find proper expression in existing partisan journals and that a vibrant Orthodox press was the need of the hour:

> The circumstances of the times urgently demanded resistance, required for it the full vigor of the sincere and fearless word ... finally, following the well-known protest of the 116 rabbis, the opposition was opened and it was candidly declared that the time had come for an independent organ whose candid and open intention would be solely to defend the interests of Orthodox talmudic Judaism. ...[17]

While he expressed the hope that the journal would never permit polemic to sink to the level of personal invective, Enoch declared that he would not shy away from honest debate and would endeavor to confront the manifold challenges arising with regard to Jewish religious life. The journal was designed to provide its readership with ideological guidance rooted in the Jewish tradition

---

16 See Duckesz, *Chachme AHW* (Hamburg, 1908), 123 and 126, and his *Iwoh Lemoshaw,* 117. Enoch had attended the Universities of Würzburg and Erlangen and had studied at the yeshiva of Ettlinger's teacher, the illustrious Abraham Bing of Würzburg, A colleague of R. Moses Sofer, referred to by the latter, *Responsa Ḥatam Sofer, Ḥoshen Mishpat,* nos. 34 and 35, and *Yoreh De'ah,* no. 343, as *ḥaveri*—"my friend" and *amiti*—"my colleague," Bing headed a yeshiva which was, at the time, a foremost center of rabbinic scholarship. See Moses L. Bamberger, *Ein Blick auf die Geschichte der Juden in Würzburg* (Würzburg, 1905), 12–13, and R. Abraham Bing, *Zikhron Avraham* (Pressburg, 1892), Introduction, 7–9.

17 Samuel Enoch, "Prospectus eines neu erscheinenden Organs zur Wahrung der Interessen des orthodoxen Judenthums" (Hamburg and Altona, 1845), 1. Cf. *TZW* 2 (1846), 98. The protest of the 116 rabbis is discussed below, note 27.

and with authoritative answers to questions of Jewish law penned by competent rabbinic scholars. As editor, Enoch pledged that careful attention would be directed to Jewish education and to the pivotal role of the school in the development of religious commitment and responsible citizenship. The journal sought to include news items of interest to the religious community, particularly information that served to bolster and strengthen Orthodoxy since one of the major aims of the journal was to give a new measure of confidence to the Orthodox and to demonstrate to all that Orthodoxy could achieve "the respect of the world."[18]

Indeed, throughout the duration of its publication the journal served first and foremost as an apologia for Orthodoxy. Countless articles were devoted to discussions of the role of religion in the modern world.[19] Particular attention was focused on the changing role of the rabbinate, on the selection of candidates to fill rabbinic positions, and on the new functions of the various communal institutions.[20] Several authors sought to analyze the changing relationship of the home to the community and one writer discussed the emancipation of women.[21] Orthodox response to the challenge of political emancipation and defense of the patriotism of the Orthodox community were recurring themes.[22]

As had been promised from the very inception, considerable space was devoted to matters pertaining to education. An attempt was made to analyze the effects of political developments on the evolution of the German educational system and to examine the merits of separation of Church and school.[23] Elementary and high schools, seminaries for the training of teachers and rabbis, yeshivot and adult education were all discussed in numerous contributions appearing over the years. Several articles discussed the role of parent and teacher in the learning process, teaching techniques, methods of

---

18 Enoch, "Prospectus," 2.
19 Typical examples are "Orthodoxes Judenthum und Gegenwart," *TZW* 3 (1847), 53, 59, 65–66 and 70; "Ein Wort über Gegenwart," *TZW* 8 (1852), 96–98 and 103–104; and "Zeitgeist," *TZW* 8 (1852), 98–100.
20 *TZW* 3 (1847), 97–101, 105–108 and 193–95; 4 (1848), 57–58, 67–68, 73–75, 81–82, 289–90, 297–98, 329–30, 338–39, 345–46, 369–70 and 377–78; 6 (1850), 9–12 and 27–30; 9 (1853), 41–43; and 10 (1854), 97–99 and 101–102.
21 *TZW* 3 (1837), 65–68.
22 *TZW* 3 (1847), 73–75 and 91–92; 4 (1848), 137–39, 147–49, 154–57, 165–66, 172–73, 241–43, 251–52, 278, 361–63 and 372–73; 5 (1849), 187–88, 209–12, 264–65 and 385–87; 6 (1850), 65–68, 93–96 and 97–99; 8 (1852), 3, 6, 14, 18–19, 22–23, 25–26, 30, 33–34, 37–38 , 47.
23 *TZW* 4 (1848), 254–68, 274–75, 284–85, 294, 315–18, 324–26, 333–34 and 339–41; and 6 (1850), 193–94.

teaching religious values and text books.[24] Of interest are descriptions of the religious schools in Halberstadt and Moisling, and of the thriving yeshiva in Pressburg, whose graduates occupied prominent rabbinic positions, particularly in Hungary.[25]

In response to the writings of exponents of Reform, the *Zionswächter* published numerous articles devoted to the explication of traditional beliefs and discussions on the divinity and authority of both Scripture and the Oral Law.[26] The very first issue of the journal contained an open letter bearing the signature of an Orthodox partisan, R. Benjamin Z. Auerbach of Darmstadt, addressed to the prominent scholar R. Solomon J. Rapoport of Prague, urging Rapoport to add his signature to the formal document of protest against the Brunswick Conference.[27] Similarly, many polemics published in early editions of the journal were part of a general attempt to discredit the Reform rabbinic conferences.[28] Editorials in the *Zionswächter* also vehemently opposed participation in the Conference of Theologians convened by Zacharias Frankel.[29]

Considerable space was devoted to discussion of the major halakhic controversies of the time. The controversy with regard to circumcision and the question of *metzitzah*,[30] in particular, were discussed at length.[31] Halakhic

---

24 *TZW* 3 (1847), 4, 11–20, 28, 34–37, 41–44, 109–10, 117–19, 227–28, 301–302, 317–18, 363–65, 374–75, 381–82; 5 (1849), 65–66, 92–93, 115–16, 137–38, 145–46, 155–56, 169–72, 212–14, 243–45, 319, 325–26, 329–31, 405–406 and 411–12; 6 (1850), 52–53, 57–59, 73–77, 77–79, 85–87, 102–103, 131–34, 170–73, 177–81 and 194–97; 8 (1852), 17–18 and 21–22; 9 (1853), 5–6 and 81–83; and 10 (1854), 81–82 and 85–86.

25 *TZW* 3 (1847), 131–32, 140, 203 and 211–12; and 5 (1849), 169–72.

26 For example, *TZW* 3 (1847), 273–74, 281–82, 289–90 and 306; 6 (1850), 33–34; 7 (1851), 5, 7 and 11; and 9 (1853), 2, 3, 6 and 8.

27 Formal protest of the Orthodox against the Reform conferences was organized in the form of a written manifesto entitled *Shelomei Emunei Yisra'el*. The manifesto was published in 1845 in a small pamphlet containing both a Hebrew and a German text and bearing the signatures of 77 Orthodox rabbis. The manifesto was published in English translation by the British *Voice of Jacob* 5 (1845), 136–37 and 142–43 and republished shortly thereafter in the American journal, *The Occident* 3 (1845), 146–49 and 198–201. Over the years, additional signatures to the manifesto were obtained and, subsequently, reports in the periodical literature refer to the document as the "protest of the 116 rabbis." See *Voice of Jacob* 5 (1845), 219, and *STN*, no. 10. By 1868, the number of signators was over 300. See *Der Israelit* 9 (1868), 287, and cf. Salomon Schreiber, ed., *Iggerot Soferim* (Vienna, 1933), vol. I, no. 60, 85.

28 *TZW* 3 (1847), 201–203, 209–10 and 217–18.

29 *TZW* 3 (1847), 81–83.

30 *Metzitzah* is part of the circumcision procedure involving suction of the blood from the wound and from the vessels flowing into the wound.

31 *TZW* 2 (1846), 285–90, 333–34, 377–78, 393–99, 400–404 and 409–10; and 3 (1847), 371–75, 378–80, 387–88, 403–404, 411–12 and 417–19.

problems stemming from the proliferation of civil marriage were the subjects of several articles appearing over the years.[32] While at times echoes of the bitter conflicts between Reform and Orthodox factions reverberated in the pages of the journal, Enoch strove to maintain the discussion on a dignified level, and lapses into invective and strident partisanship were rare.[33] In the contemporary Reform press, the *Zionswächter* was frequently the subject of derision. Particularly sharp responses which appeared in the *Zionswächter* were often evoked in response to such criticism.[34]

Most journals of this genre resembled newsweeklies in their coverage of events in the religious and cultural life of the Jewish community. The news columns of these publications were devoted to matters of religious and academic interest, rather than to general topical events. The same journals featured scholarly discussions of matters of both theoretical and practical interest in the style of a scholarly journal rather than that of a magazine. In the *Zionswächter,* as in most of these Jewish journals, news items assumed secondary importance although considerable space was given to reports of events of significance to the religious community, to intracommunal struggles of Reform and Orthodox groups and to developments in the Holy Land. As an increasing number of Jewish periodicals were founded in many different localities, there developed a network of periodicals. These periodicals supplied one another with news of their local communities on a reciprocal basis. This informal arrangement developed into a system tantamount to an international news service. Each publication felt free to report items of local news which appeared in other publications.[35] During this period the *Zionswächter* served journals in other countries as a source of news of events and developments within the German Orthodox community.[36]

The *Zionswächter* constitutes a unique source for the historical study of the development of German Orthodoxy. At that time few detailed news reports of Orthodox communal functions appeared elsewhere in the press. Many reports in the *Zionswächter* record the Orthodox view with regard to the background of clashes which erupted between Orthodox and Reform

---

32   *TZW* 3 (1847), 129–30; 5 (1849), 57–58, 66–68 and 75–77; 6 (1850), 207; and 8 (1852), 26–27 and 30.
33   See, for example, *TZW* 3 (1847), 23 and 61; and 5 (1849), 373.
34   *TZW* 3 (1847), 21; and 4 (1848), 46–47, 103, 338 and 392.
35   Mevorah, "Effects of the Damascus Affair," 58–61.
36   See for example, ibid., 59 n. 62; and *Voice of Jacob* 5 (1845), 245; 6 (1846), 11–12; and 7 (1847), 200.

groups in various cities. More significant is the chronicle of the reactions of the Orthodox community to the political upheavals of the years 1847–1848.[37] The journal is an important source for information regarding the leading personalities of German Orthodoxy. Of particular interest are the lengthy articles describing the ceremonials in Hamburg attendant upon the twenty-fifth anniversary of Ḥakham Isaac Bernays's service in the rabbinate of Hamburg.[38] Noteworthy are descriptions of services arranged by R. Ettlinger in commemoration of special events and the texts of German and Hebrew prayers composed by him for those occasions.[39] The early career of R. Samson Raphael Hirsch may be followed in a series of news items depicting his departure from Emden, his accomplishments in Moravia, and his move to Frankfurt.[40] The journal also contains reports on the activities of R. Azriel Hildesheimer in Eisenstadt.[41]

The mid-nineteenth century was a period in which the sermonic style of both Protestant and Jewish clergymen underwent a marked change. As has been well documented,[42] the nineteenth century saw the rise of a new style of Jewish preaching in which the sermon underwent changes in both structure and substance. These mirrored the transformation that had occurred at the time in the preaching style of the Christian clergy. The change manifest in the style of Reform preachers, at first, gradually came to be reflected among the Orthodox. Functioning, in a sense, as a journal of record, the *Zionswächter* serves as an interesting historical source for the changes in sermonic style taking place in the Orthodox rabbinate. There is evident a lessening of emphasis on biblical exegesis and a structuring of the sermon around specific moralistic themes. Thus, for example, in the pages of the *Zionswächter* one finds sermons in the old style by R. Abraham Samuel Benjamin Sofer (known as *Ketav Sofer*)[43] alongside the many sermons of Salomon Cohn and Israel Schwarz[44] and the

---

37 *TZW* 3 (1847), 175, 181, 308–10 and 316; 4 (1848), 314–15 and 319; and 5 (1849), 1–5, 11–14, 17–21 and 172–73.

38 *TZW* 2 (1846), 362–64, 373–76 and 391.

39 *TZW* 3 (1847), 327–28; 4 (1848), 70–71, 79 and 172–73.

40 *TZW* 3 (1847), 23, 46, 189, 239–40 and 253–54; 4 (1848), 109–11, 117–19, 158–59, 181, 199, 261, 278, 365–66 and 372–73; 7 (1851), 4 and 19; and 9 (1853), 15.

41 *TZW* 9 (1853), 8 and 75; and 10 (1854), 99–100.

42 Alexander Altmann, "The New Style of Preaching in Nineteenth-Century German Jewry," in *Studies in Nineteenth-Century Jewish Intellectual History*, ed. Alexander Altmann (Cambridge, MA: Harvard University Press, 1964), 65–116.

43 *TZW* 3 (1847), 130–31, 149–50, 234–35 and 257–59.

44 For example, *TZW* 5 (1849), 257–64 and 273–76.

numerous contributions of R. Jacob Ettlinger,[45] all of which manifest a more contemporary style.

Poetic translations as well as original verse were a regular feature of the magazine. Many issues contained selections from Scripture and the liturgy rendered into German verse.[46]

There were few significant academic contributions published in the *Zionswächter*; serious scholarship was reserved for the Hebrew journal. The magazine, however, published brief articles on Jewish history written in a popular vein, and short biographies of personalities, such as Saadia, Ibn Ezra, Maimonides, and Abravanel.[47] While comparatively few articles appearing in the *Zionswächter* were of serious scholarly consequence, the journal did play an important role in fostering recognition of Jewish scholarship among its readership by publicizing scholarly works, acclaiming societies devoted to Torah study and calling for higher academic standards in religious and educational institutions. In addition to editorials emphasizing the importance of enhanced study of the Talmud, the journal included several articles advocating more intensive programs of adult education, discussion of the importance of general studies, and a call for the study of Jewish history.[48]

The *Zionswächter* came to play a vibrant part in the social and religious life of the Orthodox community. Noteworthy is an attempt by the editor to use the journal as a means of aiding Sabbath observers in their efforts to obtain employment.[49] Also of significance was the magazine's role in promoting charitable endeavors and centralizing charitable collections.[50] Within the Orthodox community the journal was received with acclaim, no small part of which stemmed from the realization that the periodical had brought an added measure of self-confidence and prestige to Orthodoxy.[51]

---

45 *TZW* 1 (1845), 117–18, and 125–27; 2 (1846), 309–13; 3 (1847), 1–3, 9–11, 153–54, 169–70 and 305–309; 5 (1849), 161–68, 201–205, 353–55 and 363–65; 6 (1850), 46–47, 68–71, 163–65 and 169–70; 7 (1851), 9–11; 8 (1852), 45–46, 49–50 and 73–75; and 10 (1854), 17–18, 23–24, 57–58, 61–63, 73–74 and 77–78.

46 See the lengthy poem by J. Schwarz, "Assaf und Tirza," *TZW* 5 (1849), 108–10, 117–18, 122–24, 133–34, 147, 156–57, 173 and 188–89.

47 *TZW* 3 (1847), 4, 156, 157, 396–98 and 419–22; 5 (1849), 23, 71–72, 324–25, 331–34, 347–49 and 394–98; 7 (1851), 16–17, 21–22, 26–27, 30–31, 34 and 38–39; and 9 (1853), 26–27, 30–31, 34–35 and 91–92.

48 *TZW* 2 (1846), 2 and 241–45; 3 (1847), 83–84, 301–302 and 317–18; and 4 (1848), 145–47 and 213–14.

49 *TZW* 3 (1847), 200.

50 See for example, *TZW* 3 (1847), 344, and 9 (1853), 88.

51 *TZW* 2 (1846), 98–99; 3 (1847), 350 and 392. Cf. also 7 (1851), 13 and 18–19; and *STN*, no. 105, editorial note, "To the Reader."

The favorable reception accorded the German journal encouraged Ettlinger and Enoch to publish a Hebrew supplement as well. A lengthy editorial in the *Zionswächter*[52] heralding the new publication pointed out that the Hebrew magazine was designed to fill a void in the intellectual life of the Orthodox community. The Hebrew supplement was entitled *Shomer Tziyyon ha-Ne'eman,* a direct translation of the title of its German sister publication. Its primary objective was the furtherance and advancement of Jewish scholarship. The new publication was designed to serve as a forum of expression for rabbinic authorities who were urged to focus their attention upon contemporary religious problems. The editors called upon rabbinic scholars to investigate and analyze the novel questions of Jewish law and ethics which had arisen in the modern age. It was contemplated that the deliberations of these scholars would be published in the pages of the new journal. Publication, it was hoped, would itself engender scholarly debate. Thus, it was envisioned that the availability of a forum for publication would foster an atmosphere of study and scholarship and would encourage formulation of reasoned responses to these pressing issues. The editors expressed the hope that the new magazine would awaken within the Jewish community "a more enthusiastic endeavor ... to cultivate religious studies and to be concerned for their growth and development."[53]

The goals of the new magazine were inscribed on its masthead in succinct phrases: "To raise the prestige of Torah and tradition and to remove stumbling block[s] from the path of faith." The masthead proclaimed that the journal was sponsored by a "society of rabbis and scholars who stand in the breach safeguarding the holy charge." The editorial functions were performed by R. Enoch in close collaboration with R. Ettlinger. Material appearing in the journal was subdivided into four categories: theoretical inquiries; novellae and commentaries; responsa; and parables and belles lettres.

Rabbinic scholars were quick to endorse the new literary undertaking, and the periodical soon boasted an impressive roster of contributors. Articles were authored by prominent rabbis residing in Germany, Hungary, France, Poland and Palestine. The foremost contributor was R. Jacob Ettlinger, himself, whose numerous articles appeared in one hundred and fifty issues of the journal and who maintained a lively exchange with many of the writers. There were several contributions authored by R. Ettlinger's father, Rabbi Aaron Ettlinger of Karlsruhe, and many articles written by his brother, Rabbi Leib Ettlinger of Mannheim. Frequent contributors were R. Moses Schick of St. Georgen, known

---

52 "An das Publikum," *TZW* 2 (1846), 97–99.
53 Ibid., 99.

as *Maharam Shik*, a prominent Hungarian halakhic decisor, and a rabbinic scholar, R. Jacob Koppel ha-Levi Bamberger of Worms.[54] Other noted rabbinic scholars whose writings were published in the journal include R. Gabriel Adler of Oberdorf, R. Levi Bodenheimer of Krefeld, R. Joel Dembitzer of Krakow, R. Wolf Hamburger of Fürth, R. Azriel Hildesheimer, then of Halberstadt, R. Saul Horowitz of Tarnopol, R. Baer Oppenheim of Eibeschütz, R, Hayyim Joseph Pollack of Trebitsch, R. Abraham Reizes and R. Pinhas Schiffer of Lemberg, R. Getschlik Schlesinger of Hamburg, R. Simon Schreiber of Mattersdorf, R. Abraham Sutro of Münster, R. Zelig L. Schick of Pressburg and R. Abraham Wechsler of Schwabach. R. Ettlinger made available for publication in the journal scholarly communications addressed to him by the preeminent halakhic scholar of the day, R. Akiva Eger, and by his own former teacher, R. Abraham Bing.[55] Responsa written by R. Moses Sofer (known as *Ḥatam Sofer*) were made available by two of the latter's former disciples.[56] In all, the journal was representative of the finest rabbinic scholarship of the traditional mold.

Shomer Tziyyon ha-Ne'eman succeeded in generating a lively exchange of ideas among the various contributors. Frequently, discussion on a particular topic would continue for several issues with various scholars presenting their own views with regard to the specific problems raised. In many issues R. Ettlinger published a series of brief responses to questions addressed to him via the forum of the magazine. The scholarly debate encouraged by the publication was one of its most valuable achievements and served to enhance the prestige of talmudic study.

Of the numerous halakhic responsa published in the journal, a large number pertained to problems of the modern world. Noteworthy are several discussions regarding the permissibility of travel by train on the Sabbath.[57] Several responsa on halakhic controversies related to innovations introduced by the Reform movement were first published in the pages of *Shomer Tziyyon haNe'eman*. These included discussions of the mode of performance of *metzitzah* [58] and *peri'ah*,[59]

---

54 A useful biography of this relatively unknown distinguished rabbinic scholar is to be found in Nathan Raphael Auerbach, "Rabbi Jacob Koppel ha-Levi Bamberger," *HaMa'ayan* 15, no. 4 (1975), 3–11.

55 *STN*, nos. 31, 77, 78 and 100.

56 *STN*, nos. 48, 95 and 154.

57 *STN*, nos. 23, 24 and 154.

58 *STN*, nos. 5, 12, 20, 21 and 93–98.

59 *STN*, no. 218. *Peri'ah*, an essential component of the circumcision procedure, consists of removal of the mucous membrane covering the glans and its retraction in order to uncover the corona.

recitation of *kaddish*[60] and observance of the Second Days of the Festivals.[61] Of particular significance are a series of contributions by Rabbi Abraham Sutro of Münster dealing with halakhic ramifications of Reform innovations in the synagogue. Among the specific questions discussed are the permissibility of the use of an organ, recitation of prayers by the congregation in unison, mixed choirs, cantilation, the necessity of calling individuals to the Reading of the Law by name, prayer in the vernacular and confirmation ceremonies.[62]

Remarkable in a rabbinic journal of this genre was its orientation toward modern-critical scholarship. R. Jacob Ettlinger, the moving spirit behind the magazine, was himself keenly interested in the scientific study of texts.[63] This concern is reflected in the material published in *Shomer Tziyyon ha-Ne'eman*. Examples of contributions in this area are an article by R. Ettlinger discussing the authenticity of a volume of responsa attributed to Rashi,[64] and the scholarly articles contributed by R. Jacob Koppel ha-Levi Bamberger of Worms as well as the latter's study of Targum Jonathan on the Pentateuch.[65] On the basis of previously unpublished manuscripts, Bamberger edited prayers composed by R. Samson Bacharach for publication in the journal.[66] Among the most valuable features of *Shomer Tziyyon ha-Ne'eman* were the numerous manuscripts of medieval scholars published in the magazine. Most notable of these were: responsa of Sherira Gaon and Hai Gaon copied from manuscripts in the British Museum;[67] correspondence of Maimonides's son Abraham;[68] responsa of Rabbenu Asher, known as *Rosh*, and his son Rabbi Judah;[69] and the writings of R. Eliezer bar Nathan of Mainz, known as *Ravan*.[70] It is interesting to note that selections of an important nineteenth-century scriptural commentary first appeared in this journal. R. Jacob Mecklenburg published

---

60 *STN*, no. 167.

61 *STN*, nos. 176–77 and 180–82.

62 *STN*, nos. 144, 153, 154, 175, 214, 215 and 217.

63 See, for example, *Arukh la-Ner, Niddah*, introduction; J. Ettlinger, letter of approbation to Raphael Nathan Nata Rabbinowicz, *Dikdukei Soferim, Berakhot* (Munich, 1868); and Judah Rosenberg, ed. *Kovetz Ma'asei Yedei Geonim Kadmonim* (Berlin, 1856), iv, 46–77.

64 *STN*, nos. 1–9.

65 *STN*, nos. 11–15, 56, 58, 61, 63, 68, 70–71, 80–81, 83, 87, 89 and 105.

66 *STN*, nos. 54, 55, 59, 60, 66, 69, 74, 75 and 78. R. Samson Bacharach was the author of *Teshuvot Ḥut ha-Shani* and father of R. Jair Hayyim Bacharach, author of *Teshuvot Ḥavot Ya'ir*.

67 *STN*, nos. 106–109 and 111–17.

68 *STN*, nos. 111–18.

69 *STN*, nos. 16–17.

70 *STN*, nos. 128–29 and 190–93.

addenda to his *Ha-Ketav ve-ha-Kabbalah* in several issues of *Shomer Tziyyon ha-Ne'eman*.[71] This material was later included in the second edition of his work (Königsberg, 1852).

Considerable material in the journal was devoted to liturgical topics. A brief item appeared pertaining to the laws of prayer,[72] as well as several articles containing glosses of R. Jacob of Lissa's popular prayerbook *Derekh ha-Ḥayyim*.[73] In what may be viewed as the second period in the journal's publication, following a one-year interruption, the magazine featured regular publication of manuscripts found in the Hamburg library under the title "Hamburg Treasures." These included numerous liturgical poems and commentaries on prayers written by medieval scholars. Particularly noteworthy was the publication of prayers authored by Rabbi Bahya[74] and Rabbi Kalonymos,[75] as well as liturgical poems for the Festivals authored by Judah Halevi[76] and Abraham Ibn Ezra.[77]

The editors of *Shomer Tziyyon ha-Ne'eman* were eager to foster the study of the Hebrew language. Several issues of the journal featured selections of Moses Ibn Ezra's *Sefer ha-Tarshish* copied from a manuscript in the Hamburg library.[78] In an introductory note to these selections, the editors emphasized their wish to contribute to the enhancement of Hebrew literary style and their "desire to disseminate over the face of the world … the light of our holy language from its hidden treasures."[79] An article on Hebrew grammar by Solomon Dubno appeared in nos. 22–23 of the journal. Of interest is a thirty-two stanza poem extolling the beauties of the "Hebrew language, choice among tongues,"[80] and a brief article calling for a revival of Hebrew.[81] A brief poetic accolade by Isaac Weiner illustrates the readership's awareness of the contribution made by *Shomer Tziyyon ha-Ne'eman* to the revival of the Hebrew language.[82]

---

71 *STN*, nos. 17–21.
72 *STN*, no. 41.
73 *STN*, nos. 26–28 and 125.
74 *STN*, nos. 145–47.
75 *STN*, nos. 195–96.
76 *STN*, nos. 131 and 137–38.
77 *STN*, nos. 137–39.
78 *STN*, nos. 106–24.
79 *STN*, no. 106. The note concludes: "For only in the aggrandizement of Torah and the flowering of the idiom of our language will the faithful guardians of Zion achieve their desire."
80 *STN*, nos. 183–84.
81 *STN*, no. 198.
82 *STN*, no. 44.

From the purely literary viewpoint, it is noteworthy that the magazine featured numerous poetic contributions on a wide variety of subjects. Of interest are a lengthy Hebrew narrative poem entitled "Faithful of the Land,"[83] several poems authored by R. Simon Schreiber,[84] the many contributions of Moses Landau[85] and a tribute to an anonymous patron of Torah study in Altona.[86] Several writers also contributed scholarly riddles and enigmas. Occasionally, Hebrew sermons were included in the journal,[87] as well as eulogies, such as a memorial address in tribute to R. Solomon Eger,[88] and a dirge on the occasion of the death of the noted philanthropist and supporter of the settlements in the Holy Land, Zevi Hirsch Lehren.[89]

The magazine served as a forum for publication of a wide variety of articles attacking the Reform movement. These ranged from brief exhortatory letters to more lengthy and detailed statements of Orthodox views.[90] Noteworthy is a lengthy article in defense of traditionalism which appeared in a number of issues in the novel form of a dialogue between a father and son.[91] Many articles and letters indicate that the journal came to serve as a rallying point for the Orthodox.[92] Joining in R. Ettlinger's opposition to the Reform movement, rabbis of the Jewish community in Jerusalem hailed *Shomer Tziyyon ha-Ne'eman* as the guardian of tradition.[93] A letter addressed to R. Ettlinger by members of the Sephardic rabbinate of Jerusalem declares: "You from there, and we from here, shall stand on guard to strengthen our Torah, the religion of Moses and Israel."[94] This orientation evoked a responsive chord in at least segments of the readership of *Shomer Tziyyon ha-Ne'eman*. R. Jacob Mecklenburg, for example, commended the editors for combating the lethargy of the Orthodox

---

83 *STN*, nos. 14–19.

84 *STN*, nos. 143–44.

85 *STN*, nos. 164, 169–70, 173–74, 194 and 212.

86 *STN*, no. 43. Cf. *TZW* 2 (1846), 2; and 3 (1847), 83–84.

87 *STN*, nos. 119–20, 175–78 and 191–93.

88 *STN*, nos. 121–23.

89 *STN*, no. 170.

90 See, for example, Eliezer Lipman, "An Open Proclamation on Behalf of Torah," *STN*, nos. 1–5; Solomon Z. Klein, "A Soft Answer to a Harsh Vision," *STN*, nos. 10–11 and 13–14; and Israel Budak, "Regarding the Opponents of Maimonides, of Blessed Memory, in our Generation," *STN*, nos. 28–30.

91 "A Conversation between a Father and Son Regarding the Vulgar who Malign Early Scholars, of Blessed Memory," *STN*, nos. 35–37, 39–42, 44 and 46–50.

92 *STN*, nos. 32–33, 44, 105, 110, 113, 126 and 162.

93 *STN*, no. 137.

94 *STN*, no. 10.

and hailed the "guardians of Zion" who had "girded themselves to awaken those who sleep and to arouse those who slumber lest they be ensnared in the traps of the enemies of the Lord."[95]

R. Ettlinger considered belief in the restoration of Zion to be at the heart of a Jew's faith. The anticipation of Israel's spiritual rebirth as foreseen by the Prophets was the hope and dream that had sustained Israel throughout the centuries. Any attempt to eradicate this belief would deal a mortal blow to Jewry. In his anti-Reform polemics, Ettlinger emphasized that rejection of the belief in the restoration of Zion was the symbol of the final parting of the ways. The very choice of the name, "The Faithful Guardian of Zion," for both his German and Hebrew publications indicated that he deemed belief in Zion to be an issue of central importance. It was here that the ramparts must be manned. As R. Ettlinger himself declared:

> The belief in Israel's future rebirth in splendor and glory [and] the erection of an altar in Zion ... stands in the forefront of our wishes and hopes and constitutes the principal content of the prayers which we daily direct heavenward. ... [H]er enemies notwithstanding, we shall place the hope of a future return [to Jerusalem] at the summit of our wishes. Let us, as faithful guardians of Zion, guard God's royal residence against any attack on its honor and great significance.[96]

Love of Zion was one of the central motivating forces of R. Ettlinger's life. From his earliest youth he sought to give concrete expression to this sentiment and was eager to assist in any endeavor to improve conditions in the Holy Land.[97] R. Ettlinger's deep commitment to the Land of Israel found expression in the pages of both *Shomer Tziyyon ha-Ne'eman* and the *Zionswächter.* In both journals, matters relating to the welfare of the Holy Land were featured prominently. These publications played an all-important role in establishing the needs of the *yishuv* (Jewish settlement in Palestine) as a matter of priority and vital concern to diaspora Jewry.

---

95 *STN*, no. 17. See also Abraham Sutro's remarks in *STN*, nos. 17 and 175.

96 "Zions Wiedergeburt," *TZW*, 10 (1854), 17–18.

97 See, for example, Heimann Kottek, *Geschichte der Juden* (Frankfurt am Main, 1915), 443; Mordecai Eliav, "Regarding the History of the *Batei Maḥaseh* in Old Jerusalem," *Sinai* 61 (1967), 298–315; and his *Ahavat Tziyyon ve-Anshei Hod: Yehudei Germaniah ve-Yishuv Eretz Yisra'el be-Me'ah ha-Yod-Tet* (Tel Aviv, 1970), 121 and 125 n. 11; and Joseph Unna, "The Testament of Rabbi Jacob Jukuv Ettlinger, of Blessed Memory," *Ha-Ma'ayan* 12, no. 2 (1972), 39.

Articles concerning Palestine publicized in the *Zionswächter* fall into three categories: news items, descriptions of conditions in the country; and appeals for funds. Brief news reports appearing in every second or third issue of the journal underscored the problems faced by the settlers and their economic difficulties. Constant mention of the Holy Land served to heighten the reader's sense of identification with Palestinian Jewry.[98] Occasionally, a longer article featured a description of a journey to Palestine or of conditions in the various Palestinian communities.[99] *Shomer Tziyyon ha-Ne'eman* also featured descriptions of the conditions in the Palestinian settlements.[100]

The journals were of major importance in attempts to raise funds for the Holy Land. The year 1846 was a time of famine and exceptional hardship for inhabitants of Palestine. The *Zionswächter* gave extensive coverage to the plight of the *yishuv* during this period. An appeal for funds signed by Sephardic chief rabbi R. Chaim Abraham Gagin, known as the *Rishon le-Tziyyon*, depicts the desperation of "the precious sons of Zion ... their tongue cleaves to their palate for a piece of dry bread."[101] Subsequent issues publicized appeals signed by the *Pekidim* and *Amarkalim* of Amsterdam, the Sephardic rabbinate of Tiberias and Safed and the *Kolel Perushim* of Jerusalem.[102] R. Ettlinger and the communal leaders of Altona issued a special appeal designating the *Pekidim* and *Amarkalim* as the central agency supervising the forwarding and distribution of these funds.[103]

---

98 Cf. a report in *TZW*, 4 (1848), 280, regarding Ettlinger's eulogy in memory of the Palestinian Sephardic Chief Rabbi Chaim Abraham Gagin, in which the writer observes that the gathering demonstrated the essential unity of the Jewish people: "Ein zahlreiches Publikum gab abermals den Beweis wie ... die Gesamtheit Israels sich als ein ganzes betrachtet, miteinander fühlt, miteinander leidet, aber auch hofft, Söhne eines Volkes, Kinder eines Gottes." See also Jonathan Wittkower, "An Elegy for Everlasting Memorial," *STN*, no. 57.

99 *TZW*, 2 (1846), 87–88 and 196; 3 (1847), 324–25, 332–33, 341–42, 347–48, 354–55, 366–67 and 405–406; 6 (1850), 7 and 30; 7 (1851), 3–4, 7–8, 11–12 and 24; and 10 (1854), 20 and 24.

100 *STN*, nos. 165–66 and 178–79.

101 *TZW*, 2 (1846), 88.

102 *TZW* 2 (1846), 273–76 and 306–307. The *Pekidim* and *Amarkalim* constituted an organization which served as an agency for the collection of funds on behalf of the Jews of Palestine. In 1824 this organization was designated by the Jerusalem rabbinate as the exclusive agency for collection of funds on their behalf throughout Western Europe. Palestinian immigrants from various European countries banded together to form their own communities and institutions which were known as *kolelim*. These *kolelim* obtained financial support primarily from Jewish communities in their countries of origin. *Kolel Perushim*, established in the nineteenth century, was composed of disciples of the Gaon of Vilna.

103 *TZW* 2 (1846), 347–48. See also 3 (1847), 94; and 4 (1848), 30. R. Ettlinger's efforts were noted by *Voice of Jacob* 6 (1846), 37.

In the following years, the *Zionswächter* continued to underscore the financial straits of the communities in the Holy Land.[104] In 1854, the *yishuv* was again faced with an emergency. A communication from leaders of Congregation Jeschurun of Jerusalem entitled "The Tear of the Oppressed," appearing in no. 175 of *Shomer Tziyyon ha-Ne'eman*, described the poverty and destitution of the Jerusalem community:

> At this moment the condition of all the inhabitants has deteriorated greatly [and has regressed] ten steps backwards. It is a year of famine and inflation of all foodstuffs. … The entire populace wail in their misfortune, they all cry, all loins are atremble, young and old alike, calling out for bread. Know you that like unto this year there has never been.

A plea for assistance signed by the Jerusalem rabbinate was published in no. 180 of *Shomer Tziyyon ha-Ne'eman*, with the addition of a personal appeal authored by R. Ettlinger. Signing himself "one who pleads on behalf of the impoverished holy flock," R. Ettlinger urged his coreligionists: "Have pity and mercy on the thousands of souls of your unfortunate brothers and sisters who faint with hunger on the holy ground. … Do multiply your contributions. …" Concurrently, an eloquent appeal by R. Ettlinger was also published in German in the *Zionswächter*.[105] Subsequent issues of the journal included reports of collections undertaken in various communities and news regarding conditions in Palestine.[106] The last available issue of the *Zionswächter*, dated December 29, 1854, contains a report of monies collected for Palestine in Lübeck.[107] A large part of these funds were sent directly to the Holy Land by R. Jacob Ettlinger himself. It is noted that a Palestinian emissary, Eliezer Bergmann, had encouraged the women to make a special contribution to the Holy Land at the time of the baking of *ḥallot* (Sabbath loaves) and that this had become a widespread practice among women in the Altona vicinity.[108] The report concludes with the observation that the generous response to these appeals on the part of German Jewry testifies to the enduring nature of Israel's national character and to the vitality of its commitment to the Holy Land.

---

104 See for example, *TZW* 7 (1851), 51–52; and 8 (1852), 91–92.

105 *TZW* 10 (1854), 49.

106 *TZW* 10 (1854), 51, 64, 71–72 and 91–92.

107 *TZW* 10 (1854), 104.

108 Cf. remarks of the Palestinian emissary; Moses Sachs, *Ha-Maggid* (1862), 83. See also M. Eliav, "The Journeys of R. Moses Sachs as an Emissary of the *Batei Maḥaseh*," *Sinai* 62 (1968), 179 n. 35.

In 1851, the Sephardic rabbis and the *kolelim* of Jerusalem bestowed upon R. Ettlinger the honorific title of *Nesi Eretz Yisra'el* (Prince of the Land of Israel), in recognition of his efforts on their behalf and of his single-minded striving "for the purposes of the settlement of the Land of Israel, for the sake of Heaven, with no ulterior motive whatsoever." A copy of the certificate of investiture was included in the *Zionswächter*.[109] A brief introductory comment noted that R. Ettlinger's manifold activities had been crowned with success in the past and that hopefully the new office would serve to enhance his efforts to stimulate the interest of his coreligionists in the life and work of the Palestinian community.[110]

Many editions of the Hebrew journal featured learned contributions, novellae and responsa authored by Jerusalem scholars and rabbis.[111] Rabbi Isaac Prague of Jerusalem, a disciple of R. Moses Sofer, was a very frequent contributor.[112] Several articles by R. Simon Deutsch, also a former disciple of R. Moses Sofer, were published during the years 1852–53.[113] Of particular interest are the scholarly articles of R. Nachman Nathan Koronel, a native of Holland who settled in Israel in 1834 and became one of the founders of *Kolel Hod*.[114] R. Koronel contributed his notations of variant talmudic textual readings found in old manuscripts that had come into his possession.[115] He also contributed an unpublished scholarly note on the commentary of Ibn Ezra[116] and a manuscript of a concise halakhic treatise authored by an early-day talmudic commentator, R. Eliezer bar Nathan (*Ravan*).[117]

It may thus be seen that during the ten-year period in which it was published, *Shomer Tziyyon ha-Ne'eman* was instrumental in forging links

---

109 *TZW* 7 (1851), unnumbered page following p. 44. A facsimile of the document is to be found in Jacob Ettlinger, *Haggadah shel Pesaḥ, Minḥat Ani* (Jerusalem, 1972), seventh of the unnumbered pages.

110 *TZW* 7 (1851), 44.

111 *STN*, nos. 143, 154–58, 177, 185–88, 207 and 218.

112 *STN*, nos. 135, 140, 144, 148, 149, 154, 161, 166, 169, 170, 176, 179, 186, 192 and 216. Notes by R. Ettlinger are included in Prague's article in *STN*, no. 144 and are reprinted in *Binyan Tziyyon he-Ḥadashot*, no. 173. R. Ettlinger's response to Prague's queries in *STN*, no. 154 appears in *STN*, no. 155 and is reprinted in *Binyan Tziyyon he-Ḥadashot*, no. 124. For biographical information on Prague, see Eliav, *Ahavat Tziyyon*, 250–51.

113 *STN*, nos. 137, 143, 149, 150 and 154.

114 See Eliav, *Ahavat Tziyyon*, 149–50. *Kolel Hod*, established in the nineteenth century; was composed of immigrants from Holland and Germany (*Hod: Holland und Deutschland*).

115 *STN*, nos. 134, 139, 147 and 164.

116 *STN*, no. 155.

117 *STN*, no. 190–93.

between members of the scholarly community in the Holy Land and their colleagues in Europe. The importance of both this Hebrew journal and its German-language counterpart in strengthening the bonds between the Jews of Palestine and the Diaspora should not be underestimated.

These two periodicals were of marked importance in the development of German Orthodoxy. The failure of modern scholars to assess their significance constitutes a serious lapse, particularly because the debate generated by the emergence of the Reform movement was conducted for some decades in the periodical literature.[118] Numerous scholarly works were authored by leading exponents of the *Wissenschaft des Judentums;* but learned tomes were not the appropriate means for the dissemination of new ideas among the masses. Newspapers and journals, with their lighter style, briefer articles and periodic exposure, provided ideal media for publicizing and popularizing religious innovations. To be sure, for a great number of readers, the periodicals were of interest primarily as a source of information, diversion and entertainment, and only secondarily because of their theological content. Yet, precisely because the influence was subtle and indirect was its effect more pronounced. Thus, for example, the *Allgemeine Zeitung* enjoyed unusual success on the popular level and consequently was one of the most powerful instruments for advancing Reform ideology. Until the appearance of the traditionalist publications fostered by R. Ettlinger, no comparable media were available to the Orthodox. *Der treue Zionswächter* and *Shomer Tziyyon ha-Ne'eman* were significant not so much because of the fact that they presented a response to Reform views as that they provided the Orthodox public with alternative reading material. They were effective primarily for their role in the struggle of the Orthodox for containment of the Reform movement, rather than as a means of spreading Orthodoxy among those who were leaving the fold.

An additional observation should be made. Assessment of the degree of success of the *Zionswächter* depends upon one's vantage point. To the more sophisticated columnists of the *Orient* and the *Allgemeine Zeitung,* the *Zionswächter* appeared to be a second-rate journalistic endeavor, never quite attaining the standards of literary competence which the former set for themselves and, hence, they tended to react to it with a measure of disdain. Yet, on a very fundamental level, this Orthodox journal did indeed meet the challenge of the Reform publications: it was written in fluent German and its table of

---

118 W. Gunther Plaut, *The Rise of Reform Judaism* (New York: World Union for Progressive Judaism, 1963), 10–26.

contents included belles lettres, poetry, and scholarly essays. The successful accommodation to the modern world which was to be accomplished under the leadership of Rabbis Hirsch and Hildesheimer is a matter of historical record. The first step in this direction was taken at an earlier date by R. Jacob Ettlinger. The fact that a man of his ilk, a halakhist and talmudist, who was entirely a representative of the old school, had chosen to foster a "modern" magazine constituted a significant milestone in Orthodoxy's adaptation to a changing world.

The pioneering work of Rabbis Ettlinger and Enoch convinced the Orthodox of the crucial role played by communications media in the modern world. The journalistic tradition of the Orthodox press initiated in Altona was continued in several publications founded in the latter half of the nineteenth century. Shortly before the *Zionswächter* ceased to exist, R. Samson Raphael Hirsch announced his intention to found a new Orthodox journal devoted to "the furtherance of Jewish spirit and Jewish life in home, community and school." This periodical, a monthly called *Jeschurun*, was published from October 1854 to September 1870. *Jeschurun* served as a forum to circulate Rabbi Hirsch's own views as well as other articles and news of general interest to the Orthodox community. A publication which was destined to have a greater impact on the wider community was *Der Israelit*, an Orthodox weekly which first appeared on May 15, 1860 under the editorship of R. Marcus Lehmann. *Der Israelit* was published uninterruptedly until 1939, and exerted considerable influence on the development of German Orthodoxy.

A more direct line of influence may be traced from the Altona periodicals to another important journalistic venture. In June 1870, at R. Azriel Hildesheimer's initiative, an Orthodox weekly, *Die jüdische Presse*, was founded in Berlin. The first editors of the journal were R. Samuel Enoch, Gustav Karpeles and Jacob Hollander. Karpeles, a noted writer and scholar, was a graduate of the Breslau Rabbinical Seminary and, apparently, his association with the more traditionalist Hildesheimer faction was not without its difficulties. Accordingly, he relinquished his editorial responsibilities after only a few months in October 1870. Jacob Hollander, a native of Altona and a disciple of R. Ettlinger, had come to Berlin to continue his studies under Hildesheimer and was subsequently called to the rabbinate of Hanover in 1871. Since R. Enoch lived in Fulda, at an even greater distance from Berlin, Hollander served as principal editor of *Die jüdische Presse* until 1873. From 1873 to 1875 R. Enoch edited *Die jüdische Presse* in Fulda. Following R. Enoch's demise, the editorship of the paper from 1876 to 1882 was assumed by Seligmann Meyer. From 1883 until his death in 1910 Hirsch Hildesheimer, R. Azriel Hildesheimer's son, edited the journal. *Die jüdische Presse* continued to appear until 1923. In its final years of publication it was the official organ of the Mizrachi party.[119]

The close connection between *Die jüdische Presse* and the *Zionswächter* is readily manifest in the fact that both the first principal editors of *Die jüdische Presse* had an intimate relationship with R. Ettlinger. Jacob Hollander had been one of R. Ettlinger's outstanding students. Jacob's father, Rabbi Isaiah Hollander, had been a prominent Altona *dayyan* who, for decades, had served the Altona community in close association with R. Ettlinger.[120] The productive collaborative venture of Rabbis Enoch and Ettlinger has already been noted. With both these men at the helm of his new periodical, R. Hildesheimer was certainly justified in noting, as he did in an article appearing in its second edition,[121] that *Die jüdische Presse* was the spiritual heir of the *Zionswächter.* In the spirit of its predecessor the *Zionswächter,* R. Hildesheimer declared, *Die jüdische Presse* would be dedicated to the interests of "true Judaism" and would endeavor to serve as a "guardian of Zion."

One of the most striking resemblances in the editorial policy of the two periodicals was the positive manner in which both journals addressed themselves to questions relating to the Land of Israel. *Die jüdische Presse* has been regarded as the most "Zionistic" in orientation of the many periodicals that appeared in Germany before the emergence of political Zionism.[122] In respect to its advocacy of the cause of the settlements of the Land of Israel, *Die jüdische Presse* was continuing a tradition which, as has been noted, characterized both the *Zionswächter* and *Shomer Tziyyon ha-Ne'eman.*

Rabbi Ettlinger's own evaluation of the signal contribution of the periodicals published in Altona, the *Zionswächter* and *Shomer Tziyyon ha-Ne'eman,* is included in his introductory remarks to *Arukh la-Ner* on tractate *Sukkah.* He emphasizes the significance of the *Zionswächter* as a means of combating the Reform movement but indicates clearly that the Hebrew journal was intended "for another objective, to serve as a literary link for scholars from distant countries to make known to one another novellae and commentaries, laws and queries with regard to matters of importance, and also to send one another responsa, to sift and clarify laws ..." Thus, from the very outset, the German-language journal was focused on defense of Orthodoxy and negation

---

119 M. Eliav, "The 'Jüdische Presse'—The Newspaper of Rabbi Azriel Hildesheimer," *Sinai* 65 (1969), 222–23.
120 Duckesz, *Chachme AHW,* 128–29.
121 June 24, 1870. Cited in Eliav, The 'Jüdische Presse,' 223.
122 Ibid., 222–23.

of Reform whereas its Hebrew supplement, while equally devoted to these goals, was more positive in orientation. It is not surprising that, as a result, the German journal contains but few contributions of either literary or scholarly significance. Yet, the Hebrew journal is replete with articles of lasting value. Many of the responsa published therein were subsequently included in responsa collections and were cited in the works of later rabbinic scholars. Consequently, a demand for copies of issues of this journal continued long after they ceased to circulate and caused them to become collectors' items. The republication of *Shomer Tziyyon ha-Ne'eman* in New York, 1963, is evidence of its enduring interest and value as a rich treasury of Jewish scholarship.

From the perspective of time there is one important point regarding the early Orthodox publications that merits particular note. The individuals who were involved in those journalistic endeavors were imbued with a sense of mission and perceived their literary activities as a significant facet of their role as watchmen guarding their communities. There was a clear understanding and appreciation of the awesome power of the written word and the concomitant responsibility incumbent on writers and publishers.

It is related that one evening the hasidic sage Reb Naphtali of Ropshitz met a watchman making his rounds and asked him, "For whom are you working?" After answering, the man turned to the rabbi and inquired: "And for whom are you working, Rabbi?" The *Ropshitzer* was thunderstruck. He walked alongside the man for a bit and then asked him, "Will you work for me?" "Yes," the man responded. 'I should like to, but what would be my duties?" "To remind me," responded Reb Naphtali, "to remind me."

CHAPTER 3

The Circumcision Controversy in Classical Reform in Historical Context

Toward the close of the nineteenth century, a gathering of rabbinic leaders took place in the city of St. Petersburg. The primary issue on the agenda was the official stance to be taken *vis-à-vis* Jewish children who had not been circumcised, that is, whether such children were to be officially registered as Jews in the communal records. The virtually unanimous response of the assembled rabbis was absolutely to forbid registration of uncircumcised boys as Jews. Clearly, their intent was to adopt this measure as a strategy designed to induce assimilated parents to acquiesce to the circumcision of their sons. The sole dissenting voice was that of R. Hayyim Soloveitchik of Brisk. R. Hayyim duly noted that an uncircumcised male is forbidden to partake either of *terumah* or of sacrificial offerings and that, if he does not undergo circumcision upon reaching the age of majority, he incurs the punishment of *karet*. He then proceeded to protest vigorously that there is no halakhic provision that would serve to support the view that an uncircumcised male be treated differently from other transgressors who are not excluded from the Jewish community.

Relating this incident, his grandson, the late Rabbi Joseph B. Soloveitchik commented that both from a pragmatic and socio-political standpoint as well as religiously, as a *hora'at sha'ah* (a temporary emergency ruling), the decision of R. Hayyim's colleagues was entirely justified. However, from the vantage point of pure halakhah, R. Hayyim was entirely correct in his ruling; as the *Ish ha-Halakhah*, the champion of pristine halakhic purity, he was not willing to sacrifice truth even for a noble purpose.[1]

---

1 R. Joseph B. Soloveitchik, "Ish ha-Halakhah," *Talpiyot* 1 (Nissan-Tishrei, 1944), 707. Rabbi Soloveitchik does not give a date for this rabbinic gathering. Vladimir Levin in his unpublished doctoral dissertation, "Jewish Politics in the Russian Empire During the Period of Reaction 1907–1914" (PhD Dissertation, Hebrew University of Jerusalem, 2007),

Culturally, Russian society was fifty years behind Western Europe. It took Russia fifty years to catch up to the social upheavals and assimilationist trends of the West. The problem confronting the rabbis in St. Petersburg was one with which their colleagues in Germany, France, and Hungary grappled a half-century earlier and which led to the eruption of one of the most searing controversies between adherents of Orthodoxy and Reform—a controversy that has been aptly described as "the classic modern instance of ritual ambivalence."[2] The ambivalences and strong emotions reflected in the controversy did not abate with the passage of time and their lingering echoes are still audible in current literature.

THE FRANKFURT CONTROVERSY

The controversy between exponents of Orthodoxy and Reform centered on the actual rite of circumcision. Concurrently, another debate raged primarily within the internal Orthodox community itself regarding the practice of *metzitzah*[3]—a debate that is still very much alive and contentious to this very day.

In recent years, extensive discussions of the circumcision controversy and the numerous published rabbinic opinions it spawned have been authored by

---

discusses the Rabbinic Commission of 1910 convened at the behest of the Ministry of Internal Affairs and the several preliminary meetings of rabbis in Warsaw and Vilna from 1908–1910. The controversy over registration of uncircumcised boys as Jews was on the agenda (see especially ibid., 257–259). The rabbinic assembly described by Rabbi Soloveitchik may well have been one of these preliminary gatherings or may have been a discussion regarding policy that took place at an earlier time.

Cf., however, R. Joseph Saul Nathanson, *Sho'el u-Meshiv, Mahadura Tinyana*, part 3, concluding section of responsum no. 64, who refers to the Frankfurt controversy and emphatically declares that an uncircumcised male should not be accorded religious acknowledgement as a Jew because disdaining circumcision in contrast to other transgressions places a person beyond the pale of the community.

2   Lawrence A. Hoffman, *Covenant of Blood: Circumcision and Gender in Rabbinic Judaism* (Chicago and London: University of Chicago Press, 1996), 2.

3   Traditionally, as explicitly recorded in the Mishnah, *Shabbat* 133a, the circumcision ritual consists of three distinct acts: (1) *milah*, excision (*ḥittukh*) of the thick foreskin; (2) *peri'ah*, retraction and removal of the underlying mucous membrane covering the glans in order to uncover the corona; and (3) *metzitzah*, suction of blood from the wound and from the blood vessels flowing into the wound. In conjunction with this controversy, objections were also raised regarding the customary method of performing *peri'ah* with the fingernail. However, the issue of *peri'ah* did not engender as much furor as did the debate concerning *metzitzah*. Regarding *peri'ah* see Moses Bunim Pirutinsky, *Sefer ha-Berit* (New York, 1972), 183–84, 206–13.

Jacob Katz (in Hebrew and translated into English)[4] and by Andreas Gotzmann (in German)[5] and for that reason only the briefest summary of the salient facts will be presented here. At the time of the controversy the various governmental jurisdictions in Germany required every national to profess a religion. Baptism was required for Christian children; circumcision was required for Jewish males. Functionaries of the religious communities, priests, ministers and rabbis, were responsible for registration of children born to their respective communicants. The controversy erupted in 1843 in Frankfurt am Main when a member of the Frankfurt Jewish community, a banker named E. Flörsheim,[6] declined to circumcise his son, but nevertheless presented the virtually unprecedented request that the child be registered as a Jew in the communal records.

The event occurred after the Frankfurt public health authorities had, on February 8, 1843, promulgated an ordinance requiring that circumcision performed by a *mohel* (religious functionary) must be conducted under medical supervision. The wording of the regulation, "Jewish citizens and residents insofar as they wish to have their children circumcised" (*"Israelitische Bürger und Einwohner, insofern sie ihre Kinder beschneiden lassen wollen"*) implied that the decision to circumcise a child might be but an option to be exercised at the parents' discretion and not a necessary prerequisite for membership in the

---

4 Jacob Katz, *Ha-Halakhah be-Meitzar: Mikhsholim al Derekh ha-Ortodoksiyah be-Hithavatah* (Jerusalem: Magnes Press, 1992), 123–83; idem, *Divine Law in Human Hands: Case Studies in Halakhic Flexibility* (Jerusalem: Magnes Press, 1998), 320–402.

5 Andreas Gotzmann, *Jüdisches Recht im kulturellen Prozess: Die Wahrnehmung der Halacha im Deutschland des 19. Jahrhunderts* (Tübingen: Mohr Siebeck, 1997), 251–302. See also Robert Liberles, *Religious Conflict in Social Context: The Resurgence of Orthodox Judaism in Frankfurt am Main, 1838–1877* (Westport, Conn: Greenwood Press, 1985), 52–61.

6 The exact form of the banker's surname is unclear. The *Allgemeine Zeitung des Judenthums* (*AZdJ*) 8 (1844), 405, spells the name "Floisheim." Josef Meisl, "Zur Geschichte der jüdischen Reformbewegung," *Monatsschrift für Geschichte und Wissenschaft des Judentums* 69 (1925), 42, refers to the banker as "Flersheim." Katz, *Divine Law*, 322, employs the spelling "Flörsheim."

The press of the day intimated that Flörsheim was motivated by a desire for acceptance in non-Jewish society. An ironic Frankfurt news item reported that Flörsheim, whose request instigated the circumcision controversy, sought admission to the Casino, a club which generally excluded Jews. A Christian banker's contemptuous response was *"Wir wollen keine Juden, keine beschnittene und keine unbeschnittene"* ("We want no Jews, neither circumcised ones, nor uncircumcised ones"), and Flörsheim's candidacy for membership was unanimously rejected. See *AZdJ* 8 (1844), 405. Liberles, 239 n. 17, on the basis of an item in *Der Orient* 1 (1840), 7, reports that, in point of fact, members of the Rothschild Family who were Orthodox had been admitted to the Casino in 1838 and that later references in *Der Orient* 5 (1844), 178, 207, confused Flörsheim with the Rothschilds.

community. Despite the efforts of Rabbi Salomon Trier, the elderly rabbi of Frankfurt, to persuade the city Senate to declare that an uncircumcised child not be recognized as a Jew, the Senate refused to intervene and the ensuing internal Jewish debate developed into a heated controversy that engulfed the entire Jewish community in Germany.[7]

The issue was exacerbated because it was perceived not as a matter limited to a single rebellious individual but as part of a radical Reform agenda. Prior to this incident, a number of Jewish laymen had founded the Frankfurt Society for the Friends of Reform (*Verein der Reformfreunde*) and by September 1842 (before the promulgation of the public health ordinance and the Flörsheim incident) their agenda had become a matter of public knowledge. The initial unpublished statement of the *Reformfreunde* platform consisted of five principles, amongst them an explicit declaration that they did not consider circumcision binding either as a religious obligation or as a symbolic act. Although the subsequent publication of the founding principles reduced those principles to three in number and omitted the reference to circumcision, the *Reformfreunde* were perceived as spearheading a concerted attack on the rite of circumcision.[8]

The covenant of circumcision is not only endowed with religious meaning but also serves as a symbol of identification with the community of Israel. Unique among mitzvot, circumcision—the mark of the covenant—is so powerful a symbol that Spinoza, in his *Tractatus Theologico-Politicus*, although by no

---

7 See Liberles, *Religious Conflict*, 52–61. For Rabbi Trier's own account see Salomon A. Trier, ed., *Rabbinische Gutachten über die Beschneidung* (Frankfurt am Main, 1944), vii–xii.

8 For an incisive analysis of the *Reformfreunde*, see Michael A. Meyer, "Alienated Intellectuals in the Camp of Religious Reform: The Frankfurt *Reformfreunde*, 1842–1845," *AJS Review* 6 (1981), 61–86. See also, the detailed account in David Philipson, *The Reform Movement in Judaism*, 2nd ed. (New York: MacMillan, 1931), 107–39 and cf. Liberles, *Religious Conflict*, 43–52. Meyer notes that although the three-year history of the *Reformfreunde* appears to be of but limited historical interest, this small group gave rise to a significant body of literature and "reflects currents and tendencies of considerably broader measure and of larger duration" (61). Zunz predicted correctly, in a letter of October 5, 1843, that "... the Frankfurt Reform requires no violent Petichat Ha-Arez in order for it to perish" but he was not quite right in his assertion that "in a year people will not be talking about it any more." See Nahum N. Glatzer, ed., *Leopold Zunz: Jude–Deutscher–Europäer* (Tübingen, 1964), 224, cited in Meyer, "Alienated," 65 n. 7.

Liberles, *Religious Conflict*, 54–55, 57, hypothesizes that the impetus for the 1843 Frankfurt circumcision ordinance can be traced to the *Reformfreunde* and points out that one of their prominent members, the influential physician Dr. Heinrich Schwarzschild, was later appointed a member of the Health Department Board itself. If Schwarzschild influenced the Board to promulgate the ordinance, the wording "*insofern sie ihre Kinder beschneiden lassen wollen*" was intentionally precise. Cf. Gotzmann, *Jüdisches Recht*, 256 nn. 9, 10.

means did he endorse such particularity, acknowledged that "the sign of circumcision is, as I think, so important, that I could persuade myself that it alone would preserve the nation forever."[9] Little wonder that the controversy over circumcision within the Reform movement in the mid-nineteenth century was fierce and pitted advocates of Reform against one another—as well as against those outside that nascent movement. The bitterness of the debate was fueled at least as much by the need for expression of ethnic identity as by religious ideology.

Yet vehement opposition to circumcision persisted despite its pivotal role in forging a sense of Jewish identity. The opposition did not arise in a vacuum. Perceived by outsiders as tangible evidence of otherness, circumcision was viewed with a strange fascination as at one and the same time both barbaric and mysterious. It may be demonstrated that much of the then vocal criticism of circumcision among both Jews and non-Jews can be traced to the vicious attack on circumcision in the writings of the French intellectual elite of the eighteenth century. During the period before the French Revolution and in its aftermath, the ritual came under ever increasing attack from outside the Jewish community.

Perception of the teachings and religious observances of Judaism as outmoded and primitive was rooted in the currents of anti-Semitism that permeated intellectual circles of that era. During the eighteenth century, "the century of Voltaire," France developed an intelligentsia that unabashedly expressed pronounced anti-Jewish sentiments. By the end of the century, their influence had spread throughout Europe. In Germany, Immanuel Kant's hostility to Judaism and his characterization of the Jewish religion as obsolete and lacking in morality was emblematic of the thinking of his time. The only possibility for social rehabilitation of the Jews, according to Kant, lay in their rejection of unedifying rituals and acceptance of "purified" religious concepts. Nor was Kant's younger friend and sometime student, Johann Gottfried von Herder, commonly regarded as a liberal and philosemite, incapable of expressing anti-Jewish comments. Herder disparaged what he termed "pharasaism" and disdained halakhic distinctions as ponderous hairsplitting.[10] Deprecatory attitudes such

---

9 Benedict Spinoza, *The Chief Works of Benedict de Spinoza*, vol. 1, trans. R. H. M. Elwes (New York: Dover Publications, 1951), 56. *Sefer ha-Ḥinnukh 2*, states that circumcision is designed "to separate [Israel] from the nations in the form of their bodies as in their souls." Both Ramban, *Commentary on the Bible*, Genesis 15:18, and R. Jacob Emden, *Migdal Oz, Bereikhah Elyonah* 2:20, assert that Israel is preserved from extinction in the Diaspora by virtue of the covenant of circumcision.

10 The ambiguities and ambivalences surrounding Emancipation in France are described in Arthur Hertzberg, *The French Enlightenment and the Jews* (New York: Columbia University Press, 1968). An excellent portrayal of the German climate of thought is found in Paul

as these were internalized by acculturated Jewish intellectuals in their desperate quest for acceptance in a society that had always rejected them as alien.

To be sure, opposition to the ritual of circumcision was often rooted in anti-Semitic bias and prejudice. However, that opposition was also an outgrowth of newly developing attitudes toward the body, together with scientific and medical advances as well as anthropological studies of myths and rituals of primitive societies.

THE ASSAULT UPON CIRCUMCISION

During this era, circumcision in general did indeed become the focus of strident negative attention. It is important to understand the extent to which anti-circumcision feelings permeated the cultural and intellectual milieu of Western Europe to better ascertain the extent to which those sentiments influenced Reform ideologues. A wide range of meanings were imputed to the practice and numerous analyses of its social implications as a marker of differentness were advanced. The full-scale virulent cultural assault on the rite in nineteenth century Germany may be assessed in terms of five distinct factors: (1) medical, (2) anthropological, (3) socio-political, (4) demonic and (5) aesthetic.

1. Medical

In the latter part of the nineteenth century, as governmental authorities began to supervise various aspects of public health, circumcision came under increasing medical scrutiny. It was often Jewish physicians themselves who brought the subject of the ritual and its attendant dangers to the attention of the authorities. A ubiquitous argument against circumcision was that it constitutes an unnecessary surgical procedure that endangers the health of the infant. The incidence of tragic complications and even deaths associated with circumcision was publicized and exaggerated.[11] A manual for *mohalim*

Lawrence Rose, *German Question/Jewish Question: Revolutionary Antisemitism from Kant to Wagner* (Princeton, NJ: Princeton University Press, 1992); see especially, 90–132.

11 See Liberles, *Religious Conflict*, 55, 245 n. 116. See also Katz, *Divine Law*, 323 and the references to the polemical literature, in particular, J. Bergson, *Die Beschneidung von historischen kritischen und medizinischen Standpunkt* (Berlin, 1844) and M.G. Salomon, *Die Beschneidung, historisch und medizinisch Beleuchtet* (Braunschweig, 1844). See also Samuel Kohn, *Ot Berit* (Cracow, 1903), 147–56.

prepared by Dr. Ph. Wolfers of Lemforde, Westphalia, championed retention of circumcision but nonetheless, noting the medical dangers, recommended governmental supervision of circumcision and the banning of *metzitzah* upon pain of a fine.[12]

With the emergence of bacteriology as a science, concerns regarding the practice of *metzitzah* became increasingly vocal. Between 1805 and 1865 outbreaks of syphilis and tuberculosis in several European cities were attributed to infected *mohalim*.[13] Following allegations that the practice of *metzitzah* led to infant fatalities, civil authorities in a number of cities, including Vienna, Cracow and London, banned the act.[14] In some instances the charges were disputed. Thus, in the celebrated case of a Viennese *mohel* accused of infecting children upon whom he had performed *metzitzah*, upon examination, the *mohel* showed no sign of the illness contracted by the children and consequently he was completely exonerated.[15] Similarly, the Orthodox periodical *Der treue Zionswächter* publicized views of medical experts defending *metzitzah* as medically harmful neither to the patient nor to the practitioner and, to the contrary, as having a positive therapeutic value.[16] Be that as it may, the possibility of danger could not be ruled out and the need for constant vigilance and supervision of *mohalim* (optimally self-regulatory rather than governmental) was acknowledged.

Ironically, in the United States, in the later decades of the nineteenth century, physicians outside the Jewish community became convinced of the medical benefits of circumcision and circumcision of neonates was routinely recommended.[17] Since then, scientific opinion has vacillated and the pendulum continues to shift to and fro with regard to the therapeutic value of circumcision.[18]

---

12 See Katz, *Divine Law*, 358.

13 David L. Gollaher, *Circumcision: A History of the World's Most Controversial Surgery* (New York: Basic Books, 2000), 28–29. Cf. allegations regarding *metzitzah*-related deaths in London reported in Alexander Tertis, *Dam Berit* (London, 1901), 1 and ibid., 3–9, reports of infections associated with circumcision in several European cities.

14 See Aaron Friedenwald, "Circumcision—in Medicine," in *Jewish Encyclopedia*, vol. 4 (New York: Funk & Wagnalls, 1906), 100 and Immanuel Jakobovits, *Jewish Medical Ethics* (New York: Bloch Publishing Company, 1967), 338 nn. 36, 37.

15 See Katz, *Divine Law*, 360.

16 *TZW* 3 (1847), 417–18.

17 See Gollaher, *Circumcision*, 73–108.

18 Ibid., 161–176 and J. David Bleich, "Circumcision: The Current Crisis," *Tradition* 33 (Summer 1979), 46–49, 61–63.

2. Anthropological

Further erosion in the perceived sanctity of circumcision resulted from the claim that circumcision was a borrowed rite that did not originate among Jews.

With increased knowledge of distant parts of the globe and exotic cultures beginning in the Age of Discovery during the late fifteenth and sixteenth centuries, Europeans became aware that various primitive tribes in Africa, the Americas and Australia practiced circumcision-like rituals. At first, some writers speculated that these primitive peoples were linked to ancient Israel, perhaps by virtue of being members of the lost tribes. Others later turned the theory around in claiming that circumcision originated in ancient and primitive civilizations and that Jews, in adopting the ritual, had merely imitated the practices of ancient Egypt.[19]

The English Deists, followed by Voltaire, popularized the notion that the Jewish custom stemmed from Egypt.[20] Indeed, Greek and Roman writers had voiced the same argument in bygone days. Voltaire, quoting classical sources, repeatedly asserted that the Jews, an "ignorant crude people," were plagiarizers who borrowed everything in their culture from others and adopted all their religious rites from the Egyptians.[21] This view was reiterated in the writings of the influential orientalist Johann David Michaelis.[22]

J. H. F. Autenrieth, Chancellor of the University of Tübingen, published an influential work on circumcision in 1829[23] in which he advanced the thesis that circumcision represents a primitive act performed as a surrogate for human sacrifice. Subsequently, anthropologists formulated an evolutionary hypothesis positing that society passed through three stages: magic, religion and science. Religious circumcision, they maintained, retained magical elements and was essentially an initiation rite, a primitive people's sacrificial act, namely, the sacrificing of a part of the body to divine powers in order to redeem the community.[24] If circumcision was merely a borrowed practice, objections to its abolition lost their cogency.

---

19 See Gollaher, *Circumcision*, 53–54.

20 S. Ettinger, "Yahadut ve-Yehudim be-Einei ha-De'istim ha-Angliyim be-Me'ah ha-18," *Zion* 29 (1964), 184–88; L. Tonney, *Voltaire and the English Deists* (New Haven, CT: Yale University Press, 1930), 170–71, 173.

21 Hertzberg, *The French Enlightenment and the Jews*, 303, citing Voltaire, *Philosophical Dictionary*, vol. 1, ed. and trans. Peter Gay (New York: Harcourt, Brace & World, 1962), 62, 201, 499.

22 See Gotzmann, *Jüdisches Recht*, 255.

23 *Abhandlung über den Ursprung der Beschneidung* (Tübingen: Heinrich Laupp, 1829).

24 See Gollaher, *Circumcision*, 54–55, citing, for example, James Frazer, "The Origin of Circumcision," *Independent Review* 4 (1904–1905), 204–18. Cf. Howard Eilberg-Schwartz,

3. Socio-Political

The medical and anthropological arguments were seized upon and embellished by anti-Semitic French intellectuals in their campaign of social ridicule and mockery of Jewish practices, an endeavor for which circumcision provided a ready target. In references to Jews, those writers invariably included the adjective "circumcised" to accentuate their differentness. Circumcision was the distinctive mark of otherness. Spinoza was quite correct in observing that the laws which caused Jews to separate themselves from other nations drew down upon them "universal hate."[25]

Classical sources—a literature in which Voltaire was steeped—attacked circumcision viciously and accused Jews of hatred of others. Tacitus charged that Jews, obstinately devoted to one another, harbored an implacable hatred for the rest of mankind.[26] The animus of Jews toward others was believed to be rooted in the latter's uncircumcised state. Juvenal, describing the repugnance Jews felt toward Roman laws, claimed specifically that they had been taught by Moses in a secret book not to lead an uncircumcised man to water. This categorization of Jews was repeatedly echoed by Voltaire in his portrayal of Jews as people who hate all other men and are fanatically intolerant. That they themselves are, in turn, universally detested, Voltaire averred, is the direct result of their peculiar laws and was reinforced because of their animosity "toward the uncircumcised Romans."[27]

The tone of such remarks is remarkably akin to the comments of a district procurator (in November 1793) denouncing the Jews of Lorraine and their alien practices. He noted: "It is the inhumane law of these people that the

---

The Savage in Judaism: An Anthropology of Israelite Religion and Ancient Judaism (Bloomington, IN: Indiana University Press, 1990), 141–76, who notes a current diminishing interest in ethnographic data on circumcision but himself argues in favor of the comparative perspective. He focuses on what he terms the "priestly" understanding of circumcision in presenting a highly conjectural theory based on a symbolic exegesis of biblical passages rooted in his acceptance of the documentary hypothesis. For recent anthropological literature see Sander L. Gilman, *Jews in Today's German Culture* (Bloomington, IN: Indiana University Press, 1995), 121 n. 14.

25 Spinoza, *Chief Works*, 1, 55.

26 Tacitus, *Histories*, 5.5.8–9. See also M. Whittaker, "Jews and Christians: Graeco-Roman Views," *Cambridge Commentaries on Writings of the Jewish and Christian World: 200 B.C. to A.D. 200* (Cambridge: University Press, 1984), 22–23, 83.

27 Hertzberg, *The French Enlightenment and the Jews*, 302–3, citing Voltaire, *Oeuvres complètes*, vol. 12, ed. Louis Moland (Paris: Garnier, 1870), 159–63. Hertzberg, 10, quite correctly observes that, "An analysis of everything that Voltaire wrote about Jews throughout his life establishes the proposition that he is the major link in Western intellectual history between the anti-Semitism of classic paganism and the modern age."

newborn male infant is to be bloodily operated upon as if nature herself were imperfect" and then proceeded to scoff at their long beards, devotion to a dead language and mischievous laws that commit them to make usurious loans.[28]

The extent to which circumcision became a theme of ridicule and a symbol of all that was backward and constricting to the spirit of political freedom and enlightenment may be seen in the words of a poem that achieved a popular currency. The author of the poem, "*Déclaration des Droits de l'Homme et du Citoyen*" (1789), wrote:

> Rien ô ma chère liberté
> Ne peut te circoncire.
> (Nothing, oh my dear liberty,
> Is able to circumcise you).[29]

Precisely at a time when German Jews wished to emphasize their similarities to their countrymen rather than their differences from them, the spotlight on circumcision as a sign of inalienable otherness was experienced by them as a painful embarrassment.[30] Moreover, the social critique of circumcision was often expressed in the context of political objectives. Johann David Michaelis maintained that circumcision originated as a formal prerequisite for citizenship in the Israelite nation, not as a practice of religious significance. If Jews desire to become integrated as citizens of Western nations, it was argued, distinctive physical marks were no longer appropriate.[31] This attitude found its most

---

28 Cited in Robert Anchel, *Napoléon et les Juifs* (Paris: Les Presses Universitaires de France, 1928), 18.

29 See Zosa Szajkowski, "Jewish Religious Observance, during the French Revolution of 1789," *YIVO Annual* 12 (1958–9), 221.

30 The manner in which circumcision was conflated with anti-Jewish sentiment and hence viewed as not merely an embarrassment but even as a political hindrance is reflected in a popular apocryphal anecdote regarding the career of Eduard Lasker, a prominent Prussian Jewish jurist, politician and one-time supporter of Bismarck. Commending Lasker for his financial acuity, Bismarck turned to him and, it is alleged, remarked, "By right, you should be a member of the cabinet." "My right to a seat in the cabinet," Lasker is said to have replied, "was cut off when I was eight days old."

The persistence of circumcision as an anti-Semitic trope is evident in a mocking and menacing postcard titled "*Une bonne petite retouche, Eine kleine Nachbesserung*," circulated in the French colony of Algeria in approximately 1900. See Patrick Hirt, "Die Dreyfus-Affäre und der Französische Antisemitismus," *Abgestempelt: Judenfeindliche Postkarten auf der Grundlage der Sammlung Wolfgang Haney*, eds. Heimut Gold and Georg Neuberger (Frankfurt-am-Main: Umschau/Braus, 1999), 359. See also the reproduction of the postcard in color, ibid., 153.

31 Cf. Liberles, *Religious Conflict*, 55.

articulate exponent in the radical Reform spokesman Samuel Holdheim whose evolving view of circumcision became increasingly negative. In an answer to questions addressed to him by a Reform society in Arad in 1848, Holdheim emphatically advised abrogation of the ritual in stating:

> ... protest must be lodged against circumcision, the expression of an out-lived idea. It testifies to something which is not true—yes, something which is, in fact, denied by all Israelites who have become self-conscious. The Jew today believes by no manner of means that he, through the accident of his descent from Abraham stands in a close special relationship to God and that he is obligated to give physical evidence of this closer relationship by a sign in the flesh. I am opposed to circumcision on principle and declare every Jew who confides in my religious insight and conscientiousness absolved from all obligation in this matter. Yes, I declare every Jew who neglects to have his son circumcised because of his larger belief to be a true and complete Jew.[32]

4. Demonic

Perhaps the most bizarre of the anti-Semitic canards associated with circumcision was the demonic allegation that Jews, if empowered, would forcibly circumcise others.

---

32 Cited in Philipson, *The Reform Movement*, 280.
　　For an analysis of Holdheim's earlier writing on circumcision, *Über die Beschneidung zunächst in religiös-dogmatischer Beziehung* (Schwerin: C. Kürschner, 1844), see Robin E. Judd, "Samuel Holdheim and the German Circumcision Debates," in *Redefining Judaism in an Age of Emancipation: Comparative Perspectives on Samuel Holdheim (1806–1860)*, ed. Christian Wiese (Leiden: Brill, 2007), 127–142. In this monograph Holdheim focused on the distinction between what he termed religious law and religious truth as well as on questions of communal and rabbinic authority. In castigating his colleagues for their recourse to civil authorities during the heated controversy, he charged them with harboring a political rather than religious motive, namely a desperate wish "to retain their diminishing control" (see Judd, "Samuel Holdheim," referring to *Über die Beschneidung*, 70–88). Judd fails to note that Holdheim's own detached view of the significance of circumcision led him to misinterpret and misjudge his colleagues' deep-seated and genuine anguish and concern over the possible abandonment of a rite they believed to be of fundamental religious import. A dispassionate observer would recognize that the issue of circumcision was indeed a rare instance in which questions of power and authority played no role in the response of the defenders of the rite. Proponents of circumcision, whether Orthodox or Reform, were prompted by emotion. The question of rabbinic power was irrelevant; at issue was a core matter of faith.

As with most of the common anti-Semitic myths regarding Jewish ritual, the accusations bore no relationship whatsoever to the truth of Jewish practice. Blood ritual accusations ran counter to strict prescriptions of Jewish law forbidding the admixture of any liquid other than water in preparation of *matzot*,[33] not to speak of the prohibition against ingesting blood.[34] So too did this accusation fly in the face of halakhic rulings that discourage the circumcision of non-Jews.[35]

But mythic fears feed on other fodder. Perhaps, in the case of circumcision, this fairly widespread misapprehension traces its roots to the biblical narrative (Genesis 34) concerning Simeon and Levi and the circumcision and subsequent annihilation of Shechem son of Hamor, his father and his people. The statement of Hamor and Shechem, "Only herein will the men consent unto us to be one people, if every male among us be circumcised as they are circumcised" (Genesis 34:22), may have been perceived as an ongoing demand which, if in power, Jews would insist be fulfilled as a precondition for peaceful coexistence with those not of their faith.

Whatever their provenance may have been, in the Middle Ages when blood libel accusations proliferated, the tales often included accounts of how Jews first circumcised the Christian children whom they later killed to utilize their blood for ritual purposes. For example, accounts of the martyred "Little Hugh of Lincoln," found murdered in 1255, related that he had been beaten, his nose had been broken and he had been circumcised before his death. The child Simon, later beatified as Saint Simon of Trent, was found dead in Trento, Italy in 1475. Engravings and woodcuts celebrating Simon's martyrdom graphically depict Jews circumcising the lad—focusing on the cutting of his genitals with a large knife—while ghoulishly inflicting other wounds on his body and bleeding him to death.[36]

---

33 Blood is one of the seven liquids enumerated by the Mishnah, *Makhshirin* 6:4. The admixture of any one of those liquids or of fruit juice with water renders dough *hametz*. See *Shulḥan Arukh, Oraḥ Ḥayyim* 462:1 and commentaries *ad locum*.

34 *Keritut* 22a and Maimonides, *Mishneh Torah, Hilkhot Ma'akhalot Assurot* 6:2.

35 See *Beit Yosef, Yoreh De'ah* 266; *Levush, Yoreh De'ah* 363:5; *Taz, Yoreh De'ah* 363:3. Cf. *Shakh, Yoreh De'ah* 363:8. Cf., however, *Shulḥan Arukh, Yoreh De'ah* 268:9, and *Teshuvot ha-Rambam*, vol. 1, ed. R. Joshua Blau (Jerusalem: Mekitzei Nirdamim, 1958), no. 148, reprinted in *Iggerot ha-Rambam*, ed. R. Isaac Shilat (Ma'aleh Adumim, Israel: Ma'aliyot, 1987), 212–14.

36 Gollaher, *Circumcision*, 38–39. In 1965, the Roman Catholic Church withdrew the cult of Saint Simon. Regarding Simon of Trent see R. Po-Chia Hsia, *Trent 1475: Stories of a Ritual Murder Trial* (New Haven, CT: Yale University Press, 1992).

Despite the passage of time these accusations continued to be given credence. In seventeenth-century England, one Samuel Purchas wrote that

> One cruell and (to speak the properest phrase) *Jewish crime* was usuall amongst them, every yeere towards Easter ... to steale a young boy, *circumcise him,* and after solemn judgment, making one of their own Nation a Pilate, to crucifie him out of their divellish malice to Christ and Christians.[37]

Another English source, an account of the trial of Jacob of Norwich, accused him and his accomplices of "Stealing away, and Circumcising, a Christian child."[38]

Hateful stories of this genre which served to exacerbate xenophobic fears of mysterious Jewish rituals resurfaced with a renewed vigor during the tumultuous years preceding and following the French Revolution. Prominent among eighteenth century French clerical intellectuals who repeated medieval calumnies against the Jews was Abbé Charles Louis Richard. When a Parisian Jewish banker by the name of Liefman Calmer bought a barony in 1774 and attempted to appoint priests to two benefices on that land, Richard denounced Calmer and asserted that no Jew had a right to make appointments to Church offices. In Richard's essays he denounced the Jew as "A born and sworn enemy of all Christians" but in anonymous pamphlets he went much further. Richard composed a letter purportedly authored by "the rabbi of the synagogue of the Jews of Metz" addressed to Mordecai Venture whom he described as "the rabbi of the synagogue of Paris" in which the rabbi of Metz related that he planned to convene a Sanhedrin to "instruct" Calmer not to appoint any priest to a benefice unless that priest had been circumcised. In his pose as a rabbi, Richard also imaginatively put into the mouth of Voltaire the recommendation that Abbé Guénée, a defender of the Jews, be circumcised and further expounded on why the holder of a benefice conferred by a Jew required circumcision.[39]

After the Revolution, the Catholic Church conducted a well-organized campaign designed to persuade the legislature to abandon proposals for Jewish emancipation and to provoke uprisings against the new regime. Jews were blamed for the new regime's decrees against the Church. Counter-revolutionaries

---

37 Cited in Gollaher, *Circumcision*, 40.
38 Ibid., 40.
39 See Hertzberg, *The French Enlightenment and the Jews*, 250–52.

argued that Protestants and Jews supported the new regime and together they would discriminate against Catholics. In popular pamphlets the strongest warnings were issued against Jewish usurers who would compel Christians to forsake their faith. In this context, one newspaper writer went so far as to write that it was quite possible that within thirty years all Christians would be forced to undergo circumcision: "*Qui peut nous assurer, que nous ne serons pas forcés de nous faire tous circoncire avant trente ans?*"[40]

Similarly, in the course of the debates on the question of admitting Jews to citizenship, Camille Desmoulins ironically ventured to suggest that, in the event the Jews were to become citizens, circumcision might well become a condition of admission of any gentile to that status.[41] Desmoulins may have made his remarks in jest, but Jean François Rewbell of Alsace, a bitter opponent of emancipation of the Jews, was pleased to seize on this remark and wrote to Desmoulins that the remarks concerning circumcision had given him pleasure.[42]

Whether or not Rewbell took literally the canard that Jews would force circumcision on non-Jews, it was evident that he deemed the threat a useful and powerful symbol demonstrating what he considered to be at the heart of the insidious danger of accepting Jews as equal citizens. He proclaimed that the teachings of the Jewish religion were incompatible with non-Jewish society: "You'll see it is not I who excludes the Jews; they exclude themselves." Only when Jews would be prepared to leave the synagogue, renounce their particularistic practices and follow the customs of their neighbors, he argued, should their acceptance as citizens be considered.[43]

In all likelihood, intelligent individuals did not take these calumnies seriously but they were effective weapons in the arsenal of anti-Semites, useful in fanning the flames of enmity, stirring the primitive fears of the masses and whipping up a frenzy of hostility toward Jews. As the historian Arthur Hertzberg points out in the case of Richard, these writers took not only the "high roads" of theological

---

40 See Szajkowski, "Religious Propaganda against Jews during the French Revolution of 1789," *Proceedings of the American Academy for Jewish Research* 38 (1959), 105. Cf. idem, "Jewish Religious Observance," *YIVO Annual* 12: 221, who describes the strange report of one newspaper that the deputy Jean-Sylvain Bailly (1736–93) had felt prompted to go to the synagogue and have himself circumcised. He notes that during the Reign of Terror the district attorney of Strasbourg publicly attacked the practice of circumcision and a Jacobin publication urged a general prohibition of the rite.

41 Hertzberg, *The French Enlightenment and the Jews*, 331, citing Léon Kahn, *Les Juifs de Paris pendant la révolution* (Paris: P. Ollendorff, 1898), 44–45.

42 Hertzberg, *The French Enlightenment and the Jews*, 355.

43 Ibid., 355.

anti-Semitism but also the "low roads of traditional anti-Semitism" in pandering to the crude ethnic hatreds of the masses.[44]

5. Aesthetic

The combination and culmination of the varied medical, anthropological, social, and demonic arguments against circumcision brought into play and strengthened another fundamental element—the aesthetic. In Hellenistic society antagonism to circumcision was rooted in an abhorrence of mutilating the body; the circumcised male was an affront to Greek aesthetics. Circumcised men were not permitted to participate in Greek athletic games. To avoid embarrassment at *gymnasia* and public baths some Jews even underwent painful surgical procedures designed to disguise or reverse their circumcision.[45] During the eighteenth and nineteenth centuries, the Greek idealization of the "natural" male form reappeared in Germany and Austria in the writings of anatomists. Decircumcision came to be viewed as signifying the return to the beautiful and the healthy.[46]

---

44 Ibid., 252.

45 See *Book of Jubilees*, 15:33–34. Attempts at reversal of circumcision by "drawing in" the foreskin—a technique the Greeks called *epispasmos*—is expressly forbidden in the Jerusalem Talmud, *Pe'ah* 1:1. For a description of this process and other methods of decircumcision see Gollaher, *Circumcision*, 16.

46 Sander L. Gilman, "Decircumcision: The First Aesthetic Surgery," *Modern Judaism* 17 (1997), 202. Noteworthy is also Gilman's published lecture, *The Visibility of the Jew in the Diaspora: Body Imagery and Its Cultural Context* (Syracuse: Syracuse University Press, 1991). Commenting on nineteenth century anti-Semitic stereotyping, Gilman notes that in *fin-de-siècle* Berlin there were self-conscious Jews who resorted to cosmetic rhinoplasty and he comments as well on Freudian interpretations that explore the relationship between the nose and the genitalia.

Anti-Semtic stereotyping of circumcision as a sign of ugliness was as well not absent in nineteenth-century British literature. Nathaniel Hawthorne visited London in 1856 as a guest for dinner at the home of the city's Jewish lord mayor David Salomons. His attention was arrested by the mayor's beautiful sister-in-law. He was appalled, however, by the mayor's brother whom he described in his *English Notebooks* as follows:

> But at the right hand of this miraculous Jewess, there sat the very Jew of Jews, ... he was the worst, and at the same time the truest type of his race, ... and he must have been circumcised as much as ten times over. I never beheld anything so ugly and disagreeable, and preposterous, and laughable, as the outline of his profile, it was so hideously Jewish, ... I rejoiced exceedingly in this Shylock, ... for the sight of him justified me in the repugnance I have always felt towards this race.

See *The English Notebooks by Nathaniel Hawthorne*, ed. Randall Stewart (New York: The Modern Language Association of America, 1941), 321, cited in Elliott Horowitz, "As

The barrage of strident criticism created an atmosphere of distaste toward circumcision and the result was a visceral recoil from the ritual on the part of many Jews. Yearning to be accepted and desperate for integration within the general society, assimilated German Jews were quick to gauge social and religious practices by the reaction of their non-Jewish peers and to view their own lives through the prism of non-Jewish eyes. However, it was not only their desire for acceptance and wish to curry favor with the non-Jewish citizenry that influenced their self-perception; they themselves had internalized a new set of values. Educated in Western schools, steeped in Western culture, influenced as that culture was by both classical and Christian values and teachings, assimilated Jews developed an aesthetic temperament attuned to Western society. To the extent that they thought of religion, they tended to emphasize its rational, spiritual and aesthetic aspects in which they could see no place for an "irrational" physical rite.[47] Thus, it was not simply that Christians found the ritual of circumcision strange, German Jews themselves began to express revulsion toward it.

The language used during this era by *Jewish* critics of circumcision is revealing in the sheer vehemence of its rhetoric. Gabriel Riesser said of circumcision: "This repugnant ceremony, insofar as it is to be regarded as religious, must thoroughly disgust every cultured sensibility. ..."[48] Felix Adler in the United States described the ritual as "simply barbarous in itself and certainly barbarous and contemptible in its origin."[49] And, in what has come to be a well-known passage in his private correspondence to Zunz, Abraham Geiger wrote:

> The fact remains that it is a barbaric, gory rite which fills the infant's father with fear and subjects the new mother to harmful emotional strain. The sense of sacrifice, which in days long past lent an aura of consecration to this ceremony, has long since vanished from our midst; nor is so brutal a thought deserving of perpetuation. True, in the olden days religious sentiment may

---

Others See Jews," in *Modern Judaism: An Oxford Guide*, ed. Nicolas de Lange and Miri Freud-Kandel (Oxford: Oxford University Press, 2005), 421. See also Elliott Horowitz, "The People of the Image," *The New Republic*, September 25, 2000, 45.

47 See Michael A. Meyer, "*Berit Milah* within the History of Reform Judaism," in *Berit Milah in the Reform Context*, ed. Lewis M. Barth (New York: Central Conference of American Rabbis, 1990), 143–44.

48 Meyer, "Alienated," 77, citing, in translation, Riesser's comments as found in M. A. Stern, "Briefe von und an Gabriel Riesser," *Zeitschrift für die Geschichte der Juden in Deutschland* (o. s.) 2 (1888), 55.

49 Cited in Salo W. Baron, "The Modern Age," in *Great Ages and Ideas of the Jewish People* (New York: Random House, 1956), 366.

have clung to it; at present, however, its only foundations are habit and fear, and we surely have no desire to dedicate temples to either.[50]

The practice of *metzitzah*, in particular, aroused the most forceful expressions of aesthetic repugnance. One word reappears over and over again in the recorded medical reports: the German word *ekelhaft*—a word connoting repulsiveness to the point of nausea. The aesthetic recoil is often more emphatic than the medical concern. Thus, Dr. Wolfers of Lemforde, in his 1831 study of circumcision, declared that *metzitzah* had no therapeutic value and was an *"ekelhaft"* practice.[51] The same expression is found in a report of Viennese medical experts who investigated *metzitzah* and concluded that *metzitzah* "is superfluous, of no utility or purpose, disgusting (*ekelhaft*) and to some extent even detrimental."[52] Again, the same word was utilized in his corroborating testimony by Dr. Wertheim, chief physician in the Jewish Hospital in Vienna. Wertheim stated that *metzitzah* is "disgusting" (*ekelhaft*) and added that "its roots are in unclean soil" (*"auf schmutzigen Boden wurzelndes Herkommen"*).[53] Although virtually all assimilated German Jews had long since abjured the practice of oral *metzitzah*, the frequent and numerous derogatory references to *metzitzah* as primitive and repulsive carried over to other aspects of circumcision as well. This contributed to an aura of distaste and to a nimbus of negativity that hovered over the practice of circumcision.

ALTERNATIVE RITUALS

Traditionalist rabbis did not succeed in harnessing the aid of the secular state and hence, registry of uncircumcised children in Jewish community records was permitted. But the number of Jews who, in fact, took advantage of that option was not large. Astonishingly, despite continuing and pervasive negative propaganda, the overwhelming majority of even assimilated German Jews continued to practice circumcision. In this one area the radicals lost the battle. Despite the initial Frankfurt challenge, the overwhelming

---

50 Abraham Geiger, *Nachgelassene Schriften*, vol. 5, ed. L. Geiger (Berlin: Gerschel, 1875), 181–82. For the English translation see *Abraham Geiger and Liberal Judaism: The Challenge of the Nineteenth Century*, ed. Max Wiener and trans. Ernst J. Schlochauer (Philadelphia: Jewish Publication Society, 1962), 113–14.

51 Cited in Katz, *Divine Law*, 359.

52 Ibid., 362, citing documents published by Menahem Mendel Stern in the periodical *Kokhvei Yitzḥak* (Vienna, 1845), 38–43.

53 Katz, *Divine Law*, 362.

majority of liberal rabbis opposed the *Reformfreunde* platform and supported retention of circumcision.[54]

As early as 1821, Olry Terquem, a French proponent of Jewish religious reform, writing under the pseudonym Tsarphati, expounded on the dangers of circumcision and proposed that the ritual of circumcision be replaced by a purely symbolic ceremony.[55] At the height of the Frankfurt controversy, a teacher of religion at the Frankfurt Philanthropin school, Josef Johlson, under the *nom de plume* Bar Amithai, published a pamphlet, *Über die Beschneidung in historischer und dogmatischer Hinsicht: Ein Wort zu seiner Zeit. Den Denkenden in Israel zur Prüfung vorgelegt* (Frankfurt am Main, 1843), in which he advocated abolition of circumcision and substitution of another ceremony. Johlson prepared a rubric for such a ceremony, prospectively termed "The Sanctification of the Eighth Day," designed as an egalitarian ritual suitable for both male and female infants.[56] Abraham Geiger also privately expressed the hope that a new ritual might be found to replace circumcision in the religious life of the Jew.[57] In more recent times, the idea of devising a new ritual of initiation into the Jewish community was advanced by Mordecai M. Kaplan.[58] Nevertheless,

---

54 At the Reform rabbinic conferences of 1844–46, there was great reluctance to place an open discussion of the matter on the agenda. Although Rabbi Mendel Hess of Saxe-Weimar introduced a resolution declaring that, although circumcision is "universally considered sacred," there should be no "external coercion and exclusion" and those who do not choose to practice the rite "are to be considered members of the Jewish community," the motion was tabled and the subject removed from consideration lest the topic arouse too impassioned a debate. See Philipson, *The Reform Movement*, 154. A physician's rather strange suggestion that circumcision caused venereal disease and impotence and that the ritual therefore be abandoned or fundamentally altered was briefly discussed at a closed session at the 1845 Frankfurt conference and summarily rejected. Again, at the Breslau conference in 1846, the role of circumcision was not disputed. The practice was taken as a given and a series of regulations designed merely to enhance the safety and hygienic aspects of the ritual was adopted. See Philipson, *The Reform Movement*, 216–17 and Meyer, *Response to Modernity*, 138–39.

55 Olry Terquem, *Deuxième Lettre d'un Israélite français. Projet de réglementation concernant la circoncision* (Paris, 1821), 8, cited in Philippe-Éfraim Landau, "Olry Terquem (1782–1862), Régénérer les Juifs et Réformer le Judaïsme," *Revue des Éudes Juives* 160 (January-June 2001), 179. Although Terquem did not convert, he married a Catholic and his five children were all baptized. See Landau, "Olry Terquem," 175.

56 See Michael A. Meyer, *Response to Modernity*, 123, 423 n. 86. See also idem, "The First Identical Ceremony for Giving a Hebrew Name to Girls and Boys," *Journal of Reform Judaism* 32 (Winter 1985), 84–87.

57 Geiger, *Nachgelassene Schriften*, vol. 5, 202–3.

58 Mordecai M. Kaplan, "Toward the Formulation of Guiding Principles for the Conservative Movement," in *Tradition and Change*, ed. Mordecai M. Waxman (New York: Burning Bush Press, 1958), 304–6.

no novel rite of covenant was ever formally adopted and the ancient ritual of circumcision remains the only universally accepted Jewish sign of initiation.

In concluding remarks in his responsum regarding circumcision included in Rabbi Trier's volume of published responsa concerning the Frankfurt controversy, the eminent halakhic authority, Rabbi Jacob Ettlinger, emphasized that ultimately it is history that testifies to the abiding validity of the commandments: "Judaism itself, as it has endured in uniformity for thousands of years in all ends of the civilized world, bears witness to the inviolability of its content and structure."[59] Currently, more than a century and a half later, despite renewed protestations of a vocal minority,[60] circumcision remains the most practiced Jewish ritual worldwide, with the possible exception of burial rites.

It is evident that for many Jews there remains an unarticulated, almost unconscious, deep religious attachment to circumcision as the quintessence of identity as a Jew. Lawrence Hoffman, in a sensitive discussion of current controversy concerning circumcision, acknowledges the tenacious hold the ritual continues to have even over those with only marginal association with the Jewish community. To his mind, the response of early Reform to attempts to abolish the ritual was remarkable in that, "Nowhere else, to the best of my knowledge, were the reformers so adamantly tied to their past as in the case of circumcision."[61] Similarly, in the contemporary world, he regards the persistent practice of the ritual even by its ambivalent critics as no less remarkable. Hoffman attributes this phenomenon to the perception of some individuals that circumcision is a "manifest assertion of Jewish continuity with the past." But he concedes that for others, including many who find the ritual distasteful,

---

59 Jacob Ettlinger, *Rabbinische Gutachten*, 37.

60 The renewed challenge to circumcision focuses once again on the medical argument that circumcision is possibly dangerous and, at best, medically neutral. However, emphasis is now placed on the pain caused to the helpless infant and the procedure is decried as an unwarranted genital mutilation and physical abuse which, as is claimed by some, results in harmful behavioral and psychological consequences. Moreover, among advocates of an egalitarian Judaism, the perception of circumcision as inherently sexist has led to further denigration of the practice. See, for example, Hoffman, *Covenant of Blood*, 213–20; Ronald Goldman, "Circumcision: A Source of Jewish Pain," *Jewish Spectator* (Summer 1997), 16–20; Lisa Braver Moss, "Circumcision: A Jewish Inquiry," *Midstream* 38 (1992), 20–23; and, more recently, the various essays and discussions included in *The Covenant of Circumcision: New Perspectives on an Ancient Jewish Rite*, ed. Elizabeth Wyner Mark (Hanover, NH: Brandeis University Press, 2003), 157–203. In sharp contrast, one should note the recent development of a Reform program to train and certify ritual circumcisers. See Lewis M. Barth, "Introducing the Reform Mohel," *Reform Judaism* 13 (Fall 1984), 18–19, 32.

61 Hoffman, *Covenant of Blood*, 9.

it is retained "out of a sense of obligation to Jewish tradition and a sign of their belief that the covenant with God continues."[62]

Jacob Katz has described the persistence of the practice of circumcision as "a collective reaction, a form of 'ritual instinct,' which was not accompanied by a well thought-out intellectual process."[63] Other thinkers, informed by kabbalistic teachings, might attribute the phenomenon to the presence in Jews, even if faint, of a divine spark (*nitzotz Eloki*) and argue that in their innermost hearts many Jews continue to acknowledge that circumcision is an inalienable part of Jewish identity, or what a modern writer has called "the cut that binds."[64] Traveling in Russia in the 1970s, this writer learned how simple, untutored Jews relate to circumcision when a Russian Jew, with tears in his eyes, told her, "My grandsons have not yet been *geyiddished*." In colloquial Yiddish the term *zu yiddishen* ("to make into a Jew") means "to circumcise."[65]

The practice retains a historical, almost mystical, hold over the Jewish people that is perhaps best expressed in the liturgy accompanying the circumcision ritual itself. The ritual is described as an eternal symbol to the Jew of sanctification unto the Lord who "has set His statute in his flesh and sealed his offspring with the sign of the holy covenant. … And it is said He has remembered His covenant for ever, the word which He commanded to a thousand generations … unto Israel for an everlasting covenant."

ENDURING LITERARY STEREOTYPES

Current literature reflects lingering echoes of the ambivalences and strong emotions engendered by the conflicts over circumcision. Two striking examples from contemporary popular fiction may serve as illustration.

Philip Roth's 1986 novel, *The Counterlife*,[66] garnered almost universal acclaim on the part of literary critics.[67] Writing in *The New Yorker*, the author

62 Ibid., 220.
63 Katz, *Divine Law*, 355.
64 Barbara Kirshenblatt-Gimblett, "The Cut that Binds: The Western Ashkenazi Torah Binder as Nexus Between Circumcision and Torah," in *Celebration: Studies in Festivity and Ritual*, ed. Victor Turner (Washington, D.C.: Smithsonian, 1982), cited in Jonathan D. Sarna, *American Judaism: A History* (New Haven, CT: Yale University Press, 2004), 26.
65 Cf. Gilman, *Jews in Today's German Culture*, 74, 120 n. 7.
66 Philip Roth, *The Counterlife* (New York: Farrar Straus & Giroux, 1986).
67 See, for example, the remark of Robert Alter, "Defenders of the Faith," *Commentary* 84 (July 1987), 54, "It is, I believe, Roth's best book to date."

and critic John Updike, in a nuanced but generally favorable review, pointed to what he personally found to be a jarring and discordant note and wrote, "I wished I had liked the ending better."[68] In the concluding section of the novel, the protagonist, in an imaginative exchange of correspondence with his estranged wife, now pregnant with their child, writes that, if the child to be born is male, he will insist that she accede to his wish that the child be circumcised. The non-Jewish British wife, whose family are genteel anti-Semites, is portrayed as remonstrating that her estranged husband, totally atheistic and non-observant, merely wishes to harass and torment her. But the protagonist, Nathan Zuckerman—Roth's alter-ego—is vigorous in his advocacy of the ritual. To Updike, the white Anglo-Saxon Protestant reviewer, the circumcision argument is overwrought and such a request on the part of "a narrator so scornful of church and synagogue" is indeed "a strange twist."[69] What Updike fails to grasp, but what a knowledgeable Jewish reviewer would have understood, is that, although Roth has no progeny, Roth—a Jew whose grandparents were Eastern European immigrants and whose mother lit Sabbath candles—if he did have a child, would, in all likelihood, not feel that the child was "his" were the child not to be circumcised.[70]

---

68 John Updike, "Wrestling to Be Born," *The New Yorker* 63 (March 2, 1987), 109.
69 Ibid., 109.
70 In his novel, Roth underscores the role of circumcision in reinforcing a sense of identity for an ambivalent Jew living in an unwelcoming environment through the blunt words of Nathan Zuckerman:

> Circumcision makes it clear as can be that you are here and not there, that you are out and not in—also that you're mine and not theirs. ... Circumcision confirms that there is an us and an us that isn't solely him and me. England's made a Jew of me. ... A Jew without Jews, without Judaism, without Zionism, without Jewishness, without a temple or an army or even a pistol, a Jew clearly without a home, just the object itself, like a glass or an apple [323–4].

Cf. the much later correspondence published in "An Exchange," *The New Yorker* 74 (December 28, 1998–January 4, 1999), 98–99. Mary McCarthy—as does Updike—finds the circumcision motif to be much ado about nothing. She comments:

> Then all that circumcision business. Why so excited about making a child a Jew by taking a knife to him? I have nothing against circumcision; the men of my generation were all circumcised—a *de-rigueur* pediatric procedure—and my son's generation, too. ... And if Nathan Zuckerman *isn't* a believing Jew, why is he so hung up on this issue?

"The Circumcision,"[71] a German short story written in an entirely different tenor, is authored by a German jurist and fiction writer, Bernhard Schlink. Schlink, whose best-selling novel *The Reader*,[72] is a Holocaust-related narrative, has also written several short stories which reveal a remarkable fascination with Jewish themes. "The Circumcision" describes a love affair between a non-Jewish young German student and his New York Jewish paramour. The German youth feels impelled to undergo circumcision although the Jewish woman has made no such request, nor, to his distress, does she even notice that he has undergone the surgical procedure. To the reader, it is evident that Schlink is presenting a fictionalized portrayal of lingering feelings of foreignness and differentness that come to the foreground in non-Jewish perceptions of the mystique that surrounds circumcision.[73] In his discussion of circumcision as both a physical and metaphoric

---

Noteworthy is the reply of Roth:

> I think you also fail to see how serious this circumcision business is to Jews. I am still hypnotized by uncircumcised men when I see them at my swimming pool locker room. The damn thing never goes unregistered. Most Jewish men I know have similar reactions, and when I was writing the book, I asked several of my equally secular Jewish male friends if they could have an uncircumcised son, and they all said no, sometimes without having to think about it and sometimes after the nice long pause that any rationalist takes before opting for the irrational.

Roth's acknowledgment of the ambivalent and somewhat irrational reaction of secular Jews to questions regarding circumcision is mirrored in a brief rumination on circumcision of a son authored by a younger contemporary Jewish writer, Michael Chabon, "The Cut," included in his essay collection, *Manhood for Amateurs: The Pleasures and Regrets of a Husband, Father, and Son* (New York: HarperCollins, 2009), 21–27.

71 In Bernhard Schlink, *Flights of Love: Stories*, trans. John E. Woods (New York: Pantheon, 2001), 197–255. The original German is "Die Beschneidung," in *Liebesfluchten: Geschichten* (Zürich: Diogenes, 2000), 199–255.

72 Bernhard Schlink, *The Reader*, trans. Carol Brown Janeway (New York: Random House, 1997). The original German is *Der Vorleser* (Zürich: Diogenes, 1995).

73 Cf. Sander L. Gilman's detailed discussion, *Today's German Jews*, 71–108, of the current German literary interest in Jewish topics and, in particular, the numerous ambivalent references to circumcision. An earlier version of Gilman's discussion was published in Sander L. Gilman, "Male Sexuality and Contemporary Jewish Literature in German: The Damaged Body as the Image of the Damaged Soul," in *Reemerging Jewish Culture in Germany: Life and Literature Since 1989*, ed. Sander L. Gilman and Karen Remmler (New York and London: New York University Press, 1994), 210–49. In that volume see also Jack Zipes, "The Contemporary German Fascination for Things Jewish: Toward a Jewish Minor Culture," 15–17; Marion Kaplan, "What is 'Religious' among Jews in Contemporary Germany?" ("In Germany most books about Jewish life are bought by non-Jews"), 83–84; and Katharina Ochse, "'What Could Be More Fruitful, More Healing, More Purifying?' Representations of Jews in the German Media after 1989," 118–20.

sign of Jewish identity, Sander Gilman notes that "In German popular culture of the 1980s the sign of circumcision marked the group fantasy about the hidden nature of the male Jew's body. . . . And for German Jews, the internalization of the sense of their body's difference cannot be underestimated."[74] Schlink's story does indeed reflect a phenomenon that is characteristic of the German experience.

At the close of the nineteenth century, the French historian Anatole Leroy-Beaulieu commented that the Jew is seen throughout Europe as "the circumcised pariah."[75] At the beginning of the twenty-first century, even when pariah status is eschewed, the idea of circumcision as a barrier separating the alien from the indigenous remains. Spinoza's observations regarding the importance of circumcision—both its distancing effect on strangers and its salutary effect on preservation of the Jewish people—have been amply confirmed by modern history.

---

74 Gilman, "Male Sexuality," 75–76.
75 Anatole Leroy-Beaulieu, *Israel Among the Nations: A Study of the Jews and Antisemitism*, trans. Frances Hellman (New York: GP Putnam's Sons, 1895), 229.

CHAPTER 4

Clerical Robes: Distinction or Dishonor?

A seasoned traveler and prolific writer, Israel Cohen, commented wryly, "In matters of assimilation I have found in all my travels that no Jews are so assimilated as the Rabbis in their professional garb."[1] In the 1930s, visiting Paris, Cohen was bemused and somewhat unsettled by the appearance of the spiritual leaders he met. In Paris, he described a vast and lofty synagogue in which

> On the left, in their pews, were the Chief Rabbi of Paris and an assistant Rabbi, and on the right, in solitary dignity, the Chief Rabbi of France, with the red ribbon of the Legion of Honor conspicuous on his long black soutane—all three wearing round flattish hats like French priests.[2]

Later, having journeyed to Provence, Cohen remarked more caustically concerning the garb of the rabbi he encountered in Avignon, a clergyman who had studied at the Rabbinical Seminary in Paris:

> Suddenly there entered the figure of a young priest. At least, I would have thought from his attire that it was a priest, had I not been told a few moments before by the little dame that the Rabbi would be coming very shortly, for, except that he had no cross, he was clad exactly like a Catholic cleric—with a long black soutane reaching to his feet, a black silk sash round his waist, a flat black billy-cock on his head, and a square jabot of beautiful lace on his breast. Evidently the writ of the *Shulchan*

---

1 Israel Cohen, *Travels in Jewry* (London: Edward Goldston, 1952), 309. Israel Cohen is the author of works on the history of Zionism, the well-known *History of the Jews in Vilna* (Philadelphia: Jewish Publication Society of America, 1943), as well as the volumes *The Journal of a Jewish Traveler* (London: The Bodley Head, 1925) and *Travels in Jewry*.
2 Cohen, *Travels in Jewry*, 309.

Aruch, in the matter of eschewing the garb of Gentiles, did not run in Provence nor, as I found later, in other matters too. But the face of the minister, with its fringe of beard, and especially his nose, were unmistakably Jewish.[3]

Similarly, of the synagogue in Marseilles on *Rosh ha-Shanah*, Cohen noted at the head of the thronged aisles "the Rabbi, clad from head to toe exactly like a padre."[4]

Israel Cohen's remarks reflect a palpable tension in traditional circles surrounding the issue of rabbis officiating in clerical robes. To many, such attire contributed to the dignity and solemnity of worship services and served to bring the synagogue more into consonance with a modern Western European aesthetic; to others, such garb was but symptomatic of the regnant assimilatory trend.

EMERGENCE OF A NEW STYLE

The areas of controversy between Orthodox and Reform factions in the nineteenth century are legend. Less well-known is the extent to which the nascent Reform movement influenced synagogue practice in the traditionalist sector even while the Orthodox leadership was engaged in combating Reform. In response to the challenge of Reform two diametrically opposite approaches are discernible. There were many who, in the course of time, counseled total and complete rejection of any innovation, even the most innocuous. As Reform became more radical, the attitude of extreme caution and circumspection became ever more pronounced in those circles.

Tracing Christian influence on early German Reform Judaism, the scholar of Reform history, Michael Meyer, observes forthrightly:

The early reformers thought that some adjustment to the Christian model was expected of them and their own aesthetic and religious sensibilities, conditioned by exposure to Christian practices, drove them in the same direction. They seldom found reason to oppose pouring Jewish

---

3 Ibid., 313.
4 Ibid., 323. Cf. Cohen's depiction of the ecclesiastical vestments of the rabbis in Rome (265), in Turin of "four other ministers in full canonicals—their hats adorned with gold braiding" (282), and in Barcelona of the "*Hazan*, who wore a tall black hat and a scarlet band round his black robe while officiating" (345).

content into Christian forms. In fact, unlike the orthodox, they regarded this transfusion as the best way to preserve the contents of Judaism in a Christian environment.[5]

Nineteenth-century traditionalist rabbis were no less astute than Meyer in their assessment of Reform practice. Accordingly, in 1866, when 67 Hungarian rabbis signed the decree issued earlier by a rabbinical conference in Michalowitz condemning various ritual innovations in synagogues—clearly going beyond the demands of Halakhah in their decision—their action was motivated not only by the perceived threat of further Reform encroachments but also by the conviction that many of these innovations were, in essence, Christological in nature.[6]

At the opposite side of the spectrum, there were those rabbinic authorities who maintained that the only hope for Orthodoxy lay in some form of accommodation and who therefore manifested a willingness to incorporate unobjectionable aspects of the Reform agenda. This stance expressed itself in one of two different attitudes: reluctant concession and compromise or approval and welcome. Some conceded that, in an age of spiritual crisis, compromises involving relatively minor religious issues might be sanctioned. Concerning matters in which an innovation had strong popular appeal and entailed no halakhic prohibition but simply deviation from accepted custom, they were prepared to permit concession in order to preserve communal unity. Others expressed a far more positive attitude in acknowledging that some developments of Reform were salutary, were worthy of emulation and hence were to be harnessed in the service of tradition. Reform was to be defeated by its own weapons.

The decision of a number of Orthodox rabbis to officiate in clerical robes has been commonly viewed as an emulation of a Reform practice perceived by the laity as enhancing the dignity of the services.[7] Although disdained by

---

5 Michael A. Meyer, "Christian Influence on Early German Reform Judaism," in *Studies in Jewish Bibliography, History, and Literature in Honor of Edward I. Kiev*, ed. Charles Berlin (New York: Ktav, 1971), 300.

6 The rabbinical meeting was held in November 1865 and led by Rabbi Hillel Lichtenstein and Rabbi Chaim Sofer. The official transcript of the Michalowitz rulings and the list of signatories is included in R. Akiva Joseph Schlesinger, *Lev ha-Ivri* (originally published in Lvov, 1868; republished Jerusalem, 1924), part 2, 62b-65b. In addition to the Hungarian rabbis, R. Chaim Halberstam of Sanz and R. Yitzchak Isaac of Zidetchov also signed the decree.

7 I am indebted for a number of these sources to Mr. Zalman Alpert of the Yeshiva University Gottesman Library and to Professor Shnayer Z. Leiman both for personal discussion and

many decisors as a practice that bordered on—or actually impinged upon—the prohibition recorded in Leviticus 18:3 (a proscription against adoption or emulation of gentile practices), clerical robes were, however, worn by a number of renowned Orthodox authorities.

Historically, this innovation definitely predates the Reform movement. Seventeenth-century Sephardi rabbis in Holland and England wore clerical gowns and white collar bands, a form of Western clerical dress similar to the black Geneva gown and white bands of the Calvinist or Reformed church. If indeed those vestments resembled the attire of jurists or academics, and even if intentionally modified, there is no gainsaying their obvious similarity to Christian clerical garb.[8] Interestingly, a picture of Gershom Mendes Seixas, prominent native-born United States colonial era *ḥazan*, painted around the time of the American Revolution of 1776—well before the emergence of the Reform movement—shows him in a black gown with a white collar and two white bands. The historian Jonathan Sarna writes of this portrait, "Nothing in this miniature (artist unknown) identifies Seixas as a Jew, but his collar does identify him as a cleric."[9]

Recent studies present evidence of distinctive dress adopted by rabbis in Italy in the second half of the eighteenth century.[10] Apparently, that garb, which was entirely different from Catholic vestments, was adopted by Italian rabbis under the Northern European Sephardi influence, an area in which Protestantism was the dominant religion. The clothing also strongly resembled Italian academic and medical garb but, gradually, as those classes discontinued its wearing, the robes became viewed as exclusively clerical garb.[11]

---

for his essay "Rabbinic Openness to General Culture in the Early Modern Period in Western Central Europe, in *Judaism's Encounter with Other Cultures: Rejection or Integration?*, ed. Jacob J. Schacter (Northvale, NJ: Jason Aronson, 1997), 146–216. See especially 170, n. 56.

8 See Alfred Rubens, *A History of Jewish Costume* (New York: Crown Publishers, 1973), 159–178. See also Meyer, "Christian Influence," 301 n. 9 and Leopold Löw, "Die Amtstracht der Rabbinen," *Gesammelte Schriften* (Szegedin: Alexander Bäba, 1898), vol. IV, 217–34.

9 Jonathan D. Sarna, *American Judaism: A History* (New Haven, CT: Yale University Press, 2004), 34.

10 See Asher Salah, "How Should a Rabbi Be Dressed? The Question of Rabbinical Attire in Italy from Renaissance to Emancipation (Sixteenth-Nineteenth Centuries)" in *Fashioning Jews: Clothing, Culture and Commerce*, ed. Leonard J. Greenspoon (West Lafayette, IN: Purdue University Press, 2013), 9–66 and another version of this study, Asher Salah, "Rabbinical Dress in Italy" in *Dress and Ideology: Fashioning Identity from Antiquity to the Present*, ed. Shoshana-Rose Marzel and Guy D. Stiebel (London: Bloomsbury, 2015), 55–68.

11 See Salah, "Rabbinical Dress," 59–60.

THE NINETEENTH CENTURY

Similar attire became prevalent among Ashkenazi rabbis only in the early nineteenth century. In England, an engraving of Rabbi Solomon Hirschel (c. 1805) shows him in traditional fur hat and clerical bands, apparently Sabbath garb, and a painting (1808) in a black robe, white bands and three-cornered black hat, probably weekday dress.[12] An engraving of Napoleon's Sanhedrin (1807) shows the 45 ecclesiastical members all attired in clerical robes and long white bands.[13]

The wearing of clerical robes was a practice adopted virtually unanimously by early protagonists of Reform. Israel Jacobson, often referred to as the father of Reform Judaism, instituted many innovations in the private synagogue, Temple of Jacob, that he established in Seesen, Westphalia, in 1810. A description of the elaborate dedication ceremonies on July 17 of that year notes the presence of hundreds of guests and a processional led by officers of the Israelite Consistory followed by "all the rabbis present, walking in pairs, in their clerical robes, and the Christian clergymen similarly."[14] Eight years later when officiating at services of the Hamburg Temple, the first formal Reform house of worship, the preachers all donned clerical garb.[15] Thereafter, the wearing of canonicals became one of the distinguishing characteristics of Reform clergy.

In Germany, clerical robes (known as *Talar*[16] [robe] and *Beffchen*[17] [bands]) were also worn by a number of highly prominent Orthodox rabbis,

---

12 Rubens, *A History of Jewish Costume*, 168.

13 Ibid., 169.

14 See the report, "Feyerliche Einweihung des Jacobs-Tempels in Seesen," *Sulamith* 3, no. 1 (1810), 300, which reads, *"Dann gingen paarweise alle gegenwärtige Rabbiner in ihrem geistlichen Ornat, und eben so die christliche Geistlichkeit."*

15 Cf. Michael A. Meyer, *Response to Modernity: A History of the Reform Movement in Judaism* (New York: Oxford University Press, 1988), 61.

16 On the terms *Talar* and *Ornat* see note 47.

17 Commonly, the gown was accompanied by bands or *Beffchen* that some claimed represented the tablets of the Ten Commandments and were therefore known as "Moses tablets." See note 41 and accompanying text. These bands were not at all of Jewish provenance and were indeed to be found as part of the garb of various professional groups and religious denominations. The bands themselves are strips of cloth, at times black with white borders, more frequently white, sometimes wide, sometimes narrow, sometimes embroidered, sometimes not, sometimes long, and sometimes short. See Raymond Apple, "Robes & the Rabbis," *Oz Torah* (March 2012), http://www.oztorah.com/2012/03/robes-the-rabbis. Occasionally, the rabbinic clerical gown was worn with a kind of jabot or dickie. A jabot is worn today by vergers in some churches. It is also worn by many judges in European countries. Female U.S. Supreme Court Justices Ruth Bader Ginsburg and Sonia Sotomayor frequently wear jabots

including *Ḥakham* Isaac Bernays in Hamburg,[18] R. Jacob Ettlinger in his youth,[19] R. Samson Raphael Hirsch throughout his rabbinate with the exception of his tenure in Nikolsburg[20] and R. Seligmann Baer Bamberger.[21] Of these, R. Bamberger, who makes no mention of the matter in his writings, reportedly defended this innovation as a reluctant concession to liberal sectors of the Würzburg community made in order to prevent more severe infractions of Jewish law.[22]

In one article, Isaac Heinemann notes that "in contrast to both his teachers Hirsch wore a rabbinical gown with white bands."[23] In another essay, he states pointedly that *Ḥakham* Bernays wore black bands, not the white bands worn by R. Hirsch which were associated with Christian clergy.[24] However, that observation is not quite accurate. While, as noted, both *Ḥakham* Bernays and R. Jacob Ettlinger wore robes, and the portrait of *Ḥakham* Bernays does indicate that he wore black bands with a white trim, the portrait of Rabbi Jacob Ettlinger shows that R. Ettlinger wore white bands[25] as did many other

---

with their robes. See Adam Liptak, "The Newest Justice Takes Her Seat," *New York Times*, September 8, 2009, A12.

18 See the portrait of Ḥakham Bernays in *Jubiläumsnummer des "Israelit"* (Frankfurt am Main, 1908), 8.

19 See the portrait in Ulrich Bauche et al., eds., *Vierhundert Jahre Juden in Hamburg* (Hamburg: Dölling & Galitz, 1991), 309.

20 See Leiman "Rabbinic Openness," 197 and 197, n. 130. For a report of R. Hirsch's practice in Nikolsburg of wearing a frock-coat and white tie on the Sabbath, and of negative communal reaction to his garb and to his concern with rabbis' sartorial appearance, see David Feuchtwang, "Samson Raphael Hirsch als Oberlandesrabbiner von Mähren," *Jubiläumsnummer des "Israelit,"* 21.

21 There is no extant portrait of Rabbi Bamberger. According to family tradition, he refused to allow himself to be photographed. See Yitzchak Adler, "Minhagei ha-Rav Yitzḥak Dov ha-Levi Bamberger Zatzal ve-Hanhagotav," *Ha-Ma'ayan* 19, no. 2 (1979), 33 and Benjamin S. Hamburger, *Nesi Ha-Leviyyim: Toldot Rabbenu Rid ha-Levi me-Wurzburg* (Bnei Brak, 1992), 562 (published in *Kitvei Rabbenu Yitzḥak Dov ha-Levi Mi-Wurzburg*, ed. Zevi Bamberger [Long Beach, 1992]).

22 Shnayer Z. Leiman, "Rabbi Joseph Carlebach—Wuerzburg and Jerusalem: A Conversation between Rabbi Seligmann Baer Bamberger and Rabbi Shmuel Salant," *Tradition* 28, no. 2 (Winter 1994), 60; cf. Hamburger, *Nesi Ha-Leviyyim*, 536 and 536 n. 16.

23 Isaac Heinemann, "Samson Raphael Hirsch: The Formative Years of the Leader of Modern Orthodoxy," *Historia Judaica* 13 (1951), 46–47.

24 Isaac Heinemann, "Ha-Yaḥas she-bein S. R. Hirsch le-Yitzḥak Bernays Rabbo," *Zion* 16 (1951), 87. Heinemann observes elsewhere, "Supplementary Remarks on the Secession from the Frankfurt Jewish Community under Samson Raphael Hirsch," *Historia Judaica* 13, no. 1 (April 1951), 124, that the very learned and elderly Torah scholar, R. Moses Mainz who later opposed R. Hirsch on the issue of secession, did not approve of the clerical robes R. Hirsch wore.

25 See note 19.

Orthodox rabbis, including R. Nathan Adler, R. Hirsch's predecessor in his first ministerial position in Oldenburg.[26]

R. Nathan Marcus Adler, who served as rabbi in Oldenburg and Hanover and assumed the office of Chief Rabbi in Britain in 1845, introduced a new style of Ashkenazi rabbinical attire into England, a long black robe and round black velvet cap.[27] On occasion, his son, R. Hermann Adler, sported bishop's gaiters.[28] R. Hermann Adler was a Companion of the Royal Victorian Order (CVO) and it was said of him that "with his black garb, gaiters, the insignia of the Victorian Order like a pectoral cross upon his chest, it was difficult to tell the Rabbi from the bishops. Edward VII spoke of him as 'my Chief Rabbi,' and under him the United Synagogue seemed to be the Jewish branch of the Anglican establishment."[29] However, according to another report, in order to ensure that the CVO insignia not look like a cross, R. Hermann Adler had a slit made in his rabbinical robe to conceal a section of the CVO insignia.[30] Following the rabbinical conference in 1856 in Paris, the French rabbis formally adopted clerical robes that were similar to those of French Catholic priests, with slight modifications.[31]

R. Morris Raphall, Orthodox rabbi of New York's Congregation Bnai Jeshurun, championed an accommodationist Orthodoxy. Having previously served in England, he brought Anglicized Orthodox services to the United States with an emphasis on decorum and dignity. In the mid-1860s, his congregation adopted formal clerical garb for rabbi and cantor.[32] As to be expected, prominent American Reform rabbis Isaac Mayer Wise[33] and Max Lilienthal[34] are all pictured in formal clerical garb quite similar to that of Raphall.

---

26 See Rubens, *A History of Jewish Costume*, 172 and cf. the portrait in H. D. Schmidt, "Chief Rabbi Nathan Marcus Adler (1803–1890), Jewish Educator from Germany," *Leo Baeck Institute Year Book* 7 (1962), unnumbered page following p. 306. In both portraits Rabbi Adler is shown wearing robes. In the latter portrait it is very evident that the bands are white.

27 See Rubens, *A History of Jewish Costume*, 172.

28 Ibid., 173.

29 Chaim Bermant, *The Cousinhood* (New York: The Macmillan Company, 1971), 370. See also Rubens, *A History of Jewish Costume*, 173, plate 254.

30 Raymond Apple, "Hermann Adler: Chief Rabbi," in *Noblesse Oblige: Essays in Honor of David Kessler OBE*, ed. Alan B. Crown (London: Vallentine Mitchell, 1998), 131.

31 See Rubens, *A History of Jewish Costume*, 161 and 173. Cf. Meyer, *Response to Modernity*, 169–170.

32 Sarna, *American Judaism*, 95–96.

33 Ibid., 97.

34 Ibid., 115.

GOVERNMENTAL INTERVENTION

Curiously, in Germany, the issue of rabbinical clerical garb attracted the attention of governmental authorities.[35] At times, seemingly minor points of dissension provoke disproportionately vehement emotional responses. In the celebrated dispute over the appointment of Abraham Geiger to a position in the Breslau rabbinate the issue of Geiger's rabbinical robe occupied a central role.

At the heart of the controversy between the newly-appointed radical Reform ideologue Abraham Geiger and Rabbi Salomon Tiktin, the Orthodox incumbent, were fundamental questions of theology and Halakhah, questions regarding the binding authority of talmudic law and the role and function of rabbis. However, in the course of the struggle, communal and civil officials focused as well on details of Geiger's comportment. Among the practices adopted by Geiger, which were deemed by his antagonists to be in contravention of the Prussian Cabinet Decree of 1823 that prohibited any innovation in synagogue service was the wearing of clerical robes. At one point, King Friedrich Wilhelm IV himself was petitioned to decide whether Geiger's rabbinic gown represented "an unjustifiable imitation of Christian custom." While loathe to involve himself in a dispute over Jewish ritual, the king did declare that imitation of Christian church customs in a Jewish house of worship would not be tolerated.[36]

Opponents of Geiger, both Jewish and Catholic, argued that it was not permissible for a rabbi to wear distinctive robes of office. Breslau civil authorities reported to the Prussian Ministry that, although Geiger's robes were not identical to those of Christian clergy, they had ordered him not to wear a clerical gown and to remain "true to Jewish tradition." Geiger himself was cautious and requested a Catholic priest, Heinrich Förster, as well as a Protestant preacher, Ludwig Falk, to certify that the robe he wore was not identical to those worn by Christian clergy during church services.

---

35 Of particular interest are two recent studies of this subject. Anselm Schubert, "Liturgie als Politik. Der Rabbinertalar des 19. Jahrhunderts zwischen Emanzipation und Akkulturation," *Aschkenas* 17, no. 2 (2007), 547–563, and Auguste Zeiss-Horbach, "Kleider machen Leute. Der Streit um den Rabbinertalar in Bayern im 19. Jahrhundert," *Aschkenas* 20, no. 1 (2010), 71–118, draw on archival sources in their respective analyses and demonstrate the extent to which the controversy over rabbinic vestments was motivated by political and sociological considerations.

36 Max Wiener, *Abraham Geiger and Liberal Judaism: The Challenge of the Nineteenth Century,* trans. Ernst J. Schlochauer (Cincinnati, OH: Hebrew Union College Press, 1981), 28.

In a rebuttal presented to the Ministry, Geiger further stated that "no religious precept prescribed specific garb for a synagogue functionary." Rabbinic clothing was solely a matter governed by personal taste. Since the rabbi was not a state official, he maintained, the government had no right to regulate garb that simply reflected the sartorial taste of a private citizen.[37]

The authorities nonetheless insisted that, although he was not a state official, the rabbi might not wear vestments that met with the disapproval of a major segment of the Breslau Jewish community. Apparently, Geiger defied that ruling and continued to wear his rabbinical gown. The matter came to a head on a public occasion. Initially, the officers of the congregation and Geiger were invited to attend a formal welcoming reception and church service in honor of the inauguration of the new mayor of Breslau. The officials of the community were informed that the invitation extended to Geiger as their spiritual leader was rescinded. The Minister of State had been informed that appearance of a rabbi in church would offend the Christian worshipers and, of even greater concern, attendance of Geiger at a Christian service in a rabbinical gown would offend the opposition party in his own community.[38]

To an onlooker it appeared, in the words of Max Wiener, that "the problem of the cut of the rabbinic gown was a detail of ludicrous pettiness."[39] It is, however, of more than passing interest that, in noting the distress with regard to the gown on the part of both traditional Jews in Breslau and the Christian laity, the issues raised by non-Jewish authorities regarding imitation of Christian custom precisely paralleled the halakhic considerations later raised by those rabbinic authorities who decried the wearing of the *Talar*.

The reactions of the Ministry in Breslau were not typical of the attitude of civic authorities in other locales in Europe. In a number of jurisdictions, the authorities enacted regulations explicitly requiring rabbinic officials to wear ecclesiastical robes. The intent of these rules was to further the agenda of those civil regimes that wished to encourage acculturation and modernization of the Jewish population and, accordingly, sought to foster the development of a modern rabbinate patterned upon the model of the Christian clergy. Thus, as early as 1807, when Napoleon convened the Sanhedrin, the members were explicitly instructed not to appear at the proceedings unless clothed in specified

---

37 Ibid., pp. 29–30. The complete text of Geiger's letter is published in Ludwig Geiger, *Abraham Geiger, Leben und Lebenswerk* (Berlin: G. Reimer, 1910), 86–88.
38 See Wiener, *Abraham Geiger*, 30–31.
39 Ibid., 33.

vestments: black silk robes and cloaks, white bands and three-cornered hats—
the garb of French *Abbés*.[40]

Not much later, in 1823, in Baden, a state in which some 17,000 Jews
resided, a government official prepared a programmatic detailed list of recommendations designed to transform the nature of the rabbinic profession, specifically urging appointment to the rabbinate of individuals who had studied
in a German gymnasium and encouraging the adoption of the vernacular in
sermons and improvement of decorum in the synagogue. Included in the list of
recommendations was the introduction of a distinctive professionally appropriate garb for rabbis and prayer leaders. Apparently, at a later time, an Orthodox
rabbi suggested that, in order to differentiate between the clothing of rabbis
and that of Christian clergy, rabbis should wear a navy blue robe rather than a
black one. Later, in several German states, a designated professional apparel—
Amtstracht—was prescribed for rabbis. In Württemberg, the required clothing
for rabbis was a black robe, black velvet skullcap, and white collar bands which
were known as "Moses tablets."[41] Those vestments were to be worn by the
rabbis at all formal services, including confirmations, weddings and funerals.[42]

Similarly, in Denmark as well, government authorities were involved
with the question of clerical garb. Abraham Alexander Wolff was appointed
the Danish Chief Rabbi in 1828 and occupied that office until his demise
in 1891. On October 11, 1828, the Jewish community received a document
from the Danish Chancellery stating: "After proposals from him [the rabbi]
and the explanation of the same given by the Representatives and on further representation from the Danish Chancellery, His Majesty will determine
an official dress which should be worn on all his official ceremonies. ..."[43]

---

40 See Anselm Schubert, "Liturgie als Politik," 549 n. 13, citing the text, as found in Renée
    Neher-Bernheim and Elisabeth Revel-Neher, "Une iconographie juive de l'époque du grand
    Sanhédrin," in *Le grand Sanhédrin du Napoleon*, ed. Bernhard Blumenkrantz and Albert
    Soboul (Toulouse: Privat, 1979), 134. The regulations were explicit: "Art. I: *Aucun membre
    composant L'Assemblée du Grand Sanhédrin ne pourra entrer en séance s'il ne s'est pas conformé
    au costume prescrit. Ce costume consiste en u habillement complet en noir, manteau de soie de
    même couleur, chapeau à trois cornes et rabat.*"

41 See Adolf Lewin, *Geschichte der badischen Juden seit der Regierung Karl Friedrichs (1738–
    1909)* (Carlsruhe: Komissionsverlag der G. Braunschen Hofdruckerei, 1909), 211–212 and
    212 n. 1. Cf. Meyer, *Response to Modernity*, 103.

42 For examples of specific rules regulating the garb of rabbis and cantors, see F. F. Mayer,
    Sammlung der württembergischen Gesetze in Betriff der Israeliten (Tübingen: Fues, 1847),
    104–105.

43 See Hanne Frøsig Dalgaard, "Rabbinical Vestments," *Danish Jewish Art—Jews in Danish Art*,
    ed. Mirjam Gelfer-Jørgensen, trans. W. Glyn Jones (Copenhagen: Rhodos, 1999), 174.

Apparently, the incumbent rabbi addressed the matter of rabbinical attire promptly upon beginning his ministry in the spring of 1829, for by July 21, 1829, a Royal Decree formalized the sartorial requirements:

> Whereby the official dress proposed by Dr. A.A. Wolff, priest in the Jewish Community in Copenhagen, consisting of a velvet biretta, a black gown of silk or wool trimmed with strips of velvet, and also a belt and white bands instead of a ruff, is graciously authorised as the official dress for the priest in the said community in Copenhagen.[44]

Not surprisingly, in some locales, there was a negative reaction to the proposals regulating rabbinic attire. In Bavaria, church officials found the similarity of rabbinic garb to church vestments to be offensive. As a result, they sought to enact regulations prohibiting adoption of rabbinic garb that was identical to Protestant cassocks.[45] Nevertheless, many liberal rabbis living in Catholic areas eventually adopted a modified attire that resembled the Catholic soutane, while in other areas it was commonplace for rabbis to wear the black *Talar* of the Protestant clergy.[46]

The interest of the civic authorities in Baden in the professional conduct of rabbis and the insistence on a prescribed *Amtstracht* sheds light on the fact, noted earlier, that at least in his youth, Rabbi Jacob Ettlinger wore a clerical robe. R. Ettlinger was a formal *Rabbinats-Candidat* (candidate for the rabbinate) as is evident from a printed address he delivered on August 24, 1824 on the occasion of the birthday of Duke Ludwig of Baden.[47] In 1825, R. Ettlinger was appointed Rabbi of the Mannheim *Klaus* and, in 1827, he was appointed District Rabbi (*Kreisrabbiner*) of the Ladenburg area.[48] As a candidate for the rabbinate and later in those positions it would have been deemed necessary that

---

44 Ibid., 174. Dalgaard notes that "There is no explanation of how the actual question of dress might have arisen." See also the source cited ibid., 381 nn. 25 and 26.

45 See Zeiss-Horlach, "Kleider machen Leute," 71–118.

46 See Schubert, "Liturgie als Politik," 561–562 and Lewin, *Geschichte der badischen Juden*, 212 n. 1. Schubert suggests that the term *Rabbinerornat* was employed for the French style cassock whereas the term *Rabbinertalar* was employed for garments in the German Protestant style. However, in most sources the terms are used interchangeably. See Zeiss-Horlach, "Kleider machen Leute," 73 n. 4.

47 *Rede gehalten zur Feier des höchesten Namensfestes Seiner Königlichen Hoheit des Grossherzogs Ludwig von Baden in der Haupt-Synagoge zu Karlsruhe* (Carlsruhe, 1824).

48 Isak Unna, *Die Lemle Moses Klaus-Stiftung in Mannheim*, vol. II (Frankfurt am Main: J. Kaufmann, 1909), 39–40.

he wear the prescribed *Amtstracht*. However, one cannot claim with assurance that R. Ettlinger wore the robe only as a concession to the civil authorities of Baden. The lithograph of R. Ettlinger in a clerical robe is clearly that of a young man. However, Ferdinand Heylandt's portrait of R. Ettlinger was printed in Hamburg in 1840 and the Hebrew inscription beneath the picture identifies R. Ettlinger as Rabbi of Altona, a position he assumed in 1836.[49] Although it is unlikely that R. Ettlinger continued to wear the robe in later years and, indeed, later portraits do not show him in a clerical robe, there is no conclusive indication that he ceased to wear such garb.

THE HALAKHIC QUESTION

The halakhic issue posed by clerical robes is by no means insignificant. The seminal halakhic treatment of the question of wearing professional robes as well as the explication of the prohibition of Leviticus 18:3—"and in their statutes (*u-be-ḥukkoteihem*) you shall not walk"—is the responsum of the fifteenth-century authority R. Joseph Colon, *Teshuvot Maharik*, no. 88. In that detailed responsum, *Maharik* asserts that the essence of the prohibition is an admonition not to mimic non-Jewish practices for the purpose of assuming the guise of a gentile in whole or in part. Encompassed within the parameters of the prohibition is, first and foremost, any non-Jewish practice in the form of a *ḥok*, that is, a practice lacking a rational or pragmatic purpose. Since such acts have no rational basis, their adoption by Jews can only be motivated by a desire to emulate gentiles. Other forbidden practices involve matters representing some form of immodesty or manifestation of a characteristic antithetical to humility. Here, again, any compromise of standards of modesty and humility might be suspected of being rooted in cultic practices and is *ipso facto* deemed to be emulation of non-Jews. Accordingly, any practice that furthers a legitimate purpose and does not involve either immodesty or self-aggrandizement is permitted. In response to the specific query of his interlocutors, *Maharik* sanctioned the wearing of the professional robe known as *cappa* by Jewish practitioners, apparently jurists or physicians, because it served the perfectly rational purpose of identifying the wearer as a legitimate practitioner worthy of honor and patronage.[50] *Maharik's* position is accepted by *Rema, Yoreh De'ah* 178:1.

---

49 See note 19.
50 *Maharik's* responsum is addressed to two individuals one of whom was the celebrated R. Judah Messer Leon, a professor at the University of Padua Medical School.

R. Elijah of Vilna, *Bi'ur ha-Gra, Yoreh De'ah* 178:8, disputes *Maharik's* position and forbids any emulation of non-Jewish practice even if the practice is designed to serve a perfectly rational purpose. *Bi'ur ha-Gra* permits gentile garb and the like only in circumstances in which "we would wear them even without the non-Jews [doing so]." According to *Bi'ur ha-Gra*, adopting a sartorial style or practice in emulation of non-Jews is forbidden even if undertaken for a pragmatic purpose unless it is manifestly evident that Jews would independently have adopted the practice.

Although many individuals were prepared to wear academic robes in reliance upon *Maharik's* permissive view, canonicals donned by Jewish clergy aroused wide opposition because those garments were, or were perceived to be, distinctively Christian in provenance.

The bulk of the halakhic discussions concerning wearing clerical robes centers on the vestments worn by cantors. It was the wearing of clerical robes by cantors and choristers that was formally prohibited by the Michalowitz decree of 1866 (perhaps because the Hungarian rabbis did not even entertain the possibility that rabbis in their locale might desire or be pressured to don canonicals).[51] Some of the sharpest condemnations of this practice are found in halakhic responsa authored by Hungarian authorities such as, for example, R. Moses Grunwald, *Arugat ha-Bosem, Oraḥ Ḥayyim*, no. 31, R. Eliezer David Grunwald, *Keren le-David, Oraḥ Ḥayyim*, no. 13, R. Chaim Sofer, *Maḥaneh Ḥayyim, Oraḥ Ḥayyim*, no. 2 and R. Judah Aszod, *Yehudah Ya'aleh, Oraḥ Ḥayyim*, no. 39.[52]

A brief negative reference to cantorial robes is also found in the writings of R. Jacob Ettlinger. This statement has generally been overlooked and is not cited in the halakhic literature on the topic because of its appearance in an infrequently consulted source. The comment is found at the conclusion of a responsum authored by R. Ettlinger that appeared in the rabbinic journal that he edited, *Shomer Tziyyon ha-Ne'eman*, no. 167, dated 15 Kislev 5614

R. Elijah of Vilna, *Bi'ur ha-Gra, Yoreh De'ah* 178:7, finds *Maharik's* position identical to the much earlier position of *Ran, Avodah Zarah* 11a, who regards all such matters as rooted in pagan practices. The twentieth-century rabbinic scholar, R. Moshe Feinstein, *Iggerot Mosheh, Yoreh De'ah*, I, no. 81, opines that, if it is established with certainty that there is no idolatrous root or association, a practice having no rational purpose is permissible according to *Ran* and *Rema* but nevertheless forbidden by *Maharik*.

51 See *Lev ha-Ivri*, part 2, 63a.

52 See also the extensive array of sources cited by Akiva Zimmermann, *Sha'arei Ron: Ha-Ḥazzanut be-Sifrut ha-She'elot u-Teshuvot ve-ha-Halakhah* (Tel Aviv: Bron Yachad, 1992), 11–20.

(December 16, 1853). R. Ettlinger's responsum was subsequently included by him in his collected responsa, *Binyan Tziyyon*, no. 122. However, the republished responsum omits the concluding sixteen lines of the material published in *Shomer Tziyyon ha-Ne'eman*. As a result, while the responsum in *Binyan Tziyyon* focusing on questions relating to recitation of *kaddish* is widely known, few are aware of R. Ettlinger's concluding remarks concerning a proposed regulation limiting worship services to one central synagogue and specifying professional attire appropriate for individuals who lead the prayer services.

Shomer Tziyyon ha-Ne'eman, no. 167, features an exchange of views between R. Baer Oppenheim of Eybeschutz and R. Ettlinger. Rabbi Oppenheim presents a query he had received with regard to certain synagogue regulations and details his response based upon his own halakhic determinations and recommendations. Rabbi Oppenheim's interlocutor had recommended that synagogues employ a designated cantor to lead services and that that individual be attired in "garments designated for prayer" in accordance with the comments of *Magen Avraham, Orah Hayyim*, 53:7. R. Oppenheim applauds this suggestion and endorses the recommendation that the prayer leader don distinctive garments. R. Oppenheim adds that he favors the appointment of a designated cantor in order to prevent the congregation from calling upon unkempt and illiterate individuals whose appearance and comportment mar the synagogue service.

In the immediately following article, R. Ettlinger presents a sharp rejoinder, prefacing his remarks with a caustic comment (that is also omitted in the *Binyan Tziyyon* version).As editor of the journal, he had acquiesced to R. Oppenheim's desire to publish his responsum in *Shomer Tziyyon ha-Ne'eman* even though it included statements that he deemed to be inappropriate. However, R. Ettlinger states that he felt duty-bound to respond since most of what R. Oppenheim had written was simply inaccurate.

Throughout R. Ettlinger's rejoinder he emphatically rejects any proposed innovation with regard to recitation of *kaddish* and, addressing R. Oppenheim directly, he declares, "I am altogether astonished at how you can describe as a wonderful and proper innovation the changing of a Jewish custom which has been followed in all parts of Germany and Poland for over 300 years." To effect such a change, R. Ettlinger adds, is "to walk in the footsteps of the Reformers of our time who have changed the form of prayer and have introduced this custom."

In a concluding statement addressing the propriety of a regulation stipulating that only a designated cantor wearing special garb be permitted to lead the services, he declares that there is absolutely no halakhic basis for instituting such a practice. Assuredly, he notes, it is unsuitable to select a prayer leader whose reading skills are wanting or whose clothes are sullied; it is quite simple to enact a regulation to that effect. However, he strongly disparages a regulation insisting that the prayer leader wear distinctive vestments that "usually are fashioned in accordance with gentile practices." Such a proposal is the mere aping of a Christian custom.

R. Oppenheim compared a cantor who prays without special garments to a priest who performed the sacrificial service in the Temple without his priestly vestments. R. Ettlinger disdainfully rejects such a comparison. Since Jewish practice has already ordained a distinctive garb for the prayer leader, namely, the *tallit* (prayer shawl), no other special garments are necessary. The *tallit* was ordained "by our predecessors, whose little finger is thicker than our loins," writes Rabbi Ettlinger, "and one should not seek to be more pious than they were."[53]

Decrying the wearing of cantorial robes similar to those of Catholic priests, the twentieth-century authority R. Yehudah Leib Zirelson, *Teshuvot Ma'arkhei Lev, Yoreh De'ah*, no. 44, protests "the repugnant and forbidden following of gentile practice" in wearing vestments that are "specifically associated with the ritual of an alien religion."[54] The Sephardi authority, R. Ovadiah Hadaya, *Yaskil Avdi*, V, *Oraḥ Ḥayyim*, no. 15, sanctioned the sartorial practice of Turkish cantors because their robes were identical to the distinctive rabbinic garb of that country. However, he ruled against wearing cantorial vestments that are similar to Christian ecclesiastical garb.[55]

---

53 As noted, in his youth R. Ettlinger himself wore a robe. For a possible explanation of his conduct see note 54.

54 Despite these vehement remarks, it appears that, on occasion, Rabbi Zirelson himself wore clerical robes. For a picture of Rabbi Zirelson in such vestments, see David Winitsky, *Bessarabiah ha-Yehudit be-Ma'arkhoteha: Bein Shtei Milḥamot Olam 1914–1940*, vol. II (Jerusalem, 1973), 504. Presumably, Rabbi Zirelson accepted the contention that the rabbinical clerical robe in vogue was quite different from Christian garb.

55 In this context, a letter dated 10 Elul 5759 (September 13, 1959) in the archives of Heichal Shlomo written by Rabbi Maurice Jaffe, Executive Director of Heichal Shlomo, to Rabbi M. J. E. Wohlgelernter (Ittamar), General Secretary of the Chief Rabbinate of Israel, is worthy of note. A cantor and choir had appeared at an event in Heichal Shlomo attired in clerical robes. Thereupon, the Chief Rabbinate issued a directive dated 21 Av 5759 (August 25, 1959), forbidding officiants at Heichal Shlomo from wearing vestments similar to those worn by Christian clergy. The letter reports that the wardens of Heichal Shlomo requested a meeting with the Chief Rabbinate for reconsideration of that ruling. I thank Professor Shnayer Leiman for bringing this letter to my attention.

   As noted, many halakhists insisted that rabbinic robes differ markedly from those of Christian clergy. Thus, it is ironic to record the attitude of a Danish Chief Rabbi in this

There is but scant halakhic discussion of rabbinical—as distinct from cantorial—clerical robes. One significant source is *She'elot u-Teshuvot Matteh Levi*. Apparently, although he himself wore canonicals, R. Marcus Horovitz, rabbi of the Communal Orthodox Community in Frankfurt, appears to have been greatly discomfited thereby. In his responsa, *Matteh Levi*, II, *Oraḥ Ḥayyim*, no. 6, he questions why the practice of wearing robes has been accepted and observes that, in light of the admonition of Leviticus 18:3, wearing clerical robes poses a greater halakhic problem than does the use of an organ. An organ might be employed in connection with a concert of secular music, he avers, whereas the clerical robe is used exclusively for religious purposes. Forthrightly, he adds, "*Were it not that gentile clergy wear such garments, without any doubt whatsoever, we would not do so.*"[56] Nonetheless, although not explicitly stated, his conclusion appears to be that wearing canonicals does not constitute a biblical violation.

A similar conclusion is implicit in the writings of R. Azriel Hildesheimer. Responding to the decree against clerical vestments for cantors and choristers issued in Michalowitz, R. Hildesheimer conceded that adoption of the practice of wearing clerical garb in imitation of the prevalent non-Jewish practice entails a serious infraction. Nevertheless, he seems to be inveighing against the assimilatory intent rather than pronouncing the existence of an objective prohibition against the act. He proceeds to acknowledge that there may be a more laudable impetus prompting adoption of such a practice. In locales in which the observant were constrained to accept such a compromise in order to maintain communal harmony and avoid more serious deviations, such conduct, asserted R. Hildesheimer, should not be stigmatized, in the manner of the rabbis of Michalowitz, as "a grave prohibition."[57]

---

regard. Hanne Frøsig Dalgaard, who authored a study of rabbinical vestments, recounts in detail her communications on this subject with the former Danish Chief Rabbis Bent Melchior in 1989 and Bent Lexner in 1995. In a letter dated August 9, 1996, Rabbi Bent Melchior commented: "My father [Chief Rabbi Marcus Melchior (1897–1969)] very categorically insisted that the long velvet strips on the Chief Rabbi's dress should be parallel to those of the bishops, so the second Rabbi had his velvet strips cut off at chest level." See Dalgaard, "Rabbinical Vestments," 381 n. 40. Dalgaard further notes that this can be seen in the photograph of Rabbi Bent Melchior's ordination in Copenhagen Synagogue in 1963 as shown in her article, 378, figure 307.

56 Emphasis added.

57 See Israel Hildesheimer, *Gesammelte Aufsätze*, ed. M. Hildesheimer (Frankfurt am Main, 1923), 20 and 25–26. Rabbi Hildesheimer urged rabbinic colleagues to issue a joint announcement protesting the Michalowitz rulings. However, since his colleagues failed to act, he published a protest under his name alone. Hildesheimer's views were published

Almost a hundred years later, a similar line of reasoning was offered by Jacob Rosenheim, an ardent champion of the approach of Rabbi Samson Raphael Hirsch. Commenting on R. Hirsch's wearing of canonicals, Rosenheim suggests that, "however non-Jewish and out of place they may strike us in the Jewish service," R. Hirsch's practice constituted a carefully considered strategy. R. Hirsch's decision to develop a worship service aesthetically appealing to the laity of his time underscores his awareness that "any restriction not definitely required by the Din [law] might have been in the true sense of the word a *ḥumra de'ati lidei kula* [a stringency that leads to a laxity]."[58] Nevertheless, Rosenheim unhesitatingly recommends that, under later, changed circumstances, this practice be abandoned:

> The present-day generation also is acting in the spirit of Hirsch by reject-ing some of the above-mentioned concessions in social life, made neces-sary by the conditions of the time, as *hora'at sha'ah* [need of the hour]. The conditions that created them having disappeared—owing to the life-work of Hirsch—*it would be absurd to cling religiously now to canonicals or similar things.*[59]

THE TWENTIETH CENTURY

Writing in the twentieth century, R. Hayyim Ozer Grodzinski deems the wearing of canonicals to be prohibited as a matter of normative Halakhah and declares that wearing clerical robes by rabbis constitutes a biblical offense even according to *Maharik* who was permissive with regard to distinctive garb worn by members of other professions. He cites R. Chaim Pelaggi, *Sefer Ruaḥ Hayyim, ot 2,* to the effect that the wearing of clerical robes similar to those of priests is "a bad and odious custom." Therefore, even if the garments have been intentionally altered to differentiate them from Christian clerical garb, the practice should be abolished. R. Grodzinski mentions that *Matteh Levi* and others wore clerical robes and yet found the practice to be personally repugnant

---

in five issues of the *Israelit* in 1866 in an article entitled "Die Beschlüsse der Rabbiner-Versammlung zu Mihalowitz" and were later included in his collected works. See Jacob Katz, *A House Divided: Orthodoxy and Schism in Nineteenth-Century Central European Jewry*, trans. Ziporah Brody (Hanover: Brandeis University Press, 1998), 83 and 295 n. 33.

58 See Jacob Rosenheim, *Samson Raphael Hirsch's Cultural Ideal and "Our Times,"* trans. I. E. Lichtigfeld (London: Shapiro, Vallentine & Co., 1951), 59–60.

59 Ibid., 62, emphasis in original.

and concludes that one who has the power to do so should prevent the practice in his community.[60]

Rabbi Salomon Breuer's willingness to continue the Hirschian practice of wearing a clerical robe as well as to deliver sermons in the vernacular and to endorse the male choir were significant factors in his election in 1890 as successor to his father-in-law R. Samson Raphael Hirsch.[61] When, however, R. Joseph Jonah Zevi ha-Levi Horovitz of Hunsdorf (later known as the *Frankfurter Rav*) was elected rabbi of the *Frankfurt Israelitische Religionsgesellschaft* (IRG) in 1928, succeeding R. Salomon Breuer, his refusal to wear canonicals created quite a stir. R. Horovitz's daughter relates that when a member of the Board raised the matter after the Horovitz family had arrived in Frankfurt, the rabbi pointedly looked at his watch and asked, "When is the next train to Hunsdorf?"[62] A perhaps apocryphal account relates that, subsequently, in a vestibule of the synagogue where the rabbi and functionaries placed their personal effects, R. Horovitz came upon a box on which were inscribed the words *"Evangelischer Geistlicher"* ("evangelical clergyman") and inside of which lay a clerical robe intended for the rabbi. For R. Horovitz the inscription was further evidence of the Christian provenance of such attire.[63]

---

60 See R. Hayyim Ozer Grodzenski, "Be-'Inyan Malbush Talar," in *Shiloh: Kovetz Zikkaron*, ed. R. Shlomoh Yosef Zevin (Jerusalem and Antwerp, 1983), 167–168. This responsum is reprinted in the supplementary volume of *Aḥi'ezer*, vol. IV (Bnei Brak: Netzah, 1986), *Likkutim*, no. 38, 38–39. In that edition, an unsigned note appended to the responsum, p. 40, states that the provenance of the responsum has been challenged. The compiler claims that the only reason for the note is simply that there was no original of the responsum, only an unsigned copy not in the author's handwriting. However, the inclusion of the responsum in *Shiloh* without comment by the editor, Rabbi Zevin, deservedly recognized as a meticulous scholar, would indicate that R. Zevin was convinced of its authenticity.

61 Jacob Rosenheim, *Zikhronot*, trans. from German by Chaim Weisman (Tel Aviv: She'arim, 1955), 38.

62 Personal communication of Mrs. Judith Zimmerman, July 26, 2001.

63 Personal communication of R. Joseph Elias, July 26, 2001. Rabbi Elias was raised in Frankfurt and heard the narrative while he was yet a youth.

   I am indebted to Dr. Elliot Bondi, grandson of Rabbi Joseph Breuer, for informing me of an unpublished letter by R. Joseph Breuer discussing his own decision not to wear clerical robes in the United States in contrast to the practice of R. Hirsch in Frankfurt. R. Joseph Breuer maintained that for R. Hirsch in nineteenth-century Germany wearing a robe was essential as part of his efforts to foster dignified and aesthetically pleasing services. Rabbi Joseph Breuer was wont to emphasize that all things must be understood in historical perspective and one must be attuned to the sensibilities of people in the new environment of the United States; policy determinations must take into consideration prevalent cultural and social norms. As noted, even in Germany during the period in which R. Joseph Jonah Horovitz served as rabbi in Frankfurt he did not wear a clerical robe. Once the precedent

Nonetheless, at least some rabbinic decisors refused to rule that wearing clerical robes is absolutely forbidden and that it is necessary to forfeit a rabbinical position if wearing such vestments is a condition of employment. In 1957, Rabbi Baruch Horovitz, a grandson of *Matteh Levi* and currently *rosh yeshiva* of Yeshivat Dvar Yerushalayim, faced the possibility that acceptance of a post in a congregation in Manchester, England that had adopted Anglicized services would require him to wear canonicals. Rabbi Horovitz solicited the opinion of R. Zevi Pesach Frank, then Chief Rabbi of Jerusalem. Rabbi Frank responded by issuing a permissive ruling in writing. Consequently, R. Baruch Horovitz informed the Synagogue Board that, if wearing canonicals was a necessary condition of his employment, he would acquiesce to their request. However, upon assuming the post, he reiterated his reluctance, procrastinated, and, offering instead to wear "rabbinicals," proceeded to don a rabbinical frock-coat. In the course of time, the members of the Board gradually, albeit unwillingly and grudgingly, came to terms with his recalcitrance.[64]

---

had been abandoned, to reinstate the practice at a later date in the United States, where few Orthodox rabbis wore canonicals, would have been quite strange.

It may be noted that beginning in 1919, during the lifetime of his father, Rabbi Joseph Breuer served as rabbi of the oldest synagogue in the community, the Frankfurt *Klaus*. The *Klaus* was not officially affiliated either with the general community or with the separatist IRG and the services were less formal; there was no choir and the rabbi did not wear clerical garb. Thus, Rabbi Joseph Breuer had not worn canonicals in Frankfurt. See David Kranzler and David Landesman, *Rav Breuer: His Life and His Legacy* (Jerusalem: Feldheim, 1998), 78 n. 28. In the brief period 1933–1934, when Rabbi Joseph Breuer served as rabbi of the small Hungarian community in Fiume, Italy it is most unlikely that he wore a clerical robe.

64 Personal communication of Rabbi B. Horovitz, July 18, 2001.

Earlier in his career, Rabbi Arie Folger, since June 2016, Chief Rabbi of Vienna, Austria, served for a six-year period as senior rabbi of the Jewish community of Basel, Switzerland. Rabbi Folger relates that during that time, despite his personal predilection not to do so, he wore canonicals in accordance with the regnant communal practice. Later, as senior rabbi of the Jewish community of Munich, Germany, he chose instead to don a rabbinic frock-coat (as had Rabbi Baruch Horovitz in Manchester). Recently, the question of the rabbi wearing a clerical robe was reconsidered in Basel. Ironically, Rabbi Folger received a halakhic query form a former congregant seeking clarification with regard to whether a change is appropriate or whether such a proposal should be rejected since it is contrary to the synagogue's established practice or *minhag*. Personal communication of Rabbi Arie Folger, September 11, 2017.

It is noteworthy that, decades earlier, discomfort with canonicals was expressed by congregants who hailed from Russia and Poland. The Machzike Hadath synagogue in London was founded in 1891 by newly-arrived Eastern European immigrants who did not approve of the religious practices of the Anglo-Jewish community and sought to establish a synagogue that would adhere to more strictly Orthodox standards of worship. The Machzike Hadath ritual rules stipulated that "the Rav, Preacher, Reader or *Shamas* may not wear such

The unpublished correspondence between R. Frank and R. Horovitz merits citation in detail because it delineates nuances of the issue of clerical robes and places the matter in perspective.[65] In his letter to R. Frank dated Rosh Chodesh Tevet 5757 (December 4, 1956), R. Horovitz enumerates several relatively minor halakhic problems with regard to the rabbinical position he had been offered, including the height of the enclosure surrounding the women's gallery, the use of an organ in conjunction with weekday weddings, and the request that the rabbi wear a clerical robe. Noting that there are both lenient and stringent views in the published halakhic literature with regard to each of those questions, R. Horovitz emphasized specifically that the majority of rabbis in Germany, including his own grandfather the *Matteh Levi* and R. Samson Raphael Hirsch, wore the *Talar*, but added that he was also aware of the stringent views recorded in *Darkei Teshuvah* 178:18. In a brief but immediate reply, dated Tevet 6, 5757 (December 10, 1956), R. Frank is explicit in ruling that, in light of the situation as described by R. Horovitz and particularly since the problems involved matters regarding which *Matteh Levi* and R. Hirsch had ruled leniently, it is permissible for him to accept the position. Indeed, R. Frank recommends that he do so posthaste in order that he may be enabled to "achieve great things and benefit the community." It is, however, clearly evident that R. Frank viewed the matter as a sanctionable and necessary leniency rather than an optimal practice. He expresses the hope that "in the course of time," when R. Horovitz "will become established and well-accepted by them [the congregants], he should do whatever is in his power" to improve the conditions of his service.

In a second letter to R. Frank, written a year later (October 8, 1957), R. Horovitz again raised the issue of clerical robes but this time in a more nuanced and complex manner. He related that, initially, in accordance with R. Frank's advice, he had informed the lay leaders of his congregation that, if wearing canonicals was made an absolute condition of employment, he would be prepared to acquiesce in the matter. However, because of his discomfort and reluctance to wear the robe, he had donned a rabbinic frock-coat and postponed dealing with the issue of wearing a clerical robe from

---

Canonicals which may appear as if in imitation of non-Jewish clergy." See Bernard Homa, *A Fortress in Anglo-Jewry: The Story of the Machzike Hadath* (London: Shapiro, Vallentine & Co., 1953), 110. So strong was their antipathy to clerical robes that in 1910 on the occasion of the reconsecration of the synagogue, when the then Chief Rabbi Hermann Adler was invited to speak, in deference to the Machzike Hadath practice Rabbi Adler did not don canonicals for the ceremony. Ibid., 73.

65 I am indebted to R. Horovitz for his further personal communication of January 2, 2002 and for his graciousness in providing me with copies of this correspondence. All citations are my translation of this correspondence.

month to month. R. Horovitz then spelled out the considerations that influenced his course of action." I felt," he wrote, "that it was my obligation to oppose the trend of imitation of the [religious] customs of the [gentile] nations with every vigor for that is one of the chief causes of assimilation; accordingly, upon me, too, rests the obligation to refrain from anything associated with this."

Secondly, from a personal vantage point, R. Horovitz added, he simply found it difficult, or as he put it in quotation marks, "le-hitlabesh," that is, "to costume himself" or "to masquerade" in that manner, while performing his rabbinical functions because he felt that to do so would constitute "farcical conduct with regard to the words of the living God." Finally—expressing a sensitivity in which he was ahead of his time—R. Horovitz commented that, quite apart from halakhic considerations, the practice "creates a barrier between the rabbi and his congregation" and results in a negative impact upon a rabbi's effectiveness in ministering to the spiritual needs of his congregants. As a consequence of those various considerations he had not acted on his original concession. The members of his congregation, however, maintained that the issue was causing strife and quarrelsomeness and might impede his efforts in dissemination of Torah teaching. R. Horovitz once more turned to R. Frank for advice, noting that his instinct was to continue to conduct himself in accordance with his own principles because, despite the ongoing contention, even the dissident members of the congregation desired him to remain as their rabbi and his tenure was no longer in jeopardy.

From R. Frank's second reply, dated 15 Kislev 5718 (December 8, 1957), it is abundantly clear that R. Frank strongly disfavored wearing robes and accordingly he recommended that R. Horovitz procrastinate with regard to implementation of the practice for as long as possible. R. Frank states forcefully, "Regarding what they ask of you to wear garments that are not in accordance with your spirit, as long as it is feasible to push off this matter and not to fulfill their demand, it is a mitzvah to be scrupulous with regard to this." Nevertheless, continues R. Frank, R. Horovitz is certainly not obligated to resign his post on account of this issue because

> In my opinion, there is a benefit in your office, [i.e.,] to attract the heart
> of the youth to fear of Heaven and perhaps also to Torah and "this is all
> of man"[66] and the purpose of his creation for which he has come to this

---

66 Ecclesiastes 12:13.

world. Because of this, it is worthwhile to expend great effort for the merit of the community is a great beneficence to man and in this manner you will merit eternal bliss.

R. Horovitz's personal perspective expressed in the late 1950s became a more common feeling among many members of the Orthodox British rabbinate decades later. A number of factors contributed to the attitudinal change. The Anglo-Jewish rabbinate was attracting more individuals who had studied for an extended period in yeshivot in England or in Israel and, accordingly, both identified with more staunchly traditionalist elements of the community and were more concerned with halakhic minutiae. Moreover, and perhaps even more significantly, the entire cultural fabric of society had undergone a profound transformation with even conservative Britain becoming a country with less insistence on formality in dress and ritual.

This development is evidenced in an interesting item included by the late R. Immanuel Jakobovits, former British Chief Rabbi, in *Dear Chief Rabbi*, a selection from his wide-ranging correspondence. In 1982, R. Jakobovits received a query from a rabbi serving in a United Synagogue pulpit who, together with his cantor, wished to dispense with the use of clerical gowns. Rabbi Jakobovits commented upon the tension that had begun to surround this practice and noted "the growing tendency among younger rabbis to discard clerical garb including cap and gown."[67] In his brief rejoinder, he also reported that he had been approached by the senior honorary officers of the United Synagogue who strongly urged maintaining the "traditional wearing of canonicals at all religious services."[68] Rabbi Jakobovits observed that, while the established practice enhanced the dignity of the rabbinate, in some instances practices that had become "traditions" might well be counterproductive and alienate younger "more religiously committed" rabbis

---

67 Jeffrey Cohen, ed., *Dear Chief Rabbi: From the Correspondence of Chief Rabbi Immanuel Jakobovits on Matters of Jewish Law, Ethics and Contemporary Issues 1980–1990* (Hoboken, NJ: Ktav, 1995), 275. Changing trends in the Anglo-Jewish rabbinate are evident in an article titled "On the Clerical Collar" published in the *Jewish Review* 7, no. 184 (September 30, 1953), 3, in which Chaim Pearl notes that in a 1925 photograph of British ministers, 40 of 48 wore Roman collars, part of the garb of the United Synagogue's clergy, whereas in 1953, only 14 out of 60 ministers were wearing the clerical collar.

It should be noted that Rabbi Jakobovits himself, rather than the usual clerical black gown, wore a blue academic gown that to cognoscenti was recognizable as such.

68 Cohen, *Dear Chief Rabbi*, 275.

and laymen. He therefore suggested that the matter be deferred for further discussion among representatives of the rabbinate but recommended that, pending a consensus, individual rabbis not depart from the regnant practice. The salient point in Rabbi Jakobovits's response is the clear recognition that it is the younger and religiously more committed who are uncomfortable with clerical garb and might, as a consequence, be discouraged from participating in worship at congregations of the United Synagogue and from serving in the ranks of its ministry.[69]

Shortly thereafter, the issue of canonicals became a heatedly debated topic among members of the British rabbinate.[70] At the time, Rabbi Jonathan Sacks, then Principal of Jews' College, wrote candidly:

> In the case of canonicals it was originally and undoubtedly an imitation of the Church: a gesture which announced in the strongest possible terms that with civil emancipation, Jews were as good as the gentiles when it came to the external trappings of religion.[71]

He pointed out that opposition to the practice was most vociferous among those who viewed it as a hallmark of Reform Judaism. Presciently, he declared that in the coming years, even in the secular world, adherence to Establishment culture would wane and asserted that as far as Jewry is concerned, "We would serve ourselves and others better by recovering our authenticity."[72]

In present-day England, the bylaws of the (Orthodox) United Synagogue continued to stipulate that canonicals were obligatory attire for clergy when officiating at services, but the regulation was more honored in the breach than in the observance. In 1998, imposition of this mode of dress upon guest rabbis officiating at weddings in synagogues that continued to adhere to the practice had become a source of contention.[73] It was ironic, but perhaps hardly surprising, that, at a time when clerical robes had already been discarded by the great majority of functionaries among Reform clergy,[74] they were still cherished by the British United Synagogue which remained a bastion of conservatism.

69 Ibid.

70 See Rabbi Jonathan Sacks, "Response: The Rabbinate," *L'Eylah*, 2, no. 5 (Spring 5743 [1983]), 23–24 and "Zero Response: The Rabbinate," *L'Eylah* 2, no. 6 (Autumn 5744 [1983]), 21–24.

71 Sacks, "Zero Response," 22.

72 Ibid., 23.

73 See Ruth Rothenberg, "New Rabbis' Distress Over Need to Dress to Impress," *The Jewish Chronicle* (London), November 20, 1998, 19.

74 Accurate data on the wearing of robes in American Reform congregations is difficult to obtain but it is generally believed that, although the majority of Reform functionaries in

Nevertheless, some fifteen years later, upon stepping down from his position as Chief Rabbi, Rabbi Sacks, in a valedictory address articulating the role of religion in the twenty-first century, noted that the British synagogue had become transformed. Services were more informal and, "Rabbis no longer wear canonicals."[75]

---

the United States do not wear clerical robes throughout the year, many still do so on the High Holy Days. Personal communication of Sue Ann Wasserman, then Director of the Department of Religious Living, Union of American Hebrew Congregations (currently rabbi of Temple Beth David of the South Shore, MA), August 7, 2001. Several past surveys of worship practice in the Reform movement failed to address the question. However, "Unpublished Worship Survey 2000," conducted by the Commission on Religious Living and the Commission on Synagogue Music of the Union of American Hebrew Congregations, included one question asking which of the following was used by worship leaders when conducting services: a *kipah*, a *tallit*, or a robe, and whether this was a matter of individual choice or congregational policy. The responses to this question indicated that 78% of worship leaders wore a *kipah* and a *tallit* while only 38% wore a robe. In terms of congregational policy, 14% of congregations required the worship leader to wear a *kipah*, 16% required a *tallit* and only 12% required a robe. I am indebted to Sue Wasserman for a copy of that unpublished survey.

In 2001, this writer conducted a very informal and limited inquiry in the form of a brief email questionnaire seeking information regarding the prevalence of robes among Reform and Liberal functionaries in the United Kingdom. I am very grateful to Dr. Tony Bayfield, then Chief Executive of the Reform Synagogues of Great Britain, currently President of what is now known as the Movement for Reform Judaism, who suggested the questionnaire and graciously assisted in forwarding it to members of the Reform and Liberal clergy in England. I received answers from 24 respondents, 8 of whom were women. The sample is too small to be significant but it should be noted, as Tony Bayfield commented, "I can't think why those who do reply should be a biased sample on this issue, so whatever percentage response you get should reflect the whole" (email communication of August 10, 2001). Nine of the twenty-four respondents wrote that they never wear clerical robes. Of those, two had worn robes in the past, but did so no longer. Nine respondents wrote that they wore a traditional *kittel* on the High Holy Days, while another nine answered that they wore white robes on the High Holy Days. Only seven of the twenty-four respondents replied that they wore robes when conducting weekly services. However, fifteen of the twenty-four noted that they wore robes when officiating at weddings and/or funerals (of these, only nine wore the robes for weddings, fifteen for funerals). Of interest, in response to the query of where the robes were purchased, most of those who wore robes replied that they obtained them from purveyors of religious supplies, three from purveyors of academic garments, and one directly from a supplier of the Church of England. One female respondent wrote, "I think you should have included a question 'I don't wear robes because . . .,'" and added the following pointed comment, "I do not wear robes because I do not feel that it is appropriate for me to wear special garments which separate me from the congregation. I am a rabbi and not a priest. On the High Holy Days I wear a *Kittel* because it is appropriate to the High Holy Days and which [sic] may be worn by any Jew at this time."

75 R. Jonathan Sacks, *A Judaism Engaged with the World* (London: Office of the Chief Rabbi, 2013), 4.

CONCLUSION

Clearly, attitudes regarding the wearing of clerical attire by members of the rabbinate have undergone several changes. It is quite plausible that the initial adoption of distinctive clerical garb by rabbis in Holland and Italy aroused little objection because of the similarity of the garments adopted by rabbis to those of physicians and jurists. Later, when such professional clothing was no longer common, the similarity to Christian practice was more pronounced and hence was decried as emulation of gentile practices. As the attire became increasingly identified with Reform clergy, whose intention was indeed to pattern themselves upon church practice, Orthodox opposition became more vociferous. In contemporary times, in which formal attire by clergy of all denominations is increasingly abandoned, the rabbinical gown has by and large fallen into disuse.

It is not at all surprising that trends in clothing and apparel change rapidly over time. Elegant robes of yesteryear may today appear pompous and off-putting. One should not be astonished that ritual practices patterned upon popular modes of conduct are subject to shifts and fluctuations. Yesterday's high fashion very soon becomes outmoded.

But, from a Jewish point of view, are rabbinic robes a distinction or a dishonor? In Italy the rabbinic clerical garb may have come to be viewed as Jewish rather than Catholic since "no priest ever dressed like an Italian rabbi."[76] Elsewhere, it was clearly seen as resembling Protestant garb and sometimes deemed an offensive imitation of church practice.[77] In England, in particular, where Jewish ministers also took to wearing a Roman clerical collar the practice was incontrovertibly patterned on the dress of the Christian clergy of that country.

Asher Salah is correct in concluding that clerical garb was not a central issue in early counter-Reform debates as may be inferred from the fact that some Orthodox authorities adopted such dress. He misses the point, however, in assuming that there were no objections to such attire during the first half of the nineteenth century.[78] While not a central issue, refusal on the part of religious authorities to accept the wearing of clerical robes with equanimity predates the Michalowitz protests. Even the non-Orthodox commented ironically on the evolving sartorial style. As early as April 1823, in a letter to a friend, the

76 Salah, "Rabbinical Dress," 63.
77 See note 44.
78 See Salah, "Rabbinical Dress," 63.

sharp-witted Heinrich Heine, with his keen eye for hypocrisy, mocked the new Reform preachers in his satirical bent. He was suspicious of their motivation and, admitting that "we no longer have the power to wear a beard, to fast, to hate …," scoffed at the theatrical recostuming of Judaism "wearing white bands in place of a beard."[79] Some twenty years later, the Orthodox District Rabbi of Sulzburg wrote similarly that *Beffchen* may symbolize the white beards of rabbis of the past—beards that perhaps represented maturity and wisdom—but *Beffchen* may be worn by a callow youth and do not represent anything at all.[80] More significantly, one should bear in mind the discomfiture with wearing the robe expressed by Rabbi Bamberger[81] and the critical reaction to specific details of the dress of Rabbi Samson Raphael Hirsch.[82]

One may indeed wonder why Rabbi Hirsch, who staunchly championed strict adherence to prescriptions of rabbinic law and reviled changes in ritual, scathingly excoriating even those who would eliminate recitation of *piyyutim*—poetic sections of the prayer service whose omission is not at all forbidden by Halakhah—should have embraced the wearing of a clerical robe.

An insight into his motivation may perhaps be gleaned from a two-part article penned by his contemporary, Rabbi Dr. Hermann Lipschutz, and published in R. Hirsch's journal, *Jeschurun*. In his depiction of the rabbinate, "*Die moderne Rabbinismus*" (The Modern Rabbinate), part I, "*Wie er ist*" (As It Is), Lipschutz derides the typical modern clergyman, bedecked in robe and white bands, proud possessor of a doctorate and elegant preacher, but lacking even a minimal competence in rabbinic or talmudic learning.[83] In a sequel, R. Lipschutz then articulates his vision of the ideal modern rabbinate, "*Wie er sein soll*" (As It Should Be), and depicts an individual learned in every aspect of rabbinic law in the manner of an old-time rabbi, but outwardly modern; an individual in essence, in thought, act, and teaching, identical to the traditional rabbi of yore but different in his external demeanor. In relating to the outer world the old-time rabbi was ineffective; in that respect alone, argues R. Lipschutz, was his image deficient. But,

---

79 Heinrich Heine, *Säkularausgabe. Werke, Briefwechsel, Lebenszeugnisse*, vol. 20. *Briefe 1815– 1831* (Berlin: Akademie-Verlag, 1970), 72.

80 See Rabbi Emanuel Dreyfuss, "Über die Amtstracht des Rabbinen," *Der treue Zionswächter* 2 (1846), 296–298. Rabbi Dreyfuss, the author of *Oraḥ Meisharim* (Müllhausen, 1848) was the last rabbi of Sulzburg. Following his demise in 1886, the seat of the district rabbinate was transferred to Freiburg.

81 See note 22.

82 See note 24.

83 *Jeschurun* 10, no. 8 (1864), 277–283.

unfortunately, this lack of understanding for the outer trappings of modernity and Western culture had alienated many congregants and caused them, mistakenly, to view the traditional rabbi as irrelevant to their lives.[84]

It was this misperception that R. Hirsch was determined to correct. He was eloquent in his espousal of unadulterated religious practice and effusive in his reverence for rabbinic scholarship but was, at the same time, passionate in advocating a rabbinate that would demonstrate an understanding and acceptance of the cultural trends of the time. Thus, the idea of a rabbi garbed in the clerical attire of the day yet upholding Torah and mitzvot in all their splendor appealed to his imagination as but another way to render Orthodoxy attractive, to stem the then rising tide of defection to Reform and to demonstrate the viability of a forward-looking Orthodoxy. Rabbi Hirsch's intent in wearing the robe was *le-hagdil Torah u-le-ha'adirah.*

In this context, one must emphasize that R. Hirsch's teacher, R. Jacob Ettlinger, a preeminent talmudist and unimpeachable, revered halakhic authority, had himself worn a robe. With that precedent, Rabbi Hirsch need have had no qualms regarding the halakhic permissibility of the practice.

Nevertheless, to many other Orthodox figures wearing of canonicals remained a distasteful, even servile, mimicry of other religions. They saw no merit in an attempt to change Jewish practice in any manner in order to make it more aesthetically appealing.

In the years since the sociological and religious controversies of the nineteenth century the Jewish people have experienced global catastrophe and cataclysmic upheavals. Among the many transformations that time has wrought, thankfully, many of today's youth have regained a healthy measure of Jewish pride. The late Michael Wyschograd related that, several decades ago, a group of his peers used to travel regularly from their Brooklyn neighborhood to classes at Columbia University. Upon exiting the subway at Broadway and 116th Street they would surreptitiously remove their *yarmulkes* before entering the awe-inspiring precincts of the campus. A generation later, however, his own son tells of regularly observing bareheaded students stepping out of the subway station and donning *kippot* as they near the Columbia campus. The distinctive head-covering is no longer perceived as a badge of shame and a source of self-consciousness but as a symbol of privileged identification and a claim to distinction.[85]

---

84 *Jeschurun* 10, no. 9 (1864), 302–308.

85 Cf. this writer's comments on Jewish pride in "The Future of American Orthodoxy," *Jewish Action* 59, no. 1 (Fall 1998), 38.

In the twenty-first century, in an era in which many among the Jews who visit the synagogue have rediscovered an appreciation of their heritage, they unabashedly seek to pray in the manner consecrated over the ages. Their garb—and the garb in which they see their religious functionaries attired—is a head covering, *tallit* and *tefillin*. Regarding Jews wearing such garb the Talmud teaches[86] that the scriptural passage testifies, "And all the peoples of the earth shall see that the name of the Lord is called upon you"[87] and they may justifiably be hailed as "Israel in whom I will be glorified."[88]

---

86 See *Berakhot* 6a, *Megillah* 15b, *Sotah* 17a, *Menaḥot* 35b and *Ḥullin* 89a.
87 Deuteronomy 28:10.
88 Isaiah 49:3.

CHAPTER 5

Intermarriage in the Early Modern Period

From late antiquity through the Middle Ages and until the early modern period most Jews lived a segregated, isolated, life—"Lo, it is a people that shall dwell alone, and shall not be reckoned among the nations" (Numbers 23:9)—and marital liaisons between Jews and members of other faiths were limited. With the Industrial Revolution, settlement of the Western Hemisphere, and the significant socio-economic and religious transformations that followed in the wake of the Enlightenment and the French Revolution, the incidence of intermarriage rose inexorably until, by the mid-nineteenth century, intermarriage became an endemic phenomenon of Jewish life in Western Europe. Today, in the early twenty-first century, the rate of intermarriage has risen to an all-time high in virtually every country with the exception of the State of Israel. In the United States well over fifty percent of Jewish marriages involve a non-Jewish partner. In the European areas of the FSU taken in totality, the rate is sixty-five percent; in the Russian Republic it is above seventy-five percent.[1] Manifold factors, including political emancipation, international migration, urbanization, and the increasing secularization of society have affected this process. The beginnings of this trend and the various initial responses to it within the organized Jewish religious community warrant detailed examination.

SOCIO-POLITICAL CHANGE, CIVIL MARRIAGE AND PATTERNS OF INTERMARRIAGE

Throughout the medieval period regulation of marriage was exclusively within the jurisdiction of ecclesiastic authorities. In France, marriages were

---

1 Sergio Della Pergola, "Jewish Out-Marriage: A Global Perspective," *Jewish Intermarriage Around the World*, ed. Shulamit Reinharz and Sergio Della Pergola (New Brunswick, NJ: Transaction, 2009), 14–15 and 26–27. Arthur Ruppin, *The Jewish Fate and Future*, trans. E. W. Dickes (London: Macmillan, 1940), 105, contends that despite religious proscriptions mixed marriages between Jews and Christians were frequent in the first thousand years of the Christian era but ceased after the Crusades.

brought under the auspices of the state in 1792; in the Habsburg Empire this occurred almost a decade earlier. As civil governments became increasingly involved in the regulation of matrimony, concerns were raised with regard to conflicts that might emerge between civil statutes and the religious practices of the various denominations.

On January 16, 1783 Joseph II issued an *Ehepatent* decreeing that henceforth with regard to marriage and divorce civil law would govern all his subjects and would govern the actions of religious authorities. In the wake of this decree the renowned Rabbi Ezekiel Landau of Prague, known as *Noda bi-Yehudah*, whose preeminence was widely acknowledged, was called upon to draft a statement of Jewish matrimonial law in order to identify disparities between the Jewish and civil codes governing such matters. In 1785, Rabbi Landau penned a brief tract in German outlining the fundamental prescriptions and proscriptions of Jewish family law and included a detailed comparison of the Habsburg civil code and Jewish law.[2] That work is succinct and comprehensive but little-known even among rabbinic scholars. Rabbi Landau's request that Jews be permitted to abide by their own religious laws and practices was granted.[3] Although the document, couched in reverential and laudatory terms, repeatedly thanks the emperor for his graciousness and praises the sagacity

2 The German manuscript titled *Das mosaisch-talmudische Eherecht* was published with an introduction and notes by Alexander Kisch (Leipzig: M. W. Kauffmann Verlag, 1900). A Hebrew translation by a grandson of Rabbi Landau, Zeev Wolf Sheinblum, bearing the title *Ḥukei ha-Ishut al pi Dat Mosheh ve-ha-Talmud*, was published in Munkács (Mukačevo) in 1901 and later appended to Yekutiel Aryeh Kamelhar's biography of Rabbi Landau, *Mofet ha-Dor*, 1st ed. (Munkács, 1903) and 2nd ed. (Pietrkov, 1934). The treatise is also reprinted in Aryeh Leib Gelman, *Ha-Noda bi-Yehudah u-Mishnatto*, 3rd ed. (Jerusalem, 1970), 109–126.

3 In introductory comments to Rabbi Landau's monograph, *Eherecht*, 4–5, Kisch notes that initially, in response to Rabbi Landau's request, a government commission of December 4, 1785 sought to modify some aspects of matrimonial law relating to Jews but later government decrees of March 4, 1786 and August 12, 1788 failed to incorporate those amendments. Not until 1791 under Leopold II were adjustments made to the law in the spirit of Rabbi Landau's recommendations and then confirmed in the legal code promulgated in 1811 as exceptions for Jews (*Ausnahmen für die Judenschaft*).

For Rabbi Landau's positive relationship with the rulers Maria Theresa and Joseph II, see Sharon Flatto, *The Kabbalistic Culture of Eighteenth-Century Prague: Ezekiel Landau (the 'Noda Biyehudah') and his Contemporaries* (Portland, OR: Littman Library of Jewish Civilization, 2010), 50–52. Charles W. Ingrao, *The Habsburg Monarchy 1618–1815* (Cambridge: Cambridge University Press, 1994), p. 119, notes that Joseph II's benign treatment of Jews as evidenced in his 1782 edict of Tolerance and his waiving of the *Leibmaut*, a tax levied only on Jews and cattle, did not garner popularity and that he was derided by Christians of all persuasions as "Emperor of the Jews."

of his laws, Rabbi Landau does not hesitate to draw attention to instances in which requirements of Jewish law would necessitate adherence to overriding religious prescriptions. For example, although Jewish authorities could in good conscience conform to civil regulations regarding authorization to marry, in the event that a couple marry in contravention of those rules—an occurrence that he assures will be unlikely—they might be subject to a civil penalty but, from the standpoint of Jewish law, since the marriage is valid, the parties would require a Jewish religious divorce, or *get*, to dissolve the union. Similarly, were a married man to take a second wife, the marriage, although prohibited by Jewish law as well as by civil law, would nevertheless be valid and hence would require a *get* for its dissolution.

Rabbi Landau enumerated the consanguineous marriages permitted by Jewish law but prohibited by the state and commented that it would not be appropriate for Jewish authorities to forbid such unions. Rabbi Landau emphasized that Jewish law permits agency in connection with marriage and divorce but has explicit and strict rules concerning persons who may be designated as agents as well as provisions governing the mode of designation. For that reason, he asserted, employment of agency must be approved by rabbinic authorities who are expert in the law.[4] With regard to mixed marriages, Rabbi Landau faced no serious problem. The civil code of Joseph II declared a marriage between a Christian and an individual of another faith to be invalid. Rabbi Landau did, however, add a caveat: "This law conforms to Jewish law provided that the man or woman are by birth of another religion *as explained in section four*" (emphasis added).[5] In the referenced section Rabbi Landau carefully noted that if the husband or wife were of Jewish birth and later converted, the original marriage would require a Jewish religious divorce for its dissolution. With respect to a mixed marriage, the inference is that if a man, born Jewish but converted to Christianity, were to marry a Jewish woman subsequent to his apostasy, that marriage would *not* be invalid in the eyes of Jewish law and would require a *get*.[6]

Since the Austrian regime avowedly professed Christianity and, as noted, its civil code did not countenance mixed marriage, rabbinic authorities were generally sanguine in complying with its provisions. The situation in France was different and the need to respond to an inquiry regarding intermarriage presented the Jewish community with a serious challenge. In convening the

---

4 See Gelman, *Ha-Noda bi-Yehudah u-Mishnatto*, 119.
5 Ibid., 118.
6 Ibid., 113.

Assembly of Notables in 1806 and the Grand Sanhedrin in 1807, Napoleon sought to delineate the respective spheres of religion and state and to pressure rabbinic authorities to subordinate Jewish religious law to the French civil code.[7] The Jewish delegates were in a quandary. They knew full well that they must answer craftily in order to assure the regime of their unwavering loyalty and must exercise caution lest they reveal any semblance of distinctiveness in their religious law.

Of the twelve questions placed before the Assembly of Notables, the first three dealt with matters of marriage and divorce.[8] In responding to the first two questions, namely, whether it is lawful for a Jew to take a second wife and whether divorce is valid even when not decreed by the courts of justice, the rabbis were able to answer with ease. Polygamy is unlawful by virtue of an eleventh-century rabbinic enactment and Jewish law permits divorce. Noting that a civil divorce was required by Jewish authorities prior to execution of a religious divorce, the Notables felt constrained to add—for diplomatic reasons, but incorrectly in terms of Jewish law—that the divorce would not be valid if not previously pronounced by the French code. In their answer to the second question, the Notables further stated unequivocally "the law of the State is the supreme law."[9]

---

7 See Jay R. Berkowitz, "The Napoleonic Sanhedrin: Halachic Foundations and Rabbinical Legacy," *CCAR Journal* 54 (Winter 2007), 12–14. Berkowitz notes that it was precisely in the arena of marriage that conflicts between religion and state first came to the foreground. Following promulgation of the 1792 French law, protocols for non-Catholic unions had not yet been established and Jews continued to conduct only religious ceremonies. Napoleon now instructed rabbis not to perform a marriage ceremony unless there was proof of a prior civil ceremony before a government official.

8 For the text of the questions to the Notables and their answers see M. Diogene Tama, *Transactions of the Paris Sanhedrim* [sic], trans. F. D. Kirwan (London: Charles Taylor, 1807), 149–156, 179–195, and 201–207.

9 It is instructive to compare this formulation with the measured and fearless comments of Rabbi Landau in his *Ḥukei ha-Ishut*, responses to sections 1–9 of the Habsburg code. See notes 3–5 and accompanying text. In all fairness, one should recognize the more delicate situation faced by the French delegates in the period following the disruptions of the Revolution and the Reign of Terror and confronted by the awe-inspiring presence of Napoleon and his advisors. Simon Schwarzfuchs, *Napoleon, the Jews and the Sanhedrin* (London: Routledge & Kegan Paul, 1979), 82, notes that Napoleon had stated clearly that he wished the Sanhedrin not only to rule that the religious marriage ceremony could take place only subsequent to a civil ceremony but that the Sanhedrin should encourage mixed marriage as well. See also Robert Anchel, *Napoléon et les Juifs* (Paris: Les Presses Universitaires de France, 1928), 211.

Unlike the French civil marriage law, the Habsburg *Ehepatent* did not provide for civil ceremonies; rather, it allowed marriage to remain under the aegis of the clergy of the respective denominations. However, with regard to both the Habsburg code and the French code, despite all efforts to gloss over discrepancies, halakhic problems arose because of

The real difficulty was posed by the third question: May a Jewess marry a Christian or a Christian woman a Jew? Or does religious law allow Jews to marry only among themselves? The attempt to answer this question without compromising Halakhah while yet appeasing the authorities split the delegates to the Assembly. In their evasive answer the Notables equivocated. They declared that the biblical prohibition was limited to heathen peoples and did not extend to Christians who are monotheists.[10] However, in practice, rabbis would not solemnize such unions and hence, from the standpoint of Judaism, such intermarriage was not possible. The Notables were careful to observe that in this respect rabbinic law paralleled church law.[11] Nevertheless, the Notables did concede that such unions were valid civilly and might be dissolved civilly without need for a religious divorce.

Significantly, the answer to the third question as formulated by the Sanhedrin was substantially different from that of the Notables. No reference whatsoever was made to the problematic assertion regarding the biblical prohibition. The statement read as follows:

> The great Sanhedrin declares that marriage between Israelites and Christians, contracted according to the laws of the 'Code Civil,' are, from a civil standpoint, binding and valid, and, although such marriages can not be invested with the religious forms, they shall not entail any disciplinary punishment (anathema)."[12]

The Sanhedrin was careful not to state that intermarriage was valid even *post factum*, but merely that, if contracted, it was civilly binding.[13]

---

contradictions between civil law and Halakhah. Schwarzfuchs, *Napoleon, the Jews and the Sanhedrin*, 191, reports increasing neglect with regard to Jewish religious divorce in France. For a discussion of rabbinic efforts to resolve some of the issues see Zevi Jonathan Kaplan, "The Thorny Area of Marriage: Rabbinic Efforts to Harmonize Jewish and French Law in Nineteenth Century France," *Jewish Social Studies: History, Culture, and Society* (n. s.) 3 (Spring/Summer 2007), 59–72.

10 Whether intermarriage with all non-Jews or only with members of the Seven Nations is biblically proscribed is a matter of disagreement among early-day authorities. Rambam, *Hilkhot Issurei Bi'ah*, 12:1–2, rules that the biblical prohibition applies to all non-Jews; R. Jacob ben Asher, *Tur, Even ha-Ezer*, 16:1, limits the biblical prohibition to the seven nations. Such unions are rabbinically prohibited according to all codifiers. See *Avodah Zarah* 36b and *Sanhedrin* 82a.

11 See Schwarzfuchs, *Napoleon, the Jews and the Sanhedrin*, pp. 70–71.

12 For the French original see A. E. Halphen, *Recueil des lois, décrets, ordonnances ... concernant les Israélites depuis la Révolution de 1789* (Paris, 1851), 25.

13 This important point is correctly emphasized by Berkowitz, "The Napoleonic Sanhedrin," 15, in his assessment of the impact of the French Sanhedrin. Schwarzfuchs, *Napoleon, the*

Despite Napoleon's clear agenda regarding the active promotion of intermarriage, the possibility of contracting a civil marriage was not, in and of itself, a motivation for intermarriage but the institution of civil marriage definitely did make such unions less difficult for the parties involved. In countries where there was no civil marriage as, for example, in Prussia prior to 1846, in order to marry a Christian the prospective spouse had to convert. Technically, such marriages were not intermarriages since both partners were Christians at the time of marriage but, since the conversions were usually only *pro forma*, those marriages are generally regarded as intermarriages. The early nineteenth century witnessed an ever-increasing number of Jews marrying out of the faith with or without a conversion ceremony. To illustrate the extent of this phenomenon and to humanize the dry statistics it is instructive to examine particular examples as well as patterns of mixed marriage in Germany, Britain, Austria, the United States, and Australia during this early period.

In the course of the year 1786 Berlin high society witnessed a curious and prolonged legal drama involving the contested will of the wealthy Jewish entrepreneur Moses Isaac who had stipulated at the time of his death ten years earlier that, if any of the five children who were beneficiaries of the will were to convert, he or she would forfeit any share in his estate. A charitable trust was also established for impecunious relatives. Two sons had successfully appealed to King Frederick the Great to uphold the terms of the will and exclude their two sisters who had converted and then married Christian noblemen. The sisters sued in civil court to invalidate the will. The court ruled in their favor but a higher court reversed the decision and then, the same year, a third court reversed the decision of the second court. In a further reversal, the new ruler, Frederick William II, confirmed the terms of the will and the sisters were disinherited. Reacting to public outrage, the brothers arrived at a private settlement with their sisters involving the transfer of a considerable sum of money to them. The ironic denouement of the saga unfolded later when one of those brothers converted and his children were excluded from the estate. Finally, by the mid-nineteenth century, only one of the Isaac children remained Jewish and even his children became apostates, with the result that the ultimate beneficiaries of the will

---

Jews and the Sanhedrin, 95, cites the speech of Rabbi David Sintzheim delivered at the closing meeting of the Sanhedrin and his outspoken words: "You have recognized the validity of certain civil acts, but you have admitted their religious incoherence."

and the charitable endowment were predominantly Moses Isaac's Christian descendants.[14]

Reflected in this case is the milieu of acculturated wealthy Jewish families and their generational struggles in *fin-de-siècle* eighteenth-century Berlin at a time when the incidence of intermarriage subsequent to conversion to Christianity was increasing markedly. As evident in this case, parents fought the trend with every means at their disposal. Frequently, their weapons were financial. Emotional bonds played a role as well as can be seen, for example, in the decision of the *salonnière* Henrietta Herz who postponed conversion until the death of her mother and of Moses Mendelssohn's daughter Dorothea who did not convert during her father's lifetime.[15]

As was the case with regard to the Isaac family in Berlin, during this period the conversion of women was more common than that of men and, when it occurred, was usually a prelude to intermarriage. The higher incidence of female over male converts in the late 1700s was reversed by the 1830s.[16] While accurate statistics are unavailable, it is estimated that converts to Christianity in Berlin in the early nineteenth century numbered about one-eighth of the Jewish population. What is distinctive about these converts and their intermarriages is not the number of individuals involved but their characteristics. Defections from Judaism had always occurred, but usually on the part of marginal figures. This wave of conversions emanated from the elite strata of the community drawn from the wealthy and the intelligentsia.[17] Of these, the particular circumstances of the salon women were exceptional and for that reason their motivations will be examined subsequently.

The picture in England at this time was similar in some respects but the general attitude to conversion and exogamy was more nuanced and

---

14 At the time of Moses Isaac's death in 1776 only six of his ten children were alive and one had been disinherited. For a fuller discussion see Warren I. Cohn, "The Moses Isaac Family Trust—Its History and Significance," *Leo Baeck Institute Year Book* 18 (1973), 267–280.

15 Upon her conversion Dorothea claimed to have seen a smiling apparition of her departed father looking down upon her baptism. See Carola Stern, *"Ich möchte mir Flügel wünschen": Das Leben der Dorothea Schlegel* (Hamburg: Rowohlt, 2000), 195. Was this a delusional fantasy, wish-fulfilling and exculpatory in nature?

16 Deborah Hertz, *Jewish High Society in Old Regime Berlin* (New Haven, CT: Yale University Press, 1988), 238.

17 See Jacob Katz, *Out of the Ghetto: The Social Background of Jewish Emancipation, 1770–1870* (New York: Schocken Books, 1978), 105 and 121–122 and accompanying notes. Cf. Alfred D. Low, *Jews in the Eyes of the Germans: From the Enlightenment to Imperial Germany* (Philadelphia: Institute for the Study of Human Issues, 1979), 179–181.

conservative. One of the earliest Jews to gain prominence after the reset-tlement, Samson Gideon, did not convert but married out of the faith and reared his children as Christians; nevertheless, he did not achieve his life-long ambition of being raised to the nobility. Social interaction and intermarriage were to be found among the wealthiest and the most impoverished strata of Jews; the masses, however, retained a strong group identity.[18]

The early generations of the British branch of the Rothschild clan loy-ally strove to resist the lure of intermarriage. Hannah, daughter of Nathan Mayer, was the first to convert and marry a Christian in a church, but as was often the case with her Berlin coreligionists, did not do so until 1839, after her father's demise.[19] Approximately forty years later, another Hannah Rothschild, daughter of Baron Mayer Amschel and a fabulously wealthy heiress, married Lord Rosebery in church subsequent to a civil ceremony but did not convert. Unsurprisingly, the ceremony was deemed a "great scandal" in the eyes of Christians. As noted in the London *Jewish Chronicle*, news of this alliance shook the Jewish community:

> If the flame seized on the cedars, how will fare the hyssop on the wall? If the leviathan is brought up with a hook, how will the minnows escape? ... A sad example has been set ... should we suppress the cry of pain heaved forth from the soul?[20]

Hannah, although happily married to a Christian, continued to attend services in London's Western Synagogue, fasted and prayed on the Day of Atonement, and lit Sabbath candles. Her funeral was arranged by the Ḥevra

---

18 See Todd M. Endelman, *The Jews of Britain, 1656 to 2000* (Berkeley, CA: University of California Press, 2002), 66–67 and Chaim Bermant, *The Cousinhood* (New York: The Macmillan Company, 1971), 11.

19 Bermant, *The Cousinhood*, 36 and 145.

20 *Jewish Chronicle*, July 10, 1877, cited in Bermant, *The Cousinhood*, 155. The highly sen-sational nature of the public reaction to this marriage is evidenced in its reverberations across the ocean in the United States. When Helen Wise, daughter of Isaac Mayer Wise, eloped with James Molony, a Christian, and was married by a Unitarian minister, the Cincinnati *Enquirer's* report (May 10, 1878), "Cupid Conquers," contrasted this fur-tive elopement to the splendid festivities in England when "the richest maiden in all Israel" married Lord Rosebery. See *The Enquirer*, May 10, 1879, unnumbered pages, small collections 13082 AJA, cited in Ann C. Rose, *Beloved Strangers: Interfaith Families in Nineteenth-Century America* (Cambridge, MA: Harvard University Press, 2001), 77 and 234.

Kaddisha (burial society) and she was buried in the Rothschild family vault in Wilesden Cemetery. Her husband wrote candidly that this added to his grief:

> There is, however, one incident to this tragedy only less painful than the actual loss; which is that at the moment of death the difference in creed makes itself felt and another religion steps in to claim the corpse. It was inevitable and I do not complain: and my wife's family have been more than kind. But none the less it is exquisitely painful.[21]

To Emma Goldsmid Montefiore, wife of Nathaniel Montefiore, intermarriage was anathema. She became reconciled to her daughter Charlotte's marriage in 1884 to a Christian, Lewis McIver, only after a rabbi in Germany was found who was willing to solemnize a marriage between a Jew and a Christian. In deference to his mother, her son Claude postponed marriage to his second wife, Florence Ward, for several years until after his mother's death. Florence then underwent a nominal conversion—"she was willing to adopt my label."[22] Claude pointed out that his mother's attitude toward intermarriage might appear to be inconsistent since in her home she had surrounded her children with non-Jewish men and women and had encouraged extensive social contact with their Christian peers. Emma claimed later that she did not hesitate to do so because she had looked upon marriage between non-Jews and her own children "as an utter impossibility."[23]

---

21 Cited in Bermant, *The Cousinhood*, 163. Cf. R. O. A. Crewe-Milnes, *Lord Rosebery* (London: Harper & Brothers, 1931), I, 367–370.

22 Lucy Cohen, *Some Recollections of Claude Goldsmid Montefiore, 1858–1938* (London: Faber&Faber, 1940), 35 and 72–73.

23 Ibid., 31. The climate of opinion in intellectual circles, however, both among Jews and Christians, was changing radically. Informed of the marriage of Charlotte to Lewis McIver, Dr. Benjamin Jowett, the eminent Greek scholar and Master of Balliol, wrote to her brother Claude:

> I am very glad to hear of your sister's marriage. . . .
> I think it quite right that the wall of distinction between Jew and Christian should be broken down. Has it not lasted long enough? In idea it has already broken down, for all intelligent persons are agreed that in the sight of God there is no distinction of race or caste . . . as a custom it will long continue. . . . But it would also be wrong to do violence to natural affection for the sake of always insisting upon them [distinctive customs]. It seems to me that Jewish society in England is too narrow to allow of Jews only marrying within limits of their own community, and that they would be placed at great disadvantage if such a rule were enforced. (Ibid., pp. 35–36).

Efforts of parents to discourage intermarriage by imposing financial disincentives continued into the early twentieth century. Samuel Montagu, Lord Swaythling, himself a devout Jew, father of six daughters and four sons, died a wealthy man saddened by his children's abandonment of traditional Judaism. He sought to curtail his daughters' association with "'Liberal Judaism' the objects of which I strongly disapprove"[24] by withholding three-fourths of their share in his estate if they persisted in that movement. Persist they did, with his daughter Lilian becoming one of its foremost leaders.

The will further stipulated that all bequests were subject to the provision that the children "shall respectively at my death be professing the Jewish religion and not be married to a person not professing the Jewish faith."[25] The problematic halakhic outcome of such a policy is reflected in the unfolding of events in the life of Samuel Montagu's son Edwin. Edwin Montagu, a distinguished parliamentarian and one-time Secretary of State for India, had long abandoned the Orthodoxy of his childhood. Although he claimed, "I will always be a good 'Jew' according to my lights," he also declared, "I firmly believe that to look for a wife from one set of people is wrong as it would be to say you should look for a wife among blue-eyed women."[26] When he later proposed to Venetia Stanley, although both were agnostics, he suggested that she convert. She was forthright:

> Were I to be washed a thousand times in the waters of the Jordan and to
> go through any rite and teaching that the strictest Jewish creed involves,

---

Some twenty years later similar sentiments were penned by Lord Arthur Balfour in a letter to a colleague:

> The Jews are not only a most gifted race, but have proved themselves ready and anxious to take part in the national and civic life of the countries where they are settled. But, from my point of view, it is an undoubted disadvantage that they do not intermarry with the rest of the population; and I think so, not because I dislike the Jews, but because I admire them; and I think that their rigid separation in this respect from their fellow-countrymen is a misfortune for us. If they think it wrong, I do not, of course, complain of their obeying what they hold to be a binding law; but I must be permitted, from my own point of view, to regret their decision.

Cited in Ronald Sanders, *The High Walls of Jerusalem: A History of the Balfour Declaration and the Birth of the British Mandate for Palestine* (New York: Holt, Rinehart and Winston, 1984), 118–119. Strikingly, Jowett favored intermarriage for the benefit of Jews, while Balfour wished intermarriage to be fostered for the benefit of Christians.

24 Bermant, *The Cousinhood*, 207.
25 Ibid., 253.
26 Ibid., 250 and 254.

I should not feel I had changed my race or nationality. I go through the formula required both because you want it for your mother's sake and also (I am going to be quite honest) because I think one is happier rich than poor. ...

Is it race or religion you care about, or merely the label? If race, then you are debasing it by marrying me, whatever I do. Religion, you know I care nothing about and shan't attempt to bring up my children in.[27]

The token conversion that preceded their marriage was clearly a charade.

The situation with regard to mixed marriage in Austria during the nineteenth century differed because of one essential legal provision. Although civil marriage existed in Austria, marriage between Jews and Christians remained forbidden by law. For a Jew and Christian to be united in marriage, one of the parties had to renounce his or her religion and be classified as belonging to the neutral category of *konfessionslos* (without religious affiliation) or convert to the religion of the other. Intermarriage statistics are not a reliable index of the rate of endogamy since they are confined to those who married *konfessionslos* individuals and do not include those who converted to Christianity prior to marriage and thus elude statistical discovery. Thus the intermarriage rate in nineteenth century Vienna appears lower than in other western European locales but the conversion rate to Christianity is higher.[28] Anti-Semitism was endemic in Vienna and many professions were closed to non-Christians. Clearly, many Jewish men converted in order to advance their careers or for purposes of enhanced social integration. Most Jewish converts to Christianity were young and single, and more than half of the men chose to affiliate with Protestant denominations although Vienna was predominantly Roman Catholic. Many of the women who converted were drawn from the poorer segments of the population and probably converted to marry men they met at their places of employment.[29] Factors inhibiting increase in the rate of intermarriage were, on the one hand, the hostile anti-Semitic environment that reduced social contact and, on the other hand, the vital Jewish cultural life and steady stream of immigrants from Galicia who rarely intermarried. Surprisingly, in the late nineteenth century there was a significant number of reversions to Judaism on the part of former

27 Ibid., 254–255. Cf. the account in S. D. Waley, *Edwin Montagu: A Memoir and an Account of his Visits to India* (Bombay: Asia Publishing House, 1964), 57–59 and 66–69.

28 Marsha L. Rozenblit, *The Jews of Vienna, 1867–1914: Assimilation and Identity* (Albany, NY: State University of New York Press, 1983), 128–135.

29 Ibid., 136 and 139–140.

converts to Christianity, perhaps because conversion had not been effective in advancing their acceptance in society or as a point of honor in the face of rising anti-Semitism.[30]

How were these patterns reflected on the other side of the ocean? The celebrated political writer and satirist Ludwig Börne, who himself underwent baptism in 1818 in order to improve his material prospects, predicted that Judaism would disappear altogether if only mistreatment and persecution were to cease. He pointed to a children's fable in which the sun and the wind vie as to who is mightier. In the narrative, a hurricane wind cannot succeed in forcing a traveler to remove his coat, but the sun in its warmth and brightness prevails and he casts the coat aside. The Jewish wanderer wrapped in the cloak of Orthodoxy, wrote Börne, will not yield to hurricane or onslaught, but "the sun will now radiate in America" and there Jewish separateness will end.[31] Although countless numbers of Jews who settled in America left their Orthodox roots, Judaism remained a vital faith in America despite daunting challenges.[32] In surveying intermarriage in the United States, this stubborn tenacity remains evident until the mid-twentieth century.

In the colonial period intermarriage by settlers was often prompted by the scarcity of available Jewish marriage partners. The first known Jew to marry a Christian was Solomon Pietersen in the year 1656. He may or may not have converted, but his daughter was baptized.[33] While many more intermarried in the following decades and their connection to Judaism was severed, there were individuals who did retain ties to their community. Some remained active in synagogues in their places of residence, others even traveled long distances in order to join coreligionists for the High Holy Day services. It was not uncommon for intermarried men to arrange for the ritual circumcision of their non-Jewish sons. Although there is no precise data, by the mid-eighteenth century the incidence of intermarriage was relatively high—varying probably from ten to fifteen percent of the population—but the marriages usually took place without either side converting.[34]

---

30 Ibid., 129 and 146. It is noteworthy that in Prague where Jews were accepted as equals in Prague's German society there was a virtual absence of conversion to Christianity. See ibid., 232 n. 14.

31 Ludwig Börne, *Gesammelte Schriften* (Vienna: Tendler, 1868), vol. VI, 13.

32 See the incisive introductory comments of Jonathan D. Sarna, *American Judaism: A History* (New Haven, CT: Yale University Press, 2004), xiii-xv.

33 See Sarna, *American Judaism*, 8. Arthur Hertzberg, *The Jew in America* (New York: Simon and Schuster, 1989), 28, states that Pietersen had converted to the Dutch Reformed Church and became a notary public, a position that required taking an oath "on the true faith of a Christian."

34 See Sarna, *American Judaism*, 24–28. Cf. Jacob R. Marcus, *Early American Jewry* (Philadelphia: Jewish Publication Society of America, 1953), vol. II, 504. In contrast, in the

In the post-revolutionary era, intermarriage rates rose; estimates of intermarriage are as high as 28.7 percent of all marriages during the years between 1776–1840, double the rate of the colonial period. The situation was exacerbated by the fact that the influence of synagogue officials was weak and the openness of American society made enforcement of strict religious rules virtually impossible.[35] In the immediately following decades, matters were further complicated by the growth of the American Reform movement and the development of diverse streams of religious practice. However, subsequently, other factors resulted in a decrease of intermarriage rates. In the last decades of the nineteenth and the beginning of the twentieth centuries wave upon wave of immigrants flocked to the United States. The mass immigration of the time consisted of more tightly-knit families of Eastern Europeans who arrived and settled in contiguous areas and, as a result, intermarriage rates plummeted. That situation changed drastically in the twentieth century as native-born Americans replaced the immigrant generation and America became a predominantly secular society.[36]

The situation in colonial America was not unique. Almost invariably, in countries in which the Jewish population was sparse intermarriage rates were high. Thus, for example, intermarriage was rampant in the pioneering Australian community in which men outnumbered women, but many of the Christian women converted and raised their children as Jews. Among the first Jewish convicts who came to Australia there were approximately nine men to every woman. Rabbi Aaron Levy of the London *bet din* traveled to Sydney to supervise the execution of a divorce and appears to have performed Australia's first conversion to Judaism, that of a woman who had previously married a Jewish convict, John Moses, in a Christian ceremony in 1826. The couple was subsequently married under a *ḥuppah* in 1831 and have present-day

European countries in which civil marriage was not legally valid intermarriage rates were somewhat lower.

35 See Sarna, *American Judaism*, 44–45. Sidney M. Fish, "The problem of Intermarriage in Early America," *Gratz College Annual of Jewish Studies* 4 (1975), 85–95, presents the intriguing text of a halakhic inquiry dated 1785 concerning problems of intermarriage encountered by Philadelphia congregants. The inquiry, composed in Hebrew and Judeo-German, was addressed to Rabbi Saul Lowenstamm of Amsterdam.

36 See Nathan Goldberg, "Intermarriage From A Sociological Perspective," in *Intermarriage and the Future of the American Jew. Proceedings of a Conference Sponsored by the Commission on Synagogue Relations of the Federation of Jewish Philanthropies of New York* (New York, 1964), 36–39.

Jewish descendants.[37] Later, in the mid-nineteenth century, young Jewish men journeyed to Australia in pursuit of gold but young Jewish women did not follow in their footsteps and the rate of intermarriage increased.[38] In Scandinavian countries, the small Jewish communities never developed a strong religious infrastructure and intermarriage rates soared even prior to the twentieth century.[39]

THE BERLIN INTELLIGENTSIA AND SALON SOCIETY

The phenomenon of intermarriage among members of the Berlin intelligentsia, as well as among the salon women of the day, merits particular attention because, due to their prestige and high visibility, those marriages engendered disproportionate psychological feelings of defeatism in the Jewish community.[40]

In the absence of precise statistical evidence, historians have differed widely in their assessment of the extent of the incidence of conversion and intermarriage in late eighteenth-century Germany as well as to whether or not the number of conversions declined after the Prussian edict of emancipation in 1812. In her detailed discussion of this topic, Deborah Hertz[41] analyzes valuable newly-available data. Ironically, a degree of statistical corroboration is provided from data compiled with German efficiency by the *Amt für Sippenforschung*, the Nazi Party's office for genealogical records. Accurate information was required for zealous implementation of the "Aryan Clause" adopted by Nazi party agencies. In addition to parish records of Jewish conversions for the years prior to 1933, a second card index, *Judenkartei*, was compiled for marriages between converted Jews and Christians from 1800 to 1846, the years in which there was no civil

---

37 John S. Levi and G. F. J. Bergmann, *Australian Genesis: Jewish Convicts and Settlers, 1788–1850* (Adelaide: Rigby, 1974), p. 218 and Hilary L. Rubinstein, *The Jews in Australia: A Thematic History* (Port Melbourne: William Heinemann Australia, 1991), vol. I, 98, 237–8 and 299–300.

38 Rubinstein, *The Jews in Australia*, p.98.

39 David Vital, *A People Apart: A Political History of the Jews in Europe 1789–1939* (New York: Oxford University Press, 2001), 315, and Solomon Grayzel, *A History of the Jews* (Philadelphia: The Jewish Publication Society of America, 1947), 707.

40 Cf. the comments of A. Menes, "The Conversion Movement in Prussia During the First Half of the 19th Century," *YIVO Annual* 6 (1951), 203.

41 Hertz, *Jewish High Society*, 224–243. See also the account in her later book *How Jews Became Germans: The History of Conversion and Assimilation in Berlin* (New Haven, CT: Yale University Press, 2007), 2–10 and the graphs, 224–226.

marriage in Prussia. Statistics derived from careful analysis of the records corroborates the fact that there was a steep rise in the number of conversions in the last decades of the eighteenth century (between 1770–1779 the number of converts was eighteen percent higher than between 1760–1769; the number in the 1780s was ninety-three percent higher than in the 1770s; and the number in the 1790s was fifty-six percent higher than in the previous decade) and during the first third of the nineteenth century the instance of intermarriages continued to increase despite sporadic declines.[42] Female conversions in the late eighteenth century were more numerous than male conversions. In particular, adult conversions of individuals in their twenties were predominantly female.[43] Comparison of the conversion records and intermarriage records is instructive and, while not conclusive, definite patterns emerge. More women than men converted and married Christians. The women also tended to marry men of a higher social class. By all measures of outmarriage in comparison with endogamous marriage, the Berlin rate for 1700–1809 was especially high, twice as high as the intermarriage rate in the United States before 1840 and twice as high as the rate in Germany a century later.[44]

The obvious question that confronts us is what caused the sudden surge in the number of conversions and intermarriages in the early eighteen hundreds and why it occurred in that particular segment of the community. In salon society Jews and Christians were brought together in a social setting in a manner that was unprecedented. In those drawing rooms intellectuals, officials, nobles, writers, and artists met in an atmosphere of ease and cordiality and forged close relationships with their Jewish hostesses.[45] To what extent were the salons a factor in the abandonment of Judaism? According to one study of twenty women closely associated with Berlin salons, at least seventeen converted and ten intermarried.[46] The salons were certainly the place where introductions of Jewish women to gentile men took place and where romantic intimacies were encouraged. Much has been written regarding the bohemian lifestyle of

---

42 Hertz, *Jewish High Society*, 227–229.

43 As noted, by the 1830s the predominance of female over male converts was reversed. See ibid., 238.

44 Ibid., 240–243. Hertz (243 n. 56) records the theory of Jacob Jacobson, the archivist of German Jewry, that the state's limitation of the number of Jewish marriages was a major factor accounting for the high rate of conversion and intermarriage.

45 See Jacob Katz, *Out of the Ghetto*, 56 and Michael A. Meyer, *The Origins of the Modern Jew: Jewish Identity and European Culture in Germany, 1749–1824* (Detroit: Wayne State University Press, 1967), 102–114.

46 See Hertz, *Jewish High Society*, 244. See also the discussion, ibid., 209–210 of the questionable conversion of another of the women, Jente Stieglitz.

the intellectuals, often celebrated in print, the atmosphere of sexual freedom in those circles, and the loose morals common among the nobility.[47] There were, however, other far more complex factors that brought about a seismic change in values that gave rise not only to the conduct of the *salonnières* but also to the assimilatory trend that began to affect an ever-widening sector of the Jewish population. As the eighteenth century drew to a close and the nineteenth century unfolded, society became radically transformed. In terms of the intermarriage issue attention should be focused on changes in (1) the socio-economic conditions, (2) the intellectual climate, (3) educational patterns, and (4) the institutions of courtship and marriage.

1. Socio-economic Conditions

In the era of the American Revolution, the French Revolution and the ensuing Napoleonic regime, the possibility of political emancipation for Jews was entertained even in countries where similar political upheavals had not yet occurred. However, true political equality was elusive and social integration was not achieved. For many, as Jacob Katz pointedly remarks, "The expectation of future equality could in no way substitute for the shortcomings of the present."[48] The frustrations wrought by prejudice against Jews, on the one hand, and the allure of glamorous social opportunities and the prospect of professional advancement, on the other, were the factors that motivated individuals such as Eduard Gans and Ludwig Börne to convert. As Heinrich Heine, another famous apostate, phrased it, the baptismal certificate was "the ticket of admission to European culture."[49]

In instances of conversion and marriage among the salon Jewesses a striking pattern is discernible. The converted women were often from wealthy families; the Christian men enjoyed the higher estate of nobility but hailed from families that were experiencing a shortage of capital as a result of economic reversals that occurred in the last decades of the century. Thus, the unions often reflected an exchange of wealth for status.[50]

---

47 See ibid., 208 and 217–220. See also Genevieve Bianquis, *Love in Germany*, trans. James Cleugh (London: F. Muller, 1964), 10–12, 23–45, 110–111, and 182–183.

48 Katz, *Out of the Ghetto*, 104.

49 Cited in Max Brod, *Heinrich Heine: The Artist in Revolt*, trans. Joseph Witriol (New York: New York University Press, 1957), 232.

50 See Hertz, *Jewish High Society*, 214–215. Hertz further notes (244–255) that data concerning the conversion of female domestic servants and their illegitimate progeny is sparse, but it appears that these women tended to convert in their twenties whereupon, after marriage, obstacles to their continued residence in Berlin were removed and their place in the social structure became more stable.

2. The Intellectual Climate

Among intellectuals in salon society rationalism and deism were fashionable. The notion that, at their core, Judaism and Christianity did not fundamentally differ was gaining currency to such an extent that David Friedlander, one of the most prominent personalities in Berlin Jewish society, could suggest that the "creed of the Church corresponds to the principles of our faith in spirit, if not in wording." Accordingly, in an anonymously published pamphlet addressed to Provost Teller, Friedlander proposed in the name of several members of the Jewish community that Jews would convert to Protestantism if they would not be required to accept certain Christian dogmas.[51] In the prevailing climate of opinion, transfer of loyalty from one faith to another was made to seem less than momentous and the sense of betrayal had lost its sting.

At the turn of the nineteenth century there was a shift in the *Zeitgeist* as the Romantic movement began to hold sway and intellectuals rejected the rationalism of the previous generation. The Romantics, in turn, developed a nationalistic and, at times, markedly anti-Semitic mindset. Paradoxically, there were those among them who became enamored of the dark-haired, foreign, exotic Jewish women; attraction and seduction led to intermarriage.[52]

3. Educational Patterns

The daughters of the wealthy Jewish merchants and bankers were quite acculturated and a number of the salon women in particular boasted impressive educational attainments. Often more educated than their husbands,[53] they perfected their German, spoke French, learned to play the harpsichord and piano, and were *au courant* with the literature and drama of the day. They studied with tutors, read widely, and the conversation of the intellectuals they entertained at the salons broadened their cultural horizons. As opposed to those educational achievements, their Jewish education was rudimentary at best.[54]

---

51 *Sendschreiben an seine Hochwürden, Herrn Oberconsistorialrath und Probst Teller zu Berlin, von einigen Hausvätern jüdischer Religion* (Berlin, 1799). The quoted passage is on p. 61.

52 Hertz, *Jewish High Society*, 147.

53 See the interesting references in Katz, *Out of the Ghetto*, 236 n. 11. Cf. Heidi Thomann Tewarsen, *Rahel Levin Varnhagen: The Life and Work of a German Jewish Intellectual* (Lincoln: University of Nebraska Press, 1998), 23–26.

54 Henrietta Herz knew the Hebrew alphabet well enough to teach it to Alexander and William von Humboldt. See Low, *Jews in the Eyes of the Germans*, 189–190. Rahel Varnhagen wrote notes in Hebrew script to her brother Ludwig Robert (who also converted), probably when communicating private financial information. See Lothar Kahn, "Ludwig Robert: Rahel's

The discrepancy between the secular knowledge and Jewish learning of the women was striking.[55] Commendably, from its inception, leaders of the Reform movement were attentive to the religious aspirations of women but they did not foresee a curriculum of study of Hebrew language and literature as a realistic option for the fairer sex. Indeed, an early Reform sympathizer, Aaron Chorin, wrote that such an endeavor would be nothing less than absurd since the Hebrew language "could have no appeal whatsoever to their [the women's] spirit."[56]

Alone among the assimilated (and, in his case, converted) intelligentsia of the time, Heinrich Heine, in a hauntingly beautiful poem, "Jehuda ben Halevy," pointed to the crux of the tragedy of the acculturated Jewish woman's alienation from her rich heritage and to the solution to the problem. In his typically incisive and witty style he described such a woman:

"Strange!" she adds in further comment,
"That I never heard the name of
This great poet that you speak of,
This Jehuda ben Halevy."

And I answered her as follows:
Dearest child, your lack of knowledge
Is quite sweet, but shows the defects
Of the French-type education

That the boarding schools of Paris
Give to girls, those future mothers
Of a freedom-loving people,
Who are thoroughly instructed

On old mummies, or the pharaohs
Who were stuffed in ancient Egypt . . .
Or the pigtailed lords of China . . .

Brother," *Leo Baeck Institute Year Book* 18 (1973), 189. Henrietta studied the English, Italian, Spanish, Swedish, Greek, and Latin languages and their literature. Although Meyer, *Origins*, 105, records that, in her youth, Henrietta's Jewish knowledge extended to reading the Bible in Hebrew with commentaries, later in her life there appears to have been no further study of Judaism. Cf. the comments of Brod, *Heinrich Heine: The Artist in Revolt*, 101–102.

55   Hertz's analysis of the significance of this discrepancy, *Jewish High Society*, 187–191, is flawed. She may be correct in ascribing greater weight to social factors but simply fails to appreciate the significance of the void in Jewish education.

56   Aaron Chorin, *Ein Wort zu seiner Zeit: Über die Nächtstenliebe und den Gottesdienst* (Vienna, 1820), 47.

All of this crammed into them,
Clever girls! But, oh ye heavens—

If you ask them for great figures
In the golden age of glory
Of the Arabic-Hispanic
Jewish school of poetry—

If you ask about the trio
Of Jehuda ben Halevy
And of Solomon Gabirol
And of Moses Ibn Ezra—

If you ask about such figures,
Then the children stare back at you
With their goggling eyes wide open—
Like cows along a hillside.

I'd advise you, my beloved,
To make up what you've neglected,
And to learn the Hebrew language;
Drop the theatre and concerts,

Go devote some years of study
To this subject—you'll be able
To read all of them in Hebrew,
Ibn Ezra and Gabirol

And of course Halevy also—
The triumvirate of song who
Once evoked the sweetest music
From the harp that David cherished.[57]

---

57 Translated by Hal Dryen. Included in *The German Jewish Dialogue: An Anthology of Literary Texts 1749–1943*, ed. Ritchie Robertson (New York: Oxford University Press, 1999), 102–103.

It was decades later that serious attention was given to Heine's simple expedient "Go devote some years of study." Responding to an inquiry from Amsterdam on how to design an educational curriculum, Samson Raphael Hirsch advocated that the program for girls be essentially identical to that of boys. Hirsch wrote:

People forget that Channah and Devorah assuredly understood Channah's prayer and Devorah's song. [They forget that] the salvation of future generations of our men, of our homes and our children depends on our winning

Far more puzzling to this writer is the lacuna in the religious experience of these women. Aside from formal training or textual study, an observant life-style affords religious knowledge and experience in myriad ways. Experiences of Sabbath, Holy Days, and, indeed, of daily life suffused the lives of traditional women no less than of men even if book learning was not part of their upbringing.

Describing the vision in his mind's eye of his mother blessing the Sabbath candles long after her death, the Anglo-Russian Jewish poet Philip Max Raskin wrote:

> And yet ev'ry Friday when twilight arrives
> The face of my mother within me revives;
> A prayer on her lips, "O Almighty, be blessed,
> For sending us Sabbath, the angel of rest."
> And some hidden feeling I cannot control
> A Sabbath light kindles deep, deep in my soul.[58]

It is apparent that Moses Mendelssohn's daughter Dorothea, despite having grown up in the Mendelssohn household, came away with no such memories. Nor does one find expressions of nostalgia in the memoirs of her friends. Their Judaism is depicted as lifeless and filled only with burdensome restrictions. One can only wonder, was their home life so devoid of religious flavor and fervor or was antipathy to their childhood so intense that they repressed even its noblest aspects and excised them from their consciousness?

Perhaps it was the void in their education and experience coupled with awe and admiration for the celebrated writers they met that led them to an exaggerated over-idealization of German culture and to accept as their own

---

over the hearts of our future wives and mothers for the sancta of our people. However, the hearts of our daughters can be stirred for the sancta of Israel only if we teach them to slake their spiritual thirst from the original sources. Then, on the basis of their own appreciation, they will prefer Isaiah and Amos to Goethe and Shakespeare. And this, with God's help, we have been able to do [in Frankfurt]. *If you wish to provide for your future, do not forget your daughters.* (emphasis added)

See Mordecai Breuer, "Iggerot me'et ha-Rav S. R. Hirsch," *Ha-Ma'ayan* 29, no. 1 (5749), 33. The letter, translated from German to Hebrew by M. Breuer, is reprinted in *Parnes le-Doro: Hitkatvut Eliezer Liepman Prins im Ḥakhmei Doro*, ed. Mayer Herskovics and Els Bendheim (Hoboken, NJ: Ktav, 1992), 36–38. The letter is dated May 26, 1867; the Frankfurt *Realschule* whose curriculum is described therein was opened in 1853.

58 "Kindling the Sabbath Light," *Songs of a Wanderer* (Philadelphia: Jewish Publication Society of America, 1917), 92.

those writers' assessment of Judaism. If Friedrich Schleiermacher, the eminent preacher and theologian, declaimed the virtues of Christianity as the religion of the heart and portrayed Judaism as a petrified mummy,[59] who were they to disagree? Thus, one finds Henrietta Herz, his close friend,[60] echoing his sentiments and speaking of the Jewish religion as a prosaic practice of mechanical observances,[61] Dorothea Schlegel expressing her disdain for ancient Judaism, "which I very much abhor,"[62] and Rahel Varnhagen asserting that, "The human soul is by nature a Christian."[63] All three of them not only converted but declared that they had turned to Christianity for emotional fulfillment and spiritual solace.[64]

Remarkably, it was a non-Jewish author and frequenter of the salons, Bettina (Brentano) von Arnim, who wrote with respect and enthusiasm about the Jew who became transformed on the Sabbath and, entering his home as a priest, invoked God's blessing upon his family and his people.[65]

4. Courtship and Marriage

Quite obviously, any discussion of intermarriage must recognize the pivotal role of romantic love and sexual attraction. Myriad rabbinic laws governing social intercourse between men and women evidence the Sages' realistic understanding of the overwhelming power of the human sexual drive and the compelling nature of man's emotional makeup. Rabbinic restrictions on food and wine cooked by non-Jews reflect an appreciation of the strength of those drives and feelings and a consequent effort to minimize opportunities for undesirable social interaction. The various *halakhot* betray a fear that social intimacy may lead to physical intimacy and, in the case of Jews and non-Jews,

---

59   See Michael A. Meyer, "Reform Jewish Thinkers and their German Intellectual Context," in *The Jewish Response to German Culture*, ed. J. Reinharz and W. Schatzberg (Hanover, NH: University Press of New England, 1985), 69–70. William von Humboldt who favored complete political equality for Jews nevertheless had a similarly negative view of the Jewish religion. Once Jews were fully emancipated and acculturated he believed that they would abandon the Jewish religion. See Low, *Jews in the Eyes of the Germans*, 135–137.
60   See Hertz, *Jewish High Society*, 175–176 and 255.
61   Meyer, *Origins*, 105–106.
62   In a letter to Schleiermacher, cited ibid., 96.
63   Cited in Solomon Liptzin, *Germany's Stepchildren* (Philadelphia: Jewish Publication Society of America, 1944), 14.
64   Stern, *"Ich möchte mir Flügel wünschen"*, 231–236.
65   Liptzin, *Germany's Stepchildren*, 24; cf. Low, *Jews in the Eyes of the Germans*, 188–190.

to intermarriage and abandonment of Judaism, the dreaded consequence spelled out in the scriptural admonition "for he will turn thy son from following Me" (Deuteronomy 7:4).

One of the novel trends in society at the close of the eighteenth century was an enhanced emphasis on romantic love and the erotic experience in the founding of a family. Marriage based on free choice and romantic love was the new ideal. In a more traditional society, marriages of children were arranged by parents who focused primarily on rational, economic and social considerations.[66] Of course, there had always been marriages that came about as a result of mutual romantic attraction. But in the modern era this was projected as the ideal.

In their own choices and decisions the salon women were influenced by the attitudes of the Romantic school. However, they were the exception rather than the rule. For the overwhelming majority of German Jewish families, the traditional pattern persisted and for the next one hundred years arranged marriages remained commonplace. As was the case with their gentile counterparts, economic and social interests predominated and marriages were viewed as contracts between families rather than as the free choice of individuals.[67] Arranged marriages promoted endogamy and intermarriage rates were relatively low. Apparently, the richest and poorest intermarried more than others: the richest paid for the privilege of entering gentile high society; the poorest women sought non-Jewish husbands because they could not afford the dowries demanded by Jewish men.[68] During the twentieth century, particularly after World War I, the romantic view of marriage gradually became the norm.

---

66 Jacob Katz, *Tradition and Crisis: Jewish Society at the End of the Middle Ages* (New York, 1971), 268–269, notes that in the new social climate even marriages contracted on the basis of economic and social factors were made to appear as if based on romantic attraction. Katz theorizes that Moses Mendelssohn, who was introduced to his wife by mutual friends, sought to emphasize the element of personal attraction in everything pertaining to his match. His daughter Dorothea left her husband and children for the sake of love, taking the romantic ideal to its extreme. Hertz, *Jewish High Society*, 199 n. 177, points out that, ironically, Katz's example of a non-arranged marriage is that of Moses Mendelssohn but Mendelssohn himself arranged the marriages of his own children.

67 See Marion A. Kaplan, "For Love or Money: The Marriage Strategies of Jews in Imperial Germany," *Leo Baeck Institute Year Book* 28 (1983), 263–300. Kaplan describes the manner in which lip service was paid to the role of sentiment and love, if only by covering up arranged marriages and camouflaging the negotiations to appear as if meetings had taken place by coincidence. Her description illustrates the view of Katz, n. 62, but applies the strategy to a much later period of time.

68 Ibid., 237 and 275 n. 58.

As social contacts between Jews and non-Jews became more common and religious ties concurrently became weaker, it was the romantic impetus that emerged as the major factor in intermarriage.

With the decline of the salons in the second decade of the nineteenth century some of these factors receded in significance. However, the educational/experiential factor and the romantic element remained the essential factors affecting the escalating rate of intermarriage. As the sociologist Marshall Sklare noted about American Jews and as doubtless applies to most contemporary mixed marriages, "The Jew who intermarries, then, generally does so because he wishes to *marry* rather than because he wishes to intermarry."[69] Those concerned with the corrosive effect of intermarriage could disdainfully dismiss as opportunists or crass materialists their coreligionists whose actions were motivated by pragmatic considerations. When, however, the intermarriage was motivated by considerations of love and personal fulfillment, a clash of ideals came into play. Free choice, personal happiness, and romantic love constituted worthy ideals enshrined in the modern mindset. Love triumphed over adversity, persecution, and even incarceration. As Richard Lovelace expressed it:

> Stone walls do not a prison make,
> Nor iron bars a cage;
> If I have freedom in my love
> And in my soul am free,
> Angels alone, that soar above,
> Enjoy such liberty.[70]

Opposition to an intermarriage when the couple had deeply rooted feelings for one another came to be viewed as an act of insensitivity bordering on cruelty.

Rabbis—even Reform clergy—could preach about duty and the need for "loyalty to an ancestral faith" that called for denying even a "great love,"[71] but when that loyalty was not ironclad the battle was usually lost. Such loyalty flourished only where the soil was watered with knowledge and emotion. Only those who had grown to experience "*Ashreinu, mah tov ḥelkeinu u-mah yafah*

---

69 Marshall Sklare, *America's Jews* (New York: Random House, 1971), 201.

70 "To Althea From Prison," in *British Verse*, ed. Daniel V. Thompson (New York: The Macmillan company, 1916), 61.

71 Samuel Schulman, *CCAR Yearbook* 19 (1909), 322. See also see note 113 and accompanying text.

yerushateinu" ("Fortunate are we, how goodly is our portion, and how beautiful is our heritage") could be expected to make sacrifices for that heritage.

THE RESPONSE OF THE RELIGIOUS ESTABLISHMENT

Orthodox spokesmen were unanimous in their adamant opposition to inter-marriage.[72] Consistent with a clear halakhic stance rejecting conversion for the purpose of marriage,[73] in the early stages of the modern period, the over-whelming majority refused, at least nominally, to countenance conversion for the sake of marriage. With the passing of time, the halakhic controversy centered upon permissibility of conversion for the purpose of marriage, the sincerity and commitment of prospective converts motivated by the desire to marry a Jewish partner, as well as upon the prohibition against marrying a woman with whom there is a suspicion of a sexual liaison prior to conversion, and whether the conversion of a spouse after a civil marriage has taken place or subsequent to the birth of children is encompassed within that prohibition. Questions of seriousness of intent, sincerity of commitment to religious prac-tice, and mental reservations that might invalidate the conversion dominate the halakhic debate.

In the eyes of most ideologues within Reform circles opposition to inter-marriage remained a "red line" not to be breached. However, conversion for the sake of marriage was not only welcomed but encouraged. In contrast, among the Orthodox, the halakhic discussion was limited to recognition of extenuat-ing circumstances in accepting a candidate for conversion motivated by con-venience rather than conviction and the *post factum* validity of conversions for ulterior motive when there is no intent of abiding by the precepts of Judaism.[74]

---

72 The thought of joining a Jew in marriage with an unconverted non-Jew was not entertained by any Orthodox decisor, performance of an intermarriage ceremony was never counte-nanced and even presence at such a ceremony or celebration was censured. As Ḥakham Bernays phrased it, from the Jewish perspective, mixed marriages are "in the realm of the unthinkable." See his "Gutachten betr. die Mischehe, erstattet im Jahre 1843," appended to Eduard Duckesz, "Zur Biographie des Chacham Isaak Bernays," *Jahrbuch der Jüdisch–Literarischen Gesellschaft* 5 (1907), 322.

73 See Rambam, *Hilkhot Issurei Bi'ah*, 13:14 and *Shulḥan Arukh, Yoreh De'ah*, 268:12.

74 Even when the conversion is proper and valid there remains a question with regard to whether it is permissible for the convert to enter into a marriage with a Jew with whom the convert had cohabited prior to the marriage. For a discussion of conflicting positions regard-ing that question as well as of conversion following a civil ceremony, see J. David Bleich, *Contemporary Halakhic Problems*, vol. I (New York, 1977), 286–292.

Decisors such as R. Jacob Ettlinger, *Binyan Tziyyon*, no. 149 and R. Isaac Schmelkes, *Teshuvot Bet Yitzḥak, Yoreh De'ah*, II, no. 100, remained adamant in rejecting prospective converts motivated by the desire to marry a Jewish partner. A twentieth-century permissive view was espoused by Rabbi Ben-Zion Uziel, *Mishpeti Uzi'el, Even ha-Ezer*, no. 18, but was strongly opposed by Rabbi Abraham I. Kook, *Da'at Kohen*, no. 154 and *Ezrat Kohen*, no. 14. Some authorities were prepared to grant leeway in determining sincerity of purpose and sanctioned conversions when confronted by a couple who had undergone a civil marriage or when there was a threat of apostasy if the marriage were not to be condoned.[75] Also debated was the question of a *bet din* accepting converts with questionable motivation in order to forestall their acceptance by Reform clergy and the consequent halakhic problems that would arise if the children of such a female convert then wished to marry other Jews.[76]

A complex problem with regard to the validity of even Orthodox conversions, once performed, if entered into for reasons other than religious conviction, centers upon the question of mental reservations with regard to acceptance of observance of commandments. The talmudic rule is that even insincere conversions, once performed, are valid. *Ritva* and *Nemukei Yosef*, in their respective commentaries on *Yevamot* 24b, explain that even conversions prompted by ulterior motivation are assumed to engender a decision to accept the obligations of Judaism. From their comments it may be inferred that if, however, mental reservations do remain present they do indeed invalidate the conversion.[77]

---

75 See the responsa of Rabbi Shlomoh Kluger, *Tuv Ta'am va-Da'at*, I, no. 130; R. Eliezer Deutsch, *Pri ha-Sadeh*, II, no. 3; and Rabbi Yehi'el Ya'akov Weinberg, *Seridei Esh*, vol. III, no. 50. Cf., however, the conflicting view of R. Meir Arak, *Imrei Yosher*, I, no. 176.

76 One of the earliest such discussions is the negative view of R. Azriel Hildesheimer, *Teshuvot Rabbi Ezri'el, Yoreh De'ah*, no. 234, countering the permissive stance of R. Mendel Kirshbaum, a Frankfurt *dayyan*, expressed in his *Menaḥem Meishiv*, no. 42.

77 Rabbi Schmelkes, *Bet Yitzḥak, Yoreh De'ah*, no. 100, argues that the conversions of individuals who, despite formal affirmations to the contrary, fail to abide by the provisions of the dietary code and laws of family purity are invalid. R. Dov Ber Kahana, *Dvar Avraham*, III, no. 28, questions whether in contemporary society, where pressure for conformity in religious practice is absent, a determination to abide by religious strictures is reached. R. Hayyim Ozer Grodzinski, *Aḥi'ezer*, III, no. 26, secs. 2–3 and no. 28, concludes that the status of converts with ulterior motives remains doubtful until their general comportment testifies to their acceptance of mitzvot. Much later, Rabbi M. Feinstein, *Iggerot Mosheh, Yoreh De'ah*, I, no. 160, advances considerations defending the validity of such conversions but in several other responsa writes that public desecration of halakhah vitiates the oral acceptance and hence such conversions are invalid. See *Iggerot Moseh*, I, *Yoreh De'ah*, no. 174 and *Even ha-Ezer*, II, no. 4 and III, no. 4.

In the years following 1848, mixed marriages were formally legalized in Denmark with the condition that the offspring be reared in the Lutheran faith. Intermarriage became permissible in many parts of Germany and was permitted in Hamburg. In many such areas the civil authorities requested an advance declaration by the prospective parents regarding the choice of religion for their offspring but permitted a subsequent change of mind.[78]

Problems with regard to the progeny of mixed marriages proliferated. At the Brunswick conference, Reform leaders pronounced mixed marriages to be permitted provided parents were allowed to raise their children in the Jewish faith. No elaboration regarding the status of such children was included in that resolution. In response, Orthodox authorities found it necessary to clarify the halakhic position. A definitive statement in the German language was issued by Rabbi Jacob Ettlinger and published in *Der treue Zionswächter* of June 28, 1850.[79] Rabbi Ettlinger emphasized that, according to Jewish law, children of a Jewish mother are Jewish even if the father is a non-Jew and children of a non-Jewish mother are non-Jews even if the father is Jewish and that those halakhic provisions are not subject to change by parental stipulation. Male children of a Jewish father and a non-Jewish mother who have undergone circumcision are not recognized as Jews unless they have also undergone formal conversion. Conversion of a non-Jewish mother following the birth of a child does not alter the non-Jewish status of previously born progeny. Moreover, although Judaism recognizes no distinction between children born in or out of wedlock insofar as mutual rights and obligations of parents and children are concerned, nevertheless, children of mixed marriages regardless of sex are recognized only as children of the mother, not of the father, even if the father converts to Judaism subsequent to their birth. This statement merely presented elementary halakhic facts synopsizing rulings recorded in the Talmud and Codes and reflected no innovative interpretations.[80] Similar statements were publicized by other rabbinic authorities.[81] Formulation of those statements

---

78 Salo W. Baron, "Aspects of the Jewish Communal Crisis in 1848," *Jewish Social Studies* 14 (1952), 116–117.

79 "Gutachten des Herrn Oberrabbiner Ettlinger in Altona über die religiösgesetzliche Wirkung der Mischehe," *TZW* 6 (1850), 207.

80 See *Avodah Zarah* 36b; Rambam, *Mishneh Torah*, *Hilkhot Issurei Bi'ah* 12:1 and 12:7; *Shulḥan Arukh*, *Even ha-Ezer* 16:1–2.

81 Cf. Baron, "Aspects of the Jewish Communal Crisis," p. 117. See also R. Tzevi Hirsch Chajes, *Minḥat Kena'ot* in *Kol Sifrei Maharatz Ḥayes*, vol. 2 (Jerusalem: Divrei Hachamim, 1958), 996–998, note and *Kuntres Aḥaron*, 1032–1035. Cf. the later statement signed by 133 Orthodox rabbis publicized in *Der Israelit* 12 (1871), 568–569.

and dissemination of the rulings in the vernacular is simply a reflection of the escalating religious problem.[82]

As noted earlier, Jewish men married to non-Jewish women often insisted on the ritual circumcision of their male children even without opting for their conversion.[83] Personal and communal tensions were exacerbated in the unfortunate cases in which rabbinic authorities were constrained to refuse burial in a Jewish cemetery to a child born to a non-Jewish woman married to a Jewish man who simply declared the child to be Jewish without formal conversion— even if the child had been circumcised.[84] Indeed, halakhic proscriptions related to burial and cemetery privileges were frequent sources of contention subsequent to an intermarriage. The non-Jewish partner of a Jew was routinely denied burial in a Jewish cemetery in accordance with the provisions

---

82 Cf. the unsigned comments in *Der Orient* 11 (1850), 171–172.

    Rabbi Ettlinger was rabbi of Altona when that city was under Danish rule. Of interest is the citation of Rabbi Ettlinger's statement published in the *Zionswächter* in the course of an early twentieth-century controversy in Copenhagen where it had become customary for the progeny of mixed marriage to assert Jewish status solely on the basis of parental agreement at the time of their marriage. In defending his opposition to this practice, R. Tobias Lewenstein, the Orthodox Rabbi of Copenhagen, appended a Danish translation of Rabbi Ettlinger's statement, pointing out that the latter was an eminent authority who had served as the "Danish rabbi in Altona." See Moses Lewenstein and Salomon Ehrmann, "Rabbi Tobias Lewenstein," in *Guardians of Our Heritage, 1724–1953*, ed. Leo Jung (New York: Bloch Publishing Company, 1958), 474–475.

83 For the response of American Orthodox rabbis in the 1840s to questions regarding the halakhic status of progeny of intermarriage and the circumcision of non-converted male children see I. Harold Sharfman, *The First Rabbi: Origins of Conflict Between Orthodox and Reform: Jewish Polemic Warfare in Pre-Civil War America: A Biographical History* (Malibu, CA: Pangloss Pr., 1988), 113–119.

    Rabbi Bernard Illowy, serving a congregation in New Orleans in the 1860s, ruled against the circumcision of unconverted children of Jewish fathers and non-Jewish mothers. Rabbi Marcus Lehmann, the editor of *Der Israelit*, published in Mainz, Germany, concurred with Rabbi Illowy's decision. See *Der Israelit* 5, no. 52 (December 28, 1864), 683–684. That position was forcefully endorsed by Rabbi Azriel Hildesheimer and publicized in *Der Israelit* 6, no. 3 (February 1, 1865), 57–59. Addressing the same issue, Rabbi Zevi Hirsch Kalischer adopted an opposing view, very strongly favoring such circumcision. The correspondence of Rabbis Hildesheimer and Kalischer has been published in *She'elot u-Teshuvot Rabbi Ezri'el, Yoreh De'ah*, nos. 229–230. See also *Sefer Milḥamot Elokim: Being the Controversial Letters and the Casuistic Decisions of the Late Rabbi Bernard Illowy Ph.D.*, published by his son, Dr. Henry Illowy (Berlin, 1914), 189–201, which includes media reports of the controversy in both English and German as well as Rabbi Illowy's halakhic discussion in Hebrew.

84 See the monograph authored by Baruch Schick, *Dat va-Din* (Temesvar, 1903) describing the heated controversy surrounding one such incident as well as the halakhic discussion of R. Chaim Eleazar Schapiro, *Teshuvot Minḥat Elazar*, III (Bratislava, 1922), no. 8.

of *Shulḥan Arukh, Yoreh De'ah* 362:5. The resultant emotional anguish experienced by the marriage partners gave rise to acrimonious disputes and, at times, to attempts—usually futile—to bring pressure to bear upon communal officials to permit exceptions to existing rules.[85]

The stance with regard to burial of the Jewish partners to an intermarriage was more complex. Apostates are excluded from burial in a Jewish cemetery.[86] Other transgressors are accorded burial but in the case of notorious sinners interment is permitted only at some distance from other graves. Nevertheless, the community, or the *Ḥevra Kaddisha*, has the authority to deny burial in the communal cemetery to an egregious transgressor. Local authorities are empowered to enact extra-statutory measures *le-migdar milta*, that is, to apply sanctions in order to prompt transgressors to return to observance and/or to avoid continued erosion of religious practice among others in the community.[87] However, there seem to have been few instances of a formal edict barring Jews who had married non-Jews from burial in a Jewish cemetery.[88]

---

85 Of particular interest is the well-known responsum of Rabbi David Zevi Hoffmann, *Melammed le-Ho'il*, III (Frankfurt am Main, 1932), no. 8, concerning the propriety of converting a non-Jewish woman in order to make it possible for her to be buried in the Jewish cemetery in which her child, who had been converted by his Jewish father, was buried. In that case it was claimed that were her application for conversion to be denied, the woman would become mentally deranged.

86 See R. Yechiel Michel Tucatzinsky, *Gesher ha-Ḥayyim* (Jerusalem, 1960), III, 274–275. See also R. Moshe Sofer, *Teshuvot Ḥatam Sofer, Yoreh De'ah*, no. 341. Cf., however, R. Ben-Zion Meir Chai Uziel, *Mishpetei Uzi'el*, vol. I (Jerusalem, 1947), no. 6, sec. 8.

87 *Gesher ha-Ḥayyim*, III, 274–275.

88 In the twentieth century Rabbi Joseph B. Soloveitchik is quoted as having reported that his father, Rabbi Moshe Soloveitchik, declared that it was "established custom (*minhag Yisra'el*)" to bury someone who had intermarried outside the fence of the Jewish cemetery. See Rabbi Moshe Sternbuch, *Teshuvot ve-Hanhagot*, vol. II (Jerusalem, 1994), no. 516. The most stringent exclusionary response to an individual who has intermarried was adopted by the Syrian community of Brooklyn, New York. In 1935 that community enacted a ban against any conversion for purposes of marriage. The ban was reaffirmed in 1946, 1972, 1984 and 2006, and in 1984 and 2006 it was adopted by other "Near Eastern Jewish communities" in various locales in the United States. According to the enactment of 1946 and subsequent affirmations, the intermarried individual was not to be accorded burial in the communal cemetery. See S. Zevulun Lieberman, "A Sephardic Ban on Converts," *Tradition* 23, no. 2 (Winter 1988), 22–25 and Sarina Roffé, *Brooklyn's Rabbinical Takana Prohibiting Syrian and Near Eastern Jews from Marrying Converts* (Master's Thesis, Touro College, 2006), 41 and 43.

The by-laws of a number of Orthodox synagogues excluded intermarried individuals from membership. Many of those synagogues restricted burial in their cemetery to members only. Hence, for those communities, burial of a person who had intermarried was a moot issue. A prime example is K'hal Adath Jeshurun of Washington Heights, New York,

At the other end of the spectrum, in addressing the issue of intermarriage, Reform thinkers were confronted by a profound dilemma. Basic to their welt-anschauung was a firm belief in a universalist ethos and the need, above all, to demonstrate to their compatriots an assurance of absolute loyalty to the laws of the state as well as a commitment to the brotherhood of mankind and the equality before God of all humanity. Passages in the prayerbook implying distinctions between Israel and the nations, such as in parts of the Morning Blessings, the first paragraph of the *Aleinu* prayer, and the phrase "*ve-lo netato le-goyei ha-aratzot*" ("And you did not give it [the Sabbath] ... to the nations of the lands") in the Sabbath service were the first to have been excised from their prayerbook. The blurring of differences and the crumbling of barriers was their aim. Intermarriage presented a crucial test. Were they prepared to endorse the ultimate fusion of Jews and non-Jews?

Their earliest public tackling of this thorny question took place at the first Reform rabbinical conference in Brunswick in 1844. In their formal resolution, Reform spokesmen went beyond the Paris Sanhedrin in candidly accepting intermarriage but with one proviso:

> that the intermarriage of Jews and Christians and, in general, the intermarriage of Jews with adherents of any of the monotheistic religions is not forbidden provided that the parents are permitted by the State to bring up the offspring of such marriage in the Jewish faith.[89]

---

where an uncircumcised or intermarried individual is excluded from membership and burial in the congregational cemetery, until recently, was limited to members. Officers of the Ḥevra Kaddisha report that, under current circumstances, burial of an uncircumcised or intermarried individual would not be countenanced in their cemetery.

Indeed, while exclusion of the intermarried individual from burial is rare, there are several recorded cases of the Ḥevra Kaddisha denying burial rights to persons who refused to be circumcised or to Jewish male children whose parents declined to have them circumcised. See R. Chaim Chizkiyahu Medini, *Sedei Ḥemed, Ma'arekhet ha-Mem*, sec. 88. Schick, *Dat va-Din*, p. 6, relates that when R. Samson Raphael Hirsch assumed his position in Frankfurt am Main he objected to the Ḥevra Kaddisha's acquiescence in the burial of uncircumcised individuals. The majority of latter-day decisors follow the established rule that uncircumcised Jews should be buried in the Jewish cemetery, but at a distance from other graves. See the discussion of R. Yekutiel Yehudah Greenwald, *Kol Bo al Aveilut* (New York, 1956), 194–195.

89 *Protokolle der ersten Rabbiner-Versammlung abgehalten zu Braunschweig* (Brunswick, 1844), 73. Mendel Hess, chief rabbi of Saxe-Weimar, twice tried to add a provision permitting a rabbi to solemnize such marriages but the motion was not carried. See ibid., 70 and 73. Pointed rabbinic criticism of this specific resolution of the Brunswick conference is found in R. Moses Schick, *Teshuvot Maharam Shik, Yoreh De'ah*, no. 331 and R. Judah Aszod, *Teshuvot Yehudah Ya'aleh, Oraḥ Ḥayyim*, no. 6. Rabbi Aszod goes so far as to caution that rabbis who passed such a resolution might soon permit incest.

Nevertheless, paradoxically, the vast majority of Reform leaders retreated from this initial position and returned to a clear and, at times, vehement anti-intermarriage policy. Even Ludwig Philippson, who had crafted the Brunswick resolution, modified his views considerably[90] and, as we shall see, others were outspoken in their refusal to sanction a mixed marriage with the result that later conferences and synods in Breslau, Augsburg and the United States could not agree on a unanimous resolution addressing the question.[91]

The response of Reform ideologues to this issue underscores a fundamental misconception regarding early Reform. It is a fallacy to view the partisans of Orthodoxy and Reform as standing at polar opposites of the spectrum of opinion with the traditionalist rabbis at one end and their Reform antagonists on the other. The situation at that time was entirely different. On one end stood staunch guardians of tradition; at the other stood advocates of total assimilation—individuals such as Olry Terquem, the Salon Jewesses, Eduard Gans, and David Friedlander who envisioned a grand union of deists of all faiths and the ultimate disappearance of Judaism as a religion separate and apart from others. Friedlander speculated what the requirements might be should "we decide to choose the great Protestant Christian community as a place of refuge."[92] Gans envisioned a utopian age in which Jews would live among the nations without distinctive identity "as the river lives on in the ocean."[93]

In stark contrast to this liberal ideology, early Reform rabbis took a middle-of-the-road position endeavoring to eliminate what in their eyes were the unseemly and inappropriate elements of rabbinic Judaism in order to attain respect and acceptance of their fellow citizens while simultaneously seeking to assure and defend the continuity of the Jewish faith. No wonder that a woman such as Rahel Varnhagen who had abandoned Judaism viewed Reform efforts with disfavor. Writing of the father of the Reform movement, Israel Jacobson,

---

90 Philippson later wrote, "Religion must pronounce against mixed marriages. ... It must be conceded that they contribute as well toward the weakening of true religiousness and sincerity in matters of faith." See *Israelitische Religionslehre* (Leipzig, 1865), vol. III, 250.

91 A motion to endorse the Brunswick resolution was tabled at the Augsburg Synod. See *Verhandlungen der Zweiten Israelistischen Synode zu Augsburg: vom 11. bis 17. Juli 1981* (Berlin, 1873), 109–110.

92 *Sendschreiben*, 63.

93 Eduard Gans, "Halbjähriger Bericht im Verein für Cultur und Wissenschaft der Juden (April 22, 1822)" in S. Rubaschoff, "Erstlinge der Entjudung. Drei Reden von Eduard Gans im 'Kulturverein,'" *Der jüdische Wille* 2 (1919), 109–15. Cited from a translation by J. Hessing in *The Jew in the Modern World: A Documentary History*, ed. Paul R. Mendes-Flohr and Jehuda Reinharz (New York: Oxford University Press, 1980), 192.

she remarked, "People like us cannot be Jews. I only hope that Jacobson with all his money does not bring about a Jewish reform here. I am afraid the vain fool will."[94]

In point of fact, among the majority of classical Reform thinkers, even among those who espoused radical reforms in other areas, opposition to intermarriage remained firm and the actual performance of a mixed marriage ceremony by a rabbi was censured. In an address before the Leipzig Synod in 1869, Abraham Geiger presented the formal report of the committee on intermarriage. While reiterating the Reform position that such marriages were valid, the committee recommended that intermarriage not be encouraged; rather, entrance into the Jewish religion of the prospective non-Jewish partner "be less difficult ... than otherwise."[95] Similarly, Joseph Aub, speaking in the same venue, described mixed marriages as "far removed from the ideal of marriage" and did not hesitate to add that to ask for solemnization of such unions by a Jewish clergyman smacked of insincerity.[96]

Sentiments similar to these were more forcefully expressed in America by Isaac M. Wise. Wise was not known for ideological consistency but he was vociferously proud of his Judaism in its Americanized version and repeatedly expressed his conviction that the majority of intelligent people would eventually turn to Judaism which was destined to become the universally accepted religion.[97] In public lectures on intermarriage, later published in the *American Israelite*, he asserted that no religious law forbade marriage between a Jew and any monotheist. Nonetheless, he warned that at the then current juncture of history "no Jewish minister has a right to sanction the marriage of a Hebrew man or woman to a person outside of the Jewish faith." For a rabbi to perform such a marriage would be "a mere mockery" and "to act the part of an ordinary actor—to go through a performance and pronounce formulas and benedictions to parties who believe in neither" and would be "to make a comedian of

---

94 Letter from Rahel, dated June 13, 1814, to Markus Theodor Robert, cited in Hannah Arendt, *Rahel Varnhagen: The Life of a Jewess*, ed. Liliane Weissberg, trans. Richard and Clara Winson (Baltimore, MD: John Hopkins University Press, 1997), 180.

95 *Referate über die der ersten israelitische Synode zu Leipzig überreichte Anträge* (Berlin, 1971), 187–88. For translations of portions of the discussions see Moses Mielziner, *The Jewish Law of Marriage and Divorce in Ancient and Modern Times and its Relation to the Law of the State* (Cincinnati: Bloch publishing company, 1884), 50–51.

96 *Referate*, 193.

97 James G. Heller, *Isaac M. Wise: His Life, Work and Thought* (New York: Union of American Hebrew Congregations, 1965), 537–539.

himself."[98] Recognizing that establishing a uniform policy was desirable, Wise urged that the matter be brought before a Reform synod.

Even stronger were the remarks of David Einhorn in response to a controversy regarding mixed marriage. Einhorn explicitly rejected belief in the sanctity of the Jewish bloodline, but faith in the prophetic mission of Israel prompted his adamant opposition to intermarriage. Accordingly, he declared that mixed marriages are "to be strictly prohibited even from the standpoint of Reformed Judaism" and was emphatic in pronouncing: "To lend a hand to the sanctification of mixed marriage is, according to my firm conviction, to hammer a nail into the coffin of the tiny Jewish race with its high calling."[99]

The son-in-law and successor of David Einhorn and the architect of the Pittsburgh platform, Kaufmann Kohler, played a formative role in the American Reform movement and delineated his theological views in elaborate detail. In his assessment of what he deemed to be the providential mission of Christianity and Islam, he was bold in pointing to their shortcomings and in predicting an eschatological era in which Israel would ultimately prevail as a "world-uniting faith." Universalist motives, he stated, necessitated "Israel's particularism." Therefore, on the question of intermarriage, Kohler stood firm:

> Yet just because of this universalistic Messianic hope of Judaism, it is still imperative, as it has been throughout the past, that the Jewish people must continue its separateness as a "Kingdom of priests and a holy nation," and for the sake of its world mission avoid intermarrying with members of other sects unless they espouse the Jewish faith.[100]

In the mid-nineteenth century the striking exception to this position was that of Samuel Holdheim,[101] one of the most outspoken German Reform

---

98 Ibid., 570–571. See *American Israelite* 25, no. 37 (March 14, 1879), 4; 30, no. 25 (December 14, 1883), 4; and 30, no. 26 (December 21, 1883), 21.

99 David Einhorn, "Die Beschlüsse der Rabbiner-versammlung," *The Jewish Times* 1, no. 45 (1869–70), 11. Einhorn's views were expressed in principled disagreement with the opinions of Samuel Hirsch published earlier in the latter's "Darf ein Reformrabbiner Ehen zwischen Juden und Nichtjuden einsegnen?," *The Jewish Times* 1, no. 27 (1869–70), 9–10; no. 28 (1869–70), 10–11; no. 30 (1869–70), 9–10; no. 31 (1869–70), 10; no. 32 (1869–70), 10; no. 33 (1869–70), 10; no. 34 (1869–70), 10; no. 35 (1869–70), 11; no. 36 (1869–70), 13.

100 Kaufmann Kohler, *Jewish Theology, Systematically and Historically Considered* (New York: The Macmillan company, 1918), 445–446.

101 For an incisive analysis of the distinctive philosophical interpretations of Jewish universalism espoused by Einhorn and Holdheim and their differing views on the question of

rabbis, a prolific author and fierce polemicist, articulate, learned and unsparingly honest. In the annals of the Reform movement the name of Holdheim stands second in significance only to that of Abraham Geiger. Of the two, Holdheim was the more consistent, and hence more radical, reformer. His personality is particularly interesting in that his intellectual trajectory parallels the movement for practical Reform. From Orthodoxy as a youth he moved gradually to a modified talmudism, then to a renunciation of the Talmud, culminating in a rejection of the eternally binding authority of the Bible itself. In the wake of publication of his opinions on the raging controversies of the day—the Geiger-Tiktin dispute, and the furor over the Hamburg Prayerbook—Holdheim, then chief rabbi of the Grand Duchy of Mecklenburg-Schwerin, published his initial writings on marriage in his most significant work, *Über die Autonomie der Rabbinen und das Prinzip der jüdischen Ehe: Ein Beitrag zur Verständigung über einige das Judenthum betreffende Zeitfragen* (Schwerin, 1843). Holdheim's incentive for presenting this work was the political situation in Mecklenburg-Schwerin. The Prussian government was contemplating promulgation of an Act of Incorporation for its Jewish subjects under which they were to be incorporated into separate communities of their own. Holdheim had pleaded against such actions, deeming such legislation a step backward. The Jews, he maintained, did not desire special statutes; they wished to be governed by the same laws as the native citizenry.

Holdheim's major thesis in the *Autonomie* is that Jewish religious, ethical and humanistic institutions must be kept rigidly apart from the national and political elements of Judaism; he classified the laws of marriage and divorce as belonging to the latter category. With the destruction of the independent Jewish commonwealth, he argued, Jewish nationality ceased to exist and since then Jews constitute a religious community with no political aims of their own. In all political questions they are identical to all other citizens of the state in which they dwell. Consequently, the autonomy of the rabbi in judicial matters must be terminated; the rabbi's autonomy must be confined to the religious sphere.[102] Religious and civil questions must be distinguished and the religious regulations concerning marriage, a civil act, must be supplanted by the civil law.

---

mixed marriage see Christian Wiese, "Samuel Holdheim's 'Most Powerful Comrade in Conviction': David Einhorn and the Debate Concerning Jewish Universalism in the Radical Reform Movement," in *Redefining Judaism in an Age of Emancipation: Comparative Perspectives on Samuel Holdheim (1806–1860)*, ed. by Christian Wiese (Leiden: Brill, 2007), 364–370.

102 Holdheim, *Autonomie* (Schwerin, 1843), vii and 14–16.

Religion adds sanctity to marriage, he conceded, but does not provide its legal basis.[103] In the *Autonomie*, Holdheim was following the precedent set by the Paris Sanhedrin and its downplaying of the ethnic character of Judaism. His teachings reflect classical Reform ideology; namely, that the mission of Judaism is purely religious and has no national or political overtones. Holdheim contended that the purely religious laws were eternal whereas those of a political or national character were but temporary. Following this line of interpretation, he argued that many laws which applied during the time of Jewish statehood are no longer binding upon Jews in the Diaspora. He went further than most of his colleagues in classifying almost all laws of ritual, prayer, diet, ceremony and holidays as nationalistic.[104]

Curiously, although in this work Holdheim clearly rejected the authority of talmudic law and described its approach to marriage and divorce as primitive and unacceptable—"*es ist für uns unbrauchbar geworden*" ("for us it has become useless")[105]—he sought to ground his argument on talmudic reasoning and precedent. No wonder that the book, the literary sensation of the year, provoked vociferous debate. As was to be expected, moderate conservative figures such as Graetz, Zunz, and Frankel[106] were joined in their condemnations by Orthodox partisans who challenged Holdheim's strained and haphazard appeal to rabbinic sources whose authority he himself rejected.[107] In time, Holdheim

---

103 Ibid., 137–165. For the debate between Zacharias Frankel and Holdheim regarding the legal nature of Jewish marriage and an analysis of Holdheim's misconceived attempt to base his theories of marriage as a purely civil act on talmudic sources and reasoning see David Ellenson, *After Emancipation: Jewish Religious Responses to Modernity* (Cincinnati: Hebrew Union College, 2004), 139–153. Ellenson, 153, notes that Frankel cast aspersions on Holdheim's motivations and argues that, in propounding his thesis, Holdheim was prompted by opportunistic considerations and the desire to advance the cause of political emancipation.

104 Holdheim, *Autonomie*, 26–28.

105 Ibid., 154 n. 113 and cf. ibid., 258–261.

106 See Emanuel Schreiber, *Reformed Judaism and its Pioneers* (Spokane, WA: Spokane Printing Company, 1892), 199–201.

107 In a pamphlet entitled *Zweite Mittheilungen aus einem Briefwechsel über die neueste jüdische Literatur* (Altona, 1844), R. Samson Raphael Hirsch threw the gauntlet:

> If you have recognized the Talmud as a falsehood be honorable men and as honorable men gather together the old folios to a great funeral pile on the grand market of modern Europeanism and let the consuming flames of eternal truth engulf the words of falsehood and deception. If you have recognized the Talmud and rabbis as liars, then, as honorable men, have nothing more to do with them. (p. 9)

Cf., also, ibid., 12, 26–27, 35, and 42, for R. Hirsch's critique of Holdheim's misinterpretations of rabbinic law and misleading citation of sources.

no longer tried to bolster his arguments regarding marriage with talmudic dialectic and his Reform position became more logically tenable.

For the last sixteen years of his life Holdheim was the spiritual leader of the separatist Berlin Reform Congregation, the most radical Reform community in Germany. In that capacity he introduced extensive ritual innovations discarding everything he deemed to be particularistic and anachronistic in traditional Judaism in favor of an enlightened universalism and, in 1849, acquiesced to moving congregational worship services from the Sabbath to Sunday. It was during that period that he publicized his views on intermarriage,[108] proceeded himself to perform wedding ceremonies for intermarrying couples, and published his address to one such couple.[109] Having placed marriage squarely in the sphere of the state, Holdheim yet had to account for its religious character. When he did, he was moved to formulate a new theological approach and adopted a humanistic interdenominational perspective. Holdheim now advocated the need to substitute "the holy God and Father of humanity for the holy God of Israel, the holy human race for the holy people, the covenant between God and humankind for the covenant between God and Israel."[110]

In an anonymously published satirical *ad hominem* attack, *Teshuvot be-Anshei Avon— Holdheim ve-Re'av be-Mikhtavim Sheloshah Asar* (Frankfurt am Main, 1845), Pinchas Menachem Heilprin noted that in Judaism marriage had always been under religious rather than civil jurisdiction and taunted Holdheim:

"According to the law of Moses and Israel" we have heard in connection with *kiddushin* [matrimony]. We have never heard "according to the law of the king and the usage of the nations." (p. 71)

Recourse to arguments from the marriage ceremony in debate with Holdheim was ironic, to say the least, for it was precisely the traditional marriage ceremony that Holdheim disdained. In one of his tracts regarding marriage Holdheim observed, *en passant*, that the standard religious ceremony would soon no longer be necessary nor would one require the customary *huppah*, or bridal canopy. Holdheim's castigated the *huppah* as an unaesthetic, outmoded oriental custom and bitterly disparaged the traditional ceremony. See his *Vorschläge zu einer zeitgemässen Reform der jüdischen Ehegesetze* (Schwerin, 1845), 27.

108 *Gemischte Ehen zwischen Juden und Christen. Die Gutachten der Berliner Rabbinatsverwaltung und des Königsberger Konsistoriums beleuchtet* (Berlin, 1850).

109 *Einsegnung einer gemischten Ehe zwischen einem Juden und einer Christin in Leipzig* (Berlin, 1849).

110 *Gemischte Ehen*, 64–65. Cf. the analysis of Andreas Gotzmann, "From Nationalism to Religion: Holdheim's Path to the Extreme Side of Religious Reform," in *Redefining Judaism*, 58–61.

For Holdheim, the crux of the problem of intermarriage was the question of liberty of conscience. He considered that principle to be essential and fundamental to true religion and therefore, if people freely chose to marry one another regardless of their religion of birth, a rabbi should not refuse to officiate at such a union.[111]

Holdheim's willingness to sanction intermarriage did not become a mainstream position in the Reform movement of his time. In the nineteenth century, in Germany the only notable figures who adopted that policy were Mendel Hess and Bernhard Wechsler. Among Reform rabbis in the United States who officiated at mixed marriages in the following decades were Samuel Hirsch, Emil G. Hirsch, Solomon Sonnenschein, Isaac S. Moses, Max Landsberg, and Jacob Voorsanger.[112] In 1909, after extensive debate, the Reform rabbinate again affirmed the position that mixed marriage was to be discouraged. On behalf of a committee appointed to study the matter, Samuel Schulman, in a lengthy address, dwelled on the reasons for refusing to sanction mixed marriage and, in particular, on the tension between love and duty. Expressing compassion and consideration for the heartrending conflict "between a great love and a loyalty to an ancestral faith," he nevertheless was unequivocal in stating that "we can not conceive the possibility ... of a Rabbi, the representative of the synagogue, consecrating such a marriage."[113] The wording of the resolution proposed by Schulman's committee, namely, "that a rabbi ought not officiate at marriage between a Jew or Jewess and a person professing a religion other than Judaism, inasmuch as such mixed marriage is prohibited by the Jewish religion and would tend to disintegrate the religion of Israel,"[114] was modified by Hyman Enelow and the resolution passed by the CCAR was much milder. The resolution adopted stated that "mixed marriages are contrary to the tradition of the Jewish religion and should therefore be discouraged by the American

---

111 See Immanuel H. Ritter, "Samuel Holdheim: The Jewish Reformer," *Jewish Quarterly Review* 1 (1889), 213. See also the discussion of Wiese in *Redefining Judaism*, 336–337. It is interesting to compare this position of Holdheim to the emphasis on absolute freedom of conscience expressed 130 years later by Professor Alvin J. Reines of Hebrew Union College in his advocacy of polydoxy, "Polydox Judaism: A Statement," *Journal of Reform Judaism* 27 (Fall 1980), 47–55.

112 See Schreiber, *Reformed Judaism*, 240 and cf. Michael A. Meyer, *Response to Modernity: A History of the Reform Movement in Judaism* (New York: Oxford University Press, 1990), 458 n. 91.

113 *CCAR Yearbook* 19 (1909), 322 and 325.

114 Ibid., 174.

rabbinate" but did not call for sanctions against a rabbi who performed an intermarriage.[115] During the next one hundred years the issue of intermarriage was again and again at the forefront of Reform deliberations. In practice, if not in theory, the Reform rabbinate reversed its previous stance and, in ever-increasing numbers, began to participate in interfaith ceremonies.[116] But that is a topic for another paper.

AN AFTERWORD

Reality must be faced forthrightly; but reality dare not be permitted to trump an ideal. A social historian would certainly assert that exogamy is a hallmark of an open society and hence virtually inevitable in our age. The prospect of wide-spread intermarriage is presciently described by Rashi in his commentary on Song of Songs. The *Zohar, Terumah* 144a, states, "That which was, that which is and that which is destined to be … all are [to be found] in Song of Songs." Rashi, in his interpretation of the allegory, charts a historical progression in the verses of Song of Songs. In the eighth and final chapter he finds allusions to the protracted period of exile and incisively focuses upon the specter of inter-marriage. Commenting on verses 8:8–10, he portrays two alternative stances available to Jews in the Diaspora: they may resolve to make themselves into an impermeable wall refusing any incursions of intermarriage or they may suc-cumb to the enticement of alien knocks on the door and behave as "a door which revolves upon its hinge and when knocked upon it opens" ("[*im delet hi*] *ha-sovevet al tzirah u-be-hakish aleha hi niftaḥat*"). In a concluding remark, Rashi depicts Israel responding with the resounding declaration, "*Ani ḥomah*"

---

115 Ibid., 170. For the debate on the issue see ibid., 174–184. This resolution was adopted in 1909 and reaffirmed in 1947.

116 For the heated debate in the 1970's, see "Mixed Marriage: A Mixture of Ideas," *CCAR Journal* 20, no. 2 (Spring 1973), 15–54. Cf. the discussion on changing attitudes in the Reform rabbinate in Sarna, 361–362 and accompanying notes; Hasia B. Diner, *The Jews of the United States, 1654 to 2000* (Berkeley: University of California Press, 2006), 308–309; Dana Evan Kaplan, *American Reform Judaism: An Introduction* (New Brunswick, NJ: Rutgers University Press, 2003), 177–179; and Gerald Cromer, *"The Quintessential Dilemma": American Jewish Responses to Intermarriage* (Ramat Gan: Rappaport Center for Assimilation Research, 2004), 18–21.

Obviously, the intense debate in Reform circles reflects the vastly changed sociological reality. For an incisive comment on the extent to which nonplussed acceptance of intermar-riage has become the new norm see Ted Merwin, "'Fiddler' for Millenials," *Jewish Week*, June 27, 2014, 70.

—"I am a wall!" (Song of Songs 8:10), giving voice to a vow and assurance that there will always be faithful Jews committed "in the strength of love" to the integrity of *kelal Yisra'el* as a people.[117]

---

117 David Eichhorn, author of one of the many contemporary books focusing on the problem of exogamy, cites a passage in *Pesikta de-Rav Kahana* that appears to identify the phenomenon that serves to guarantee the sustained Jewish identity of the faithful. He dedicates his book, *Jewish Intermarriages: Fact and Fiction* (Satellite Beach, FL: Satellite Books, 1974), frontispiece, to the wisdom of a Hellenist philosopher Oenomaus of Gadara, who lived in the early years of the common era, and recounts the following tale found in the *Pesikta*:

> Oenomaus of Gadara was one of the smartest non-Jews who ever lived. Some of his acquaintances once came to him and asked, "What can we do to get the Jews to intermarry with us?" He said to them, "Keep their synagogues and schools under close observation. As long as you hear the melodious voices of happy children in their synagogues and schools, you are not going to be able to persuade the Jews to intermarry with you. But, if you ever discover that there are no longer any such happy children in the synagogues and schools, you will know that the time has come when you will be able to persuade all the Jews to intermarry."

The substantive statement is undoubtedly accurate. The problem with the citation, however, is that, while the sentiment is correct, the textual translation, unfortunately, is not. The passage is found in *Pesikta de-Rav Kahana*, ed. S. Buber (Lyck, 1868), 121a and in *Pesikta de-Rav Kahana*, ed. Bernard Mandelbaum (New York, 1962), *Eikhah*, *Piskah* 15, I, 254–55. The word *le-hizdaveg*, literally: "to mate," in the Hebrew original is translated by Eichhorn as "to intermarry." The word *le-hizdaveg* may, however, also mean "to join with evil intent" or "to combat." Occurring as it does in the context of a description of the strife between Jacob and Esau, the word means "to make war against" or "to overcome." See the comments of Mandelbaum, I, 254 n. 13, on "*le-hizdaveg*": "*la'amod keneged ba-milḥamah*"—"to oppose in war." See also the English translation of William G. Braude and Israel J. Kapstein, *Pesikta de-Rab Kahana* (Philadelphia: Jewish Publication Society of America, 1975), 279, "Can we take on this nation in battle?" See also *Pesiqta deRab Kahana: an Analytical Translation*, trans. Jacob Neusner (Atlanta, GA: Scholars Press, 1987), vol. II, 6: "Do you maintain that we can make war against this nation?"

Eichhorn's text contains an understandable but evident mistranslation. Nevertheless, the lesson he sought to impart is quite valid and, even if that source is inappropriately cited, the message conveyed is telling. See Rashi's commentary on the very next phrase of Song of Songs 8:10, "I am a wall and my breasts are as towers" in which (on the basis of *Pesaḥim* 87a) he interprets the allegory as referring to *batei knesset* and *batei midrash*, houses of prayer and houses of study. The clear implication is that the ability to respond resolutely "*Ani ḥomah*" is drawn from "houses of prayer and houses of study that nurture Israel with words of Torah."

CHAPTER 6

Military Service: Ambivalence and Contradiction

> *There are many fighters in the midst of my nation.*
> Ḥakham Isaac Aboab da Fonseca, *Zekher Asiti Le-Nifla'ot El*, Recife, Brazil, 1646.[1]

> *The profession of a soldier is the profession of an assassin.*
> Chmoul to his son, in Leon Cahun, *La Vie Juive.*[2]

> *There upon the battlefield of honor ... there also will the barriers of prejudice come tumbling down.*
> Eduard Kley and Carl Siegfried Günsburg, *Zuruf an die Jünglinge*, 1813.[3]

> *Rabbis and schoolteachers in their teaching must present military service as a sacred duty....*
> Instructions to the Westphalian Consistory, 1808.[4]

> *[W]ar is an unmitigated evil, and ... we should abstain from all participation in it.*
> Proposed resolution before the Central Conference of American Rabbis, 1935.[5]

INTRODUCTION

Is the role of a soldier that of a hero or of an assassin, a fate to be embraced or to be dreaded, a source of pride or of anguish? Living, as they did during the medieval period, a separate existence in the lands of their dispersion in which they constituted an *imperium in imperio,* Jews for a large part of their history were spurned as soldiers and spared the dilemma. But there came a time when the question was placed squarely before them.

---

1 Manuscript in the possession of the Livraria Ets Haim-D. Montezinos in Amsterdam, cited by Arnold Wiznitzer, "Jewish Soldiers in Dutch Brazil (1630–1654)," *Publication of the American Jewish Historical Society (PAJHS)* 46, no. 1 (1956),47.
2 Leon Cahun, *La Vie Juive* (Paris, 1886), 53.
3 Eduard Kley and Carl Siegfried Günsburg, *Zuruf an die Jünglinge, welche den Fahnen des Vaterlandes folgen* (Berlin, 1813), 10.
4 Gesetz-Bulletin, no. 28, *Sulamith* 2, no. 1 (1808), 6.
5 Proposed resolution before the Central Conference of American Rabbis, *Central Conference of American Rabbis Yearbook (CCARY)* 45 (1935), 66–67.

In an attempt to force the members of the Jewish community to define their relationship to the state from the vantage point of Jewish law, Napoleon, by a decree of July 10, 1806, convened the Assembly of Notables and, subsequently, on September 24, 1806, announced his decision to summon a Great Sanhedrin to convert the decisions of the Assembly of Notables into definitive and authoritative religious pronouncements. Indicative of Napoleon's desire to assure that those synods issue unequivocal declarations regarding the primacy of the responsibilities of Jews as citizens of the state is the sixth of the twelve questions placed before those august bodies: Do Jews born in France, and treated by the law as French citizens, acknowledge France as their country? Are they bound to defend it? Are they bound to obey its laws and to conform to every provision of the Civil Code?

By the time that the Paris Sanhedrin was convened, Jews had already served in the French revolutionary armies, in the National Guard and in Napoleon's forces. When the sixth question was read before the Assembly and the question of whether Jews were duty-bound to protect France was articulated, the deputies spontaneously exclaimed, "To the Death!"[6] In the course of the ensuing proceedings of the Assembly an affirmative response to the question was formally adopted by unanimous vote. Moreover, during the subsequent deliberations of the Sanhedrin, the only matter regarding which the Sanhedrin formulated a position that went beyond the previous resolutions adopted by the Assembly was with regard to this sixth question. The Sanhedrin went so far as to declare that Jews were exempt from religious obligations and strictures that might interfere with performance of military duties.

The resounding declaration of the Sanhedrin found an echo in numerous public statements in the years that followed. Yet, as Jewish nationals were called upon with increasing frequency to serve in the armed forces of their host countries, that emerging phenomenon evoked contradictory responses.

Consistent with its clear and unambivalent regard for the sanctity and preservation of human life, Judaism manifests a distinctly negative attitude toward warfare and idealizes peace as the goal of human society. Although Scripture is replete with accounts of military conquests, the taking of human life in warfare was consistently viewed as, at best, a necessary evil. Despite King David's distinction, both temporal and spiritual, he was informed, "You shall not build a house in My name, because you have shed much blood upon the earth in My sight" (I Chronicles 22:8). The ultimate utopian society was

---

6 Simon Schwarzfuchs, *Napoleon, the Jews and the Sanhedrin* (London: Routledge and Kegan Paul, 1979), 62.

envisioned as one in which "Nation shall not lift up sword against nation, neither shall they learn war any more" (Isaiah 2:4 and Micah 4:3).

Subsequent to the biblical period there are few instances of Jews voluntarily engaging in armed warfare. Although Jews can hardly be described as a militaristic people, beginning with the garrison of the Jews of Elephantine five centuries before the common era[7] and extending to the soldiers of the quasi-autonomous Jewish community of Jodensavanne, Surinam, in the New World,[8] there have been situations in which Jews served as mercenaries or as volunteers in peacetime army units.[9] Those forces constituted the exception rather than the rule. Over the centuries there have also been occasions when Jews took up arms in self-defense or in order to achieve political objectives, including military uprisings in the Roman Diaspora (115–17 C.E.), the rebellion of Mar Zutra (513 C.E.) and an eighth century rebellion in Iraq led by Abu Isa. In Europe there is ample evidence of Jews having borne arms until they lost that right sometime in the thirteenth century. A Spanish Jewish military figure who headed the armies of Grenada in the early eleventh century was the renowned Samuel ha-Nagid. There are scattered references to Jews rendering military service in Italy and Sicily in the fifteenth and sixteenth centuries. From the sixteenth to the eighteenth centuries there were also occasional instances of Jews using weapons in self-defense in Polish cities and of Jews serving, at times, in civil defense units and even in the national army.[10]

However, it is only after the Emancipation that large numbers of Jews were conscripted into non-Jewish armies. In the global wars of the twentieth century the numbers increased significantly. Thus, for example, a quarter of a

---

7 See A. E. Cowley, *Aramaic Papyri of the Fifth Century B.C.* (Oxford: Clarendon Press, 1923; repr. Osnabrück: Zeller, 1967), xv, xvi, and 12.

8 See Jacob Beller, *Jews in Latin America* (New York: Jonathan David, 1969), 107–108, and Jacob R. Marcus and Stanley S. Chyet, eds., *Historical Essay on the Colony of Surinam 1788*, trans. S. Cohen (New York: American Jewish Archives, 1974), 42–48 and 65–72.

9 Note should be taken of R. Judah Halevi's incisive statement, *Kuzari*, part V, sec. 23, categorizing the behavior of those who endanger their lives by volunteering for army service "in order to gain fame and spoil by courage and bravery" as morally reprehensible and "even inferior to that that of those who march into war for hire." Halevi's distinction between frivolous self-endangerment and self-endangerment for purposes of earning a livelihood prefigures the thesis later developed in the classic responsum of Rabbi Ezekiel Landau, *Noda bi-Yehudah, Mahadura Tinyana* (Prague, 1811), *Yoreh De'ah*, no. 10.

10 See the intriguing summary of Jewish military activity in the Middle Ages in David Biale, *Power and Powerlessness in Jewish History* (New York: Schocken Books, 1986), 72–77, and sources cited in Yitzchak Ze'ev Kahane, "Sherut ha-Tzava be-Sifrut ha-Teshuvot," *Sinai* 23 (1948), 129–134.

million Jews served in the U.S. army in World War I and over a half million in World War II; over a half million Jews were conscripted into the Soviet army in World War II; over 50,000 Jews fought in the British army in World War I and over 60,000 in World War II.[11]

When Jews first began to be conscripted into European armies in the late eighteenth and early nineteenth centuries, two sharply divergent attitudes found expression in the broader Jewish community. For observant, traditional Jews, aside from the quite cogent fear for life and limb, the terrors of the military experience were magnified by the difficulties army service posed in terms of ritual observance of Sabbath and festivals, dietary laws, Torah study, prayer and the wearing of beards and sidelocks. Little wonder that, for such persons, army service was perceived as a calamity to be avoided at all cost. In stark contrast, to liberal elements within the Jewish population service in the army represented a tangible means of demonstrating patriotic zeal and was welcomed as the key to emancipation, enfranchisement and achievement of political equality. Sadly, although much heroism was displayed and much Jewish blood was shed, nevertheless, prejudice persisted without mitigation and in far too many jurisdictions political and social equality remained a chimera.

In responsa and writings of the next century and a half both of these contradictory reactions were articulated. Most—but not all—traditionalist halakhic authorities were far more negative toward army service than might be assumed on the basis of the published record. Within the liberal sector, which initially uniformly acclaimed army service as a sacred duty, one finds striking shifts and permutations. In the changed *Zeitgeist* of the twentieth century, when pacifism became the vogue and the ideal of *dulce et decorum est pro patria mori* lost its luster, liberal ideologues sought to discover a mandate for pacifism and conscientious objection in Jewish law and tradition. Ironically, in seeking to espouse what they believed to be a non-normative halakhic stance those writers did, in fact, draw close to the normative, but seldom candidly expressed, halakhic perspective.

THE TRADITIONALIST APPROACH

1. Published Responsa

Although the published corpus of halakhic responsa devoted to the topic of military service is not unduly sparse, it provides but a veiled and hazy portrait

---

11 See "Military Service," *Encyclopedia Judaica*, vol. XI (Jerusalem, 1971), 1550.

of the traditionalist perspective. Perusal of the responsa reveals that the respondents were fully conscious of the need for utmost caution in dealing with so sensitive a subject. They grasped far too well the implications of expressing opinions inconsistent with, or even not fully supportive of, policies espoused by the governing authority. Thus, the respondents were extremely circumspect and wrote with an eye constantly over their collective shoulder. Such vigilance is evident in the cryptic nature of some comments, in the explicit expressions of concern frequently incorporated in their responsa, but most of all in what is not written.

Of the early responsa discussing the compulsory draft in the modern era the two most significant are those of R. Samuel Landau, son of R. Ezekiel Landau, included in his father's posthumously published responsa volume, *Noda bi-Ye-hudah, Mahadura Tinyana, Yoreh De'ah*, no. 74 and of R. Moses Sofer, *Teshuvot Ḥatam Sofer*, vol. VI, *Likkutim*, no. 29. Perhaps the most remarkable aspect of both responsa is the fact that discussion of the most fundamental issue is conspicuous in its absence. There is no reference whatsoever to the basic problem of complicity in an unjust or halakhically illicit war. Another responsum of R. Moses Sofer, *Teshuvot Ḥatam Sofer, Yoreh De'ah*, no. 19, is the classic source for the ruling that non-Jews are enjoined from engaging in any form of warfare other than for purposes of self-defense.[12] Yet, in his discussion of problems associated with conscription, *Likkutim*, no. 29, *Ḥatam Sofer* makes no mention of the problem of Jewish complicity in a war of aggression. Virtually all subsequent discussions of the subject similarly avoid this sensitive issue. It is not surprising that, a century later, in addressing the vexing problem of Jews fighting other Jews in opposing enemy forces, Rabbi Ze'ev Wolf Leiter, wrote that he was unable to find this question clarified in the literature of rabbinic decisors.[13]

Moreover, the one clear reference in the writings of early-day authorities to Jews fighting in non-Jewish wars is entirely ignored by later rabbinic scholars who discuss participation in military campaigns. *Tosafot, Avodah Zarah* 18b, cites a certain Rabbenu Elḥanan who comments cryptically that it is forbidden for a Jew "to be of the number of members of the army of gentiles." The omission of this source is far too glaring to have been a simple oversight. Rabbinic writers dealing with questions pertaining to military service appear to have adopted the policy of Rabbi David Sintzheim, a member of the Paris

---

12 Cf. R. Abraham Dov Ber Kahane, *Dvar Avraham*, vol. I, no. 11, and R. Menachem Ziemba, *Zera Avraham*, no. 24, sec. 10, as well as the discussion in R. J. David Bleich, *Contemporary Halakhic Problems*, vol. II (New York: Ktav Publishing House, 1983), 164–166.

13 *She'elot u-Teshuvot Bet David*, 2nd ed. (Vienna, 1932), vol. I, no. 71.

Sanhedrin, as extolled by *Ḥatam Sofer*, who said of him: "He ... knew how to answer his questioners. ... After he had revealed one handbreadth, he concealed two handbreadths."[14]

The reason for such reticence is obvious. As a result, these responsa demand careful examination by the reader with close attention to what is hinted at only between the lines. That such scrutiny is required is apparent from explicit cues embedded in the text designed to serve as red flags indicating the delicacy of the topic and underscoring the fact that some matters must remain unsaid.

In discussing cooperation or non-cooperation with the military draft, R. Samuel Landau prefaces his ruling by stressing that "It is difficult to issue a ruling in a matter that primarily entails a question of life and death. Who shall raise his head [to render a decision] in these matters?" In his concluding remarks he adds, "I know that it is difficult to rule with regard to this [question] and with regard to this our Sages, of blessed memory, said, 'Just as it is a mitzvah to say that which will be accepted, so it is a mitzvah not to say that which will not be accepted'[15] and at this time a sagacious person will be silent."[16]

Ḥatam Sofer, also addressing the question of the conscription of Jews in non-Jewish armies, states that, "Regarding this, silence is better than our speech." Referring to unspecified reprehensible actions of Jewish communal officials, *Ḥatam Sofer* resignedly comments, "Great Jewish authorities perforce looked aside and permitted those appointed by the community to do as was fitting in their eyes according to the times. And it is a time to be silent." Presumably, silence was the best response since protest would have proven unproductive. Rabbis did not have the power to reverse or rescind communal policies without creating a situation in which government authorities would become aware of Jewish reluctance to serve in the military. There was a strong probability that overt intervention on their part would give rise to serious punitive reprisals against the entire Jewish community. In such an era, the only course of action open to responsible rabbinical leadership is one involving "the choice of the lesser evil." Accordingly, *Ḥatam Sofer* concludes, "Lo, I have been exceedingly brief for it is not fitting to expand upon this subject, as is understood." [17] In a similar vein, R. Meir Eisenstadt writes of the situation facing the

---

14 Eulogy published in *Sefer Ḥatam Sofer, Derashot*, vol. I (Cluj, 1929), 80b-82a and republished in Rabbi Joseph David Sintzheim, *Minḥat Ani* (Jerusalem: Machon Yerushalayim, 1974), 30. English translation in Schwarzfuchs, *Napoleon*, p. 116.
15 *Yevamot* 65b.
16 *Noda bi-Yehudah, Mahadura Tinyana, Yoreh De'ah*, no. 74.
17 *She'elot u-Teshuvot Ḥatam Sofer*, vol. VI (Pressburg, 1864), *Likkutim*, no. 29.

rabbis: "And if perhaps they looked aside because it is not in their power to find another solution, we, what can we answer in their place?"[18]

The issues addressed in these early responsa are the right of the state to conscript soldiers and the halakhic questions posed by the manner in which the draft was initially conducted. Government authorities demanded that the community produce a given number of recruits and, frequently, Jewish communal officials were placed in charge of filling the quota. Usually the selection was carried out by means of a lottery. In some locales it was also possible for a recruit to hire a substitute. The fundamental halakhic issue raised is the dilemma posed by the classical problem of *tenu lanu ehad mi-kem* (Palestinian Talmud, *Terumot* 8:4), that is, the question of delivering a single individual in order to save the entire community. Generally speaking, one is prohibited from delivering an individual Jew for execution even in order to save the lives of many (*Mishneh Torah, Hilkhot Yesodei ha-Torah* 5:5). The case discussed in the Palestinian Talmud serves as a paradigm prohibiting the singling out of a Jew for exposure to danger or harm in order to spare others from a similar fate. Assuming that cooperation in conscription is legitimate, a second and closely related question involves the issue of how the lottery is to be conducted and whether deferments or exemptions may be granted to some individuals when such a policy would entail substituting others in their stead.

The earliest rabbinic respondent to the question of communal conscription, Rabbi Samuel Landau rules unequivocally that, "It is forbidden to hand anyone over to them" and that "There is no room to be lenient in this matter." Individuals may do all in their power to avoid the draft, provided that they have not yet been designated by name. Moreover, the community may also strive to assist such individuals in securing an exemption prior to their actual designation. However, once an individual has been identified for conscription, the community may no longer seek his exemption if such exemption would be obtained only at the expense of another person who would be taken in his stead. Such substitution is forbidden on the basis of the talmudic argument "Who says your blood is redder than his?" (*Pesahim* 25b). However, faced with a situation in which such efforts were made, R. Samuel Landau counsels, "At this time the wise should be silent." In contradistinction, R. Samuel Landau is adamant that even non-observant youths or those who mock the law may not be handed over for military service. Although such individuals may be deserving of punishment, it is nevertheless absolutely

18 *Imrei Esh, Yoreh De'ah* (Lemberg, 1852), no. 52.

forbidden to turn them over to civil authorities in order to fill the draft quota imposed upon the community.[19] R. Samuel Landau is cognizant of the difficulty of ruling in matters of this nature. Nevertheless, while fully aware of the delicacy of the situation in negotiating both with lay communal officials and with government authorities, he does not shrink from declaring categorically that if, in fact, individuals were to be handed over to the civil authorities, it would become obligatory to engage in preventive action and in public protest ("*mehuyav limhot be-yad*").[20]

In a responsum dated Sivan 1830, *Hatam Sofer*, the preeminent halakhic authority of the time, affirms the obligation of conscripted Jews to perform the services required of them. His position is based upon the premise that the power to conscript is encompassed within the ambit of the halakhic principle *dina de-malkhuta dina* ("the law of the land is the law") and flows from the power of the ruler to levy "taxes" in the form of personal service. *Hatam Sofer* affirms the right of the state to require military service from its nationals ("*Dina din u-mimeila muttal akarkafta de-kol mi she-ra'uy la-tzet u-she-ein lo ishah u-banim kefi nimus ve-hok malkhuto*"). The only members of the community who must be excused by communal leaders from the obligation imposed upon the community as a whole are students of Torah who, argues *Hatam Sofer*, on the basis of Jewish law (*Bava Batra* 8a), are free from the obligation regarding military service. *Hatam Sofer* notes that rabbinical students and occupants of rabbinical positions were usually exempted by the government[21] and adds that he himself had frequently given testimonials to such students to assist them in obtaining exemptions.

---

19 Cf. the complex and rather strained argument presented by R. Abraham Teumim, *Hesed le-Avraham, Mahadura Kamma* (Lemberg, 1857), *Yoreh De'ah*, no. 45, in favor of compelling such persons to accept induction in order to preserve observant individuals from transgression.

20 *Noda bi-Yehudah, Mahadura Tinyana, Yoreh De'ah*, no. 74. For a discussion of why Rabbi Samuel Landau demands protest against delivery of prospective soldiers to the authorities but does not demand similar protest against communal intervention to secure the release of designated individuals when substitution of others is a certainty, see R. J. David Bleich, *Be-Netivot ha-Halakhah* (New York: Ktav Publishing House, 1996), vol. I, 120–124.

21 Policy with regard to clergymen and rabbinical student exemptions differed from country to country. In France, after 1808, Jewish youths preparing to enter the rabbinate were not granted a clergy exemption. See S. Posener, "The Immediate Economic and Social Effect of the Emancipation of the Jews in France," *Jewish Social Studies* 1 (1939), 317. However, in Russia, under a decree issued in 1827, rabbis and students in rabbinical seminaries were exempt from military service. See Michael Stanislawski, *Tsar Nicholas I and the Jews: The Transformation of Jewish Society in Russia, 1825–1855* (Philadelphia: Jewish Publication Society, 1983), 19. Cf. also the comments of R. Baruch ha-Levi Epstein, *Mekor Barukh* (New York, 1954), vol. II, 1060–1061.

Ḥatam Sofer recommends utilization of a lottery system for filling the quota imposed upon the Jewish community but emphasizes that it must be equitable and that all persons suitable for military service, observant and non-observant, be included in the lottery ("*me-ha-ra'uy she-ya'amdu kulam be-shaveh lifnei ha-eidah va-yatilu goral*"). He stresses that it is absolutely forbidden to compel any person to serve in the stead of an already drafted individual, even if the replacement is a Sabbath desecrator or an immoral person. *Ḥatam Sofer* regarded such coercion as tantamount to biblically proscribed kidnapping and sale of an innocent victim. Nonetheless, he rules that it is entirely permissible—and indeed advisable—for individuals to seek exemptions or deferments and to devise ways of avoiding military service even by means of hiring a substitute or by paying a sum of money in order to secure a reprieve. Moreover, *Ḥatam Sofer* regards it as praiseworthy for fellow Jews to render every assistance to their coreligionists in order to obtain such exemptions ("*ve-kol Yisra'el meḥuyavim le-sayyo ve-yekar pidyon nafsho*").[22]

In concluding his comments, *Ḥatam Sofer* notes that it was common practice for nonobservant individuals to volunteer to serve as substitutes for conscripts in exchange for a sum of money. He rules that it is permissible to avail oneself of such an arrangement since those volunteers were unconcerned with regard to violation of religious law at home as well as in the army and, moreover, in any event, would likely make their services available to others. Using such replacements had become common practice and, given the realities of the overall situation, *Ḥatam Sofer* asserts that availing oneself of the services of these substitutes constitutes choosing the lesser of two evils ("*livḥor ha-ra be-mi'uto*").[23]

---

22 *Ḥatam Sofer's* ruling was by no means unique. Thus, for example, R. Tzevi Hirsch Chajes reports that he had occasion to advise a synagogue to pawn the synagogue lamps in order to raise funds necessary to enable prospective conscripts to avoid military service. See *Minḥat Kena'ot*, in *Kol Sifrei Maharatz Ḥayes* (Jerusalem: Divrei Ḥakhamim, 1958), vol. II, 991.

23 *She'elot u-Teshuvot Ḥatam Sofer*, vol. VI, *Likkutim*, no. 29. Sheldon Zimmerman, "Confronting the Halachah on Military Service," *Judaism* 20, no. 2 (Spring 1971), 207 and 210, errs in positing a fundamental disagreement between *Ḥatam Sofer* and Rabbi Samuel Landau and in asserting that Rabbi Landau represented a minority view in censuring the methods used by the Jewish community in filling their quotas. Both respondents categorically forbid substitution of nonobservant youths for draftees who have been designated by name. The stronger language of Rabbi Landau, "*meḥuyavim limḥot be-yad*," in contrast to *Ḥatam Sofer's* "*ha-shetikah yafah me-dibbureinu ba-zeh ve-et la-ḥashot*" may simply reflect the difference between an earlier theoretical stance and a later deterioration in communal practice at which time protest might have proven more harmful to the welfare of the greater community. While *Ḥatam Sofer* affirms that the conscripted individual has an obligation

It is quite evident that *Ḥatam Sofer* urges that military service be avoided if at all possible. Although his language is restrained, a decidedly negative view of military service and the necessity for ritual infractions inevitably attendant thereupon is manifestly evident. It should be noted that his comments appear to be directed entirely to peacetime service, since the issue of subjecting oneself to endangerment is not raised.

Similar views regarding the draft are articulated by a contemporary of *Ḥatam Sofer*, R. Moshe Leib Tsilts of Nikolsburg, *She'elot u-Teshuvot Milei de-Avot*, 1, *Ḥoshen Mishpat*, no. 4, who stresses the need to abjure preferential treatment in administering the lottery.[24] Writing in 1841, R. Meir Eisenstadt, in *She'elot u-Teshuvot Imrei Esh*, 1, *Yoreh De'ah*, no. 74, goes beyond *Ḥatam Sofer* in declaring that not only is the hiring of substitutes permissible but, from the perspective of the draftee, may be described as a mitzvah. *Imrei Esh* declares, "It is absolutely permissible and a mitzvah to do so" (*"hetter gamur u-mitzvah la'asot ken"*) and in the conclusion of his discussion he reiterates his view with the emphatic exclamation, "It is permitted and a mitzvah" (*"muttar u-mitzvah"*). In explaining why this practice is the best available solution to the dilemma, *Imrei Esh*, perhaps naively, asserts that: (a) no one compels the substitutes to transgress Torah law; (b) dietary observances need not be violated by a conscript who is willing to accept inconvenience; and (c) problems involving Sabbath observance can be resolved since Jewish law permits arms to be carried on the Sabbath under specified conditions. *Imrei Esh* also addresses the issues posed by the danger inherent in military service but concludes that volunteering for army service is not to be forbidden on the grounds that it is tantamount to suicide.[25] Nonetheless, *Imrei Esh* rules that it is forbidden to obtain substitutes by means of coercion simply because a person may not "deliver" another individual to harm, loss or inconvenience in order to be spared the burden he seeks to shift to another.

---

to serve if he cannot avoid induction, Rabbi Landau states only that once an individual has been designated the community must desist from efforts to secure a reprieve at another's expense, but is silent regarding the individual's own obligation. However, there is no explicit contradiction between the two responsa. Nor does *Ḥatam Sofer* express "the majority view" (Zimmerman, 207) with regard to the legitimacy of the draft as flowing from the power of the ruler to levy "taxes." Whether or not the prerogatives of the king ascribed by I Samuel 8 to the Jewish king (*mishpetei ha-melekh*) apply to non-Jewish rulers as well is the subject of considerable controversy among halakhic scholars. See Shmuel Shilo, *Dina de-Malkhuta Dina* (Jerusalem: Jerusalem Academic Press, 1974), 62, 64–67, 71–73, and 101.

24 Again Zimmerman errs (207) in deeming this a stronger position than that of *Ḥatam Sofer*. Exemptions are simply not discussed by *Ḥatam Sofer*; they are not necessarily forbidden.

25 See *infra*, note 37.

Many later respondents assert that it is commendable to avoid army service at all costs. As noted, *Imrei Esh*, I, *Yoreh De'ah*, no. 74, asserts that it is a mitzvah to hire a substitute. Others point to the physical danger associated with military service in ruling that it is preferable to accept employment involving desecration of the Sabbath rather than to serve in a battle zone. Thus, R. Eliezer David Grunwald of Satmar, *Keren le-David, Orah Hayyim*, no. 100, rules that when there is no threat to life, one should not seek exemption from army service by accepting a post in which Sabbath desecration is a certainty. However, one should do everything possible to avoid being sent to the battlefront, including accepting a position that will definitely entail ongoing Sabbath desecration, because "there is nothing that stands in the way of saving life." R. Mordecai Leib Winkler, *She'elot u-Teshuvot Levushei Mordekhai, Mahadura Tinyana, Orah Hayyim*, no. 174, maintains that one must assume that any wartime service will entail battlefront conditions, i.e., military service represents at least possible danger to life. Consistent with that view, he rules that unless an individual has already been selected by a draft board he should not accept a position involving Sabbath desecration in order to avoid being called up because prior to being selected there is no imminent danger.[26] However, if a person has already been selected by a draft board he may accept employment involving Sabbath desecration in order to obtain a deferment from military service since "in our day, in the awesome battle at this time, with multiple instruments of destruction and catapult stones," such service entails danger to life.[27]

Perhaps because hiring a substitute was no longer a viable option, unlike respondents of an earlier period, Rabbi David Zevi Hoffmann, *Melammed le-Ho'il, Orah Hayyim*, no. 42, was forced to confront the issue of outright evasion of the draft. Writing after World War I, Rabbi Hoffmann rules that one should not seek to evade army service on account of fear of Sabbath desecration for more "than a question of a mitzvah" is involved. Evasion of army service may give rise to the profanation of God's name (*hillul Ha-Shem*), Rabbi Hoffmann warns, "because the enemies of the Jews say that the Jews do not obey the laws of the kingdom."

---

26 Cf., however, note 49.

27 R. Moshe Joshua Judah Leib Diskin, *She'elot u-Teshuvot Maharil Diskin* (Jerusalem, 1911), *Pesakim*, no. 4, forbids a soldier to reveal an infirmity to the authorities in order to avoid army duty lest he be coerced instead to work on the Sabbath. This responsum should not be viewed as contradicting the views of *Keren le-David* or *Levushei Mordekhai* since the responsum does not appear to apply to army service during wartime. The conclusion drawn by Zimmerman (p. 209) that *Maharil Diskin* deems profanation of the Sabbath a greater evil than danger to one's life is without basis.

Although, in application, Rabbi Hoffmann's ruling is unequivocal, his views regarding military service upon which it is based are somewhat more complex. A careful reading of this responsum indicates that Rabbi Hoffmann does not deem army service *per se* to be a religious duty since he speaks of actions that might be performed by a soldier that would constitute a mitzvah "such as to save the lives of Israelites or other mitzvah" with the implication that army service in itself does not constitute a mitzvah. It is the negative outcome in the form of profanation of the Divine Name and possible attendant danger to Jews that is the focus of his concern. Rabbi Hoffmann observes that, if rabbinic decisors ruled that an individual was obligated to evade army service to avoid Sabbath desecration, the result would be widespread evasion of the draft. This would be counterproductive "for assuredly the majority would not achieve their desire and it would cause a great profanation of the Name, God forbid, for no purpose." Again the implication appears to be that his ruling is based on a pragmatic assessment of the situation at the time and realistic considerations as distinct from an idealistic position. Were it possible for Jews successfully to avoid army service the conclusion might have been entirely different. Rabbi Hoffmann's own introductory comment in delineating the problem, namely, that the question requires an answer based "not on the inclination of our heart alone" also implies that the instinctive Jewish reaction is to avoid military duty. It is noteworthy that Rabbi Hoffmann's responsum focusing on avoidance of ḥillul Ha-Shem was penned at a time when there was an upsurge of anti-Semitism in Germany and accusations were widespread that Jews had evaded the draft in large numbers or had shirked frontline service.[28]

A further query addressed by Rabbi Hoffmann in the very next responsum, *Melammed le-Ho'il, Oraḥ Ḥayyim*, no. 43, is whether it is obligatory for an individual to take advantage of a student deferment in order to delay military service and possible attendant Sabbath infractions or whether one might accept immediate army duty in order, upon completion of the tour of duty, to be able to enter into a marriage. In the case submitted to him, Rabbi Hoffmann, for a variety of reasons, rules that it is permissible not to accept the deferment.[29] Again, from the context of the discussion, it is evident that Rabbi Hoffmann is far from enthusiastic about military service. He writes to the interlocutor, who had written on behalf of his son, that delay may be unadvisable

---

28   See notes 106 and 107 and accompanying text.
29   It must be emphasized that this responsum addresses the situation of a peacetime army and involves no discussion of danger to life. In wartime an additional factor would have had to be taken into consideration, namely, preservation of life for as long as possible.

because it might result in a longer tour of duty since "it is possible that your son is not so strong at the present time and may prove inept in army service and will soon be discharged which may not be the case three years later when he will be stronger and assuredly will be taken and will be forced to remain there the entire year."[30]

R. Israel Meir ha-Kohen, *Mishnah Berurah* 329:17, rules that Jews must allow themselves to be conscripted and implies that failure of Jews to participate in the military when foreign forces attack may enrage the populace and result in loss of life. His comments certainly do not constitute a blanket endorsement of military service and a dispensation to engage in warfare under any and all circumstances; they urge acquiescence to conscription simply as a matter of *pikuaḥ nefesh* or preservation of life.[31]

There are, however, two halakhic respondents whose views differ significantly from the majority. Writing in Germany, in the nineteenth century, R. Samson Raphael Hirsch extols the positive religious duty of serving in the army in defense of one's fatherland. R. Hirsch contends that loyalty to one's country is a "religious duty, a duty imposed by God and no less holy than all the others."[32] In *Horeb*, a work devoted to the discussion of mitzvot, R. Hirsch includes this obligation in the fifth section, the section devoted to what he terms "commandments of love." Encompassed in the religious duty of a subject and citizen, he maintains, is the obligation "to sacrifice even life itself when the Fatherland calls its sons to its defense." R. Hirsch goes far beyond most rabbinic writers in positing that this obligation must be fulfilled "with love and pride." In a most remarkable statement, he declares, "But this outward obedience to the laws must be joined by the inner obedience: i.e., to be loyal to the State with heart and mind ... to guard the honor of the State with love

---

30 *Melammed le-Ho'il, Oraḥ Ḥayyim*, no. 43. The comments of Rabbi Alfred Cohen, "In this century, R. David Hoffmann (*Or Hachaim* [*sic*], 42–43) considered it the obligation of every citizen, including Jews, to participate in the army like all citizens. Even if one can get a deferment for two or three years, R. Hoffmann opposes it and says one should enlist right away," are not an accurate representation of Rabbi Hoffmann's views. See R. Alfred Cohen, "On Yeshiva Men Serving in the Army," *Journal of Halacha and Contemporary Society* 23 (Spring 1992), 30 n. 65.

31 The note below the text marked with an asterisk, "And it has already been ruled in the Gemara: 'the law of the land is the law,'" may constitute a somewhat enigmatic reference to the legitimacy of conscription. However, the form in which it appears, i.e., outside the annotations on *Shulḥan Arukh* and without the usual marginal signal makes it possible that this comment was intended for the benefit of the authorities rather than the reader.

32 *Horeb: A Philosophy of Jewish Laws and Observances*, trans. Dayan I. Grunfeld (New York: Soncino Press, 1962), sec. 609, 462.

and pride."[33] One can but wonder to what extent R. Hirsch was carried away by the rhetoric of the time and to what extent he internalized these sentiments.[34] R. Hirsch does not address the substantive question of participation in a war of aggression. However, he does conclude his remarks on patriotism with the observation that loyal citizenship is an "unconditional duty and not dependent upon whether the State is kindly intentioned toward you or is harsh."[35] The comment seems to suggest that R. Hirsch assumed that one is duty-bound to serve in the army even in an unjust war of aggression when such is the mandate of the state.

The strongest rabbinic endorsement of army service as a positive religious obligation and the sharpest rabbinic criticism of army evasion was penned by Rabbi Moshe Shmuel Glasner of Klausenberg, the author of *Dor Revi'i*, who is known as an independent-minded and unconventional scholar. Rabbi Glasner maintains that "According to the law of the holy Torah we are obligated to heed the king's command." In a play on words, Rabbi Glasner declares that Jews are obligated to pay the burden of *damim*." *Damim*, he notes, is a homonym having a double meaning, namely, "money" and "blood." Thus the word implies both a financial tax and a "blood" tax. Rabbi Glasner concludes that, although it is unlikely that soldiers will be able to avoid infraction of dietary and Sabbath regulations, "This mitzvah of observing the decree of the king supersedes all."[36]

The position of Rabbis Hirsch and Glasner is the exception to the rule. In contrast, Rabbi Ze'ev Wolf Leiter, *She'elot u-Teshuvot Bet David*, vol. I, no. 71, is much closer to the halakhic consensus in writing negatively with regard to all forms of army service. Rabbi Leiter questions the propriety of a Jew fighting a fellow Jew in opposing enemy forces and is explicit and forthright in ruling that voluntary army service on the part of an individual who has not been conscripted or compelled to enlist[37] is an unequivocally forbidden

---

33 Ibid., 462.
34 The unquestioning patriotism of Rabbi Hirsch is subjected to a pointed critique in Rabbi Howard I. Levine, "Enduring and Transitory Elements in the Philosophy of Samson Raphael Hirsch," *Tradition* 5, no. 2 (Spring 1963), 290–293. Cf. the response of Rabbi Shlomoh Eliezer Danziger, "Clarification of R. Hirsch's Concepts—A Rejoinder," *Tradition* 6, no. 2 (Spring/Summer 1964), 155–156.
35 *Horeb*, 462.
36 *Tel Talpiyot* (Moetzin, 1916), no. 104.
37 Surprisingly, *Imrei Esh, Yoreh De'ah*, no. 52, permits voluntary enlistment despite the danger to life involved. For a recent discussion of that issue see R. Yitzchak Zilberstein's article in *Kol ha-Torah*, no. 55 (Tishri 2003), 153–154.

form of self-endangerment. Giving voice to what in rabbinic writing is a rare approach,[38] Rabbi Leiter calls for resolving the dilemma by obviating the need for army service and advocates a proactive response in declaring: "The obligation devolves upon every God-fearing individual (*ḥaredi*) to labor on behalf of world peace in order that innocent blood not be spilled . . . and that warfare cease."

Jewish participation in World War II may well have been regarded in an entirely different light by rabbinic authorities. That war was waged by the Allies against a power that had targeted Jews for annihilation. Although there is scant published material devoted to the question, the military campaign to defeat the Nazis may readily be considered as an undertaking in the nature of *ezrat Yisra'el mi-yad tzar*—"rescue of Jews from the hand of the oppressor." Such a war is categorized by Rambam, *Mishneh Torah, Hilkhot Melakhim*, 5:1, as a *milḥemet mitzvah*, i.e., an obligatory war. In a previously unpublished private letter to his son,[39] the late Rabbi Yosef Eliyahu Henkin discusses volunteering for service in the United States Army in 1942. Rabbi Henkin writes that in the period prior to institution of the draft volunteerism was to be encouraged. With establishment of the draft, those who receive exemptions need not volunteer since others will be available to fight in their stead. In particular, educators who are exempt and contribute to the needs of society render vital assistance to the war effort. Rabbi Henkin does, however, recommend that those who are suited to do so should volunteer to serve as air-raid wardens. The letter lends itself to being read as a blanket endorsement of voluntary army service. In light of the consensus of rabbinic opinion that regards participation in wars of aggression to be impermissible, it may be the case that Rabbi Henkin's comments were limited to the context in which they were written, i.e., war against the Nazis who were recognized as posing a threat to Jewish survival.

2. Rulings Reported in Biographical Sources

A number of biographical studies of Eastern European authorities contain reports of emphatically negative oral pronouncements regarding army service but, understandably, those statements are not to be found in the formal

---

38 Another orthodox rabbinic figure of the time who wrote eloquently on pacifism was R. Aaron Saul Tamaret (1869–1931). See note 144 regarding an English translation of one of his sermons on non-violence.

39 This letter has recently been published by his grandson, Rabbi Yehudah H. Henkin, in his article, "Ha-Ga'on Rabbi Yosef Eliyahu Henkin Zatzal, Shloshim Shanah le-Motto," *Ha-Ma'ayan* 44, no. 1 (Tishri 2003), 75–76.

halakhic literary record. Rulings that are not committed to writing, even when transmitted by persons of unquestionable probity, lack the authoritativeness of published decisions. Oral reports often lack contextual clarity as well as nuances of meaning and expression, not to speak of their inherent unreliability because of possible misunderstanding on the part of the transmitter. Nevertheless, in this instance the oral reports must be given a high degree of credence both because they are congruent with the circumspection evident in the published material and because of the unanimity of opinion reflected in those reports.

Even the members of the liberal sector of the Jewish community did not view military service in Russia in the same positive light as did their counterparts in Western Europe for the simple reason that, in Russia, conscription was clearly neither a harbinger of civil emancipation nor a duty shared equally by all citizens; instead, it was a burden selectively imposed by the government. In the case of Jews, conscription was an integral element of a policy of Russification and forced apostasy. Until 1874, each nationality and ethnic group within Russia was governed by its own set of military regulations. In 1827, shortly after Nicholas I ascended to the throne, obligatory military service was imposed upon Jews. Under the provisions of the new regulations, a specified number of Jews were to be drafted for a twenty-five year period. Conscription began at the age of eighteen but the regulations contained a provision allowing for the taking of youths from the ages of twelve to eighteen for preparatory training. The units in which youths under eighteen served were known as Cantonist battalions. Exemptions were available for some categories of individuals and substitutes might be employed, but only other Jews were acceptable as substitutes.

Sociologically, the worst aspect of the decree was the fact that administration of the draft was placed in the hands of the Jewish communities. Jews guilty of non-payment of communal taxes or of vagrancy, or their children, were often designated for military service by the community in order to meet its quota. Individuals drafted by the community in excess of the quota for a given year might be credited to the following year's quota. Pressured to fill the heavy quota, communities often hired kidnappers (*khappers*) whose ruthless methods, including seizing children under twelve, became legendary. As has been well documented, Tsar Nicholas was driven by a missionary zeal that strongly influenced the policies of his government; tales of forced conversion and torture abound. From 1827 through 1854 some 70,000 Jews were conscripted into the Russian army; of that number, approximately 50,000 were minors.[40]

---

40   See Stanislawski, *Tsar Nicholas*, 13–34 and Salo W. Baron, *The Russian Jew under Tsars and Soviets*, 2nd rev. ed. (New York: Macmillan, 1976), 9–32. For a discussion of Cantonists'

Rabbinic authorities bemoaned the conduct of the communal officials in implementing the decree and, in isolated instances, strove to forestall acts of injustice. They were, however, powerless to defy the system. The complicity of communal officials and Jewish kidnappers in the oppressive government policies led to an unprecedented breakdown of Jewish society.[41] As might be anticipated, given the fear of reprisal and an atmosphere of terror, there is a dearth of published material in rabbinic writings regarding the plight of the Cantonists.[42]

It is well known that R. Joseph Ber Soloveitchik, renowned as the author of *Bet ha-Levi*, was a vociferous opponent of the kidnappers who, with the complicity of communal officials, sought to satisfy the demands of the Russian authorities. In his fierce opposition to this abhorrent social evil, Rabbi Soloveitchik is reported to have advocated the total dismemberment of the official *kehillot*, or communal governing structures, throughout Russia so that the Russian government would find itself with no Jewish communal body capable of executing its decrees.[43]

---

memoirs and literary works devoted to the Cantonist theme see Adina Ofek, "Cantonists: Jewish Children as Soldiers in Tsar Nicholas's Army," *Modern Judaism* 13 (1993), 277–308.

41 See R. Baruch ha-Levi Epstein's description of the "era of the sin of the community," *Mekor Barukh*, vol. II, 962–969 and 999–1003, and vol. III, 1191–1192; cf. Stanislawski, *Tsar Nicholas*, 26–34. Cf. also Kahane, "Sherut ha-Tzava," 147.

42 Indicative of the wariness of rabbinic scholars to address these matters in print is material on the Cantonists that has only now been published. In a recent article, "'Gezeirah Hi Mi-Lefanai': Derashot be-Inyan ha-Kantonistim," *Yeshurun* 12 (Nisan 2003), 695–726, Rabbi Yisrael Meir Mendelowitz incorporates the text of a number of discourses devoted to the Cantonists as they appear in an unpublished manuscript of Rabbi David of Novardok (1769–1836), author of the celebrated rabbinic work, *Galya Massekhet*. In *Galya Massekhet*, posthumously published (Vilna, 1844) by the author's son-in-law and grandson, portions of these discourses appear but with the glaring omission of explicit references to the Cantonist decree. Thus, for example, in one discourse that is published in *Galya Massekhet*, R. David of Novardok mentions a prayer assembly called in response to the troubles that had beset the community "which cannot be recorded in writing" (*Galya Massekhet*, 13a). The identical prayer assembly is described in the newly published manuscript as having been called "in order to stir the populace because of the occurrence of the decree and edict" (Mendelowitz, "'Gezeirah Hi Mi-Lefanai,'" 717). In particular, in the discourse delivered on the *Rosh ha-Shanah* immediately following the conscription edict of August 26, 1827, Rabbi David of Novardok reflects the somber and anguished mood of a stricken community of whom he writes that it is "difficult for us to recite on these holidays the [blessing] *she-heḥeyanu*" (726) and whose feelings he can best depict (718) in the words of Ezekiel 21:12, "And it shall be when they say unto you: 'Wherefore do you sigh,' that you shall answer: 'Because of tidings that are coming, and every heart shall melt and all hands shall be feeble and every spirit shall grow faint and all knees shall be weak as water. Behold it is come and shall happen. ...'" Rabbis could express such sentiments in the privacy of their congregations but, at that time, were loath to disclose them to alien eyes that might alight upon a published work.

43 Aharon Soraski, *Marbitzei Torah u-Mussar*, vol. I (Brooklyn, NY: Sentry Press, 1977), 80.

Since he did not succeed in implementing this radical solution, Rabbi Soloveitchik undertook the task of providing refuge and securing exemptions in individual cases. In particular, he was moved by the plight of the poor who bore the brunt of the edict. On one occasion, while Rabbi Soloveitchik was yet rabbi of Slutsk, he is said to have requested the local commandant to draft only youngsters who were members of wealthy families. He later explained to the distressed and angry lay leaders of Slutsk that justice demanded such a policy. The rich, Rabbi Soloveitchik pointed out, invariably succeeded in obtaining exemptions for their children by one means or another, whereas the poor were helpless and forced to endure army service with attendant exposure to persecution and often enforced baptism.[44]

The accuracy of Rabbi Soloveitchik's assessment of the situation is dramatically illustrated in the words of a popular folksong of the time:

> Rich Mr. Rockover has seven sons,
> Not a one a uniform dons;
> But poor widow Leah has an only child,
> And they hunt him down as if he were wild ...
> But the children of the idle rich,
> Must carry on without a hitch.[45]

On the basis of oral reports of his disciple, R. Naphtali Amsterdam, biographers of R. Israel Salanter, founder of the *mussar* movement, detail Rabbi Salanter's fruitless efforts to persuade government officials to abolish the harsh decree. They recount how Rabbi Salanter rescued an orphan from his abductors and the manner in which he publicly castigated those in Salant and Kovno who turned a deaf ear to the pleas of indigent women whose sons were among the victims. The day that the decree was finally rescinded Rabbi Salanter proclaimed a day of thanksgiving and was incensed at those of his disciples who

---

44 For a description of various other incidents where Rabbi Soloveitchik intervened in such matters, see ibid., 80–81.

45 Cited in translation in Baron, *Under Tsars*, 30–31; for a slightly different Yiddish version see Epstein, *Mekor Barukh*, vol. II, 964. See also ibid., 965–967 and 967 n. 2, for the exploits of R. Eliyahu Shik and for a description of efforts of other rabbinic figures to oppose the tyranny of the communal officials who surrendered children to army authorities. Regarding R. Eliyahu Shik cf. Stanislawski, *Tsar Nicholas*, 129 and the popularized account of Larry Domnitch, *The Cantonists: The Jewish Children's Army of the Tsar* (Jerusalem: Devora Publishing, 2003), 55–56.

did not on that occasion pronounce the full blessing "*ha-tov ve-ha-metiv*" with the inclusion of the Divine Name.[46]

The hasidic leader Rabbi Menachem Mendel Schneerson, known as *Tzemaḥ Tzedek*, sought to organize communal strategies to thwart the kidnappers. There is evidence that *Tzemaḥ Tzedek* asserted that the *khappers* were morally and halakhically culpable for violation of the biblical admonition, "And he that steals a man and sells him, or if he be found in his hand, he shall surely be put to death" (Exodus 21:16) and hence, in the struggle against them, even extreme measures might be countenanced.[47]

It is quite apparent that in Poland and Russia, long after mitigation of earlier harsh decrees, avoidance of army service continued to be advocated by rabbinic figures. It is common knowledge that R. Hayyim Soloveitchik of Brisk rarely issued halakhic rulings himself, preferring instead to submit the questions that were referred to him to the *dayyanim* of Brisk or other authorities. However, with regard to questions that involved possible danger of loss of life, R. Hayyim customarily departed from that practice and did not hesitate personally to issue rulings in such matters. Those rulings were invariably lenient in nature. R. Hayyim was wont to say that it was his policy to be *maḥmir* (stringent) in matters involving preservation of life, that is, his apparent leniencies in permitting matters that might otherwise be regarded as forbidden were not at all reflective of a posture of leniency but of a policy of stringency with regard to preservation of life. For example, he was lenient with regard to questions of fasting on *Yom Kippur* because of his conviction that it is necessary to be stringent in avoiding even remote danger to life.[48]

Army service and its attendant perils was viewed by R. Hayyim with great trepidation. It is related that on one occasion an individual approached R. Hayyim on a Friday with the following dilemma: His son who was

---

46 See Dov Katz, *Tenu'at ha-Mussar*, vol. I (Tel Aviv: Avraham Zioni, 1958), 204–206.

47 See Mendelowitz, "'Gezeirah Hi Mi-Lefanai,'" 443 n. 18. Cf. Domnitch, *The Cantonists*, 57–60. The hasidic leaders, R. Yitzchak of Worki and R. Israel of Rizhin prevailed upon Moses Montefiore to travel to Petersburg in order to intercede with Tsar Nicholas and urge mitigation of the harsh draft decree but Montefiore's intervention was unsuccessful. See Aaron Marcus, *Ha-Ḥasidut*, trans. into Hebrew from German by M. Schonfeld (Tel Aviv: Netzah, 1954), 213–214. For the application of the conscription decree in the areas of Poland under Russian rule and Polish Jews' fruitless efforts to mitigate provisions of the law, see also Jacob Shatzky, *Die Geshikhte fun Yidn in Varshe* (New York: Yiddish Scientific Institute [YIVO], 1948), vol. II, 74–81.

48 R. Shlomoh Yosef Zevin, *Ishim ve-Shittot* (Tel Aviv: Avraham Zioni, 1958), 63–64 and Soraski, *Marbitzei Torah u-Mussar*, vol. I, 112.

undergoing medical treatment in a nearby town was scheduled to appear before the draft board the next day for a medical examination to determine his fitness for army duty. The father questioned whether he might desecrate the Sabbath and travel to the neighboring city in an attempt to secure an exemption for his son. R. Hayyim permitted the man to travel on the Sabbath and explained his reasoning as follows: If the young man were to be taken to the army and his service were to extend over a period of years it was probable that, in the course of time, war would break out and he might be sent to the front and killed. Even a "double doubt" (*sfek sfeika*) of danger to life warranted suspension of Sabbath regulations.[49]

A similar ruling of R. Hayyim Soloveitchik, as attested to by R. Hayyim Ozer Grodzinski, is recorded by R. Baruch Ber Leibowitz.[50] When asked whether he might accept a position in an office that would involve desecration of the Sabbath in order to obtain an exemption from army service, R. Hayyim ruled permissively. However, in a situation in which an individual was able to secure an exemption only by attending a *gymnasium*, R. Hayyim ruled restrictively, declaring that, in his opinion, the latter case involved the grave transgression of the study of heretical works and hence could not be condoned even for the purpose of avoidance of danger.

Another report regarding R. Hayyim Soloveitchik's attitude toward some of the complex problems posed by army deferments is recorded in two disparate versions. During World War I, the Russian authorities granted rabbinical exemptions. Consequently, many synagogues provided letters of appointment to young men eligible for the draft. R. Hayyim was opposed to the granting of spurious letters of appointment indiscriminately lest the fraudulent nature of these appointments be discovered and the government revoke all rabbinical exemptions, thereby endangering the lives of those who actually occupied rabbinical posts. Despite the fact that his own son Ze'ev and his son-in-law, R. Hirsch Glicksman, were of draft age, R. Hayyim refused to allow them to accept the offer of several congregations in Minsk, where they at the time resided, to "appoint" them as rabbis.[51]

---

49 Zevin, *Ishim*, 65 and Soraski, *Marbitzei Torah u-Mussar*, vol. 1, 112. For a discussion of how that ruling involves an expansion of the *holeh le-fanenu* ("a patient before us") principle necessary to justify suspending biblical strictures, see R. J. David Bleich, *Bioethical Dilemmas: A Jewish Perspective* (Hoboken: Ktav Publishing House, 1998), 154–156. Cf., however, *Hazon Ish, Oholot* 22:32 and *Yoreh De'ah* 208:7.

50 *Birkat Shmu'el*, vol. I (New York, 1947), *Kiddushin* 27:6, 41.

51 Zevin, *Ishim*, 73–74, as related to him by R. Iser Zalman Meltzer.

According to another, probably more reliable, version of the narrative, R. Hayyim's motivation in refusing the letters of appointment reflected an entirely different consideration. R. Hayyim harbored a deep and abiding distrust of Czarist officialdom. He was convinced that any official record would eventually be used by the authorities to compromise the interests of persons whose names appeared in such records. He feared that recording the names and addresses of potential conscripts in conjunction with issuance of exemptions would result in that information being entered in an official file that in all likelihood would later be used to their detriment. In dealing with Czarist authorities, R. Hayyim believed that the prudent course of action was to avoid formal documentation in any guise whatsoever. The soundest protection was to remain "invisible."[52]

The extent to which army service was dreaded is also reflected in accounts of the Novardok yeshiva. In accordance with the policy espoused by Rabbi Joseph Yozel Hurwitz, the *Alter* of Novardok, students at the Novardok yeshiva disregarded all government induction orders and simply failed to report to the recruitment stations. For a period of time during World War I, the tactic succeeded and most of the students avoided detection. In 1919 the young R. Ya'akov Yisrael Kanievski, later renowned as the *Steipler*, was appointed *mashgiah* in a branch of the Novardok yeshiva established in Rogachov. There, agents of the Yevsektsia (Jewish section of the Soviet Communist party) arrested Rabbi Kanievski, and he was inducted into the

---

52 Ibid., 74 n., as related to Rabbi Zevin "by a reliable source." Rabbi Zevin suggests that R. Hayyim's attitude may have been formed by his personal experience in the Volozhin Yeshiva. So long as the Yeshiva did not come to the attention of the authorities, its operation was unimpeded. Once the Yeshiva was formally recognized by government bureaus, harassment and attempts at regulation began. The lesson to be learned was that safety was to be found in obscurity.

R. Hayyim's aversion to army service was shared by other members of his family. His grandson, the late Rabbi Joseph B. Soloveitchik of Boston and New York, was not eager to serve in the army. In 1924 he enrolled in the Free Polish University in Warsaw and in 1926 left for Berlin to continue his studies in the philosophy department of the University of Berlin. A factor influencing his decision to leave for Berlin was the possibility of being drafted into the Polish army. See Aaron Rakefet-Rothkoff, *The Rav: The World of Rabbi Joseph B. Soloveitchik* (Hoboken, NJ: Ktav Publishing House, 1999), vol. I, 26 and 68 n. 11, and Bertram Leff, "Letter to the Editor," *Torah u-Madda Journal* IX (2000), 268–269. Another grandson, the late Rabbi Moshe Soloveitchik of Switzerland (together with the late Rabbi Aaron Leib Steinman, formerly *Rosh Yeshiva* of Yeshiva Ga'on Ya'akov in Bnei Brak), fled Poland in 1937 after receiving draft notices from the Polish army and thus survived the war. See Moshe Musman, "A Reiner Mentsch, A Reiner Torah: Ha-Rav Moshe Soloveitchik zt'l," *Yated Ne'eman*, May 3, 1996, 19.

Red Army and stationed at a military camp in Moscow. A considerable sum of money was raised but efforts to secure his release by means of bribery failed.[53]

A similar aversion to military service prevailed among hasidic leaders as well. The counsel and assistance of R. Yehudah Leib Alter of Gur, better known as the author of *Sefat Emet*, and R. Yerachmiel Yisrael Yitzchak Danziger, *Rebbe* of Alexander, in avoidance of the draft became legendary. Reports of their subversion of draft regulations reached the ears of government officials whose wrath was aroused, as might have been anticipated. In an endeavor to put an end to these activities and probably to punish the rabbinic figures involved, they contrived a stratagem designed to trick the rabbis into revealing their antagonism to the draft. Agents were sent who pretended to seek advice and aid in evading military duty. The rabbinic figures in question are reported to have astutely recognized that those agents were not *bona fide* supplicants and avoided the trap that had been set for them.[54]

It is related of Rabbi Kalonymus Kalman Shapira of Piaseczno (known later as the *Rebbe* of the Warsaw Ghetto) that he exerted great effort to obtain army exemptions for his followers. He would not hesitate to expend large sums of money in bribing draft authorities in order to secure a reprieve for a conscript. Failing that, he would employ all manner of other tactics, including the use of amulets or performance of particular mystical acts, in order to spare his disciples the fate of army duty.[55]

3. Ritual Observance

For the observant, as noted, the difficulties involved in fulfilling religious obligations and observing dietary proscriptions were most worrisome aspects of army

---

53 M. Sofer, *Ḥomat Esh* (Israel, 1985), vol. I, 114–115 and 126–130.

54 A number of incidents are recorded by the popular historian Abraham I. Bromberg in his *Admorei Aleksander* (Jerusalem: Ha-Machon le-Hasidut, 1954), 93–94 and *Ha-Admor R. Yehudah Leib Alter mi-Gur, Ba'al "Sefat Emet"* (Jerusalem: Ha-Makhon le-Hasidut, 1956), 114–117. Cf. Yisroel Friedman, *The Rebbes of Chortkov* (Brooklyn: Mesorah Publications, 2003), 221–222, for a similar unsuccessful attempt on the part of the authorities to apprehend R. Yisrael Friedman, the *Rebbe* of Chortkov, in the act of advising his followers to evade conscription.

55 Aharon Soraski, "Foreword: Kalonymus Kalman Shapira, Rebbe of the Warsaw Ghetto," in R. Kalonymus Kalman Shapira, *A Student's Obligation: Advice from the Rebbe of the Warsaw Ghetto*, trans. by Micha Odenheimer (Northvale, NJ: Jason Aronson, 1991), xxv and xxxiii–xxxiv. On the use of amulets and other mystical practices for avoidance of conscription cf. note 62 and accompanying text. See also Epstein, *Mekor Barukh*, vol. II, 1061 n. 1.

service. Away from the battlefield such problems were much easier to resolve. The very first Jewish soldiers in the Western Hemisphere concerning whom a contemporaneous record is extant were Jews who served as mercenaries in the Dutch expeditionary force that arrived in Brazil in 1630. For the privilege of exemption from guard duty on the Sabbath the Jews who settled in Dutch Brazil and served in the local militia were willing to pay a fee but, nonetheless, on several occasions, the exemption was not honored.[56] In North America the environment was more tolerant. Thus, when Hart Jacobs petitioned the authorities in Philadelphia in January 1776 to be exempt "from doing military duty on the city watch on Friday nights which is part of his Sabbath," the request was granted provided that he perform "his full tour of duty on other nights."[57]

In Western Europe, when recruitment of Jews for military service began in earnest, reports from community after community in France, Austria, and Italy provide tangible evidence that ritual observance was a grave issue. In France the problem of Sabbath observance was a crucial factor in determining the reluctance on the part of Jews to serve in the army. During the period of 1790–93, the petitions of Jews from several communities for Sabbath exemptions were rejected and ultimately all Jews were forced to perform military duties on the Sabbath. Municipal authorities frequently made arrangements for provision of kosher food to Jewish soldiers but that practice was curtailed during the Reign of Terror.[58] Service in the army aroused concern among those who wore beards and sidelocks which then were popular targets of ridicule and anti-Semitic acts.[59]

---

56 Wiznitzer, "Jewish Soldiers in Dutch Brazil," *PAJHS* 46, no. 1 (1956), 40–50.

57 Arthur Hertzberg, *The Jews in America: Four Centuries of an Uneasy Encounter: A History* (New York: Simon and Schuster, 1989), 52

58 Zosa Szajkowski, *Jews in the French Revolutions of 1789, 1830 and 1848* (New York: Ktav Publishing House, 1970), 557–558, 786 and 794.

59 Ibid., 792. In some instances Jews were forced to have their beards and sidelocks publicly cut off, and they also were forced to pay the barbers for this service. A surprising exception is the case of the head of the yeshiva in Metz, Rabbi Aaron Worms, who reportedly voluntarily shaved off his beard and enlisted in the National Guard, and, upon being given a lance, proclaimed in Hebrew, "This is the day that we awaited" (ibid., 792). Rabbi Aaron Worms, the author of novellae entitled *Me'orei Or*, later, in 1815, became Chief Rabbi of Metz.

It is noteworthy that during the Polish uprising of 1831, at a time when several hundred Jews bore arms in the national army, there were several Jewish units comprised of observant individuals in the Warsaw militia who received specific dispensation not to cut their beards and sidelocks. See N. M. Gelber, "Yehudim bi-Tzva Polin," in *Ḥayyalim Yehudim be-Tzava'ot Eropah*, ed. Yehudah Slutzky and Mordecai Kaplan (Israel: Ma'arkhot, 1967), 94–95, and Shatzky, *Geshikhte*, I, 322–323.

Although a number of Jewish communal leaders in Alsace-Lorraine encouraged army service as proof of patriotic fervor, among ordinary Alsatian Jews who were traditional in observance, a lingering aversion to military service prevailed. In the Judeo-Alsatian dialect the term *reik* (empty or devoid of value) was used as a derogatory cognomen for "soldier."[60] Draft avoidance was extremely difficult since, under the provisions of Napoleon's "Infamous Decree" of March 17, 1808, unlike other Frenchmen, Jews could not hire substitutes.[61] A mystical ceremony designed to evoke divine mercy in the form of drawing a high number in the lottery and thereby escaping service gained currency. At midnight, the young man of draft age would light a lamp with oil, make a pledge to charity, and utter a prayer for exemption from the draft invoking the sage Rabbi Meir Ba'al ha-Nes and the angels Michael, Gabriel, Uriel, and Raphael. Quite obviously, aspirations for equality and civil rights had not quenched the deeply rooted distrust and fear of military service harbored by the populace.[62]

With tears in his eyes, Rabbi Ezekiel Landau is reported to have addressed the first group of Jewish recruits conscripted in Prague in May 1789. Encouraging them to remain steadfast in their fealty to mitzvot, he suggested that they exchange tours of duty with Christian comrades so that the latter would be on duty on the Sabbath and the Jews, in turn, would perform their duty on Sunday. He also urged the Jewish conscripts to observe dietary regulations for as long as possible, that is, until malnutrition became life-threatening. He urged that, even in the event of sickness, they endeavor to subsist on tea for warm liquid nourishment unless it become absolutely necessary to partake of non-kosher soup.[63] However, at the same time, Rabbi Landau expressed his awareness that their comportment as soldiers would bring honor and respect to their people and that their actions would demonstrate to the monarch the sacrificial loyalty of his Jewish subjects.[64]

---

60 Paula E. Hyman, *The Emancipation of the Jews of Alsace: Acculturation and Tradition in the Nineteenth Century* (New Haven, CT: Yale University Press, 1991), 74 and 174 n. 29.

61 Hyman, ibid., 17, observes that, since many other departments were exempt from the decree, the burden of this provision fell heavily on the Jews of Alsace-Lorraine. Regarding the question of substitutes in the French army and Jewish agents active in recruiting and pressuring individuals to serve as substitutes, see Szajkowski, *French Revolutions*, 564–565.

62 Hyman, *The Emancipation of the Jews of Alsace*, 69–70 and 174 n. 26.

63 For the text of the address see Solomon Wind, *Rabbi Yehezkel Landau: Toldot Ḥayyav u-Pe'ulotav* (Jerusalem: Da'at Torah, 1961), appendix 3, 115–116.

64 Ibid., 116. Yekuti'el Aryeh Kamelhar, *Mofet ha-Dor: Toldot Rabbenu Yeḥezkel ha-Levi Landau Ba'al ha-Noda bi-Yehudah ve-ha-Tzlaḥ* (Pietrkov, 1934), p. 82, note 6, cites a communication

Subsequent to the conquest of Mantua by Napoleon's forces in February 1797, the walls of the ghetto were razed and the Jews of Mantua were granted civil rights. Rights entailed duties, and with the privileges they received the Jews became subject to civic obligations, including army service. Members of the community turned to R. Ishmael ha-Kohen of Modena with a query regarding performance of guard duty and bearing arms on the Sabbath. R. Ishmael, in *Zera Emet*, part 3, *Oraḥ Ḥayyim, Hilkhot Shabbat*, no. 32, responded permissively, noting that refusal might endanger Jewish lives and that the city had an *eruv*. From the details of the reply it is clearly evident that R. Ishmael condones violation of religious law only when absolutely necessary.[65]

In the heat of conflict, matters became far more complicated and it required a great measure of self-sacrifice to remain meticulous in religious observance. It is particularly moving to read accounts of the lengths to which some Jewish soldiers went in order to observe mitzvot under trying circumstances. Especially noteworthy are reports of the efforts of soldiers in what was commonly considered to be the godless United States to observe religious precepts even in battle situations. Private Isaac Gleitzman, who received the Cross of Honor for "conspicuous gallantry in the field" during the Civil War, remarked that he was "prouder of never having eaten any nonkosher food or 'trefa.'"[66] Similarly, according to the diarist Emma Mordecai, the Levy brothers, Ezekiel J., who attained the rank of captain in the Richmond Light Infantry Blues, and the younger twenty-one year old Isaac J., who was killed by an exploding shell in August 1864, "had observed their religion faithfully, ever since they have been in the army, never eating forbidden food."[67] A few months

---

regarding a letter from R. Shlomo Kluger of Brody, in which Rabbi Kluger delivers a report concerning Rabbi Landau's reaction to the conscription edict. According to this account, Rabbi Landau was told that the king had announced that the Jews would be accorded great honor in that they would henceforth be able to serve in the army. Of this honor Rabbi Landau is said to have remarked that it constituted the curse alluded to in Leviticus 27:44: "And yet for all that, when they be in the land of their enemies, I will not cast them away, neither will I abhor them to destroy them utterly and to break My covenant with them for I am the Lord their God." Rabbi Landau allegedly declared that, because in the army Jews will be susceptible to violating all the dietary laws, to give Jews the honor of military service and no longer to "abhor them" and "cast them away" will be "to destroy them utterly and to break My covenant with them."

65 The text of the question is included in Baruch Mevorach, *Napoleon u-Tekufato* (Jerusalem: Mossad Bialik, 1968), part 1, 37.

66 Robert N. Rosen, *The Jewish Confederates* (Columbia, SC: University of South Carolina Press, 2000), 173. His family still has in its possession his two mess kits—one for meat and one for milk. See ibid., 421 n. 39.

67 Myron Berman, *Richmond's Jewry, 1769–1976: Shabbat in Shockoe* (Charlottesville: University Press of Virginia, 1979), 175; Rosen, *Jewish Confederates*, 199. Knowledge of

before he died, Isaac wrote to his sister telling how the brothers had purchased sufficient *matzot* to last the Passover week and that "We are observing the festival in a truly orthodox style."[68]

Although responsible halakhic authorities certainly did not maintain that mere service in the army automatically entailed exemption from religious observances, there was a marked concern to find ways and means within the Halakhah to ease the hardships experienced by the conscripts. Thus, R. Israel Meir ha-Kohen, *Ḥafetz Ḥayyim*, in the manual he prepared for Jewish soldiers, *Maḥaneh Yisra'el* (first published in 1881),[69] states his avowed intention to ascertain whether "There may possibly be found, in accordance with the law, a remedy or expedient to make matters less burdensome for them [the soldiers] in any regard because, assuredly, we perceive individuals such as these as being subject to difficult circumstances."[70] Presenting a précis of Sabbath regulations and other laws, *Ḥafetz Ḥayyim* endeavors to explain to the unlearned how to conduct themselves under duress in a manner that would diminish the

---

the rudiments of Jewish dietary law was common among the non-Jewish populace as is evident from the following charming vignette: Major Alexander Hart of New Orleans, one of the highest ranking Jewish Confederate infantry officers, was seriously wounded in his thigh by grapeshot early in the war. The surgeon wished to amputate the leg but was restrained by the mistress of the house to which Hart had been taken after the battle. She implored the doctor to delay the amputation and permit her to try to nurse Hart back to health because, she argued, so young and handsome a man should not lose a leg. After the war Hart visited his benefactress annually. Once, when her daughter-in-law complained that there was no ham on the table, the elderly lady responded, "No, there shall be no ham on my table when my 'Jewish son' is here." See Herbert T. Ezekiel and Gaston Lichtenstein, *The History of the Jews of Richmond from 1769 to 1917* (Richmond, Virginia: Herbert T. Ezekiel, 1917), 157.

68   Rosen, *Jewish Confederates*, 200. See also ibid., 115, Edward Kursheedt's letter in which he communicates, "I have not been able to see the Chanucka lights this year." For further details regarding observance of Passover and the Day of Atonement and informal Sabbath services see Bertram W. Korn, *American Jewry and the Civil War* (Philadelphia: Jewish Publication Society, 1961), 88–94.

69   I am indebted to Rabbi Samuel N. Hoenig for drawing my attention to the fact that a slim English-language manual for Jewish soldiers was distributed in the United States during World War II. That work by Moses M. Yosher, based on *Ḥafetz Ḥayyim*'s *Maḥaneh Yisra'el*, is titled *Israel in the Ranks* (New York: Yeshiva Chofetz Chaim Publication, 1943).

70   R. Israel Meir ha-Kohen, *Maḥaneh Yisra'el* (New York: Shulsinger Bros., 1943), Introduction, 8. *Ḥafetz Ḥayyim*'s concern for Jewish soldiers expressed itself in other practical endeavors as well. An open letter, "Regarding Kosher Food for Soldiers," signed by him dated 5683 (1923), emphatically underscores the interdependence and mutual responsibility of each Jew for his fellow and calls on Jewish communities to establish kosher soup kitchens for the benefit of soldiers stationed in their environs. The letter is published in S. Greiniman, ed., *Ḥafetz Ḥayyim al ha-Torah* (New York: Shulsinger Bros., 1943), 237.

seriousness and minimize the number of infractions of Jewish law. Intricate halakhic complexities are unraveled by *Hafetz Hayyim* in uncomplicated language in this remarkable work, the pages of which are suffused with *ahavat Yisra'el*, love and compassionate empathy for fellow Jews.

Mahaneh Yisra'el is singularly important in its focus not only on matters of ritual but on ethical and moral issues as well. *Hafetz Hayyim* identifies those issues as constituting the most serious challenges associated with army service. It is noteworthy that *Hafetz Hayyim* strongly recommends early marriage for recruits both in order to enable them to fulfill the mitzvah of siring children and because he believed that marital bonds would strengthen a soldier's ability to withstand the lax morals common in an army milieu.[71] Above all, *Hafetz Hayyim* seeks to raise the recruits' spirits and to bolster their self-esteem. Cognizant of the supreme effort required in order to maintain an observant lifestyle in the army, Hafetz Hayyim adds words of encouragement:

> If he [the soldier] will become valiant ... and shall see to observe the Torah in all its details at that time (*in that which is not contrary to the laws of the government*), in the future these days will be the most cherished of all the days of his life. Not as they appear to the soldier [now] in his thoughts that these times are the lowliest of his days. He will be of God's holy ones on account of this and no man free [of military obligation] will be able to stand in his precincts. ... When a person withstands a trial he becomes most exalted in stature.[72]

THE POSTURE OF THE LIBERALS

1. Early Reform—Rendering Jews Suitable for Army Service

Israel Jacobson, commonly regarded as the founder of the Reform movement, was president of the Westphalian Consistory, a principal aim of which was to institute a coherent program of religious reform. It is of more than passing interest that the most controversial of the consistorial innovations was a matter relating to military service. The relationship between participation in the armed forces and religious reform merits analysis.

---

71 Greiniman, *Hafetz Hayyim al ha-Torah*, "Davar be-'Itto," 175–187.
72 Ibid., 19–20.

In the pre-Emancipation era, Jews did not regard themselves as potential participants in active warfare. In a sermon delivered in London during the Seven Years' War on the occasion of a national day of prayer ordered by the king (in 1757 or 1758), Rabbi Hirschel Levin (Hart Lyon), Rabbi of the Great Synagogue, declared that Jews could best serve their country through prayer rather than through military service. Although, in England, the Militia Bill enacted in June 1757 subjected all citizens to military service with the quota to be filled by lottery, attempts to enforce the law were not successful. The question of whether Jews would also be subject to conscription had not yet been raised. In his remarks, Rabbi Levin discounted the possibility of benefit accruing to a country by virtue of Jewish participation in the armed forces:

> Now it is obvious that we are always obliged to pray for the welfare and prosperity of our kings.... For how else can we serve the king under whose protection we live? If we were to suggest that we serve him by fighting in his armies, "What are we, how significant is our power? ...
>
> How then indeed shall we serve our king? Our only strength is in our speech. The Sages expressed this in commenting upon Isaiah 41:14, *"Fear not, O worm Jacob*; just as the worm's power lies only in its mouth, so the power of Israel is only in its prayer."* (*Mekhilta, Be-Shallaḥ* on Exodus 14:10). It is incumbent upon us to pray for the welfare of the sovereign under whose protection we live, and for the welfare of the land in which we reside, for our welfare is bound up with theirs.[73]

In the years that followed, however, a different attitude soon came to the fore. In 1773 Rabbi Levin was appointed chief rabbi of Berlin, a post he occupied until the year 1800. It is doubtful that he would then have delivered

---

73 See "Sermon on Be-Ha'aloteka," in *Jewish Preaching 1200–1800: An Anthology*, ed. Marc Saperstein (New Haven, CT: Yale University Press, 1989), pp. 351–353, and the very informative notes, ibid., 351 nn. 3 and 4. Although he stressed the obligation of Jews to obey their kings and pray for their welfare, victory and prosperity, Rabbi Levin did not hesitate to comment upon the ethical and philosophical problems posed by military excursions. He stressed the fact that warfare engendered deplorable economic and political disruption. Nonetheless, he expressed assurance that rulers, in their wisdom, had their own compelling reasons for leading their nations into battle. Even though thousands might perish in a particular war, the monarch might feel compelled to engage in battle in order to forestall even greater bloodshed in the future. Thus, in addressing the morality of war, this traditional preacher expressed confidence in the royal leader, even while echoing the age-old messianic aspiration for universal peace. See ibid., 355 and 358.

a similar public address in Berlin because during the period of his incumbency it had become fashionable for Jews to argue that, as would-be citizens of the state, they should assume both the privileges and the duties of citizenship, including the honor of defending the fatherland by means of military service.

When, in 1655, Asser Levy petitioned for the right to serve in the militia in New Amsterdam and won this right in 1657 he did so simply because he had difficulty paying a tax in lieu of home guard service.[74] At a later time, in many European lands where Jews had lived for centuries in relative social isolation, this right was, however, welcomed as tangible evidence of political equality. In 1806, when Düsseldorf came under Napoleonic rule and the French civil code was adopted, Heinrich Heine's father gained a commission in the local civil guard. In all likelihood, he was the first Jew to hold such office in Germany since the early Middle Ages. The first day he wore the distinctive colorful uniform he celebrated the event by treating his fellow officers to a barrel of good wine.[75]

Following the promulgation of the Edict against the Civil Status of the Jews in Prussia (March 11, 1812), Prussian Jews were accorded the prerogatives and duties of citizenship, including the right to serve in the army.[76] In a burst of enthusiasm, hundreds of Jews volunteered for military service.[77]

---

74 Hertzberg, *Jews in America*, 28–29; Jacob Rader Marcus, *Early American Jewry*, vol. I (Philadelphia: Jewish Publication Society, 1951), 30–31.

75 Amos Elon, *The Pity of It All: A History of Jews in Germany, 1743–1933* (New York: Henry Holt & Co., 2002), 91; cf. Hans Brandenburg, ed., *Das Denkmal. Heinrich Heine: Denkwürdigkeiten, Briefe, Reisebilder, Aufsätze und Gedichte* (Munich: W. Langewiesche-Brandt, 1912), 62.

76 Ironically, even conservative elements in Prussia favored army service for Jews. If Jews would not participate in the struggle, they argued, Jews would benefit financially from the war while Christians were killing one another. See H. D. Schmidt, "The Terms of Emancipation, 1781–1812," *Leo Baeck Institute Year Book* 1 (1956), 33.

77 See Martin Phillippson, "Der Anteil der jüdischen Freiwilligen an dem Befreiungskriege 1813 und 1814," *Monatsschrift für Geschichte und Wissenschaft des Judentums (MGWJ)* 50, nos. 1–2 (1906), 1–21 and 220–247, for lists of Jewish volunteers who served in the military campaigns against Napoleon. Phillippson refers to the intriguing narrative of a Jewish woman, Esther Manuel (1785–1852), later known as Luise Grafemus, purportedly of Hanau, who fought against the Napoleonic forces in 1813–1814. According to her own account, confirmed in an official Russian military gazette, her husband had abandoned her and their two children and enlisted in the Russian army. In an attempt to trace him, she traveled to Berlin and then, disguised as a man, enlisted in an East Prussian cavalry regiment. Allegedly, she took part in several battles, advanced to the rank of *Wachmeister* (sergeant-major), was twice wounded and was awarded the Iron Cross by General Graf Bülow von Dennewitz. She succeeded in finding her husband in Montmartre, Paris on March 29, 1814 but he was killed by a cannonball the next day. Eventually, she returned to Hanau with great honor. See the journalistic accounts

Jews of that period believed that demonstration of willingness to sacrifice life and limb would serve as proof positive of Jewish devotion to the state and the worthiness of Jews for citizenship. As stated eloquently and unabashedly by Eduard Kley and Carl Siegfried Günsburg in the stirring call to arms they addressed to their coreligionists:

> O what a heavenly feeling to possess a fatherland! O what a rapturous idea to be able to call a spot, a place, a nook one's own upon this lovely earth. . . . There upon the battlefield of honor where all hearts are animated by one spirit, where all work for a single goal: for their fatherland; there where he is best who submits most loyally to his king—there also will the barriers of prejudice come tumbling down. Hand in hand with your fellow soldiers you will complete the great work; they will not deny you the name of brother, for you will have *earned* it.[78]

Gabriel Riesser, the passionate advocate of Emancipation, later voiced a similar sentiment: "There is only one baptism that can initiate one into a nationality, and that is the baptism of blood in the common struggle for a fatherland and for freedom."[79]

---

reported in Comité zur Abwehr antisemitischer Angriffe in Berlin and collected in *Die Juden als Soldaten* (Berlin: Sigfried Cronbach, 1896), 4.

In his account, written in 1906, Martin Phillippson, "Der Anteil der jüdischen Freiwilligen," *MGWJ* 50 (1906), 9, commented that whether Esther Manuel did indeed receive the Iron Cross as she claimed "remains unsubstantiated but is not improbable." In the course of time, because of the numerous discrepancies in her account, later writers have questioned the veracity of the facts as reported by her. There also appears to be no record of Esther Manuel's residence in Hanau at any time. Nonetheless, whether or not Esther Manuel actually served in the army she did succeed in receiving a veteran's pension. See Moritz Stern, *Aus der Zeit der deutschen Befreiungskriege, 1813–1815*, vol. II: *Luise Grafemus* (Berlin: Verlag Hausfreund, 1935), and Sabina Hermes, "Eine Tasse mit grosser Geschichte—oder: Kennen Sie Luise Grafemus?," *Der Bote aus dem Wehrgeschichtlichen Museum* 37 (1999), 29–33. See also the more recent accounts of Gerda Hoffer, *Zeit der Heldinnen: Lebensbilder aussergewöhnlicher jüdischer Frauen* (Munich: Deitscher Tachenbuch Verlag, 1999), 126–44, and Deborah Hertz, *How Jews became Germans: The History of Conversion and Assimilation in Berlin* (New Haven, CT: Yale University Press, 2007), 120–121. If, indeed, Luise Grafemus did not take part in the military campaigns, such recognition on the part of German authorities well known for their bureaucratic punctiliousness may perhaps be viewed as an even more astonishing exploit.

78 Kley and Günsburg, *Zuruf an die Jünglinge*, 5 and 10. Cited in Michael A. Meyer, *The Origins of the Modern Jew: Jewish Identity and European Culture in Germany, 1749–1824* (Detroit: Wayne University Press, 1979), 139.

79 Cited in "The Paulus-Riesser Debate," in *The Jew in the Modern World: A Documentary History*, ed. Paul R. Mendes-Flohr and Jehuda Reinharz (New York: Oxford University Press, 1980), 131.

Paradoxically, Jews who were eager to serve in the military faced a unique problem: they were ready and willing to fight alongside their non-Jewish compatriots but not all their fellow citizens were prepared to welcome them with open arms. They were ardent suitors fearful of rejection by their beloved both because of ethnic and religious prejudice and because of a perception that their religious practices would perforce interfere with proper discharge of military duties. It is for that latter reason a desire to demonstrate their suitability for military service became a motivating factor in the efforts of Jewish liberals to effect religious reforms.

The liberal view that, in order to be accepted as citizens, Jews must first adapt to the non-Jewish environment merely echoed statements openly expressed by non-Jewish writers. Jewish integration, it was believed, necessitated a reconceptualization of the Jewish religion. Judaism was portrayed as primitive and backward and it was widely assumed that Jews would have to undergo a process of *Verbesserung* or "improvement" in their religious observance and social mores if they were to participate fully in the social and intellectual life of non-Jews but that interaction and the granting of civil rights would hasten their transformation. In France in 1787, Abbé Grégoire had explicitly stated that Jews should be subject to the direction of rabbis in ritual matters and to the authority of government in civil matters but that they would assimilate and modify their religious observances when accepted into French society. "We have reason to believe," he declared, "that the Rabbis will relax upon that head when their decisions come to be authorized by necessity, and the Jew will give up his scruples when he is warranted by the infallibility of his doctors."[80] Campaigners for Jewish rights such as Wilhelm von Dohm affirmed the view that, with integration into the secular state, Jews "will then reform their religious laws and regulations according to the demands of society. They will go back to the freer and nobler ancient Mosaic Law, will explain and adapt it according to the changed times and conditions, and will find authorizations to do so alone in the Talmud."[81]

To these integrationists, persistence of virulent anti-Semitism in face of full participation in the burden of military service was not only unanticipated but unimaginable. The faulty nature of their thesis is perhaps best illustrated by an incident that occurred in 1896. When Jewish war veterans protested the continued discrimination against them, the Rumanian War Ministry responded bluntly, "The tax of blood bears no relation to the question of citizenship." Zalman Filip "Yehudim Bi-Tzva ha-Romani," in *Ḥayyalim Yehudim*, 169.

80 Abbé Henri Grégoire, "An Essay on the Physical, Moral and Political Reformation of the Jews" (London, 1791), 150, cited by Gil Graff, *Separation of Church and State: Dina de-Malkhuta Dina in Jewish Law, 1750–1848* (Tuscaloosa, AL: University of Alabama Press, 1985), 59.

81 Christian Wilhelm von Dohm, *Concerning the Amelioration of the Civil Status of the Jews*, trans. Helen Lederer (Cincinnati: Hebrew Union College–Jewish Institute of Religion, 1957), 80.

Less sympathetic was the attitude of Abbot F. M. Thiebault who had opposed Jewish emancipation when that proposal was brought before the National Assembly with the forthright argument that dietary restrictions and Sabbath laws would interfere with proper military service on the part of Jews.[82] Indeed, the charge that Jews were not suited to serve as soldiers was a common anti-Semitic slur. As expressed by Johann Michaelis, "For the power of a state does not depend on gold alone, but rather, in large part, on the strength of its soldiers. And the Jews will not contribute soldiers to the state as long as they do not change their religious views. ... As long as they observe the laws about kosher and non-kosher food it will be almost impossible to integrate them into our ranks."[83]

It is probable that it was a perceived need to negate these and similar allegations that motivated the Jewish Consistory in Westphalia to institute a controversial religious innovation. In a directive to the rabbinate dated January 17, 1810, the Consistory ruled that, contrary to accepted Ashkenazi practice, the rabbis were to declare rice and legumes to be permissible for consumption on Passover. The Consistory stated that Jewish soldiers had bemoaned the scarcity of permissible food available to them on Passover and the scant supply of *matzot* and, accordingly, requested dispensation to use peas, beans, lentils, rice and millet for their sustenance during the holiday. The Consistory noted that those foods are not leaven and that the ban on those foods dating from the post-talmudic era had been opposed by some authorities. Motivated by concern for the welfare of their brethren and by the desire that they be enabled to fulfill their civic duties with ease, the Consistory proceeded to rule that such foodstuffs were to be permitted not only to soldiers but "to every Israelite ... in good conscience."[84]

---

82 Szajkowski, *French Revolutions*, 794.

83 "Arguments Against Dohm," text included in Mendes-Flohr and Reinharz, *The Jew in The Modern World*, 38. In an ironic comment, Moses Mendelssohn responded to Michaelis that if "Christians have neglected the doctrines of their founders and have become conquerors, oppressors and slave-traders ... Jews too could be made fit for military service." See "Remarks Concerning Michaelis' Response to Dohm," in Mendes-Flohr and Reinharz, *The Jew in The Modern World*, 43. Later apologists countered these anti-Semitic arguments by predicting that with attainment of emancipation the Jewish personality itself would become transformed. In David Friedlander's opinion, if Jews achieved equality, they would become like everyone else, "physically stronger and more stupid." Cited in Meyer, *Origins*, 68.

84 The text of the directive may be found in *Sulamith* 3, no. 1 (1810), 15–17 as well as in B. H. Auerbach, *Geschichte der Israelitischen Gemeinde Halberstadt* (Halberstadt, 1866), 215–216. The Consistory had leaned heavily on the view of Ḥakham Tzevi in issuing the dispensation. The opinion of Ḥakham Tzevi is cited by his son R. Jacob Emden, *Mor u-Ketziʻah*,

In order to understand why, even when bitter controversy ensued, the Consistory persisted in advocating this innovation—as well as their decision to urge an innovation in respect to the laws of *ḥalitzah*,[85]—one must recognize the extreme sensitivity of the members of the Consistory to the issue of military service. In his initial formal audience with King Jerome on February 9, 1808, the President of the Consistory, Israel Jacobson, hastened to assure the ruler of the patriotism of his Jewish subjects and their eagerness to serve as soldiers. "It will be a pleasure for me," responded Jerome, "if, as good citizens, they furnish me with brave soldiers for my army, true servants of the state."[86] The very first royal edict of March 31, 1808 establishing the Westphalian Consistory directed the rabbis and teachers to stress that military service is a sacred duty and that one is absolved from any religious observances that are incompatible with such service.[87] Accordingly, in the consistorial order of March 15, 1809, enumerating rabbinic responsibilities, the rabbis were specifically so instructed ("*Der Rabbiner muss … den Militärdienst als eine heilige Pflicht darstellen*").[88] It is quite likely that a need to provide further assurance to the authorities in this regard prompted the Consistory to issue the dispensation regarding consumption of legumes on Passover.[89]

Oraḥ Ḥayyim 453 and *She'ilat Ya'avetz*, vol. II, no. 147. In a lengthy discussion of this topic in *Minḥat Kena'ot*, written in 1849, R. Tzevi Hirsch Chajes analyzes the view of *Ḥakham Tzevi* and explains why the conclusions drawn by the Consistory are not applicable. See *Kol Kitvei Maharatz Ḥayes*, vol. 2 (Jerusalem: Divrei Hakhamim, 1958), 1027–1030. For a discussion of a number of additional reasons advanced for the prohibition of legumes on Passover see *Encyclopedia Talmudit*, vol. XVII, 101–102.

85 See *Sulamith* 3, no. 1 (1810), 145–148. To avoid difficulties in cases in which the groom's brothers were of military age, the Consistory proposed that a conditional clause be incorporated in the marriage ceremony that would serve to circumvent the laws of *ḥalitzah* enabling the widow to remarry freely. The proposed conditional marriage was an innovation for which there was significant halakhic precedent, but such precedent was fraught with controversy. See A. H. Freimann, *Seder Kiddushin ve-Nisu'in: Me-Aḥarei Ḥatimat ha-Talmud ve-ad Yameinu* (Jerusalem: Mossad Harav Kook, 1964), 386–388, and Aaron Dov Alter Waranawski, *Ein Tn'ai be-Nisu'in* (Vilna, 1930).

86 Ludwig Horwitz, *Die Israeliten unter dem Königreich Westfalen* (Berlin: S. Calvary, 1900), 10–11.

87 *Sulamith* 2, no. 1 (1808), 6.

88 *Sulamith* 2, no. 2 (1809), 301.

89 The permissive ruling of the Consistory was defended by the junior rabbinical member of the Consistory, Menahem Mendel Steinhardt, in *Divrei Iggeret* (Rödelheim, 1812). See my "Menahem Mendel Steinhardt's *Divrei Iggeret*: Harbinger of Reform," in *Proceedings of the Tenth World Congress of Jewish Studies* (Jerusalem: World Union of Jewish Studies, 1990), 207–214, in which I argue that the "hidden reasons" to which Steinhandt alludes as motivation for the dispensation were in all likelihood the need to reassure the government with regard to the suitability of Jews for service in the military.

It is significant that, in instituting changes, the Westphalian Consistory chose to issue a broad ruling extending to all Jews rather than a narrower ruling providing only for dispensation on grounds of hardship to soldiers.[90] In contrast, in drafting its response to the sixth of Napoleon's questions concerning the duties of Jews in defense of their country, the Paris Sanhedrin formulated a position that went beyond the decisions of the Assembly of Notables and declared that soldiers are released from obligations and strictures that might interfere with military service. The Sanhedrin's mitigation of religious obligations was, in that case, expressly restricted to soldiers.[91] Moreover, the dispensation itself was circumscribed. The decisions of the Sanhedrin were recorded in both French and Hebrew texts. While the French text states that the exemption applies during the time of military service, *"pendant la durée de ce service,"* the Hebrew text limited the exemption to time of war and only to the extent that such religious obligations might interfere with performance of military duties. Thus, the Hebrew text provided for exemption "as long as they are obligated to stand on their post and to do their service in war" (*kol zman she-hem ḥayyavim la'amod al mishmartam ve-la'avod avodatam be-milḥamah*).[92]

The concern for halakhic integrity evidenced in the decisions of the Paris Sanhedrin was, to a great extent, a reflection of the influence of Rabbi David Sintzheim who, apparently, personally drafted many of the answers of the Assembly of Notables and who later served as President of the Sanhedrin.[93] At the Sanhedrin's final meeting, Rabbi Sintzheim forcefully asserted that the Sanhedrin's consent to an exemption from religious duties under certain

---

90 Graff, *Separation*, 100.

91 Schwarzfuchs, *Napoleon*, 93.

92 Graff, *Separation*, 93. The full Hebrew text is included in Mevorach, *Napoleon u-Tekufato*, part 2, 97. Cf. ibid., 115, the response to this question of the aged Rabbi Ishmael of Modena who formulated answers to the questions although he did not attend the proceedings in Paris. Rabbi Ishmael acknowledged the obligation of a Jew to serve in the army but added the caveat that the principle "the law of the land is the law" does not encompass ritual matters for which the king surely extends dispensation to inhabitants of the state. By contrast, Napoleon's own instructions dated February 1807, stated: "When some of their youth are requested to join the army, they will stop having Jewish interests and sentiments: they will acquire French interests and sentiments." See Schwarzfuchs, *Napoleon*, 100. With regard to the distinction between actual battle and peacetime maneuvers, it is instructive to note an address to Jewish draftees into the Austrian army, "Toldot ha-Zman," *Ha-Me'assef* (Berlin, 1788), 334 (cited by Graff, *Separation*, 162 n. 67), exhorting them "to serve the Lord through His commandments in the days of respite and to serve the Kaiser at the time of war and battle."

93 Regarding Rabbi Sintzheim's role and influence see Schwarzfuchs, *Napoleon*, 66–67, 202 n. 6, and 206 n. 9.

conditions applied only when the sovereign and the state were in danger. Rabbi Sintzheim was unequivocal in his concluding declaration that the laws of Israel are perfect and that "whoever betrays divine laws will soon trample underfoot human laws."[94] Rabbi Sintzheim's remarks validate the accolade accorded to him by Ḥatam Sofer:

> During his lifetime he was honored and was very close to the monarchy in Paris; he was asked a number of questions and knew how to answer his questioners … he did not allow others to rule over him, and was not seduced into following them, God forbid! After he had revealed one hand-breadth, he concealed two handbreadths. His integrity stood by him. …[95]

With the fall of Napoleon a wave of reaction swept over Western Europe. Throughout Prussia there was a move to pare down or entirely to rescind the civil rights that had been granted to the Jewish populace. Reactionaries such as Friedrich Rühs and Jacob Fries, who sought to reverse the emancipatory trend, asserted that Jews constituted a distinct nation rather than a mere religious denomination and that, as such, they were unassimilable in the body politic. In vain did Jewish apologists remonstrate that Judaism was but a religious confession, that Jews did not constitute a nation and that customs and folkways might be modified. As the national-Christian reaction reached a peak in the summer of 1819, anti-Jewish riots took place throughout Germany accompanied with cries of "Hep! Hep! Down with the Jews!"[96] During the ensuing years the pendulum swung back and forth. In the ongoing debate regarding whether Jews were fit to be citizens, the issue of military service often come to the fore. It is noteworthy that, as late as 1844, when Frederick William IV adopted reactionary policies and proposed recognition of Jews as a national minority, he sought to release them from the obligation of military service.[97]

---

94 Ibid., 95–96.

95 Translation cited ibid., 116. Graff, *Separation*, 176 n. 44, cites Simon Dubnow's condemnation of the Sanhedrin's response to the questions regarding civic patriotism in which "servility passed beyond all bounds." Ḥatam Sofer, with a perhaps more realistic appraisal of the harm that might have ensued to the Jewish nation had the Sanhedrin been more forthright, expressed his admiration of Rabbi Sintzheim's combination of cautiousness and halakhic integrity.

96 Meyer, *Origins*, 139–142.

97 Ismar Schorsch, "Ideology and History in the Age of Emancipation," in *The Structure of Jewish History and Other Essays by Heinrich Graetz*, trans. and ed. I. Schorsch (New York: Jewish Theological Seminary, 1975), 19–20.

2. Persistence of Anti-Semitism in the Army

The tragic fate of assimilationists, particularly in Germany, unfolded most dramatically in the army experience. Those individuals who wished to embrace their fatherland and render it service shoulder-to-shoulder with their fellow citizens were crudely rebuffed. The desire to demonstrate loyalty and to achieve political equality were motivating factors for Jews who welcomed army service as a privilege. Yet, the military itself all too often remained an arena in which anti-Semitism flourished. In country after country Jews served in the army but were accused of slacking and draft-dodging. Their defenders compiled list upon list detailing the Jewish contribution to military endeavors[98] and excelled in composing apologetic literature, but the stigma persisted.

Even in the comparatively tolerant United States, the canard that Jews did not pull their weight in the armed forces surfaced again and again. In the late eighteenth century, responding to aspersions cast on Jews, Haym Solomon insisted that Jews had served in the Revolutionary armies in numbers beyond their proportion to the total population.[99] Almost a century later, anti-Semitism, almost nonexistent in the United States, was aroused by the turmoil of war and is why Jews were singled out in Grant's Order No. 11. More serious than economic anti-Semitism was the charge, repeated frequently until the end of the 1800s, that Jews had not fought in the Civil War. That charge gained credibility because, in the North, a conscript could buy an exemption upon payment of three hundred dollars; in the South one needed simply to provide a substitute in order to avoid service. To counter the charge that Jews had been slackers the prominent Washington lobbyist Simon Wolf published a work entitled *The American Jew as Soldier, Patriot and Citizen* (1895) in which he listed the names of 8,000 Jewish men who had served in the Union and Confederate forces, a list that was far from comprehensive.[100]

---

98 Brief but intriguing accounts of Jewish soldiers in the armies of various European countries and a useful bibliography are included in the Slutzky and Kaplan's collection of essays *Ḥayyalim Yehudim be-Tzava'ot Eropah*. See *supra*, note 59.

99 Hertzberg, *Jews in America*, 136. In actuality (see ibid., 62), of the 2000 Jews in America at that time, almost one hundred have been identified as soldiers in the revolutionary armies. In Charleston, South Carolina, Captain Lushington's company was half Jewish and became known as the "Jew Company." See also ibid., 178.

100 Ibid., 132–136. See the extensive discussion of Grant's Order No. 11 and of "American Judaeophobia" in Korn, *American Jewry*, 121–188.

A telling example of how widespread the stereotypical image of the Jew as non-fighter had become is Mark Twain's spirited essay—part praise, part prejudice—"Concerning the Jews," published in *Harper's Monthly* 99 (September 1899). As Mark Twain himself

In the United States some Jews rose to high rank in the armed forces but religious bias was not totally absent. Uriah Phillips Levy, who ran away to sea at the age of ten and was commissioned a lieutenant of the Navy in 1817 at the age of twenty-five, was made a commodore in 1857. George Bancroft, who had been Secretary of the Navy in 1845–1846, testified that at the time he had refused to give Levy a command because of "a strong prejudice in the service against Captain Levy, which seemed to me, in a considerable part attributable to his being of the Jewish persuasion" and, as Secretary of the Navy, Bancroft stated, he had felt obliged to take into consideration "the need for harmonious cooperation which is essential to the highest effectiveness" of the armed forces.[101]

In France, as well, Jews attained positions of prominence in the army throughout the course of the nineteenth century. During the Third Republic, as many as twenty-three Jews rose to the rank of general.[102] Nonetheless, anti-Semitism was prevalent in the army as is best exemplified by the notorious case of Captain Alfred Dreyfus in which the superficial veneer of acceptance was rudely torn away to reveal a morass of bias and hostility simmering beneath the surface.

Prejudice against Jews in the army was even more blatant in Germany. False accusations and canards about Jewish cowardice prompted Ludwig Philippson, editor of *Die Allgemeine Zeitung des Judentums*, to collect and publish the names of all German Jews who had served on the front lines during the 1870 Franco-Prussian War.[103] Despite the fact that thousands of Jews had

---

predicted, that essay aroused a storm of protest and pleased almost no one. Jewish critics acknowledged Twain's respect for Jewish accomplishments but berated his many factual errors and were incensed because of the credence he lent to the common reproach that Jews are willing "to feed on a country but don't like to fight for it" ("Concerning the Jews," 534). Twain subsequently conceded that he had erred and, before including the essay in *The Man That Corrupted Hadleyburg and Other Stories and Essays* (New York and London: Harper & Brothers, 1900), added a postscript to his essay titled "The Jew as Soldier," in which he admitted his and others' ignorance of the facts, attempted to correct the record of the Jew's "gallant soldiership in the field" and concluded that "the Jew's patriotism was not merely level with the Christian's but overpassed it" (*The Man That Corrupted Hadleyburg*, 282).

101 Hertzberg, *Jews in America*, 100. It is noteworthy that Levy remained loyal to his religious heritage. The Spanish-Portuguese congregation, of which he was a member, thanked him for transporting to New York on his ship a wagonload of earth from the Holy Land for use in burials.

102 "Military Service," *Encyclopedia Judaica*, vol. XI, 1561.

103 *Die Juden als Soldaten*, Introduction, i.

participated and hundreds had suffered casualties, the slurs persisted. Even subsequent to promulgation of the new emancipation law of 1871 effective for the entire Reich, German Jews continued to be excluded from the officer corps. In Prussia, they were refused commissions even in the reserves. This was a serious disadvantage in German society in which military status played an all-important role and in which an army commission was a prerequisite for a serious career in government. None of the close to 30,000 Jews who had served in the army since 1880 and who had appropriate educational qualifications was promoted to the rank of officer although several hundred Jews who had converted were given commissions.[104] "For every German Jew there is a painful moment that he remembers his entire life: the moment he is first made fully conscious that he was born a second-class citizen. No ability and no achievement can free him from this."[105] These are the words of Walther Rathenau, later to become a German foreign minister, who was humiliated by his inability to receive an officer's commission and by the fact that upon his discharge from his mandatory year of military service he had only attained the rank of a mere lance corporal.

The situation in the German military did not substantially improve with the passage of time. Emblematic of the status of the Jews at the time is the case of Max Rothmann, a Berlin neurologist whose father and grandfather had been decorated in the Wars of 1815 and 1870, respectively, and whose elder son fell on the Western Front in 1914. Nonetheless, Rothmann's younger son's application to the Prussian cadet academy was rejected because, as the deputy war minister wrote, "Since your son adheres to the Jewish faith, the War Ministry regrets that it must reject your application."[106]

In World War I, 12,000 German Jewish soldiers died on the battlefield. Yet, the extent to which prejudice persisted is most strikingly apparent in the infamous *Judenzählung* (census of the Jews) ordered by War Minister Wild von Hohenborn in 1916 to determine the number of Jews who served on the front-lines as opposed to those who served in the rearguard. The census disproved the calumnies and demonstrated that eighty percent had served on the frontlines.

---

104 Elon, *Pity of It All*, 219, 223 and 248.
105 Walther Rathenau, *Zur Kritik der Zeit* (Berlin: S. Fischer, 1912), 189.
106 Elon, *Pity of It All*, 337. See the detailed account in R. Vogel, *Ein Stück von Uns: Deutsche Juden in deutschen Armeen, 1813–1976. Eine Dokumentation* (Mainz: v. Hase & Koehler, 1977), 65–70. The officer corps' policy appeared to change because of the exigencies of war in 1914 but by 1916 there was a recrudescence of anti-Semitism. See Ruth Pierson, "Embattled Veterans: The Reichsbund Jüdischer Frontsoldaten," *Leo Baeck Institute Year Book* 19 (1974), 141 n. 9.

Not only did the War Ministry fail to make the results public, but the findings were also distorted by anti-Semitic agitators.[107]

Anti-Semitic propaganda dating from the early 1900s in Germany focused upon alleged Jewish ineptitude and unsuitability for military service. Popular postcards abounded presenting caricatures of Jews exhibiting exaggerated stereotypical Jewish features, hooked noses and dark curly hair, and portrayed those individuals being turned away at recruitment centers because of their pronounced physical weakness, extreme shortness of stature, etc. A typically nasty cartoon postcard depicts *"Der kleine Cohn,"* a tiny naked Jewish specimen measuring barely half the minimum height required for induction. The purpose of those hateful caricatures was to defame Jews and to foster a climate of opinion in which a military career, and perhaps also the subsequent possibility of high government office, would remain off bounds to Jews.[108]

3. Jew Against Jew

Challenged with regard to their preparedness to defend their country, the Assembly of Notables, in reply to Napoleon's sixth question, intimated that Judaism created no national bond and was but a religious confession. The love of French Jews for their fatherland is so powerful, they stated, that a French Jew feels himself a foreigner even among English Jews: "To such a pitch is this sentiment carried among them that ... French Jews have been seen fighting desperately against other Jews, the subjects of countries then at war with France"—and, impliedly, this gave rise to no special problem.[109]

This statement in itself is highly significant. In the first place, it reflects egregious servility. In offering unnecessary and gratuitous assurance of their

---

107 Vogel, *Ein Stück von Uns*, 148 ff; Pierson, "Embattled Veterans," 142–143. The calumny of seeking rearguard service dogged Jewish soldiers everywhere. Instances of similar allegations in the United States Army were much rarer but did occur. A chronicle of Richmond's Jewish soldiers during the Civil War notes the following incident with regard to Marx Mitteldorfer of the First Virginia Cavalry: During one battle a member of the company jeered that Jewish soldiers were wont to fire and then fall back. Mitteldorfer challenged the accuser to follow him and proceeded to ride so far to the front that the captain had to recall him lest he mistakenly be shot by his own comrades. Thereafter he was known by the sobriquet "The Fighting Jew." See Ezekiel and Lichtenstein, *Jews of Richmond*, 183.

108 Cristoph Glorius, "'Unbrauchbare Isidore, Manasse und Abrahams': Juden in deutschen Militärkarikaturen," in *Abgestempelt: judenfeindliche Postkarten auf der Grundlage der Sammlung Wolfgang Haney*, ed. Helmut Gold and Georg Heuberger (Frankfurt am Main: Umschau/Braus, 1999), 222–226.

109 M. Diogene Tama, *Transactions of the Parisian Sanhedrin*, trans. F. D. Kirwan (London, 1807, repr. Cincinnati: Hebrew Union College Press, 1956), 24.

allegiance, the delegates to the Assembly were quite willing to compromise Jewish self-respect. Secondly, and more importantly, their response represents a fundamental shift in Jewish self-identification and anticipates the philosophical stance of later assimilationists who renounced Jewish peoplehood, utterly denying the existence of the ethnic and national dimension of Judaism.

Perhaps even more so than any other statement of the Assembly, this assertion fails to reflect truthfully the sentiments of most Jews. For many a Jewish soldier the very thought of engaging in combat against a fellow Jew was unsettling. While the quite serious halakhic question was seldom raised in public, on occasion, ethical and emotional qualms were expressed at the prospect of Jews going to battle against their coreligionists.[110] In the United States during the Civil War, Jews faced the dilemma not only of fighting fellow Jews but of fighting fellow Jews of their own country and possibly even of their own immediate family. Thus, for example, John Proskauer served in the Union Army, but his son, Major Adolph Proskauer, joined the Confederate forces. During the Battle of the Wilderness in May, 1864, Major Proskauer was close enough to his father, who was in charge of the commissary of the opposing force, to ask him for food.[111] With Jews arrayed on both sides of the conflict, a number of both Orthodox and Reform spokesmen passionately affirmed allegiance to opposing forces. Isaac M. Wise chose the path of neutrality and silence motivated in part, he claimed, because beloved kinsmen were to be found in both camps.[112]

Some 200 Jews bore arms in the Greco-Turkish War of 1897. In the wake of the hostilities, Saul Tschernichowsky composed a poem, "*Beyn ha-Metzarim*," depicting two brothers, one fighting for the Turks, the other for the Greeks, who meet in the dead of night and shoot one another and only "In the light of the lightening shot did each one his brother recognize"—"*Le-or brak ha-yiriyah ish et ahiv hikkiru*." Whether or not there is a historical basis for the poem has not been ascertained but it is highly plausible that Tschernichowsky was moved to portray the drama of such a tragic confrontation by a story that reached Odessa during the war.[113] In any event, several years thereafter, in the Balkan Wars of

---

110 This reaction is more emotional than purely halakhic. There are numerous sources indicating that taking of the life of a non-Jew is encompassed within the prohibition against homicide. See *Ra'avan, Bava Kamma* 111b and *Kesef Mishneh, Hilkhot Rotzeah* 2:11. See also *Mekhilta, Mishpatim* 4:58. For a discussion of the severity of the transgression see *Meshekh Hokhmah, Parashat Mishpatim*, s.v. *ve-yitakhen*. Cf., however, *Taz, Yoreh De'ah* 158:1 as well as *Bet Me'ir, Even ha-Ezer* 17:2.

111 Berman, *Richmond's Jewry*, 175.

112 See Korn, *American Jewry*, 32–55 and James G. Heller, *Isaac M. Wise: His Life, Work and Thought* (New York: Union of American Hebrew Congregations, 1965), 335.

113 A. Moaisis, "Yehudim bi-Tzva Yavan," in *Hayyalim Yehudim*, 182.

1912–1913, Jews did face coreligionists in battle. There is a record of a meeting between King Constantine and Rabbi Jacob Meir, Chief Rabbi of Salonika, in the course of which the king praised the contributions of his Jewish soldiers and specifically pointed to the fact that they had fought against fellow Jews in the enemy camp as compelling evidence of their genuine loyalty.[114]

During World War I patriotism bordering on chauvinism found expression in the writings of liberals on both sides of the conflict. One may contrast the remarks of Hermann Cohen in Germany regarding "Jews who can battle for our Fatherland, … the land of intellectual freedom and ethics"[115] with those of Theodore Reinach in France concerning French Jews who "risk health, youth, life in order to liberate a freedom-loving France."[116] The halakhic and ethical problems involved in fighting against coreligionists were suppressed by those nationalists. On the other hand, although Simon Dubnow found himself supporting the Russian war effort, he gave voice to his abiding sorrow over the prospect of Jews battling other Jews.[117]

The devastation caused by the First World War was incalculable. More soldiers were killed in World War I than in any previous war and countless civilians died from starvation and resultant disease. Millions continued to suffer from physical and psychological wounds. Exposure to massive casualties and overwhelming feelings of despair shattered the emotional wellbeing of soldiers who had fought in trenches and, for many, lasting mental illness was a legacy of the war.[118]

The veterans continued to be haunted by their experiences. One veteran expressed the melancholy reality:

> The older I get, the sadder I feel about the uselessness of it all, but in
> particular the deaths of my comrades. … I thought I had managed all

---

114 Ibid., 183.

115 Cited in Gunther W. Plaut, *The Growth of Reform Judaism* (New York: World Union for Progressive Judaism, 1965), 78.

116 Ibid., 80.

117 See Koppel S. Pinson, "Simon Dubnow: Historian and Political Philosopher," in Simon Dubnow, *Nationalism and History: Essays on Old and New Judaism*, ed. Koppel S. Pinson (Philadelphia: Jewish Publication Society, 1958), 24.

The phenomenon of Jews facing other Jews on the opposing side in the trench warfare of World War I was sufficiently common for the following apocryphal story to circulate: A puny Jewish soldier was successful in taking several enemy soldiers prisoner. When the occurrence repeated itself, his superior officer became suspicious. The soldier explained that Jewish practice requires a quorum for recitation of memorial prayers on the anniversary of the death of a loved one. He added that, when there was a lull in the fighting, he simply called out, "I have *yahrzeit*; I need a *minyan*" and forthwith a number of Jewish soldiers came over to his side.

118 Louis Breger, *Freud: Darkness in the Midst of Vision* (New York: John Wiley and Sons, 2000), 243 and 250–253.

right, kept the awful things out of my mind. But now I'm an old man and they come back out from where I hid them. Every night.[119]

Those who had killed others in battle were unable to shake the memory. Not atypical is the account of one shell-shocked soldier being treated with hypnosis who wept and made trigger movements with his right forefinger while at the same time crying out: "Do you see, do you see the enemy there? Has he a father and a mother? Has he a wife? I'll not kill him."[120] If those who had taken the lives of other soldiers were haunted by the recollection, how much more poignant and painful was the experience of the Jew who may inadvertently have slain a coreligionist.

One such episode is detailed in a recent film, *Shanghai Ghetto*, which depicts the experiences of German refugees in Shanghai. In one scene, a woman named Evelyn Rubin reminisces regarding her experiences in the ghetto and presents a vivid portrayal of her late father, Benno Popielarz. A World War I veteran who had been decorated for valor and suffered the remaining years of his life from the effects of a war wound, even when transported to Buchenwald, her father had simply been unable to believe that despite his loyalty and patriotism he would be subject to the anti-Jewish Nazi decrees. Pointing to a picture of her father in his uniform, Evelyn Rubin relates one terrible event that occurred during the war of which her father often spoke. One day, during face-to-face combat, he and the soldier opposite him raised their rifles and took aim simultaneously. Her father fell to the ground wounded but, at the same time, his opponent was hit as well. As the other soldier fell, her father distinctly heard him call out, "*Shema Yisra'el.*" The knowledge that he might have killed a fellow Jew left her father with a pain that could not be assuaged.[121]

---

119 Quoted in Richard A. Gabriel, *No More Heroes: Madness and Psychiatry in War* (New York: Hill and Wang, 1987), frontispiece.

120 Cited in Eric J. Leed, *No Man's Land: Combat and Identity in World War I* (Cambridge: Cambridge University Press, 1979), 107. For decades, Freud and many other psychoanalysts failed to appreciate the long-term effect of these adult traumas. See the discussion in Breger, *Freud*, 252–268. Breger portrays the manner in which actions and thoughts associated with armies and war permeated the consciousness of Europeans in the years before World War I. Interestingly, elsewhere (ibid., 192–193), Breger incisively comments upon the repeated occurrences of militaristic terminology in Freud's own writings regarding himself and his colleagues and questions the appropriateness of battle imagery in Freud's version of the history of the psychoanalytic movement.

121 In a personal communication (November 19, 2003), Evelyn Rubin informed me that the incident occurred at the Battle of Verdun. The story left a profound impression on her because her father spoke of it frequently when she was a young child and, after his death, her mother continued to retell the narrative and to speak wistfully of her husband's deep anguish and remorse at having shot a fellow Jew.

It was following World War I, at a time when some individuals began to confront the enormity of the atrocities of war, that Rabbi Ze'ev Wolf Leiter forthrightly addressed the emotion-laden topic of Jew fighting against Jew. Rabbi Leiter cites a narrative recorded by Josephus describing how Jews were coerced into doing battle against fellow Jews which, writes Josephus, is "against our religion." Rabbi Leiter also refers to Or Zaru'a, Avodah Zarah, chap. 1, no. 132, which addresses halakhic problems attendant upon fighting against enemies among whom Jews reside. Probably because he was writing subsequent to the conclusion of World War I, after hostilities had come to an end, Rabbi Leiter could permit himself to address a topic others had avoided and regarding which, as noted, he writes, "I have not seen this law clarified in the writings of rabbinic decisors."[122] Rabbi Leiter's responsum prefigures the changing attitude to warfare that was to be expressed widely in the coming decades.

4. Pacifism and Twentieth-Century Reform Writers

A pronounced shift in the attitude of exponents of Reform Judaism toward warfare and military service becomes apparent in the twentieth century.[123] That

I am indebted to Dr. Jonathan Helfand for drawing my attention to the description of a similar incident dating from the much earlier period of the Napoleonic wars. In a forceful and moving manner, the author of the account records the emotional reaction of a Jew confronting the agonizing possibility of shooting a coreligionist and remarks as well on the mystical resonance of the words "Shema Yisra'el." La Sentinelle Juive, réponse à la dix-septième lettre de la correspondance dite israélite de Tsarphati (Paris, 1839), authored by Alexandre Créhange, is a fifteen-page pamphlet responding to the reformist essays written by Olry Terquem (Lettres Tsarphatiques). In defending the use of Hebrew for prayer, Créhange tells the following:

… près du champ de bataille de Dresde, en 1813, j'ai eu l'indicible joie de sauver la vie à un soldat ennemi [italics in the original] qui dans sa détresse avait prononcé avec désespoir les mots magiques Chema Israël, dans l'impossibilité de secourir tous les malheureux qui s'offraient à ma vue, j'ai dû borner mon action à celui qui venait de s'adresser à mon cœur avec le langage [sic] irrésistible de ma religion; deux mots m'ont suffi pour conserver la vie à un frère, un fils à son père. Je défie tous nos réformateurs de me donner littéralement, l'équivalent de ces deux mots en aucune langue. (15)

122 She'elot u-Teshuvot Bet David, vol. I, no. 71. Although the responsum published in Bet David is undated, a handwritten earlier draft of the responsum in the possession of his son, Rabbi Abba Leiter, is dated 9 Tevet 5684 (December 17, 1923). I am indebted to Rabbi Abba Leiter for providing me with a copy of the handwritten responsum.
123 For a detailed discussion of social policies advocated by the Reform movement at this time, see Leonard J. Mervis, "The Social Justice Movement and the American Reform Rabbi,"

shift constituted nothing less than a one hundred and eighty degree reversal of policy from advocating military service as a sacred duty to endorsement of absolute pacifism.

During World War I, the Central Conference of American Rabbis (CCAR) overrode a passionate minority of its members in refusing to endorse the position that acceptance of the tenets of Judaism constitutes valid grounds for conscientious objection. The Conference stated that an individual who asserts that Jewish religious teaching is the basis for his claim to exemption from military service "does so only as an individual, inasmuch as historic Judaism emphasizes patriotism as a duty as well as the ideal of Peace."[124] At the time, several rabbis went on record as disagreeing with that proposition. One of these, Martin Zielonka, argued that while he himself was not a pacifist he believed that Jews were obliged to "protect the honest and sincere conscientious objector who places his objections upon a religious ground" and maintained that the biblical verse "What man is there that is fearful and faint-hearted; let him go and return unto his house, lest his brethren's heart faint as well as his heart" (Deuteronomy 20:8) should be interpreted as grounds for excusing conscientious objectors.[125]

In the wake of World War I, sentiment in America in general and among many Christian groups in particular became increasingly anti-war. A similar attitudinal progression was reflected in the gatherings of the Reform leadership. While a stance of absolute pacifism was not adopted, the proceedings of the Conference reflect unrelenting opposition to war. A 1924 CCAR resolution stated, "Because we love America ... for this reason we urge upon our fellow citizens ... that ... they adopt an uncompromising opposition to war. We believe that war is morally indefensible."[126] During that period the Conference established a Standing Committee on Peace which functioned from 1925 until 1942 when it was incorporated in the Commission on Justice and Peace.[127] In practical terms, the CCAR lent its support to a series of measures designed to lead to cessation of warfare and proclaimed: "We believe in the outlawry of war by the nations of the earth. We support all movements which conscientiously

---

part I: "The Central Conference of American Rabbis," *American Jewish Archives* 7 (1955), 171–230. On pacifism in the Reform movement, cf., also, Michael A. Meyer, *Response to Modernity: A History of the Reform Movement in Judaism* (New York and Oxford: Oxford University Press, 1988), 313.

124   *CCARY* 27 (1917), 174–75.
125   Ibid., 176.
126   *CCARY* 34 (1924), 91.
127   Ibid., 93 and Mervis, "Social Justice," 189.

and honestly strive to that end."[128] Accordingly, the Conference advocated America's participation in the Permanent Court of International Justice, endorsed Senator Borah's program to ban war and endorsed international conferences leading to disarmament.[129] Compulsory military training programs in schools and colleges were strongly condemned:

> We reaffirm our opposition to the militarization of our schools and colleges by compulsory military training. We advocate in all educational systems an increasing emphasis on the comity and partnership of nations and, rather than the extollation of military prowess, the glorification of the heroes who have made for peace and progress.[130]

In 1932, the prominent Reform spokesman Stephen Wise expressed "everlasting regret" for his pro-war stance during World War I and pledged "without reservation or equivocation" never to bless or support any war whatsoever again.[131] Another influential Reform ideologue, Abraham Cronbach, was an uncompromising pacifist[132] who crusaded for the total renunciation of warfare. An ever greater proportion of Reform clergy became convinced that religious imperatives mandated a policy of refusal to bear arms under all circumstances since "war is a denial of all for which religion stands."[133] In 1935, the issue of pacifism was placed squarely before the Conference. The Committee on International Peace asked the Conference to declare that "henceforth it stands opposed to all war and that it recommends to all Jews that, for the sake of conscience, and in the name of God, they refuse to participate in the bearing of arms."[134] After prolonged debate this recommendation was, however, tabled for further study. While espousing pacifism in general, a majority of Reform rabbis insisted on the right to self-defense in the event of invasion.[135] They continued to oppose compulsory military training and any educational policies designed to promote warfare. A majority now claimed that conscientious objection by Jews on religious grounds was valid.[136]

---

128 *CCARY* 38 (1928), 85.
129 Mervis, "Social Justice," 189–90.
130 *CCARY* 38 (1928), 86.
131 Cited in Mervis, "Social Justice," 189.
132 See Meyer, *Response*, 302 and Mervis, "Social Justice," 216. Maurice Eisendrath, also an outspoken pacifist, became executive director of the Union of American Hebrew Congregations in 1943. See Meyer, *Response*, 355.
133 *CCARY* 45 (1935), 60.
134 Ibid., 67.
135 Ibid., 76.
136 *CCARY* 46 (1936), 67.

With the rise of the Hitlerian forces, the pacifist position of many of those rabbis was modified. In 1939, the Conference officially noted the distinction between innocent and aggressor nations.[137] Subsequently, when the United States entered the war, the CCAR, with few dissenting votes, expressed "complete support for our country in its present war" and declared, "We believe that God is on the side of Justice and that it is His will to see a tyrant-free world."[138]

Anti-war sentiment again rose to the forefront in the Reform movement in the mid-1960s as opposition mounted to American involvement in Vietnam. The Reform movement soon became the most outspoken Jewish organization decrying United States military activity in Southeast Asia. A 1965 resolution of the Union of American Hebrew Congregations urging a cease-fire and negotiated peace settlement represented what was at the time a minority position in the United States among Jews and the general public. After the Six-Day War, some Reform clergy found difficulty in opposing American policy in Vietnam while at the same time urging support for Israel. However, Reform clergy and laity remained in the forefront of demonstrations and protests against the Vietnam conflict.[139]

The emphasis in Reform ideology in favor of pacifism in the 1930s and later the opposition to the Vietnam conflict in the 1960s prompted an attempt on the part of Reform thinkers to find precedents and sources in Jewish law and teaching that would serve as a mandate for pacifism and conscientious objection to military service.

In the intense debate on pacifism before the annual convention of the CCAR in 1935 a tentative resolution placed before the assembly proclaimed:

> ... the time has come to change the traditional attitude of our faith toward war. We realize to the full the seriousness of this change we propose, and we adopt it because of our belief that the spirit of Israel, the first faith and people to love peace and pursue it, necessitates such a vital change in the text and letter of our historic attitude. In the past Israel has made the distinction between righteous and unrighteous wars. In the light of the foregoing, we believe that this distinction has no reality for our day. And we are now compelled to adopt as our belief, and as the basis for action of our

---

137 *CCARY* 49 (1939), 147–48.
138 *CCARY* 52 (1942), 106. Cf. the remarks of Judah Magnes, an ardent pacifist who supported the allies in World War II, cited in Plaut, *Growth*, 160.
139 See Meyer, *Response*, 366–367; *CCARY* 76 (1966), 19; and 82 (1972), 21–24.

religious followers and ourselves, the principle that war is an unmitigated
evil, and that we should abstain from all participation in it.[140]

Several discussants at the Conference questioned these sweeping gener-
alizations regarding historical Jewish attitudes to war and urged further scholarly study of the subject.[141] The following year, Abraham Cronbach presented
the Conference with a paper, "War and Peace in Jewish Tradition," in which
he had assembled a vast array of sources regarding this topic in biblical and
talmudic literature.[142] Cronbach wished to demonstrate that Jewish tradition
encompasses teachings which can be applied at various points "on a modern-
istic scale" ranging from extreme militarism to extreme pacifism. He claimed,
incorrectly, that the moral differentiation between wars of aggression and wars
of defense is a distinction of which the tradition is not conscious.[143]

Vigorous Reform opposition to the Vietnam conflict in the 1960s spurred
renewed interest in this subject and a number of studies appeared emphasizing the teachings of Judaism that lend themselves to pacifist interpretation.[144]
Some writers sought to demonstrate that alongside the normative halakhic
position there was a position that refused to condone violence even in extreme

---

140 *CCARY* 45 (1935), 66–67.
141 Ibid., 71, 73 and 76.
142 *CCARY* 46 (1936), 198–221. See also Cronbach, *The Quest for Peace* (Cincinnati: Sinai
Press, 1937).
143 *CCARY* 46 (1936), 206 and 221. For halakhic sources demonstrating distinctions between
defensive and offensive wars, see the discussion of the legitimacy of warfare in R. Shlomoh
Yosef Zevin, *Le-Or ha-Halakhah: Ba'ayot u-Berurim* (Tel Aviv: Avraham Zioni, 1957), 1–18.
144 See, for example, Reuven Kimelman, "Non-Violence in the Talmud," *Judaism* 17, no. 3
(Summer 1968), 316–334; Everett E. Gendler's translation of Aaron Samuel Tamaret,
"Passover and Non-Violence," *Judaism* 17, no. 2 (Spring 1968), 203–210; and Sheldon
Zimmerman, "Confronting the Halakhah on Millitary Service," *Judaism* 20, no. 2 (Spring
1971), 204–212. Preoccupation with the question of the morality of the Vietnam conflict
characterized intellectual discourse among the Orthodox as well as is evidenced in the
exchange of opinion in Michael Wyschograd, "The Jewish Interest in Vietnam," *Tradition* 8,
no. 4 (Winter 1966), 5–18, and Charles S. Liebman, "Judaism and Vietnam: A Reply to
Dr. Wyschograd," *Tradition* 9, no. 1–2 (Spring/Summer 1967), 155–160; the survey of
Charles S. Liebman, "The Orthodox Rabbi and Vietnam," *Tradition* 9, no. 4 (Spring 1968),
28–32; and more general studies, including Solomon Simonson, "Violence from the
Perspective of the Ethics of the Fathers," *Tradition* 10, no. 2 (Winter 1968), 35–41; Joseph
Grunblatt, "Violence and Some Aspects of the Judaic Tradition," *Tradition* 10, no. 2 (Winter
1968), 42–47; and Leo Landman, "Civil Disobedience: The Jewish View," *Tradition* 10,
no. 4 (Fall 1969), 5–14. See also Isaiah Leibowitz, "The Spiritual and Religious Meaning of
Victory and Might," *Tradition* 10, no. 3 (Spring 1969), 5–11, for a pertinent discussion
prompted by the Israeli Six-Day War.

situations.[145] One writer posited "an undercurrent of non-violence which grew alongside the Halakhah (and even in it at one point). ... At times this position was at the forefront ... at others, it remained the view of small groups."[146]

The view that it was necessary to abandon the traditional attitude of Judaism toward war as expressed by the CCAR in 1935 persisted. Only now the position was stated more baldly:

> We have faced the tradition and have found its normative halakhic position wanting. ...[147] We cannot accept its normative patterns as the only meaningful expression of God's demands on us as Jews. As liberal Jews, we cannot accept the notion that the *memrah* and the *mitzvah* are always heard in the *din* given by the *g'dolei ha-dor*.[148]

Yet in order to anchor the emerging liberal position in Jewish tradition, Reform writers argued that the longstanding non-normative halakhic view must now be affirmed.

Ironically, the position a number of these writers espoused was hardly one that differed from what is, in reality, the normative halakhic position. Sheldon Zimmerman wrote:

> Thus, although we find ourselves not to be pacifists (and there is a pacifist trend in Judaism as seen by the non-violent tradition), we cannot countenance any military forms of violence in this country or by this country where no *clear* issue of self-defense of *home* and *family* can be established. ... Thus, some of us find ourselves differing with the normative halakhic position.[149]

Zimmerman found himself conflicted because of his own misunderstanding of the halakhic sources. The position he himself articulated is much closer to the normative halakhic view than to the non-normative. Zimmerman and other liberal writers who addressed this issue were attacking a straw man and disputing a tradition that they misconstrued.

---

145 Kimelman, "Non-Violence," 323.
146 Zimmerman, "Military Service," *Judaism* 20 (1971), 211. As noted earlier, misunderstanding the view of R. Samuel Landau, *Noda bi-Yehudah, Mahadura Tinyana, Yoreh De'ah*, no. 74, Zimmerman (210) assumed there was a contradiction between the ruling of Rabbi Landau and that of his contemporaries.
147 Zimmerman, "Military Service," 212.
148 Ibid., 211.
149 Ibid., p. 212.

Certainly, as Isaiah Leibowitz wrote, while there is no enthusiasm for military prowess *per se* in Judaism, Halakhah recognizes that, when war is necessary, "legitimate value is attached to one who fulfills his responsibilities in this area of human reality...."[150] Yet, in most instances, warfare is not legitimate and is not condoned by Halakhah. The normative halakhic view of the Vietnam conflict does not differ significantly from the view espoused by Zimmerman. Indeed, as aptly expressed by Rabbi Joseph Grunblatt:

> If a Viet Cong takeover of South Vietnam cannot be considered a clear and present military danger to the United States[151] it would make this war a *milchemet reshut* for America, which is not permissible for a *Ben Noach*. One may question whether the Halakhah and *Daat Torah* have been considered by those supporting our government's policies in Vietnam.[152]

In the final analysis, one comes back full circle. Neither patriotic enthusiasm that extols warfare nor absolute pacifism that precludes self-defense is reflective of the Jewish tradition. The view that for Jews in our day, and for Noahides at any time, there is no legitimate discretionary war appears to be the normative halakhic position as accepted by the majority of halakhic authorities.[153] Perhaps in the contemporary historical epoch, in which the horrors perpetrated by the ravages of warfare have shocked our society to its foundation and the ethical dilemmas of political aggression in the name of patriotism are confronted more forthrightly, articulation of the halakhic view need not be hampered by apologetic obfuscation and halakhic objections to complicity in participating in a war of aggression need no longer be relegated to the sphere of *Torah she-be-al peh*.

---

150 Leibowitz, "The Spiritual and Religious Meaning," 7.

151 In point of fact, absent considerations of self-endangerment, Jews are required to intervene in order to rescue Jewish victims of aggression. Insofar as the Noahide obligation is concerned, there is disagreement with regard to whether intervention on behalf of a third party is mandatory or merely discretionary. See Zevin, *Le-Or ha-Halakhah*, 17.

152 Grunblatt, "Violence," 46.

153 Zevin, *Le-Or ha-Halakhah*, 17. Cf. Bleich, *Contemporary Halakhic Problems*, vol. II, 159–165, and vol. III (New York: Ktav Publishing House, 1989), 4–10. It must, however, be noted that *Ḥazon Ish, Oraḥ Ḥayyim, Mo'ed* 114: 2, astutely observes that a halakhically objectionable war may rapidly be transformed into a legitimate war, at least insofar as conscripts are concerned. War, by its very nature, creates danger to human life. Thus, even a war of aggression is a source of danger to the aggressor. Therefore, argues *Ḥazon Ish*, once hostilities have commenced any combatant who does not have the power to call for a cease fire is, in effect, engaging in an act of self-defense.

A POLITICAL ASIDE—ALL-JEWISH BATTALIONS
IN NON-JEWISH ARMIES

During an age in which civic and social equality were the anticipated goals prompting participation in military endeavors, promotion of all-Jewish army units would have been counterproductive. Such units would have served to affirm difference precisely when the desire was to assert commonality. However, from time to time, efforts were made to establish all-Jewish battalions in order to achieve entirely different objectives.

Whether or not one's personal value system, in consonance with that of the Sages, regards weapons in a negative light ("They are but a disgrace," Mishnah, *Shabbat* 63a), it would be naïve not to recognize that in society in general an undeniable mystique surrounds the accoutrements of war, such as uniforms, arms and medals. Similarly, an aura of power and authority is associated with military personages. The phenomenon of former generals rising to positions of civilian prominence even in peace-loving democracies is familiar to all. An acute awareness of those factors and the recognition that military exploits bestow a measure of political and social influence on participants served as motivating considerations for those who sought to promote the establishment of all-Jewish battalions in both World Wars.

During World War I two diametrically opposite perspectives regarding Jewish participation in the conflict emerged among Zionist leaders. In Palestine, Ben-Gurion and Ben-Zvi proposed the formation of a Jewish Legion attached to the Turks on the side of the Central Powers. Initially approved by the Turkish authorities who rapidly rescinded their approval, the project ended in the imprisonment and deportation of the Jewish volunteers. In contrast, Jabotinsky and others proposed the formation of a Jewish Legion to fight on the side of the Allies in order to free Palestine from the Turks.

The Zion Mule Corps, organized in 1915 and composed in part of Russian Jewish immigrants to Britain, fought under a battalion flag of their own. Later, two battalions attached to the Royal Fusiliers, consisting mainly of Jewish volunteers from America, were sent to Egypt and fought under their own flag in the campaign to conquer Palestine. It was hoped that, if Jews fought as a national unit, as cobelligerents, they would later gain the right to advance claims at the peace table. The presence of such a Jewish military unit fighting for Palestine, hailed as "the first Jewish army since Bar Kochba," had great emotional resonance to Jews throughout the world.[154] Those

---

154 Hertzberg, *Jews in America*, 231–232.

sentiments are captured in a poem published just before a large contingent of American volunteers left to join the Legion:

> The swords of many nations
> Have made of thee a prey,
> The feet of many strangers
> Have worn thy stones away;
> But harken, O Jerusalem,
> And hear a joyful sound—
> The tread of Jewish warriors
> On their ancestral ground!
> Arise and sing, Jerusalem,
> Who art no longer dumb;
> O citadel of David,
> The sons of David come![155]

During the Second World War, a Jewish Brigade Group was formed to serve alongside the Allied forces as an independent Jewish national military unit. From 1940 on, many Jews served in the British East Kent Regiment in Jewish companies primarily involved in guard duty and not fully equipped. In 1944, those units together with new volunteers and a number of Jews serving in other sections of the British army were incorporated into an independent Jewish Brigade of approximately 5,000 soldiers. The Brigade took part in assaults against the Germans and later played an important role in caring for Jewish survivors of the concentration camps and ghettos.

Winston Churchill, no stranger to political nuance and keenly attuned to the import of propaganda and symbol in boosting morale, had his own agenda in favoring the organization of the Jewish Brigade as a distinct and recognizable body. In a telegram sent to President Roosevelt, Churchill demonstrated sympathetic understanding of the unique nature of Jewish involvement in the struggle against the Nazis and that "surely ... of all other races" Jews qua Jews had the right to strike at the Germans. Therefore, he concluded, the assembling of a Jewish regimental combat team with its own flag "will give great satisfaction to the Jews when it is published ... [and] would be a message to go all over the world."[156]

---

155 Cited in the fascinating, albeit partisan and subjective, account of Elias Gilner, *War and Hope: A History of the Jewish Legion* (New York: Herzl Press, 1969), 177.

156 Martin Gilbert, *The Second World War: A Complete History*, rev. ed. (New York: Henry Holt & Co., 1991), 576. The story of the exploits of the Brigade is recounted in Bernard M. Casper, *With the Jewish Brigade* (London: E. Goldston, 1947).

As was the case with regard to the Jewish Legion, the formation of the Jewish Brigade was the culmination of efforts on the part of Zionist leaders to enhance the status of the *yishuv* and to promote the political aims of Zionism. The Zionist leadership well understood the powerful psychological and political impact that would result from the existence of Jewish fighting units. In forming the Jewish Legion and the Jewish Brigade, deeply rooted ambivalences toward warfare and the military were overcome by the desire of ardent Zionists to achieve overriding aims, namely, the realization of nationalist aspirations and, with regard to the Brigade, the elimination of a threat to the very existence of the Jewish people.

AFTERWORD

Plato, in the *Republic* (V, 466), suggests that in the ideal state men and women who go out to the battlefield should take children along as spectators in order to enable them to observe and to learn "this trade like any other" and to familiarize themselves with their future duties. Men who are destined to become warriors, Plato argues, should see something of warfare in childhood.[157]

Plato articulates the very antithesis of a Jewish educational perspective. The extent to which his model differs from a Jewish one is exemplified by a *bon mot* current among European Jews. When the German Emperor William I passed away, an elderly officer was given the honor of carrying the deceased Kaiser's sword on a cushion in the funeral procession. Berlin Jews characterized that distinction as "*goyishe naches*" (satisfactions of the gentiles).[158]

---

157 The notion of a warrior profession was taken to an extreme in the morally twisted writings of the Nazi ideologue Alfred Rosenberg who foretold that a new German church would replace the crucifix with the symbols of the warrior-hero: "Reverence for the soldier fighting for the honor of his people is the new, recently developed living sentiment of our time … the new religion of national honor. … The man and the hero in the field-gray under his helmet shall become one and the same person. Then the road shall be opened for the German national religion of the future. …" See Alfred Rosenberg, *Myth of the Twentieth Century*, cited in Salo W. Baron, *Modern Nationalism and Religion* (New York: Meridian Press, 1960), 83.

158 Theodor Reik, *Jewish Wit* (New York: Gamut Press, 1962), 61. The currency of this expression is reflected in its use as the opening gambit in S. N. Behrman's depiction of 1937 Europe, *The Burning Glass* (Boston and Toronto: Little Brown & Co., 1968), 3–5. Militarism was a favorite target of Jewish folk humor. See Reik, *Jewish Wit* 60–63. Reik (60) cites a line of Heine's poetry, "*Lebenbleiben wie das Sterben für das Vaterland is süss*" ("To remain alive as well as to die for the Fatherland is sweet") that demonstrates Heine's vestigial

In point of fact, the Jewish educational ideal represents a reinterpretation and transformation of the notion of the military hero. Thus, a characteristic aggadic commentary on Song of Songs 3:7–8 states:

> "Behold his bed, which is Solomon's; threescore valiant men are about it, of the valiant of Israel. They all hold swords, being expert (schooled) in war [*melumadei milḥamah*]." *Melumadei*—schooled—*she-melamdim et beneihem, ve-limadetem et beneikhem*—that they teach their children, and you shall teach them unto your children; *milḥamah*—war—*milḥamtah shel Torah*—the war of Torah.[159]

The sole instruction in battle commended by rabbinic teachers is to hone the minds of students so that they become expert in intellectual struggle and strive for the truth and knowledge necessary to triumph in the "war" of Torah.

Jewish response in underscoring a reverence for life in contradistinction to the ideal of military honor extolled in German society.

159 *Yalkut Shim'oni, Shir ha-Shirim* 986. For rabbinic teachings interpreting the might of the hero (*gibbor*) in a spiritual rather than material sense, see Eliezer Berkovits, *With God in Hell: Judaism in the Ghettos and Death Camps* (New York and London: Sanhedrin Press, 1979), 142–154.

CHAPTER 7

The Testament of a Halakhist

R. Jacob Lorbeerbaum of Lissa was an eminent rabbinic authority whose prolific writings exerted far-reaching influence on talmudic and halakhic scholarship. His literary legacy includes a personal statement addressed to his children in the form of a last will and testament. As a classic expression of the ideal of talmudic scholarship this document possesses considerable historical value. A striking feature of the testament is the emphasis placed upon business ethics.

At the turn of the nineteenth century in Poland, in a generation rich with talmudic scholars, R. Jacob ben Jacob Moses Lorbeerbaum of Lissa stands out as an authority of exceptional renown. His commentary on *Shulḥan Arukh, Yoreh De'ah* (Lemberg, 1799) established his reputation at an early date and it is by the name of this work, *Ḥavvat Da'at*, that he became known to posterity. Both this volume and his magnum opus, *Netivot ha-Mishpat*, are fundamental texts with which no serious student of rabbinics is unacquainted.

In his intellectual pursuits R. Jacob of Lissa followed an illustrious family tradition. He was a great-grandson of *Ḥakham Tzevi* Ashkenazi. His grandfather, Nathan Ashkenazi, was numbered among the coterie of "Sages of the *Klaus*" of Brod and his father, Jacob Moses, was rabbi of Zborow.[1]

R. Jacob of Lissa's date of birth is unknown.[2] As a young man he lived in Stanislav and journeyed to Tisminitz to study under the aegis of R. Meshullam Igra.[3] During these years he began his literary activity while attempting to support his family by business enterprise. Following severe commercial reversals he was compelled to accept a rabbinical post in the town of Monasterzyska,

---

1 Abraham Isaac Bromberg, *Ha-Gaon R. Ya'akov Lorbeerbaum mi-Lissa* (Jerusalem, 1957), 9. Some novellae of Jacob Moses of Zborow were published by his son and appended to *Mekor Ḥayyim* (Zolkiev, 1807).

2 Isaac Lewin, "Le-Toldot ha-Gaon Ba'al Ḥavvat Da'at Z.T.L.," in *The Leo Jung Jubilee Volume*, ed. Menachem M. Kasher et al. (New York: The Jewish Center, 1962), 167. It is possible that R. Jacob was born after his father's demise and therefore was also named "Jacob." Cf. Bromberg, *Ha-Gaon R. Ya'akov*, 10.

3 Cf. Shevach Knobel, *Gerem ha-Ma'alot* (Lemberg, 1914), 14 and 24 n. 32.

where he founded a yeshiva. Thereafter he was appointed rabbi of Kalusz,[4] and subsequently, in 1809, he accepted a call to become *Av Bet Din* of Lissa (now Leszno, Poland).[5] After the death of R. David Tevele in 1792 the rabbinate of Lissa remained vacant for seventeen years until the appointment of R. Jacob Lorbeerbaum. A community of prominence in the Jewish world, Lissa could boast of an elite group of scholars and of the generally high level of talmudic learning attained by its inhabitants. *Ḥavvat Da'at* himself attests to the intellectual caliber of the community in an address in which he underscores that "here especially ... everyone knows what is forbidden, for there is no ignorance in this place."[6]

Rabbi Jacob's association with the Lissa congregation appears to have been mutually satisfactory. The years he spent in Lissa were a period of prolific literary productivity. In communal affairs he emerged as an articulate and vigorous leader championing the cause of Orthodoxy against the rising Reform movement.[7] Despite the high esteem in which he was held as rabbi of the community, in the year 1824, R. Jacob Lorbeerbaum left Lissa for Galicia. His sudden departure from Lissa has long been shrouded in mystery.[8] Some scholars claimed that Rabbi Jacob's militant opposition to the Reform movement had evoked enmity within the *kehillah* and that it was this antagonism which had induced him to leave his position.[9] Others averred that the communal leaders had expressed their displeasure with the personal life of their rabbi. The purpose of *Ḥavvat Da'at's* journey to Galicia had been to effect there the divorce of his wife. It was said that the congregation criticized their rabbi on this score.[10]

---

4 Lewin, "Le-Toldot," 167, gives the approximate date as 1791. See Lewin, "Le-Toldot," 167 n. 2, for identification of the city as Kalush, Galicia rather than Kalisz, Poland, as erroneously listed in various biographical sketches.

5 The communal officials of Lissa resolved to offer the Lissa rabbinate to the anonymous author of *Ḥavvat Da'at* purely on the strength of the scholarship evidenced in that authoritative work. They apparently had no other knowledge of, or further information concerning, R. Jacob. See the rabbinical contract sent by the Lissa community, published in Lewin, "Le-Toldot," 174.

6 Cited by Bromberg, *Ha-Gaon R. Ya'akov*, 25.

7 See the responsum of R. Jacob Lorbeerbaum included in *Eleh Divrei ha-Berit* (Altona, 1819), 76–82. Cf. Bromberg, *Ha-Gaon R. Ya'akov*, 40–42.

8 Naphtali Z. Chachamowicz, in an introductory note to the Breslau, 1849 edition of *Naḥalat Ya'akov*, notes that Rabbi Jacob left Lissa "on account of certain undisclosed reasons that were known at the time only to select individuals in that city." Financial considerations were not the motivating factor for his departure. Louis Lewin, *Geschichte der Juden in Lissa* (Pinne, 1904), 218, records that his initial salary was increased substantially.

9 Bromberg, *Ha-Gaon R. Ya'akov*, 46–48.

10 Salomon Schreiber, ed., *Iggerot Soferim* (Vienna, 1933), sec. 1, 88 n. 1.

Recently, new sources have been uncovered which shed light on the entire episode. Several letters from R. Akiva Eger to the Lissa community regarding his colleague R. Jacob Lorbeerbaum clarify the course of events. Apparently, Rabbi Jacob had travelled to Galicia in order to arrange his divorce and, judging the matter to be of lengthy duration, had sold many of his belongings. His intention to return was, however, clearly evident in the conditional contract drawn up between himself and the congregation and deposited with R. Akiva Eger. Subsequently, hostile elements within the community sought to lower the rabbi's salary. It may have been this faction which brought Rabbi Jacob's immigration status to the attention of the government. Be that as it may, the *Landrat* (regional government) issued a ruling denying R. Jacob Lorbeerbaum re-entry to Lissa on the grounds that he was of foreign citizenship and, having sold his belongings, had forfeited the right of residence. The intervention of R. Akiva Eger was successful in uniting the Lissa congregation in the cause of their rabbi. However, the civil authorities again denied R. Jacob permission to return and attempts to revoke this governmental decision proved fruitless.[11]

For a number of years Rabbi Jacob resided in Kalusz, once more assuming rabbinical duties there. Thence he moved to Stryi, Eastern Galicia, where he served as district rabbi until his death in 1832. It is noteworthy that, despite the fact that he never returned to Lissa and that he subsequently accepted other positions, he continued to the last to sign himself as Rabbi of Lissa.[12] In his testament (section 26) he urges his children to notify the congregation of Lissa of the day of his decease inasmuch as it was the custom of that community to recite a *Kel male raḥamim* (memorial prayer) publicly on every festival in memory of their deceased rabbis.[13]

R. Jacob Lorbeerbaum's writings span the vast array of Jewish law and lore. They range from definitive works on halakhah and talmudic novellae to scriptural commentaries whose content is exegetic, homiletic and aggadic and which include frequent references to mystic doctrines. Of primary importance are those of his writings which are concerned with practical aspects of halakhah. *Ḥavvat Da'at* is a commentary on *Shulḥan Arukh, Yoreh De'ah* 69–201; *Mekor Ḥayyim*

---

11 Lewin, "Le-Toldot," 169–174. Tireless in his attempts to reinstate his colleague as rabbi of Lissa, R. Akiva Eger continued to admonish the heads of the Lissa community not to accept the governmental decree as final, "not to be silent regarding this and not to despair of the matter." Ibid., 185.

12 Bromberg, *Ha-Gaon R. Ya'akov*, 53.

13 Lewin, *Geschichte der Juden*, 220 n. 4, cites the memorial tribute to R. Jacob Lorbeerbaum included in the Lissa Synagogue record book.

is a commentary on *Shulḥan Arukh, Oraḥ Ḥayyim*, 429ff. with notes on the commentaries *Turei Zahev* and *Magen Avraham*; *Netivot ha-Mishpat* is a commentary on *Shulḥan Arukh, Ḥoshen Mishpat*. *Torat Gittin* and *Bet Ya'akov* are commentaries on *Shulḥan Arukh, Even ha-Ezer* and the talmudic tractates *Gittin* and *Ketubot* respectively. *Kehillat Ya'akov* is a collection of discussions on various topics appearing in *Even ha-Ezer* and *Oraḥ Ḥayyim*.

Rabbi Jacob of Lissa wrote individual commentaries on the five *megillot* which are referred to inclusively as *Imrei Yosher*. His well-known commentary on the Passover Haggadah is entitled *Ma'aseh Nissim*. He also composed a short compendium of *dinim* (laws) printed as part of his arrangement of the prayer-book under the title *Derekh ha-Ḥayyim*. Known as the "Lissa Rav's Siddur," this work enjoyed great popularity and has been reprinted a number of times. Various writings, sermons on the Pentateuch, responsa, novellae and glosses on the Talmud were posthumously published in *Naḥalat Ya'akov* and *Emet le-Ya'akov*. The former work also contains the text of his last will and testament.[14]

REFLECTIONS OF A PERSONALITY

This testament reveals the ethical character and personality of R. Jacob Lorbeerbaum. After its initial publication (Breslau, 1849), it was reprinted together with the testament of R. Akiva Eger (Warsaw, 1875) and frequently thereafter. Mitnagdim and hasidim alike cited its provisions and held it in high regard. The hasidic sage, R. Yehiel Danziger of Alexander, adopted it as his own and enjoined his followers "to observe with the force of a testament the will of the honored Jacob of Lissa of blessed memory."[15]

1. Study of Torah

The emphasis on the primacy of Torah study is hardly novel. The significant point is that the advice, while couched in affirmative language, is in actuality an admonition against acceptance of the educational philosophy and methodology which were widespread at the time. In effect, the testament offers a critique of pilpulism, undirected study, and lack of concern with halakhic application.

---

14 Originally published in Breslau, 1849, a photo offset edition of this work was published in New York, 1961.

15 Bromberg, *Ha-Gaon R. Ya'akov*, 6.

2. Attitude to Hasidism

R. Jacob Lorbeerbaum spent most of his life in Galicia—then a stronghold of Hasidism. Some of the statements in the testament reflect his critical attitude towards hasidic practices. He cautions his sons to shun a life of constant rejoicing and gaiety and to disregard "those who say that it is meet that one be in joy all of one's days" (sec. 8)—an obvious allusion to Hasidism. In contrast to hasidic views regarding asceticism, Rabbi Jacob favors self-abnegation and urges his sons not to let a month pass without fasting (sec. 14). Particularly pointed are his comments regarding kabbalistic *kavvanot* (meditations) and secrets. Although he valued study of the *Zohar,* he insisted that in prayer one should bear in mind the literal meaning of the words and the *kavvanot* prescribed by the *Shulḥan Arukh.* In contemplating kabbalistic secrets there is too great a danger of "cutting the saplings." Particularly incisive is his indictment of contemporary teachers of the Kabbalah:

> Nowadays, one cannot rely on any person for instruction in this discipline, particularly [not] on those who have not become saturated with Talmud and Codes and who, nonetheless, have pretensions to this discipline. Do not believe and do not consent and do not listen to even a minor matter which proceeds from them. (sec. 9)

These views notwithstanding, in practice, *Ḥavvat Da'at* was not a militant opponent of Hasidism. His position was close to that of those mitnagdim who joined forces with the hasidim in a concerted effort to stem the tide of the Haskalah and Reform movements. His primary concern was that his disciples assume the responsibility of active leadership in Orthodoxy. Regarding two of his hasidic students who accepted rabbinical positions he wrote: "Is it not fitting that students of descendents of the Besht find a means to fence the breach in Germany?"[16] Indicative of the fact that *Ḥavvat Da'at* was not an extreme mitnaged are his most cordial personal relationships with hasidic leaders such as R. Bunim of Peshischa and the Maggid of Kosnitz. His son-in-law, Eleazar ha-Kohen of Plotosk, and his granddaughter's husband, David Dov Meisels, were both prominent hasidim of the *Kotzker Rebbe.* Indeed, many of his former students were active proponents of Hasidism.[17]

---

16 Ibid., 127–28.
17 Ibid., 127–28.

3. Attitude to the Rabbinate

Rabbi Jacob exhorts his sons to be wary of accepting an appointment to the rabbinate (sec. 7). This is not merely a token admonition. It reflects a deeply-rooted attitude of *Ḥavvat Da'at*.[18] As noted, he himself accepted his first post in Monasterzyska only after his commercial endeavors had failed and he had no alternative means of sustenance. His negative view of rabbinical office persisted throughout his life, doubtless bolstered by the many disappointments he experienced in Lissa. In his final wishes, he adjures his sons:

> On the tombstone do not write either "Rabbi" or "Gaon" for perhaps I have sinned by assuming the role of rabbi for I was not worthy of it. Why, then, should my sin be remembered constantly?

The reason for the testator's attitude is of paramount importance: it is his seriousness as *posek* and his grave concern lest there be any error in halakhic decision. It is instructive to compare the testament with his remarks in the introduction to *Ḥavvat Da'at*:

> I did not compose this work for self-aggrandizement, nor for the purpose of rendering halakhic decisions for I, myself, know that I am not competent to render decisions. ... Accordingly, I have called this work *Ḥavvat Da'at* [expression of opinion], its name indicating of it that I wrote it solely to express opinion and not, God forbid, to establish halakhah.[19]

He was no less concerned with regard to rendering judgment in monetary disputes, fearing that a possible error might cause unlawful financial loss to one of the litigants. This concern manifests itself in his further instruction to his sons that in the event that one of them should accept a rabbinical office he should stipulate in advance that his decisions on litigation be accepted as a form of arbitration "whether it be in accordance with the law or in error" rather than in the guise of a purely halakhic decision.

---

18 It is noteworthy that Rabbi Jacob's close friend and colleague, R. Akiva Eger, also expressed a strong antipathy to holding rabbinical office. In one letter he wrote: "All my life I have detested the rabbinate. ... True, many have been rabbis before me and many will yet be. Lo, many have crossed strong seas in boats and many more will. That does not make the sea safer. ... Each day my life is a misery because of the rabbinate." Schreiber, *Iggerot Soferim*, 11–13.

19 Included in *Shulḥan Arukh, Yoreh De'ah*, vol. I (reprinted, New York, 1953), following p. 602.

It is of interest to note that R. Jacob Lorbeerbaum's grandson, R. Abraham Teumim, did accept a rabbinical position in the town of Zborow, Galicia. It is related that Rabbi Jacob cautioned his youthful grandson to be well-acquainted with the calendar for, to the uneducated layman, such knowledge serves as an indication of the rabbi's scholarship. Furthermore, he is said to have charged the youth: "If you desire to be a rabbi you must be able to swallow needles point-first without emitting the slightest sigh and without batting an eyelash."[20]

4. Halakhic Rulings and Observance of the Law

A number of provisions of the testament shed light on the halakhic opinions of *Ḥavvat Da'at*. Examples are his stringencies regarding smoking on the first day of the festivals (sec. 10), the qualified view he takes of shared ownership of an *etrog* (sec. 15), and his insistence upon a separation of six handbreadths between graves (sec. 26).[21]

The testament clearly reveals that Rabbi Jacob was thoroughly attuned to the ethical implications of the law and, paralleling his careful guardianship of the minutiae of observance, was a concern regarding all facets of ethical conduct. For him meaningful study and *shmirat ha-mitzvot* (observance of the commandments) must ultimately mold personality. The folk-stories and legends surrounding *Ḥavvat Da'at's* own life portray him as a man of humility who shied away from all public expression of honor.[22] In light of his repeated exhortations regarding humility and "study for the sake of Heaven" one should note that his own books were originally published anonymously and that he requested that all laudatory titles be omitted from his tombstone.

THE TESTAMENT: SELECTIONS

It is written in the Torah, "For I have known him, to the end that he may command [may give a testament to] his children and his household after him, that

20 Bromberg, *Ha-Gaon R. Ya'akov*, 70.
21 The inscription on the reverse side of R. Jacob Lorbeerbaum's tombstone reads: "There shall be an empty space the size of a cubit of six handbreadths on each side of this grave for thus was the testament of the author of *Sefer Ḥavvat Da'at* who lies here." See Lewin, *Geschichte der Juden*, 222 n. 1. Of particular interest is a similar insistence on the part of his great-grandfather *Ḥakham Tzevi* in a ruling regarding local burial practices addressed to the communal leaders of Amsterdam. Tzevi Ashkenazi, *She'elot u-Teshuvot Ḥakham Tzevi* (Amsterdam, 1712), no. 149.
22 Bromberg, *Ha-Gaon R. Ya'akov*, 65–68.

they may keep the way of the Lord. ..." (Genesis 18:19). Now, if the giving of a testament to one's descendants brings about the love of the Lord, blessed be He, then it is meet and proper for every person to have before him in written form words which touch upon the ways of God and the fear of Him so that this shall be left for his progeny after him. Perhaps they will be receptive to his message, so that he will thereby merit to have his soul bound up in the bond of life. Consequently, I have resolved to write down rules of conduct which affect the fear of the honored and revered Name.

1. My beloved sons! The first thing regarding which a person is judged is Torah study. You should have a regular study period each day for Scripture and Mishnah. Although our Sages said, "The Babylonian Talmud is blended of them all," they had already previously been saturated with Scripture and Mishnah. Besides, the evil inclination to learn for an ulterior motive has no dominance over the study of Scripture and Mishnah. Even though you have not seen me do so, in my youth I did so; but in my old age time was treacherous to me; I was very much occupied, so that I was not able to fulfill that which was in my heart.

2. Should you be privileged to become Torah scholars, schedule for yourselves each day the nonanalytic study of not less than one folio of Gemara following the order of the Talmud, in addition to a period of analytic study. This shall be an inviolable rule. Should you become proficient enough to discuss novellae of Torah study, schedule one hour every day for penetrative study, for the essential query will be, "Did you engage in discussions of wisdom?" Your penetrative study should be with a view to establishing harmony with the halakhah— not like the customary kind of casuistry prevalent in our generation through our many sins.

3. Study a folio or a page of *Shulḥan Arukh, Oraḥ Ḥayyim* each day and see to it that you be well-versed in the laws, for most of the laws of *Oraḥ Ḥayyim* are encountered at times when it is impossible for a person to investigate or to consult a scholar. I have already composed a book containing the order of prayer accompanied by all the laws in order to acquire merit for my soul. Also establish a study period in the holy *Zohar* every Sabbath. Repeat and repeat again all that you study, for on the basis of studying a thing one time it is impossible to remember it, as it is stated in *Eruvin* 54, "The cunning hunter will not last long ..."

4. Study the Psalms according to the literal meaning of the words many times over, and let it be fluent in your mouths with the commentary of Rashi, so that you will understand well when you recite [the Psalms] as a supplication. Be careful to recite five chapters every day—no less—for through this the heart becomes instilled with ardor for the service of the Lord, Blessed be his Name. Long ago David requested that [this recitation] be deemed comparable to engaging in the study of the tractates of *Nega'im* and *Ohalot* and in this there is no question of ulterior motivation.

5. See to it that you study so that you be properly proficient in the laws pertaining to the establishment of anticipated menstrual cycles, for through our many sins this halakhah has been well-nigh forgotten among Israel. ...

6. Supervise well the teachers of children, for through our many sins the holy Torah and its students have become greatly diminished and must be sought like hidden treasures. Do not leave little children among the big ones, for through our many sins the generation is unchaste, and they teach them base and empty things. Especially on the Sabbath and the holidays place additional supervision upon your children that they do not mix with insolent children, for this requires great vigilance, and you must warn the teachers exceedingly about this. When they reach the age of eight or nine, see to it to study one tractate with them in order. The children should review it constantly until it is fluent in their mouths, for having studied one's lesson one hundred times is not the same as [having studied it one-hundred-and-one times]. Moreover, see to it that the children understand the manner in which laws are derived from that which they have studied. Should you be privileged to become Torah scholars, you will yourselves understand the goodness of learning.

7. Strive greatly to avoid accepting a rabbinical appointment. For if the Ancients whose hearts were open wide as the door of a hall said of themselves [with regard to this], "Of my own free will I am going to meet death," what are we—most bereft of orphans—to say after them? And should you be compelled by great need to do so, be careful to request at the very outset, as you arrive in the city, that they accept [your decision] upon themselves whether it be in accordance with the law or in error. Likewise, if you are accepted [to render] judgment in some place, state at the outset that the parties to the

litigation should accept you whether the decision be in accordance with the law or in error—inasmuch as error is very frequent. Or say to the parties prior to the close of the litigation that you are judging merely according to your own discretion: "It is possible that we may have erred, therefore, accept [the decision] whether it be in accordance with the law or in error."

8. My beloved children! How exceedingly should you further yourselves from mirth and merriment! For how can man rejoice, when every day he hastens to sin! If a man's life were forfeit to a mortal king how could he rejoice on Purim or on a festival? All the more so when he merits the death penalty by the requirement of the King of kings, the Holy One, Blessed be He! Do not listen, then, to those who say that it is meet that one be in joy all of one's days. For all this belongs to the scheming of the evil inclination, since merriment and levity accustom a person to sexual license. In all melancholy there is advantage except that at the time of the performance of a precept or [at the time of] Torah study a person should concentrate and rejoice in the heart, but not with the accompaniment of levity, for levity is a very evil trait.

9. In prayer think of the literal meaning of the words and, when mentioning the honored and revered Name, think of what is explained in *Shulḥan Arukh, Oraḥ Ḥayyim*. With respect to contemplation of the mysteries according to the wisdom of the Kabbalah particular vigilance and caution is needed, lest one come to cut the saplings. Nowadays, one cannot rely on any person for instruction in this discipline particularly [not] on those who have not become saturated with Talmud and Codes and who nonetheless have pretensions to this discipline. Do not believe and do not consent and do not listen to even a minor matter which proceeds from them. We have never heard of anyone who had a true understanding of this discipline, except for those who were very keen of intellect, such as Nachmanides and Rabbi Isaac [Luria], and similar individuals, the memory of the righteous be a blessing. In spite of that, however, their main subject of study was the Talmud and the Codes, as explained in the books of Nachmanides and Rabbi Solomon ben Aderet, q.v.

10. My beloved sons! Be extremely meticulous with respect to the prohibition of the produce of the new harvest, as well as with respect to smoking tobacco on the first day of a festival and things of a like nature—matters which touch upon a biblical prohibition. In matters

of this sort, which touch upon a biblical prohibition, one cannot rely upon the leniencies espoused by the latter-day scholars in order to defend the custom, for Rabbi Nissim has already written in his responsa that we must not rely on our own judgment with respect to something which touches upon a biblical prohibition. However, regarding a matter which involves merely a rabbinic prohibition, such as dregs of the produce of the new harvest, which involves merely the factor of being an emulsifier and similarly smoking tobacco on the second day of the festival and in similar instances, one may rely on them.

11. How extremely distant should you keep yourselves from the character trait of pride! The Sages stated with double emphasis, "Exceedingly, exceedingly be humble and meek of spirit, for the hope of man is vermin." If a person thinks of his sins, which are so numerous that they overpower him, he will surely flee the trait of pride, for a sinner has nothing of which to be proud. Always bear in mind, though you be men of money and wealth, that all is in the hands of God. Always imagine to yourselves that all the misfortunes and tragedies conceivable in the world have already befallen you. After all, it is possible—for you see with your own eyes that people are smitten with many accidents and injuries, and you, too, are formed out of mortal substance just as they. By means of this concept you will dispel the traits of pride and anger. For can your heart be staunch, can your hands be strong, when the sore injuries which are man's destiny enter your recollection? Stay away even from beautiful clothing—for how can it occur to a sinful person, whose destiny is suffering, to adorn himself?

14. Although it is meet for a person to spend all his days in fasting and mortification of the flesh, as we find that the *tanna'im* fasted on account of minor and insignificant matters until their teeth became blackened, what shall we, rebellious and sinful people, respond to them? What can we do for atonement? It would certainly be proper for us to fast and castigate ourselves to the point of death! However, inasmuch as the generation is frail—especially you whom I know to be frail of constitution so that you cannot castigate yourselves—nevertheless see to it that a month does not pass without fasting unless you recognize in yourselves frailty. In such a case increase your study of Torah and performance of good deeds, as our Sages, of blessed memory said, "If a person has committed bundles of transgressions let him perform bundles of good deeds."

15. Do not, God forbid, be stingy in fulfilling a precept. When the Feast of Tabernacles arrives, see to it that each one purchase for himself an individual *etrog* for his own use or in partnership with some learned person who knows how to transfer property on condition of subsequent return, and one should say to the other expressly: "I am giving it as a gift on condition of subsequent return," in accordance with the opinion of the Gaon whose words are cited in *Hagahot Maimoniyot* on Maimonides's *Code, Laws of the Lulav.* Even though he has there raised a question regarding this view, nonetheless, I agree with his opinion and in my novellae I have resolved the question he has raised. Especially [should one do so] since one should meet the requirements of all the schools of thought and not rely on the congregational *etrog.* Similarly, for every single precept, study every halakhic regulation at its proper time in *Shulḥan Arukh, Oraḥ Ḥayyim,* so that you shall know all the laws clearly.

17. I hereby admonish you to schedule a study session in books of ethics each day. Through our many sins our heart has become petrified, and by means of the books of ethics, the petrified will become softened.[23] The general rule is: for the sake of the Lord! See to it, and act accordingly, that the greater part of the twenty-four-hour span be spent in Torah study, in scheduled lessons, as our Sages, of blessed memory, have said, "Minimize your business activity and engage in Torah study."

18. How exceedingly should you take heed not to speak any evil about a person, even though he do the deed of Zimri, for certainly your heart well knows that among you, too, there are evil things, and perhaps the evil which is in you overweighs the evil which is in him, and how can you dare to speak evil about your fellows? Especially since the greatness of the sin of evil speech is known—its guilt is too great to be forgiven!

19. When a person is ushered in for judgment, he is asked: "Have you been honest in business?" Consequently, you should have one basic rule in financial matters: whenever you have any scruple with regard to a monetary dispute which you have with another person, do not decide independently, but consult a scholar—even though all of you

---

23 This provision of the "holy testament" of Rabbi Jacob of Lissa is cited by R. Isaac Blaser, *Sha'arei Or,* section 5, included in *Or Yisra'el* (London, 1951), 4.

be scholars—for a person does not see wrong in himself. And if your fellow man's money should come into your hands, without his knowledge, and you have a monetary claim against him, do not say: "Since it has come into our hands, we have taken possession of it—and I will not inform him at all, but will seize it in lieu of what is owed to me by him." And even by asking the opinion of a scholar do not rule it permissible for yourselves, for the "first one is righteous in his litigation, then comes his fellow and subjects him to questioning." And even if, in your opinion, the obligation is clear—perhaps he has a claim of a possible previous debt against you—[do not rule it permissible] until you notify him and tell him: "Know that so and so much of yours is in our possession and now let us go to court together." Our Sages, of blessed memory, have said in *Berakhot*, chapter 1, with respect to Rav Huna whose four hundred barrels of wine turned sour, that the Sages considered it a sin on his part that he did not give the sharecropper the tendrils, although he said to them, "Did he give me anything?" Certainly, Rav Huna said the truth and the sharecropper did steal many times that amount from Rav Huna, nevertheless they said, "Steal in the wake of a thief and taste the flavor of theft." Of course, this was because he had not notified the sharecropper, for had he done so with the knowledge of the sharecropper he would not at all have been at fault. For a person is entitled to assert his rights. This is what they meant by saying "in the wake of a thief." However, if one notifies one's fellow, it is permitted; whereas without notifying him it is forbidden, even upon consultation with a learned man. For so long as the defendant is not present it is impossible he know, "whether the first is righteous in his litigation." Besides, he may possibly have a claim against him stemming from a previous debt, and perhaps through the questioning of the second party in the presence of the scholar, the matter will be clarified. Moreover, if the matter becomes known it may lead to a desecration of the Divine Name. ...

20. Should you be privileged to become Torah scholars study the laws of usury with thorough analysis before embarking upon commercial activity, so that you may be proficient in all their regulations, for a person may easily stumble in a business activity, with respect to the prohibition of usury and all the more so in lending activities. Before embarking upon any business transaction, a person should weigh the matter in his mind as to whether it touches upon the prohibition of usury, for a person may

easily err in this, as in selling on credit for a price above the value, and many things of a similar nature which do not lend themselves to detailed enumeration. For those laws a great deal of study is required inasmuch as [usury] is a halakhah of great severity.

21. How exceedingly do I admonish you to desist very, very much from having others rely on your trustworthiness, so as not to cause suspicion to fall upon you. Besides rationalization in these things is frequent especially in view of the sway that the lust for money exercises. Consequently, be very careful not to get into such a situation—unless it should prove entirely impossible to avoid it.

22. Furthermore, I admonish you not to cause any person to take an oath, God forbid. Is it then a trifling matter, that which is written in this regard, "Turn aside from the tents of these evildoers?" And if the Merciful One has called such a person an evildoer, it is better that one lose all one's money rather than that one be an evildoer for one hour before the Lord. And should a person have an obligation of an oath towards you, substitute for it the acceptance of a *herem*—for thus you will avoid damage. In any event, he who is suspect with regard to a *herem* is suspect also with regard to an oath, and by a *herem* you will not commit a misdeed, for anyone who robs his fellow of his money merits to be put in *herem* by law. It should be all the more self-understood that you should not swear in contradiction of any person in any monetary matter, unless it be a time of severe need.

23. Distance yourselves greatly from entering into litigation and, should you have any disagreement with your fellows, settle the matter by compromise and do not bring the matter to litigation for the ignominy of litigation is great. See also, my children, the doctrine of the Sages, of blessed memory: "Jerusalem was destroyed solely because they insisted on the rigidity of Torah law in their disputes." And if they attributed the destruction of Jerusalem to this, how fitting is it, then, to desist from it as far as humanly possible!

24. I also admonish you that, should you have any dealing with any person who does not understand well, explain the matter clearly and cause him to understand every detail. Do not say: "What matter? He has agreed, and agreed is agreed." Do not entertain such an idea, for you may easily transgress the prohibition "Do not deceive. ..." And what of the maxim of the Merciful One, "Love your neighbor as yourself"? One should merely do everything according to the same justice one

asks for oneself. And what is disagreeable to you do not do to others. Take heed not to borrow more than the amount of money you possess for nothing impedes God from granting succor, whether with much or with little. Should you not be able to conduct business with a small quantity of money, then accept the money in return for a share of the profit but not as a loan.

26. Select for me a place where there is an empty space the size of a cubit of six handbreadths on each side, for our Sages were very particular about this. Throughout the seven days of mourning gather ten learned men in your houses to study Mishnah and have them say prior to the study: "We are studying for the merit of his soul." Thereafter, you should recite *Kaddish.* Afterwards schedule for yourselves the study of Mishnah for one entire year, and do likewise on every *yahrzeit,* and say that it is for the merit of my soul. Eulogize me, and if you cannot do so yourselves hire eulogizers, inasmuch as our Sages, of blessed memory, were very particular about this, and certainly, they were not particular about it because of mere vanity. Certainly, it has some benefit though there is none among us who knows its extent, but their mind was broader. Notify the community of Lissa immediately of the day of my decease, inasmuch as they have a beautiful custom with respect to their deceased rabbis—they recite a *Kel male raḥamim* for them publicly on every festival. I ask the Torah scholars to study Mishnah for my sake every year, for the merit of my soul, and their reward will be doubled by Heaven.

27. On the tombstone do not write either "Rabbi" or "Gaon," for perhaps I have sinned by assuming the role of rabbi, for I was not worthy of it. Why, then, should my sin be remembered constantly? After all, the angels cover their feet, so that the sin of the calf be not remembered. Only my name alone should be inscribed. Write "the author of," followed by the titles of the books I have authored, for if but one good item be found in the entire book it deserves to be mentioned as a merit.

28. All the novellae which I have produced in halakhah and aggadah appear according to my meager intellectual faculties to be true. I have repeated them to a number of outstanding scholars, who have praised them. My request of you is that you see to bring them to publication and should the merit of my ancestors cause you to become scholars too, then test my words by the penetrative powers of your minds, and select what you consider best assigning it the priority of being printed.

However, even that which does not seem right in your eyes do not erase from the book—for the words of the Torah are poor in one spot and rich in another. And when you bring my words to publication [write my name on the book]. Even though I myself did not write my name on the book, for through our many transgressions hatred and jealousy reign in our generation, and perhaps some will say, "This one, too, is among the authors!" and without thorough study will scorn it whereas, not knowing the author's name, they will look deeper into it. I hope with God's help that after deeper study they will find good things in it. However, now that many of my writings will have been printed and, with God's help, accepted, when you publish, write my name on the work. After all, is it a trifling matter that which David said, "Let me dwell in Thy tent forever"? Our Sages, of blessed memory, explained this as meaning that when a halakhic concept is recited in a person's name, his lips move in the grave. Likewise, see to it to print once again the published works, and to my book *Netivot ha-Mishpat* add the notes I have written in the margins.

29. I have in my possession works composed by my father, my master, the remembrance of the righteous be a blessing. Select such good and choice things which you find therein and bring them to publication. You will certainly be amply rewarded for this for my soul knows exceedingly the immense longing my father, my teacher, of blessed memory, had that this should come to pass. Fast and do thorough repentance before God on his *yahrzeit* each year, for the merit of the sons is of avail to atone for the sins of their parents.

CHAPTER 8

Between East and West: Modernity and Traditionalism in the Writings of Rabbi Yehi'el Ya'akov Weinberg

A preeminent twentieth-century halakhist, Rabbi Yehi'el Ya'akov Weinberg (1884–1966) stands out as a singular personality venerated by, and exercising a profound influence upon, both traditionalist and acculturated sectors of the Orthodox community. Born in Ciechanowiec, he became known as a talmudic prodigy in his youth during his years of study at the yeshivot of Mir and Slabodka. He served with distinction as rabbi of the Lithuanian town of Pilwishki until 1914, at which time he emigrated to Germany where he pursued studies at the Universities of Berlin and Giessen. He received a PhD from the University of Giessen for a thesis on the Masoretic text of the Pentateuch and was appointed to the faculty. Later he established residence in Berlin and assumed the post of rabbi in the Charlottenburg district. In 1924 he joined the faculty of the Berlin *Rabbinerseminar für das Orthodoxe Judentum* and was subsequently appointed its rector in 1931. During the pre-World War II era, he was viewed as the major halakhic authority for German Orthodoxy and, after the war, upon settling in Montreux, Switzerland, he was regarded as one of the few surviving halakhic authorities who remained on the European continent. While continuing to be a champion both of *mussar* and of traditional talmudic scholarship, Rabbi Weinberg was a keen advocate of the appropriation and integration of modern academic scholarship within the framework of traditional Torah study.

The discerning reader will find a synthesis of East and West revealed in Rabbi Weinberg's several volumes of responsa, *Seridei Esh*, as well as in his essays and homiletical writings. These writings reflect depth and breadth of scholarship, independence of thought, and penetrating insight in carefully formulated positions regarding social, technological, and philosophical questions of the day. They consistently manifest a reverence for time-hallowed values combined with an understanding of the temper of the age.

Many of the questions addressed to Rabbi Weinberg arose from intramural tensions between diverse segments of the Jewish community. Among Rabbi Weinberg's essays and homiletical writings are also historical sketches that reveal his critical approach as an analyst of the Jewish religious movements and trends of his time.

An analysis of these and other writings of Rabbi Weinberg serves to illustrate his unique method of combining the new with the old in preserving tradition in the face of modernity. A study of the writings of a revered Torah authority undertaken by someone who was not privileged to have had personal contact with the author of those writings must, of necessity, be flawed and limited. Hence this endeavor, which is an attempt to present an analysis of some of the written works of Rabbi Weinberg, his *Torah she-be-ktav*, is sorely lacking in the added dimension of *Torah she-be-al-peh*, direct oral transmission. A cursory glimpse at the biographical writings of colleagues, students and disciples of Rabbi Weinberg reveals a force of personality, of which only a glimmer can be obtained from the written word alone.[1] Yet the written word, naked and unadorned, has a life of its own.

---

1 See, for example, Chanan Lehrmann, introduction to J. J. Weinberg, *Das Volk der Religion: Gedanken über Judentum* (Geneva: Éditions Migdal, 1949), 9–18; Eliezer Berkovits, "Rabbi Yechiel Yakob Weinberg Satzal, My Teacher and Master," *Tradition* 8, no. 2 (1966), 5–14; idem, "Sirtutim le-Ishiyuto shel Mori ve-Rabbi," *Ha-Darom* 24 (1966–67), 6–11; David Ben-Davied, "Kavim li-Demuto shel ha-Rav Weinberg Zatzal be-Tor Posek," *Ha-Darom* 24 (1966–67), 12–15; C. D. Chavel, "Mi-Tzror Mikhtavim shel ha-Rav Weinberg Zatzal," *Ha-Darom* 24 (1966–67), 16–20; Samuel Atlas, "Ha-Gaon Rabbi Yeḥi'el Ya'akov Weinberg Zatzal: Kavim li-Demuto," *Sinai* 58 (1966): 281–92; Shilo Rafael, "Ha-Gaon Rabbi Yeḥi'el Ya'akov Weinberg Zatzal: Gadol u-Posek," *Sinai* 58 (1966), 293–296; Gabriel Chaim Cohen, "Devarim le-Zikhro shel Harahag Dr. Yeḥi'el Ya'akov Weinberg Zatzal," *De'ot* 31 (1966–67): 7–18; Avraham Abba Weingort, "Mi-Derekh Limmudo shel ha-Rav Yeḥi'el Ya'akov Weinberg," *De'ot* 31 (1966–67), 19–22, also published in *HaPardes* 41, no. 9 (June 1967): 38–41; Moshe·Stern, "Ish ha-Eshkolot," *De'ot* 31 (1966–67): 23; Hayyim H. Grinberg, *Mi-Gedolei ha-Dor* (Tel Aviv, 1967); Kalman Kahane, *Ḥeker ve-Iyun: Kovetz Ma'amarim*, vol. II (Tel Aviv: Mossad Yitzchak Breuer, 1967), 174–188; Moshe Auerbach, "Ha-Gaon R. Yeḥi'el Ya'akov Weinberg Zatzal be-Ḥever Morei Bet ha-Midrash le-Rabbanim be-Berlin," in *Sefer ha-Zikaron le Morenu ve-Rabbenu ha-Gaon Yeḥi'el Ya'akov Weinberg Zatzal, Rosh Bet ha-Midrash le-Rabbanim be-Berlin*, ed. Ezriel Hildesheimer and Kalman Kahane (Jerusalem: Keldheim, 1969), 359–361; and Ze'ev Hayyim Lipschitz, "Hirhurim al ha-Ish bi-Tekufato: Kavim li-Demuto shel ha-Ga'on Maran R. Yeḥi'el Ya'akov Weinberg, Zatzal," in Hildesheimer and Kahane, *Sefer ha-Zikaron*, 363–387. For personal, anecdotal

In analyzing R. Weinberg's views on the subtle interaction of different factors in Jewish communal and intellectual life, interpretive opinion may differ. This writer has therefore used direct citation liberally in order to present R. Weinberg's thinking in his own words so that the reader is free to reach independent conclusions, at least on the basis of the sources selected as representative of his thinking. Unfortunately, the distinctiveness and stylistic beauty of R. Weinberg's expression of the rabbinic idiom in flawless modern Hebrew cannot be reproduced in translation.

I

1. The Writings

Despite the loss of many of his writings during the war, R. Weinberg left a considerable body of published material. His major *oeuvre*, four volumes of *Seridei Esh*, was published in Jerusalem by Mossad Harav Kook. The first three volumes appeared during his lifetime in 1961, 1962, and 1966, respectively, and the fourth was published posthumously in 1969 with an introduction by Rabbi Shilo Rafael. In addition to responsa, they contain talmudic novellae, scholarly studies on rabbinics, and essays on Jewish intellectual history. His *Meḥkarim ba-Talmud* (Berlin: Bet ha-Midrash leRabbanim, 1937) included in *Seridei Esh*, vol. IV, 10–137, illustrates his mastery of both traditional and modern talmudic scholarship. Many of his essays and aggadic commentaries are collected in the Hebrew *Li-Perakim* (Bilgori: Chovevei ha-Agada ve-ha-Drush be-Warsha, 1936; second, revised edition, Jerusalem: Kiryah

reminiscences and data regarding R. Weinberg's youth see H. L. Gordon, "Aḥarei Mitato," *Ha-Do'ar*, 21 Shevat 5726 (February 11, 1966), 235 and Z. Mateson, "Ha-Tragedyah shel Adam Gadol," *Ha-Do'ar*, 12 Adar 5726 (March 4, 1966), 284–285, with additional notes by I. Smolar, *Ha-Do'ar*, 12 Adar 5726 (March 4, 1966), 285. Hitherto unpublished talmudic novellae, responsa, and correspondence of R. Weinberg have appeared in *Ḥiddushei Ba'al "Seridei Esh" ha-Ga'on ha-Rav Yeḥi'el Ya'akov Weinberg Zatzal al ha-Shas* (Jerusalem, 1995). That work, edited by Rabbi Abraham Abba Weingort, also contains a commentary, *Gaḥalei Esh*, by the editor as well as a valuable biographical essay. Regrettably, that significant volume of R. Weinberg's writings did not appear until after the material in this chapter was originally published. Marc Shapiro's extensive study, *Between the Yeshiva World and Modern Orthodoxy: The Life and Works of Rabbi Jehiel Jacob Weinberg, 1884–1966* (London: Littman Library of Jewish Civilization, 1999), was published subsequent to the appearance of the original version of this chapter in the proceedings of the Orthodox Forum. An intimate portrayal of Rabbi Weinberg, including many fascinating vignettes, is presented in a recent volume edited by Rabbi Abraham A. Weingort, *Zikhronot ha-Seridei Esh: Pirkei Zikhronot ve-Siḥot shel ha-Ga'on ha-Rav Yeḥi'el Ya'akov Weinberg Satral* (Jerusalem, 2019).

Ne'emanah, 1967). A shorter collection of essays in German was published in *Das Volk der Religion: Gedanken über Judentum* (Geneva, 1949). Additional novellae, articles, and essays appeared in various Hebrew, Yiddish, and German periodicals. The title of R. Weinberg's collection of responsa, *Seridei Esh*—Survivors of the Fire, or *Remnants from the Fire*—reflects his perception of himself as a brand plucked from the flames, a refugee, a survivor of a lost and bygone world. Rabbi Weinberg was tormented in the post-war years by the anguish of a survivor who had witnessed the death and destruction of so much that was beloved to him. He was painfully conscious of the fact that the responsa and novellae that he succeeded in publishing were but a remnant of his voluminous writings, the lion's share of which had been lost during the war. Yet, he harbored a hope that his work would serve as a memorial to cherished colleagues and to a Torah institution over which he had been privileged to preside.[2] The title is, however, appropriate in more ways than one. There is a poetic, lyrical strain in R. Weinberg's prose, a passion and enthusiasm that leaps from the page. The embers are aglow with fire.

The personality of R. Weinberg emerges as a configuration of intriguing paradoxes: a *Litvak* imbued with hasidic fervor, an East European culturally ill at ease in Berlin but who had acquired profound understanding of Western scholarship, an exacting halakhic scholar with a flair for aggadic interpretation, a thinker who fully understood modern theories but who remained firmly rooted in traditionalist values.

The numerous personal comments interspersed in R. Weinberg's various writings provide more than biographical data; they are windows through which the character of the author shines forth. They represent a chronicle of the life experiences of an individual who lived alone but who manifested an unusual talent for friendship and collegiality as well as an overriding sense of responsibility toward people and community. His early essays show vitality, vigor and engagement in the political and ideological ferment of the times. The responsa composed during the years he spent in Berlin represent a period of communal leadership during which a wide array of duties devolved upon him and a period during which he was besieged by demands upon him as a communal rabbi, as a lecturer in, and head of, the *Rabbinerseminar* and as the foremost halakhic arbiter for German Orthodoxy. The writings dated during the years following World War II betray the shifting moods and depression of years of struggle and torment during which "*lulay Toratekha sha'ashu'ai oz avadeti*

---

2 *Seridei Esh* (hereafter S. E.), vol. 1, introduction, 3.

be-onyi"—"were it not that Thy Torah was my delight, then I would have perished in my affliction." Writings of later decades reveal the relative isolation of his years in Switzerland when he assuaged his loneliness[3] and narrowed the distance from centers of Torah scholarship by "speaking in learning" through the medium of letters and responsa, in which he maintained a lively interchange with young and old, with representatives of diverse religious factions and alignments, with students, scholars, and rabbis in all corners of the globe. During his last years, occasional comments regarding failing health cloud the generally mellow tone of letters that impart advice and encouragement to those who sought his guidance. Throughout, there is a cordiality that is paradigmatic, a sense of appreciation, patience, and consideration for all who consult him, whether learned laymen or venerable scholars, combined with a genuine empathy toward friends and colleagues and, even more strikingly, a particular delight in nurturing the aspirations of young scholars who devoted their energies to Torah study.

Two character traits of R. Weinberg's that were recognized in him by his contemporaries are repeatedly reflected in his written works and are of crucial importance in assessing his role as a pivotal intellectual personality who bridged two diverse intellectual traditions. R. Weinberg was fiercely independent in spirit and uncompromising in his commitment to intellectual honesty. He was unstinting in his praise of those qualities in others, and it is from his praise of others that one gains insight into his own character.

R. Weinberg's breadth of intellect and subtlety of perspective precluded susceptibility to partisan influences. He refused to be confined within the constraints of social or political factions. In his description of the signal attributes of the late R. Chanoch Ehrentreu of Munich, one finds a portrayal that is also self-reflective:

> He related to everyone with understanding and with affection. Constantly, and in every situation, he sought to find the Jewish kernel, the Jewish spark, without distinction between trend and trend or between party and party. I know that there are people among us who will not perceive an unmitigated praise of the departed in pointing out this fact. On the contrary, they tend to denigrate receptivity to everyone as a form of compromise and insistently demand of every brother and fellow Jew a clear and definite stand in the nature of "are you with us or against us?"[4]

---

3 In a letter to R. Symcha Elberg, the editor of *Ha-Pardes,* R. Weinberg wrote that during his later years correspondence with intimates constituted "the single pleasure in my loneliness." See *Ha-Pardes* 40, no. 8 (May 1966), 39, and cf. *Ha-Pardes* 40, no. 9 (June 1966), 39.

4 *Li-Perakim,* 229. The address was delivered in Berlin in 1926.

Individuals such as Ehrentreu, emphasizes R. Weinberg, exemplify the eternal unity of the Jewish people. When called upon, they are ready to express their views unequivocally, but "an overflow of love of Israel"[5] determines the course of their public conduct and pronouncements.

Elsewhere, R. Weinberg praises R. Abraham Abba Reznik, a successor in the rabbinate of Pilwishki, for having a quality of honesty that prompted him to admit the cogency of a counter-argument or critique—and even to praise the individual whose critical comments had sharpened his own understanding.[6] Here, again, R. Weinberg's assessment of a colleague focuses upon a trait that characterized his own personality. His writings are replete with references to the critical comments of friends and colleagues and to insights and corrections based on newly perused sources. A disciple wrote of R. Weinberg that he had never seen an individual of comparable stature who admitted the validity of a question or criticism or acknowledged the insightful comments of students with such regularity.[7]

2. East and West

R. Weinberg's homiletical and aggadic writings almost in a confessional vein betray the deeper levels of his emotional and intellectual experience. Most significantly, they illustrate his attachment to the yeshivot and the *mussar* tradition and his constant awareness of the tension between the atmosphere of the yeshivot and the lifestyle of German Orthodoxy.

As an expatriate from Eastern Europe, despite the passage of time, R. Weinberg continued to feel somewhat of an outsider in Berlin. His sense of dislocation and non-belonging did not fade even subsequent to his assumption of positions of authority and prominence. A certain prejudice toward some Western and/or German characteristics finds subtle and not so subtle expression in his writings and East-West tensions echo in passages scattered throughout his homiletical and literary essays.

Thus, Rabbi Weinberg's description of various groups of Jews of widely disparate background and demeanor living together in cosmopolitan Berlin

---

5 Ibid., 229. Cf. an interesting personal portrayal of Ehrentreu by Gershom Scholem, *From Berlin to Jerusalem*, trans. Harry Zohn (New York: Shocken, 1988), 120–121.

6 Abraham Abba Reznik, *Klei Sharet* (Netanya, 1987), Introductory Essay by Rabbi J. J. Weinberg, 1.

7 Berkovits, "Siritutim," 7. Cf. the comments of Grinberg, *Mi-Gedolei ha-Dor*, unnumbered pages, section "Modeh al ha-Emet"; Atlas, "Ha-Gaon Rabbi Yeḥi'el Ya'akov Weinberg," 283; and Kahane, *Ḥeker ve-Iyun*, vol. II, 187.

betrays a hyper-sensitivity. A trace of prejudice even may be detected in a passage portraying the Western Jew in whom, although "the countenance is apparently already frozen, one may yet discern the marks of a Jew, the brightness of eyes and the radiance of a Jewish face."[8] Elsewhere, commenting on an aggadic statement, "R. Helbo in the name of R. Huna said: When a man leaves the synagogue, he should not take long steps. Abaye said: This is only when one goes *from* the synagogue, but when one goes *to* the synagogue, it is a pious deed to run" (*Berakhot* 6b), R. Weinberg contrasts the manner in which East European Jews rush to their familiar houses of prayer with the exaggerated dignity manifested by Western Jews who enter the portals of imposing edifices comporting themselves as if preparing for an audience with the monarch on a state occasion. There is more than a touch of satire and pain in the ironic portrayal of the disdain with which the Western Jew looks down on his "uncouth" Eastern brother's behavior.[9] The hurt is more evident in a description of a scenario in which Jews from different countries meet on a broad promenade in Berlin but barely acknowledge one another's presence:

> If, on occasion, a Western Jew extends his hand to greet his brother, the Eastern Jew—how cold is this hand! Should he look at his face and say a few words to him, how alien is his glance and the tone of his voice, how alien it is to him![10]

An anecdote related by R. Weinberg and recorded by a former student who personally heard the story from him underscores how alert R. Weinberg was to what he perceived as a deeply ingrained prejudice harbored by German Jews toward East European Jews. In the summer of 1920, R. Weinberg visited Königsberg. A young couple approached him at his hotel with the request that he perform a marriage ceremony on their behalf. The young woman was Esther Marx, daughter of a prominent Königsberg banker; her fiancé was a

---

8 *Li-Perakim*, 31.

9 Ibid., 177.

10 Ibid., 32. The perception of a barrier preventing understanding between East and West and of an accompanying strangeness is found again in R. Weinberg's depiction of the burial of a leading Lithuanian philanthropist in Homburg, a town in the environs of Frankfurt: "Here in a foreign land, an exile from his home ... Alone in a strange place, among people strange to [him]. ..." Ibid., 250. Cf. Hermann Schwab's description of the tensions between Eastern and Western Jews in *The History of Orthodox Jewry in Germany*, trans. Irene R. Birnbaum (London: The Mitre Press, 1950), 107–108, which concludes, "And so they lived side by side as strangers until the hurricane seized them and flung them together into the abyss."

young man from Eastern Europe who later gained renown as the Nobel Prize-winning author, Shmuel Yosef Agnon. They explained to R. Weinberg that they were unable to seek out a local rabbi to perform the ceremony since the young woman's father, an influential person and a pillar of the Orthodox community, was adamantly opposed to the marriage. Convinced that, come what may, the couple were determined not to go their separate ways, R. Weinberg acceded to their request and performed the marriage on Lag b'Omer of that year.

A number of years later, R. Weinberg once more found himself in Königsberg. Mr. Marx sought him out in the synagogue and expressed plea-sure at meeting him. Marx informed him that he was now most pleased with his daughter's match. His son-in-law had proved himself to be a devoted hus-band and a God-fearing individual. He proceeded to express his appreciation to R. Weinberg and offered a sum of money as an honorarium for having performed the marriage. R. Weinberg responded that when he had performed the ceremony he had had no thought of a fee and would not now accept remuneration. Marx then asked him to accept the proffered money as a contribution to a charity of his choice. R. Weinberg insisted, however, that Marx himself forward the money to some charity and, if he wished, have a receipt sent to him in Berlin. Explaining his course of conduct, R. Weinberg continued, "He surely thought to himself that I, as a rabbi from Eastern Europe, would accept the money and keep it for myself." R. Weinberg's projection onto Marx of a stereotyped prejudice toward the rapacious *Ostjude* is indicative of his own feelings after many years of sojourn in Western Europe. The former student reports having heard the story in 1934—twenty years after R. Weinberg established residence in Germany.[11]

On the other hand, on a purely intellectual level, R. Weinberg developed a regard and respect for German Orthodoxy and expressed satisfaction that East European Jewry was beginning to develop an appreciation of the Western

---

11 As related from personal experience by Dr. Reuvain Avineri, "Nesu'in shel Agnon," *Ma'ariv* (May 6, 1988). I am indebted to Professor Shalom Carmy for drawing my attention to this source. Interestingly, Scholem, *From Berlin to Jerusalem*, 125, describes meeting Agnon and his fiancée before their wedding:

> At that time Agnon was about to marry Esther Marx, the beautiful daughter of what might be described as one of the most aristocratic Orthodox Jewish families of Germany a family whose fame has endured to this day. Esther Marx had two qualities I deemed especially memorable in those days: she was as much a confirmed atheist as she was an admirer and master of the Hebrew lan-guage—surely a rare combination among German Jews. She spent that winter at Starnberg, and Agnon proudly showed me her postcards, which were written in flawless calligraphy and almost flawless Hebrew.

Orthodox renascence. He well understood the subtle interplay in which liberal Jews flattered and patronized East European Jews at the expense of German Orthodoxy. To R. Weinberg it was apparent that secularists could afford to patronize East European Jews who posed no threat to them, whereas their antagonism to the German Orthodox stemmed from a discomfiture at the synthesis of scrupulous religious observance and worldly culture that the latter group had achieved and which presented a challenge to the secularists' own weltanschauung.[12] For his part, R. Weinberg urged that due respect and recognition be accorded to the accomplishments and contributions of revitalized German Orthodoxy for "also from the great rabbis of Germany is there much for us to learn. Only if we strive to learn from all that is good and beneficial, beautiful and noble from all of our great rabbis together, whether they be in the East or in the West, only then will we be truly ennobled and successful, and the Name of Heaven be hallowed by us."[13]

The echoes of the East-West tensions and the potential for intellectual stimulus in an East-West nexus is poignantly expressed in an essay in which R. Weinberg describes a failed attempt at cross-cultural fertilization. In a eulogy on the death of R. Benjamin Milakowsky, the rabbi of the Russian-Polish Jewish congregation in Königsberg, delivered in 1929, R. Weinberg depicts Rabbi Milakowsky's vast erudition as the quality that prompted R. Yitzhak Elhanan to recommend his candidacy as successor to the ministry of Malbim. Always attuned to the ironies of a situation, R. Weinberg notes,

---

12 *Li-Perakim*, 232. Cf. R. Samson Raphael Hirsch, *The Collected Writings*, vol. 6: *Jewish Communal Life and Independent Orthodoxy* (New York: Philipp Feldheim Inc., 1990), 121–122.

13 *Li-Perakim*, 234. Cf. also ibid., 283, on what is lacking in Western Jewry, and ibid., 302–316 on the characteristics of the Kovno community. The latter essay, originally published in German, in *Jeschurun* 6 (1916), reflects an earlier, less optimistic view of an East-West synthesis; see, especially, p. 316, in the comments on rabbis of the "old" school: "It is the old yeshiva that gave them to us. The new college will not give us their like. It is not in its ability to do so. Let our brethren in Germany bear this in mind. ... For God's sake, for God's sake, do not take from us, what is in our purview, what remains yet for us as a refuge. Be cautious!" R. Weinberg's modified later view may be seen as the result of a change that took place in the intellectual atmosphere in the ensuing decade as a result of his own active participation in the *Rabbinerseminar*. On the efforts to introduce both the analytic method of talmudic study as taught in Lithuanian yeshivot and *mussar* ideology into the *Rabbinerseminar* on the part of R. Weinberg and his predecessor as rector, R. Avraham Eliyahu Kaplan, see Moshe Avigdor Shulvass, "Bet ha-Midrash le-Rabbanim be-Berlin," in *Mosdot ha-Torah be-Eropah*, ed. Samuel K. Mirsky (New York: Ogen, 1956), 695 and 703–704, and Isidor Grunfeld, *Three Generations: The Influence of Samson Raphael Hirsch on Jewish Life and Thought* (London: Jewish Post Publications, 1958), 78–79.

In this Lithuanian rabbinic personality, the Königsberg community acquired a representative of Torah Judaism, an ambassador of the old *bet midrash* in the modern cultural capital. In the city of Kant there settled a representative of Abaye and Rava, Ravina and Rav Ashi, with a residence permit in his hand.[14]

However, in that instance, the experiment failed. The attempt to transplant the Lithuanian Torah style to German soil did not bear fruit. R. Benjamin Milakowsky did not succeed in training a cadre of students. R. Weinberg writes of an earlier time when Malbim served as rabbi of Lithuanian and Russian émigrés in Königsberg, when R. Israel Salanter sojourned there briefly, and when R. Jacob Zevi Mecklenburg was rabbi of the German congregation. At the time, it appeared as if a creative intellectual symbiosis might emerge. However, when Rabbi Milakowsky assumed his post, times had already changed. A new group of lay leaders had emerged and the youth of both the Russian and the German communities had little interest in the Talmud study that was the forte of Rabbi Milakowsky. R. Weinberg, nevertheless, concluded even these words of criticism on an affirmative note. His own observation was that the post-World War I generation was experiencing an awakening of Torah study.[15] The goals of Rabbi Milakowsky would yet be realized after his passing. The East-West nexus would yet bear fruit.

R. Weinberg's feelings regarding Western Jews influenced his attitude toward their innovative educational institutions. Although he valued the contributions of the *Rabbinerseminar*, he did not believe the Seminary was the ideal place of study for all students. He writes candidly of a young man who had become one of his most beloved disciples and of how he had originally sought to dissuade the youth's family from sending him to study in Berlin. He had told the young man's mother:

> The people of Poland are not like the people of Germany. The people of Germany have long become accustomed to the cold atmosphere. Their stomach has become habituated and it is easy for it to digest various studies. Those, however, who have been raised in the atmosphere of Polish ḥasidut, a Judaism that is warm and fervent, are open to grave danger if they cross over to the chill atmosphere of German Jewry that is not capable of warming others of a different temperament.[16]

---

14 Ibid., 245.

15 Ibid., 346–347.

16 "Le-Zikhro," in *Yad Sha'ul: Sefer Zikaron al Shem ha-Rav Doktor Sha'ul Weingort Zatzal*, eds. J. J. Weinberg and P. Biberfeld (Tel Aviv, 1953), 5.

Moreover, R. Weinberg believed that the Lithuanian yeshivot were peerless institutions for training in advanced Talmud studies. When his disciple Saul Weingort was completing his ordination examination at the *Rabbinerseminar*, R. Weinberg advised him to pursue further studies in Eastern Europe:

> I have one request of you: that afterwards you travel to the Yeshiva of Mir or the Yeshiva of Slabodka. There you will devote all your time, day and night, to sacred subjects and only to sacred subjects. ... It is my desire to bring you to the wellspring from which I myself drank. Now that you have satiated yourself more than sufficiently with European culture, it is your obligation to return to the pure and holy wellspring of the yeshivot. There you will attain the gates of wisdom and enhanced knowledge of our holy Torah.[17]

Among the Lithuanian yeshivot, there was one in particular with which R. Weinberg identified and upon which he looked with pride and love, namely, the yeshiva of Slabodka. R. Weinberg composed a series of articles on the thought, methodology, and leadership of the *mussar* movement, as well as on the controversy surrounding that movement. These essays are remarkable both for their scholarly presentation of historical data[18] and for their trenchant critical analysis.[19] Nevertheless, the author's personal bias and subjectivity is evident throughout these writings. R. Weinberg's articles represent an assessment of a movement authored by an ardent protagonist, not by a disinterested observer. Thus, R. Weinberg describes the Slabodka yeshiva as having achieved the epitome of excellence. To R. Weinberg, Slabodka under the spiritual guidance of Rabbi Nathan Zevi Finkel[20] achieved a "wondrous synthesis"[21] in the creative combination of penetrating talmudic scholarship and profound *mussar*. Prior to that time, students who wished to pursue talmudic studies enrolled in various yeshivot and those whose goal was the attainment of higher levels of piety and spirituality sought out the presence of a *tzaddik* or spent hours of meditation in a *mussar* conventicle. After the closing of Volozhin, Slabodka assumed pride of position as a center of talmudic study that attracted students of the

---

17 Weinberg and Biberfeld, *Yad Sha'ul*, introduction, 7.
18 See especially *S. E.*, vol. 4, 276–284.
19 See especially ibid., 333–340.
20 1849–1926. He established the yeshiva in Slabodka in 1882.
21 *S. E.*, vol. 4, 328.

highest caliber.[22] In Slabodka there was, however, no cleavage or dichotomy between scholarship and piety. The ideal was an integrated personality. In the opinion of R. Weinberg, the *Alter* of Slabodka had reached a pinnacle of success in creating "a unified and perfect synthesis of keen and penetrating *lomdut* and elevated and purified *mussar*—a synthesis the like of whose purity and depth existed in no other place."[23]

All his life R. Weinberg also looked back with nostalgia on the years he had spent as rabbi of Pilwishki. The West might provide sources to slake one's thirst for knowledge but only in the East was the very air permeated with Torah. R. Weinberg bemoaned the fact that, unlike the Polish *shtetl*, the small Lithuanian Jewish towns did not find a poet laureate to record and extol their character. Writing of Pilwishki, R. Weinberg stated:

> The primary strength of the Lithuanian town was in the creation of an atmosphere totally permeated with spiritual values and high aspirations for human perfection in the acquisition of knowledge of the Torah. The air of the Lithuanian town was saturated with love of Torah. All, from the great scholars to the simple folk, saw in the study of the Torah the goal of life and the essence of life. This love spurred the laymen to cause their daughters to marry Torah scholars and to support them and it is this love that prompted even the poor and impoverished to share their meager bread with youths who studied in the *bet ha-midrash* of the town....
>
> The *bet midrash* was akin to a terrestrial Garden of Eden in which dwelled men of stature who derived pleasure from the light which burst forth from every folio of the Gemara. The Torah study of the great diligent scholars did not contain anything at all of the asceticism that is cut off from reality, that rejects life and seeks refuge in the world of the imagination.
>
> The Lithuanian Jew was by nature overflowing with vigor and loved life with every thread of his soul, but he wished for a life worthy of its name, a life in which there is fulfillment of the claims of heart and spirit. In Torah he found the only path to perfection, to enrichment of thought, to purification of character ... in a word, to a life of the elevation of man above the beast.[24]

---

22 Ibid., 326.
23 Ibid., 328
24 *Klei Sharet*, introduction, 4–5.

The Holocaust left an indelible mark on R. Weinberg. There are wounds from which there is no complete recovery.[25] In his despair and pain at the destruction the Nazi hordes had wrought on the Lithuanian towns, he wrote: "Who could ever have thought, who could have let cross his mind, the dreadful thought that a devastating end would come to this Jewry, not to leave of it a remnant or a refuge? Behold, oh Lord, and consider to whom have they, the evil ones of the human race, done this!"[26]

Elsewhere, R. Weinberg expressed his opinion that it was appropriate for the Jewish community to designate a memorial day for the "rabbis and martyrs of Israel who had been killed, slaughtered, and burned for the Sanctification of the Name, to remember the souls of these martyrs on that day."[27] R. Weinberg was the only halakhic authority of stature to call for a Holocaust commemoration of this nature.[28] Such a memorial was necessary not only to give due honor to the departed but in order that future generations not forget the devastating losses of our people during this time when the black Nazi evil enveloped the countries of Europe. Of those who preached forgiveness, a philosophy of let bygones be bygones, R. Weinberg wrote, "Rather let them advise the cursed wicked ones that they do as did the executioner of R. Hananya ben Teradyon: 'He then too jumped and threw himself into the fire' (*Avodah Zarah* 18a)."[29]

---

25 See Zorach Warhaftig's moving personal account of a series of meetings with R. Weinberg, both before and after World War II, as recounted in his *Palit ve-Sarid be-Yemei ha-Sho'ah* (Jerusalem: Yad Vashem, 1984), 343–346. Warhaftig describes R. Weinberg's flawed assessment of the Nazi threat before the war, his utter desperation following *Kristallnacht,* and his pitiful, shattered mental and physical state in the aftermath of the war. Cf. R. Weinberg's own description of his terrible ordeal, *Yad Sha'ul,* introduction, 8–13 and S. E., vol. II, 64. Commenting on why he does not favor a reception in honor of the publication of S. E., R. Weinberg notes that, apart from his shunning public displays, "In the final analysis, one must not forget that my work, S. E., memorializes the terrible Holocaust that occurred to our people. How can one rejoice while the terrible mourning has not been mitigated even minutely? Perhaps it is the forgetfulness that is found among us that enables us to live and accomplish and be creative." See letter published in *Ha-Pardes* 40, no. 9 (June 1966), 38–39.

26 *Klei Sharet,* 5.

27 S. E., vol. 2, no 30, 53 n.

28 Establishment of a formal day of commemoration was actively opposed by ranking halakhic scholars. See the analysis of this controversy in Immanuel Jakobovits, "Some Personal, Theological and Religious Responses to the Holocaust," in *Remembering for the Future: The Impact of the Holocaust and Genocide on Jews and Christians* (Oxford: Pergamon Press, 1988), vol. III, 177–185.

29 S. E., vol. 2, 53 n. Cf., also, *Yad Sha'ul,* 10, and his comments on the Warsaw ghetto uprising. Agony over the fate of Holocaust victims only heightened R. Weinberg's sensitivity to the history of Jewish persecution and martyrdom. Cf. a characteristic homiletic comment of R. Weinberg on *Sukkah* 45a, in which he portrays the grandeur of Jewish self-sacrifice, as recounted by Berkovits, "Sirtutim," 10.

The sole consolation he found was the reestablishment of yeshivot in the United States and *Eretz Yisra'el*. It was to the abiding impact and influence of the towering personalities of the *mussar* movement[30] and to the devotion to Torah of Eastern European Jewry that R. Weinberg credited this renaissance:

> The love of Torah on the part of the Lithuanian Jew was a firm foundation in his soul and was absorbed in his blood and all his limbs. Therefore, Lithuanian Jewry merited what it merited: The creation of Torah values and intellectual values from which the entire people sustained itself and continues to sustain itself.[31]

II

The primary factor leading to the development of a chasm between rabbinic leaders and the masses of Jews was the fact that the great majority of the populace lived in an entirely different world from that of the Torah scholars. Individuals firmly ensconced within the four ells of halakhah, who spent their lives steeped in Torah, had little knowledge and understanding of the mental frame of reference employed by those whose lives had moved far from these traditional parameters. Beginning with the stirrings of the Enlightenment and continuing until contemporary times, the issues with regard to which a wide abyss of noncomprehension has arisen include the problems of belief in an age of secularism and religious skepticism, aspirations inspired by nationalism as expressed in Zionist ideology and desire for return to the Land of Israel, the university experience on the part of students, the sensibilities of women moved by feminist concerns and the need for innovation and change in institutional structures within the community.

An examination of the views of R. Weinberg illustrates the extent to which he was alert to the ideological, social, and communal problems that confronted the Jewish community of his day.

1. Zionism and the State of Israel

Opposing factions cannot engage in meaningful dialogue if they fail to understand one another's basic premises. Just as individuals who speak different

---

30 *S. E.*, vol. 4, 312.
31 *Klei Sharet*, 5.

languages require an interpreter to facilitate communication, people whose intellectual and social frames of reference are vastly different may be well served by an interpreter who is able to explain the disparate motivations and hesitations of one group to the other. R. Weinberg's intimate association with the yeshivot and their leaders and his receptivity to, and interest in, the Zionist enterprise rendered him exceptionally suited to be the individual who served as an interpreter to both sides. This was a function he consciously sought to perform throughout his life, beginning with youthful writings in which he depicted understanding as the key to rapprochement, later published under the title "The Path to Communication (*Verstendigung*) with Orthodoxy" (1917),[32] and culminating in his celebrated letter to Ben Gurion on the "Who is a Jew?" issue (1959).[33]

From its earliest beginnings, the Zionist movement engendered an emotionally charged controversy within the traditional rabbinate. Within the rabbinic community, a minority embraced its visionary program while the majority were wary of its nonreligious orientation and secular leadership. Moreover, many prominent rabbinic figures expressed adamant opposition both to its immediate agenda and its long-range goals.[34] As the movement grew in popularity, its redemptive allure captured the imagination of young people in all sectors of the Jewish community and attracted a following even within the ranks of yeshiva students. As a counterbalance to the growing secular Zionist movement, religious Zionists established the Mizrachi movement in 1902 while the non-Zionist Orthodox founded Agudath Israel in 1912.

An independent person by nature, Rabbi Weinberg remained above the fray of party politics throughout the greater part of his life and did not identify with either Mizrachi or Agudath Israel. It is true that as a young man he was active in the *Maḥazikei ha-Dat*, a prominent Orthodox yeshiva-based movement that was a precursor of Agudath Israel.[35] Subsequently, he enjoyed

---

32 First published in 1917 as a series of articles in Yiddish in *Dos Yiddishe Vort* and republished in pamphlet form in Hebrew in Lodz in 1922. Also republished together with other essays in *Et Aḥai Anokhi Mevakesh* (Bnei Brak: Netzaḥ, 1966), 49–76.

33 See *S. E.*, vol. 4, 379–385 and *Et Aḥai*, 87–100.

34 See Jacob J. Schacter, "Haskalah, Secular Studies and the Close of the Yeshiva in Volozhin in 1892," *The Torah u-Madda Journal* 2 (1990), 128 n. 121, for an excellent note on the response of various prominent rabbinic authorities to the *Ḥibbat Tziyyon* movement and early Zionist aspirations.

35 See Aaron Suraski, "Mi-Toldotav," in *Et Aḥai*, 18. On the relationship of *Maḥazikei ha-Dat* and the Agudath Israel, see Rabbi Hayyim Ozer Grodzenski, *Aḥiʿezer: Kovetz Iggerot*, ed. A. Suraski (Bnei Brak: Netzaḥ, 1970), vol. I, 279–284.

a close relationship with leaders of the Agudath Israel and became a regular contributor to the Agudist press. His articles appeared frequently in publications such as the Hebrew *Ha-Modiʻa* of Poltava, the Yiddish *Dos Yiddishe Vort* and the *Togblatt* of Warsaw, and *Dos Vort* of Vilna as well as the German *Israelit* of Frankfurt and *Jeschurun* of Berlin. It is also evident that, at that time, he disapproved of affiliation with Mizrachi since such affiliation would have been tantamount to disassociation from preeminent rabbinic leaders of the day.[36] He did, however, recognize the need for creation of an effective Orthodox organizational infrastructure[37] and did not minimize the contributions of the nascent Agudath Israel in that endeavor.

During those years, one of his chief concerns was the desire to foster mutual understanding between the various factions and, in particular, to explain the motivations underlying the intensity of feeling on the part of opponents of the secular Jewish political movements. The religious mentality, he argued, eschews tolerance, not out of narrow-mindedness, but because of a depth of commitment that leads to an equation of tolerance with indifference. "Tolerance—a modern invention!" he wrote. "I can love my brother or hate him; but under no circumstances am I, or can I be, tolerant of him. From my brother I *demand*—and have the privilege to demand—that he not deny me the opportunity to love him properly, as one loves a brother. ... Not manners and restraint but warmth of feeling, not tolerance and indifference but love and brotherhood we ask and demand of you!"[38]

Ruminations regarding the early religious Zionist movement are recorded in a tribute to Rabbi Yitzhak Yaʻakov Reines that R. Weinberg authored, originally in German, soon after Rabbi Reines's death in 1914. R. Weinberg certainly did not refuse to be identified with a personality such as Reines[39] and did not hesitate publicly to express his admiration for him even though he did not find himself fully in agreement either with Reines's educational theories or his political agenda.

As a perceptive and sensitive person, R. Weinberg was keenly aware of the pain of those individuals destined to suffer the "fate of great individuals in Israel

36 *S. E.*, vol. 4, 357.

37 *Et Aḥai*, 70–74.

38 Ibid., 58–59.

39 To the contrary, he notes he was "privileged to be close to Reines and a friend of his," *S. E.*, vol. 4, 358. The essay on Reines appeared in several German journals and was later translated into Hebrew by R. Weinberg, published in *Li-Perakim*, 326–336, and republished in *S. E.*, vol. 4, 353–359.

graced with extraordinary talents and burdened with Jewish *mazal* (luck),"[40] individuals whose lives ought one day to be recorded in a "chronicle of the afflicted in Israel."[41] He unreservedly admired Reines's scholarship, his written and spoken words, his enormous vitality and sacrificial communal activism as well as his independence of spirit, vision, and idealism. But he understood only too well the chain of events that had led to the isolation and unhappiness that marked Reines's life.

Reflecting familiarity with the causes of socio-religious ferment in Eastern Europe, R. Weinberg describes the conflict within the Jewish community in the early days of the Zionist movement. The community had already been sundered by the Enlightenment; pious Jews had become overly defensive in reaction to purveyors of Russian culture who sought to achieve forced Russification and assimilation; and antagonism between modernists and traditionalists had grown to warlike dimensions.[42] With the advent of Zionist ideology, the community became further fragmented. The fiery enthusiasm and passion of Zionist youth was blunted by the opposition of rabbinic leaders based in part upon their lack of trust in activists who were not loyal to the traditions of Judaism. Caught in the middle were young rabbis who found themselves torn "between two magnets," drawn to the vibrancy and glamour of the new movement but anchored by allegiance to the rabbinic luminaries who were its opponents.

It was against this background that Reines announced himself as an advocate of Zionism. Reines's move was prompted by sincere conviction and boundless love of fellow Jews.[43] To his colleagues in the rabbinate, however, his actions were those of a traitor. R. Weinberg delivers his own unequivocal evaluation of Reines's position. Notwithstanding the sincerity of Reines's conviction, R. Weinberg believed that Reines had committed a grievous error in parting company with the eminent rabbinic scholars of the day and in deviating from the policies established by them.

The extent to which R. Weinberg was moved by Reines's quandary is evident in the manner in which he repeats a discussion with Reines regarding Reines's vain attempts to heal the breach that developed between himself and

---

40 S. E., vol. 4, 359.

41 Ibid., 355.

42 Incisive is R. Weinberg's description of how offended were the faithful East European Jews at the insinuation that their learned sages needed to be taught etiquette. They felt wounded to the core as would be "the feeling of an aristocrat by birth to whom a wealthy *noveau riche* boor would preach correct behavior and teach the rules of manners and proper conduct." Ibid., 355.

43 Cf. Reines's own comments, *Shnei ha-Me'orot* (Pietrkow, 1913), part 2, 27.

his colleagues. R. Weinberg recounts how Reines commiserated with him: "Surely Torah scholars should not have turned a deaf ear when he approached them to plead the case of a movement that gave promise for the rescue of Jewish lives." At the very least, he argued, with passion, their reaction should have been comparable to that customarily forthcoming in the case of an *agunah* problem in which the authority consulted can find no basis for a favorable response. In such cases the response is to seek the advice of others. Affected by the torment reflected in those words, R. Weinberg repeated the complaint to one of Reines's opponents and the latter responded: "He came to us to organize activity, not to ask advice. Why did he not come before he took such a drastic public step?" R. Weinberg concludes:

> Surely, justice was on the side of the older rabbis. Whoever does not understand this, whoever does not want to understand the spiritual premise of their pure and innocent hearts does not understand anything. On the other hand; it is a dreadful wrong to dispute the righteousness of the aged Reines, of blessed memory. His intent was also pure and innocent.[44]

R. Weinberg recognized that it was psychologically impossible for rabbinic leaders to join forces with someone who had broken ranks and publicly espoused policies that they had decried. Hence, for Reines, the early years of the Mizrachi movement he founded were inevitably doomed to be years of painful disappointment. R. Weinberg presents a moving portrayal of how, although hurt and wounded in the political fray, Reines continued to admire and revere the rabbinic personalities who all but ostracized him. Events develop a momentum of their own and Reines found himself increasingly isolated. The scholars with whom he could have communicated spurned him and, although to the youth of the Zionist Congresses he was a patriarchal figure, he was nevertheless a remote hero whose language they did not at all comprehend. He continued to be a visionary but—in R. Weinberg's opinion—one who lived in a dream world, ineffective in both his educational[45] and Zionist endeavors.

---

44   S. E., vol. 4, 357. Cf. *Shnei ha-Me'orot*, part 2, 22–23 and 49.

45   S. E., vol. 4, 359. R. Weinberg was an open critic of Reines's educational philosophy. R. Weinberg relates that after he had delivered a guest talmudic discourse at Reines's yeshiva, the aged Reines asked him his opinion of the yeshiva from which, stated Reines, had emerged, "scholars, strictly religious Jews, enlightened Jews, good Zionists, according to my pattern ... Obviously, I answered his enthusiasm with gloomy silence. I did not want to destroy his last dream with my wicked doubts" (359).

Whether or not R. Weinberg's own political views regarding either the Mizrachi or the general Zionist movement changed significantly during the ensuing years, his writings began to reflect an increasing sympathy for the Zionist enterprise. In one of his essays he profiles two diverse sets of personalities: the traditional religious Jew versus the assimilated liberal Jew and the traditional religious Jew versus the idealistic self-sacrificing ḥalutz (Zionist pioneer). With regard to the first pair, there is no difficulty, claims R. Weinberg, in preferring one over the other: obviously, a Jewish personality must be selected over a secular one. With regard to the second pair, it is difficult to negate the contribution of either member of the pair. Truth and fairness, writes R. Weinberg, demand a positive assessment of the character traits of the nationalist Jew who has rebuilt the Land with his blood and sweat and prepared a haven and place of refuge for his fellow Jews. How is it possible to harbor disdain or ingratitude toward these pioneers, asks R. Weinberg, when they have literally sunk their youth and their health into the malarial swamps in order to transform the Land of Israel into a fruitful Eden?[46]

Most indicative of R. Weinberg's sympathy for Zionist aspirations is his remarkable essay devoted to an assessment of Theodor Herzl. Few, if any, East European rabbinic scholars would have expressed in writing a favorable portrayal of the assimilated Herzl. Yet, R. Weinberg did not hesitate to write that he saw Herzl as a prophetic visionary and spiritual personality. The title of the brief sketch encapsulates the message: "Herzl Ish ha-Dat" (Herzl, the Man of Religion).[47] R. Weinberg suggests that Herzl was a "great ba'al teshuvah [returnee], a pioneer of the great era of teshuvah in Judaism." He perceives Herzl's idealism as emanating from the deep recesses of a spiritual personality and is convinced that "in his innermost being he was totally of a religious nature."[48] R. Weinberg distinguishes between Herzl the statesman and Herzl the poet and finds the statesman to be rooted in the world of reality and the poet to be rooted in the world of faith.

This essay is briefer and less structured than R. Weinberg's other writings and consists merely of a series of vignettes: Herzl dispensing charity; Herzl at his father's gravesite; Herzl meeting the common folk in Vilna; Herzl, with

---

46 See undated essay "Ye'ud ve-Ya'ad (Ha-Hit'orrerut ha-Le'ummit)," in Li-Perakim, 77.
47 "Herzl, Ish ha-Dat" was published in Ha-Olam 29 (July 18, 1935), 460–461. It is instructive to compare this essay with Isaac Breuer's "Epilog zum Tode Dr. Herzls," Der Israelit 45, no. 61 (August 1, 1904), 1295–1299. Cf. also Isaac Breuer, Concepts of Judaism, ed. Jacob S. Levinger (Jerusalem: Israel Universities Press, 1974), 3, 302–307, and 318 n. 18.
48 Ha-Olam, 460.

tears in his eyes, accepting a scroll of the Torah from Rabbi Shlomoh ha-Kohen of Vilna. R. Weinberg writes that, to the masses, the name "Herzl" became a symbol of "future, hope and faith."[49] The reader readily perceives that R. Weinberg was not unaffected by the Zionist dream.[50]

Following the cataclysmic events of the Holocaust that left a decimated European Jewry in their wake, R. Weinberg looked upon the establishment of the State of Israel in 1948 as a sign that Divine favor had not departed from the Jewish people. He was unreserved and unambivalent in describing the founding of the State as a providential event of unsurpassed magnitude. He hailed

> the great event that occurred to the Jewish people for the first time after a lengthy exile of two thousand years. I see in this the work of miracles of a higher Providence that stood by us in our time of sorrow, the like of which there has not been since Israel became a nation. Following the destruction of the greater segment of our people, "From the Lord this has been, it is wondrous in our eyes"[51]: the union of nations opposed to one another and fighting one another with fury and with hatred such as the Russian people and the American people for purposes of a common endeavor, that is, the founding of a Jewish State. I have already spoken publicly at a large public assembly regarding these miracles and wonders.[52]

---

49 Ibid., 461. Cf. *Das Volk der Religion*, 79.

50 R. Weinberg's growing sympathy for Zionist aspirations was not unnoticed by colleagues on the faculty of the *Rabbinerseminar*. Both Auerbach, *Sefer ha-Zikaron*, 360, and Mario Offenberg, "Adass Jisroel: Orthodox und aufgeklärt," in *Adass Jisroel, die jüdische Gemeinde in Berlin (1869–1942). Vernichtet und Vergessen*, ed. Mario Offenberg (Berlin: Museumspädagogischer Dienst, 1986), 34–35, describe the variegated Seminary faculty during the 1930s as including passionate adherents of both Mizrachi and Agudath Israel. Partisans of Mizrachi sought to win over R. Weinberg to their political viewpoint but, despite the attraction he felt to their cause, R. Weinberg remained critical of the Mizrachi. In an ironic riposte typical of his personality, R. Weinberg is reputed to have said: *"Mizrachis Essen schmeckt zwar besser, doch das von Aguda ist kosherer ... Ihr Mizrachi-Leute werdet im Jüdischen Staat Gott die Gleichberichtigung gewähren. Doch ich bin überzeugt, herrschen last ihr ihn nicht."* See Isi Jacob Eisner, "Reminiscenses of the Berlin Rabbinical Seminary," *Leo Baeck Institute Year Book* 12 (1967), 45 and Offenberg, "Adass Jisroel," 36.
While R. Weinberg remained politically independent and unaffiliated throughout his life, Kalman Kahane, *Ḥeker ve-Iyun* 2:182, remarks on his particular sympathy for Poalei Agudath Israel, a party whose ideology combined elements of both Mizrachi and Aguda in a manner that R. Weinberg may well have found appealing.

51 Psalms 118:23.

52 *S. E.*, vol. 2, no. 70, 186. Cf. *Das Volk der Religion*, 80.

R. Weinberg's essay, "Religion and State in Israel," written in 1949, can only be understood as reflective of the words of the psalmist: "When the Lord returned the returning of Zion we were as dreamers" (Psalms 126:1). R. Weinberg dreamed glorious dreams of the fledgling country. He glorified the Israeli soldiers, "grandchildren of the Maccabees, soldiers of the Bar Kochba army, who in renewed partnership with the students of Rabbi Akiva have taken up the battle for the Holy Land interrupted two thousand years ago,"[53] envisioned the establishment of a social welfare system rooted in biblical teachings and anticipated a new golden age of Arab-Jewish cultural cooperation. Perhaps most utopian of all were his hopes that the secular pioneering spirit would be transformed into a religious one and that a spiritual revival would ensue. Herzl had awakened the hopes of Jews with the charge that the Jewish State could become a reality: "If you will, it is no dream." In the heady first days of the State, R. Weinberg believed that the time had come to proclaim: "If we will, the Messiah is a reality."[54] The only cloud he saw on the horizon was the suggestion on the part of some that the Israeli government adopt a policy of separation of "church" and state, a policy that had gained wide currency in Western democracies. However, R. Weinberg expressed his conviction that ultimately such a policy would not be endorsed by the majority of Israelis and that even those whose political allegiance was to the socialist parties were, at heart, too intimately attached to the fundamentals of Judaism to accept a political modality that would sunder religion and nationality in the State of Israel.

As the years passed, he continued to express lavish praise of the achievements of the developing State and, despite its secular character, he viewed it as endowed with a measure of sanctity. R. Weinberg wrote:

> To a Jewish person whose soul is not yet completely frozen there is no need to explain the full blessing that the State of Israel has brought us. This, our State that has renewed itself in the ancient land of the fathers, has brought revival and political independence to the Jewish people who dwell in Zion and to us, the dispersed of Israel in strange lands, honor and glory. The debate born of the question of whether to recognize a secular State that, to our great sorrow, is not founded upon the basis of Torah and mitzvot fades like smoke in the face of the existing reality of a sovereign Israeli government with a powerful security force that with unparalleled

---

53 *Das Volk der Religion*, 83.
54 Ibid., 87.

self-sacrifice protects our lives and the lives of our children within the country as well as our honor and our rights outside of it.

The renewed country is holy to us, not only because of its essential holiness derived from the word of our God and the God of our fathers and because of the sacred mitzvot that are dependent upon it. It has become even more sanctified by the holiness of Jewish blood, the blood of our pioneers who sank their blood and sweat in the accursed malarial swamps to transform them into flourishing, blossoming Edens for us and for those who follow us. It has been sanctified by the blood of our heroes, fighters of the battle of our people for conquest of the land and its freedom, in order to establish for the oppressed, a haven of refuge and a saving remnant in the land of the fathers for the oppressed, faint and persecuted nation.[55]

R. Weinberg sought occasions to encourage and applaud efforts on behalf of *aliyah*. A typical example of his thinking are the remarks appended to a halakhic discourse in honor of the *bar mitzvah* of the child of an intimate disciple:

In the Torah it is said: "For man is as the tree of the field." Man is like unto a tree. Just as for a tree there are two factors [needed] for its growth and development, the earth in which it is rooted and the air in which it lives and [grows] and which it breathes, so for his spiritual growth, a man requires the land in which he is born and rooted and the atmosphere of the environment which he imbibes and from which he lives and develops. In the land of Israel we had both factors, a holy land, the land of our fathers: Abraham, Isaac and Jacob, the land of the prophets and the holy *tanna'im* as well as the sacred air of the holy land. "The air of the Land of Israel makes one wise," say the Sages. We who have been born in the Diaspora, in a foreign land, where even the air is foreign and the surroundings are foreign, have no possibility to live and exist as Jews save by means of the fact that we have established for ourselves synagogues and houses of study and academies in which the air has been hallowed with the sanctity of the Torah. When we sit in the synagogue and in the house of study and are engaged in prayer and Torah, we breathe into ourselves the spirit of Torah and in this merit we are able to exist despite the fact that we dwell in a foreign land. But for a Jew, it is good that he traverse and settle in the Land of Israel where all is holy and all is Jewish, the land, the air, the surroundings, the home, the marketplace, et cetera.[56]

---

55 *S. E.*, vol. 4, 375.
56 *S. E.*, vol. 3, no. 84, 272.

Nevertheless, R. Weinberg remained a sharp critic of secularist ideal-ization of a state devoid of religious heritage. Here, too, his views are clearly expressed in a homiletical comment in which he pointed to a contradic-tion between the verse "Moses commanded us the Torah an inheritance of the congregation of Jacob" (Deuteronomy 33:4) and the verse "And I shall give it unto you for an inheritance" (Exodus 6:8). Deuteronomy 33:4 posits the Torah as the inheritance of the Jewish people, whereas the reference in Exodus 6:8 is to the Promised Land as the inheritance. R. Weinberg suggests that prior to his demise, Moses "revealed that the secret of Jewish existence is not contingent upon the Land but upon the 'Torah commanded unto us by Moses."[57] The inheritance of Israel is the Torah rather than the Land. The Land is indeed described as an inheritance, but only in an instrumental sense. R. Weinberg concludes, "The inheritance that is the basis of our life and our existence is solely the Torah and we need not be embarrassed in the presence of scoffers but must proclaim unequivocally that the national territory is the Torah. … In this we are distinct from every nation and people. Whoever does not acknowledge this denies the fundamental principle of Judaism."[58]

It was precisely because of his belief in the operation of Divine providence in the establishment of the State of Israel that R. Weinberg was concerned lest the moment of destiny be lost. His sorrow at the establishment of the State of Israel as a secular polity governed by an alien system of law rather than by halakhah and influenced by the cultural values of Europe and America rather than by Torah teachings was not the pain of a passive observer saddened at an absence of religiosity but the anguish of a visionary who feared the loss of a historic opportunity for salvation. As a realist, he was aware that a state founded on secularist military and political aspirations need not necessarily endure. Survival of the state can be assured only as a phenomenon of salvation which, in turn, is unlikely to be associated with a state devoid of spiritual and cultural integrity. Adoption of Hebrew, even the idiom of the Bible, as the national lan-guage cannot suffice to establish the spiritual integrity that merits salvation. Hence, denial of the religious and prophetic ethos of Judaism is tantamount to national suicide. For Jews there can be no other culture than that of "the religion of Moses and Israel. … The ultimate outcome of the development of secular identity and abandonment of accepted halakhah is disintegration. …"[59] Moreover, although he recognized that a modern state cannot engage in religious coercion, he was equally convinced that only by assuming a public

57 Ibid., no. 77, 258.
58 Ibid., no. 77, 258.
59 S. E., vol. 4, 374.

posture of identification with authentic Jewish values would it be possible for the Jewish State "to be assured that the entire Jewish world would recognize and acknowledge its sovereignty."[60]

The attitude of those observant Jews who were unable to identify joyously with the resurgence of Jewish sovereignty in Israel was sympathetically explained by R. Weinberg as reminiscent of the elders in the days of Ezra and Nehemiah, who feared that the new Temple and the service performed therein would not attain the quality of sanctity and spirituality manifest in the First Temple.[61] Similarly, the trepidation among contemporary Jews that the new State might not lead to a spiritual rebirth could not be stilled:

> *Galut* (exile) yet continues and extends. It has gone up with us to the land of the fathers and we have not as yet succeeded in freeing ourselves from its bonds. ... When we see a large number of the Jewish youth in the land influenced by the false worship of coarse and cruel materialism and adopting an atheistic materialistic weltanschauung we taste the taste of embittered *galut*.[62]

R. Weinberg cautioned that the State dare not risk further alienation of religious Jewry for, in the final analysis, it is that segment of the Jewish people alone of whose allegiance the State of Israel can be assured:

> They are more important for the preservation of the State than the millions and millions of dollars of the American United Jewish Appeal. It is they who bear aloft the banner of Jewish culture and preserve Judaism in its pristine form. It is they who stood firm in times of trouble and tribulation and national calamity, who stood up to the test in all spiritual crises. ...
>
> A fateful question stands before us. Do we wish to continue the historic tradition and remain a great Jewish people renewing its youth and ancient glory, or, heaven forfend, to break the historic chain and cease to be a Jewish people? But—we have not yet lost our hope (*od lo ovdah tikvatenu*), the very old hope. There will yet arise a new generation with the song of renaissance, the spiritual renaissance, in its mouth.[63]

---

60 Ibid., 374.
61 R. Weinberg's comments are based on his interpretation of Ezra 3:12.
62 S. E., vol. 4, 376.
63 Ibid., 379.

His positive attitude to the State lends an added measure of poignancy to R. Weinberg's occasional critical statements. Unlike the chastisements of many other rabbinic leaders who held themselves aloof from the State, his criticisms were the warnings of an insider and fellow-traveler. By 1959, when he was among the individuals whose opinion Ben Gurion solicited during the "Who is a Jew?" crisis, he was forthright in expressing his fears that the State might fail to fulfill the challenge of the times and that its secular orientation might damage or dilute the character of Judaism in a manner that would be deleterious to the fate of the Jewish people.

R. Weinberg's response to Ben Gurion's question contains no earth-shattering revelation or revolutionary insight. Assuredly, his reply, which is entirely consistent with halakhic norms, is exactly what was to be anticipated to emanate from the pen of any halakhic decisor. But R. Weinberg's words in response to the "Who is a Jew?" question of the 1950s, forceful, passionate, and emotional as they were, acquire an added measure of significance in light of the manner in which questions of intermarriage, Jewish identity, and the issue of "Who is a Jew?" continually resurface on the political agenda.

With regard to the question of conversion, R. Weinberg presents an intriguing line of argument.[64] Ethnic identity is determined by biological relationships that are not subject to change or to subjective determination. Consequently, observes R. Weinberg, when Göring proclaimed that it was he personally who would subjectively determine who was to be designated as an Aryan, he made himself into a laughing-stock in the eyes of the world. In the theological sense, however, conversion is an entirely valid concept. It is a process whereby an individual who professes one corpus of belief undergoes a religious transformation and expresses allegiance to another series of faith-commitments. In an analogous manner, nations grant citizenship to a foreigner and thereby bestow upon him rights of nationality through the process of naturalization. Such a civic act does not transform ethnicity but merely changes legal status and secures certain prerogatives. However, Judaism is unique in that it alone among the religions of the world is an amalgam of religion and ethnic identity. Conversion to the religion of Judaism serves also to entitle the proselyte to the rights and prerogatives associated with Jewish descent. Adherence to the religion of Judaism entails membership in the community of Israel despite the absence of a genetic tie. Accordingly, the Sages ruled that converts who bring the first fruits to the Temple can also include the phrase "our God and the God of our fathers" in the accompanying dedicatory declaration.[65]

---

64 Ibid., 380–381.
65 *Mishneh Torah, Hilkhot Bikkurim* 4:3.

R. Weinberg presents an ideological underpinning for this phenomenon. In Jewish teaching, the spiritual and ethical are of paramount importance. For the nation founded by Abraham and Sarah, who are viewed also as the father and mother of converts,[66] "biological race took the form and shape of spiritual-cultural race."[67] Individuals who adopt the ethical and religious teachings of Abraham and convert to his religion cleave to the spiritual race he founded and become fused with the spiritual stock that forms the foundation of Jewish nationality. The determinant characteristic of such conversion is not national identity, but attachment to a spiritual heritage.

R. Weinberg notes that Jewish law requires total identification with the spirit of the people of Israel: "Hence conversion can be effected only in the manner of religious conversion, in acceptance of the religion of Moses and Israel, in absorbing the spirit of Judaism in heart and soul and in acceptance of its values and its lifestyle. Another type of conversion does not exist."[68] An individual who is converted by any means other than that established by the Torah remains a non-Jew. This is not a matter that is subject to change by government fiat:

> Whoever is born a gentile or is born to a gentile mother remains a gentile. Neither the Jewish government nor the *Knesset* is able to make him into a Jew. Only the Torah of Judaism decides who is a Jew and who is not a Jew. It is not in the power of a political government or of a constitutional institution to make a determination contrary to the law of the Torah and it does not redound to the honor of the Jewish government to testify falsely that one who is not a Jew is a Jew.[69]

R. Weinberg cautions Ben Gurion not to tamper with Jewish identity by denuding Judaism and robbing it of its unique character. In the past, he notes, there have arisen false interpreters of Judaism who sought to deny its national dimension. To erase the religious dimension is equally spurious and destructive: "Judaism is a merger of two components, the imprint of Judaism, 'who is like unto your people, a singular people in the land?,' on one side, and 'who has chosen us from among the nations and given us a Torah of truth,' on the other. Exponents of Reform in the early years of that movement cut the coin into two;

---

66 Ḥagigah 1:3.
67 S. E., vol. 4, 381.
68 Ibid., 382.
69 Ibid., 382.

they took out one side and the coin became devoid of value. Do we want to erase what is on the other side and invalidate the Jewish coin?"[70]

Any attempt on the part of the State to alter the halakhah of conversion is doomed to failure. Concern for the honor of the government of Israel prompted R. Weinberg to urge Ben Gurion to rescind the newly enacted registration statute, since such a law could only turn the Israeli government into an object of ridicule. R. Weinberg concludes:

> Nationalistic conversion, so to speak, has no logical meaning and has no value whatsoever. No Jewish community, and no Jewish institution in this world, will accept such an unaccepted convert who is armed with an identification certificate of a government that conducted itself contrary to the Torah of Israel.
>
> We are truly and sincerely concerned for the honor of our Jewish government, this government that has arisen for us after thousands of years of exile, tribulations, wanderings and dispersions. Therefore in all sincerity we advise it to remove the directives for the laws of registration of the birth of adults and children that were conceived in an hour of conceit and to forget them entirely.[71]

R. Weinberg further argues that enactment of an Israeli registration statute that alters standards of identification as a Jew will have a shocking effect on Jews all over the world. The rabbinate's fears are not exaggerated, writes R. Weinberg:

> The fear that enactment of the law of registration according to the intent of the Minister of the Interior will encourage and speed the process of assimilation that is connected with intermarriage stands in all its awesomeness. We, the rabbis of the Diaspora, fight with all our might against mixed marriages with a clear recognition that they constitute the decisive

---

70 Ibid., 383.

71 Ibid., 383. These words of caution are interesting in light of a related but different controversy that has arisen with regard to a conversion performed in Israel in the case of Paula Cohen, in which the conversion certificate was stamped "conversion valid only in the Land of Israel." To be sure, the conversion certificate had the imprimatur of the *bet din* of Rabbi Goren and not of the Israeli government. However, the concept of a conversion according to halakhah being linked to a residence requirement or, in any manner, differing from universally accepted halakhic norms arouses consternation. See Moshe Ish-Horowicz, "The Case of Mrs. Paula Cohen and her Children," *Jewish Law Annual*, 11 (1994), 171–194 and David Horovitz, "Israeli Conversion Rejected," *Jerusalem Post*, February 3, 1989, 20.

cause of total assimilation and abandonment of the Jewish community. We have seized methods of defense against this epidemic that has broken out in Western countries. We disqualify those who marry a non-Jew from any matter involving holiness and forbid the circumcision of a child born of a non-Jewish mother. These methods of protection frighten and restrain any individual who is frivolous in matters of marriage but does not want to exit from the body of the Jewish people.

Now a frivolous individual can legitimize himself and his children with the license of the Jewish government. He only has to appear before the Israeli consul in the Diaspora or the registration office in the Land of Israel and to affirm with sincerity that he and his children are Jews.... Did the Prime Minister not consider the destructive result of this registration law upon the Judaism of the Diaspora?[72]

In concluding his remarks, R. Weinberg reiterates his belief in the providential destiny of the State and his conviction that the only meaningful future for the State of Israel is one in which historical continuity is not denied. The Jewish State must be worthy of its name:

The State of Israel is in our eyes the final step in the fulfillment of the national-religious hope of countless generations, who suffered and were persecuted and slaughtered and killed for the sake of their faith....

What do we want? Not authority and not special privileges. Only that the Jewish State be a Jewish State....[73]

2. Feminist Concerns

R. Weinberg's lifelong championship of the cause of women's education was quite unusual. In his sensitivity to feminist issues he was, in many respects, ahead of his time. In our day, responsiveness to feminist concerns is taken for granted. Indeed, a person who is unresponsive to such concerns is likely to be branded a reactionary. This, assuredly, was not always the case. Social and religious concerns of women have become matters of topical discussion only in recent years. Yet as early as 1925, close to a century ago, R. Weinberg called attention to the issue of women's education as a matter of critical importance.

---

72 S. E., vol. 4, 383–384.
73 Ibid., 384–385.

Later he was to extol the Beth Jacob movement as "the most splendid accomplishment of our time"[74] and in 1949 he dedicated his collection of essays, *Das Volk der Religion*, to Sara Schenirer and to the ninety-three Beth Jacob girls who allegedly suffered martyrdom rather than submit to defilement by the Nazis.[75] In various responsa that he authored over a period of decades, he consistently exhibited sensitivity to the feelings, sensibilities, and religious stirrings of women.

However, while all of these facts are certainly noteworthy, there is one respect in which R. Weinberg's writings about women are truly remarkable. With regard to virtually any social problem, it is possible to adopt either a minimalist or a maximalist approach. For example, one may seek to alleviate the plight of the homeless by means of moderate reforms and appeals to charity or one may opt for no less than a sweeping system of welfare legislation designed to provide employment, housing, and social benefits for all. Insofar as education of women is concerned, individuals may have recognized the need for a basic educational program simply in order to hold assimilation arid intermarriage at bay. R. Weinberg did not advocate a minimalist approach of that nature. From the time of his earliest involvement in this issue, he advocated comprehensive change in order to provide intellectual challenge and satisfaction for women no less than for men. He was aware that in the modern world women were gradually achieving a sense of equality in all aspects of secular life and that to grant them anything less in the religious sphere was both perilous to the welfare of the community and indefensible in terms of the justified demands of women themselves. He well realized that women must not be given cause to regard themselves as second-class citizens within the Jewish community.

In 1925 R. Weinberg wrote a short essay eulogizing a prominent, highly educated woman, Esther Rubinstein of Vilna. This brief contribution is of interest primarily because of its focus upon educational goals. The essay was contributed by R. Weinberg to a commemorative volume issued in memory

---

74 S. E., vol. 3, no. 93, 297.

75 The veracity of this incident has been seriously challenged. See the interesting discussion of Judith Tydor Baumol and Jacob J. Schacter, "The Ninety-three Bais Yaakov Girls of Cracow: History or Typology," *Reverence, Righteousness and Rahamanut: Essays in Memory of Rabbi Dr. Leo Jung*, ed. Jacob J. Schacter (Northvale, NJ: Jason Aronson Inc., 1992), 93–130. The authors of that article record the doubts that have been expressed (see, especially, 101–104), but their own conclusion serves to cast doubt upon the doubts. Their argument is, however, not compelling. The veracity of the incident remains a matter of serious doubt, particularly since a number of those who deny that the martyrdom took place were themselves closely associated with the individuals who publicized the original report.

of Esther Rubinstein on the first anniversary of her death.[76] R. Weinberg was always quick to acclaim the accomplishments of women of talent. In this instance, he did not hesitate to write that Esther Rubinstein had been respected by all segments of the Jewish community, including scholars of the *bet midrash* and yeshiva, and to declare that her comprehensive Torah knowledge was of such caliber that it would have been worthy of note even in a man whose life was exclusively devoted to Torah study. He acknowledged her breadth of knowledge, her mastery of the written word and oratorical skills, and her readiness to articulate her views publicly so that, ultimately, people became so accustomed to her presence, that "her silence aroused more astonishment than her speech."[77] He noted with pride that she was a rare example of a deeply religious woman who played a prominent role in the public arena and yet retained a fundamental and deeply rooted modesty. Witnessing the spiritual turmoil experienced by the Jewish community in the wake of the First World War, she felt compelled to assume a public posture in order to arouse the broader community from its lethargy and to agitate for serious attention to the religious education of women. He extolled Esther Rubinstein for having taught by personal example that religiosity and intellectuality need not represent an irreconcilable dichotomy for women and for having raised her voice to criticize a society in which women were discouraged from serious cultivation of scholarly and· intellectual pursuits.

In this essay, R. Weinberg makes it abundantly clear that the issue of women's education constituted one of the most pressing questions on the agenda of the Orthodox community. In concise but quite direct language, R. Weinberg expressed the conviction that "education of girls is the most difficult of our problems. It is with this problem, in particular, that we who are zealous and faithful to the standard of our heritage struggle in the open and in the recesses of our hearts." He recognized the need for creative leadership in this major area

---

76 "Eshet ha-Mofet," in *Sefer Zikaron le-ha-Rabbanit Ester Rubinshteyn*, ed. S. L. Citron (Vilna, 1925), 9–12. The learned Esther Rubenstein was the daughter of the rabbi of Shaki and was married to Rabbi Isaac Rubinstein, an interesting personality who was appointed crown rabbi of Vilna in 1910. Rabbi Rubinstein was one of the few government-appointed rabbis who possessed rabbinic credentials, but despite these qualifications, or perhaps, in part, because of them, his appointment aroused controversy.

77 Ibid., 9. R. Weinberg (ibid., 11) records Esther Rubinstein's interpretation of the phrase *Kol kevudah bat melekh penimah*—"The entire glory of the king's daughter is within" (Psalms 45:14)—which is usually cited to illustrate that the parameters of a woman's life should be limited to nonpublic functions—to the effect that ultimately, it is the inner world of a woman that constitutes her true glory and adornment.

of concern. There was a need to forge new paths (*kvishat derekh*); once forged, there was a need for guidance in traveling that path and for "a lamp to illuminate the crossroads." R. Weinberg sought to kindle hope and awaken a sense of destiny. Perhaps the single most noteworthy comment in this essay is his concluding remark in which he expresses the hope *cum* prayer that the memory of the accomplished Esther Rubinstein remain a "symbol for *massa-nefesh*, for aspiration."[78] Although R. Weinberg did not reach the point of developing detailed curricula for women, his appreciation of the extent of their yearning and aspiration may have been a factor contributing to change in the dominant cultural milieu.

Two responsa of R. Weinberg concerning women, one addressing the question of mixed singing and the other regarding the celebration of a *bat mitzvah*, are well-known and frequently cited. Less well-known and often ignored are the caveats R. Weinberg attached to these landmark decisions and the precedents upon which they are based.

Responding to a query regarding the propriety of a *bat mitzvah* celebration, R. Weinberg dismisses the argument against instituting such a celebration based on the fact that it is not a time-hallowed practice. He writes:

> In truth, however, this is no argument. In previous generations it was unnecessary to be preoccupied with the education of girls for every Jewish person was filled with Torah and fear of Heaven. Moreover, the atmosphere in each and every city in Israel was filled to capacity with the flavor and spirit of Judaism. Girls who were raised in a Jewish home imbibed the spirit of Judaism without doing anything and practically absorbed Judaism from their mothers' breast. Now the generations have become radically transformed. The atmosphere of the street removes any spark of Judaism from the heart of every boy and girl. Girls are educated in non-Jewish schools or in secular schools that do not take pains to implant love of the Torah of Israel and of the holy customs of authentic Judaism in the heart of their students. ... Indeed, it is a very painful matter that, insofar as general education is concerned, regarding instruction in languages, secular literature, sciences, and humanities, there is concern for girls just as for boys, whereas with regard to religious education, biblical studies, the ethical literature of the Sages and the practical mitzvot regarding which women are obligated, there is utter neglect. Fortunately, the

---

78 Ibid., 12.

great Jewish leaders of the previous generation recognized this failure and established institutions of Torah and religious encouragement for Jewish girls. The establishment of a great and comprehensive network of Beth Jacob schools is the most splendid accomplishment of our age. Sound logic and the obligation of fundamental pedagogic principles would practically mandate that one also celebrate attainment of the obligation of mitzvot on the part of a girl. Discrimination between boys and girls with regard to the celebration of maturity is an affront to the human feelings of the adolescent girl, who in other respects, as it were, has been accorded the privileges of emancipation.[79]

R. Weinberg, however, ruled that the *bat mitzvah* celebration should be observed in the home, or in a synagogue hall, but not in the sanctuary proper. In this, he is in agreement with an earlier ruling of R. Moses Feinstein, *Iggerot Mosheh, Orah Hayyim*, no. 104.[80] Nevertheless, R. Weinberg advocated that the rabbi attend the festivities and deliver an address encouraging the *bat mitzvah* celebrant to further strengthen her religious commitment and to aspire to marry a learned and pious husband. R. Weinberg emphasizes that there was strong reason to permit and to encourage the practice of *bat mitzvah* celebrations in such a guise even in accordance with the view of the Gaon of Vilna who had ruled very restrictively with regard to innovations involving possible infraction of the prohibition against adopting any practices that might be deemed *hukkat ha-goy*.[81]

---

79 *S. E.*, vol. 3, no. 93, 297.

80 In a personal letter to Rabbi Elberg published in *Ha-Pardes*, R. Weinberg states emphatically that his view regarding the *bat mitzvah* celebration is identical to that of Rabbi Feinstein. See *Ha-Pardes* 40, no. 10 (July 1966), 36.

81 *S. E.*, vol. 3, 297. R. Weinberg was, in effect, assuring that the ceremony be used as a means of promoting traditional values and constitute the very antithesis of a Reform innovation. Creative compromise that defuses communal tension can serve to resolve halakhic questions while also promoting educational goals. In 1830, when confirmation was a subject of a heated controversy in Germany, Rabbi Jacob Ettlinger, who at the time served as *Klaus* Rabbi in Mannheim, ruled against instituting confirmation ceremonies but suggested to the Baden Jewish Council that they introduce a public examination day with a formal assembly that would serve a social and pedagogical purpose similar to that of the confirmation ceremony but avoid the halakhic problems associated with taking of an oath as well as the question of *hukkat ha-goy*. See Mordecai Eliav, *Ha-Hinnukh ha-Yehudi be-Germaniyah be-Yemei ha-Haskalah ve-ha Emantzipatziyah* (Jerusalem: The Jewish Agency, 1960), 269. See also Adolf Lewin, *Geschichte der badischen Juden seit der Regierung Karl Friedrichs (1738–1909)* (Karlsruhe: H. Bissinger, 1909), 256–257 and Berthold Rosenthal, *Die jüdische Volksschulen in Baden* (Frankfurt, 1934), 155. On opposition to confirmation on halakhic grounds, see

A further reason militating against *bat mitzvah* celebrations in the synagogue proper, R. Weinberg maintained, was the need to eliminate any shred of suspicion that the celebration was instituted in emulation of Reform practices. He distinguished sharply between the question of the permissibility of introducing *bat mitzvah* celebrations and the propriety of use of an organ in the synagogue. The latter he regarded as halakhically proscribed because of its Reform provenance. Although R. Weinberg expressed concern that, even in the case of *bat mitzvah* celebrations, it was necessary to avoid even inadvertent association with Reform innovations, he reasoned that the home celebration of the *bat mitzvah* clearly constitutes a private religious event far removed from the public celebrations of Reform.

A further consideration militating against celebration of the *bat mitzvah* ceremony in the sanctuary of the synagogue itself is the halakhic principle that the synagogue proper may be utilized only for liturgical purposes.[82] Although the *bat mitzvah* ceremony may serve pedagogic and religious purposes, the ceremony does not fall within the ambit of practices that it is permissible to conduct within a synagogue. It was upon this consideration that Rabbi Moses Feinstein's ruling against *bat mitzvah* ceremonies in the synagogue was predicated.

It should be noted that elsewhere R. Weinberg discusses the question of use of synagogues for lectures or concerts. The question arose in the period prior to World War II when the gathering of Jews in other locales was not a viable option. In granting limited permission for such activities as a temporary

---

R. Abraham Sutro, "Od be-Inyan Hithadshut be-Bet ha-Knesset," *STN* 175 (1854), 348–349. Subsequently, in Altona, Ettlinger remained opposed to confirmation ceremonies but instituted an "öffentliche Religionsprüfung," a formal public religious examination. It was Ettlinger's wont to participate in the public examinations and to address the students in the rhetoric of the day concerning their duties as Jews and as citizens. A correspondent to *Ha-Maggid*, June 22, 1870, 186, reports on a ceremony held in Altona in the year 1870 in which the aged Rabbi Ettlinger participated.

Mordecai Breuer, "Perakim be-Toldot Rabbi Shimshon Rafa'el Hirsch," *Ha-Ma'ayan* 12, no. 2 (1972), 61 n. 25, relates that he heard from his teacher, Rabbi Shlomoh Adler, that he had seen a published text of a discourse delivered by Rabbi Ettlinger in honor of a *bat mitzvah* celebration. However, Yehudah A. Horovitz, ed., *She'elot u-Teshuvot ha-Arukh la-Ner*, vol. II (Jerusalem: Dvar Jerushalayim, 1989), 107 n. 1, quite correctly points out that there exists no record of any such publication. The discourse given by Rabbi Ettlinger was on the occasion of a public religious examination that was conducted in lieu of the confirmation exercises required by the Danish government. A Hebrew translation of the latter discourse may be found ibid., 145–148.

82 See *Shulḥan Arukh, Oraḥ Ḥayyim* 151.

dispensation, R. Weinberg carefully circumscribes his ruling in order to assure that the activities will not violate the sanctity of the synagogue and, even with those limitations, emphasizes, "I declare explicitly that this dispensation applies only during the present time, which is an emergency situation as is well-known, and, please God, when the Almighty will improve our situation we will, with the help of God, continue to be meticulous with regard to the sanctity of the synagogue in all its rigor."[83]

R. Weinberg concludes his discussion with two significant comments. He enunciates as a general rule of thumb that with regard to such matters the question of motivation is crucial. The salient question is whether the intent of those introducing the new practice is for the sake of Heaven or whether they seek imitation of liberal trends. Secondly, and more significantly, R. Weinberg emphasizes that with regard to the *bat mitzvah* celebrations a case can be made both pro and con. All the more reason, he cautions, for mutual understanding and respect. Among the pious, many respond to questions involving proposed ritual or liturgical changes in a manner that is not subject to reasoned debate. Quite appropriately, "the Jewish heart that is attached to the tradition of parents and teachers recoils before any change whatsoever in religious conduct." However, underscores R. Weinberg, such individuals should not be oblivious to the fact that those who wish to institute the *bat mitzvah* celebration are also motivated by religious zeal and emotional attachment to Judaism and that, in their case as well, "their heart beats with trembling to strengthen the religious education of Jewish girls who, on account of the circumstances of life in this age, have a special need for spiritual strengthening and ethical encouragement when they reach the age of mitzvot."[84]

R. Weinberg's responsum is comprehensive but hardly innovative. What is striking is the balanced treatment of different facets of the question, the sympathetic appreciation of diverse positions and, above all, the keen sensitivity to, and profound concern for, the feelings and sensibilities of women.

In another important responsum, R. Weinberg addressed the question of mixed singing. The Gemara, *Berakhot* 24a, states, "A woman's voice is a sexual incitement" and a number of halakhic restrictions pertaining to women's singing are predicated upon the postulation of an erotic quality associated with the female voice.[85] In accordance with those principles, *Ḥatam Sofer*, writing in the nineteenth century, ruled explicitly that mixed choirs comprised of men

---

83 S. E., vol. 2, no. 12, 28.
84 S. E., vol. 3, 298.
85 See *Shulḥan Arukh, Even ha-Ezer* 21:1 and *Oraḥ Ḥayyim* 76:3.

and women choristers are prohibited.[86] Nevertheless, various discussions have appeared in the responsa literature addressing the limited circumstances in which it may be permissible for men to listen to the singing of women.[87]

As has been noted, knowledge of R. Weinberg's permissive ruling regarding one facet of this issue is widely disseminated. However, the specific situation in which his comments apply, the hesitations he articulates in his account of his own initial negative reaction, and the ultimate dispositive consideration he advances are frequently overlooked. In order to understand this responsum, it is imperative to examine closely the fine points of the discussion. The responsum is paradigmatic of the balance of scholarship, judgment, caution, and innovation R. Weinberg brought to bear upon halakhic issues of practical moment to the Jewish community.

After World War II, leaders of *Jeschurun*, a Jewish youth organization in France, asked R. Weinberg whether it was permissible for them to continue to sponsor social and educational programs in the course of which male and female participants join in communal singing. The interlocutors were prompted to seek R. Weinberg's guidance because of criticism of their activities on the part of individuals who maintained that *Jeschurun*'s non-segregated activities were, in themselves, a departure from the accepted norms of Jewish tradition and that mixed singing, in particular, constituted an egregious violation of halakhah.

In his reply, R. Weinberg does not merely provide halakhic sanction for this practice: R. Weinberg is forceful, eloquent, and persuasive in endorsing and commending the activities of *Jeschurun*. He endorses and showers praise upon their programs and forcefully urges their continuance. He expresses full support for the policies of *Jeschurun* as suitable for the times and, indeed, as the only approach capable of success in the France of his day. Nevertheless, R. Weinberg is in no way dismissive of the gravity of the question from the

---

86 *Teshuvot Ḥatam Sofer, Ḥoshen Mishpat*, no. 190.
87 See sources cited in J. David Bleich, *Contemporary Halakhic Problems*, vol. II (New York: Ktav, 1983), 147–150. Cf. Saul J. Berman, "Kol Isha," in *Rabbi Joseph H. Lookstein Memorial Volume*, ed. Leo Landman (New York: Ktav, 1980), 45–66, who claims that R. Weinberg's ruling on this matter represents a return to the understanding of the principle "A woman's voice is a sexual incitement" reflected in the writings of early-day scholars. An analytic examination of that halakhic principle is beyond the scope of this paper. It may, however, be noted that there would have been no reason for R. Weinberg initially to have expressed astonishment upon observing the practice in Germany or later to invoke the principle of *et la'asot* (see n. 94 and accompanying text), if he believed the practice to be consistent with the plain meaning of the text as understood by the classic commentators.

vantage point of halakhah and tradition or of the validity of opposing views. He writes, "The *haredim* assuredly have what to base themselves upon."[88] He then proceeds to discuss with meticulous concern the technical halakhic aspects both of the general question of the acceptability of non-segregated social programs and of the specific question of the permissibility of women singing in mixed groups.

R. Weinberg candidly records his own initial negative reaction and ensuing protest when, upon moving to Germany, he discovered that it was common practice in observant homes in that country for all members of the family, female as well as male, to join in singing *zemirot* on the Sabbath even when guests were present. He was soon informed that such conduct had been sanctioned by both Rabbi Samson Raphael Hirsch and Rabbi Azriel Hildesheimer. He notes that, even with such assurances, "I was not satisfied"[89] and continued to seek recorded sources that might provide a basis for sanctioning the practice. Moreover, although he responded affirmatively to the question before him and, as will be seen, he deemed the critics of *Jeschurun* to be misguided and short-sighted, he appended an important caveat to his ruling, namely, that those women who demur from participating in mixed singing are to be accorded every respect, "for, in the final analysis, they are seized of the custom of our sainted fathers who were careful not to permit women [to sing] even holy *zemirot* [in mixed company]."[90]

R. Weinberg bases his halakhic leniency regarding the issue of mixed singing on a number of considerations. Some authorities cite the talmudic dictum, formulated in an entirely different context, to the effect that "two voices are not heard"[91] simultaneously and, applying it in this context, they conclude that, when the female voice is not distinctively audible, mixed singing is not forbidden. R. Weinberg himself advances a stronger argument for sanctioning mixed singing of sacred songs. He argues that listening to the female voice is forbidden only when it is likely to arouse prurient interest. Sacred songs are sung, not for the purpose of deriving sensual pleasure, but in order to arouse religious feeling and fervor; accordingly, in such context, the sound of a female voice is not likely to be provocative.[92]

---

88 S. E., vol. 2, no. 8, 13.

89 Ibid., 16.

90 Ibid., 17. Cf. *Maharam Shik, Even ha-Ezer*, no. 53, and *Iggerot Mosheh, Orah Hayyim*, I:26, on the teaching "Whosoever is stringent in such matters should be spoken of as holy."

91 See *Rosh ha-Shanah* 27a and Rashi, *Megillah* 21b.

92 See also R. Weinberg's succinct statement "holy *zemirot* do not arouse thoughts of sin," S. E., vol. 2, no. 14, 30, as well as other authorities who follow this line of reasoning cited in Bleich, *Contemporary Halakhic Problems*, vol. II, 150.

Most telling is the concluding argument presented by R. Weinberg. It is from this final consideration that it becomes apparent that R. Weinberg deemed the question to involve an issue that might be resolved permissively in case of necessity but that such a ruling would be far from indisputable. In light of the significant halakhic controversy concerning the points at issue, a lenient ruling might in a particular time and locale be mandated by wisdom, but practices instituted pursuant to that ruling must be recognized as dictated by circumstance and not as a mode of behavior to be espoused indiscriminately.

R. Weinberg observes that, in issuing a ruling regarding this question, the broader ramifications of a complex situation must be taken into consideration. Youth organizations such as *Jeschurun* had a record of phenomenal success in inspiring youth to return to observance of Torah. He recognized that the organization's programs merited endorsement because of their proven value. More significantly, it was necessary to beware lest adoption of stringent standards cause the youth to be alienated from Torah and mitzvot. Forthrightly, R. Weinberg states:

> In countries like Germany and France, women would feel disgraced and deprived of their rights if we would forbid them to participate in rejoicing over the Sabbath by singing holy *zemirot*. This is evident to anyone familiar with the character of women in these countries. A stringent ruling could cause women to become disaffected from religion, Heaven forfend.[93]

In light of these pedagogic and social realities, R. Weinberg discusses the principle developed on the basis of talmudic exegesis of Psalms 119:126, "*Et la'asot la-Shem*"—"It is time to accomplish for the Lord, they have made void Thy law." He emphasizes that in matters of halakhah the principle may be invoked, but only by the Sages of the Talmud. Nevertheless, he avers, the underlying principle may legitimately be relied upon with regard to the question of mixed singing of religious songs since that involves "no absolute prohibition (*issur gamur*) but rather a pious custom and practice of modesty."[94]

The historical and sociological comments R. Weinberg adds regarding the approach of different rabbinic authorities to these matters are instructive. He expresses the opinion that the rabbis of Poland and Hungary who protested

---

93 *S. E.*, vol. 2, 17.
94 Ibid., 16.

against mixed singing did not have a proper understanding of the cultural milieu of French Jewry and did not fully comprehend the deterioration of religious observance that had occurred in France. Accordingly, their counsel, if heeded, would only endanger the success of existing religious educational enterprises. Moreover, states R. Weinberg, "the great sages and Torah scholars of Lithuania and Poland" were unsuccessful in retaining the religious allegiance of the youth "because they did not know how to adjust education to the conditions of the time."[95] In contradistinction, he asserts, the rabbinic leaders in Germany were "knowledgeable and experts in the field of education,"[96] and, in particular, they succeeded "in the education of girls and young women more so than did the great Torah scholars of other countries. In Germany we see educated women zealous for the Jewish religion and enthusiastically observing mitzvot." As a consequence, R. Weinberg concludes, he would fear to deviate from the policies earlier established by the German rabbis, and declares, "Therefore, I myself do not dare to forbid what they permitted."[97]

It was precisely R. Weinberg's insightful understanding of the reasons for the success of *Jeschurun* that constituted the motive underlying the particular halakhic leniency under discussion. He describes in detail various aspects of the French Jewish cultural and social milieu that contributed to the high rate of assimilation. He underscores the fact that, in France, adolescents were involved in a demanding and absorbing program of secular studies with virtually no exposure to Torah study. The little Torah study in which they participated was hardly vital or stimulating. As a result, Jewish youth possessed of a modicum of spiritual aspiration felt themselves socially isolated:

> The root cause of the sad and foul situation created in France is, in my opinion, the feeling of loneliness that presses upon the heart of Jewish

---

95 Ibid., 14.

96 Ibid., 14. R. Weinberg relates that, upon returning from a visit to Berlin during which he had observed Rabbi Hildesheimer lecturing to young women, R. Israel Salanter stated that, were a Lithuanian rabbi to introduce such classes, he would quite correctly be dismissed from his post. Nonetheless, he declared, would that his portion in the world-to-come be like that of the great and saintly Rabbi Hildesheimer. R. Weinberg adds that the distinction between Lithuania and Germany reflects the principle of *et la'asot la-Shem*. Cf. the report of these comments of Rabbi Israel Salanter in Rabbi Yitzhak Ya'akov Reines, *Shnei ha-Me'orot*, part 2, 46. Offenberg, "Adass Jisroel," 36, notes the pioneering efforts on behalf of education of women undertaken by individuals associated with the *Rabbinerseminar*, such as Azriel Hildesheimer, Moses Auerbach, and Leo Deutschlander.

97 *S. E.*, vol. 2, 16–17.

youth. The Jewish boy or girl feels alone and abandoned with no spiritual anchorage in the home or in the family of [his or her] parents and relatives. The home and the family of our brothers in France is empty of the heritage of their fathers and of their tradition of a living, vital Jewish way of life; they contain no sign of life in the spirit of Judaism.[98]

The key to the success of an organization such as *Jeschurun* lies in the fact that it presents this youth with a Judaism that is vibrant and attractive; it provides Torah study and religious teaching within the context of a social setting. Social activities, meetings, and excursions create an atmosphere of conviviality and warmth. Study sessions and religious services are conducted in a manner designed to foster self-pride. The activities of the youth group counteract the feelings of despondency and depression Jewish youth experience in the general community. In such a setting, insistence upon standards of conduct that would be viewed by the young women in the group as humiliating and demeaning and as relegating them to an inferior status would undermine the very basis of the organization's success.

It is significant that R. Weinberg concludes with a very sharp criticism of those who oppose *Jeschurun*'s activities. Not only do such individuals blind themselves to reality, not only are they without any influence whatsoever on youth of the community at large, not only are they guilty of "concentrating in their narrow circle and paying no attention to the process of assimilation that is wreaking havoc even among the strictly religious," but in their self-absorption, they will lose their own children for "they do not worry the worry of the morrow for the religious future of their children." Even the children of the strictly religious attend non-Jewish schools and there is no guarantee that they will withstand the tide of assimilation.[99] Little wonder then that R. Weinberg's "permissive" ruling was more than permissive; R. Weinberg ruled that continuation of such activities was mandatory.[100] The responsum concludes with the statement: "It is the command of the hour to create a circle of religious

---

98 Ibid., 14.

99 Ibid., 17. In the course of time this sector of the community did develop their own network of schools in which it was appropriate for them to set their own stringent standards of religious conduct.

100 In a personal communication to R. Elberg, *Ha-Pardes* 41, no. 5 (February 1967), 38, R. Weinberg notes with obvious satisfaction that R. Kalman Kahane had informed him that R. Abraham I. Karelitz (*Ḥazon Ish*) had also counseled with regard to the activities of Ezra, the youth organization of Poalei Agudath Israel, that no one should undertake measures that might undermine its effectiveness.

young men and young women, a youth organization with contagious zeal ... to conquer hearts and raise weakened spirits."[101]

Evident in both responsa is R. Weinberg's awareness of the need to enhance women's religious experience, particularly in an age in which their daily life was influenced by Western cultural trends that were antithetical to Torah values. He recognized that, given the socio-religious realia of the day, synagogue attendance assumed an importance far greater than in earlier generations, particularly as far as women were concerned. Accordingly, he urged that every effort be made to foster such attendance and assure that women not be made to feel excluded. He cautions: "If the women will stay in the house and not come to the synagogue, the teachings of Judaism will become entirely forgotten to them. ... In our days women take great exception if they are distanced from houses of prayer. Indeed, in our day, for women and mothers, attendance at synagogue prayer services constitutes the fulfillment of Judaism."[102]

It is noteworthy that in some respects the comments of R. Weinberg regarding youth groups and women singing remain germane. It is a question whose resolution is dependent on the intricacies and complexities of each specific locale and the circumstances prevalent at any given time. Certainly, non-participation in singing is experienced by some young women as a great deprivation. Nonetheless, where educational standards are higher than those of the French community described by R. Weinberg, the situation may be somewhat altered. Of interest in this regard are comments on mixed singing in the context of the Israeli Bnei Akiva movement to be found in Rabbi S. Aviner, "Be-Inyan Shirat Na'arot," in *Am ke-Lavi: Inyanei Halakhah* (Jerusalem, 1983), sec. 333, I, 290; idem, "Histarfut le-Tenu'at No'ar Me'urevet," in *Gan Na'ul: Pirkei Tzniyut* (Jerusalem, 1985), 118–120; and idem, "Be-Inyan Bnei Akiva," in *Mi-Kedem le-Beit-El* (Jerusalem, 1990), sec. 47, 174–175. Rabbi Aviner urges "constant striving for improvement" with regard to this practice (*Am ke-Lavi*, 290).

101 S. E., vol. 2, p. 17.
102 Ibid., no. 14, 30. Cf. also S. E., vol. 3, no. 95, 301, his warning that in establishing standards of female attire, the rabbi should on no account "provoke a quarrel that will discourage women from synagogue attendance."

In light of the importance he attached to synagogue attendance by women, one cannot but wonder what the response of R. Weinberg would have been to a controversial question of the latter part of the twentieth century, namely the propriety of women's prayer groups. It is evident that he would have been open to understanding the motives and the aspirations of those who, in all sincerity, advocate the practice as a vehicle of expression of deep religious feeling, and he would have been cognizant of the impact of changing cultural mores. Nonetheless, the countervailing considerations of absence of precedent, defense for tradition in all forms of communal life and ritual, and the concern not to create a rift with tradionalist sectors and to shatter the unity of the overall community would also have been significant factors in any ruling he would have issued. To suggest what his ruling might have been would thus be presumptuous and purely speculative.

R. Weinberg's responsa on the question of women's suffrage and women serving in elected office are also revealing. From the two brief responsa that refer to this topic, it is evident that R. Weinberg believed that, from the perspective of halakhah, there was ample ground for a permissive policy.[103] Since he maintained that the considerations of those who ruled restrictively with regard to this question were extra-halakhic in nature, he declared that this was an issue in which social and pragmatic considerations should play the decisive role. R. Weinberg observes that those rabbinic authorities who ruled restrictively were concerned that active leadership of women in communal affairs was a practice that ran counter to Torah teachings of modesty.

His responsa reflect not only the view that this area is one in which sociological realia play a definitive role but also that it is an area in which social acceptability is relative in nature rather than absolute. It is noteworthy that in his responsum dated 1932, R. Weinberg writes in strong language that "Assuredly, it is appropriate to prevent women's participation in communal leadership and elections insofar as possible,"[104] whereas in the responsum authored in 1951 he merely notes that those who rule restrictively are motivated by considerations of piety and religious practice. Since he believed that no normative halakhic rules were involved, he concluded with the pragmatic observation that this particular question would resolve itself in the course of time: "Let us leave the matter to time, which will decide."[105]

R. Weinberg was always sympathetic to the plight of women whose anguish and suffering in cases of marital breakdown was aggravated by halakhic difficulties. His concern for *takkanat bnot Yisra'el* ("rectification [of the status] of Jewish daughters") is expressed repeatedly. Moreover, quite apart from his concern for the well-being of individual women in such predicaments, he was wary lest failure to defend the rights of victimized women lead to defamation of halakhic Judaism and concomitant desecration of the Name of Heaven.

During the early part of R. Weinberg's lifetime, the modern-day *agunah* problem arising from situations in which a recalcitrant husband refuses to execute a religious divorce had not reached its present tragic proportions. The individual cases in which his assistance was sought were related to the more conventional types of *agunot*, that is, situations involving halakhic criteria for identification of a corpse or for declaring a missing person to be deceased in

---

103 *S. E.,* vol. 2, no. 52, 104, dated 1932, and *S. E.,* vol. 3, no. 104, 322, dated 1951.
104 Ibid., 104.
105 *S. E.,* vol. 3, 322.

order to accord the woman permission to remarry[106] or situations involving validation of a divorce in the absence of documentation.[107] In the tradition of rabbinic decisors since time immemorial, he consistently "made every effort to seek support for permissive rulings on behalf of an *agunah*."[108]

With the dramatic rise in the incidence of divorce in the 1950s and 1960s, the modern-day *agunah* problem became greatly exacerbated. R. Weinberg was attuned to the gravity of the situation and deemed it imperative that rabbinic decisors not ignore this pressing issue. In 1966 one of R. Weinberg's disciples, Rabbi Dr. Eliezer Berkovits, authored a monograph entitled *Tn'ai be-Nesu'in u-be-Get*, in which he advocated adoption of a form of conditional marriage as a comprehensive remedy for the modern-day *agunah* problem. Berkovits enjoyed a particularly close relationship with his mentor. It was Berkovits who, with great difficulty and inconvenience to himself, preserved many manuscripts of R. Weinberg's novellae and responsa during and immediately after the war years.[109] Although Berkovits's work is prefaced by introductory comments authored by R. Weinberg, those remarks do not contain an explicit endorsement of Berkovits's proposal but commend the work to the attention and study of rabbinic scholars.[110] Subsequently, in an article on this topic published in *No'am*, R. Menachem M. Kasher publicized a later letter from R. Weinberg in which the latter expressed his regret for having written the introductory comments incorporated in Berkovits's book. In this later communication, R. Weinberg writes, "Due to my physical weakness, I am not at all able to investigate this grave question that is of utmost importance to our society and I regret that I wrote that letter."[111] Moreover, R. Weinberg claims, he had been unaware of the publication *Le-Dor Aharon* (New York, 1937), containing a prohibition signed by leading American rabbis forbidding any form of conditional marriage.[112]

Berkovits's proposal is based upon a previous proposal advanced by a group of French rabbis in the early years of the twentieth century and firmly rejected by leading scholars of the previous generation, including R. Isaac Elhanan Spektor, R. Hayyim Ozer Grodzinski, R. Me'ir Simhah of Dvinsk,

106 Ibid., 32–36.
107 Ibid., no. 42, 46–51.
108 Ibid., no. 12, 32.
109 S. E., vol. 1, 1.
110 "Divrei Hakdamah," published in Eliezer Berkovits, *Tn'ai be-Nesu'in u-be-Get: Birurei Halakhah* (Jerusalem: Mossad Harav Kook, 1966), unnumbered pages, 1–4.
111 Cited in Menachem M. Kasher, "Be-Inyan Tn'ai be-Nisu'in," *No'am* 12 (1969), 347.
112 Ibid., 347.

and R. Abraham of Sochatchow, author of *Avnei Nezer*.[113] In his original letter, R. Weinberg noted that he had not been sufficiently well to undertake a detailed study of Berkovits's work but claimed that Berkovits's proposal incorporated significant modifications of the remedy suggested by the French rabbis and that these modifications served to obviate objections to the earlier proposal. According to Kasher, Berkovits offers no specific text for the condition to be incorporated in the groom's declaration and Berkovits's proposal parallels the earlier French one in all salient points.[114] Accordingly, concludes Kasher, it is impossible to draft an acceptable condition on the basis of Berkovits's exposition.

R. Weinberg's letter to Kasher leaves unclear a fundamental question, that is, whether he had at any time fully investigated the original French proposal. At the time that he wrote the prefatory comments to Berkovits's monograph, R. Weinberg apparently believed that the halakhic objections to the French proposal could be overcome by modifications of the condition. He may well have assumed that the rabbinic objections were based primarily upon policy considerations and concern for debasement of the sanctity of the marital relationship were a situation to be created in which a decree of civil divorce would retroactively nullify the marriage in the eyes of Jewish law. Accordingly, he states that the original proposal for use of conditional marriage as a remedy was rejected by rabbinic authorities at a time when there had been but isolated cases of recalcitrant husbands withholding a *get*. In the interim, the situation had deteriorated markedly, and the problem had become one facing the entire Jewish community. The increasing number of women who contracted a second marriage without benefit of a *get* raised the specter of ever-increasing instances of *mamzerut*. Under such circumstances, R. Weinberg explicitly declared, radical solutions must be explored.

R. Weinberg keenly appreciated the urgent need for study, deliberation, and, hopefully, action to ameliorate the plight of the *agunah*:

> All know the severity of the problems that have arisen in our time, both in Israel and in the Diaspora, problems that have found no solution and that endanger marriage and destroy the sanctity of families in Israel. It is appropriate for the great scholars of our generation to deliberate concerning them. . . .

---

113 Ibid., 339–341.
114 Ibid., 342–343.

Therefore, I say one cannot pass over in silence or in passivity the prevalence of this calamity and there is urgent need to investigate the possibility and vital need for remedies to remove terrible stumbling blocks from wide circles and even from the circles of faithful Jews.[115]

Whatever the cogency of Kasher's critique of Berkovits's proposal on halakhic grounds, a report by Kasher that the situation had not deteriorated, but had even improved, is astonishingly contrafactual.[116] Putting aside the question of R. Weinberg's acceptance of Berkovits's halakhic conclusions, R. Weinberg certainly did not delude himself into thinking that the situation was improving.

R. Weinberg's concern for the status and dignity of women is also reflected in comments he authored in conjunction with questions concerning the edict of Rabbenu Gershom prohibiting polygamy. R. Weinberg writes that it was designed to ameliorate problems faced by women involved in plural marriages and to improve women's status and, accordingly, it served to silence their justified complaints and to blunt the scorn of non-Jews in that they would no longer be able to claim that "in Jewish law the woman is considered but a Canaanite slave. And how great a disgrace that has been!"[117]

In a responsum regarding the question of granting a man dispensation to remarry in the form of a *hetter me'ah rabbanim* (dispensation of one hundred rabbis), R. Weinberg dismisses the request with the remark that in the case in question, the man's claims are simply not justified halakhically. Moreover, he comments, a controversy does exist with regard to a specific halakhic question, namely, whether or not a man may be granted such a dispensation in an instance in which his wife has been childless for a ten-year period. He notes that, in general, the rabbis of Lithuania and Germany did not grant the dispensation on the basis of ten years of childlessness, but that it was common for rabbis of Poland and Galicia to do so. While, in such cases, R. Weinberg personally refused to join in a dispensation, he did not protest against those who did so since he could not dispute the fact that there was halakhic precedent for such action. However, in the case brought to his attention, he maintained that the halakhic requirements for such dispensation had not been met and, therefore,

115 "Divrei Hakdamah," *Tn'ai be Nesu'in*, unnumbered pages, 1–2. Regarding R. Weinberg's constant keen interest in all developments in this area and fear of remedies that would undermine halakhic standards, see his letters in *Ha-Pardes* 40, no. 8 (May 1966), 38–39 and no. 9 (June 1966), 38–39.

116 *No'am*, no. 12: 350–351.

117 *S. E.*, vol. 2, no. 6, 18.

there existed no halakhic grounds for the dispensation and concluded with the observation that "In general, we must be assiduous with regard to *takkanat bnot Yisra'el* that they not be abandoned."[118]

3. Faith in an Age of Doubt

Doubt is endemic to the modern age. It would have been impossible for R. Weinberg to be unaware of the ubiquitous challenge to religious faith. Accordingly, it is not surprising that the theme of faith and doubt is addressed in several of his essays. The first chapter of *Das Volk der Religion* is entitled "Glaube und Unglaube,"[119] and the essay on "Religious Renascence" in *Li-Perakim* begins with a section subtitled "Emunah u-Kefirah" (Faith and Heresy).[120]

Those essays are poetic rather than rigorously argued and, in all likelihood, their rhetoric appealed to but a narrow audience. Indeed, R. Weinberg discounts the purely analytic and logical Maimonidean approach to questions of belief and focuses on psychological considerations that affect intellectual perspective. In practice, he sees limited value in addressing crises of religious faith by means of direct philosophical discussion. He was convinced that solutions to questions of religious belief are more likely to be found in the realm of emotional and psychological experience.

R. Weinberg well understood the factors that foster skepticism and why it is that persons nurtured by Western culture and influenced by its value system question and struggle with certain aspects of religious law and teaching. It is at times the case, he observed, that, paradoxically, sincere qualms of faith born of intellectual integrity are indicative of a yearning and propensity for belief. In this regard R. Weinberg was wont to relate an incident of a man who was called upon to recite the *kaddish* (memorial prayer) at a memorial service for victims of the Holocaust but found himself emotionally unable to recite the traditional prayer. Instead, he uttered anguished, rebellious, and almost blasphemous words. R. Weinberg remarked that this person was moved to so desperate an outburst precisely because, in reality, he was possessed of a deep-seated faith, that is,

---

118 Ibid., 18.

119 *Das Volk der Religion*, 19–29.

120 *Li-Perakim*, 139–154. At first glance, the German text "Glaube und Unglaube" appears to be a verbatim translation of the Hebrew "'Emunah u-Kefirah." See, however, *Das Volk der Religion*, 20, for additional remarks modifying somewhat the antiphilosophical comments of the Hebrew.

because of his abiding belief in the reality of Divine justice, that person was unable to fathom its seeming absence. R. Weinberg's disciples testify that R. Weinberg's response to individuals struggling with such doubts was consistently understanding and sympathetic and that he shunned apologetics or evasive replies.[121]

First and foremost, R. Weinberg emphasizes that faith is nurtured in an atmosphere of intense and lively learning. He refers to the passion and intensity of Torah study that, to a Jew, constitute the quintessential religious experience. Discussing the religious apathy of post-war European Jewry, he bemoans the fact that they have never experienced Torah "study that is entertaining and intellectually enticing."[122]

In counseling individuals whose intellectual grounding in Torah is meager, R. Weinberg stresses the benefit of social interaction. As already noted, he greatly appreciated the pedagogic importance of youth groups that generate an atmosphere of belonging and cohesiveness in the firm belief that the activities of such groups foster religiosity and spirituality. R. Weinberg notes that there is yet another way of dispelling religious doubt, namely, by means of religious experience that is self-validating. Striking is R. Weinberg's autobiographical assertion that an inspired teacher can induce such a religious experience. Describing his own reaction to a stirring discourse of R. Isaac Blaser, R. Weinberg writes:

> It would appear to me that whoever did not merit to hear a discourse such as that of R. Isaac Blaser does not know the taste of the genuine religious experience. At times, I think in my heart that there is no need for proofs of the truth of religion. A religious experience that generates excitement in the heart and soul constitutes the clearest and most convincing proof.[123]

Conversely, R. Weinberg cautions that disillusionment with religious people often results in disillusionment with religion. The disappointment that ensues when spiritual leaders fail to live up to the highest standards of ethics and probity can have a deleterious effect upon belief.[124] In an age in which religious association is tenuous at best, it is all the more necessary, notes R. Weinberg, to be on guard lest by acts of commission or of omission situations be permitted to arise which would further weaken religious commitment.

---

121 Cohen, *De'ot* 31:17 and ibid., n. 45.
122 *S. E.*, vol. 2, no. 8, 14.
123 *S. E.*, vol. 4, 307.
124 See the lengthy discussion in ibid., 317–322.

R. Weinberg was exacting in the standard of probity that he demanded of those who were spokesmen on behalf of Orthodoxy. His sharpest censure was directed against public figures who hypocritically cloaked themselves in the garb of religion and piety yet conducted themselves in an unethical manner. With pain and anguish, he wrote:

> Deceit grows and increases. ... It is clear to me that the question of the survival of our people and our State is contingent upon spiritual purity and elevation of the ethical standard. Those who are stringent with regard to *kashrut*, *shatnez*, customs of the synagogue and the like, but openly and brazenly violate fundamental canons of ethics and human etiquette cause the estrangement of people of our times from religion and the observance of mitzvot. It is the greatest misfortune that activism for purposes of disseminating Torah and observance of mitzvot has become a source of livelihood. ... We ought to prostrate ourselves upon the graves of "the *maskilim*" (enlightened ones) who fought against hypocrites and ask their forgiveness for impugning their honor. They fought for the truth with self-sacrifice. Now everyone wishes to court popularity among people and makes peace with sycophants and with audacious authorities and with minor *Admorim* who have nought whatsoever in their world. We will, Heaven forfend, sink into oblivion, if we do not arouse ourselves from the dust of falsehood and flattery.[125]

R. Weinberg was concerned lest Judaism be portrayed publicly in a manner that might arouse intellectual disdain. He was attuned to the sense of honesty and straightforwardness that animates youth and to their disappointment when they detect or suspect dishonesty in religious practices. He understood the modern mentality that eschews hypocrisy. Thus he strongly discouraged the issuance of *hetterim* (permissive rulings) enabling businesses to operate on the Sabbath day by means of utilization of legal devices that could be perceived as legal fictions circumventing the spirit of the law and thus lead to denigration of halakhah and desecration of the Divine Name.[126]

---

125 From a letter to S. Z. Shragai, dated Montreux, 1952, published in *Ba'ayot Aktu'aliyot le-Or ha-Halakhah: Gedolei Yisra'el Meshivim le-R. S. Z. Shragai*, ed. Abraham Bick (Jerusalem: Mossad Harav Kook, 1993), 58–59. Cf. also the comments of Berkovits, "Rabbi Yechiel Yakob Weinberg," 13–14.

126 See, for example, *S. E.*, vol. 2, no. 155, 374.

Likewise, in a complex and serious case involving a question of *mamzerut* regarding which R. Weinberg had consulted R. Iser Yehudah Unterman, R. Weinberg rejected Rabbi Unterman's suggestion of a solution that would appear to the untutored as but a circumvention of the law. Rabbi Unterman had proposed a possible remedy for removing the onus of bastardy based on a proposal of R. Shalom Mordecai Schwadron, *Teshuvot Maharsham* I, no. 9, involving the retroactive annulment of a marriage. Under relevant provisions of biblical law, a husband may appoint an agent to deliver a bill of divorce to his wife and yet retain the prerogative of nullifying the agency in order to invalidate the divorce. An agent, unaware of the fact that his authority to deliver the bill of divorce had been nullified, might, in good faith, present the bill of divorce to the wife. In order to prevent the unfortunate consequences of such a scenario, Rabban Gamaliel the Elder promulgated a decree forbidding annulment of the agency other than in the presence of the agent. Moreover, Rabban Gamaliel ordained that any annulment other than in the presence of the agent be itself null and void. Although there is no rabbinic authority to validate a biblically invalid divorce, Rabban Gamaliel employed the principle "Everyone who betroths a wife does so in accordance with the intention of the Sages"[127] in declaring the marriage to be retroactively annulled, that is, Rabban Gamaliel decreed that nullification of the agency other than in the presence of the agent serves to annul the marriage retroactively.

The proposal to legitimatize a child who had already been born a *mamzer* called for the husband to appoint a proxy to deliver a bill of divorce to his wife; the husband would then proceed to annul the proxy other than in the presence of the messenger. Since the marriage is retroactively annulled, the subsequent liaison between the wife and another man does not constitute adultery and the issue of their union are not deemed *mamzerim*.[128] R. Weinberg underscores his reluctance to endorse such proposals to ameliorate even so grave a social problem as *mamzerut* because the inevitable effect of such strategies is to render halakhic rulings a subject of derision in the eyes of the masses. He asserts: "Since we are battling to strengthen the laws of the Torah and their sovereignty in the State of Israel, it is forbidden for us to suggest matters that are not acceptable to common sense and that greatly undermine [Jewish law]."[129]

---

127 *Gittin* 32a.

128 For a discussion of this proposal and of some modifications thereof as well as of the halakhic difficulties posed thereby, see Bleich, *Contemporary Halakhic Problems* (New York: Ktav, 1977), vol. I, 162–167.

129 From a responsum of R. Weinberg addressed to Rabbi Unterman and published in R. Iser Yehudah Unterman, *She'elot u-Teshuvot be-Araba'ah Ḥelkei Shulḥan Arukh* (*Mi-Ktav Yad*) (Jerusalem: Ariel, 1993), *Even ha-Ezer*, 12, sec. 3, 265.

In discussing the permissibility of circumcising a child of a non-Jewish mother and a Jewish father, R. Weinberg cautions that even those authorities who ruled permissively with regard to this question did so only in situations in which the parents intended to convert the child and the circumcision was undertaken for purposes of conversion. Other than in the context of conversion, the circumcision of a non-Jewish child is forbidden—and the conversion itself, emphasizes R. Weinberg, is not always permitted. In instances in which the mother herself has not undergone a valid conversion and the family is not observant of Sabbath and dietary laws, R. Weinberg rules that conversion of the child is null and void. The Gemara sanctions conversion of a minor lacking capacity to assent on the grounds that conversion represents a distinct benefit for him. However, argues R. Weinberg, if the child is not reared in a religious environment, conversion cannot be regarded as an unmitigated benefit. Consequently, R. Weinberg rules against permitting circumcision of a son born to a gentile mother and adds the following remarks:

> In my opinion, your honor should stand firm and not permit circumcision of the son of a gentile woman so that all should know that a child born to a non-Jewish mother is an absolute gentile. Whoever marries a gentile woman gives birth to gentile children and there is no solution for these children unless they convert when they reach the age of majority or unless the parents oblige themselves, at the very minimum, to rear the young child according to the laws of Israel with a kosher diet and observance of the holy Sabbath. Then it may be permissible to permit circumcision for purposes of conversion.[130]

Elsewhere, writing with regard to a similar matter, R. Weinberg notes that rabbis must protect Jewish values with courage and fortitude and not permit

---

130 S. E., vol. 2, no. 160, 378–379. This is also the position of R. Isaac Schmelkes, *She'elot u-Teshuvot Bet Yitzḥak, Even ha-Ezer*, no. 29, sec. 11; R. David M. M. Babad, *She'elot u-Teshuvot Ḥavatzelet ha-Sharon*, vol. I, no. 75; R. Abraham I. Kook, *Da'at Kohen*, nos. 147–148 (Jerusalem: Mossad Harav Kook, 1969); and R. Isaac J. Weisz, *She'elot u-Teshuvot Minḥat Yitzḥak*, vol. III, no. 97. See also R. Gedalia Felder, *Naḥalat Tzevi*, vol. I (New York, 1978), 24, and R. Joel Schwartz, *Madrikh la-Ger* (Jerusalem: Dvar Jerushalayim, 1990), 40–41. An opposing position is presented by R. Mordecai Horowiz, *She'elot u-Teshuvot Matteh Levi*, vol. II, nos. 54 and 55; R. David Horowitz, *She'elot u-Teshuvot Imrei David*, no. 172, sec. 2; and suggested by R. Judah L. Graubart, *She'elot u-Teshuvot Ḥavalim ba-Ne'imim*, vol. IV, no. 30. Cf., also, the correspondence of R. Azriel Hildesheimer and R. Zevi H. Kalischer, included in *Teshuvot Rabbi Ezri'el*, vol. I (Tel Aviv, 1969), *Yoreh De'ah*, nos. 229 and 230, in which R. Hildesheimer rules restrictively and R. Kalischer rules permissively.

brazen violation of the law. Acceptance of inauthentic conversions, he contends, fosters disrespect for Judaism: "Conversion conducted by liberals is, in truth, but a tasteless charade; it also arouses mirth among [even] the best of Christians. Whoever marries a female convert of this genre knows in his heart that by his actions he is throwing dust in the eyes of people."[131]

R. Weinberg was particularly sensitive to the need for scrupulousness in conducting proceedings of rabbinic courts both because such is demanded by halakhah and because of the need to preserve the dignity and reputation of rabbinic tribunals. He also urged rabbinic courts to strive for arbitration designed to provide equitable relief unachievable by means of application of the letter of the law. In counselling such a policy R. Weinberg refers not only to the talmudic statement, *Sanhedrin* 6b, declaring compromise to be preferable in the interest of restoring harmonious relations between the litigants but also cites the statement of *Bava Kamma* 100a establishing an obligation to conduct oneself in accordance with a standard that extends beyond the letter of the law as well as the statement of the Sages, *Bava Metzi'a* 30b, in which they declared, "Jerusalem was destroyed because they ruled therein according to Torah law … and they did not rule beyond the letter of the law."[132]

R. Weinberg himself adds that he was wont to quote the biblical passage, "For that is his covering only, it is his raiment for his skin: wherein shall he sleep? And it shall come to pass, when he cries unto me, that I will hear; for I am gracious" (Exodus 22:26) in stressing that the Torah depicts the plight of the poor man in most moving terms in order to alert the creditor to the fact that, although from the purely legal perspective he is not obliged to return the surety that has been given to him, nevertheless, the Torah demands that the creditor forego his right and respond with compassion to the plaintive plea, "wherein shall he sleep?"[133]

R. Weinberg did not merely counsel such a policy as a preferable course of action: in one instance in which he feared that untempered application of the provisions of the law would cause the litigant to lose his livelihood, he urged the judges to recuse themselves unless the parties were able and willing to accept a conciliation in achieving resolution in the form of *pesharah* or compromise. The Talmud, *Sanhedrin* 7a, exhorts a judge to picture himself always as if a sword is hanging over his head. R. Weinberg expressed the fear that the "sword" could become a weapon to destroy an individual's livelihood.[134] He recognized full well that the same "sword" could destroy the *bet din* itself and

---

131 *S. E.*, vol. 3, no. 100, 317.
132 See ibid., no. 65, 232.
133 Ibid., 232.
134 Ibid., 232.

the principles it represents if its decisions were to be perceived as producing suffering and misery.

In this context it is noteworthy that, despite the fact that Judaism was embattled, R. Weinberg always counseled adoption of a public stance of pride and abjuration of apologetics. He wrote disparagingly of those whose response to anti-Semitic canards was to organize public lectures and commission scholarly works in an endeavor to demonstrate that the verities of Jewish teaching are acknowledged even by non-Jews. He felt deeply ashamed and slighted by such endeavors. "Who asked you to apologize on my behalf?," he wrote, and urged all members of the community to respond with dignity and self-pride and not to adopt a defensive posture:

> Judaism and apologetics—there are hardly any other two concepts that are more contradictory to one another than these. The concept of apologetics is so very strange and unsuitable to the character of Judaism whose first appearance in the world was with so much Divine might and with a powerful striving to pour out its spirit upon all flesh: "As I live ... surely with a mighty hand ... and with fury poured out, will I rule over you." (Ezekiel 20:33). In such language does the prophet speak in the name of God.[135]

R. Weinberg derides "the modern Jew, a Jew possessed of only one verse of the Torah" as a caricature. He recounts an incident in which a noted author extolled the Torah's contribution to civilization of the concept "And you shall love your neighbor as yourself" (Leviticus 19:18) and proceeded to declare that as long as there exists a need for armed forces in any country, as long as one soldier yet stands guard, Judaism had not fulfilled its destiny. R. Weinberg challenges the writer, pointing out that Judaism also taught, "Unto a stranger you may lend upon usury" (Deuteronomy 23:21) and "You shall save alive nothing that breathes" (Deuteronomy 20:16). He concludes: "The Torah is not dear to us because of some verses that find favor in the eyes of the enlightened, so to speak. The entire Torah, as it is, with all its verses and every crownlet is equally dear to us. A scroll of the Law that is missing even a point of the letter *yod* is rendered unfit."[136]

R. Weinberg cautions that ideas that are in vogue and thought to be progressive may be disdained in the future; concepts that are now considered to be of peripheral value may be viewed as significant at a later time. Intellectual modes and trends are short-lived. To tailor the Torah to suit the fickle intellectual fads of each era is not only forbidden, but also counterproductive.

---

135 *Li-Perakim*, 300.
136 Ibid., 295.

As for anti-Semitism, it is motivated by illogical considerations and therefore apologetics will, in any event, not eradicate this scourge.[137]

4. Secular Studies and Academic Jewish Scholarship

R. Weinberg was aware as well of a problem common to his own time, namely, the high rate of disaffection of youth from traditional backgrounds that resulted in situations in which they felt that their desire for a broader education was being forcibly denied to them.[138] R. Weinberg's consciousness of the debilitating effect of such deprivation is evident in his writings regarding educational curricula. R. Weinberg was, himself, no stranger to academic disciplines and their methodology is reflected in his own scholarship.

As might be anticipated, R. Weinberg's mastery of talmudic scholarship is reflected primarily in his responsa and novellae. His competence in general academic Jewish scholarship is reflected in writings such as his *Kuntres ha-Idit*,[139] and his studies on the Mishnah[140] and the *Targumim*.[141] His familiarity and engagement with philosophical writings is apparent in his numerous essays and homiletical writings.[142] However, R. Weinberg was not an intellectual schizophrenic. Singular in all these works is the extent to which they reflect a personality in which all these areas of scholarly endeavor were integrated and synthesized. His *lomdut* and his academic attainments merged in scholarly endeavors in which rabbinic scholarship grounded in deep faith and piety was enriched by modern critical methodology.[143] Because of the unusual intellectual synthesis achieved by R. Weinberg, his writings discussing the role to be accorded secular studies in the educational curriculum and intellectual endeavors of a Torah scholar are particularly instructive.[144]

---

137 Ibid., 295. This attitude did not preclude his giving answers to serious questions regarding the relationship of Jews and non-Jews, as well as explication of difficult passages that might lead to genuine misunderstanding. See, for example, ibid., 166–167, his comments regarding the disqualification of non-Jews from serving as witnesses and S. E., vol. 3, no. 66, 232–233, his discussion of a frequently misunderstood reference to property rights of non-Jews found in *Rema, Shulḥan Arukh* 156:5.

138 *Li-Perakim*, 113.

139 S. E., vol. 4, 10–137.

140 Ibid., 222–266.

141 Ibid., 267–275.

142 See, for example, *Li-Perakim*, 121–154, and S. E., vol. 4, 337–338, 360–374.

143 See, for example, *Li-Perakim*, 142–167.

144 Joseph Safran, *Pirkei Iyun be-Toldot ha-Ḥinnukh ha-Yehudi: Meḥkarim u-Berurim be-Ḥinnukh ha-Yehudi le-Or ha-Mekorot*, vol. 3 (Jerusalem: Mossad Harav Kook, 1993), chap. 8, 327–341, presents a cursory outline of aspects of R. Weinberg's contributions as educator.

R. Weinberg was fully conscious of the magnetic attraction of the intellectual currents of the age and the powerful tug of intellectual curiosity. In the course of a eulogy describing a favored disciple, R. Weinberg expressed himself in words that may be taken as self-revealing and even self-descriptive. R. Weinberg writes that his departed student, R. Saul Weingort, regretted spending precious time in the pursuit of secular studies but "perceived himself compelled to do so, whether because of the needs of the time that had changed from what [they] had been in bygone eras or whether *because of the passion for knowledge that pulsated in his heart,* he wished to acquire for himself the knowledge that it is possible for a person of our times to attain."[145]

R. Weinberg's own understanding of the allure of intellectual pursuits permeates his analysis of the revolutionary aspect of the contribution of Rabbi Samson Raphael Hirsch. R. Weinberg is sharp in his critique of revisionist writers who sought to portray R. Hirsch's openness to secular studies as a form of compromise or as the choice of a lesser evil as a concession to the times. It has been claimed by some that R. Hirsch's advocacy of secular studies for Jews in Germany was a product of his recognition of the economic exigencies that made pursuit of such studies essential for those who found it necessary to seek their livelihood in commerce or in the practice of a profession. They maintained that R. Hirsch instituted such studies in the school he founded simply because of the necessity to comply with government educational regulations.[146] R. Weinberg regarded such categorization of R. Hirsch's educational policy as a perversion of historical truth. R. Weinberg asserted that R. Hirsch sincerely favored a "synthesis of Torah and worldly studies (*derekh eretz*) in the broadest sense of that term."[147] Nevertheless, R. Weinberg emphasized,

---

145 *Yad Sha'ul*, 17. Emphasis added.
146 See unsigned article "Das Bildungsideal S. R. Hirschs und die Gegenwart," *Der Israelit* 35 (August 30, 1934), 5, and Jacob Rosenheim, introduction to R. Samson Raphael Hirsch, *Be-Ma'aglei Shanah*, vol. 1 (Bnei Brak: Netzah, 1965), 12–18, 31–33. Regarding changing currents in German Orthodoxy, see also Schwab, *Orthodox Jewry in Germany*, 128.
147 *S. E.*, vol. 4, 366. These remarks were included in R. Weinberg's introductory essay on Hirsch published in the Hebrew edition of Hirsch's writings, issued by Netzah, *Be-Ma'aglei Shanah*, vol. 3 (Bnei Brak: Netzah, 1966). However, an unsigned editorial note appended to these comments (16) presents the contradictory analysis of Jacob Rosenheim and of R. Baruch Ber Leibowitz, *Birkat Shmu'el*, vol. 1, *Kiddushin* no. 27, to the effect that Hirsch's policy was a concession to the times. The unsigned publisher's preface to *Be-Ma'aglei Shanah*, vol. 3, p. 10, portrays R Weinberg's point of view on this matter as that of a *da'at yaḥid*, an individual, minority opinion. But see Rabbi Eliyahu Meir Klugman, "Kuntres ve-Yehi bi-Yeshurun Melekh: Toldot u-Pirkei Ḥayyim," in R. Samson Raphael Hirsch, *Shemesh Marpeh*, ed. E. M. Klugman (Brooklyn: Mesorah Publications, 1992), 327,

R. Hirsch did not espouse the view that secular studies were necessary in order to achieve intellectual perfection or even a well-rounded personality; rather, R. Hirsch stressed that Torah was the repository of supreme wisdom and contained within itself all significant teachings and values. Secular studies might be of assistance to a person in explicating the truths of Torah, but the Torah, in and of itself, is self-sufficient. Indeed, writes R. Weinberg, "No religious Jew can be comfortable with the notion that if he has learned only a great deal of Torah, he cannot be deemed to have attained a high cultural standard or that he must seek culture beyond Torah for the enrichment of his personality. Thus, in the writings of R. Hirsch no word can be found that might lead to the conclusion that he understood Judaism and general culture as constituting complementary values."[148] Hirsch did not endeavor to make the Torah *salonfähig*, but to bring the *Salon* to Torah; he did not wish to introduce Jews to drawing-room society, but to introduce *Salon* society to the *bet midrash*.[149]

Despite the value R. Weinberg placed upon secular wisdom, his comments regarding the primacy of Torah scholarship are unequivocal. In articulating his conviction that, in his day, there could no longer be any conceivable halakhic

---

unnumbered note, as well as his general discussion of Hirsch's philosophy of *Torah im Derekh Eretz* (Torah and Worldly Studies), 327–35.

In his championship of Hirsch's views in face of revisionist interpretations, one finds a striking example of R. Weinberg's sensitivity to East-West prejudices and differences of perspective. In comments that appeared originally in German, in *Nachalath Zwi* (1937), later republished in his *Das Volk der Religion*, 69–70, R. Weinberg responds to the claim (advanced in *Israelit* 35 [1934]) that Hirsch advocated a *Realschule* education only to enable laymen to pursue business careers. R. Weinberg rejects such a limited interpretation of Hirsch's outlook and adds:

> Ob in Hinblick auf die Grösse Rabb. Hirsch seine solche Form der Legalisierung nötig war, ist wirklich nur eine Frage des guten Geshmacks. Eine solche Deutung aber verzerrt die gigantische Gestalt Hirschs und reduziert sie auf die Figure eines verdienstvollen Rabbiners und Lehrers, der für seine süddeutschen Baale Batim eine Realschule gründet, damit sie den Olam Haseh als Grosskaufleute geniessen können und doch nicht des Olam Habah verlustig zu gehen brauchen.
>
> Für uns aber, und ich sage es mit stolzer Betonung—für uns "Ost-Juden" bedeutet Rabbiner Hirsch viel mehr, und wir glauben auch ihn besser verstanden zu haben.
>
> Vielleicht wird mancher gutter Frankfurter, der Rabb. Hirsch quasi also ein Privateigentum ansieht, uns die Legalität abstreiten so zu sprechen; aber jeder, des Hirschs Grösse verspürt, darf ein Bekenntnis zu ihm ablegen.

148 *Das Volk der Religion*, 73. Cf. S. E., vol. 4, 368.
149 *Das Volk der Religion*, 67.

impediment to delivery of sermons in the language of the country, R. Weinberg noted that rabbinic opposition to preaching in the vernacular had indeed been expressed in some locales during a period of time in which the vast majority of the Jewish population in those areas spoke Yiddish and liberal elements had sought to speed assimilation and acculturation of the masses by exposing them to both written and spoken German and by denigrating Yiddish as an inferior language. However, he argued, at a time when the masses had already become fully fluent in the vernacular and it was obvious that the sole motive in utilizing the language of the country in sermons was to enhance communication with the audience in order to impart Torah teachings, there could no longer be any objection whatsoever to such a practice. In characteristic fashion, R. Weinberg does not equivocate and boldly expresses his assurance that "were the *Ḥatam Sofer*, of blessed memory, alive in our present era, he would certainly have rejoiced greatly to see the religious rabbis of Germany fighting the machinations of false enlightenment of secular studies by means of the German language. Everything depends upon the purpose and the desired result."[150]

R. Weinberg follows these remarks with an insightful comment on how, as a matter of practical strategy, one should react to secular blandishments in the context of clarifying priorities and setting standards:

> In general, there are two methods of fighting against the false enlightenment of secular studies. One method involves prohibition and ban and raging battle against it. The second method involves mental disrespect and belittling its honor and reinforcement of love and regard for the sanctity of our true wisdom, which is our life and the length of our days. For example, if one sees a modern rabbi who is not knowledgeable in Torah but is fluent in the language of the country and learned in secular studies, it is necessary to publicize the limitations of his knowledge of Torah and to berate him for the meagerness of this knowledge and not to publicize his worldly attainments, for in the [latter] manner one ascribes importance to them. Similarly, if an individual appears who is a Torah scholar and also secularly educated, one should honor him for his Torah and pay no attention to his secular attainments, as if they did not at all exist.[151]

---

150 *S. E.*, vol. 2, no. 149, 364.

151 Ibid., 364. See also *Ha-Pardes* 40, no. 7 (April 1966), 4, for R. Weinberg's pithy comments regarding those who prefer the title "doctor" over that of "rabbi." See *S. E.*, vol. 2, no. 30, 53 n., R. Weinberg's assertion that among the graduates of the *Rabbinerseminar* there were pious individuals for whom secular attainments were secondary in nature and who made

A devotee of the *mussar* movement, one of the first writers to analyze its thought as a systematic ideology, and an admirer of the works of Rabbi Hirsch, R. Weinberg develops a most intriguing comparison of these two philosophical approaches. R. Weinberg maintained that both Rabbi Samson Raphael Hirsch and Rabbi Israel Salanter had, each in his own unique manner, sought to foster the development of a deep and conscious spirituality (a "religious enlightenment"—*haskalah dattit*) and to teach the way in which Torah, which is coextensive with life, could be the source for fulfillment of all personal, social, and cultural aspirations. In this manner both Rabbi Hirsch and Rabbi Salanter sought to present an attractive alternative to the intellectual currents of the Enlightenment. Both were critical of the religious society of their time in which superficial and mechanical performance of mitzvot had replaced spirituality. Living in a society permeated with Western culture, Hirsch endeavored to demonstrate that all culture can be viewed through the prism of Torah values since Torah is the wellspring of all spiritual creativity. Of the two, claimed R. Weinberg, Rabbi Salanter's formulation was closer to the sources; however, R. Hirsch's methodology and approach were more suited to those raised in the West.[152]

In his own day, under somewhat altered circumstances, R. Weinberg advocated emulation of the pioneering strategies of R. Hirsch in adapting to changing conditions and in formulating pedagogic modalities designed to promote more intensive Jewish education. Certainly, he was aware of the extent to which most Western Jews are acculturated and recognized that ostrich-like burial of one's head in the sand and denial would not change the sociological reality:

> Truly, the Jew of our times already stands head and shoulders in another world, a world rich in spiritual creativity, with an agenda for scientific advancement and an enhanced standard of living, with poetry and music, literature and philosophy. All these visions entice, attract and captivate Jews whose religious consciousness is not deep and is not even properly founded.

---

use of their academic titles only in dealings with the civil authorities or the assimilated. See also *S. E.*, vol. 3, no. 75, 256, where R. Weinberg expresses approval of an individual who, despite his accomplishment in secular scholarship, concentrates upon Torah study, "for that is our life and the length of our days and the Almighty has in His world but the four ells of halakhah" and it is in the merit of assiduous Torah study that fame and honor in Israel is attained.

152 *S. E.*, vol. 4, 372. Cf. *Das Volk der Religion*, 76.

The Jew of our times[153] is bound by thousands of ties to this new world in both commercial and industrial pursuits as well as in communal affairs and in matters of education and professional training in schools and halls of academe. This is a fact that cannot be denied or negated with pursing of lips, with sighs and tears. The solutions proposed by those of small mind and narrow perspective will not serve to build a bridge and a passage to safety for a confused and bewildered generation. My counsel is to heed and accept instruction from a great teacher in Israel who underwent the test and was greatly successful. Certainly his approach and educational methodology require a new formulation[154] that is more suited to the values of the time and the needs of the Jewish soul [that is] thirsty for complete mastery and deep knowledge of the sources of Torah. However, the direction and the goal charted by the great teacher retain their full force.[155]

R. Weinberg does not spell out the specific changes that he advocates in R. Hirsch's educational approach. But his reference to the desire for "complete mastery and deep knowledge of the sources of Torah" is an indication that he

---

153 The text of this essay as it appears in Hirsch, *Be-Ma'aglei Shanah*, vol. 3, 22, has the interpolation of the phrases "to the extent that he is not immersed in study of Torah and is not bound to the style of life that pulses in its tents." This volume of *Be-Ma'aglei Shanah* was published by Netzah Publishing Company shortly after the death of R. Weinberg. One hopes that the additional phrases were added with the consent of R. Weinberg during his lifetime and do not constitute revisionism of Weinberg (in an essay deploring revisionism of Hirsch).

154 The text in *Be-Ma'aglei Shanah* has an editorial note suggesting that the new formulation should include abolition of all forms of coeducation, both in formal and informal settings. R. Weinberg might well have agreed, in principle, to that suggestion—particularly for schools in Israel. However, he does not make that statement explicitly in any of his own writings.

155 *S. E.*, vol. 4, 373. Toward the end of his life, R. Weinberg was sorely troubled by the opposition to general studies increasingly prevalent in Orthodox circles. A characteristic expression of his concern is reflected in a personal communication, dated 1964 (Letter cited in "Sarid ha-Esh," *Ha Ma'ayan* 6, no. 3 [Nisan 1966]: 66):

> If my health permits, I will ... publish articles on German Jewry. To my distress, it has no successor in other countries, not even in *Eretz Yisra'el*. ...
> The circles that oppose the ideology of the Gaon R. S. R. Hirsch, of blessed memory, respond with animosity to any article in which they detect a whiff of science. R. S. R. Hirsch and R. A. Hildesheimer emerged in opposition to those circles. As is known, their intent was for the sake of Heaven. In our day as well, the situation is such that it is necessary for us to emphasize that science is not scorned by us if it does not involve rejection of the yoke of tradition or denial of the fundamentals of faith. In my opinion, it devolves upon those who are of German extraction to maintain steadfastly the ideology of *Torah im Derekh Eretz* in its broadest form and not be drawn after the zealots who trample it underfoot.

opts for an intensification of the talmudic curriculum. His lifelong interest in the rabbinate pervades his writings on this topic. Thus he also lauds the earlier efforts of Rabbi Azriel Hildesheimer to develop a cadre of rabbis who would be intellectually equipped to serve as mentors to an educated laity:

> In return to the sources of Judaism, in analysis and study of Talmud and codes and the vast geonic and rabbinic literature, [Hildesheimer] perceived the greatest surety for returning the splendor of Judaism to its original state.... But he demanded of his students that they not abandon work in the field of the science of Judaism in accordance with the principles of tradition. He argued that, in our day, it is not sufficient that rabbis know a chapter in the rulings of the permitted and the forbidden, the dietary code and *trefot*, the impure and the pure, which certainly are the foundation of foundations of the life of Judaism. Rather, it is necessary for them to stand before the larger world and demonstrate the correctness of Judaism and its eternal truths in the face of secular science. As bearers of the word of God, it is the obligation of rabbis to explain to the [Jewish] nation and to the world the view of Judaism with regard to all problems of ethics, law, and social reform with which the new generation struggles. It is their obligation to demonstrate that Judaism is not merely a compendium of religious laws and customs but is a decisive spiritual force in the life of humanity. Of course, they may not leave any problem or challenge on the part of natural science without a suitable and convincing reply.... It is not possible for a rabbi in our day to evade [the problems] and shrink in a corner of his study.... He must know what is transpiring around him in the world of science and literature, the intellectual trends that constantly evolve from epoch to epoch. Without systematic training and without knowledge of the language of modern intellectual thought, he will not be able to find the path and the spiritual connection to the inner world of the youth and the members of the new generation.[156]

Rabbi Hildesheimer envisioned the creation of "an institution that would develop a religious intelligentsia"[157] in the manner of previous generations that boasted of luminaries such as Sa'adiah Gaon, Maimonides, and Nahmanides, scholars who had mastered Torah and the secular wisdom of the day. His mission was to produce a new group of Torah leaders and scholars who would

---

156 *S. E.*, vol. 1, introduction, 2.
157 Ibid., 2.

expound Torah ideology as it relates to the broadest range of ethical and social questions, in a mode and manner that would appeal to modern intellectuals.[158]

Such aspirations had not yet become actual. The synthesis of *Torah im Derekh Eretz* heretofore achieved, maintained R. Weinberg, was far too narrow. He sought the development of a synthesis of faith and secular wisdom that would express itself in a broad academic perspective. His goal and aim was the development of a creative interaction of Torah and secular studies and its expression in a sophisticated intellectual manner. Of the synthesis to which the modern Torah community should aspire, he wrote:

> It is impermissible that this synthesis should be confined in narrow and minuscule borders, such as the invention of a Sabbath belt in order to make possible the carrying of house keys on the Sabbath, or the discovery of a cream for shaving without a razor, and the like. Rather this endeavor is broad and deep, and thus it is required and compelled to be. It is your responsibility to continue it in this direction: not merely utilization of technical means born of Western progress in order to conceal our Jewishness or to still the conscience, but penetration to the depth of the sources and plumbing them anew for the purpose of flowering of the spirit and a complete synthesis of Torah and life.[159]

However, in contrast to most proponents of the *Torah im Derekh Eretz* approach, R. Weinberg was well aware that the attempt to achieve such a synthesis was not without problems. The potential for a conflict of values was real:

> Deference toward the tradition on the one hand and a feeling of respect toward scientific investigation on the other hand generate a singular problem that is not the estate of free-thinkers to whom reverence for tradition is foreign and who are arrogant in their scientific knowledge, nor is it the problem of the devout whose eyes only gaze in one direction. In exchange for the comfort of absence of problems, [members of] this latter group are compelled, however, to accept upon themselves the charge of disdain for culture and laziness of thought.
>
> This problem does not lack an identifiable tragic aspect. But loyalty to Judaism does not imply the comfort of absence of knowledge

---

158 Ibid., 2.
159 *Li-Perakim*, 233.

and investigation; rather, it implies a greater burden of obligations and responsibility—obligations vis- à-vis the great ones of the past and the treasures of their spirit and responsibility vis- à-vis the youthful generation that seeks fresh spiritual sustenance. As the inner burden increases, so will the powers of creativity become stronger.[160]

With total confidence born of deep faith and firm knowledge, R. Weinberg was certain that solutions to all such problems could be found and he was convinced that ultimately the struggle would bear fruit. Out of struggle and challenge, new intellectual forces are born. Just as there is ferment and challenge in the study of Torah, so, too, would the challenge of modernity prove to be a source of creative tension. The challenge of culture and modernity would engender a creative response and give rise to an efflorescence of Torah thought.[161] Similarly, with regard to academic scholarship in Jewish studies, he believed that, if pursued by those whose background and training in rabbinics was of a high caliber, the creative combination of modern critical scholarship and talmudic erudition would lead to scholarly productivity that would itself serve as an enhancement of Torah.

Throughout his life R. Weinberg manifested a sustained interest in academic Jewish scholarship. Upon completion of his graduate studies at the University of Giessen, he accepted a post at the university as a *Dozent* in Jewish studies and research assistant to Professor Paul Kahle. Kahle later acknowledged the assistance of R. Weinberg in his own work.[162] A study, "The Mishna Text in Babylonia," published in 1935, includes fragments from the *Genizah* jointly edited by Kahle and R. Weinberg.[163] It is noteworthy that in a

---

160 Ibid., 232–33.
161 Ibid., 232–33.
162 Paul Kahle, *Die Masoreten des Westens*, vol. I (Stuttgart: Kohlhammer, 1927), 78, and vol. II (Stuttgart: Kohlhammer, 1930), 3.

    For a reference by R. Weinberg to Kahle in the context of a discussion of the *Targumim*, see S. E., vol. 4, 269–270. Noteworthy is R. Weinberg's concurrence with some observations of Kahle while disputing a conjecture of Kahle regarding the Letter of Aristeas, secs. 30–33. Although he disputes Kahle's conjecture entirely on the basis of internal textual evidence, R. Weinberg was surely aware that acceptance of Kahle's point would have served to cast doubt upon the integrity of the Hebrew text of Scripture.
163 *Hebrew Union College Annual* 10 (1935), 185–222. Publication of R. Weinberg's work in a journal such as the *Hebrew Union College Annual*, which was sponsored by a Reform institution, may seem incongruous. However, examination of the format in which the article is presented is instructive. The title appears in capital letters; immediately following, in smaller point type, is the subtitle "Fragments from the Geniza edited and examined by

responsum authored by R. Weinberg in response to the question of whether it is permissible to lecture on Jewish law at a non-Jewish university, R. Weinberg reports that his earliest consideration of the matter occurred when he confronted the identical issue at the time of his appointment as an instructor in Jewish studies at the University of Giessen.[164]

Striking is the fact that R. Weinberg's academic expertise is reflected not only in articles of an academic nature but also in a number of his halakhic responsa. In a discussion of the obligation of married women to wear a covering over their hair, he incorporates a lengthy linguistic analysis of biblical terms and their Aramaic equivalents in the *Targumim*.[165] R. Weinberg's linguistic proficiency and thoroughgoing familiarity with the pertinent scholarly literature on this topic reflects a standard of competence not usual among talmudists. His extensive discussion of the attitude of halakhah toward secular courts of law (*arka'ot shel akum*)[166] contains a masterful analysis of rabbinic sources interwoven with historical data and presents what he describes in his own words as "a new method of talmudic exegesis incorporating an historical approach to the law itself, clarifying the historical background of the foundation of the Mishnah, its development and its final formulation."[167]

R. Weinberg's particular academic interests centered upon philological studies of classical biblical translations, the Masoretic text of the Pentateuch, and the redaction of the Talmud. He sought to encourage and legitimize similar scholarly investigations among Torah scholars as an accompaniment to traditional rabbinic scholarship. With regard to rabbinic scholarship itself, R. Weinberg considered the rigorous methodology of the traditional analytic approach as essential for an understanding of Talmud. Nevertheless, he was convinced that scientific scholarship could yield many valuable insights as

---

P. Kahle and J. Weinberg." This, in turn, is followed by an indication of Section I, bearing the title "Introduction and Edition of the Texts by P. Kahle." The left running head contains only the name "P. Kahle." Throughout the article, the first person pronoun is used repeatedly. Clearly, the submission to *Hebrew Union College Annual* was that of Kahle.

Although this article was intended to be the first of a series in which Kahle would be responsible for "the philological publication of the text" while R. Weinberg would analyze "the importance of these fragments for the history of the Mishna text" (ibid., 191), only one further article by Kahle was actually published. It appeared under the title "The Mishna Text in Babylonia, II," *Hebrew Union College Annual* 12–13 (1937–1938), 275–325.

164 S. E., vol. 2, no. 92, 229–233.
165 S. E., vol. 3, no. 30, 84–91.
166 Ibid., "Arka'ot shel Akum," 357–375.
167 Ibid., 375.

well. In promoting a synthesis of traditional *lomdut* and modern scholarship, R. Weinberg wished to dispel misunderstandings that existed in both camps. He sought to defend traditional rabbinic scholarship from its denigrators and was critical of those whose historical studies had failed to capture the essence of talmudic dialectic: "Like surgeons they sliced up the Talmud as though it were a mummified corpse. … This kind of science … has failed to locate the Talmud's soul and has not recognized that the immanent core of the Talmud is none other than the perpetual striving to clarify fully and exhaustively each and every concept and to enable their future development."[168]

Although, on occasion, he faulted rabbinic scholars who failed to take advantage of the fruits of scholarly investigation, R. Weinberg was first and foremost a champion of rigorous talmudic dialectic that he chooses to refer to as *pilpul*.[169] Writing to a scholar who had completed a study of the sources of Rambam's rulings utilizing what R. Weinberg termed the "single method that leads to the truth," R. Weinberg was careful to emphasize:·

> However, I will not deny what is in my heart. My opinion is not like that of modern scholars that all works of *pilpul* are vain toil. That is not the case! The attempts of the best of the sages, of blessed memory, served to develop Torah and talmudic thought and to clarify and elucidate talmudic concepts. … If not for our great rabbis, the geniuses of the latter generations, the study of Gemara would have become a dry and boring subject. They transformed it into a sea of wisdom and understanding in which every talent finds a place for expression.[170]

---

168 *Li-Perakim*, 118, and Shalom Carmy, "R. Yehiel Weinberg's Lecture on Academic Jewish Scholarship," *Tradition* 24, no. 4 (Summer 1989): 20. This excerpt is from a lecture of R. Weinberg's included in *Li-Perakim*, 115–120. Professor Carmy's excellent introduction, notes, and translation of this essay were published in *Tradition* 24, no. 4 (Summer 1989), 15–23. The translation of the quotations from that essay is that of Professor Carmy.

169 Over the centuries the term *pilpul* has been used to describe a variety of differing and diverse methodologies of Talmud study. The word has been used both as a term of approbation and as a term of derision. Indeed, in Lithuanian circles, the term was frequently used as a pejorative description of a dialectical method involving imaginative analogies and far-fetched attempts to find commonalities underlying diverse principles. R. Weinberg uses the term approvingly to describe the analytic method of the Lithuanian yeshivot whose methodology involved clarification of definitions and meticulous attention to shades of meaning reflected in the nomenclature of both talmudic texts and statements of early commentators as well as careful comparison and contrast of talmudic principles. Many would abjure use of the term *pilpul* as a description of the latter methodology.

170 *S. E.*, vol. 3, no. 133, 356. R. Weinberg also commented frequently on the intellectual freshness and vitality engendered by *pilpul*. Cf. for example, ibid., no. 74, 251, where R. Weinberg

Addressing students of the *Rabbinerseminar*, R. Weinberg was even more emphatic:

> To be sure, it has been decided in the school of that narrow science which is cramped into its disciplinary four cubits that an investigation which is based on the halakhah and which discusses only the literature of halakhah does not count as science and hence should be rejected. They think that such an investigation can be dismissed by the descriptive term "*pilpul*" and they · regard it as something that has passed and disappeared from the world. ... If the meaning of "scientific investigation" is the clarification of concepts, the extrapolation from cognate ideas of the fundamental concepts and their logical and methodical construction, then it is difficult to grasp precisely why a discourse on talmudic ideas which presents them in the formal framework of formulated clarified concepts should not be worthy of the name "science." Particularly you, *rabbotai*, insofar as you have the regular opportunity to find yourselves in the smithy of the halakhah, must reject with both hands the claim that the method called "*pilpul*" is unscientific. ...[171]
>
> Already David Hoffmann, one of the founders of the science of Talmud, stood up against the attitude of contempt adopted towards *pilpul*, noting that the essence of the Talmud, its mode of instruction and proof, is *pilpul*. Whoever eschews *pilpul* will not escape from the logical conclusion that he must reject the Talmud too.[172]

However, there do exist severe limitations upon use of the methodology of *pilpul*. *Pilpul* should never be misapplied, contends R. Weinberg, by utilizing it to resolve textual difficulties in the writings of *rishonim* (early-day scholars) in a manner that contradicts the meaning of talmudic sources. R. Weinberg quotes a comment of Rashba who remarks that it is preferable to declare that Rambam overlooked a talmudic source than to interpret Rambam in a manner that perverts the meaning of the talmudic text. R. Weinberg writes:

> In my opinion, the efforts of some authors to defend Rambam from criticism by means of radically distorting lengthy talmudic disquisitions

---

suggests an answer to a problem on the basis of *pilpul* and then proceeds to offer a more direct explanation. In light of R. Weinberg's explicit praise of the use of *pilpul* within the proper parameters, Berkovits's remarks, *Tradition* 8, no. 2 (1973), 6, are puzzling. Of course, strictures regarding inappropriate and incorrect use of *pilpul* are another matter entirely.

171 *Tradition* 24, no. 4 (Summer 1989), 19.
172 Ibid., 20.

through the use of sharp *pilpul* runs counter to the simple truth. It is preferable to leave Rambam as is than to distort what is explicit in the Gemara in opposition to his view.[173]

Pilpul should never be used to obscure the literal meaning of the talmudic discourse, the true import of which is most difficult to discern. "Indeed," writes R. Weinberg, "there is nothing more difficult than ascertaining the plain meaning of the *sugya*. The simple, plain meaning (*ha-peshat ha-pashut*) is a matter that is most hidden, and obscure."[174]

Suited as it is for clarification of talmudic concepts, *pilpul* is not suitable for the resolution of difficulties and discrepancies with regard to matters of style and language. Verification and comparison of manuscripts, as well as philological and historical studies, are the modes of investigation suited for linguistic analysis of a text. The essential prerequisite for the scholar is the availability of an authoritative text. However, comments R. Weinberg:

> It is well-known that, in previous times, those who published the works of early scholars were not very meticulous and did not go to any trouble to find other manuscripts by means of which they would have been able to preserve the works from gross errors. It is not profitable to enter into involved explanations solely in order to resolve what are really the errors of writers and copyists of books.[175]

To illustrate the fact that establishing a correct textual reading could obviate difficulties in interpretation, R. Weinberg recounted an anecdote concerning Rabbi David Zevi Hoffmann. A scholar had suggested to Rabbi Hoffmann a method of resolving problems posed by a difficult passage in the text of the Bartenura commentary on the Mishnah on the basis of an ingenious *pilpul*. Rabbi Hoffmann responded that he was convinced that there was simply a misprint in the text. R. Hoffmann quipped that after his demise, when this individual arrives in heaven he will be welcomed, not by the Bartenura, but by the

---

173 *S. E.*, vol. 2, no. 162, 381.
174 *Meḥkarim ba-Talmud*, introduction, iii.
175 *S. E.*, vol. 3, no. 127, sec. 18, 346.

typesetter of the Romm edition of the Mishnah whose typographical error he had so well succeeded in defending.[176]

The publication of newly discovered manuscripts of *rishonim* was welcomed by R. Weinberg, who noted that use of such manuscripts might obviate strained and unconvincing interpretations of a text.[177] At greater length he emphasized that publication of critical editions of the works of *rishonim* constitutes a crucial area of scholarship and ought to engage the attention of rabbinic scholars. Decrying the fact that text-critical studies had been neglected by the vast majority of latter-day talmudic scholars, R. Weinberg expressed a firm conviction that, at times, existing textual inaccuracies contributed to unnecessary difficulties in the formulation of halakhah and that research in this field "would open before us a clear road to understanding the words of our Sages, of blessed memory, and the true intent of the teachings of the *rishonim*."[178]

Works of *rishonim* predated the printing press and were preserved by repeated copying of manuscripts. As an inevitable result, copyists' errors proliferated over the course of centuries. As noted, a seemingly minor inaccuracy in copying a text could result in an alteration of the meaning that might have significant ramifications. Early publishers of the texts of classical *rishonim* did not examine the manuscripts they used with a critical eye and, as a result, errors became enshrined in the printed text and, in the course of time, came to be regarded virtually as sacred writ.[179] R. Weinberg points out that scholars such as *Maharshal* and *Shakh* were meticulous in striving to establish correct textual readings. *Shakh* did not hesitate to rule contrary even to *Bet Yosef* and *Rema* in an instance in which he found evidence that their ruling was based on what he believed to be reliance upon a corrupt manuscript. In that instance, even when challenged by *Taz*, *Shakh* did not withdraw from his position.[180] The Gaon of Vilna, R. Weinberg adds, toiled throughout his life to establish accurate textual

---

176 S. E., vol. 1, p. 364. Berkovits, "Rabbi Yechiel Yakob Weinberg," 7–8, writes that he personally heard the anecdote first from Dr. Wohlgemuth of the *Rabbinerseminar* faculty and, on frequent subsequent occasions, from R. Weinberg who was fond of repeating the story.

177 S. E., vol. 2, no. 12, 22 n.

178 S. E., vol. 3, 401–402. See also ibid., 252–253, 346–347.

179 R. Weinberg points to examples of a common form of printing error in which the typesetter misses several lines of text because the first word of the line or phrase in each case begins with the identical word and thus the ellipsis is not readily noted by the printer. See ibid., 402, n.

180 The reference is to *Shakh, Yoreh De'ah* 94:15, in which *Shakh* maintains that *Bet Yosef* and *Rema* relied upon the Venice edition of *Semak*, whereas the correct reading is to be found in

readings and the importance of those endeavors was fully appreciated by the Gaon's disciples: "And long ago, the Gaon R. Hayyim of Volozhin noted regarding our great teacher, of blessed memory, that 'he brought us out of the darkness of errors to light.'"[181]

This pursuit, although championed by the Gaon of Vilna, suffered from neglect on the part of later scholars. With a changing intellectual climate, R. Weinberg believed that a new era of scholarship could commence:

> At the present time, science has progressed and reached a stage in which critical study of sources is feasible. Bibliographical science has properly established the various extant manuscripts of early scholars. Thus there is now a possibility to produce scientific editions of the sources of halakhah with notes regarding variant textual readings. ... There is virtually no work of the early scholars, of blessed memory, that does not require such an approach.[182]

In a detailed discussion included in the third volume of *Seridei Esh*, R. Weinberg demonstrates the importance of such an understanding by giving specific examples by way of citations from *Halakhot Gedolot, Sefer ha-Terumah, Hiddushei ha-Ra'avad* on *Bava Kamma* and *Issur ve-Hetter* of Rema. R. Weinberg seeks to validate a number of proposed emendations in these works on the basis of linguistic evidence ("clear to anyone who has an intuitive linguistic sense")[183] and by corroboration in the form of parallel statements in a host of works of other *rishonim*. As his final example, R. Weinberg discusses a suggested emendation in the text of *Ra'avad* and describes his elation at finding corroboration of his thesis in a new edition of *Ra'avad* based upon a manuscript found in the British Museum:

> From comparison with the manuscript, the validity of my emendation became clear to me and I gave praise and thanks to the Almighty that I had been privileged to find the true teaching of our teacher, the *Ra'avad*, of blessed memory.[184]

---

the Cracow edition of that work. *Taz, Yoreh De'ah* 94, *Daf haAharon*, dissents sharply and is answered by *Shakh, Yoreh De'ah* 94, *Kuntres Aharon*.

181 *S. E.*, vol. 3, 403, citing R. Hayyim of Volozhin, introduction to Commentary of R. Elijah Gaon of Vilna to *Zera'im*.

182 *S. E.*, vol. 3, 403.

183 Ibid., 404.

184 Ibid., 408.

R. Weinberg was firmly convinced that this was but an isolated example and that further critical examination of texts would enhance rabbinic scholarship:

> This method of investigation of halakhah is not yet widespread among great rabbis. But it is an obligation to make [this method] well-known and to popularize it among the ranks of talmudic scholars in order to establish the investigation of Talmud and halakhah on a strong scientific foundation as was understood by the great teachers of previous generations, such as our great teacher, the Gra, of blessed memory.[185]

As accurately stated in the above citation by R. Weinberg himself, this type of meticulous critical textual study was not (and is not) common among scholars of the traditional mold. In this regard, R. Weinberg's own investigations are unique. Most significant is his desire that this type of scientific scholarship be conducted *al taharat ha-kodesh* (with ideological purity).[186] Only those who possess the requisite appreciation and understanding of traditional rabbinic scholarship are capable of transmitting that learning to others and it is they who are qualified to harness the methodology of modern scholarship in order to enhance talmudic scholarship.[187] In the 1930s he expressed the hope that this "double vocation" would be assumed by students of the *Rabbinerseminar* who would thereby render a singular contribution to the Jewish community by filling the one lacuna existing in traditional yeshivot.[188] Decades later, in Montreux, he continued to encourage rabbinic scholars to turn their attention to this area of scholarship and, at that time, urged nothing less than preparation of a critical edition of the Talmud itself in declaring, "In my opinion, there is an obligation to fill this lacuna by a new publication of the Talmud with all the variant readings and commentaries."[189]

---

185 Ibid., 408.
186 Nevertheless, R. Weinberg was receptive to the scholarly insights of individuals whose ideology he could not share. Theological differences did not mar his friendship with Professor Samuel Atlas who taught at Hebrew Union College. R. Weinberg's notes on Atlas's work are included in the latter's edition of *Ḥiddushei ha-Ra'avad al Bava Kamma* (New York: Feldheim, 1963), 362–385. In a letter published in Atlas, *Netivim be-Mishpat ha-Ivri* (New York: American Academy for Jewish Research, 1978), 154, R. Weinberg notes that, despite the criticism to which he had been subjected for so doing, he did not regret including a responsum to Atlas in S. E., vol. 2, no. 78.
187 A fine example of the methodology advocated by R. Weinberg is found in his own textual-halakhic analysis, S. E., vol. 1, 364–369. See, in particular, the concluding paragraph.
188 *Tradition* 24, no. 4 (Summer 1989), 22.
189 S. E., vol. 3, no. 74, 253.

5. Rabbis and Communities

R. Weinberg was preoccupied with the need to maintain effective communal structures in order to assure Jewish continuity. He was neither an ivory tower theoretician nor naive in his assessment of the power politics of communal life. Consequently, he was alert to the problems involved in attempts to bring idealistic visions to realization in the face of communal inertia. These concerns are reflected in several of his essays exploring changing aspects of lay and rabbinic leadership in the twentieth century, as well as in responsa addressed to rabbis who turned to him with practical problems stemming in greater or lesser degree from an absence of communal cooperation and initiative.

R. Weinberg appreciated the pivotal role of the rabbi in the internal workings of the community and consistently manifested concern for those engaged in the active rabbinate and empathy with individuals "on the firing line."[190] He looked back upon his own first position as rabbi of Pilwishki with appreciation for having been privileged to serve a community suffused with Torah scholarship and love of learning combined with a reverential and affectionate regard for its spiritual leaders. He was not unaware of the fact that many of his own disciples were not nearly so fortunate in their professional placement and that consequently their frustrations and difficulties were far greater. In later years, as a lecturer and subsequently as the rector of the *Rabbinerseminar*, R. Weinberg found himself in the position of advocate for, and mentor to, numerous students who aspired to a rabbinic career. The founder and first head of the *Rabbinerseminar*, Rabbi Azriel Hildesheimer, viewed the training of future rabbis as an essential factor in safeguarding embattled Orthodoxy in an age of assimilation and communal disintegration.[191] While this was not his sole aim in founding the *Rabbinerseminar*, it was undoubtedly his major aspiration. Ideological activism remained central to the ethos of the *Rabbinerseminar* and is reflected·as well in many of R. Weinberg's writings.

---

190 See, for example, S. E., vol. 2, 104, 171, 284, 334, and vol. 3, 237 and 256. Cf. R. Weinberg's heartfelt expression of concern for a young rabbi faced with a grave halakhic problem that might jeopardize his position. R. Weinberg writes, "My primary worry is on account of the rabbinic interlocutor. ... The above rabbi awaits my response with crushed spirit." *Shevet me-Yehudah (mi-Ktav Yad)*, 262.

191 See Meir Hildesheimer, "Ketavim be-Dvar Yesod Bet ha-Midrash le-Rabbanim be-Berlin," *Ha-Ma'ayan* 14, no. 2 (1974), 14–15. Cf. Auerbach's account of the seriousness with which the Seminary's faculty deliberated regarding recommendations of candidates for rabbinic office, in full awareness of their dual responsibilities to both candidate and congregation, and of the pivotal role played by R. Weinberg in those discussions. Auerbach, *Sefer ha-Zikaron*, 361.

R. Weinberg's analysis of the functions and authority of the rabbinate is an interesting example of the manner in which he formulated classical concepts in modern terminology, while giving the new terminology an interpretation that went beyond its conventional meaning and thus led to a new understanding of classical notions.[192] In conformity with the historic parameters of rabbinic office, R. Weinberg presents four broad areas of rabbinic activity: (a) scholarly pursuits, (b) legal-judicial functions, (c) hortatory, and (d) pastoral duties.

First and foremost, the rabbi is responsible for dissemination of Torah; his primary function is to "raise many disciples" (*Avot* 1:1). Contrary to common contemporary misconception, historically, the positions of rabbi and *rosh yeshiva* were not separate and distinct. In the major German and French centers of Jewry, communal rabbis functioned primarily as expositors of the Talmud. *Pnei Yehoshu'a* and *Hafla'ah* of Frankfurt am Main, R. Yonatan Eybeschutz of Metz and Hamburg, *Sha'agat Aryeh* of Metz, and *Noda bi-Yehudah* of Prague were all renowned as exemplary teachers of Talmud. Among Ashkenazi Jewry, the official designation of the chief rabbi of a community was "head of the judicial court and *rosh yeshiva—Abad ve-Ram.*" During the Middle Ages, cities acquired fame as centers of Jewish learning because of the students who flocked to study Talmud at the feet of the rabbi of the city. In Sephardi centers in the Balkans and Turkey, the rabbi was known by the title *Marbitz Torah,*—"disseminator of Torah."[193] The primary function of the rabbi, declares R. Weinberg, is to serve as teacher and fill the role model of *talmid ḥakham.*

The second function of the rabbi is to act as halakhic decisor and counselor in all matters of the daily life of the individual and the community. As a halakhic authority, the rabbi is the final arbiter on questions of *kashrut* and synagogue ritual, as well as the judge of domestic, financial, and commercial disputes.

The third rabbinic function is to serve as preacher, primarily on Sabbaths and festivals. It is significant that R. Weinberg does not minimize or marginalize this rabbinic function. Many rabbinic scholars view the public *derashah,* or discourse, as being of minor import and tend to denigrate the preacher. As a devotee of the teachings of Rabbi Israel Salanter and his disciples, who followed R. Salanter in his emphasis on the hortatory value of sermons, as well as of the modern German Orthodox ideologues who placed great significance on

---

192 See his essay, "Ha-Rabbanut be-Yisra'el, Tafkideha ve-Samkhuyoteha," S. E., vol. 4, 341–344.

193 See R. Weinberg, ibid., 342, who cites the study of Meir Benayahu, *Marbitz Torah* (Jerusalem: Mossad Harav Kook, 1953).

development of homiletical skills and urged rabbinical training in the oratorical arts,[194] R. Weinberg was attuned to the inspirational potential inherent in effective sermons as a vehicle for the dissemination of religious teachings.

Elsewhere, R. Weinberg writes of the *derashah* or sermon as an educational tool possessing unparalleled emotional and inspirational potential and laments the deterioration of this art form in the hands of those who had turned public addresses into occasions for vapid and arid sermonizing:

> The crown of the *derashah* has fallen because of the neglect of great scholars who left the arts of speech fallow to the minds of lesser individuals. It may return to be a subject for academic and artistic study if it will once more be fructified by creative thinkers. Then it will be seen that the *derashah* can serve as the *shofar* for the great leaders of the people and its wise men—a direct mode of influence of personality upon the heart.[195]

It was the use of the *derashah* in such a manner, R. Weinberg attests, that galvanized the followers of R. Israel Salanter during the early days of his public activity in Vilna. R. Salanter was unique in his ability to attract and engage the attention of heterogeneous audiences composed of scholars and of the untutored masses. It is related by his disciples that when a public address by R. Salanter in Vilna was announced, capacity audiences thronged the assembly hall and it was, at times, necessary to convey R. Salanter above the heads of the crowd to the speaker's podium. R. Salanter's masterful oratory became a model for emulation by his disciples. Personalities such as Rabbi Jacob Joseph (acclaimed as the chief *darshan* of Russia), Rabbi Isaac Blaser, and Rabbi Naphtali Amsterdam achieved renown as orators in their own right, but each received his early training in oratorical skills in the crucible of Rabbi Salanter's *bet midrash*.[196]

R. Weinberg does not, however, limit his interest to the narrow confines of stylized Western sermonics. He is open, rather, to the broad sweep of aggadic material and the vast resources in the literature of Bible, Jewish thought, philosophy, mysticism, and poetry available to a learned rabbi. He remarks that the Sages speak of "*dor dor ve-dorshav ve-ḥakhamav*"—"each generation and its

194 S. E., vol. 1, introduction, 2.
195 S. E., vol. 4; pp. 288–289. See also R. Weinberg's essay on the sermon, "Ba-Bayit u-ba-Ḥutz," *Ha-Modiʿa* 4, no. 26 (March 22, 1913), 414, cited in the publisher's introduction to the first edition of *Li-Perakim* (Bilgori, 1936), 1–4.
196 S. E., vol. 4, 288–89.

interpreters (preachers)[197] and its scholars" (*Sanhedrin* 38a). Each generation, he writes, has its own interpreters and different ages have different styles of teaching and preaching. The wise men of each era must find the idiom and the style appropriate to their milieu. But while the superficial style of the *derashah*, or sermon, is flexible and changeable, the inner content and purpose must be in conformity with Jewish teachings and values. Herein, writes R. Weinberg, lies the particular charge to the rabbi. He must fashion a sermon in modern idiom while preserving its eternal content, utilizing the podium for transmission of Jewish ideas and not of alien values. "Since the *derashah* has a great and unmediated effect upon the broad masses," he concludes, "it requires special training and development. It is appropriate for rabbis to devote their best energies to its improvement and perfection in content and form."[198]

Finally, rabbis perform significant pastoral functions. It is in his comments upon this aspect of rabbinic service that R. Weinberg injects his own genre of interpretive *ḥiddush*. He describes the rabbi's role as protector of the poor, the aged, the sick, and the bereaved, emphasizing the rabbi's responsibility for both the spiritual and material welfare of his charges. East European Jews, R. Weinberg writes, tend to view these functions, described by German Jews as *Seelensorge* (pastoral duties), somewhat disdainfully as an assumed affectation imitative of the pastoral role of non-Jewish clergymen. However, to R. Weinberg, this view is flawed. The practice of lovingkindness or *gemilat ḥasadim*, one of the three pillars which support the world (*Avot* 1:2), includes activities such as visiting the sick, comforting the bereaved, and the like. It devolves upon the rabbi to assure their proper fulfillment as religious acts.

Indeed, argues R. Weinberg, the unique character of Judaism is its embodiment of religious laws governing not only ritual or theological matters but

---

197 This is a play upon the Hebrew word *dorshav*, having a dual meaning connoting both "its interpreters" and "its preachers."

198 S. E., vol. 4, 342. Cf. ibid., 288–89. R. Weinberg discusses, ibid., 342–43 n., the emphasis placed by the Sages on aggadic interpretation. He cites *Avot de-Rabbi Natan*, chap. 29: "He who has in his hand *midrash* but not *halakhot* has not tasted the taste of wisdom; he who has in his hand *halakhah* but not *midrash* has not tasted fear of sin. He used to say: He who has in his hand *midrash* but has not in his hand *halakhot* is a mighty man but is not armed; he who has in his hand *halakhot* but has not in his hand *midrash* is weak but is armed; he who has both in his hand is mighty and is armed." R. Weinberg adds that the recorded *midrashim* constitute the public discourses on the weekly Torah portion delivered by the Sages of the Talmud. He cites Zunz's research on the *derashah* and Philo's assertion that it was customary even during the period of the Temple for discourses to be delivered in conjunction with the public reading of the Bible and prophets.

extending to every detail of daily life. In Judaism, the ideal of "love thy neighbor" becomes concretized in a series of specific acts. Rabbinic Judaism has been subjected to criticism for promoting dry legalism rather than lofty philosophic sentiments. All too often, comments R. Weinberg, such sentiments remain empty phrases, whereas what appear to be formalistic religious obligations transform "love thy neighbor" and similar injunctions into a living reality. Seemingly prosaic laws create a matrix of observance that invests life with a dimension of spirituality and holiness. A state of being is created, writes R. Weinberg, such that "the pure religiosity of modern spiritual seekers with all their phrases regarding filling the hollowness of the soul will never achieve."[199] It is this that the Sages understood to be the great animating principle of the Torah.[200] Unlike Christianity, Judaism emphasizes "we will do and we will hear" (Exodus 24:7), that is, that concrete acts ("we will do") lead to understanding ("we will hear") and ultimately to fashioning an environment in which spirituality becomes a reality. It is in the fulfillment of his pastoral duties that the rabbi preserves the all-important mundane aspect of religious communal life. In observance of mitzvot reflecting concern for one's fellow man, Jews express the supreme sanctification of the Divine Name. If the rabbi is to be the teacher of all facets of Torah and the role model representing a religious personality, he must serve as the guardian of observance of the Torah's laws governing lovingkindness, because those laws embody the Jew's unique method of concretizing Torah teaching.[201]

R. Weinberg recognized that the ability of a rabbi to serve as a teacher and spiritual mentor is commensurate with his success in relating to the social and emotional needs of his congregants. The ability to arouse and to express love and affection is necessary in order that a personal relationship flourish. "Whoever wishes to influence others," writes R. Weinberg, "must be extravagant with his energy, his time, his honor, and his money. ... He must be extravagant with love for people."[202] Such a relationship must be established with all members of the community. The rabbi dare not wait for those who are distant

---

199 Ibid., 343.

200 *Shabbat* 31a.

201 S. E., vol. 4, 344.

202 *Li-Perakim*, 113. R. Weinberg appreciated the manner in which an individual such as R. Meir Schapiro, "the most popular rabbi of our times," stirred the emotions of the masses and won and sustained their loyalty. Ibid., pp. 261–262. R. Weinberg writes that he had been so overcome with grief over the death of R. Meir Schapiro that he was unable to complete delivery of his eulogy.

from Judaism to find their way back. Rather, he must seek them out and initiate the process: "It is our obligation to pursue each and every one who is distancing himself from our people. ... In most cases, the thirst for life and knowledge have distanced him from us. It depends upon us to return him to the good. ... 'From the mountain to the people' [Exodus 19: 14]—that is the obligation of every rabbi and leader."[203]

Constant conflict in community affairs between older elements of the populace and the younger generation give rise to a tension to which R. Weinberg was keenly attuned. In this matter as well, R. Weinberg was sensitive to the legitimate concerns and interests of both sides. There are recurring references to this tension in his homiletical writings and it is evident that this was an issue in which he had more than a merely abstract interest. In those conflicts, he manifested a concern and sympathy for the strivings of the younger generation. As he phrased it on one occasion: "We are all, my young friends, subject to a spiritual travail unknown to our [i.e., the older] generation, one which even its imagination could not depict. And, although we all suffer, the greatest share is borne by our youth!"[204]

In particular, he understood the need to allow for originality and creativity on the part of the new generation. It was not enough for the young to continue to walk along already trodden paths. There must be new vistas for them to discover on their own. In assessing R. Samson Raphael Hirsch's innovative approach to the interpretation of ritual in Judaism, R. Weinberg wrote that youth "wish to receive this Torah not merely as something that they acquire by inheritance from their fathers, but from a deep inner experience and from independent choice. They yearn to achieve a receiving of the Torah and acquisition of faith through their own merit and through God's kindness to them."[205]

Similarly, in his writings on Zionism, he portrayed the turmoil experienced, in particular, by youthful rabbis upon whom the Zionist enterprise had a magnetic effect: "Their young heart was attracted to the place where all is inspired and vital, hopeful and striving, loving and beloved." The youth, more so than other segments of the population, chafed at the restraints placed on their nationalistic fervor by the elder members of the rabbinate.[206]

His empathy with the younger generation also led R. Weinberg to form personal relationships with younger scholars. In particular, during the last years

---

203 Ibid., 113.
204 Ibid., 116, and *Tradition* 24, no. 4 (Summer 1989), 18.
205 "Mishnato shel R. S. R. Hirsch Zatzal," *De'ot* 9, no. 46, reprinted in *S. E.*, vol. 4, 361.
206 *Li-Perakim*, 333 reprinted in *S. E.*, vol. 4, 357.

of his life spent in Montreux, he maintained close contact with a number of young scholars and it was they who were among his keenest mourners and who felt most sharply the pain of his passing.[207]

In the wake of World War I, Lithuanian Jewry achieved a measure of communal autonomy. Under the newly independent regime, communal structures were reshaped and a redistribution of power occurred within the community. The youth, invigorated and heady at the prospects of emancipation and independence, eagerly assumed control of communal institutions and sought to displace their elders from positions of leadership in synagogal, educational, and administrative bodies. The elders, in turn, looked with disfavor upon the "young Turks" as radical upstarts. When invited to address the community of Pilwishki, the site of his own first rabbinic position and a city split asunder by internecine tensions, R. Weinberg seized the occasion to mediate between the opposing factions and to express his own views on communal cooperation.[208]

In underscoring the need for a community to adhere to the biblical model "with our young and with our old shall we go,"[209] R. Weinberg penetrates beyond the superficial, facile explanations emphasizing the linkage of conservatism with the aged and enthusiasm with youth to an understanding of the deeper motivations and aspirations that underlie the conflicting agendas usually pressed by these two groups standing at opposite poles of the human life cycle.

Any power struggle between young and old is likely to reflect a desire on the part of the old to hold on to the reins of authority, to protect the status quo and not to relinquish the perquisites of a dominant oligarchy, coupled with the stolidity and inertia that are emblematic of individuals whose reactions and mental processes have become rigidified over the course of decades. But R. Weinberg recognized that, frequently, there are also deeper forces at play. Years of experience, toil, and disappointment upon disappointment take their toll as well. Even if elders maintain an optimistic stance and continue to dream idealistic dreams, when the opportunity for realization of cherished hopes presents itself, older people often find that "the passive element triumphs and a spirit of lethargy overpowers them. Weakened, we lose spiritual forces that serve as a stimulus to turn faith and hope into active forces full of lively energy, creators of fact, builders of worlds."[210] When confronted by such despondency

---

207 Cohen, "Devarim le-Zikhro," 17–18.
208 *Li-Perakim*, 273 n.
209 Exodus 10:9.
210 *Li-Perakim*, 277.

and inaction, young people feel choked and crushed. Creative stirrings are deadened; constructive energies are stymied; and imaginative plans and programs are curtailed. The old cling to the tired ways of the past, while the youth feel they are being cheated of a brighter future.

R. Weinberg was even more troubled because, as power oscillates back and forth between young and old, there emerges a more profound source of conflict. The old tend to be conservative in their orientation; they are fixated upon tradition and homeland, hearth and family. At times, this is simply a manifestation of the weakness of age: people for whom the future holds no allure find solace and comfort in memories of the past. There are, however, elders who do not lack intellectual and spiritual vigor and whose breadth of spirit does not preclude their sharing the reins of leadership with youth. Nevertheless, they are conservative in orientation but theirs is a conservatism "that in the purity of its form is not born of weakness, but is symptomatic of cultivation and maturity of spirit."[211] Their judgment is usually more disciplined and sound. The young are often blinded by the dazzle of the new; their "spirit is caught by the external glitter and they do not have the ability to penetrate to the essence of a novel phenomenon."[212] The perspectives of the young are colored by personal ambition and aspiration. The old, endowed with experience upon which they can reflect as well as with a keener sense of the fleeting nature of human life, are better able to distance themselves from immediate concerns and hence to judge affairs and their consequences in a more objective, dispassionate and considered manner.

If a community is to grow and flourish, harmony between young and old is essential. The young must be afforded an opportunity for assertive creativity and must be permitted the full advantages of freedom and autonomy. The old must be respected and heeded because of their balanced wisdom and guardianship of the nation's sancta. For redemption to occur, it is necessary to seek out the elders, as indicated in Scripture, "Go and gather the elders of Israel."[213] But only with the coalescence of all forces of the nation will regeneration occur, as again indicated in Scripture, "with the insolence of the clamorous youth, and with the stubbornness of the weeping elders."[214]

---

211 Ibid., 281.

212 Ibid., 281.

213 Exodus 3:17.

214 *Li-Perakim*, 285. The reference to weeping and clamor is based on Ezra 3:12, "But many of the priests and Levites and heads of families, who were old men who had seen the first house with their eyes, when the foundation of this house was laid, they wept with a loud

The heightened antagonism between various ideological factions was also viewed by R. Weinberg as a destructive force that would ultimately result in disintegration of the greater community. For ideological as well as pragmatic reasons, R. Weinberg counseled assiduous pursuit of harmonious relations.[215] He urged appeasement and accommodation for the sake of peace, at times upon one faction, at times upon another. In particular, R. Weinberg recognized that the groups he referred to as *yere'im* ("God-fearing") or *haredim* ("strictly religious") would not compromise their position on certain basic issues. Stubborn resistance to their concerns would, in all likelihood, have deleterious effects on the community at large.[216] However, he cautioned, it is the rabbi who must decide when to accede to the demands of one group or another; he must not allow the laity to dictate policy.[217] At the same time, he exhorted rabbis not to jeopardize tenuous communal harmony if it was at all possible to accommodate diverse factions. For example, although he did not consider granting women the right to vote on synagogue matters to be halakhically proscribed, he maintained that their participation in administration of communal affairs was "contrary to the custom of Israel and the teachings of Israel in communal life" and "should be prevented as much as possible." He nevertheless urged compromise in the face of an insistent faction since the issue of women voting did not, in his opinion, warrant disruption of communal peace and unity.[218]

---

voice; and many shouted aloud for joy." In developing his theme, R. Weinberg uses this text as an instance of a historic occasion on which old and young responded differently to the challenge of rebuilding the Temple at the time of Ezra and Nehemiah. Even among the older sector of the community, there were two groups, those who wept and whose nostalgia for the past overpowered them and those who shouted aloud for joy and were able to join forces with the youth in inaugurating a new era.

215 In addressing himself to strife between rabbinic organizations as well, R. Weinberg counseled adoption of a conciliatory approach and encouraged cooperative ventures. He took exception to the tone of sharp censure in articles critical of a rabbinic organization that had appeared in *Ha-Pardes* and urged the editor of that journal to exert his influence with "mild words" and to be aware that "error is not yet sacrilege or betrayal." See letter published in *HaPardes* 40, no. 10 (July 1966), 37.

216 See, for example, S. E., vol. 2, no. 14, 30, where he concludes, "The result of this quarrel might be the destruction of the community."

217 Cf. *Li-Perakim*, 193–194.

218 S. E., vol. 2, no. 52, 104. Elsewhere, regarding the *mehitzah*, or barrier separating the women's section in a synagogue, he counsels, "If it is possible to make an improvement, it is certainly a mitzvah to make an improvement, but one should not generate a serious quarrel and destroy an association of the Godfearing for a *hiddur mitzvah* [an enhancement of a mitzvah]." Ibid., no. 11, 21.

In discussing questions relating to cremation, R. Weinberg ruled that even in areas in which burial of the ashes in the cemetery is permitted by the local community, the rabbis and *ḥevra kaddisha* are forbidden to participate in the burial. Similarly, the *ḥevra kaddisha* may not assist in the purification, or *taharah*, of an individual who directs that his remains be cremated. The reasoning is obvious. In face of contravention of law and prescribed religious practice, under no circumstances may the rabbi or *ḥevra kaddisha* lend their sanction to an act that might be construed as exculpatory. Thus R. Weinberg concludes with an exhortation to the rabbi and heads of the *ḥevra kaddisha*: "I advise them to surmount all obstacles and preserve the holy character of the *ḥevra kaddisha* of the great community of Berlin which has already been privileged to sanctify the Name of God in public and to make our holy religion beloved among all sectors of the great city. ..."[219]

On the other hand, when consulted regarding the custom of some mourners not to rend their clothes but instead symbolically to tear a necktie, he agreed with the interlocutor that one should permit the tie to be torn in order that the requirement of rending garments not be forgotten. The people concerned should be informed that tearing a tie does not fulfill the requirement of the law and be advised to tear old clothes if they wish: "But, in general, one must be careful not to create a quarrel on account of these matters, and [the Sages] long ago declared that one is obligated to conduct oneself according to the custom of the locale on account of quarrels" (*Pesaḥim* 50b).[220]

---

219 Ibid., no. 124, 284. As the practice of cremation became increasingly common among non-Jews during the latter part of the nineteenth and early twentieth centuries, the practice gained a measure of popularity among liberal Jews as well. Orthodox authorities were unanimous in prohibiting cremation, but a major controversy arose over the permissibility of interring cremated ashes on the cemetery grounds. R. Weinberg, ibid., 283, cites the conflicting views of Rabbi Meier Lerner and Rabbi Chanoch Ehrentreu. Rabbi Lerner and the vast majority of rabbinic authorities of Hungary, Poland, and Lithuania forbade interment of the ashes. A collection of the condemnatory responsa was published by Rabbi Lerner in his *Ḥayyei Olam* (Berlin, 1905). On the other hand, R. Chanoch Ehrentreu and R. David Zevi Hoffmann did permit interment of the ashes in a separate section of the cemetery, but forbade any participation of the *ḥevra kaddisha*. In the preceding responsum, *S. E.*, vol. 2, 278, R. Weinberg is forceful in expressing his chagrin over any concession with regard to interment of the ashes, "And I may attest in all the lands of the East not a single rabbi would ever allow this." For a bibliography of halakhic sources regarding this controversy, see Michael Higger, *Halakhot ve-Aggadot* (New York, 1932), 181–183. Instructive statistics regarding cremation practices may be found in Falk Wiesemann, "Jewish Burials in Germany: Between Tradition, the Enlightenment and the Authorities," *Leo Baeck Institute Year Book* 37 (1992), 29.

220 *S. E.*, vol. 2, no. 121, 278.

When no actual halakhic violation was involved, R. Weinberg was always careful to indicate that any response must be predicated upon the conditions prevailing in a particular area. For example, when asked if it is proper to call an uncircumcised son and his father to the reading of the Torah on the occasion of the son's *bar mitzvah* in a situation in which the father was also guilty of public desecration of the Sabbath, R. Weinberg responded that, since no absolute halakhic prohibition was involved, the matter must rest upon the judgment of the local rabbi. The rabbi must carefully consider the ramifications of the policy to be adopted. Under certain circumstances, a stringent and censorious posture might influence such individuals to mend their ways; on the other hand, there are situations in which stringency might result in the total alienation from Judaism of the individuals concerned. The rabbi, who is familiar with the details, must strive to exercise judgment in accordance with his knowledge of the particular circumstances prevalent in his community and make a decision on the basis of which policy will have the most salutary effect on the future lives of all concerned.[221]

Nevertheless, with regard to questions arising in connection with intermarriage and Reform innovation, R. Weinberg refused to consider any concession whatsoever. For example, he ruled that it was forbidden to inter a non-Jewish spouse in a Jewish cemetery even in instances in which there was danger that, as a result, the husband might abandon Judaism entirely.[222] He also ruled that one may not call a man who is intermarried to the reading of the Law or count him in a quorum for purposes of public prayer.[223]

Similarly, with regard to matters in which there was the slightest possibility that leniency or compromise might be misinterpreted as a concession to Reform or liberal Judaism, R. Weinberg's rulings were unfailingly stringent. Thus, for example, in response to a query as to whether a non-Orthodox rabbi might lecture in an Orthodox synagogue even if it was agreed that he would refrain from discussing matters of a religious nature, R. Weinberg's answer was a firm negative. He declared that, in general, lectures regarding secular matters were out of place in a synagogue.[224] Permission for a rabbi to deliver a discourse on a general theme in the synagogue is based upon the presumption that his comments will be religiously edifying. Such a presumption is not warranted, asserts R. Weinberg, in the case of a non-Orthodox clergyman. More

---

221 Ibid., no. 10, 21.
222 Ibid., no. 123, 281.
223 Ibid., no. 6, 12. Cf. S. E., vol. 4, 383.
224 See *Oraḥ Ḥayyim* 15.

significantly, R. Weinberg refused to countenance relaxation of communal standards since there existed a firmly established policy throughout Germany not to permit Reform speakers to address Orthodox congregations.[225]

In discussing the use of an organ at religious ceremonies even outside of the synagogue, R. Weinberg asserts that it is prohibited to adopt any practice that emulates the practices of heretics. Earlier, R. David Zevi Hoffmann, *Melammed le-Ho'il, Orah Hayyim*, no. 16, had prohibited the use of the organ in conjunction with prayer services because the organ had become identified as a symbol of Reform innovation. Any religious ceremony involving the use of the organ, asserts R. Weinberg, might be misinterpreted by the masses as a capitulation to Reform innovation. Consequently, he rules unequivocally that Orthodox leaders may not modify existing traditions and that any innovation whatsoever involving an organ "may not be permitted under any circumstances." He concludes that a policy of strictness in such matters is the most effective strategy in assuring the survival of Orthodoxy: "Experience has demonstrated that whoever was self-sacrificing in preserving the customs of the ancient ones was privileged to sanctify the Name of Heaven in public and caused the strengthening of religion and of Judaism in general."[226]

A similar posture is manifested in a responsum addressed to Rabbi Leo Jung in 1954 regarding recitation of English hymns in the course of synagogue services. R. Weinberg observes that there is certainly no halakhic prohibition against recitation of hymns in the vernacular. However, he counsels strongly against introduction of the practice. Not only will the stringently Orthodox, who are opposed to any manner of synagogue innovation, construe such action as a concession to Reform, but the change would be inherently unwise for both religious and pedagogic reasons: "Indeed, due to our many transgressions, there remains no place for unadulterated Judaism other than in the synagogue. Therefore we must be meticulous that there the holy tongue reign supreme."[227] Use of Hebrew, he argues, will enhance the services and serve as an impetus to encourage people to study the holy tongue. However, most significantly, in matters such as these, R. Weinberg warns, a rabbi must be exceedingly cautious lest his synagogue serve as a negative example for others and provide them with a model that may lead to further innovation of a prohibited nature. The

---

225 S. E., vol. 2, no. 13, 28.
226 Ibid., no. 80, 204.
227 Ibid., no. 9, 17.

principle of scrupulous adherence to tradition must be followed in all matters of synagogue ritual.[228]

Reverence for communal tradition and appreciation of the sanctified nature of liturgical customs permeates R. Weinberg's responsa. Instructive are his comments on the recitation of *kiddush* in the synagogue on Friday night. He advises a rabbi in whose congregation the custom had lapsed to reinstate the practice and not stand on his dignity:

> For the honor of God and the honor of the Sages who instituted this custom is greater. ... Moreover, there is therein an aspect of communal education and public sanctification of the Sabbath and it adds grace and the beauty of holiness to the ushering in of this holy day. Perhaps, then, some will be aroused to repent and to recite *kiddush* in their homes as well. In any event, it is not correct to make our community separate and distinct from other Jewish communities that are accustomed to reciting *kiddush* in the synagogue and which also sell the privilege of donating wine for *kiddush*. This mitzvah is very beloved to those who fear God and cherish mitzvot and Heaven forfend that it be abolished.[229]

As will be shown, sentiments such as these shaped R. Weinberg's approach in many facets of halakhic decision-making.

6. Caution and Conservatism in Halakhic Decision-Making

R. Weinberg was considered to be one of the preeminent European halakhic decisors and questions were addressed to him from far and wide. His responsa encompass all areas of Jewish law. In some cases, such as issues involving electrical stunning prior to *shehitah*[230] and exhumation of the dead,[231] his comprehensive

---

228 Ibid., 17.

229 Ibid., no. 157, 377. R. Weinberg advises the reintroduction of *kiddush* in the synagogue despite the fact that its recitation in the synagogue was the subject of considerable dispute among early authorities. *Rosh, Pesaḥim* 10:5, opposes the practice and *Shulḥan Arukh, Oraḥ Ḥayyim* 269:1, rules that it is preferable not to recite the *kiddush*. Although R. Weinberg cites these negative sources and nevertheless defends that practice on halakhic grounds, he insists on the reintroduction primarily because the practice has become a hallowed tradition and "it is not correct" to render one congregation "separate and distinct from other Jewish communities."

230 See below, note 237.

231 *S. E.*, vol. 2, no. 125, 284–322. Comments of R. Moshe Mordecai Epstein, R. Chanoch Henoch Eiges, R. Yecheskel Lipschitz of Kalish, and R. Abraham I. Karelitz (*Ḥazon Ish*) are appended to the responsum, ibid., 322–327.

studies of the question constitute a *tour de force*. But despite his creativity and innovativeness in talmudic dialectic. R. Weinberg was cautious and conservative in matters of halakhic decision-making (*pesak*). He consistently followed the rulings of the recognized latter-day scholars and often deferred even to leading scholars among his own contemporaries. The fear and trepidation with which a decisor approaches a complex halakhic decision is an emotion which is readily discernible in R. Weinberg's writings. Even in the absence of recorded differing opinions, he often declined to act on his own initiative. Thus, responsum after responsum concludes with the comment that his ruling should be relied upon only if his colleagues concur. In explaining his trepidation, R. Weinberg wrote that if *Ḥatam Sofer* stated that he was prepared to render a permissive ruling with regard to a grave matter only with the consensus of other leading scholars, then "all the more so," must such be the policy "of an insignificant person such as myself."[232] Accordingly, even with regard to matters in which R. Weinberg had invested an inordinate amount of time and energy in investigating every aspect of the question under discussion, he refused to issue a ruling on any major issue regarding which there was no precedent without the benefit of concurring opinions of other authorities. Describing his tenure as rector of the *Rabbinerseminar* during which time the burden of queries addressed to him was immense, he notes, "I strove with all my strength and with painstaking investigation to issue clear rulings and, when faced with serious questions, I sought the corroboration of the great scholars of the generation."[233] For example, in responding to a query involving the complex halakhic question of performance of the *ḥalitzah* ceremony by an amputee, R. Weinberg writes, "Since this is a novel matter that has not been explicated by latter-day scholars, and [since] the matter is a very grave one, I do not wish to issue a ruling to be implemented in practice until the great rabbis of the generation agree with me."[234]

The question of whether or not a couple united in matrimony solely on the basis of a civil ceremony require a religious divorce (*get*) to dissolve the relationship was the subject of considerable controversy among rabbinic authorities during the early part of the century. R. Weinberg wrote extensively on the matter and maintained, as did Rabbi Hayyim Ozer Grodzinski of Vilna, the preeminent halakhist of the era, that it is permissible for the couple to remarry without execution of a religious divorce. Rabbi Rosen, the Rogatchover *gaon*, disagreed sharply. Although he categorically rejected the line of reasoning

---

232 *S. E.*, vol. 3, no. 120, 333.
233 *S. E.*, vol. 1, introduction, 3.
234 *S. E.* vol. 3, no. 49, 168. Cf. ibid., no. 42, 151.

propounded by the Rogatchover, and despite the already published concurring opinions of other renowned halakhic authorities, he declined to issue a ruling in accordance with his own opinion. Many years later, after Word War II (and after the death of the Rogatchover), R. Weinberg did agree to issue a permissive ruling under similar circumstances but only in conjunction with a court of three authorities or upon the agreement of Chief Rabbi Herzog and his *bet din*. Moreover, he further insisted that in each instance in which such a problem presented itself, a new ruling was to be required.[235]

The most striking example of the great deference R. Weinberg paid to the opinion of contemporary Torah scholars is found in his investigation of a complex question relating to *shehitah*. On April 21, 1933, the Nazi government decreed that animals must be anesthetized prior to slaughter. The decree effectively abolished *shehitah* throughout the German Reich since halakhah prohibits consumption of animals maimed prior to slaughter. Subsequently, there was much pressure on halakhic authorities to seek new procedures that might satisfy the requirements of German law. Rabbinic decisors investigated the halakhic permissibility of electronarcosis, that is, stunning of the animal by electric shock, before *shehitah*. The salient questions were whether such stunning inflicted organic injuries that rendered the animal a *terefah* or whether it caused internal bleeding that would preclude later draining of blood through soaking and salting in the prescribed manner. At the request of his colleagues in Germany and, subsequently, of Rabbi Hayyim Ozer Grodzinski of Vilna as well as Rabbi Meir Schapiro of Lublin, R. Weinberg prepared a detailed monograph devoted to an analysis of the halakhic issues posed by the contemplated procedure.[236]

The project was dual in nature, involving both investigation of the scientific facts and halakhic analysis—a project for which R. Weinberg's talents were eminently suited. R. Weinberg's comprehensive study of this issue is remarkable both for its masterful, incisive treatment of the halakhic sources and for its extensive and meticulous investigation of the scientific data.

---

235 See ibid., no. 22, 47 and ibid., no. 51, 198. He considered the reasoning of the Rogatchover, in this instance, to be an example of the ingenious analytic methodology of the Rogatchover that was often idiosyncratic and not compelling in halakhic *pesak*. See ibid., 46. More significantly, cf. his remarks in S. E., vol. II, no. 31, 67, in which he criticizes the Rogatchover for not following precedents in *pesak*. Cf. also R. Ovadiah Yosef, *She'elot u-Teshuvot Yehaveh Da'at*, vol. 2, no. 26, 103, n. For another instance in which R. Weinberg disagreed with, but deferred to, the Rogatchover, see S. E., vol. 3, no. 144, 157.

236 S. E., vol. 1, 6.

The East European Torah authorities ultimately determined not only to prohibit any change whatsoever in the practice of *sheḥitah* but also to ask R. Weinberg not to publish his study lest publication in some manner betray to the government authorities that there was even a remote possibility of a degree of concession that would allow for even minor variation of the *sheḥitah* process.

Despite the extensive amount of time and effort invested in his research and writing, R. Weinberg acceded to the request of the Torah scholars not to publish this work. Only decades later, with the publication of his first volume of responsa *Seridei Esh* in 1961, did R. Weinberg publish this material. By that time, Germany had long been defeated and controversy surrounding the nature of *sheḥitah* had abated. Correctly or incorrectly, R. Weinberg believed that *sheḥitah* was no longer under attack as being inhumane. The publication of R. Weinberg's views and his correspondence with other scholars regarding this subject serves to clarify many points of halakhah, as well as to illuminate a number of intricate talmudic *sugyot*. The material is also of significant historical and sociological interest.[237] The fact that R. Weinberg withheld publication of such a major work for so long a period of time is of considerable moment and underscores the extent to which he felt bound by the views of the preeminent Torah scholars of his generation.[238]

---

237 This enormously complex subject is dealt with in detail in S. E., vol. 1, 4–172 and ibid., appendix, 370–92. An English version of the explanatory preface written by R. Weinberg upon publication of the responsum in S. E. may be found in Robert Kirschner, *Rabbinic Responsa of the Holocaust Era* (New York: Shocken, 1985), 38–50. See also the two-volume study published by the Gur Aryeh Institute for Advanced Jewish Scholarship, *Edut Ne'emanah: She'elot u-Teshuvot al Ma'avak ha-Sheḥitah bi-Eropah*, vol. 1 (Jerusalem: Gur Aryeh, 1974) and Michael L. Munk and Eli Munk (religious research) and I. M. Levinger (medical aspects), eds. *Shechita: Religious and Historical Research on the Jewish Method of Slaughter*, vol. 2 (Jerusalem: Gur Aryeh, 1976), with extensive bibliography. Regarding the publication of R. Weinberg's study of this question, see also Grinberg, *Mi-Gedolei ha-Dor*, unnumbered pages, section "Keniyah le-Gedolei ha-Torah." In the body of his responsum, R. Weinberg presents an argument permitting stunning. However, in his prefatory remarks in S. E., he states that despite the many experiments conducted, he was unable to determine conclusively on the basis of the scientific data "that the electric current did not cause lethal injury or damage sufficient to render the slaughtered animal's internal organs *terefah*." He further declares that, even if permissible as a matter of halakhah, no changes should be instituted in the manner in which *sheḥitah* is performed and enumerates a number of considerations upon which that policy is predicated. See S. E., vol. 1, 7.

238 Another remarkable instance of R. Weinberg's deference to East European authorities was his acquiescence in the decision to abandon a 1933 plan to transfer the *Rabbinerseminar* to Palestine. See Moshe Auerbach, "Zikhronot (3)," ed. Nathan Rafael Auerbach, *Ha-Ma'ayan* 22, no. 1 (Tishri 1981): 5 n. 105, and 13–14 n. 116, as well as the extensive discussion in

A disciple of R. Weinberg has noted that his teacher's conservatism in *pesak* did not parallel his creativity in talmudic learning and scholarship and has speculated with regard to whether or not this conservatism stemmed from a deeply rooted psychological malaise. He questions, "Was it justified caution or over-anxious hesitancy? Was there a *Derekh* in that, or was it again a fear that had its root in some aspect of his personality?"[239] Whatever the tragedies and torments of R. Weinberg's life may have been, and setting aside speculations regarding the unconscious, his approach to *pesak* is readily understandable as a logical consequence of a number of conscious considerations that are explicitly and repeatedly articulated by R. Weinberg. These considerations are: (1) reverence for Torah scholars, (2) meticulous devotion to tradition in all its manifestations, (3) individual versus national needs, and (4) his own expressed view of the vastly different roles of analytic research and the freedom of inquiry permitted in such endeavors as opposed to halakhic decision-making with its rigid canons and parameters.

1. Reverence for East European Torah Authorities

R. Weinberg's years of study in Mir and Slabodka and his concentration upon intensive Talmud study and *mussar* ideology during that period constituted his most profoundly influential life experience. He remained convinced that total immersion in Talmud study emblematic of the yeshivot of Eastern Europe was the ideal environment for development of Torah knowledge.

Christhard Hoffmann and Daniel R. Schwartz, "Early but Opposed—Supported but Late: Two Berlin Seminaries which Attempted to Move Abroad," *Leo Baeck Institute Year Book* 36 (1991), 267–304. See also Daniel Schwartz, "Beyn Berlin, Lita, ve-ha-Mizraḥ ha-Raḥok: Al Kamah She'elot u-Teshuvot ve-Tikun be-Hashmattah," *Kiryat Sefer* 64, no. 3 (1992), 1077–87; and the pointed remarks in R. Weinberg's letter, ibid., 1086–87.

Apparently, at approximately the same time, R. Weinberg entered into some negotiations with the United Synagogue in London, England regarding the possibility of his accepting a position as a *Dayan* on the London *Bet Din*. See M. E. Abramsky, "Maran Rav. Y. Abramsky and the London Beis Din," *Yated Neeman* (August 25, 1995), 14; and cf. *S. E.*, vol. 1, 380, the letter of R. Hayyim Ozer Grodzinski, dated 6 Kislev 5695 (November 13, 1934). Decades later, the possibility of R. Weinberg accepting a post in London arose once again. Accompanying comments by I. Smolar, *Ha-Do'ar*, 12 Adar 5726 (March 4, 1966), 285, there is a reproduction of a postcard written in R. Weinberg's hand, dated 1 Adar 5712 (February 27, 1952). In a note appended to this postcard, R. Weinberg reports that he had been chosen as Head of the London *Bet Din*, but that "the matter yet remains in doubt because of age and lack of strength."

239 Berkovits, "Rabbi Yechiel Yakob Weinberg," 13.

The philosophy of the *mussar* movement was an equally strong molding force in the development of his thinking. R. Weinberg internalized *mussar* teachings to such an extent that he himself attested that, at times, he had difficulty unravelling which elements of the *mussar* concepts that he developed in his essays were the received teachings of his mentors and which were the product of his own further elaboration and development of their seminal ideas. In a note appended to his presentation of several discourses of the *Alter* of Slabodka, Rabbi Nathan Zevi Finkel, R. Weinberg writes that since decades had passed since he had heard those talks as a young man: "It is obvious that there are additions and omissions. For the omissions, I have regrets; for the additions, I have no regrets. … The fundamentals are etched deeply in my memory and they fructified my own thinking; mine are his."[240] Elsewhere, he adds, "I was yet young at the time of the talks. Only when I matured did I perceive to what extent his ideas were exalted and how profound were his thoughts. At the time we did not appreciate the depth of what he said in the course of his talk. These words were not merely a *mussar* discourse but profound, eye-opening insights."[241]

In consonance with *mussar* teaching, R. Weinberg had the deepest reverence for rabbinic personalities whose piety was commensurate with their learning. It was second nature for him to defer with willing subordination to authorities whom he regarded as repositories of virtue, guardians of tradition and the embodiment of Torah wisdom. It was this mindset that shaped his thinking and formed the basis on which he fashioned his own approach to halakhic decision-making.

In a peripheral comment included in one of his responsa, R. Weinberg includes an evaluation of the personality of Rabbi Abraham Isaiah Karelitz, known as *Ḥazon Ish*. At first reading, one might dismiss this passage as a hagiographic panegyric reminiscent of the writing currently in vogue in a certain genre of popular histories of *gedolim* (great scholars). It would be an error to read these comments in that manner. Piety and devotion to meticulous and honest scholarship were R. Weinberg's highest ideals. Of *Ḥazon Ish*, he writes:

> Regarding what you asked concerning the greatness of the Sage, the preeminent pious scholar, author of *Ḥazon Ish*, of blessed memory—

---

240 *S. E.*, vol. 4, 312 n. He notes that Rabbi Y. Sarna, *rosh yeshiva* of Slabodka, "the friend of my youth," correctly observed that his labeling of the essay in question "Talks" might mislead the reader into thinking that these were verbatim transcriptions and the purpose of his note on their second publication was to obviate any such misconception.

241 Ibid., 310.

[he manifested] sound and lucid powers of reasoning, depth of investigation and love of the plain meaning. He distanced himself from scintillating casuistry where it had no anchor in inference from the text and, most importantly, he sat in his chamber tens of years and went through the entire Talmud together with the [writings of] the early scholars and the codes with diligent penetrating study until every halakhah was clear to him. In his great piety, he did not venture to disagree with early scholars; rather, he toiled to substantiate their words. However, this toil did not lead him to perversion of reason or distortion of the text. ... His empathy for early scholars flowed from his staunch faith that the Divine spirit dwelled in their house of study. The Gra permitted himself, at times, to depart from the words of the early scholars in interpretation of the Mishnah. Not so the Ḥazon Ish, of blessed memory. Assuredly, he was the greatest scholar of the generation in the area of halakhah and his piety enhanced him with a splendor of holiness. There was not another comparable to him in our generation, or in the previous generations since the time of the Gra.[242]

To such an individual, he felt bound to defer in *pesak*, not out of psychological weakness, but out of strength of conviction.

2. Devotion to Tradition

R. Weinberg was usually conservative in his rulings regarding communal matters. To the extent that these rulings reflect policy considerations, they reflect a deeply rooted concern for the preservation of time-hallowed communal practices and structures. R. Weinberg notes that Rabbi Eliyahu Hayyim Meizel of Lodz[243] was known for his extraordinary kindliness and dauntless championship of the poor[244] and, at the same time, as an uncompromising rabbinic leader and arch-conservative. It would be an error, contends R. Weinberg, to assume that Rabbi Meizel's gentleness and soft-heartedness stood in opposition to his zealousness and that he was an individual who harbored conflicting and contradictory character traits:

[Rabbi Meizel's] zealousness did not flow from a feeling of strictness or irascibility but was based upon ... recognition of the deep obligation

---

242 S. E., vol. 3, no. 72, 249.

243 S. E., vol. 4, 345–352.

244 Ibid., 348–349.

to fight and to take risks for truth and justice. If you will, gentlemen, this, too, is compassion! Pure zealotry, that which is aroused in a holy and sincere heart, is but compassion in another form. Every mitzvah or custom that has become beloved and sanctified by the people is not a "dry body," but a living entity that is saturated with the blood and tears of all the generations. ... There is not even a trivial custom that cannot awaken some slumbering memories, that does not move some string of the heart.

Accordingly, every idea is not simply a theoretical construct but rather a living organism. ... Can one who possesses a sensitive heart watch the death or the wounding of a living, ethical organism? R. Elya Hayyim possessed a sensitive heart and it was impossible for him to stand by the blood (blood of fathers, blood of generations!) and be silent. ...

It is possible that, in the eyes of the reader, my judgment will appear to be a strange paradox, a form of forced, convoluted truth. ... What wonder ... if a giant of the spirit such as R. Elya Hayyim, unto whom every custom was dear as his life, was not able to bear in silence and observe with equanimity some from among his brothers and his people, trampling and wounding living beings, plucking and cutting fresh living roses? What wonder? And if he came to anger, if there were heard from his mouth antagonistic expressions, this was surely but anger that arose from a deep pain; these were but responses evoked by anguish and compassion—anguish for the anguish of the living sanctity that had been trampled underfoot and compassion for his brethren whom he saw so doing.[245]

It would be naive to assume that these words are simply descriptive of the merits of a colleague R. Weinberg sought to eulogize in writing. Rather, they reveal that to which R. Weinberg himself aspired and the values to which he subscribed.

3. Individual versus National Needs
In matters relating to the State of Israel rather than merely to individuals, R. Weinberg espoused a more aggressive and innovative approach to halakhic decision-making. He recognized that, while in dealing with problems posed by an individual or by a local community a decisor might in good conscience rely only upon established precedent, the selfsame problem arising in the State of

---

245 Ibid., 51.

Israel could well become a matter of pressing need to the entire nation. Such ramifications, he believed, demanded that the decisor refuse to bow to precedent and rule upon his convictions, at least when he finds support for that position in the writings of earlier scholars. Most revealing is his posthumously published letter regarding performance of autopsies in the State of Israel. In this private communication to the late R. Kalman Kahane, R. Weinberg expresses a clearly permissive view in forcefully stated language, however, with the reservation that "I do not now wish to issue a halakhic ruling, but you may use this letter as, in your wisdom, you see fit."[246]

R. Weinberg hardly takes an unusual or innovative position in arguing that the *Noda bi-Yehudah*'s principle of permitting an autopsy in an instance of *ḥoleh le-faneinu* (lit., "a patient before us")[247] has a different connotation in modern times. In an era of instantaneous communication throughout the entire world, the definition of *ḥoleh le-faneinu* extends far beyond the parameters of that which is directly "before us."

What is remarkable, however, is the emphasis placed by R. Weinberg on additional considerations in reaching his permissive decision. He questions the continued viability of a modern state in which medical science would be unable to benefit from knowledge gained by means of autopsies. R. Weinberg distinguishes sharply between the restrictive ruling he issued in the past to a private physician[248] and a policy decision to be rendered on behalf of the entire State of Israel. In the latter case, it is evident that he believes a far more aggressive stance is mandated. He writes emphatically:

> We will, with the help of God, be able to preserve the Torah if we demonstrate that our Torah is a Torah of life. This consideration is sufficient to lighten the severity that is inherent in this matter, particularly since there are great rabbis who rule leniently in the matter. ... Indeed, nowadays, when the question affects the community of Israel and the State of Israel, I am unable to prohibit. ...
>
> I have expressed my opinion to your honor openly, and I will not deny to your honor, that if the matter were dependent on me, and if I were the preeminent authority of the generation in halakhic decision-making, I would permit the universities to conduct autopsies in the case of doubtful and questionable maladies.[249]

---

246 *Teḥumin* 12 (1991), 384.
247 *Noda bi-Yehudah, Mahadura Tinyana, Yoreh De'ah,* no. 210.
248 *S. E.,* vol. 2, no. 119.
249 *Teḥumin* 12 (1991), 384.

As noted, this opinion of R. Weinberg was published only posthumously—a fact that, in itself, is significant. Even with regard to this issue, R. Weinberg had noted that he was indicating the decision he would have rendered were he the "preeminent authority of the generation in halakhic decision-making." In all likelihood, this represents but another example of an instance in which R. Weinberg once more deferred to those among his colleagues whom he considered to be the final arbiters of halakhah.

4. The Distinction between Decision-Making (*Pesak*) and Theoretical Analysis (*Ḥakirah*)

While ever mindful of the obligation to bow to authoritative precedent in matters of halakhic *pesak*, R. Weinberg was, of course, committed to free and unfettered inquiry in study and analysis of classical texts. To a critic who had noted that some of R. Weinberg's novellae on a specific topic contradicted the interpretation of recognized latter-day scholars; R. Weinberg responded:

> Indeed, what of it? Does this not constitute the way of Torah, [i.e.,] to debate and to establish new interpretations even in opposition to the views of the greatest of the latter-day scholars? Only with regard to practical halakhah is it forbidden for us to disregard the words of the great scholars, of blessed memory, whose wisdom was broader than ours and we are all worthless by comparison to them. However, with regard to theoretical inquiry and explication of concepts, we have the option of establishing new interpretations and formulating opinions that they did not apprehend. For every Jewish person whose soul was present at Sinai received his portion in the Torah and in Torah interpretation. This is indisputable.[250]

R. Weinberg carefully distinguishes between the respective roles of authority and innovation in academic Torah study and the manner in which the tension between them ultimately redounds to the benefit of the student and to enhancement of Torah scholarship. In the course of doing so, he presents an insightful interpretation of Avot 6:6: Among the forty-eight ways in which Torah is acquired, the Sages enumerate "debate of the students and faith in Sages" (*pilpul ha-talmidim* and *emunat ḥakhamim*). On the surface these

---

250 S. E., vol. 3, no. 9, 27. Cf. also ibid., no. 97, 115, R. Weinberg's concluding comment, "I know that my words are contrary to many of the latter-day scholars. ... I decided to clarify the matters according to the sources of the early-day scholars."

"modes of acquisition" appear to be contradictory in nature. However, suggests R. Weinberg:

> If one would not have faith in the Sages or if one would peruse their words lightheartedly or with foolish arrogance, saying with conceit, "They did not understand," one would not struggle at all to penetrate and to substantiate the words [of the Sages] of blessed memory. But, in the end, it becomes clear that we have erred and not they. Therefore, it is indeed one of the paths of wisdom to have faith that they have not erred, Heaven forfend, for it is only we who are short-sighted and small-minded. However, simply to have faith and not to exhaust the mind with study and reflection, but merely to say, "They knew and we are able to rely on them unthinkingly," that, too, is not correct. Rather, it is necessary to debate and refute and question as if they were people such as us. Then one achieves additional depth of understanding and scholarly acuity. Accordingly, both elements together, faith in Sages and debate until the end, result in acquisition of Torah. And the Almighty delights in the debate of Torah.[251]

III

There is little in R. Weinberg's work that is trailblazing. His responsa, while they are the product of a consummate halakhist, are well within the mainstream of the tradition in which he writes. He fully accepts the axiological principles of the halakhic system and, in the spirit of *"yikov ha-din et ha-har"*—"let the law bore through the mountain," accepts any and all conclusions compelled by sources and precedents.

One seemingly incongruous comment of R. Weinberg is worthy of note. In a responsum in which he addresses the question of whether a daughter born to a Jewish mother and a non-Jewish father is permitted to marry a *kohen*, he remarks that "this prohibition causes me great anguish."[252] Taking these words out of context, one might presume that R. Weinberg's anguish reflects an extrinsic ethical concern, personal sympathy, or sociological sensitivity that renders the prohibition unpalatable. However, R. Weinberg proceeds to discuss the technical halakhic grounds on which his discomfort rests.

---

251 Ibid., no. 97, 115. See R. Weinberg's further citation of *Gittin* 6b to the effect that even partial attainment of truth of Torah delights the Almighty.

252 Ibid., vol. 3, no. 54, 200.

Despite what he believes is the weight of early authority to the contrary, *Shulḥan Arukh* and the Gaon of Vilna rule restrictively. R. Weinberg's "great anguish" is caused by the fact that, purely from the methodological perspective of the canons of halakhic decision-making, he has difficulty with the normative formulation of *Shulḥan Arukh*.

Modernists have criticized the halakhic mentality that "ends up deciding basic questions of war and peace and human dignity by the same terms in which one approaches the kashrut of a chicken."[253] Questions pertaining to the *kashrut* of a chicken and human dignity are indeed approached in one and the same manner by the halakhist. The modernist fails to understand that such a stance does not minimize the importance of questions of human dignity but maximizes the importance of the *kashrut* question. The *kashrut* question is treated with the utmost seriousness. Both are encompassed within the parameters of halakhah and the ethical considerations that underlie and permeate the halakhah. Of course, the halakhist is moved by compassion for the human situation. But he approaches the halakhah from within its own frame of reference. R. Weinberg's comment regarding the law that vexes him is not prompted by categories or considerations external to halakhah. The halakhist experiences "great anguish" when he fears that canons of halakhah and *pesak* have not been correctly applied.[254]

In the halakhah and the aggadah R. Weinberg sees a comprehensive self-contained system of ethics. The aggadah gives expression to "a veracity that stands most high, far above the veracity of the intellect."[255] Both together, halakhah and aggadah, express the beauty and truth of Torah:

> Both of them, both halakhah and aggadah, are a hidden treasure of the Creator of the universe who chose the Jewish people and gave it His Torah. We have no permission to prefer one over the other. How beautiful is the allusion given to us by our Sages, of blessed memory, "For I ... will be unto her a wall of fire [roundabout] etc." (Zechariah 2:9)—the fortified wall of the halakhah round about the holy flame of the aggadah.[256]

---

253 Yehudah Mirsky, letter to the Editor, *First Things* (October 1991), 3.

254 Cf. R. Weinberg's comments, *S. E.*, vol. 2, no. 65, 106: "Is it an insignificant matter to permit that which has been accepted as forbidden? Does the matter depend solely upon the feeling of compassion?"

255 *Li-Perakim*, 211.

256 Ibid., 212, commenting on *Bava Kamma* 60b.

R. Weinberg's open-mindedness rendered him capable of functioning as an intermediary interpreting ideas and values of one sector of the community to another.[257] Thus, he defended Zionist aspirations to the non-Zionist Orthodox while explicating the fears of the religious to secular nationalists; he was an advocate of women's rights while cautioning innovators regarding concerns of the devout; he emphasized the significance of text-critical scholarship to rabbinic scholars while underscoring the fundamental importance of analytic study and *pilpul* to academics; and, in the communal sphere, he strove for accommodation and harmony while standing guard to protect hallowed traditions. In times such as ours, when factionalism and dissension have split Orthodoxy into camps of left, right, and center, a personality such as that of R. Weinberg illuminates the manner in which divisions may be healed.

R. Weinberg was not afraid to meet new challenges and did not retreat from innovative positions. He knew the failings the *yere'im* and *ḥaredim* sometimes exhibited and their occasional narrowness of focus or scope, but he also understood and valued their loyalty and reverence for Torah and tradition and their sacrificial devotion. He understood that disdain for the new was often a hesitation born of fear of destruction of the old, a hesitation born of devotion and love. In 1960, R. Weinberg responded to an interlocutor from the

---

257 An instructive anecdote illuminates the manner in which the unique personality of R. Weinberg was esteemed by diverse sectors of the fractious Orthodox community. When R. Weinberg's body was brought to Israel for burial, two competing groups came to meet the cortege which was accompanied by disciples who had transported the departed from Switzerland to Jerusalem. One group, headed by the then minister of the interior, Chaim Moshe Shapiro, a former student, and the then minister of religion, Zorach Warhaftig, a friend and son of an intimate friend, intended to bury R. Weinberg, as instructed, in the Sanhedriyah cemetery in a plot adjacent to the graves of the late Chief Rabbi Herzog and other rabbis associated with the Mizrachi. A second group of yeshiva youth appeared on the scene together with the elderly and frail R. Yeheskel Sarna, *rosh yeshiva* of Hebron Yeshiva, who had declared, "His place is among his colleagues, the luminaries of Torah, *mussar*, and hasidism in the section of the scholars and saints on *Har ha-Menuḥot*." The yeshiva youth succeeded in diverting the cortege to *Har ha-Menuḥot*. See Warhaftig, *Palit ve-Sarid*, 34–7, and cf. Lipschitz, *Sefer ha-Zikaron*, 387. See also Weingort, *Zikhronot*, 164–166.

Daniel Schwartz, "Early but Opposed," 283, reports that, during his lifetime, R. Weinberg himself remarked that had he moved to Israel he would not have been regarded as a peer by prominent rabbinic scholars, but would have been dismissed as "but another German *Doktor*." R. Weinberg was, of course, universally recognized as an outstanding talmudic and halakhic scholar. Nonetheless, R. Weinberg's comment may not have been merely a self-deprecatory statement but a somewhat exaggerated reaction born of a realistic assessment of the Israeli scene. In life, R. Weinberg represented and advocated a religio-cultural expression of Judaism that his colleagues may not have been prepared to endorse, or to be perceived as endorsing. In death, it was easier to accord him honor.

United States who consulted him for guidance in reacting to a suggestion of government officials that animals be rendered unconscious by some form of gas prior to *shehitah*. As noted, this was a matter that R. Weinberg had researched and studied extensively. In a very brief responsum, R. Weinberg reviewed recent literature on the topic and mentioned the discussions of the Swiss rabbinate regarding the use of a substance called "necromal" for this purpose. He noted that Rabbi Breisch in his *Ḥelkat Ya'akov*, Rabbi Weiss in his *Minḥat Yitzḥak*, and, earlier, Rabbi Meisels in his *Mekadshei Ha-Shem* had all ruled against this innovation. R. Weinberg concluded with the following remarks:

> According to my opinion, one should not seek permissive rulings from rabbis who are halakhic authorities for I know that this permissive ruling will not be acceptable to some of the God-fearing who do not want, under any circumstances, to make changes in the practices of *shehitah* customary from time immemorial. In a conversation I had with the great Gaon R. Menachem Ziemba, may the memory of the righteous and holy be blessed, and may the Lord avenge his blood, he said to me, in his wisdom, that this issue will be determined not by scholars of halakhah, but by scholars of mysticism and kabbalah, namely, the *Admorim* (*Rebbes*) of the Hasidim, and they will not agree to any leniency whatsoever. Therefore, let the matter rest. For such a permissive ruling will lead to dissension and to the fashioning of two *Torot* in Israel.[258]

R. Weinberg would not countenance any innovation that carried with it the potential for splitting the community.

R Weinberg's exhortations regarding the danger of fissure, and of the tragedy inherent in making two *Torot*, did not stem from a lack of courage or a fear of factions on the right or on the left but from a deep-seated love and appreciation of the grandeur of *Kelal Yisra'el*:

> Ten Jews enter one house of prayer with *lulavim* and *etrogim* in their hands. They are imprinted with the imprint of a marked and united Jewish congregation. Each one of the ten feels with all his heart and soul his association with this congregation and at the same time he experiences his own personal religious life of the spirit. In the joint format of the religious enterprise each one invests his personal spiritual riches, cleaves to the

---

258 S. E., vol. 3, no. 90, 285.

congregation and realizes his private essence. Let us imagine to ourselves this sublime fantasy: The giants of Judaism of the earliest generations (*tanna'im* and *amora'im*), and of the intermediate generations (Rambam, Rav Y. Halevi, *Ra'avad*), and the later generations (the Baal Shem Tov and the Gra), as well as the last generation (Rav Y. Salanter, Rav Hirsch, the various *Admorim*) join in one gathering to pray with the congregation and to observe the mitzvah of "taking the *lulav*." Whoever looks at this lofty assembly will be astonished at the sight of this spectacular picture: generations and generations, diverse factions and trends, differing systems, coalescing into one whole unit whose beginning is situated in a generation of ancient times and whose end concludes with the Jew who has this day completed his thirteenth year. And that young lad of thirteen, at the moment when he grasps the *lulav* in his hand and joins with that quorum of hundreds of generations and their luminaries, feels a total harmony and an absolute compatibility between himself and them. How great and powerful is the pleasure of religious bliss in the feeling of the lad of thirteen in knowing that the *lulav* that he is taking into his hand is the very same *lulav* grasped in the hand of the father of the nation, our father Abraham, the first Jew, and that this very *lulav* is placed in the hand of every born Jew, whether he is in Morocco or in Yemen, in Berlin or in Radun, in Frankfurt or in Gur, in Jerusalem or in Rome.[259]

---

259 From an essay on "Religious Renascence," first published in *Ha-Olam* 27–30 (1926) and included in *Li-Perakim*, 153. Cf., also, his comments on the uniqueness of *kelal Yisra'el* in his explication of the talmudic comment, *Berakhot* 6a, "And I shall make you a singular unit in the world as it is said, 'And who is like unto Your people Israel, a unique nation in the land.'" R. Weinberg writes: "There are things in the world that it is not possible to define by analogy or example.... That of which there is only one single and singular sample, how is it possible to depict by analogy? The terrestrial globe is the terrestrial globe. The universe is the universe. Jews are Jews." See *Li-Perakim*, 172.

CHAPTER 9

Liturgical Innovation and Spirituality: Trends and Trendiness

For I know that Thou wilt not be appeased by a plethora of words nor wilt Thou be found by the breath of the lips, but only by a broken spirit, trembling soul and softened heart. . . .
Deliver me from the troubles, distresses and evils of this world . . ., both those that are known to me and those that are hidden from me, which separate me from Thee and drive me away from Thy service.

R. Bahya ben Joseph ibn Paquda, "Bakashah," appended to *Ḥovot ha-Levavot*

INTRODUCTION

Prayer—involving, as it does, the paradoxical attempt of a finite being to approach the *En-Sof* and to enter into communication with a transcendent God—is fraught with theological tension. The difficulties facing the worshiper have been recognized from time immemorial. Small wonder, then, that the Psalmist's plea, "Oh Lord open my lips that my mouth may declare Your praise" (Psalms 51:17), acknowledging the need for assistance in facilitating prayer, was incorporated by the Sages as a prefatory petition[1] to be recited before approaching God in the *Amidah* prayer.[2] The Deity to whom prayer is addressed must be beseeched not only to answer prayer but even to enable prayer itself to become a possibility. The Talmud relates that *ḥasidim ha-rishonim*, the pious men of ancient times, were wont to spend an hour in preparation before engaging in prayer and another hour in meditation thereafter.[3]

---

1 *Berakhot* 4b and 9b.
2 The *Amidah* or *Shemoneh Esreih* (Eighteen Benedictions) is referred to in the Talmud as *Tefillah* because it is the quintessential prayer.
3 *Berakhot* 32b.

Foremost medieval Jewish philosophers and theologians stressed the perils and dangers of careless prayer. Explicit and emphatic are the oft-cited admonitions of Maimonides[4] and Ibn Ezra[5] in their respective explications of the verse in Ecclesiastes 5:1, "Be not rash with your mouth, and let not your heart be hasty to utter one thing before God: for God is in heaven and you upon earth; therefore let your words be few." Closer to our own era, within the devotional movements of more modern times, hasidic teachers[6] and exponents of *mussar*[7] alike dwelt upon the obstacles that must be overcome in finding suitable modes of prayer.

If a significant period of time elapses during which one is unable to pray in a meaningful manner, "there accumulate in one's heart numerous stumbling blocks that produce an inner heaviness of the spirit" writes Rav Kook. Only when the gift of prayer is restored do the barriers disappear, but they do not disappear "all at once; it is a gradual process."[8] The difficulties encountered in expressing oneself in prayer, the obstructions—psychological and religious, personal and social—that virtually everyone experiences at one time or another, need not be belabored. A popular Ḥabad hasidic melody set to Yiddish lyrics gives voice to this commonly experienced frustration: "*Essen esst zikh un trinken trinkt zikh; der khisoren iz nor vos es davent zikh nit.*" Essentially untranslatable, a paraphrase would be: "Eat, it's easy for us to eat; and drink, it's easy for us to drink; the problem is that it's just not at all easy for us to *daven*."[9]

---

4 *Guide for the Perplexed*, I, chap. 59.

5 Commentary on Ecclesiastes 5:1.

6 See, for example, sources cited in Norman Lamm, *The Religious Thought of Hasidism: Text and Commentary* (Hoboken, NJ: Yeshiva University Press, 1999), chap. 6: "Worship, Service of God," 175–218, especially 197–198, the translation of a passage of R. Levi Yitzhak of Berdichev, *Kedushat Levi, Va-Etḥanan*, s. v. *o yevu'ar*, that concludes, "Hence there are two aspects to prayer: the prayer itself, and a prayer for the ability to pray [properly]."

7 See the earlier text much beloved of devotees of the *mussar* movement, R. Moshe Hayyim Luzzatto, *Mesillat Yesharim*, chap. 17, on preparation for prayer, concentration and avoidance of distraction. See also R. Israel Salanter, *Or Yisra'el*, no. 28 and R. Yitzhak Blaser, *Netivot Or* published with *Or Yisra'el* (London, 1951), 121; Dov Katz, *Tenu'at ha-Mussar*, 2nd ed. (Tel Aviv: A. Zioni, 1944), vol. II, 302; and R. Simchah Zisel Ziff, *Ḥokhmah u-Mussar* (New York, 1958), 65 and 215–216.

8 *Olat Re'iyah* (Jerusalem: Mossad Rav Kook, 1963), I, 11.

9 See Samuel Zalmanov, ed., *Sefer ha-Niggunim* (Brooklyn: Hevrat Nihoah, 1949), 57 and 97. R. Shalom Ber Butman relates that the late *Lubavitcher Rebbe*, Rabbi Menachem Mendel Schneerson, who inveighed against wasting time in sleep, was wont to sing this stanza with a slight variation, "*Essen esst zikh un shlofen shloft zikh*" ("Eat, it's easy for us to eat; and sleep, it's easy for us to sleep").

Yet when a contemporary writer states that "Religious worship is a particularly acute problem for the modern individual,"[10] the statement does not reflect the hubris of a modern writer who is convinced that present-day man faces novel predicaments and who is unaware that in seeking meaningful modalities of prayer moderns are engaged in reinventing the wheel. Commencing with the period of the Enlightenment, traditional religion has been confronted with unprecedented challenges. Contemporary Western culture, predominantly secular in nature, has created an environment in which religious worship does indeed pose a "particularly acute problem." If in earlier ages the worshiper was frustrated by the daunting task of summoning emotional fortitude and of finding the appropriate words to address an awesome God, the modernist is all too often paralyzed by the notion of addressing prayer to a Deity with regard to whose existence, power or concern he or she is deeply conflicted.

Presently, at the dawn of a new millennium, increasingly large numbers of people, feeling themselves alienated and desolate in an atomized, technological universe, are endeavoring to find meaningfulness and purpose in their lives. In a secular culture devoid of a religious infrastructure this quest often expresses itself in a vague and inchoate affirmation of spiritual values. Those who find conventional religious belief difficult to accept are attracted to a form of "secular spiritualism"[11] akin to the teachings promoted in the best-selling writings of the Dalai Lama who purports to find some benefit in religion yet also asserts, "But even without a religious belief we can also manage. In some cases we manage even better."[12]

Within the Jewish community as well, the hunger of the soul that underlies the search for spirituality has motivated many who heretofore were distant from Judaism to engage in a renewed encounter with their tradition. Unfortunately, far too often, those seekers find themselves in a New-Age type of environment in which their encounter is with an amorphous syncretistic Judaism. Thus, a recent news item reports that a participant in a "Jewish Renewal" retreat described as "Living Waters ... a spiritual health spa program grounded in ancient kabbalistic teachings" avowed that the recital of the *Ave Maria* at the retreat's Sabbath services was "one of the most moving experiences of the week."[13]

---

10   Chava Weissler, "Making *Davening* Meaningful," *YIVO Annual* 19 (1990), 255.

11   Richard Bernstein, "Critic's Notebook," *New York Times*, October 7, 1999, A2.

12   Tenzin Gyatso, the Dalai Lama, and Howard C. Cutler, *The Art of Happiness: A Handbook for Living* (New York: Riverhead, 1998), 306. See also idem, *Ethics for the New Millennium* (New York: Riverhead, 1999).

13   *The Jerusalem Report*, August 2, 1999, 38. Cf. Gary Rosenblatt, "Spirituality (Whatever That Means) Is on the Rise," *The Jewish Week*, January 14, 2000, 7.

The early minor liturgical innovations and the subsequent trajectory of the nineteenth-century Reform movement as well as the return swing of the pendulum in the latter part of the twentieth century are well-known. What is sometimes overlooked or forgotten is the rhetoric that urged implementation of those reforms in the name of spirituality and enhancement of religion. An analysis of those phenomena is particularly valuable for the light it casts on the ambiguous and amorphous meanings that attach themselves to the concept of "spirituality" and on the extent to which such meanings are influenced by, and reflective of, regnant cultural trends in society at large.

MOTIVATIONS

The earliest stirrings of Reform centered on improvement of the worship service. The changes advocated involved matters extrinsic to the liturgy, that is, matters of aesthetics and comportment (the three D's: design, dignity, and decorum), as well as the language and content of the prayers themselves. From the outset, complex motivations, both assimilationist and religious in nature, were expressed candidly. Thus, it was easy for opponents to point an accusatory finger. Yet the total picture is much more subtle; a skein of contradictory considerations must be unraveled.

Ostensibly, the failings and flaws of then existing synagogal practices were the impetus for innovation. But a closer look at even the very earliest formulations of the concerns of the innovators reveals a mixture of motivation, a desire—quite possibly, sincere—for enhanced spirituality and devotion combined with an equally strong desire—quite obviously sincere—for the acceptance and regard of non-Jewish neighbors.

Perception of the teachings and religious observances of Judaism as outmoded and primitive was rooted in the currents of anti-Semitism that permeated intellectual circles of the era. During the eighteenth century, the "century of Voltaire," France developed an intelligentsia that unabashedly expressed pronounced anti-Jewish sentiments. By the end of the century, their influence had spread throughout Europe. In Germany, Immanuel Kant's hostility to Judaism and his characterizations of the Jewish religion as obsolete and lacking in morality was representative of the thinking of his time. The only possibility for social rehabilitation of the Jews, according to Kant, lay in their rejection of unedifying rites and acceptance of "purified" religious concepts. Nor was Kant's younger friend and sometime student, Johann Gottfried von Herder, commonly regarded as a liberal and philo-Semite, incapable of expressing anti-Jewish comments. Herder disparaged what he termed "pharasaism" and disdained halakhic distinctions as ponderous hairsplitting.[14] Deprecatory attitudes such as these were internalized by acculturated Jewish intellectuals in their desperate quest for acceptance in a society that had always rejected them as alien.

The imperative for change in divine worship was vigorously articulated by the forerunners and pioneers of the Reform movement, Israel Jacobson and David Friedlander. Jacobson, whose status as the father of Reform Judaism was acknowledged in the dedication of the Hamburg Temple Prayerbook (1819), was the president of the Westphalian Consistory. In 1810 Jacobson founded a synagogue in Seesen that he named the Temple of Jacob. The edifice was adorned with a belfry, the *bimah* removed from its central position and prayer was accompanied by the music of an organ. In an address delivered at the Temple's inaugural ceremony, Jacobson declaimed with a rhetorical flourish:

> What I had in mind when I first thought about building this temple was *your* religious education, my Israelite brothers, *your* customs, *your* worship, etc. Be it far from me that I should have any secret intention to undermine the pillars of your faith.... You know my faithful adherence to the faith of my fathers.... [But w]ho would dare to deny that our service is sickly because of many useless things, that in part it has degenerated into a thoughtless recitation of prayers and formulae, that it kills devotion more than encourages it.... On all sides, enlightenment opens up new areas for development. Why should we alone remain behind?[15]

But, after stressing the importance of restoring spiritually degenerated services to religious purity, Jacobson did not hesitate to mention a further consideration and admitted: "Let us be honest, my brothers. Our ritual is still weighted down with religious customs which must be rightfully offensive to reason as well as to our Christian friends."[16]

---

14 The ambiguities and ambivalences surrounding Emancipation in France are depicted in Arthur Hertzberg, *The French Enlightenment and the Jews* (New York: Columbia University Press, 1968). An excellent portrayal of the German climate of thought is found in Paul Lawrence Rose, *German Question/Jewish Question: Revolutionary Antisemitism from Kant to Wagner* (Princeton, NJ: Princeton University Press, 1992); see especially 90–132.

15 W. Gunther Plaut, *The Rise of Reform Judaism: A Sourcebook of its European Origins* (New York: World Union for Progressive Judaism, 1963), 29.

16 Ibid., 30.

In 1786 David Friedlander published his *Gebete der Juden auf das ganze Jahr*, a translation of the liturgy into German but printed in Hebrew characters because German Jews had not yet acquired facility in the reading of German. Dedicated by Friedlander to his mother and mother-in-law, the work was intended for the edification of Jewish women whose ignorance of Hebrew was taken for granted.[17] The text of this prayerbook and its brief preface extolling the merits of prayer reflect no intimation of dissatisfaction with the liturgy. But not long thereafter, in his infamous proposal to Probst Teller for a conditional merging of Judaism and Christianity, Friedlander's muddled mixture of spiritual concern and denigration of the traditional liturgy is evident in his description of the *siddur*:

> From century to century these prayers became more numerous and worse and worse, the conceptions more mystical, muddied with the principles of Kabbalah which were in direct contradiction to the genuine spirit of Judaism. ... The larger portion of our nation understands nothing of these prayers and that is a happy circumstance, because in this way these prayers will have neither good nor bad effect on the sentiment of the worshipers.[18]

In these remarks Friedlander did not limit himself to a veiled critique of the content of the liturgy; his comments include a series of unsubstantiated slurs. The formulas of the prayers composed in Hebrew, Friedlander claimed, reveal "the weakness of an aging language." The prayers, even those of thanksgiving for divine beneficence and including the benedictions recited under the wedding canopy, he characterized as "without exception" resounding with "the plaintive cry of slaves who pine for redemption." In a sweeping statement filled with innuendo, he expressed the canard that, "finally, the language in which these prayers are expressed offends not only the ear, but also mocks at all logic and grammar."[19]

---

17 Early Reform writings are striking in their commendable attentiveness to the religious needs of women. A cursory glance at the history of the nineteenth-century German Jewish community reveals the presence of a cadre of educated and sophisticated women, the Salon Jewesses, who played a prominent role in German society, but were only marginally involved in the Jewish community and many of whom intermarried. A lacuna in the education and religious experience of Jewish women is unmistakable.

18 *Sendschreiben an seine Hochwürdigen, Herrn Oberconsistorialrat und Probst Teller zu Berlin, von einigen Hausvätern jüdischer Religion* (Berlin, 1799), 34–35. This tract has been republished in an offset edition and with a Hebrew translation (Jerusalem: Zalman Shazar Center, 1975).

19 Ibid., 34–35

A marginally more temperate tone pervades Friedlander's detailed 1812 proposals for the "reformation" of Jewish worship services and educational institutions. The focus of this document is on "devotion and elevation of the soul to God." Hebrew prayers in their traditional form, he avers, are a barrier to sincere worship. To pray in a language one does not comprehend is off-putting. But for one who does understand the language the problem is even graver because the prayers, as constituted, stand "in sharpest contrast to his convictions, his aspirations and his hopes."[20] Friedlander further bemoans the substitution of quantity for quality, the dissonance between the content of the prayers and the reality of the needs of the times as well as the absence of musical accompaniment as a result of which circumstances "the knowledgeable man of religion" who seeks edification must perforce abandon the synagogue.[21]

Although it was never explicitly stated, imitation of Protestant worship was an implicit objective. A telling anecdote illustrates this fact. Josef Johlson[22] compiled one of the earliest books of hymns in the vernacular for use in a synagogue. That work, entitled *Gesangbuch für Israeliten* (Frankfurt-am-Main, 1816), attained a measure of popularity. The vast majority of these songs were taken verbatim from Protestant hymnals save that Johlson substituted the words "Lord" or "my Refuge" for each mention of the name "Jesus." Only after the book was printed was it discovered that, inadvertently, in one such occurrence the substitution had not been made. As a result, it was necessary for an entire signature of the book to be removed and replaced. This publishing mishap piquantly underscores the Christological orientation of the innovators.[23]

---

20 Jakob J. Petuchowski, *Prayerbook Reform in Europe: The Liturgy of European Liberal and Reform Judaism* (New York: World Union for Progressive Judaism, 1968), 132.

21 Ibid., p. 133.

22 A teacher of religion at the Frankfurt Philantropin school, Johlson, under the *nom de plume* Bar Amithai, later published a pamphlet, *Über die Beschneidung in historischer und dogmatischer Hinsicht* (Frankfurt am Main, 1843), in which he recommended abolition of circumcision and substitution of another ceremony. Johlson prepared a rubric for such a ceremony prospectively termed "The Sanctification of the Eighth Day" and designed as an egalitarian ritual suitable for both male and female infants. See Michael A. Meyer, *Response to Modernity: A History of the Reform Movement in Judaism* (New York and Oxford: Oxford University Press, 1988), 123 and 423 n. 86.

23 See Heinrich Zirndorf, *Isaak Markus Jost und seine Freunde: Ein Beitrag zur Kulturgeschichte der Gegenwart* (Cincinnati: Block Pub. Co., 1886), 161–162. Zirndorf adds that the historian Jost remarked, perhaps in jest, that an unemended copy of the Christological version should have been kept intact because, as a collector's item, it would one day command a handsome price.

The few rabbinic figures who responded affirmatively to the early innovations were also influenced by a variety of factors and considerations ranging from opportunism, accomodationism, naiveté and desire for containment to genuine conviction and empathy. The somewhat quixotic approach of Aaron Chorin in his early writings in support of liturgical reform[24] reveals a complexity of intent. Deep concern for the esteem of non-Jewish fellow citizens is demonstrated in his *Davar be-Itto*[25] both in the extensive discussions of the status of non-Jews in the first portion of each section of that work[26] and in his pointed remarks regarding disruptive and indecorous services that he regarded as a disgrace in the eyes of the nations.[27] But it is an entirely different motif that is pervasive throughout this brief work. Chorin argues that a conciliatory and moderate approach is essential in order to stem the loss of vast numbers of Jews who have become entirely disenchanted with Judaism. Contemporary Jews find existing religious services outmoded and alien. Aesthetically attractive public worship is the most effective way to arouse the alienated to renewed reverence of God and even "to observe the commandments."[28] Castigating the negativity of rabbis serving the established community, Chorin contrasts their forbidding stance with the midrashic portrayal of the spiritual leadership of Moses and David, both of whom are depicted as loving shepherds who nurtured their flocks with compassion and concern for the distinctiveness of each and every one of their charges. The Midrash portrays David as taking pains to give sheep of different ages food appropriate to their needs and describes

---

24 Chorin's views evolved over the years from an initial moderate support of innovation to a marked break with accepted halakhic practice. For biographical data on Chorin see Leopold Löw, "Aron Chorin: Eine biographische Skizze," in Chorin's *Gesammelte Schriften*, ed. Immanuel Löw (Szegedin, 1890), vol. II, 251–420 and Moshe Pelli, "The Ideological and Legal Struggle of Rabbi Aaron Chorin for Religious Reform in Judaism" [Hebrew], *Hebrew Union College Annual* 39 (1968) (Hebrew section), 63–79.

25 Chorin's first defense of synagogue reform was his responsum included in *Nogah ha-Tzedek* (Dessau, 1818) sanctioning the practices of the Berlin Beer Temple. In response to the attacks on him in *Eleh Divrei ha-Berit* (Altona, 1819), he published *Davar be-Itto* (Vienna, 1820). This slim book is presented in a curious format. It is comprised of three sections: a Hebrew section; a similar but not identical German section in Gothic characters entitled *Ein Wort zu seiner Zeit: Über die Nächstenliebe und den Gottesdienst*; and the identical German section in Hebrew characters. The German-language section is sharper and more condemnatory in tone than the Hebrew one. Citations in this paper will be either to the Hebrew or to the German sections as identified by their respective titles.

26 "Nächstenliebe," *Ein Wort*, 5–27 and "Sha'ar Torah," *Davar be-Itto*, 5–22.

27 *Davar be-Itto*, 43.

28 Ibid., 26–27.

how Moses followed a small kid that strayed from its flock in search of water, picked it up and carried it in his arms.[29] Those models should illustrate for us, Chorin contends, that one must exercise wisdom and understanding in guiding each individual Jew in accordance with his needs and talents and must lovingly mentor the weak and frail who flee the flock "bearing them on one's shoulder to green pastures—to the paths of faith, that they not be utterly cast aside from the paths of life."[30]

Chorin's later writings, however, emphasize not so much the need to attract the disaffected as the quest to enhance devotion. During the last weeks of his life he wrote to a conference of Hungarian rabbis in Paks:

> I need not tell you that of all the external institutions the public service demands our immediate and undivided attention. He who is faithful to his God, and is earnestly concerned for the welfare of his religion, must exert himself to rescue our service from the ruin into which it has fallen and to give it once again that inspiring form which is worthy of a pious and devout worship of the one true God. For it is not only the excrescences of dark ages which cover it with disgrace, but thoughtlessness, lack of taste, absence of devotion, and caprice have disfigured its noble outlines.[31]

Reform reconceptualization of Judaism, it has been quite correctly noted,[32] was an attempt to recast Judaism in the cultural and theological mold of the host country. In the seventeenth and eighteenth centuries the center of gravity in Protestantism moved from a God-centered faith to a focus on the individual's subjective religious conscience. The concepts of *Glückseligkeit* (spiritual contentment) and *Erbauung* (edification) became much vaunted religious goals. Following those Christian trends, Reform innovators favored retention of customs and rituals that they perceived to be spiritually uplifting and proposed innovations that they thought would enhance religious experience.

---

29 Ibid., 47–48, citing *Midrash Rabbah, Shemot* 2.
30 *Davar be-Itto*, 48.
31 Cited in David Philipson, *The Reform Movement in Judaism*, rev. ed. (New York: Ktav, 1967), 442 n. 112.
32 See Meyer, *Response to Modernity*, 17–18. In stating that, like early Lutheranism, Judaism paid little attention to the subjective religious state of the individual and regarded observance of the commandments "as an end in itself, not the means to any other," Meyer, in common with Reform thinkers of the nineteenth century, overlooks classical Jewish sources.

In doing so they remained blissfully unaware of classic sources of Jewish teaching and failed to seek guidance in the vast corpus of Jewish ethical literature. The classic early-day work *Sefer ha-Ḥinnukh* unambiguously finds moral edification to be the primary goal of particular mitzvot. According to *Sefer ha-Ḥinnukh*, the multiplicity of commandments is intended as a form of behavior modification designed to habituate man to the path of virtue. *Sefer ha-Ḥinnukh's* philosophy of mitzvot is exemplified in a number of emblematic statements that serve as a motto for the entire work:

> Know that a man is influenced in accordance with his actions. His heart and all his thoughts are always [drawn] after his deeds in which he is occupied, whether [they are] good or bad.... For after one's acts is the heart drawn....
>
> The omnipresent God wished to make Israel meritorious; therefore He gave them ... a multitude of mitzvot ... that all our preoccupation should be with them.... For by good actions we are acted upon to become good....[33]
>
> ... For the physical self becomes cleansed through [its] actions. As good actions are multiplied and as they are continued with great perseverance, the thoughts of the heart become purified, cleansed and refined.[34]

Centuries later, R. Moshe Hayyim Luzzatto expressed similar concepts in nomenclature paralleling the language of *Erbauung* and *Glückseligkeit*. Central to his thought is his description of man's goal in life as attainment of perfection through attachment to God by means of the mitzvot.[35]

The term *Glückseligkeit*, or spiritual contentment, lends itself to a wide variety of interpretations, some worldly, others somewhat otherworldly. Nevertheless, as used in theological writings, the term clearly connotes a state of spiritual well-being. The distinction between worldly success (*hatzlaḥah*) and serenity of spirit (*osher*) is emphasized in the much later comments of R. Meir Leibush Malbim in his explication of the spiritual contentment the Psalmist ascribes to the righteous.[36]

---

33 *Sefer ha-Ḥinnukh*, ascribed to R. Aaron ha-Levi of Barcelona, trans. by Charles Wengrov (Jerusalem and New York: Feldheim Publishers, 1991), no. 16, vol. I, 119–121.
34 Ibid., no. 95, vol. I, 359.
35 *Derekh Ha-Shem* (Amsterdam, 1896), chaps. 3–4.
36 Psalms 1:1. Cf. R. Samson Raphael Hirsch, *The Nineteen Letters*, trans. Karin Paritzky (Jerusalem and New York: Feldheim, 1995), second letter, 14–15, for R. Hirsch's rejection of happiness in the conventional sense as the ultimate goal of mankind.

A major contribution of R. Samson Raphael Hirsch in *Horeb* was precisely his analysis of mitzvot in a manner that stressed their ethical moment. He made use of the vocabulary and conceptual framework of the day in demonstrating the manner in which mitzvot further the goals regarded by Reform thinkers as paramount. The mitzvot that Reform regarded as superfluous R. Hirsch found to be invaluable in promoting the selfsame spirituality that the innovators found so significant. He faulted Reform ideologues for failing to appreciate the richness of their heritage and for not mining its treasures. It is this fundamental assessment that underlies R. Hirsch's sharp critique of the Reform movement.

Although many rabbinic authorities indiscriminately branded all innovators as rebels and sinners whose goal was simply to ease the burden of religious observance, some realized that the picture was not monochromatic. R. Samson Raphael Hirsch disarmingly chose to seize upon the positive motivations of the innovators even while deploring their actions. Regarding those who proposed innovations for the sake of promoting spiritual improvement he counseled, "Respect all of them, for they sense a shortcoming; they desire the good as they conceive it."[37] It was a tragedy, he maintained, that their good intentions had led to deleterious results. That occurred, he asserted, because exponents of Reform responded to the spiritual challenge of the time in a shallow and superficial manner. These individuals were satisfied, claimed R. Hirsch, with an "uncomprehended Judaism and merely to revise the outward forms of one misunderstood part of it, the Divine service and [to] remodel it according to the sentimentalities of the age"[38] rather than seeking to intensify efforts to invigorate a Judaism "intellectually comprehended and vigorously implemented."[39]

In turning our attention to specific liturgical innovations with regard to language, music, aesthetics, decorum, duration of services, recitation of *piyyut* (liturgical poetry) and fundamentals of belief, it is instructive to take cognizance of rabbinic discussions of those issues in order to appreciate the extent to which traditionalists did or did not relate to the concerns expressed by Reform writers.

LANGUAGE

The second[40] formal prayerbook incorporating liturgical reforms, *Die deutsche Synagoge*, edited by Eduard Kley and C. S. Günsburg, clearly articulated

---

37 Ibid., seventeenth letter, 243.
38 Ibid., 243.
39 Ibid., 242.
40 *Gebete am Sabbath Morgens und an den beiden Neujahrs-Tagen*, the earliest Reform prayerbook, was published anonymously, probably in 1815, without indication of city

the ardor with which the constituency to whom it was addressed embraced the German language. While the editors acknowledge a lingering fealty to Hebrew ("*Holy* is the language in which God once gave the Law to our fathers") based on a reverence for past history ("a memorial ... a sweet echo ... and venerable it will remain for everyone who still reveres the past"), they were unabashed in their passionate expression of sentiment for the German language, proclaiming:

> But seven times more holy unto us is the language which belongs to the present and to the soil whence we have sprung forth ... the language in which a mother greets her new-born child ... the language which unites us with our fellow men ... the language, finally, in which our philanthropic and just king speaks to us, in which he proclaims his law to us. ...[41]

The ensuing controversy over the language of prayer can be properly appreciated only in light of extravagant rhetoric such as this and the ideology it betrays. At issue were not the bare bones of halakhic rulings regarding the legitimacy of prayer in the vernacular but the much more profound questions of motivation and of fundamental loyalty to, and appreciation of, the sancta of Judaism.

Promotion of prayer in the vernacular was a primary issue in the agenda of worship reform. While yet in Westphalia, Israel Jacobson solicited halakhic opinions in an endeavor to validate the contemplated change. The responses of R. Samuel Eger of Brunswick, a cousin of the famed R. Akiva Eger, deploring the proposal[42] and of the Westphalian Consistory's own R. Menahem Mendel Steinhardt endorsing hymns in the vernacular and alluding to the permissibility

---

or year of publication, and consists of a number of sections that originally appeared separately and were subsequently bound together. As early as 1815, Jacobson sent copies of these prayers and of German hymns from a songbook issued in Cassel (1810 and revised in 1816) to a government minister. See Meyer, *Response to Modernity*, 49 and 406 n. 145.

41 From the preface to *Die deutsche Synagoge*, vol. I (Berlin, 1817), cited in Petuchowski, *Prayerbook Reform*, 135. The same year that this prayerbook was published, the first French Jewish periodical, *L'Israélite Français*, advocated the introduction of French language prayers. However, in France, unlike in Germany, substitution of the vernacular for Hebrew, as espoused by radicals, did not gain popular acceptance. See Phyllis Cohen Albert, "Nonorthodox Attitudes in French Judaism," *Essays in Modern Jewish History*, ed. Frances Malino and Phyllis Cohen Albert (Rutherford: Farleigh Dickinson Press, 1982), 123–124 and 132.

42 R. Samuel Eger's letter to Jacobson is published in B.H. Auerbach, *Geschichte der Israelitischen Gemeinde Halberstadt* (Halberstadt, 1866), 219–221.

of vernacular prayer in general[43] were but the first salvos in what was to become a pitched battle.

Turning the question on its head, Aaron Chorin noted that the proper question to be posed is not whether one may pray in the vernacular but whether one may pray in Hebrew, a language understood by "barely three out of ten." Chorin suggested the existence of an absolute requirement that prayer services be conducted in the vernacular in order to be understood by all.[44] Conceding that Hebrew, no less so than any other language, is subsumed in the dispensation "A person may pray in any language in which he desires" and that, in addition, Hebrew carries with it the distinction of history and tradition as well as the encomium "holy tongue," Chorin concludes that, nevertheless, it is preferable that a person pray in the language he understands as recommended by *Magen Avraham, Oraḥ Ḥayyim* 104:4. Since *Magen Avraham*'s ruling applies to an individual rather than to the community, Chorin commends as sagacious the decision of the innovators who reached a compromise in maintaining Hebrew as the language used by the cantor in chanting major obligatory prayers while introducing German in other parts of the liturgy.[45]

Chorin's final comment on the language of prayer illustrates the manner in which people who viewed themselves as the cultural vanguard and in tune with the *Zeitgeist* were yet limited and constrained by the very notions that they deemed to be enlightened and liberal. Chorin concludes his call for enhanced, aesthetically pleasing worship services with the observation that women must not be excluded from the benefits of communal prayer for gone are the barbaric ages in which women were viewed as an inferior species. "But," he asks, "in which language are such services to be conducted? Surely not solely in Hebrew, of which women do not have the vaguest notion and which has no appeal whatsoever to their spirit (*die ihr Gemüth in gar keiner Beziehung anspricht*)."[46] *Tempora mutantur et nos mutamur in eis!*

Chorin's initial moderate stance was soon abandoned. As is well known, extensive discussions regarding the use of Hebrew in religious services took place at the second Reform rabbinical conference in Frankfurt in 1845. The delegates determined that Jewish law did not require use of Hebrew as the language of prayer. A subsequent vote of 15 to 13 affirming that retention of Hebrew in

---

43 *Divrei Iggeret* (Rödelheim, 1812), 10a.
44 *Ein Wort*, 38.
45 Ibid., 39–40.
46 Ibid., 47.

public services was not necessary on other grounds led Zacharias Frankel to leave the conference and part company with the Reform movement. Insistence on preservation of Hebrew as the language of liturgy was a defining feature of Frankel's positive historical Judaism, an ideology that was later to be institutionalized in this country as Conservative Judaism. Frankel contended that the Hebrew language was integral to the essence of Judaism and still vibrantly alive in the emotions of Jews even if their knowledge of the language was deficient.[47]

At the Frankfurt conference, Abraham Adler, Joseph Kahn, Abraham Geiger, and David Einhorn made unequivocal statements endorsing prayer in the vernacular. Adler urged his colleagues to avoid sentimentality in the search for truth, to recognize that no language is sacred and instead to acknowledge that it is the content of language rather than the words that convey sanctity. Prayer in Hebrew, he contended, offered by those who do not understand the language, encourages lip service and hypocrisy. Moreover, he argued, the Hebrew language is meager and inadequate as a medium for prayer since it is lacking in vocabulary and nuances of expression and "[i]n any case, it is dead because it does not live within the people."[48] Kahn similarly claimed that there is "no pure religious impulse" inherent in a language. Although he conceded that some Hebrew must be retained provisionally, Kahn asserted that under ideal circumstances services should be conducted entirely in German.[49] Geiger confessed that, as far as he personally was concerned, prayer in German aroused him to deeper devotion than did Hebrew prayer for it is in German that "[a]ll our deepest feelings and sentiments, all our highest thoughts, receive their expression."[50] Hebrew must be viewed as a dead language, argued David Einhorn, and, assuredly, smiting the rock of a dead language will not produce living waters with which to quench people's thirst.[51] Accordingly, for Einhorn, there is no doubt that Hebrew is not

> the organ with which to express the feelings of the people. Aforetimes, prayer was only a cry of pain; a scarcely intelligible expression sufficed for

---

47 See Meyer, *Response*, 88 and 137, and Philipson, *Reform Movement*, 165–66 and 189–93.
48 *Protokolle und Aktenstücke der zweiten Rabbiner-Versammlung* (Frankfurt am Main, 1845), 45.
49 Ibid., 41.
50 Ibid., 32–33. Cf. the contention of J. Jolowicz, ibid., 38, *contra* Z. Frankel, stating that *vox populi* and *salus publica* militate for German and against Hebrew since the vast majority of the populace "think and feel in German" and have therefore turned their backs on synagogues that employ Hebrew as the language of prayer.
51 Ibid., 49.

this; but now people need a prayer that shall express thoughts, feelings, and sentiments; this is possible only through the mother tongue.[52]

It is evident from these comments that Reform abandonment of Hebrew was not motivated purely by concern for enhancement of devotion in prayer but was motivated equally by an announced desire to deemphasize nationalistic aspirations. Joseph Maier did indeed acknowledge the "nationalistic" value inherent in the phenomenon of Jews in different lands sharing a common language of prayer but asserted that any such benefit could be achieved by restricting use of Hebrew to a few brief prayers such as the *Shema* and *Kedushah* and to some Torah readings. "Anything else," he added, "I consider detrimental."[53] Jacob Auerbach more candidly asserted that the fundamental question to be addressed was "the relationship of the national to the religious element." The question, he declared, is no longer what is desirable but what is necessary "to accomplish our mission." In that respect, "History has decided; centuries lie between the national and the religious elements. . . . The purely religious element is the flower of Judaism."[54] Nevertheless, Auerbach contended, Jewish history mandates continued study of Hebrew as the language of Scripture and of the sources upon which the liturgy is based. However, he asserted, the language of devotional prayer at its core must be the vernacular.[55]

One of the few congregations to give concrete expression to this extreme viewpoint was the Berlin *Genossenschaft für Reform im Judenthum* (Association for the Reform of Judaism) whose published prayerbook eliminated almost all vestiges of Hebrew. Their prayerbook reflected the firm conviction of members of the Association that liturgy must employ only a living language whose mode of thought and expression was familiar to the worshiper.[56] Similarly, a radical group, Friends of Reform, located in Worms stated forthrightly: "We must no longer pray in a dead language when word and sound of our German mother

---

52 Ibid., 27.
53 Ibid., 39.
54 Ibid., 46.
55 Ibid., 47. One of the dissenting votes at the Conference was that of Leopold Schott of Randegg who underscored the significance of educating youth in the Hebrew language by citing Maimonides, *Commentary on the Mishnah*, Avot 2:1. Maimonides categorizes the study of Hebrew language as an example of an "easy mitzvah." In response, Gotthold Salomon countered that Maimonides "is not an unimpeachable authority (*keine unumstössliche Autorität*)." See ibid., 49–50.
56 Plaut, *Rise*, 59.

tongue are to us both understandable and attractive. These alone, therefore, are suited to lift us up to our Creator."[57]

Remarkable is the fact that proponents of Reform in Germany differed from their counterparts in other countries in the nature of their espousal of vernacular prayer. Thus, for example, in the United States, the members of the Charleston congregation who joined Isaac Harby in 1824 in petitioning for worship innovation and prayer in the vernacular[58] and, at a later date, Isaac M. Wise, in advocating rendition of selected prayers in English,[59] presented a straightforward case based on the need to understand the content of the liturgy. In contrast, the German writers exhibited an exaggerated veneration of German and gave voice to an often mean-spirited denigration of the Hebrew language.[60]

From the outset, rabbinical scholars were keenly aware of the implications of decisions regarding the language of prayer both for the individual and for the community qua community. It was precisely the *spiritual* aspect of this

---

57 Ibid., 62.

58 See the memorandum submitted to the Adjunta of Congregation Beth Elohim, in Charleston published in *A Documentary History of the Jews of the U.S. 1654–1875*, ed. Morris U. Schappes, 3rd ed. (New York: Schocken Books, 1975), 172–173.

59 James G. Heller, *I. M. Wise: His Life, Work and Thought* (New York: Union of American Hebrew Congregations, 1965), 393, 395 and 566.

60 It is noteworthy that in the opinion of the radical exponent of Reform, David Einhorn, the triumph of Reform ideology was contingent upon preservation of the German language. Accordingly, he advocated that American-born youngsters be taught German so that they might become familiar with the German philosophical background of the Reform movement. See Kaufmann Kohler, "David Einhorn, the Uncompromising Champion of Reform Judaism," *CCAR Yearbook* 19 (1909), 255. In light of his attitude toward Hebrew it is instructive to note Einhorn's assertion: "If you sever from Reform the German spirit—or what amounts to the same thing—the German language, you will have torn it from its native soil and the lovely flower will wilt." See Kaufmann Kohler, ed., *Dr. David Einhorns Ausgewählte Predigten und Reden* (New York: Steiger, 1880), 90.

Passionate espousal of the German language remained a characteristic feature of German Jews well into the twentieth century. There is an excellent literary portrayal of this phenomenon in Nathan Shaham's masterful novel, *The Rosendorf Quartet*, trans. from Hebrew into English by Dalya Bilu (New York: Grove Press, 1991). Shaham's fictional protagonist, the German writer Egon Lowenthal, who finds himself in misery as an expatriate in Palestine of the 1930s ("I am a German writer who thinks in German, writes in German, and loves and hates in German" [270]; "I am full of longing for Germany. Lines of German poetry buzz in my head, and in my heart is only a deep pain" [278]; "there is no music sweeter to my ear than the sound of the German language" [325]), expresses a view of Hebrew fully consistent with that of members of the early Reform movement when he derides his Zionist friends as "People who are content with a vocabulary of three hundred words" (270) and who "speak an artificial language" (281) and describes Hebrew as "a dead language which all of the flogging in the world will not revive" (318).

question rather than its halakhic parameters that was emphasized by authoritative rabbinic spokesmen.

With regard to some areas of dispute it may be the case that nuances of the Reform proposals were not fully appreciated by rabbinic figures because of the culture gap that existed between those rabbis and their more worldly coreligionists. However, rabbinic leaders demonstrated in their responses that, with regard to the question of use of Hebrew as the language of prayer, they were not at all unaware of issues that went far beyond technicalities of halakhah. They realized that preservation of the Hebrew language was intimately linked to the unity of the Jewish people and the preservation of the Torah.

Although R. Samuel Eger's responsum dwelt on the pivotal role of Hebrew as a spiritual bond for Jews the world over[61] and R. Akiva Eger's pronouncement was predicated upon halakhic minutiae, R. Akiva Eger was aware, no less so than his cousin, of the assimilatory motives of the innovators, of their desire to curry favor in the eyes of the nations[62] and of their "shaming our pure and beautiful language."[63]

The several contributions of R. Moses Sofer, known as Ḥatam Sofer, to the anti-Reform tract Eleh Divrei ha-Berit were the subject of much satiric comment on the part of early partisans of Reform who asserted that his rulings on vernacular prayer were contrary to talmudic law and the general tenor of his comments was abstruse and mystical, naïve and superstitious.[64] There is, however, no naiveté at all evident in Ḥatam Sofer's response to the suggestion of Aaron Chorin that the Pesukei de-Zimra (Verses of Song) be recited in the vernacular and Hebrew preserved only for recitation of the Shema and the Amidah. Ḥatam Sofer concedes that, with regard to recitation of the Pesukei de-Zimra in the vernacular, "I, too, would say that it is not such a terrible thing." However, he pointedly questions Chorin's ultimate agenda. If most congregants are able to master some Hebrew there is no need to make specious distinctions and therefore, he queries, why does Chorin "not direct them to study the holy tongue? After all, they do study the languages of the nations."[65]

61 Auerbach, Geschichte, 219–221.
62 This responsum is published in L. Wreschner, "Rabbi Akiba Eger's Leben und Wirken," Jahrbuch der Jüdisch-Literarischen Gesellschaft 3 (1905), 75–77 and in Likkut Teshuvot ve-Ḥiddushim mi-Rabbi Akiva Eger (Bnei Brak, 1968), 11–13.
63 Eleh Divrei ha-Berit, 27–28.
64 See, for example, [Meyer Israel Bresselau,] Ḥerev Nokemet Nekom Berit (Hamburg, 1819), 15; Chorin, Davar be-Itto, 46–47, and Ein Wort, 43–44; and David Caro, Berit Emet (Dessau, 1820), 52.
65 Eleh Divrei ha-Berit, 8. Jakob J. Petuchowski, Understanding Jewish Prayer (New York: Ktav, 1952), 52, concedes that the hidden agenda of Reform exponents is evidenced by the fact

An unwillingness to veer from the traditional use of Hebrew in statutory prayer does not necessarily imply that rabbinic authorities were insensitive to the advantages of self-expression in a language in which an individual is fully conversant. One of the most intransigent halakhic discussions regarding acceptability of prayer in the vernacular is that of R. Abraham Lowenstamm of Emden.[66] Yet even R. Lowenstamm explicitly adds that, following recitation of the statutory prayers, every individual should feel free to address personal prayer, thanksgiving or supplication as moved by one's spirit in any form one chooses. In offering such private prayer one should take pains that one's language be both pure and clear as befits supplication addressed to a monarch and "Of course, a prayer or thanksgiving such as this must necessarily be said in the language one understands and not in a language one does not understand, even if it is in the holy tongue."[67]

The importance of fluency and understanding in prayer was particularly well appreciated by the hasidic teacher R. Nahman of Bratslav. Although he cannot be described as emblematic of mainstream rabbinic or even hasidic thought, R. Nahman's teachings are much revered in Orthodox circles. R. Nahman urged his followers to address supplications to the Almighty daily in the language in which they were accustomed to speak. Especially when the "channels of prayer" are clogged or blocked, asserted R. Nahman, there is a need to use one's native language in order to burst the dam. R. Nahman extolled the virtue of solitude and recommended seclusion in a room or a field for a designated period of time for the purpose of engaging in solitary communion the more readily to attain single-minded devotion in service of God. R. Nahman explicitly advised:

> This prayer and conversation should be in the vernacular, Yiddish,[68] since you may find it difficult to express yourself fully in the holy tongue

that they did not make any attempt to encourage adult study of Hebrew; their obvious intent was to propagate an ideology that would divorce Judaism from its nationalistic foundations.

66 Tzeror ha-Ḥayyim (Amsterdam, 1820), "Lashon Esh," 28a-35b and "Safah Nokhriyah," 42a-53b. The second edition of Tzeror ha-Ḥayyim (Ujhely, 1868), with different pagination, has been reproduced in an offset edition (Brooklyn, 1992).

67 Tzeror ha-Ḥayyim, 52b.

68 The Hebrew text reads "be-lashon ashkenaz (be-medinatenu)," i.e., "in the German language (in our country)." The reference is obviously to Yiddish. See "Or Zoreaḥ," 4, published as an addendum to Ḥayyei Moharan (Brooklyn: Moriah Offset, 1974), where, in discussing R. Nahman's advocacy of personal prayer in the vernacular, the term "prost Yiddish," i.e., simple Yiddish, is employed.

[Hebrew]. Furthermore, since we do not customarily speak the holy tongue, your words would not come from the heart. But Yiddish, our spoken language and the one in which we converse, more readily engages the emotions, for the heart is more attracted to Yiddish. In Yiddish we are able to talk freely and open our hearts and tell God everything, whether remorse and repentance for the past, or supplications for the privilege of coming closer to Him freely from now on, or the like, each of us according to his own level. Try carefully to make this a habit, and set aside a special time for this purpose every day. ...

Even if you occasionally fumble for words and can barely open your mouth to talk to Him, that in itself is [still] very good, because at least you have prepared yourself and are standing before Him, desiring and yearning to speak even if you cannot. Moreover, the very fact that you are unable to do so should become a subject of your discussion and prayer. This in itself should lead you to cry and plead before God that you are so far removed from Him that you cannot even talk to Him, and then to seek favor by appealing to His compassion and mercy to enable you to open your mouth so that you can speak freely before Him.

Know that many great and famous *tzaddikim* relate that they reached their [high] state only by virtue of this practice. The wise will understand from this how important such practice is and how it rises to the very highest levels. It is something that everyone, great or small, can benefit from, for everyone is able to do this and reach great heights through it.[69]

Doubtless as a result of their distrust of the motives of protagonists of Reform, rabbinic respondents who addressed the issue of prayer in the vernacular tended, at times, to overstate their opposition. A prime example is the *Tzeror ha-Ḥayyim* of R. Abraham Lowenstamm of Emden. R. Lowenstamm's monograph stands out as the most systematic discussion of the halakhic questions raised by the innovations of the Hamburg Temple. However, although his halakhic analyses are comprehensive and his principal theses are

---

69 *Likkutei Moharan, Tinyana* (New York, 1958), no. 25, 301. The translation is taken from Lamm, *Hasidism*, 198–199. See also *Ḥayyei Moharan*, II, "Shivḥei Moharan, ma'alat ha-hit-boddedut," nos. 3–4, 45, in which it is reported that R. Nahman saw merit in utter simplicity in personal supplication, in the manner of a child turning to a parent or a person approaching a friend, and that he asserted that if one is but able to utter the words *"Ribbono shel Olam"* as a plea, that alone is beneficial. Cf. R. Yonatan Eybeschutz, *Ya'arot Devash* (Lemberg, 1863), pt. 2, 4a, who recommends recitation of a private confession or *viduy* in the vernacular.

cogent, his analogies and justifications are, at times, weak. Thus, in emphatic rulings confirming the necessity of retaining Hebrew as the language of prayer, R. Lowenstamm declares that accurate translation into Western European languages is not at all feasible with the result that it is entirely impossible to fulfill one's obligation with regard to prayer by reciting the *Amidah* in the vernacular.[70] Other authorities are careful to note that one who cannot read Hebrew but prays in the language he understands fulfills his duty.[71]

Addressing the question of alteration of the text of statutory blessings and prayers, R. Lowenstamm focuses particularly on the contention of the innovators that their motive for change was the desire to increase devotion and spirituality and on their claim that if the wording of prayers and blessings were to be in closer consonance with the usage of the time, prayer would become more meaningful to contemporary worshipers and the atmosphere of the services would be enhanced. R. Lowenstamm stresses that the precise wording of prayer was meticulously chosen by inspired sages whose intent was to find the vocabulary most perfectly attuned to spiritual requests. Those saintly teachers plumbed the wondrous secrets and mysteries of the metaphysical world, knew exactly how to relate them to human concerns, and understood how best to find intelligible language to describe an unknowable God. Later generations, lacking comparable wisdom, must needs rely on, and be guided by, those saintly and inspired sages.[72]

R. Lowenstamm then offers a much more dubious argument in suggesting that the matter may be understood by analogies to two separate situations. A physician prescribes various medicines and serums for a patient. Bystanders lacking medical sophistication, who neither know the properties of the medicaments nor appreciate the nature of the disease, should hesitate to tamper with the physician's prescriptions even if, for whatever reason, those prescriptions are not to their liking. Or, to take a different example, a commoner finding himself a stranger at the royal court would do well to follow the protocol and

---

70 *Tzeror ha-Ḥayyim*, 49a-b.

71 See, for example, R. Samson Raphael Hirsch, *Horeb: A Philosophy of Jewish Laws and Observances*, trans. Isidor Grunfeld, 4th ed. (New York: Soncino, 1981), no. 688, 544 and 547, who carefully stipulates that a person may pray in the vernacular only "as long as he faithfully mentions all the essential parts of prescribed forms of prayer." See his further remarks concerning *Shema* and the Torah reading. *Horeb* is noteworthy for the precision and meticulousness with which halakhic rulings are formulated. Cf. R. Tzevi Hirsch Chajes, *Minḥat Kena'ot* in *Kol Sifrei Maharatz Ḥayes*, vol. 2 (Jerusalem: Divrei Ḥakhamim, 1958), 983–984.

72 *Tzeror ha-Ḥayyim*, "Siftei Yeshenim," 20b.

instructions of the king's trusted courtiers. Aware of the obvious counterarguments, R. Lowenstamm seeks to deflect them. He admits that the selfsame examples may be employed to demonstrate the very opposite conclusion. Medicine has changed over the centuries and remedies that were once deemed beneficial are no longer in vogue. Changes have occurred in royal courts as well; in modern times rulers eschew pomp and ceremony and have adopted a far less formal mode of conduct in interaction with their subjects. In a rather feeble rebuttal, R. Lowenstamm avers that physical illnesses rather than medications have changed, whereas with regard to maladies of the soul such change has not occurred. With regard to the second analogy, he declares that one cannot possibly compare temporal kings who, as human beings, are prone to change, to the King of Kings before whom our conduct must always reflect an unchanging standard of reverence and awe.[73] Of course, in offering that final debater's point, R. Lowenstamm vitiates his own analogy. If there can be no comparison between human monarchs and the Deity in terms of present-day conduct, the analogy may be equally flawed with regard to comportment of a bygone era.

R. Tzevi Hirsch Chajes, known as *Maharatz Ḥayes*, presents a detailed discussion of various technical halakhic questions with regard to prayer in the vernacular and adds the comment that, by eschewing Hebrew, Reform leaders sinned greatly in sundering the firm bond that exists among Jews dispersed to all corners of the world

> who are yet united and intertwined with one another through the medium of the Hebrew language that is understood by them since they pray in it. This alone remains to us as a portion from all the precious things that we had in days of yore. And now these villains come to rob us of even this ornament so that there will not remain with us anything at all that can testify to the magnitude of the holiness of our people. The danger threatens that with this conduct the entire Torah will also be forgotten even from those few who yet occupy themselves with it.[74]

Maharatz Ḥayes points to an important historical precedent in the conduct of Jews at the time of Ezra. The exiles who returned from Babylon had become habituated to the language of their host country and in a relatively brief period of time had forgotten Torah and mitzvot to the point that they were no

---

73   Ibid., 20b-21a.
74   *Minḥat Kena'ot*, 984 n.

longer familiar even with the manner of celebrating the festivals and the sanctity of the Day of Atonement. Ezra sought to restore the Torah to its glory and it was precisely for that reason that Ezra introduced the weekday public reading of the Torah and, together with the Men of the Great Assembly, established a uniform liturgy. It was in this manner that Ezra assured the continuity of the Torah:

> This is the principal cause that has sustained our ancestors and us so that the Torah is yet our portion in all its details. Those … who call themselves Reformers wish to uproot everything. From this alone [abandonment of Hebrew] it is evident that their entire aim is to erase from us anything that has a connection to our holy Torah in order that we may join and make common cause with the nations in whose midst we dwell. If their spirit were loyal to the people of Israel and its God, as they constantly dare to claim in their deception … they would not dream of a ruinous matter such as this.[75]

R. Chajes emphasizes that the preservation of Torah is inextricably bound with preservation of the holy tongue. Citing the talmudic comment, *Megillah* 10b, "'and I will cut off from Babylon the name and remnant' (Isaiah 14:22)— This is the writing and the language," *Maharatz Ḥayes* concludes, "If the populace will become accustomed to pray in the language of the country in which they live, then in a short time there will be forgotten from us the writing and the language in which the Torah is written. And the Torah, what will become of it?"[76]

In one of the most inspiring passages of *Horeb*,[77] R. Samson Raphael Hirsch, advancing beyond the technical halakhic issues posed by the question of prayer in the vernacular, addresses the broader dimensions of the problem and its fundamental significance for the "spirituality" of the Jewish people. R. Hirsch's trenchant remarks reflect three fundamental points:

1. Familiarity with Hebrew is a primary educational goal. It is the first and earliest duty of a father to assure that his child become familiar with the Hebrew language of prayer. For the community, this is a *sine qua non* for preservation of its heritage.
2. Many authorities had pointed out that translation, by its very nature, must be inexact and that nuances of expression cannot be preserved.

---

75 Ibid., 984 n.
76 Ibid., 984 n.
77 *Horeb*, no. 688, 544–547.

Therefore, prayer in the vernacular leads to a loss of the benefit of the mysteries and the *tikkunim* (mystical effects) incorporated by the Sages in their prayers. R. Hirsch incisively points out that even more is at stake. The Hebrew liturgy constitutes the repository of Israel's collective religious-national thought. There is no adequate translation that is able to capture all the nuances of this world of thought and aspiration. Supplanting Hebrew with any other language, he argues, may lead to introduction into divine worship of concepts alien to Judaism with the result that foreign ideology may gain credence and even acquire an undeserved aura of sanctity.

3. Individuals have obligations to the community. Prayer in the vernacular thwarts the educational goals of the Sages and removes a principal bulwark against assimilation. In contrast, prayer in Hebrew on the part of each individual leads to the fulfillment of communal educational goals and to spiritual elevation of the community. Abandonment of Hebrew by the community, writes Hirsch, would "tend to drag down to our own level that which should raise us."[78]

In encouraging the community to be steadfast in their loyalty to the Hebrew language in prayer, R. Hirsch stresses the role of a community *qua* community and affirms his faith in the future:

A community is not in truth as a single individual. The individual may and should consider his specific circumstances; he may and should use the means which are to hand as a help in his weakness. A community, however, has to consider the future generations in everything that it does, for a community is eternal and can always be rejuvenated. A community as a community is never incapable of fulfilling its task. When the older ones cannot do it, then the younger generation enters into the ranks of the community, and in twenty years or so the general body can be rejuvenated and strengthened, the younger generation achieving that which the older one did not attain. The community carries all the sanctities of Israel for the future generations. It must therefore beware of undermining what is by no means the least important pillar of the community—namely, *Avodah*, which is communal prayer in the holy tongue."[79]

---

78 Ibid., 546.
79 Ibid., 546.

In a complete *volte face*, at the present time, virtually all Reform spokesmen repudiate the negative attitude of classical Reform vis-à-vis Hebrew. Poignant is the fact the arguments they now proffer echo precisely those of Orthodox rabbis of a century and a half ago.[80]

The trend toward reversal was already clearly evident in the 1970s in the writings of the historian of Reform liturgy, Jakob Petuchowski. Petuchowski writes appreciatively of the genius of the Hebrew language in conveying a wide variety of meaning in a few words with the result that, for the Hebraist, prayer provides a rich spiritual and intellectual experience. Petuchowski adds that even for those who do not understand the language, prayer in Hebrew affords a glimpse of what they readily perceive to be a holy language, a language that conveys an intimation of transcendence.[81] Writing from a post-Auschwitz perspective, Petuchowski endorses prayer in the vernacular only as a transient arrangement dictated by necessity while cautioning that vernacular prayer "must never become an ideology."[82]

More recently, an outspoken critic of Mordecai Kaplan's prayerbook revisions, Alan W. Miller of Manhattan's Society for the Advancement of Judaism, asserts bluntly, "The entire effort by Jews to reshape the classical Jewish liturgy since the nineteenth century has been, in my considered judgment, a huge mistake."[83] Recognizing that a radical change in our understanding of language has taken place, Miller observes:

> For the Jew to pray in English—as opposed to study or to teach in English—is to incorporate automatically the value system of that language into his worship. If we have learned anything from modern linguistics it is that no language is transparent. All language is ideological ... as Marshall McLuhan would say: "The medium is the message. ..."[84]

---

80 Before reintroduction of Hebrew had gained popularity in Reform circles, Solomon B. Freehof authored an elementary text, *In the House of the Lord: Our Worship and our Prayer Book* (New York: Union of American Hebrew Congregations, 1951), for use in supplementary religious schools. In moving words (140–143), Freehof presents precisely the argument of R. Samuel Eger for retention of Hebrew as the bond joining Jews into a common fraternity. However, Freehof takes it for granted that English will also be used extensively during the services.

81 Petuchowski, *Understanding Jewish Prayer*, 47–48.

82 Ibid., 53–54.

83 Alan W. Miller, "The Limits of Change in Judaism: Reshaping Prayer," *Conservative Judaism* 41, no. 2 (Winter 1988–89), 27.

84 Ibid., 27.

... We must go back, in all humility ... to the sources. ... To pray as a Jew is to talk as a Jew. Without a thorough grounding in that language [Hebrew], prayer may evoke or edify, but it will bear no relationship to the past, present or future of a viable ongoing Jewish people.[85]

MUSIC

The power of music in arousing the religious spirit has always been acknowledged in Judaism. Prayer was frequently accompanied by song ("to hearken unto the song and the prayer," I Kings 8:28) and the Temple service incorporated elaborate musical components. Speaking of the prophet Elisha, Scripture tells us that music was a catalyst for the prophetic spirit: "*Ve-hayah ke-nagen ha-menagen ve-tehi alav yad Ha-Shem*"—"And it came to pass when the minstrel played, the hand of the Lord came upon him" (II Kings 3:15). In the striking hasidic interpretation of R. Dov Ber of Mezritch this passage is rendered: "When the music and the minstrel became a unitary whole [that is, when the music, *ke-nagen*, became the minstrel, *ha-menagen*], then the hand of the Lord came upon him." When musician and music fuse, inspiration is present.[86]

Nonetheless, there are forms of music that are inherently inappropriate in a synagogue. In Germany the dispute over the use of the organ in the synagogue became the defining issue dividing traditionalists and the Reform elements. Introduction of the organ at services in Seesen and later in Berlin, Hamburg, and Budapest was one of the earliest Reform innovations and was followed in subsequent decades in many cities in Germany, Hungary, Austria, England, and the United States. Eventually, the growth and spread of Reform could be marked by the rising number of "organ synagogues," of which there

---

85 Ibid., 28. A recent call for revitalization of Reform worship services was issued by Eric H. Yoffie, president of the Union of American Hebrew Congregations (UAHC) at the 65th General Assembly of UAHC, in his presidential sermon, "Realizing God's Promise: Reform Judaism in the 21st Century" (New York: UAHC, December 18, 1999). Yoffie advocates "a new Reform revolution" (p. 2) that emphasizes the primacy of Hebrew and the promotion of a vigorous program of adult Hebrew literacy. Yoffie states that Hebrew, as the sacred language of Jews, is "part of the fabric and texture of Judaism, vibrating with the ideas and values of our people" and that "absence of Hebrew knowledge is an obstacle to heartfelt prayer" (p. 4). Missing from this positive statement is acknowledgment of the steadfastness of the Orthodox community that preserved Hebrew prayer so that, in R. Hirsch's words, "the general body can be rejuvenated and strengthened."

86 See Aaron Marcus, *Ha-Ḥasidut*, trans. into Hebrew from German by M. Schonfeld (Tel Aviv: Netzah, 1954), 84.

were more than thirty in the United States by 1868[87] and one hundred and thirty in Germany by the early twentieth century.[88]

The halakhic question is threefold: Is instrumental music permissible at worship services; if yes, is it permissible to make use of the instrument on the Sabbath; and, finally, may the instrument be played by a Jew on the Sabbath? With regard to use of the organ an additional question arises, namely, since this instrument is characteristically used in church services, is its use in the synagogue proscribed as a distinctively gentile practice prohibited by Leviticus 18:3? A host of halakhic authorities ruled against use of the organ at any time and against use of any musical instrument on the Sabbath, even when played by a non-Jew.[89]

Initially, Reform sympathizers permitted the use of the organ on Sabbath but only if played by a non-Jew.[90] In his *Davar be-Itto*, Chorin expounds on the effect of music in enhancing worship and promoting spirituality. Reiterating his previously expressed decision[91] permitting use of the organ, Chorin disdainfully dismisses R. Mordecai Benet's assertion that instrumental music accompanying prayer does not constitute fulfillment of a mitzvah.[92] Even someone "who understands but a little of the wisdom of the ways of the soul," writes Chorin, "must admit that the sound of an instrument has the power and force to dominate the powers of the soul, whether for joy or sadness, or whether

---

87 Meyer, *Response*, 251.

88 Ibid., 184.

89 The earliest discussions are found in *Eleh Divrei ha-Berit*, 1, 5, 18, 23, 25, 28–31, 50, 61, 76, 81, and 85; *She'elot u-Teshuvot Ḥatam Sofer*, vol. 6, nos. 84, 86, and 89; and *Tzeror he-Ḥayyim*, "Kol ha-Shir," 1a-6b. R. Chajes, in a subsequent discussion, *Minḥat Kena'ot*, 988–990, is unequivocal in ruling that it is forbidden to utilize the services of a non-Jew to play the instrument on Sabbath. R. Chajes deemed employment of a non-Jew for that purpose not only to be halakhically prohibited but also unseemly in that "it is not befitting for a non-Jew to take part in a service that is not in accordance with his belief." Cf. R. Abraham Sutro, "Be-Mah she-Ḥiddshu ha-Mitḥadshim be-Inyanei Bet ha-Knesset," *Shomer Tziyyon ha-Ne'eman*, no. 144 (5 Shevat 5613), 287 and *Shomer Tziyyon ha-Ne'eman*, no. 217 (4 Shevat 5616), 433. A later treatment of this issue is included in R. David Zevi Hoffmann, *Melammed le-Ho'il*, part 1, no. 16; see also R. Yehi'el Ya'akov Weinberg, *Seridei Esh* (Jerusalem: Mossad Harav Kook, 1962), vol. 2, no. 154; and R. Abraham Isaac ha-Kohen Kook, *Oraḥ Mishpat* (Jerusalem: Mossad Harav Kook, 1985), 49–50. The discussion of Akiva Zimmermann, *Sha'arei Ron: Ha-Ḥazzanut be-Sifrut ha-She'elot u-Teshuvot ve-ha-Halakhah* (Tel Aviv: Bronyahad, 1992), 21–46, focuses on the dispute over use of organs in Hungarian synagogues. See also Abraham Berliner, *Ketavim Nivḥarim* (Jerusalem: Mossad ha-Rav Kook, 1963); vol. 1, 173–87.

90 *Nogah ha-Tzedek*, 3–28.

91 Ibid., 21.

92 *Eleh Divrei ha-Berit*, 15.

also to give thanks, pray and sing the kindnesses and praises of God."[93] Not only is instrumental music as an accompaniment to prayer absolutely permissible, Chorin avers, but it will serve as a means of enticing many of those who have abandoned the synagogue to return. In the German section of this work, Chorin makes the sweeping statement that whatever enhances the religious spirit is not halakhically forbidden and music obviously arouses religious consciousness. Moreover, he declares, the assertion that a Christian religious practice may be proscribed on the basis of Leviticus 18:3 is not to be countenanced since that prohibition applies only to pagan ceremonies. In acid tones Chorin disparages the rabbinic establishment that disputes those views, is not open to rational argument, and, by means of ban, bell, book and candle, exercises unchallenged tyranny over the community.[94]

Delegates to the Second Reform Rabbinical Conference in Frankfurt unanimously affirmed that the organ "may and should be played by a Jew on the Sabbath."[95] During the discussion concerning the organ that took place at the Frankfurt Conference, Samuel Holdheim expressed the conviction that the contemporary synagogue with its devotional inwardness is of a loftier character than the sacrificial services it replaces. If the sacrificial service involved no desecration of the Sabbath, then certainly, argued Holdheim, instrumental music accompanying present-day services involves no desecration of the Sabbath.[96]

Proponents of the organ argued heatedly—if not very convincingly—that this instrument alone has the potential to transform the quality of worship services. Delivering a lengthy report on the question of the organ to the Frankfurt Conference on behalf of the commission on liturgy, Leopold Stein ascribed well-nigh wondrous attributes to the instrument. It might be inadvisable,

---

93 *Davar be-Itto*, 47.

94 *Ein Wort*, 42–44.

95 *Protokolle*, 151.

96 Ibid., 150. Declaring that the organ "may and should" be played on Sabbath by a Jew, Holdheim stated: "Activity that serves for such enhancement of divine worship cannot at all be biblically proscribed. We have virtually unanimously removed from our prayers the plea for return to Jerusalem and the reinstituting of the sacrificial cult and have thereby clearly stated that our houses of worship are equal to the Temple in Jerusalem ... that our divine worship, with its inwardness, is higher than the sacrificial cult, replaces it and renders it superfluous for all future time." Holdheim's statement, uttered with perfect aplomb, did not meet with any protest on the part of his colleagues at the Conference. Although present-day Reform leaders express an attachment to the Land of Israel, these sentiments have never been accompanied by affirmation of the role of the Temple. Consequently, there is a painful incongruity in current vociferous Reform demands for unimpeded access to worship at the *Kotel* for formal Reform services.

he averred, to introduce the organ into the not-yet-reconstituted worship services. Yet,

> introduction of the organ in the synagogue, even though it is not advisable [at present], is still *necessary*. For no service needs elevation as much as ours, during which somnolence and nonchalance are predominant. There is no more exalting means of encouraging devotion than the music which issues from that ... grand instrument.[97]

That emphasis on the putative role of the organ bordered on the absurd may be seen from the detailed record of the Conference proceedings. At the conclusion of the extensive report of the commission on liturgy, Jospeh Maier stated categorically that "without an organ an impressive and dignified divine service is impossible" and, consequently, "the commission has deemed [use of] of the organ in the synagogue not only permissible but *dringend nothwendig* (urgently necessary)."[98]

In the United States Isaac Mayer Wise introduced an organ in his temple in Cincinnati in 1855. Admitting that several years earlier such a step would have been considered "heretical," Wise championed the organ as a "Jewish instrument" commonly used in synagogues in Germany.[99] Contending that it was particularly suited for the expression of religious emotion, Wise termed the pipe-organ "the sublimest instrument of the world. ... It is not so much a single instrument as a multitude of them, dwelling together—a cathedral of sounds within a cathedral of service."[100]

These encomia notwithstanding, use of the organ continued to engender heated controversy even in Reform circles.[101] Many individuals continued to

---

97 *Protokolle*, 328.

98 Ibid., 316.

99 *The American Israelite* 1, no. 45 (May 18, 1855), 356.

100 *The American Israelite* 5, no. 49 (June 10, 1859), 389. For a report on opposition to introduction of the organ in the United States see I. Harold Sharfman, *The First Rabbi: Origins of Conflict Between Orthodox and Reform* (n.p.: Pangloss Press, 1988), 379–388. Sharfman, 383, cites (without source) the retort of Julius Eckman, spiritual leader of Temple Emanuel of San Francisco, when asked whether a Jew may play the organ on the Sabbath: "Fifty years hence our successors will wonder more at the question than at the reply." Ironically, Eckman's prophecy has been fulfilled but hardly in the manner that he anticipated.

101 See the bibliographic references in Philipson, *Reform Movement*, 436 n. 95. See also Phyllis Cohen Albert, *The Modernization of French Jewry: Consistory and Community in the Nineteenth Century* (Hanover, NH: Brandeis University Press, 1977), 264 and 290, for brief references to the situation in France where introduction of the organ continued to arouse

express discomfort with an obvious emulation of church practice.[102] Among protagonists of Reform, the more conservative admitted openly that the organ's Christian associations were undeniable. Isaak Noa Mannheimer stated forthrightly:

> I would never figure on an organ, even if all outward objections against it were to cease. I admit that the sound of the organ, like the sound of bells, has become too much a characteristic of the Christian church, and it is, therefore, offensive to the Jew. Honestly, in the five years since I have become unaccustomed to the sound of the organ, it would no longer quite suit my own feelings.[103]

In a moving reflection on prayer, Rabbi Joseph B. Soloveitchik notes that overemphasis on an external aesthetic is alien to the mood of the synagogue and that organ music is not only halakhically objectionable but that it conjures a spirit foreign to the traditional "worship of the heart":

> From a musical viewpoint the forms developed by the generations lack perfect structure. The Jewish melodic formula is often marked by the absence of strict form, and by sudden leaps and bounds. One who seeks harmonies and euphonies in the tunes of Jewish prayer is destined to disappointment. What can be found is stychic eruption of feeling.... Unlike the Church, Jewish Synagogues never developed architecture or decorative means with which to enchant man, to anesthetize him into a supernatural mood. They never created the illusion of standing before God when the heart seeks Him not, when the heart is, in fact, hard as stone, cruel and cynical. Our Synagogues were never in the dominion of half-darkness; the

---

opposition although it was endorsed by many delegates to the 1856 Paris rabbinical conference convened by Grand Rabbi Salomon Ullmann. In the United States controversy over introduction of the organ led to a court battle in Charleston in 1844. That incident involved a struggle over even more fundamental changes; the organ was simply emblematic of the underlying friction. See Allan Tarshish, "The Charleston Organ Case," *American Jewish Historical Quarterly* 54, no. 4 (June, 1965), 411–449.

102 Use of a guitar as an instrumental accompaniment has become the practice in a number of present-day Reform congregations. Restrictions pertaining to use of a musical instrument on the Sabbath apply to the guitar no less so than to other instruments. However, as a religiously neutral artifact of popular culture not identified with church services, the halakhic odium associated with use of the organ does not extend to the guitar.

103 Cited in Plaut, *Rise*, 44.

clear light of the sun was never hidden by narrow stained-glass windows. There never echoed the rich, polyphonic strains of the organ, and the song of the mixed choir, hidden from the eyes of worshippers, in order to create a mysterious, unworldly, mood. They never tried to extract the Jew from reality, to introduce him to spirits. To the contrary: they always demanded that prayer be continuous to life and that in it man confess the truth. For this reason the Catholic-style dramatization of prayer is so utterly alien to our religious sense, therefore the great opposition of Halakhah to so-called modernization of prayer services which erases the uniquely original in "worship of the heart."[104]

Once welcomed as the hallmark of Reform innovation, the organ has lost its popular appeal. In Great Britain, the West London Synagogue and Manchester's Park Place Synagogue both installed organs in 1858.[105] In recent years, however, an increasing number of Britain's Reform synagogues have abandoned the instrument. In a brief journalistic survey of attitudes in the British Reform movement, Simon Rocker cites reactions such as "...we prefer congregational singing. Our performances may be less polished but they are more *heimeshe*, [with an organ] the congregation was quite passive. ... [Without an organ], there is now more participation and people feel less inhibited." Respondents admitted quite candidly: "... I have always associated organs with churches. ... I'd much rather hear the beautiful voices than an electric whine"; "I suppose it [the organ] has an association with the Church of England"; and "I would say that the congregation is split fifty-fifty in favor and against. The young don't want it. They feel it is anachronistic, untraditional, and doesn't reflect anything Jewish."

Ironically, several British Reform temples have discarded the organ during most services, but retain it for the High Holy Days. A number of clergymen point out that young people, and particularly those who have attended services in Israel without an organ, have a strong preference against use of the instrument. Rodney Mariner, minister of the Belsize Square Reform Synagogue in North-West London, comments on a tension in the congregation over whether or not the instrument enhances services and reports that a growing number of congregants are in favor of its abandonment. However, adds Mariner

---

104 "Jews at Prayer," *Shi'urei Harav: A Conspectus of the Public Lectures of Rabbi Joseph B. Solove-itchik*, ed. Joseph Epstein (New York: Hamevaser, 1974), 27–28.

105 Anne J. Kershen and Jonathan A. Romain, *Tradition and Change: A History of Reform Jews in Britain, 1840–1995* (London: Vallentine Mitchell, 1995), 66; and Meyer, *Response*, 177.

(without a trace of irony), "[t]heir voice is not loud enough to wipe away 150 years of tradition, but it is loud enough to be listened to seriously."[106] Although he was not prepared to take so radical a step as to forego the organ entirely, Mariner deemed the organ too intrusive for use during the *Yom Kippur* services in their entirety. He therefore reserved the instrument for the end of the day, thereby "creating a climax to a day of prayer."

A report of the experiences of the Bournemouth Reform Synagogue is instructive. While they have not phased out use of the instrument altogether, the congregation now offers a once a month organ-less Sabbath morning service. That innovation is the result of a series of events that, Rocker writes, "you might say was an act of God." One winter, on a number of occasions, the organist was homebound because of the snow and unable to participate in the services. After their initial panic, the members of the choir found that the organ-less service was to their liking. The synagogue's minister, David Soetendorp, anticipates dispensing with the organ in the course of time but states that, for the moment, "I wouldn't want to force a revolt. I'm a believer in evolution."[107]

Evolution is apparent in attitudes toward music in the Reform movement in the United States as well. In a groundbreaking address in which he urged Reform Judaism to proclaim a new revolution and reclaim synagogue worship as the movement's foremost concern, Eric Yoffie, president of the Union of American Hebrew Congregations, singled out the role of music as the key to ritual transformation. But, bemoaning the fact that Reform congregants "have lost our voices" and that Reform worship has become "a spectator sport," the music Yoffie seeks to enhance is primarily vocal, not instrumental. He anticipates a spiritual renewal that may be engendered by means of music that is "vibrant, spiritual and community-building" if "the congregation finds its voice."[108]

Apart from the controversy over instrumental music, as early as the mid-eighteenth century, there was considerable discussion in rabbinic writings of the role, whether positive or negative, of song and the precentor.[109]

---

106 The musical tradition of that Reform temple encompasses many of the works of the nineteenth-century German composer Louis Lewandowski set for organ music.

107 Simon Rocker, "Instrumental Break," *The Jewish Chronicle* (London), October 3, 1997, 29.

108 Yoffie, "Realizing," 3.

109 While a certain musical *nusaḥ* (melody or mode) is traditional, there is latitude in halakhah for musical innovation. See Lippmann Bodoff, "Innovation in Synagogue Music," *Tradition* 23, no. 4 (Summer 1988), 90–101. Apart from questions of halakhah, the type of music that is welcomed in the synagogue, or the extent to which it is shunned, deemed inspiring or deemed inappropriate, is often influenced by external cultural trends. Thus some forms of music may be inherently inappropriate because they are overly distracting or are associated

R. Jacob Emden is censorious in the extreme of cantors of his day whose comportment detracted from public worship.[110] At a later date *Maharatz Ḥayes* wrote approvingly of some of the improvements in decorum and the conduct of services in the *Chorshulen*, but inveighed against those locales where innovators instituted halakhically proscribed mixed choirs.[111]

Melody and the role of the prayer leader as a spiritual force are the subjects of a luminous discourse by R. Nahman of Bratslav. R. Nahman emphasizes the need to judge one's fellow compassionately and to perceive the good qualities that are present even in the apparently wicked (and in oneself as well, if for no other reason than that it serves to keep depression at bay!). That concept he finds reflected in the simple meaning of the Psalmist's words "For yet [*od*] a little while and the wicked shall not be; you shall diligently consider his place and it shall not be" (Psalms 37:10), "For yet a little while"—if one spends but a little time ferreting out good qualities in others, "the wicked shall not be"— it will turn out that the wicked are not really wicked after all. A prayer leader is the *shaliaḥ tzibbur*, the messenger and agent of the congregation. As such, R. Nahman points out, the prayer leader should be a person who is capable of representing the entire community and of discerning the positive qualities, that is, the "good notes," of every worshiper. The prayer leader is charged with taking the "good notes" of each and every person and combining them into a melody[112] and only "one who has this noble talent ... who judges everyone charitably, who finds their noble qualities and forms melodies from them ... is fit to be the cantor and *shaliaḥ tzibbur* to stand in prayer before the lectern."[113]

---

with profane matters or with other religions. Cf. *Horeb*, sec. 689, 549. On changing canto-rial styles see also R. Baruch ha-Levi Epstein, *Mekor Barukh* (New York: M. P. Press, 1954), pt. 2, chap. 2, sec. 5, II, 1047–1049 and 1048 n.

110 *Siddur Amudei Shamayim* (Altona, 1745), 27a; *She'ilat Ya'avetz*, I, no. 61; and *Mor u-Ketzi'a* 53. Cf. centuries-earlier criticism of Rabbenu Asher b. Yehiel, *She'elot u-Teshuvot ha-Rosh*, *klal revi'i*, no. 22. *Amudei Shamayim* in the first section of Rabbi Emden's *siddur* printed in Altona, 1745. The citations herein are from an offset of a later unidentified edition published in New York, 1966, entitled *Siddur Amudei Shamayim le-Mahar Ya'avetz*.

111 *Minḥat Kena'ot*, pp. 990–993. The *Chorshulen* were Orthodox synagogues that featured male choirs and promoted decorous and aesthetically pleasing services.

112 In a play on words, R. Nahman adds, in typical hasidic homiletic fashion, that in the Psalm-ist's exclamation, "While I exist [*be-odi*] will I praise the Lord" (Psalms 146:2), the word "*be-odi*" may be rendered as "with *od*," i.e., "I will praise the Lord in prayer with the concept of *od*, which occurs in 'yet but [*od*] a little while and the wicked shall not be,'" meaning that prayer shall be offered with an eye to the good qualities that negate the wickedness of those on whose behalf prayer is offered.

113 *Likkutei Moharan*, I, no. 282. Regarding cantors and melody see also ibid., nos. 3 and 54.

Noteworthy in the context of the ongoing Orthodox-Reform debate over music in the synagogue is a remark found in the commentary to the prayerbook *Iyun Tefilah* of R. Jacob Zevi Mecklenburg, an articulate antagonist of Reform. The book of Psalms closes with a song calling upon an orchestra of musical instruments to join in a crescendo of praise. In the final verse the Psalmist calls out, "Let all souls [*kol ha-neshamah*] praise God, Hallelujah" (Psalms 150:6). *Iyun Tefillah* renders the verse: "Above all should the soul praise God, Hallelujah." Interpreting the word *kol* as connoting completeness and perfection, *Iyun Tefillah* explains the psalm as follows: After enumerating the various musical instruments with which praise is offered to God, the Psalmist employs the expression *kol ha-neshamah* to indicate that "superior in perfection" to instrumental music is the praise offered by the human soul.[114]

DECORUM

Mirabile dictu, there was one matter pertaining to the synagogue regarding which Orthodox and Reform partisans were in agreement: that worship services ought not be marred by unseemly conduct was undisputed; that the synagogue was deficient in this respect was undeniable. The foibles of human nature are such that lapses in decorum at prayer services have been a persistent problem over the ages.[115] But in the period immediately prior to the emergence of the Reform movement this problem was particularly acute.

From the latter part of the seventeenth through the eighteenth centuries, a general deterioration in religious sensibility took place. That deterioration was

---

114 *Iyun Tefillah, Siddur Derekh Ḥayyim im Iyun Tefillah* (Tel Aviv: Sinai, 1954), 80. *Iyun Tefillah* observes that the vocalization of the consonant with a *ḥolom* rather than with a *kametz* supports this interpretation. Cf. *Redak, Psalms, ad loc.,* who comments on the phrase *kol ha-neshamah* [rendering the phrase as if it read *al ha-kol, ha-neshamah*]: "Above all the praises is the praise of the soul and that is contemplation and knowledge of the works of the Lord, may He be blessed, as far as is in the power of the soul while it is yet in the body."

115 On the ubiquitous nature of the problem see Moshe Halamish, "Siḥat Ḥullin be-Bet ha-Knesset: Metzi'ut u-Ma'avak," *Mil'et* II (Tel Aviv, 1984), 225–251. The problem is common and ongoing and has been the subject of many essays and stories. See, for example, Chava Willig Levy, "Why There Was no Gabbai at the Regency Theater," *Jewish Action* 55, no. 1 (Fall 1994), 88 and Wallace Greene, "'In the King's Presence.' Teaching for Tefillah: A Communal Responsibility," *Ten Da'at* 12 (Summer 1999), 60–70. A characteristic anecdote relates of the wealthy mogul who left instructions with a clerk that he not be disturbed in the synagogue on the Day of Atonement unless a certain stock in which he had a considerable investment reached the figure of twenty-five. Summoned to the vestibule to receive the news, he responded, "You are late. Inside they quoted twenty-seven a half hour ago."

reflected in patterns of worship. In some of the smaller towns laxity in attendance at weekday prayer services became commonplace and communal attempts to remedy the situation by means of coercive regulations or by imposition of fines were unsuccessful.[116] Rabbinic writings of that period are replete with reports of chatter and gossip that profaned the solemnity of Sabbath and festival services and of how the synagogue had become an arena for rowdy fights and altercations.[117] R. Jacob Emden testified that "all the news and vain pursuits of the world are known and heard in the synagogue. There is even frivolity and levity, as if it were a gathering place for idlers."[118] If Reform writers were ashamed of the impression such services made on their non-Jewish neighbors, R. Emden was no less forthright in noting that in comparison to the worship service of their Christian compatriots Jewish performance was disgracefully deficient.[119]

Almost a decade before the founding of the Hamburg Temple, Moses Mendelssohn of Hamburg (not to be confused with Moses Mendelssohn of Berlin),[120] a moderate Enlightenment figure and author of *Pnei Tevel* (Amsterdam, 1872), wrote scathingly of the utter disorder prevalent in the traditional synagogue, of the fracas and rowdiness commonly found there, and of the boisterous conversation typical of a fish market.[121] It was this sorry state

---

116 Azriel Shohat, *Im Ḥilufei Tekufot: Reshit ha-Haskalah be-Yahadut Germaniyah* (Jerusalem: Bialik Institute, 1960), 144–45. Shohat (144–45) cites the wry witticism of R. Aryeh Leib Epstein of Königsburg who remarked that the synagogue is desolate, visited only occasionally as if it were a sick person. It has become the custom to visit the synagogue (*le-vaker heikhalo*) in a manner similar to that which the *Shulḥan Arukh* prescribes for visiting the sick (*le-vaker ha-ḥoleh*). Close relatives and friends visit the patient immediately and the more distant visit only after three days; those close to God, i.e., the scholars and the pious, enter immediately while those more distant attend only after three days have elapsed, i.e., on Mondays and Thursdays.

117 Ibid., p. 146 and Halamish, "Siḥat Ḥullin," 229–230.

118 *Siddur Amudei Shamayim*, 27a.

119 Ibid., 26b. A much earlier work by the late twelfth-century figure, R. Judah he-Hasid, *Sefer Ḥasidim*, ed. Judah Wistinetzky (Berlin: Mekitzei Nirdamim, 1891), no. 1589, 389, bemoans the fact that Jews suffer by comparison to non-Jews in terms of comportment at religious services and ibid., no. 224, 78, warns that synagogues in which Jews behave frivolously are fated to fall into gentile hands.

120 "Moses Mendelssohn of Hamburg" is the name chosen for himself by Moses (1781–1867) son of Mendel Frankfurter (1742–1823), R. Samson Raphael Hirsch's paternal grandfather. Although Moses Frankfurter's writings include a biting, satirical denunciation of obscurantists and fanatical opponents of Enlightenment, he was clearly opposed to any actions that would undermine allegiance to rabbinic Judaism.

121 See Noah Rosenbloom, "Ha-Yahadut ha-Mesoratit ve-ha-Reformah kefi shehen Mishtakefot be-'Pnei Tevel' le-Mendelson," in *Sixth World Congress of Jewish Studies* (Jerusalem, 1977), vol. 3, 454–455. Halamish, "Siḥat Ḥullin," 242 n. 101, errs (possibly

of affairs that later prompted him to praise the aesthetic improvements in the worship service introduced by the founders of the Hamburg Temple. In the course of time he was, however, disappointed by the orientation of the Temple leadership and their substantive changes in the liturgy. Ultimately, he concluded that those efforts had not produced the desired result of enhancing religious devotion. Although the Hamburg Temple did not formally abrogate weekday prayer, it was not open during the week; certainly the Hamburg Temple was not seen as encouraging weekday prayer. To the author of *Pnei Tevel*, it appeared that the Sabbath worshipers at the Temple gradually decreased in number and that only on the High Holy Days did the Temple membership turn out in full force. Despite this disappointment, he harbored the hope that the example set by the Hamburg Temple would serve as a spur to the communal leadership and prompt them to institute long overdue improvements in synagogue services.[122]

In this respect the Reform critique was indeed salutary. Traditionalists were prompted to ask themselves: if so many of their coreligionists were attracted to the new-style services, was it simply because they presented a less demanding form of ritual; was it solely because of the prevalent assimilatory trend; or was it because these services were satisfying a deeply-felt need? A recognition that the desire for liturgical change was to be attributed to deficiencies in the services of the traditional synagogue was intimated by R. Eliezer of Triesch in the aftermath of the establishment of the Hamburg Temple. In his second contribution to *Eleh Divrei ha-Berit* he urged his colleagues in Hamburg to examine the nature of their own services and to strive to make synagogue worship more edifying. He found poetic justice and even punishment "measure for measure"

---

confusing Mendelssohn of Hamburg with Mendelssohn of Berlin) in assuming this to be a portrayal of a Reform worship service.

122 Rosenbloom, "Ha-Yahadut ha-Mesoratit," 459–460. Others concurred in the assessment that the Hamburg Temple proved to be uninspiring. Of the Temple's spiritual leaders Moses Moser remarked in a letter to Immanuel Wolf-Wohlwill that one could learn more from a stuffed rabbi in a zoological museum than from a live Temple preacher. See Adolf Strodtmann, *H. Heine's Leben und Werke*, 3rd ed. (Hamburg: Hoffmann and Campe, 1884), vol. I, 326. Cf. Ismar Elbogen, *Jewish Liturgy: A Comprehensive History*, trans. from German into English by Raymond P. Scheindlin (Philadelphia and Jerusalem: Jewish Publication Society, 1993), 306, who errs in attributing this comment to Leopold Zunz. A selection of the engaging Moser correspondence liberally cited in Strodtmann's work has since been published by Albert H. Friedlander, "The Wohlwill-Moser Correspondence," *Leo Baeck Institute Year Book* 11 (1966), 262–99. For the comment regarding the Temple preachers see ibid., 271 and 297 for the original German. I thank Professor Michael A. Meyer for this latter reference.

in the fact that the inroads and successes of Reform were precisely in the areas in which the Orthodox were remiss:

> It is well known that the punishments of the Creator, blessed be He, are measure for measure. Since our many sins have brought it upon us that this breach occurs in matters of the synagogue and prayer we must presume that, heaven forfend, you have not appropriately honored the holy synagogue that is in your noble community. Therefore this trouble has come upon you that they seek to desanctify and profane it entirely, heaven forfend. Indeed, because of our manifold sins, it has become accepted as permissible in several congregations (and, in particular, in provinces of Germany, according to reports) to engage in idle conversation in the synagogue. Great is this stumbling block and at times people even come to shouting and quarreling and that constitutes a grievous sin.[123]

Not content to limit himself to negative self-criticism, R. Eliezer of Triesch exhorted the rabbis and spiritual leaders of the generation to adopt a positive agenda, to institute seminars and lectures devoted to strengthening interpersonal relationships and ethical conduct and to reach out with patience and gentleness, with "a soft expression and intelligent ethical reproof," even to those with whom they had religious disagreements.[124]

Even more explicit was the *mea culpa* in R. Chajes's *Minḥat Kena'ot*. R. Chajes blamed a passive and apathetic Orthodox rabbinate for the spiritual malaise of their congregations. By contrast, he noted, synagogues that had introduced reforms were gaining in numbers because the innovators were concentrating their energies on attracting a following. Their clergy were talented speakers who understood the temper of the times and, above all, were to be commended for expending time on a great deal of "activity and work for the congregation."[125] Writers such as R. Eliezer of Triesch and R. Chajes demonstrate a growing recognition among the Orthodox that the success of Reform institutions was related to lacunae in the existing traditionalist establishment and that efforts must be made to transform the atmosphere of the synagogue, albeit in an halakhic manner, to effect the desired results.

The decision of a number of Orthodox rabbis to officiate in clerical robes was an emulation of a Reform practice perceived by the laity as enhancing the

123 *Eleh Divrei ha-Berit*, 94–95.
124 Ibid., 95–96.
125 *Minḥat Kena'ot*, 1019.

dignity of services. Although disdained by many decisors as a practice that bordered on or actually infringed upon the prohibition of Leviticus 18:3, this innovation was nonetheless adopted by highly respected authorities. Among the prominent rabbinic figures who wore clerical robes were Rabbi Samson Raphael Hirsch[126] and the venerable halakhic scholar Rabbi Seligmann Baer Bamberger. Reportedly, Rabbi Bamberger defended this innovation as a reluctant concession to the liberal sectors of the Würzburg community made in the hope of preventing more serious infractions of Jewish law.[127]

A much more pervasive manifestation of Reform influence upon the traditional synagogue was the introduction of sermons in the vernacular. Ḥakham Isaac Bernays[128] and Rabbi Jacob Ettlinger[129] were the earliest Orthodox rabbis of note to preach in German. At first this development was vigorously opposed, particularly by Hungarian rabbinic authorities,[130] but, gradually, in most countries the vernacular sermon became an accepted feature of Orthodox services.[131]

The positive influence of Reform innovations on decorum in Orthodox synagogues is reflected in the formal synagogue statutes and regulations of the day. In 1810, the Westphalian Consistory over which Israel Jacobson presided published a *Synagogenordnung* (Synagogue Order), an official

---

126 Isaac Heinemann, "Samson Raphael Hirsch: The Formative Years of the Leader of Modern Orthodoxy," *Historia Judaica* 13 (1951), 46–47.

127 Shnayer Z. Leiman, "Rabbi Joseph Carlebach—Wuerzburg and Jerusalem: A Conversation between Rabbi Seligmann Baer Bamberger and Rabbi Shmuel Salant," *Tradition* 28, no. 2 (Winter 1994), 60. Regarding clerical robes see also Shnayer Z. Leiman, "Rabbinic Openness to General Culture in the Early Modern Period in Western and Central Europe," in *Judaism's Encounter with Other Cultures: Rejection or Integration?*, ed. Jacob J. Schacter (Northvale, NJ: Jason Aronson, 1997), 170 n. 56. For a more complete discussion see chapter four of this volume.

128 See Eduard Duckesz, "Zur Biographie des Chacham Isaak Bernays," *Jahrbuch der Jüdisch-Literarischen Gesellschaft* 5 (1907), 298–307.

129 Rabbi Ettlinger's sermons in German date from the very beginning of his rabbinic career. See, for example, *Rede gehalten zur Feuer des höchsten Namensfestes Seiner königlichen Hoheit des Grossherzogs Ludwig von Baden* (Carlsruhe, 1824) and Jacob Aron Ettlinger, Elias Willstätter, and Benjamin Dispeckter, *Predigten, gehalten in den Synagogen zu Karlsruhe und Bühl von den Rabbinats-Kandidaten* (Carlsruhe, 1824).

130 See Rabbi Moses Sofer, *Teshuvot Ḥatam Sofer, Ḥoshen Mishpat*, no. 197; Rabbi Akiva Joseph Schlesinger, *Lev ha-Ivri* (Jerusalem, 1904), part 1, 19a-21b; Rabbi Hillel Lichtenstein, *Teshuvot Bet Hillel* (Satmar, 1908), nos. 34, 35, and 39; "Die Beschlüsse der Rabbiner-Versammlung zu Mihalowitz," *Israelit* 7, no. 32 (August 8, 1866), 521; and Rabbi Moses Schick, *Teshuvot Maharam Shik, Oraḥ Ḥayyim*, nos. 70 and 311.

131 By the mid-twentieth century Rabbi Yehi'el Ya'akov Weinberg, *Seridei Esh*, vol. 2, no. 149, 364, was unequivocal in ruling that, in his day, when the masses were fluent only in the vernacular, there could no longer be any legitimate halakhic objection to delivery of sermons in the language of the country.

pronouncement, roughly equivalent to contemporary by-laws, designed to promote order and decorum.[132] In the ensuing decades similar regulations were adopted by many communities in Germany. Those statutes, which frequently were accompanied by a government imprimatur, were binding upon all synagogues within the community, including the Orthodox. When, as was usually the case, those regulations provided for liturgical reforms as well and were governmentally enforced they became a further source of communal factionalism. However, improvement of decorum in itself was viewed as a *desideratum* by traditionalists.

Most interesting is the fact that R. Hirsch's separatist *Israelitische Religionsgesellschaft* in Frankfurt-am-Main promulgated a *Synagogenordnung* upon the dedication of its own building in 1853 and a revised version in 1874, both of which were patterned upon prototypes enacted by Reform communities.[133] In formulating the detailed and strict rules of conduct enshrined in this code, R. Hirsch was responding to the concern for decorous and dignified behavior in the synagogue but, at the same time, he was meticulous with regard to halakhic practices. Accordingly, the *Synagogenordnung* stipulated a head covering and *tallit* for men and abstention from wearing leather shoes on the Ninth of Av and *Yom Kippur*. However, removal of shoes by *kohanim* prior to recitation of the priestly blessing was permitted only in a designated room. Reacting to similar efforts to enact rules and statutes to enhance decorum, R. Chajes writes it is "clear as the sun" that promulgation of ordinances for that purpose is permissible provided that such ordinances do not encroach upon laws prescribed by the *Shulḥan Arukh*.[134]

Notice should be taken of the Copernican revolution that has taken place with regard to what is considered appropriate synagogue behavior. In the early days of the movement for synagogue reform, Aaron Chorin wrote disparagingly of the "unbecoming swaying and reeling back and forth" and of prayer uttered in a loud, shrill voice and urged that services be purged of such disruptiveness.[135] Subsequently adopted synagogue regulations uniformly required

132 The document was published independently (Kassel, 1810) and also in *Sulamith* 3, no. 1 (1810), 366–80.

133 See Petuchowski, *Prayerbook Reform*, 123–124 and Robert Liberles, *Religious Conflict in Social Context: The Resurgence of Orthodox Judaism in Frankfurt am Main 1838–1877* (Westport, CT: Greenwood Press, 1985), 140–142. For similar regulations enacted by the consistories in France cf. Albert, *Modernization of French Jewry*, 190–191.

134 *Minḥat Kena'ot*, 993 n.

135 *Ein Wort*, 34. Cf. Karla Goldman, *Beyond the Synagogue Gallery: Finding a Place for Women in American Judaism* (Cambridge: Harvard University Press, 2000), who notes the

the worshiper to behave in a seemly manner and to refrain from unnecessary bodily motion. Even in calling individuals to the reading of the Torah there was an attempt to eliminate the coming and going of synagogue officials and to reduce the number of individuals required to leave their pews. In contrast, contemporary Reform writers celebrate the value of movement and dance in conjunction with worship.[136] Admiration for staid churchly decorum has been replaced by appreciation of hasidic warmth and exuberance.

AESTHETICS

In keeping with the desire to present an appealing religious service new emphasis was also placed upon beautifying the synagogue building. The considerations that prompted aesthetic enhancement were purportedly spiritual. However, two innovations in synagogue design introduced by Israel Jacobson in the Seesen Temple in 1810, namely, removal of the *bimah* (also known as *almemor* or *tevah*) the raised platform from which the Torah is read, from the center of the synagogue to the front of the synagogue in proximity to the Ark creating a visual effect similar to that of the church nave leading to the altar and, in more obvious emulation of church edifices, erection of a belfry were changes that bespoke a desire to imitate man rather than to draw close to God.

In an intriguing analysis of different cultural modes of expressing the quest for the numinous in prayer, Professor Lawrence Hoffman suggests that classical Reform's emphasis on imposing architecture, dignified and decorous services, and use of the sonorous organ reflect an approach to the holy in which the transcendent Deity is perceived as awesome, lofty, and distant. This rationalistic approach, Professor Hoffman suggests, was shared by

---

nineteenth-century American Jews' discomfort with "the embarrassing disorder of traditional Jewish worship" characterized by "chaotic behavior and swaying movements" (81). For sources describing the positive effects of swaying in prayer see Bernard M. Casper, *Talks on Jewish Prayer* (Jerusalem: World Zionist Organization Department for Torah Education and Culture in the Diaspora, 1958), 27–28 and Abraham Kon, *Prayer* (London: The Soncino Press, 1971), 38–39. Cf. the satiric comments of Norman Lebrecht, "The Reason Why All Our Shuls Are Swaying," *The Jewish Chronicle* (London), July 13, 2001, 27.

136 See, for example, Michael Swartz, "Models for New Prayer," *Response* 13, no. 1–2 (Fall/ Winter 1982), 35; Arthur Waskow, "Theater, Midrash and Prayer," *Response* 13, no. 1–2 (Fall/Winter 1982), 133 and 136–37; and, more recently, Joseph A. Levine, *Rise and Be Seated: The Ups and Downs of Worship* (Northvale, NJ: Jason Aronson, 2000), 64–65 and 167–68.

European Protestants and early partisans of Reform.[137] The suggestion that the imposing cathedrals, organs, and dignified services of Protestants mirrored this theological perspective of man's relationship to God is cogent. It is, however, questionable whether the motivation of Reform innovators was the product of a similar theological perspective or simply a desire to emulate Christian neighbors.

In defense of the early exponents of Reform it must be stated that the two matters may have been interrelated. A form of self-denigration born of what was perceived as "orientalism"[138] or primitivism in Judaism was clearly operative. They further presumed that what they perceived as a more advanced Western Protestant cultural aesthetic was worthy of emulation as a means of achieving a higher spirituality as well. In stark contrast is the view of R. Jacob Emden that the key to prayer is an individual's appropriate appreciation and understanding of his own self-worth both as a human being and as a Jew. In forceful and unambivalent language Rabbi Emden encourages and exhorts the worshiper to develop feelings of self-confidence and self-assurance. Since prayer can be not only a source of personal benefit but also a matter of cosmic significance, R. Emden emphasizes the import of the worshiper's awareness of the awesome power, and hence the concomitant responsibility, he has as a praying individual: "Let it not be light in his eyes that he is created in the [divine] image and form and the root of his soul is connected with the supernal world. ... If he utters a holy and pure utterance there is inherent in it the power to create effects in the loftiest heavens."[139] Confidence in the power of human prayer, writes Rabbi Emden, should be coupled with particular pride and assurance in one's status as a Jew for "Should we not take pride in this, a great, wondrous pride of which there is none greater?"[140]

Rabbinic authorities had no problem with the general desire to enhance the beauty of synagogue buildings. However, the bell tower and location of the *bimah* did pose halakhic questions. Summoning worshipers to prayer by means of a bell was considered to be a Christological practice forbidden by Leviticus

---

137 Lawrence A. Hoffman, *Beyond the Text: A Holistic Approach to Liturgy* (Indianapolis: Indiana University Press, 1987), 151–162.

138 See Kaufmann Kohler, *Jewish Theology: Systematically and Historically Considered*, augmented ed. (New York: Ktav, 1968), 470–473. See also Kohler on the Bar Mitzvah ceremony and the head covering as "a survival of orientalism," cited in W. Gunther Plaut, *The Growth of Reform Judaism* (New York: World Union for Progressive Judaism, 1965), 312.

139 *Siddur Amudei Shamayim,* 5a.

140 Ibid., 18b.

18:3.[141] The belfry was so obvious a borrowing from Christianity that it never became popular.[142] The more equivocal issue was the location of the *bimah*. Removal of the *bimah* from its central position was advocated by leading Reform spokesmen, including Aub, Geiger, Hess, Herxheimer, Samuel Hirsch, Holdheim, Hamburger, Kahn, Mannheimer, Maier, Philippson, Schwab, and L. Stein.[143]

Although in Germany introduction of the organ was the defining issue in Reform-Orthodox controversies, in Hungary location of the *bimah* became elevated into a question of ideology that became symbolic of the entire struggle for and against Reform. It was in connection with his unequivocal ruling on the impermissibility of shifting the *bimah* from its central position that Ḥatam Sofer applied his oft-quoted aphorism "*ḥadash asur min ha-Torah*"—"innovation[144] [that is, departure from accepted practice] is forbidden by the Torah"[145]—a remark that became a slogan of the traditionalists.

In actuality, this halakhic ruling is the subject of considerable dispute. The halakhic basis for placing the *bimah* in the center of the synagogue is to be found in three rulings of Maimonides: *Mishneh Torah, Hilkhot Tefillah* 11:3; *Hilkhot Ḥagigah* 3:4; and *Hilkhot Lulav* 7:23. While R. Moses Isserles (Rema), *Oraḥ*

---

141 *Minḥat Kena'ot*, 991 n.

It has been incorrectly asserted that Rabbi Yisrael Moshe Hazan, Chief Rabbi of Rome, ruled in favor of an Italian community's intention to build a clock tower with a bell for their synagogue. See the report of Yaakov Friedler, "Spain: Fountainhead of Modernization," *Jerusalem Post*, 17 April, 1992, 1C. In fact, Rabbi Hazan, *Kerakh shel Romi* (Livorno, 1876), no. 1, rules that it is permissible to place a clock that announces the hours in the synagogue courtyard. At the conclusion of his responsum (ibid., 16), he states that although no technical violation is involved he rules emphatically against placing a bell tower on the synagogue building. Rabbi Hazan was wary of Reform innovations and authored *Divrei Shalom ve-Emet* (London, 1856), a response to a British Reform pamphlet and contributed a lengthy letter of protest to the collection of rabbinic condemnations of Reform published in *Kin'at Tziyyon* (Amsterdam, 1846), 3a-17a.

142 The only other German synagogue to feature a bell tower was that in Buchau built in 1839. See Meyer, *Response*, 404 n. 115. Cf. also Michael A. Meyer, "Christian Influence on Early German Reform Judaism," in *Studies in Jewish Bibliography, History and Literature in Honor of I. Edward Kiev* (New York: Ktav, 1971), ed. Charles Berlin, 292–293.

143 Kaufmann Kohler, "Almemar or Almemor," and A.W. Brunner, "Almemar or Almemor, Architecturally Considered," in *Jewish Encyclopedia* (New York, 1906), vol. I, 431 and Leopold Löw, *Gesammelte Schriften* (Szegeden, 1899), vol. IV, 93–107.

144 Use of the term *ḥadash* (new) is a pun based upon the term's denotation of "new" grain that is forbidden as food until an offering from the newly harvested produce is brought on the second day of Passover as prescribed by Leviticus 23:14.

145 *She'elot u-Teshuvot Ḥatam Sofer, Oraḥ Ḥayyim*, no. 28. Cf. R. Jacob Ettlinger, *Abhandlungen und Reden*, 1899), 7–10, on the symbolism of the central *bimah*.

Ḥayyim 150:5, maintains that the *bimah* should be placed in a central position, R. Joseph Karo rules otherwise in his commentary on Maimonides's *Mishneh Torah, Kesef Mishnah, Hilkhot Tefillah* 11:3. He notes that in some places the *bimah* was erected at the western side of the synagogue, "... for its location in the center is not mandatory; everything depends on the place and the time." Accordingly, many authorities viewed placement of the *bimah* in the center of the synagogue as recommendatory rather than mandatory while others ruled that the *bimah* must be centrally located and considered displacement of the *bimah* to be the thin end of the wedge of Reform.[146]

The attitude generally adopted by Orthodoxy today is best reflected in two responsa authored by R. Moses Feinstein.[147] R. Feinstein rules that, in building a synagogue structure, the *bimah* should be placed in the center but that failure to position the *bimah* in the center does not invalidate a synagogue as a place of prayer. In a comment placing the issue in historical perspective, Rabbi Feinstein adds that the stringent attitude ascribed to certain Hungarian rabbinic authorities who forbade prayer in a synagogue in which the *bimah* was not located in the center was based on a *hora'at sha'ah*, an *ad hoc* temporary ruling, as a means of stemming the tide of Reform.[148] The *bimah* controversy is an instance in which a comparatively minor halakhic matter assumed exaggerated significance and, as a focal point of ideological controversy, became the banner around which the opposing forces arrayed themselves.

A far graver halakhic infraction is involved in removal of the *meḥitzah*, the barrier separating the men's and women's sections of the synagogue. If, as noted, use of the organ was the defining issue in Germany and location of the *bimah* the central point of dispute in Hungary, it was in the United States that the question of *meḥitzah* became the *cause célèbre*. The reason for this is not that the gravity of the matter was insufficiently recognized in European countries but that the vast majority of European synagogues, including the Reform and Liberal, did maintain some form of separation of the sexes until well into the twentieth century. It was in the United States that family pews

---

146 See Immanuel Jakobovits, *Jewish Law Faces Modern Problems* (New York, 1965), 43–46. See also *Minḥat Kena'ot*, 992 n. Among the prominent halakhists who prohibit removal of the *bimah* from its central position are R. Abraham Samuel Benjamin Schreiber, *She'elot u-Teshuvot Ketav Sofer, Oraḥ Ḥayyim*, no. 19; R. Judah Aszod, *She'elot u-Teshuvot Mahari Asad, Oraḥ Ḥayyim*, no. 50; and R. Naftali Zevi Yehudah Berlin, *She'elot u-Teshuvot Meshiv Davar*, vol. I, no. 15.

147 *Iggerot Mosheh, Oraḥ Ḥayyim*, vol. II (New York: 1963), nos. 41 and 42.

148 Cf. an illuminating comment on this issue in Naphtali Carlebach, *Joseph Carlebach and His Generation* (New York, 1959), 225–230. For further elaboration see also Leiman, "Rabbi Joseph Carlebach," 58–63.

were first introduced by Isaac Mayer Wise in Albany in 1851 and it was in the United States that mixed seating took root. Wise had long favored elimination of the separate seating of women in a balcony but the actual institution of mixed pews came about fortuitously when Wise's Reform congregation Anshe Emeth purchased a church building that already had family pews and Wise retained them.[149] A contemporary commentator observed that introduction of family pews in Germany would have been "a gross anomaly." Following the model of German churches in which separate seating was the norm, German Reform synagogues continued to maintain separate seating even when the *meḥitzah* was abandoned.[150] In the United States, with the spread of mixed seating to Conservative synagogues as well, the *meḥitzah* became the visible demarcation between Orthodoxy and other denominations.[151] In terms of synagogue design, removal of the *meḥitzah* is the single most significant Reform departure from Jewish law. That change acquires greater significance when it is realized that it was introduced primarily for ideological, rather than aesthetic, reasons.

With regard to questions of synagogue structure and aesthetics in general, R. Chajes's comments on communal priorities are instructive. R. Chajes deems the expenditure of vast sums of money on an imposing edifice rather than on education or care of the needy to be misguided. Indeed, on one occasion he advised a small congregation to pawn the synagogue lamps in order to raise funds to enable individuals to avoid army service. The physical and spiritual welfare of the community, including support of hospitals, freeing captives, assistance to the poor, and establishing institutions for religious education as well as for professional training, he emphasizes, all take precedence over synagogue beautification.[152]

Thus, issues of synagogue design and structure also reflect a system of values. That even aesthetic perception is influenced by one's ideological perspective is evident from a brief passage in Howard Morley Sachar's *The Course*

---

149 Heller, *Isaac M. Wise*, 160 and 213–14.

150 See Meyer, *Response*, 426 n. 107. Jonathan D. Sarna, "The Debate Over Mixed Seating in the American Synagogue," in *The American Synagogue*, ed. Jack Wertheimer (Hanover: Brandeis University Press, 1987), 364, reports that as late as the early twentieth century the Hamburg Temple, bastion of German Reform, refused a one-million-mark donation because the gift was conditioned upon introduction of mixed seating of men and women.

151 Ibid., 380 and 386. For a discussion of the halakhic issues, including responsa in Hebrew and in English translation, see Baruch Litvin, ed. *The Sanctity of the Synagogue* (New York: Spero Foundation, 1959).

152 *Minḥat Kena'ot*, 991.

of Modern Jewish History. In discussing synagogues established in the New World, Sachar notes:

> The variety of functions performed by the synagogue was not always apparent to the outsider. Thus, a Christian traveler who visited Newport's synagogue once commented with sublime misunderstanding: "It will be extremely elegant when completed, but the outside is totally spoiled by a school which the Jews [would] have annexed to it for the education of their children."[153]

That comment eloquently illustrates the influence of ideology upon the aesthetic perception of both the author and the individual he cites.

It is noteworthy that some twentieth-century writers have found the nineteenth-century Reform aesthetic a deterrent to religious spirituality. One of the criticisms of the overall tenor of Reform services centers upon a perception of the temple as a place of worship set apart and unconnected to a vital, living Judaism. One keen twentieth-century critic, Professor Eliezer Berkovits, has pointed to the nomenclature associated with temple worship. Words such as sanctuary, chapel, chants, altar, and holy ark are seen as illustrative of religious services that require consecrated props and take place in an artificial, synthetic atmosphere. In contrast to the functionality of the old-fashioned *shul* with its *tashmishei kedushah, shulḥan,* central *bimah,* and *aron ha-kodesh,* the temple artifacts, claims Berkovits, its clericalism, and its overly solemn dignity reflect an emphasis on an external aesthetic that may hide a religious vacuum. Berkovits remarks that, ironically, the temple architecture, although new and expensive, has rarely resulted in inspired artistry, whereas old synagogues, often simple in design, have become more venerable with increasing age. The ritualism and clericalism of classical Reform worship may be an appropriate style, comments Berkovits, for individuals whose renewed interest in the synagogue is motivated by a desire for conformity or by other sociological and psychological considerations but has little to do with genuine religiosity; rather, it is worship directed to a god shaped in man's own image.[154]

---

153 Howard Morley Sachar, *The Course of Modern Jewish History* (New York: Dell Pub. Co., 1963), 164.

154 See Eliezer Berkovits, "From the Temple to Synagogue and Back," *Judaism* 8, no. 4 (Fall 1959), 303–311; reprinted in Jakob J. Petuchowski, *Understanding Jewish Prayer* (New York: Ktav, 1972), 138–151. It is, of course, the constant use to which the old synagogue testifies that is the source of the veneration it evokes. Cf. the comments of Leon Wieseltier, *Kaddish* (New York: Alfred A. Knopf, 1998), 5: "There are stains in the velvet. In places it

DURATION OF SERVICES

As early as 1796, when the Amsterdam break-away congregation Adath Jeschurun introduced a number of moderate reforms, a major objective of the young intellectuals at its helm was removal of what were viewed as distracting and unnecessary additions to the prayer ritual.[155] Virtually all early Reform spokesmen who focused on liturgical issues advocated streamlining services. Enhancement of worship would be achieved, they believed, if the length of prayer services were to be shortened in order to command the unflagging attention of congregants.[156]

The negative effects of unnecessarily prolonged services are acknowledged by all. In a famous passage included in the introduction to his *siddur*, R. Jacob Emden cites in the name of "early scholars" the adage "Prayer without *kavvanah* (concentration and intentionality) is as a body without a soul."[157] Proceeding to delineate the obstacles to devotion and singlemindedness in prayer, R. Emden points to the stultifying effect of habit and the deadening quality of ritual (which he terms elsewhere as *seremoniyah be-la'az*)[158] performed in a mechanical manner *(mitzvot anashim mi-lumadah)*.[159] If it transpires that "the formula of prayer becomes almost a matter of habit in the constant use of one formula, the *kavvanah* evaporates in its habituation." The net effect of repetition is to heap rote upon rote and for the prayer to become so familiar "that the soul is not excited by it."[160]

R. Emden also recognized length of prayer services as a factor influencing devotion. Bemoaning the distressing "scandalous" proliferation of novel

---

is threadbare. This is an exquisite erosion. It is not neglect that thins these instruments. Quite the contrary. The more threadbare, the better. The thinner, the thicker."

155 Meyer, *Response*, 26; Jaap Meijer, *Moeder in Israel: Een Geschiedenis van het Amsterdamse Asjkenazische Jodendom* (Harlem, 1964), 56–57; and Isaac Maarsen, "Maamar Or ha-Emet," *Otzar he-Ḥayyim*, no. 9 (1933), 110–120.

156 See, for example, Plaut, *Rise*, 49, 155, and 181. See also Albert Cohen, "Nonorthodox Attitudes in French Judaism," 131 and 133. Cf. Geoffrey Alderman, *Modern British Jewry* (Oxford: Clarendon Press, 1992), 35 and Todd M. Endelman, *The Jews of Georgian England 1714–1830: Tradition and Change in a Liberal Society* (Philadelphia: Jewish Publication Society, 1979), 162.

157 *Siddur Amudei Shamayim*, 4b. The aphorism is found in Abarbanel, *Naḥalat Avot* 2:17 and idem, *Mashmi'a Yeshuah* 12:1.

158 *Siddur Amudei Shamayim*, 411a.

159 Isaiah 29:13, lit.: "taught by the precept of men," idiomatically connotes performance of a precept in a mechanical manner.

160 *Siddur Amudei Shamayim*, 5a.

petitionary prayers and *tehinot*, R. Emden notes that were an individual to recite all of those prayers he would have no remaining time for study or gainful employment. He adds that, if with regard to prayer in general there is a cautionary recommendation "Better a little with *kavvanah*,"[161] all the more so does this admonition apply to the verbose additions instituted in latter days whose drawbacks far outweigh their positive effects, whose harm is greater than their benefit, and with respect to which silence is preferable. Prudent communal policy with regard to such petitions, R. Emden advises, is selectivity and brevity.[162] His contemporary, R. Yonatan Eybeschutz, similarly remarks of those who continually mumble an overabundance of supplicatory prayers that, "Without *kavvanah*, any addition is a diminution."[163]

The concept of *tirha de-tzibbura*, or burdening the congregation,[164] has definite halakhic implications. However, from the halakhic standpoint, there obviously exist set parameters and limits to what may legitimately be abridged. In Reform congregations that do not feel bound by Halakhah and the requirements of basic statutory prayer and Torah reading, the question of what constitutes a reasonable shortening of the service remains open. Reform clergy tended to differ in their opinion of what constituted an adequate service. Of more than passing interest is a resolution adopted by the Touro Synagogue of New Orleans in June 1889 requiring that the Sabbath morning ritual be abbreviated to last no longer than one hour, including the sermon.[165]

In this context, it may be apposite to take note of a differing perspective based on an individual idiosyncratic reaction but offering a penetrating observation regarding the atmosphere and environment that foster spiritual responses. Milton Himmelfarb, in a personal memoir describing his own experiences during the time when he attended synagogue on a regular basis to recite *kaddish* in memory of his father, describes the difficulty he experienced in keeping repeated obligatory prayer from becoming routine and perfunctory. He comments:

> But to make the service short will not help us much. I have felt most untouched and unmoved in short services, Reform or near-Reform Conservative or Reconstructionist; and my neighbors have seemed to me equally untouched and unmoved. In fact, lengths have certain advantages.

---

161 *Tur Shulhan Arukh, Orah Hayyim* 1 and *Shulhan Arukh, Orah Hayyim* 1:4.

162 *Siddur Amudei Shamayim,* 2b-3a.

163 *Ya'arot Devash,* pt. 1, 8a.

164 See "Tirha de-Tzibbura," *Encyclopedia Talmudit,* vol. 20, 662–678.

165 Leo A. Bergman, *A History of the Touro Synagogue, New Orleans* (private pub., n.d.), 5.

In a way a long service is like a long poem. You do not want unrelieved concentration and tightness in a long poem; they would be intolerable. Length requires *longueurs*. A good long poem is an alternation of high moments and moments less high, of concentration and relaxation. In our synagogue, the heights may not be very high, but the long service does provide some ascent and descent. The short service tends to be of a piece, dull and tepid.[166]

PIYYUTIM

As noted, the desire to improve decorum and even to shorten the duration of services was heartily endorsed by traditionalists as well. Nor were the innovators on halakhic quicksand in their efforts to eliminate the *piyyutim* or liturgical poetry. However, once the theological battle had been joined on other fronts, any suggestion the innovators made was viewed with suspicion and trepidation.

The debate over recitation of *piyyut*, and particularly over its inclusion in the statutory blessings of the *Shema* and *Amidah*, dates as far back as geonic times.[167] R. Abraham Ibn Ezra's caustic critique of the *piyyutim* of R. Eleazar ha-Kalir[168] and the negative view of Maimonides[169] are well known and widely cited. Over the ensuing centuries recitation of *piyyut* had notable champions as well as fierce detractors. Among latter-day scholars, R. Elijah of Vilna eliminated most inserted *piyyut*[170] whereas R. Eleazar Flekeles was a staunch proponent of retention of all traditional *piyyutim*.[171] R. Flekeles's championship

166 "Going to Shul," *Commentary*, 41, no. 4 (April 1966), 68–69; reprinted in Petuchowski, *Understanding Jewish Prayer*, 159.
167 See the exhaustive and meticulous discussion in Ruth Langer, *To Worship God Properly: Tensions Between Liturgical Custom and Halakhah in Judaism* (Cincinnati: Hebrew Union College Press, 1998), 110–187.
168 Commentary on the Bible, Ecclesiastes 5:1.
169 *Teshuvot ha-Rambam*, vol. II, ed. Joshua Blau (Jerusalem: Mekitzei Nirdamim, 1960), nos. 180, 207, and 254. See also Langer, *Worship*, 153 nn. 167 and 168. Cf. also Maimonides, *Guide for the Perplexed*, vol. I, chap. 59.
170 Exceptions allowed by R. Elijah of Vilna during the *Amidah* include the *piyyutim* of the High Holy Days and the prayers for rain and dew. He also recited the *piyyutim* of festivals and the four special pre-Passover Sabbaths but only after completion of the *Amidah*. See *Ma'aseh Rav*, secs. 127, 163 and 205. *Ma'aseh Rav* was compiled by R. Yissakhar Ber of Vilna and first published in Zolkiew, 1808. The edition of *Ma'aseh Rav* published in Jerusalem, 1987 by Merkaz ha-Sefer incorporates anthologized comments and suggests a halakhic rationale for the practice adopted by the Gaon of Vilna; see 191–192.
171 *Teshuvah me-Ahavah*, I, nos. 1 and 90. The arguments of R. Eleazar Flekeles are based to a significant extent upon the earlier responsum of R. Jair Hayyim Bacharach (d. 1702), *Teshuvot Havot Ya'ir* (Lemberg, 1896), no. 238.

of *piyyut* is not yet tinged by the first glimmerings of the acrimonious battles over prayerbook revision.

Those intent on trimming the services focused on accretions to statutory prayer and consequently, quite naturally, on the *piyyutim*. Their suggestions were usually sweeping in nature. Chorin, who urged "cleansing" the liturgy and removal of *piyyut*, writes:

> Only a few words concerning the second category of prayers (*yotzrot*, *kerovetz*, and *piyyutim*). In the whole Talmud there is not one relevant passage concerning the nonsense of these prayers (if they deserve that appellation at all). They were generally written much later, at the time of the darkest persecutions. They bear the mark of the extreme suppression of the human spirit.[172]

It is in light of such remarks that one must read the pronouncements of authoritative rabbinic figures of the time. For example, in R. Akiva Eger's defense of the *piyyutim* of Kalir, he takes strong exception to Ibn Ezra's criticisms and endorses absolute faithfulness to the time-hallowed Ashkenazi tradition. His forceful remarks are, however, made in the context of a broader denunciation of liturgical innovations and a plea for steadfast following "in the footsteps of our fathers."[173]

Even those halakhists who did not favor retention of *piyyut* were now wary of deletion that might be misinterpreted. R. Tzevi Hirsch Chajes favored eliminating *piyyutim* and noted approvingly that many congregations in Poland and Russia had done so. Yet he counseled that matters be allowed to take their natural course, that rabbis should issue no rulings on the subject and should avoid any publicity lest the untutored become confused and fail to

---

172 *Ein Wort*, 36. Cf. the remarks of Joseph Maier in the preface to his 1861 Stuttgart Prayerbook in which he advocated "total removal" of *piyyutim*: "Science has given the verdict on those additions. They have in part, artistic and, in part, scientific or historical value, but none as far as devotion and edification are concerned. ... [T]hey were to a certain extent a substitute for the sermon. But, since to the joy and refreshment of every truly pious spirit, the sermon has returned to the House of God, the *piyyutim* have completely lost any value. Lest they continue to interfere with the dignified recitation of the prayers, and disturb devotion, their total removal has become a holy duty." Cited in Petuchowski, *Prayerbook Reform*, 161.

173 *Iggerot Soferim*, ed. Salomon Schreiber (Vienna and Budapest: Joseph Schlesinger, 1933), pt. 1, no. 35, 48–49.

distinguish between mere folkways and usages of no halakhic significance and those customs and practices that have the force of law.[174]

A completely different assessment is found in the writings of Rabbis Abraham Lowenstamm and Samson Raphael Hirsch who both sought to portray *piyyut* as a positive element in the liturgy. R. Lowenstamm points to the then recently published felicitous translation and commentary of Heidenheim[175] that render even abstruse and verbally complex poems more readily understandable. Aware of current sensibilities and that the *piyyutim* are "not desirable in our eyes in accordance with the changed responses of this era with regard to aesthetics,"[176] R. Lowenstamm argued that nonetheless the *piyyutim* continue to arouse intense religious emotion even among those who deem them to possess neither stylistic elegance nor linguistic beauty. R. Lowenstamm decries the vagaries of popular taste and notes that fashion trends soon become outdated while classics are timeless. Of attractive new literary creations that sway the masses he writes, "At the first instance of their novelty they delight those who see them; yet after they have been recited two or three times, the ear becomes attuned to them and very quickly does their glory fade. But a moment and they are forgotten."[177] In contradistinction, he avers, the *piyyutim*, composed in antiquity, despite their linguistic failings and the absence of a grace of idiom or felicity of language, are yet dear to the populace and stir the spirit, "drawing us closer to our Father in Heaven, whether because of the holiness embedded in them or because of the greatness and nobility of their composers ... time does not affect them."[178]

A more impassioned defense of *piyyutim* is offered by R. Samson Raphael Hirsch. Responding to the charge that in an era of enlightenment and emancipation it was no longer edifying to recite poetry that spoke of oppression and

---

174 Chajes, *Minḥat Kena'ot*, 992 and idem, *Darkei Hora'ah*, chaps. 6 and 7, in *Kol Sifrei*, vol. I, 238–242. Cf. the quite different response of R. Yosef Stern, *Sefer Zekher Yehosef, Oraḥ Ḥayyim* 19:3–4, who concluded that *piyyut* must be retained lest its abolition be the thin wedge leading to further, unacceptable innovation.

175 Wolf Heidenheim (1757–1832), an exegete and grammarian, established a press at Rödelheim where he published critical editions of the *siddur* and *maḥzor* that are justly acclaimed for their meticulously corrected texts, scholarly commentaries, and accurate translations.

176 *Tzeror ha-Ḥayyim*, "Bi-Yeshishim Ḥokhmah," 37b.

177 Ibid, 37 b. A similar argument ("Their worship will quickly become habitual and insipid") is presented by Solomon Jehuda Leib Rappoport, *Tokhaḥat Megulah* (Frankfurt am Main, 1845), a pamphlet written in response to the Frankfurt Rabbinical Conference, cited in Paul R. Mendes-Flohr and Jehuda Reinharz, *The Jew in the Modern World: A Documentary History* (New York: Oxford University Press, 1980), 172.

178 *Tzeror ha-Ḥayyim*, "Bi-Yeshishim Ḥokhmah," 37b.

persecution, R. Hirsch turns the tables and tauntingly poses the question: is Judaism more secure now or does it face more even pernicious dangers than previously? In the period of the Crusades, when many of the *piyyutim* were composed, Jews were threatened physically, but at that time were there ritual slaughterers who themselves violated the dietary code, butchers who profaned the Sabbath or Jewish schools that fostered abrogation of Jewish law? If the *piyyut* recited between *Pesaḥ* and *Shevu'ot* recalls the physical massacres of our ancestors then, suggests R. Hirsch, it may be appropriate to find in it a resonant plaint regarding spiritual degeneration in an era "in which rabbis among us publicly conferred about how—in a respectable manner—Torah and mitzvot could be buried."[179] R. Hirsch's more trenchant question—one that cannot fail to elicit a shiver in any post-Holocaust reader who recalls that Germany is the venue of this discussion—is, "Has such an era of brightness come to Israel everywhere among the nations that these prayers of lament no longer have a place in the synagogue?"[180]

Spirituality is enhanced, R. Hirsch contends, by arousing intimate empathetic feelings joining Jews into a community of destiny spanning the generations. The crucial mistake, he argues, is to assume that less is always better. It is the error of "Jewish 'Reform' enthroned in robe and hat ... declaring war on *piyyutim* and *yotzerot*" to assume "The prescription for creating devotion? Delete prayers!"[181] Rather, asserts R. Hirsch, acknowledging struggles and sorrows of the past, remembering the sweat and blood, sacrifice and exertions endured to preserve Torah in centuries of "outer and inner *galut*" will create bonds of solidarity and bring to life models of faith.[182]

---

179 *The Collected Writings*, English translation, vol. I (New York and Jerusalem: Philipp Feldheim, Inc., 1984), 138.

180 Ibid., 133.

181 Ibid., 132. Cf. Petuchowski, *Prayerbook Reform.*, 30, who comments on *piyyut* as an expression of *kavvanah* and cites the remarks of Gustav Gottheil, a lone Reform champion of *piyyut*, delivered at the 1869 Israelite Synod in Leipzig: "I fully recognize the rights of the present to change the prayer, but I believe that the religious consciousness of other times also has the right to find expression in our prayers. I do not believe that our time, with its cold rational direction, is especially suitable to create warm, heart-stirring prayers. And for these I would rather go back to the warmer religious sentiment of antiquity, and let it supply us with such prayers. Therefore, I must speak out against the generally condemnatory judgment against *piyyutim*."

182 *Collected Writings*, vol. 1, 138. R. Hirsch denigrated the pedantic academic study of Jewish history and literature then in vogue that he saw as breeding religious sterility. He was particularly unimpressed by scholarly interest in *piyyut*. "The true heirs" of Jewish prophets and poets, who will they be, R. Hirsch asked rhetorically, "those who repeated their prayers but forgot their names, or those who forget their prayers and remember their names?" See ibid., 343.

It would be an error to conclude that the contention of Rabbis Lowenstamm and Hirsch that *piyyutim* evoke strong emotional responses merely reflects the apologetics of anti-Reform writing of the nineteenth century. In a lecture on the sanctity of the Day of Atonement, the prominent twentieth-century rabbinic figure, Rabbi Joseph B. Soloveitchik, acknowledged, "I must admit that my philosophy of *Yahadus* is the product, not of my talmudic studies or of my philosophical training, but of my childhood *Yom Kippur* memories and reminiscences."[183] He then proceeded to relate:

> It is quite strange that the *Piyutim* recited on *Yom Kippur* played a significant role in the formation of my religious personality. My father and grandfather taught me the beauty and grandeur of *Yom Kippur*. For them the *Maḥzor* was not just a prayer book. It was more than that. It was a book of knowledge. I do not know whether modern linguists would subscribe to the philological excursions made by my father and me in the *Maḥzor*. They might consider them obsolete. Regardless of the philology, however, the essence of the liturgy, with its lofty *Aggadic* and *Halachic* aspects, became suddenly inspirational and experiential. All of the *Halachic* and *Aggadic* teachings which I absorbed as a young child have remained with me until this day.[184]

SPIRITUALITY: CLAIMS AND ASSESSMENTS

Grandiose claims were made for the spiritual and religious impact of the liturgical innovations. The editors of the second edition of the Hamburg Prayerbook (1842) praised their prayerbook for restoring "simplicity" and "dignity" to synagogue services and asserted that, as a result, "the religious sense has been revived" among many individuals for whom religion had lost its sanctity.[185] That very same year the West London Synagogue published the first edition of the *Forms of Prayer Used in the West London Synagogue of British Jews*. The editors of that prayerbook similarly claimed that they had rendered the service more dignified and intelligible by expunging sections of the liturgy that "are deficient in devotional tendency" and linguistic expressions that are "the offspring of feelings produced by oppression, and which are universally admitted

---

183 Transcript of an Elul 1974 lecture, published in *Sefer Nora'ot ha-Rav*, ed. B. David Schreiber, vol. 13 (New York, 2000), 96.

184 Ibid., 96.

185 Petuchowski, *Prayerbook Reform*, 138.

to be foreign in the heart of every true Israelite of our day."[186] So, too, laymen in Metz, eager to emulate the Hamburg model in order to "restore dignity" and avoid "oblivion, apathy and indifference" prevalent at worship services, introduced modifications in synagogue practice and sought to abolish "superannuated ceremonies, practices which choke the sublimity of our teaching and are entirely at odds with today's customs and habits."[187] Others called for renunciation of "antiquated customs" in order "to give our religion a worthier form" and for the removal of practices that have "degraded and dishonored it in the eyes of thinking men."[188]

Few of the liturgical innovators would have concurred entirely with the radical statement of the Frankfurt Friends of Reform declaring that the "practical commands, the observance of which constitutes the bulk of present-day Judaism, ... [these] external form[s] are for the most part without significance—yes, even unworthy of pure religion."[189] Be that as it may, there is more than a whiff of smugness and sanctimoniousness in these writers' conviction that their "necessary" changes in synagogue practice are all salutary and edifying and in the frequently recurring phrases "the genuine spirit of Jewish religiosity,"[190] "true religiosity,"[191] or "pure divine worship service"[192] that dot the writings of protagonists of the new prayerbooks.

To many of those individuals the "genuine Jewish spirit" and "the spirit of true religiosity"[193] were congruent with what were the dominant cultural and philosophical perspectives of the time. Unabashedly, they proclaimed that it is "the religious spirit of the present to which Judaism owes its reawakening and revitalization"[194] and naively they placed their faith in "the trumpet sound of our time."[195] Only through discarding the "husk" of antiquated ritual did they believe they would gain access to "the treasure of the kernel" and bring Judaism into harmony with what they perceived as "the genius of the modern era."[196]

The *Zeitgeist* beckoned and many were caught up in its allure. Little wonder then that the ritual and religious practices of Judaism seemed "encrusted with moldering medieval ceremonies." Above all, they feared being considered

---

186 Ibid., 140.
187 Plaut, *Rise*, 45.
188 Ibid., 51.
189 Ibid., 51.
190 Ibid., 39.
191 Ibid., 39 and 60.
192 Ibid., 42.
193 Ibid., 60.
194 Ibid., 59.
195 Ibid., 57.
196 Ibid., 59–60.

backward or culturally inferior by their Western confreres and declared candidly: "Is this possible at a time when everything blossoms and decks itself with the fresh apparel of the new age; is our faith alone to declare itself absolutely incompatible with the new age? No! No! say we."[197]

The desire to be *au courant* by accepting current modes of thought as well as a longing to be considered worthy citizens led to modifications in the content of the prayers, particularly with regard to expressions of chosenness, prayer for ingathering of exiles and references to a personal messiah. Particularistic prayers were deemed to be narrow and selfishly ethnocentric; universalist prayers were regarded as emblematic of a higher spiritual sensibility. The editors of the Berlin Reform Prayerbook (1848) articulated the new philosophy quite clearly:

> For a noble, truthful pious soul, the thought of the Father of all mankind is more stirring than that of a God of Israel. The image of God, imprinted upon every human being as a covenant-sign of divine love, has more poetry than the chosenness of Israel. The general love of a neighbor and brother, deeply imbedded in every man, has more attraction than a particular ceremonial law.[198]

Similarly, the *Reform-Freunde* in Worms declared in all honesty that they could no longer pay lip service to prayers for a return to Palestine "while at the same time our strongest bonds tie our souls to the German Fatherland whose fate is inextricably interwoven with ours—for what is dear and precious to us is embraced by her." They could no longer mourn the destruction of the Temple "for another fatherland had been ours for many years, one that has become most precious to all of us." To remember the historic fate of the destruction of the Temple does serve a purpose, "but why should we pretend a sorrow which no longer touches our hearts?" Rather, they conceded their inability to lament a historical event "in which we see the loving hand of God." In a spirit of enthusiasm and ardor, they sought to banish "untruth" from their service, to jettison "dead ballast" and to build a new temple in which a "fresh and free wind blows to animate our ambitious youth."[199]

Other writers accentuated the changing "religious needs of the times" that prompted a liturgical revision designed for "promotion of edification."[200]

---

197 Ibid., 62.
198 Ibid., 59.
199 Ibid., 61–62.
200 Petuchowski, *Prayerbook Reform*, 143–144.

Taking note of the frequent references to the concept of "edification" (*Erbauung*) as the goal and purpose of religious services, contemporary scholars have observed that the term was used in association with religious worship by German Protestant Pietists.[201] Thus, both German patriotism and Protestant theology exerted considerable influence on the ideological stance that early exponents of Reform equated with "the spirit of true religiosity."

The lofty rhetoric of the ideologues did not always appeal to the rank and file. There was a deep-seated traditionalism in many a simple German Jew, even those no longer punctilious in observance of mitzvot, which restrained them from embracing extreme innovation in synagogue services.

Abraham Geiger has been described as the most influential Reform Jewish liturgist of the nineteenth century. Adaptations of his *Israelitisches Gebetbuch* (1854) constitute the foundation of the more traditional prayerbook of Manuel Joel (1872) and the more radical text of Vogelstein (1894) and traces of his work are to be found in the *Einheitsgebetbuch* of German Liberal Jews (1929), edited by Seligmann, Elbogen, and Vogelstein, as well as in the United States in the second edition of Szold's *Avodath Yisrael* (1871) prayerbook as revised by Jastrow and Hochheimer.[202] The popularity of his liturgy may be attributed to the fact that, in practice, Geiger diverged sharply from his own very radical liturgical theory.

Geiger argued that Hebrew is no longer a living language, that Israel lives only as a community of faith, not as a people, that Amalek has become an irrelevancy and that no hope is to be associated with Jerusalem. Yet, in practice, when he published his own *siddur* in Breslau, he retained a basically Hebrew service and did not consistently revise the prayerbook to conform to his own radical theories. He had been scornful of the editors of the second edition of the Hamburg prayerbook because of their timidity but, in his own enterprise, he did not incorporate the changes (e.g., removal of *tal* and *geshem* prayers) that he had criticized the Hamburg editors for failing to implement.[203]

Whether, as his admirers have argued, the gap between Geiger's weltanschauung and his practice is to be understood in a positive light, i.e.,

201 See Alexander Altmann, "The New Style of Jewish Preaching," in *Studies in Nineteenth-Century Jewish Intellectual History*, ed. Alexander Altmann (Cambridge: Harvard University Press, 1964), 87 ff. See also note 32 in this chapter and accompanying text.
202 Jakob J. Petuchowski, "Abraham Geiger, the Reform Jewish Liturgist," *New Perspectives on Abraham Geiger*, ed. Jakob J. Petuchowski (New York: HUC Press, 1975), 42–44.
203 Ibid., 47–48.

as an expression of his sincere desire to work within the framework of a total community rather than from a limited denominational platform,[204] or whether this divergence between theory and practice should be seen as a reflection of opportunism and an absence of integrity is debatable. What is apparent is that Geiger's decision that it was desirable to opt for "accommodation of the religious needs of a large segment of the present generation"[205] lies behind the secret of his popularity as a Reform liturgist. It is the instinctive reactions of *amkha*, the common folk, who retain a Jewish spark, that ofttimes preserve us from the follies of misguided leaders and prophets.

When innovations were introduced, to what extent did they lead to fulfillment of the lofty aspirations of the liturgists, i.e., to "edification" and to "true religiosity"? In order to answer this query a brief survey of reactions of Reform writers themselves is in order. Several of those discussions were offered decades later and bring a historical perspective to an analysis of the issues.

In the preface to the 1855 Mannheim prayerbook, M. Präger, the editor, conceded that while cities such as Mannheim required compilation of a text suited to their heterogeneity, liturgical innovation in general had splintered the greater community. Reform prayer modalities were so diverse and numerous that one might "indignantly proclaim with the Prophet, '*ki mispar arekha hayu elohekha*' (Jer. 11:13)[206]—as many prayerbooks as there are cities!"[207] The

---

204 Ibid., 48–52. See also Geiger's own comments on the distinction between theorists and practitioners and the constraints upon a rabbi functioning within a communal framework in *Abraham Geiger and Liberal Judaism: The Challenge of the Nineteenth Century*, ed. Max Wiener, trans. Ernst J. Schlochauer (Cincinnati: HUC Press, 1981), 275–282.

Noting Petuchowski's discussion of the discrepancy between Geiger's theory and practice, Ken Koltun-Fromm, "Historical Memory in Abraham Geiger's Account of Modern Jewish Identity," *Jewish Social Studies* (n. s.) 7, no. 1 (Fall 2000), 116, suggests that "it is better to jettison talk of a theory/practice distinction and instead focus on how Geiger integrated significant theoretical claims about identity into practical discussions about Jewish liturgy." Koltun-Fromm's own analysis, in the opinion of this writer, is hardly compelling. He does, however, demonstrate that Geiger "blurred the historical memory" (123) and that "For Geiger, Wissenschaft was neither a scientific nor an objective study of a past. It was a motivated retrieval of that past conditioned by modern concerns about identity" (110). That Geiger's historical and liturgical writings did not always present a "scientific" and "objective" study" of the past but rather "a constructed collection of meaningful memories that fashion a usable past for decidedly modern concerns" (110) is an important acknowledgement. That foremost practitioners of the *Wissenschaft des Judentums* were not necessarily scientific or academic in their approach to liturgy has not been sufficiently recognized.

205 *Protokolle*, 70.

206 Lit.: "For according to the number of your cities are your gods."

207 Cited in Petuchowski, *Prayerbook Reform*, 152–153.

issue of liturgical uniformity dominated the agenda of three regional Reform rabbinical conferences held in Southern Germany in the 1850s. Conference delegates were caught on the horns of a dilemma, since the quest for creativity conflicted with the quest for unity and, in addition, local communities jealously sought to preserve their autonomy.[208] Because of those impediments, German Reform did not succeed in publishing a commonly accepted uniform prayer-book until the publication of the *Einheitsgebetbuch* in 1929.[209]

In the United States, a common Reform liturgy was adopted somewhat earlier. The earliest edition of the *Union Prayer Book* (*UPB*) was published in 1892, was revised by a committee and published as a prayerbook for the High Holy Days in 1894 and for Sabbaths, festivals, and weekdays in 1895.[210] However, Reform clergy acknowledged that, even after successive further revisions, the *UPB* never became a charmed medium capable of wafting souls heavenward. In 1928, Samuel S. Cohon, in a blistering critique of the infelicity of many English passages, of the "prosy homilies and stereotyped phrases,"[211] objected more fundamentally that the *UPB* did not faithfully or consistently reflect Reform theology.[212] Petitionary prayers to the Deity were replaced by vague meditations on ethical themes that conveyed the impression that they were "especially written for a people composed of retired philanthropists and amateur social workers."[213] In addition, Cohon bemoaned the manner in which congregations utilized the prayerbook, that is, he regarded absence of congregational participation as a reflection of a loss of a desire to pray.[214]

Although Israel Bettan, writing a year later, disputed Cohon's suggested emendations because he feared a further denuding the prayers of their poetry and emotional resonance in favor of a dry literalism, he fully concurred in the negative evaluation of the text of the *UPB*, particularly of passages that read like

---

208 Robert Liberles, "The Rabbinical Conferences of the 1850's and the Quest for Liturgical Unity," *Modern Judaism* 3, no. 1 (October, 1983), 312 and 315.

209 *Gebetbuch für das ganze Jahr*, ed. Ceasar Seligmann, Ismar Elbogen, and Hermann Vogelstein, 2 vols. (Frankfurt am Main, 1924).

210 Meyer, *Response*, 279. On Isaac Mayer Wise's persistent efforts for the adoption of a uniform Reform liturgy and the conflict between proponents of the respective prayerbooks of Wise and Einhorn see ibid., 258–259 and James G. Heller. *Isaac M. Wise: His Life, Work and Thought* (New York: UAHC, 1965), 302–306 and 476.

211 "The Theology of the Union Prayer Book," in *Reform Judaism: A Historical Perspective*, ed. Joseph L. Blau (New York: Ktav, 1973), 281.

212 Ibid., 265–281.

213 Ibid., 262 n. 5.

214 Ibid., 283.

sociological discourses and of those that cast a negative light on longings for a return to Zion or depicted the dispersion as a sign of blessed privilege. Far from arousing fervor, "the cure effected by early Reform gave rise to a new malady," Bettan charged, turning worshipers into passive participants, mere "weary auditors" and "languid spectators" and in consequence "our services have been immeasurably weakened."[215]

When growing frustration with the *UPB* led a number of Reform congregations to experiment with alternative texts, the results were no more inspiring. Reporting on a detailed analysis and study of thirty-three congregations' *Rosh ha-Shanah* evening services, Daniel Jeremy Silver portrays the *UBP* liturgy as inadequate to their needs, decrying its propensity for "the vague and the high-flown," its failure to provide a "richness of ideas" and the fact that the meditations are usually devoid of specific Jewish elements. However, he admits that the substitute liturgies prepared by some congregations offered similarly "over-blown language" and he confesses, "I am afraid that high-flown vagueness has a fatal fascination for our movement." Noting that 90% of the Hebrew portion of the service is recited or chanted by the rabbi, cantor or choir, he observes that this enables "the worshiper, like an opera goer, to enjoy the mood without thinking about the libretto."[216] Discussing substitutions introduced into the High Holy Day liturgy, Silver characterizes one rewritten service as "an enthusiastic, if sometimes incoherent, blend of Buber's *Tales of Rabbi Nahman* and classical Reform's social gospel."[217] Silver notes that, in general, the new prayers were vague and the "combination of fuzzy piety and fuzzy language sometimes boggled the imagination."[218]

---

215 Israel Bettan, "The Function of the Prayer Book," *Reform Judaism*, ed. Blau, 289 and 295–96. See the much later article of Lawrence A. Hoffman, "The Language of Survival in American Reform Liturgy," *CCAR Journal* 24, no. 3 (Summer 1977), 87–106, for a critique of the *UPB*'s failure to express an effective message of Jewish particularism.

216 "Do We Say What We Mean? Do We Mean What We Say?" *CCAR Journal* 24, no. 3 (Summer 1977), 133–134.

217 Ibid., 128.

218 Ibid., 126. Of even felicitous creative prayers Eugene Borowitz, *Liberal Judaism* (New York: Union of American Hebrew Congregations, 1984), 439, writes: "Seeking to reuse a creative service which once moved us greatly, we are regularly disappointed. Few things we write retain their ability to inspire us. Fewer still can bear a community's repetition week after week after week." On the use of non-halakhic forms in prayers composed in post-talmudic times and on the limited success of innovative and creative prayers in Orthodox circles as well, cf. the brief comments of Joseph Tabory, "The Conflict of Halakhah and Prayer," *Tradition* 25, no. 1 (Fall 1989), 22–23.

More recent assessments of Reform liturgy have noted the contradictory tendencies of recovery and reconstruction evident in several new prayerbooks. On the one hand, these prayerbooks reflect an attempt to recover traditional texts and to incorporate more Hebrew and, on the other hand, they exhibit a significant degree of self-censorship and radical innovation, particularly as a response to feminist agitation for a liturgy that is entirely gender free.[219] The desperate attempt to be simultaneously more traditional and more modern has produced prayerbooks that one reviewer describes as "not very rigorous theologically" and "not very inspiring."[220]

Continuing dissatisfaction within the Reform rabbinate with the *UPB* led to the adoption of a new prayerbook, *Sha'arei Tefillah—Gates of Prayer*, in 1975. This prayerbook offers several alternative liturgies, as many as ten separately themed Sabbath eve services and six different Sabbath morning services, ranging from the traditional to the radical. One of the proffered services omits any reference to God. The editors aimed for richness and diversity but many readers found the series of alternative options bewildering.[221] In response, the Reform movement determined to issue a new prayerbook which they hoped would please traditionalist elements and develop a more unified approach to synagogue worship. Those involved in editorial decisions expressed the concern that "we don't want to have a book that will feel dated in five years."[222] The new prayerbook, *Mishkan T'filah*, edited by Elyse Frishman, was published in 2002.

The return to the traditional Hebrew texts demonstrates a significant phenomenon. Creative texts fail to be as spiritually elevating as anticipated while, in the final analysis, the spare wording of the Sages is recognized as meaningful and moving. Rabbinic authorities emphasized that the words of the *Amidah* composed by the Men of the Great Assembly are ideal for prayer because each letter and syllable contains profound *kavvanot*. In the words of R. Yonatan Eybeschutz: "Every jot and tittle has within it mysteries of the Torah, secrets of

219 Arnold Jacob Wolf, "The New Liturgies," *Judaism* 46, no. 2 (Spring 1997), 235.
220 Ibid., 242.
221 Ibid., 240.
222 *JTA Daily News Bulletin*, December 23, 1999, 4. A concern for datedness is certainly not misplaced. Milton Himmelfarb, *The Jews of Modernity* (New York: Basic Books, 1973), 357, remarks: "Well, if you make revisions every twenty or thirty years, you run the risk of being irrelevant much of the time. ... [T]here is nothing so dead as the newspaper from the day before yesterday. The Twentieth Psalm speaks of chariots and horses, which no army has used for some time now. Would it be more relevant if it spoke of tanks and planes? Chariots and horses make the point quite well."

the holy *Merkavah* [Chariot], and combinations of Names from the supernal worlds, that open up the gates and are efficacious and rise up higher than the highest to the Guardian."[223] But, quite apart from their mystical properties, the words of the ancient prayers are endowed with an unusual literary quality. The *Zohar* states: "Woe unto that person who says that the Torah has come to teach us mere stories or the words of an ordinary person for, if so, we could compose in our time a Torah from the words of an ordinary person even more beautiful than all these. ... Rather, all words of the Torah are transcendent words and transcendent mysteries."[224] Yet who would deny that the Torah is indeed "the greatest story ever told" and that the stories alone are matchless? In like manner, the prayers of the Sages, immutably preserved on account of their transcendent sanctity, are, at the same time, incomparable in their pure literary power.

A glance at an entirely different, alternative type of liturgical innovation further highlights the drawbacks of classical Reform worship while at the same time it focuses our attention on what may well be the most vexing aspect of the entire Reform liturgical enterprise.

As noted, early liturgical innovators were influenced heavily by the style and manner of worship of nineteenth-century Protestantism. Quite different intellectual currents may be discerned in the *ḥavurah* movement of the 1960s. Critical of the establishment and steeped in the counterculture, the founders of the *ḥavurot* distanced themselves from the formality of mainstream institutions they looked upon as "sterile, hierarchical, divorced from Jewish tradition, and *lacking in spirituality*."[225] The emphasis in *ḥavurah* movement services is on intimacy, warmth, egalitarianism and engagement. Typically, *ḥavurah* worship takes place in a small room, the seating arrangement is circular, dress is highly informal, and services are led by various members. Although many of the prayers are recited in Hebrew with traditional *nusaḥ*, there is much room for creative interpretations and interpolations. In an analysis of one particular *ḥavurah*, Chava Weissler quite accurately focuses on the crucial importance of the social and interpersonal element in those services whose success is gauged to a large extent by the interaction of leader and followers and by participants' responses to one another. Another characteristic element of *ḥavurah* services is the reframing or reinterpretation of the prayers as a strategy for coping with

---

223 *Ya'arot Devash*, pt. 1, 8a.
224 *Zohar, Be-Ha'alotekha*, 152a, cited by R. Yitzchak Arama, *Akedat Yitzhak*, introduction to the Book of Ruth. *Akedat Yitzhak* cites this comment of the *Zohar* precisely because the Book of Ruth is acknowledged to be an exceptional literary masterpiece.
225 Weissler, "Making *Davening* Meaningful," 257, emphasis added.

what is perceived to be a "problematic liturgy."[226] Weissler points out that each week the role of the leader is to present a current and novel interpretation. The message conveyed is that meaning is fleeting and interpretation must continually be constructed anew.

This practice underscores the difficulty members experience in affirming the words of the liturgy. The *havurah* thus reflects the members' "attraction to tradition and the ambivalence regarding it"[227] and makes "doubt and ambivalence as axiomatic a part of worship as faith once was."[228] Reflecting upon the specific circular seating arrangements and the manner in which sacredness is experienced by *havurah* members through "sacralization of the interpersonal," Weissler concludes her remarks with the statement: "God is approached through human relationships; God is perhaps what happens across the circle."[229]

Weissler's comments lead us to the central, fundamental issue liturgical innovation forces us to confront, an issue beside which all other issues pale into insignificance: the question of the core beliefs and doctrines of Judaism.

FUNDAMENTAL BELIEFS

Probably no single work has had a greater impact on the average Jew over the course of millennia than the prayerbook. Jews to whom philosophical works were closed tomes, for whom the Talmud and *Shulḥan Aruch* were far too difficult, were thoroughly familiar with the words of the *siddur*. From these prayers simple Jews gleaned an awareness of, and an appreciation for, the fundamentals of faith. Belief in the messiah, in bodily resurrection, in the veracity of the prophets, and a yearning for Zion were thrice daily reinforced in the course of prayer; *meḥayeh ha-meitim, et tzemaḥ David avdekha bimherah tatzmiaḥ, shuvekha le-Tziyyon* were familiar and tangible beliefs. The Jew who cleaved to his *siddur* was a Jew whose conceptual framework was rooted in the thought-world of the Sages that the liturgy mirrored. In describing the role of the synagogue in molding a religious personality, R. Hirsch points to the common usage of the term *shul* for synagogue and remarks, "We call our houses of worship 'Schulen' [the German word for schools] and that is what they are meant to be: schools for adults, for those who have entered the mainstream of life."[230]

---

226 Ibid., 270.
227 Ibid., 276.
228 Ibid., 279.
229 Ibid., 279.
230 R. Samson Raphael Hirsch, *Neunzehn Briefe über Judentum* (Berlin: Welt-Verlag, 1919), fourteenth letter, 79–80; cf. idem, *The Collected Writings*, vol. I, 193.

Let there be no mistake. The paramount concern of the nineteenth-century rabbinic authorities who were adamant opponents of liturgical innovation was the correctly perceived challenge to faith. The pages of *Eleh Divrei ha-Berit* contain many an argument regarding halakhic minutiae but the constant refrain is a fear and trembling in the face of erosion of *"ikkarei ha-dat"* or fundamentals of faith.[231] Similarly, two months after publication of the second edition of the Hamburg Temple Prayerbook, on October 16, 1841, when Ḥakham Isaac Bernays responded with a *"Moda'ah,"* a public notice, declaring the prayerbook unfit for use in fulfillment of one's religious obligations, it was the ideological issue that was paramount. Three words appear in large, bold characters: Redemption, Messiah, Resurrection.[232] The theological concern underlying Ḥakham Bernays's response to the Hamburg Temple *siddur* was clearly aroused by the renewed assault on those cardinal doctrines reflected in its liturgical emendations.

R. Chajes, sorely conflicted over an appropriate response to the Reform movement, writes that its blatant rejection of fundamental beliefs ultimately precluded compromise. As long as minor modification of synagogue custom was at issue and innovators paid at least lip service to the teachings of the Sages, there had existed a possibility for containment and the hope of finding a *modus vivendi* through the art of gentle persuasion. Even at the outset, he admits, rabbinic authorities "recognized that they [Reform leaders] had acted with deceit and intended to uproot everything," but with Reform renunciation of the basic doctrines of Judaism there was no longer even a possibility of accommodation.[233]

Earlier, Chorin argued that the rabbis' exaggerated prohibitions, extending even to permissible matters, would in the long run lead to a blurring of boundaries and transgression of the forbidden. Rather than multiplying prohibitions as a hedge against sin, he argued, the rabbis should have ruled in accordance with "the need of the time, the place, and the generation."[234] Had they adopted a conciliatory posture, Chorin maintained, and, at the same time, in a non-strident manner correctly objected to the initial changes in the Hamburg Prayerbook with regard to ingathering of the exiles, their influence would have been salutary.[235]

---

231 See *Eleh Divrei ha-Berit*, iv, ix, 6, 12–13, 17, 22, 24, 27–28, 54–57, 67, and 90–91.
232 *Theologische Gutachten über das Gebetbuch nach dem gebrauche des Neuen Israelitischen Tempelvereins in Hamburg* (Hamburg, 1842), 14.
233 *Minḥat Kena'ot*, 1007.
234 *Davar be-Itto*, 57–58.
235 Ibid., 49–50.

A similar hypothesis was advanced a century later by Ismar Elbogen. Elbogen's history of the liturgy culminates in a survey of the liturgical controversies of the modern period in which he states that, rather than adopting a hostile position, had the rabbis "taken charge of the new movement ... who knows what the eventual development of German Jewry would have been?"[236]

An opposing view was espoused by R. Chajes who does not otherwise hesitate, when he deems it justified to do so, to take the rabbinic establishment to task. Addressing the contention that rabbis should be lenient in order to keep within the fold those whom either the blandishments or the pressures of modern life were distancing from religious observance, R. Chajes differentiates between a permissible temporary leniency (*hora'at sha'ah*) and an impermissible permanent abrogation of the law. The matter is moot, he notes, because the innovators followed a different path entirely. It was not necessary for them to tamper with references to basic beliefs such as resurrection or the messiah in order to ease the burden of ritual observance. Nor had such beliefs stood in the way of attainment of civil rights. Indeed, in an aside, R. Chajes points out that, contrary to what might have been anticipated, in Germany, the seat of greatest Reform agitation, there was renewed prejudice and anti-Semitism, whereas in France, Holland and Belgium, where innovation was not widespread, Jews enjoyed equal rights and privileges.[237]

Foresight or hindsight? Would different tactics have altered the cataclysmic process? Could Niagara Falls be reversed by gentle persuasion? Whether or not their tactics were the wisest, whether or not their rhetoric was more harmful than helpful, one thing is clear, the foremost rabbinic authorities, the *gedolei hora'ah*, were not naïve. On the contrary, it was individuals such as the Italian rabbis who were initially sympathetic to the innovators and, in *Or Nogah* and *Nogah ha-Tzedek*, lent their imprimatur to changes that appeared innocuous, who failed to recognize the dimensions of the hazard.

At the very heart of the endeavors of those engaged in the earliest experiments in worship reform was an attempt to alter the wording of the prayers to conform to the mindset and belief system of the majority of their enlightened coreligionists. To those individuals, the most troubling references in the prayerbook were the petitions for rebuilding the Temple[238] and reinstitution

---

236 *Jewish Liturgy*, 304.

237 *Minḥat Kena'ot*, 1021 and 1027.

238 Many temples prominently display a large seven-branched menorah. It has been conjectured that Reform congregations consciously introduced the seven-branched menorah into their sanctuaries because this artifact is identified with the Temple that stood in

of the sacrificial order. Later, other fundamental beliefs were also assailed. The concept of a personal messiah and the Davidic monarchy, prayers for return to Jerusalem and the ingathering of the exiles, mention of bodily resurrection, blessings that acknowledged a distinction between Jews and non-Jews[239] and between men and women as well as particularistic prayers that emphasized the chosenness of Israel aroused unease among many of their constituents. Leaders of the Reform movement argued that to give expression in prayer to doctrines that were contrary to their convictions was hypocritical and damaging to the spirituality to which divine service should aspire. The imagery and wording of some prayers was also viewed as problematic. References to angels were attacked by some as archaic and anachronistic and defended by others as merely poetic and fanciful embellishments.[240]

Conservative liturgists' alterations of the *siddur* were not as numerous or as blatant as those of Reform editors, but they, too, introduced changes that touched on matters of belief. Comfortable with references to sacrifices in times gone by but maintaining that reinstitution of the sacrificial order "cannot be made to serve our modern outlook,"[241] the editors of the Conservative 1946 *Sabbath and Festival Prayer Book* modified the *Tikkanta Shabbat* and *Mipnei Ḥata'einu* prayers by altering the tense of the verbs employed. Their approach to the fundamental doctrine of resurrection was more oblique. In a manner similar to that of editors of the Hamburg Temple Prayerbook who retained the Hebrew word *go'el* (redeemer) but translated it into German as *Erlösung*

Jerusalem. The subliminal message of a seven-branched menorah in a modern-day temple is that there is no longer a desire to rebuild the Temple in messianic times; the Temple has been supplanted by sanctuaries in the Diaspora. See Joseph Gutmann, "A Note on the Temple Menorah," in *No Graven Images: Studies in Art and the Hebrew Bible*, ed. Joseph Gutmann (New York: Ktav, 1971), 38.

239 John D. Rayner, "Ideologically Motivated Emendations in Anglo-Jewish Liturgy," *Noblesse Oblige: Essays in Honor of David Kessler OBE*, ed. Alan D. Crown (London and Portland, OR: Valentine Mitchell, 1998), 117–121, suggests that Reform practice influenced British Orthodox liturgists with regard to references to non-Jews. The examples Rayner cites, taken from (British) United Synagogue prayerbooks, are an emendation of the first stanza of the *Ma'oz Tzur* hymn and changes in the Prayer for the Royal Family. Far from supporting Rayner's thesis, these examples actually demonstrate the opposite. Both changes are minor in nature and occur in non-statutory prayers. If indeed they reflect Reform influence, the influence was quite trivial.

240 See, for example, Elbogen, *Jewish Liturgy*, 326; Cohon, "Theology," 267–269; and Bettan, "Function," 285–287 and 294–295.

241 *Sabbath and Festival Prayer Book* (n.p.: Rabbinical Assembly of America and United Synagogue of America, 1946), ix.

(redemption)[242] in order to avoid reference to a personal messiah in the vernacular, the Conservative editors retained the Hebrew *meḥayeh ha-meitim* ("who revives the dead") but rendered it in English as "who calls the dead to everlasting life." That ambiguous translation, they explicitly suggested, would be satisfactory to both liberals and traditionalists.[243] Moving from prevarication to a more definitive but still not quite honest formulation, the 1972 Conservative Prayer Book retains *meḥayeh ha-meitim* but translates the phrase as "Master of life and death."[244]

Ironically, in the latter part of the twentieth century, even as the Reform movement has veered back toward reintroduction of more traditional prayers, to an appreciation of the Hebrew language and even (in muted form) to an acknowledgement of Zion and Jerusalem in prayer, deviation in the area of doctrine has become, if anything, more marked.

Prayer in essence is a petition, plea, meditation or praise that presupposes the presence of a Supreme Being; it constitutes a dialogue, an address or appeal to God. Even those commentators who emphasize the meditative aspects of prayer in interpreting the term *le-hitpallel* as a reflexive verb connoting self-judgment recognize that the enterprise of prayer involves a perception of the individual standing before God at the moment of meditation.

Although the nineteenth-century innovators discarded the particularistic and nationalistic elements of the prayerbook, they were comfortable with conventional monotheistic beliefs and experienced no embarrassment in directing prayer to a Supreme Being. Prayers and meditations composed by classical Reform writers are unambiguously addressed to "Our father in heaven" and "merciful God." But it is precisely a belief in God, and especially in an all-powerful Almighty God whose providential guardianship is manifest and who is "nigh unto all them that call upon Him" (Psalms 145:18) that, today, is troubling to many of the laity and clergy of the Reform movement. In their denial of a personal God and the election of Israel[245] Reconstructionists parallel the radical

---

242 *Ordnung der öffentlichen Andacht für die Sabbath- und Festtage des ganzen Jahres. Nach dem Gebrauche des Neuen-Tempel-Vereins in Hamburg* (Hamburg, 1819), 44.

243 *Sabbath and Festival Prayer Book* (1946), viii.

244 *Maḥzor for Rosh Hashanah and Yom Kippur: A Prayer Book for the Days of Awe*, ed. Jules Harlow (New York: The Rabbinical Assembly, 1972), 31.

245 In the United States one of the most highly dramatized encounters involving changes in synagogue liturgy occurred at the time of the publication of Mordecai Kaplan's *Sabbath Prayer Book* (New York: Jewish Reconstructionist Foundation, 1945) in which the blessing "who has chosen us from among all the peoples" was changed to "who has drawn us (nigh) to His service" (10 and 160). This innovation aroused vociferous protest from many

exponents of Reform, while devotees of Jewish Humanism opt for a genre of humanistic, nontheistic prayer.

In non-religious Israeli circles there is a new interest in study of the sources of Jewish thought and law but, for the moment, the turn toward study of the sources is far removed from traditional Jewish belief. There, too, a number of individuals have articulated a desire for a new *siddur* that expresses the sentiments of secular Jews[246] and for development of festival rituals "from which the Lord has been erased."[247]

Moreover, quite apart from issues involving belief in God and the efficacy of approaching God in prayer, a new and grave problem with regard to the wording of the liturgy has emerged in recent decades. The desire of many in the Reform movement to develop a prayer service that is completely gender neutral has led to a thorough revision of the basic elements of the blessings and prayers. These sweeping changes cannot be viewed as mere technical adaptations or semantic alterations.[248] A work such as Marcia Falk's *The Book*

sectors of the community with one Orthodox rabbinical group excommunicating Kaplan and a public burning of the prayerbook. See Mel Scult, *Judaism Faces the Twentieth Century: A Biography of Mordecai M. Kaplan* (Detroit: Wayne State University Press, 1993), 341, 344, and 360–361, as well as Jeffrey S. Gurock and Jacob J. Schacter, *A Modern Heretic and a Traditional Community: Mordecai M. Kaplan, Orthodoxy, and American Judaism* (New York: Columbia University Press, 1996), 140–141 and 206 n. 14. It is noteworthy that a number of Kaplan's prominent colleagues on the faculty of the Jewish Theological Seminary, Louis Ginzberg, Saul Lieberman and Alexander Marx, distanced themselves from Kaplan's prayerbook. See "Giluy Da'at," *Ha-Do'ar* 24, no. 39 (October 5, 1945), 904–905. In 1945 an emendation rejecting chosenness could hardly be characterized as having been made in response to a cultural trend; Kaplan was making a forthright statement entirely consistent with his theology. David Novak, "Mordecai Kaplan's Rejection of Election," *Modern Judaism* 15, no. 1 (February, 1995), 1–19, cogently points out that Kaplan's rejection of the election of Israel flows directly from his radical theology. To continue to pay lip service to the doctrine would have been dishonest, and "whatever faults Kaplan may have had, hypocrisy was not one of them" (ibid., 2).

246 See Yael Tamir, "Mahapekha u-Masoret," in *Anu ha-Yehudim ha-Ḥilonim*, ed. Dedi Zucker (Tel Aviv: Yedi'ot Aḥaronot, 1999), 182–183.

247 Dedi Zucker, "Ha-Tzabar Ḥayyav la-Lekhet," ibid., 189.

248 See, for example, a critique of the *siddur*'s "unrelievedly masculine language," stereotyping the role of women and reflecting a male perspective in Annette Daum, "Language and Liturgy," in *Daughters of the King: Women and the Synagogue*, ed. Susan Grossman and Rivka Haut (Philadelphia: Jewish Publication Society, 1992), 183–202. Daum surveys Conservative and Reform liturgies designed to include feminist imagery and women's experiences and use of language to describe God utilizing both masculine and feminine terminology. See ibid., 197–198, for how (in what one may characterize as the spirit of the Yiddish translator who presented Shakespeare "*vertaytsht un verbessert*—translated and improved") efforts to incorporate gender-neutral language encompass biblical verses as well so that, for

of Blessings: New Jewish Prayers for Daily Life, the Sabbath, and the New Moon Festival illustrates the extent to which much current feminist liturgy celebrates a radical theology in which God is viewed, not as a transcendent Other, but as immanent in creation and inseparable from human empowerment.[249] Falk expresses fealty to Hebrew as "the heart of the heart of my work"[250] and there is moving poetry in her writing. But her newly-coined liturgical formulas, "*Nevarekh et eyn ha-ḥayyim*" which she renders as "Let us bless the source of life" and "*Nevarekh et maayan ḥayyeinu*" which she renders as "Let us bless the flow of life," are not simply innovative prayer texts; they constitute a theological statement.[251]

Thus we find ourselves in the twenty-first century, two hundred years after the advent of the movement for liturgical change, confronting a Reform liturgy that has turned almost 180 degrees with regard to some respects but that, in another respect, is further removed from the classical prayer service of Judaism than at any previous time.

The appeal of familiar ritual has long been recognized.[252] Current eagerness on the part of segments of the liberal constituency to embrace a greater amount of religious ceremonial has been attributed to several factors: an increased identification with the Jewish people and concomitant waning of

---

example, Lev. 19:17 is translated "You shall not hate your brother or sister in your heart." Daum describes the process of revision as "slow and inconsistent," but "irreversible" (ibid., 199). See also Ellen Umansky, "(Re)Imaging the Divine," *Response* 13, nos. 1–2 (Fall/Winter 1982), 110–119, who states that she is not suggesting rewriting the Bible and Talmud to make their ideas more consonant with contemporary ones but maintains that the *siddur* must be adjusted to reflect present notions lest "increasing numbers of men and women may find themselves forced to choose between membership in the Jewish community and communion with God" (ibid., 119).

249 Marcia Falk, *The Book of Blessings: New Jewish Prayers for Daily Life, the Sabbath, and the New Moon Festival* (Boston: Beacon Press, 1999). See especially the discussion, 417–423. See also Marcia Falk, "What About God?," *Moment* 10, no. 3 (March 1985), 32–36.

250 *The Book of Blessings*, xviii.

251 For these blessing formulas see, for example, ibid., 18–19 and 368–369. Noteworthy and characteristic are Falk's *Alenu*, 288–289, in praise of the beauty of the world and human power to heal and repair, and her blessing for the New Moon, 344–345, which is converted from a prayer that God renew the lunar cycle to a paean to the new moon that renews itself. Even a laudatory reviewer of Falk's work, Eric L. Friedland, "A Women's Prayer Book for All?," *CCAR Journal* 49, no. 1 (Winter 2002), comments critically on the "vaguely pantheistic" tone in which "more often than not, no God is addressed at all" (111).

252 See, for example, Petuchowski, *Understanding Jewish Prayer*, 37–39; Borowitz, *Liberal Judaism*, 410–440; and the interesting personal remarks of Morris Raphael Cohen, "Religion," in *The Faith of Secular Jews*, ed. Saul L. Goodman (New York: Ktav, 1976), 163.

embarrassment with distinctive rites; a quest for spirituality in Judaism rather than mere ethnicity; and a holistic approach to life that prompts adoption of practices that appeal to emotion rather than to rational cognition alone. There is also a newly-found recognition of the value of regulation and discipline and the sense, as Eugene Borowitz puts it colloquially, that "God deserves and our community requires rules."[253] The openness to Jewish ritual in general[254] finds particular expression in synagogue life and liturgical practice because of a renewed interest in observance of Sabbath and festivals including their distinctive prayers.

This welcome development should not, however, obscure the philosophical chasm that continues to divide liberal worship from that of halakhic Judaism. Borowitz, in his admittedly warm and appreciative endorsement of mitzvah observance, hastens to reassure his readers that the words "who has sanctified us by divine [sic] commandments and commanded us to ..." need not be taken in so literal a sense that they must fear being obligated by "the entire repertoire of Jewish ceremonial."[255] The essence of the liberal approach inheres in the commitment to personal autonomy and to the freedom to choose to accept or to desist from accepting specific observances.[256]

---

253 Borowitz, *Liberal Judaism*, 431.

254 I am indebted to Dr. Joel Wolowelsky for a telling example of the changing attitude toward ritual in the Reform movement. *The Union Haggadah: Home Service for the Passover* (n.p.: CCAR, 1923), 141, refers to "the quaint ceremony of 'b'dikas hometz—searching for leaven,' still observed by orthodox Jews." Fifty years later, *A Passover Haggadah* (n.p.: CCAR, 1974), 14, describes the search for leaven in a different manner entirely, portrays the ritual as "a dramatic and even compelling experience, particularly for children" and includes the Hebrew text of the blessing for disposal of *ḥametz*.

255 Borowitz, *Liberal Judaism*, 410.

256 Ibid., 411. Cf. the news report of reactions to the new worship initiative announced at the 1999 biennial UAHC convention. According to the *JTA Daily News Bulletin*, December 21, 1999, 2, the response was positive as long as individuals felt that the new ideas were "encouraged, and not required." As one conventioneer phrased it, the changes "don't bother me, as long as there is a choice." Cf. Frederic A. Doppelt and David Polish, *A Guide for Reform Jews*, rev. and augmented ed. (New York: Ktav, 1973), 9: "For what determines whether a custom, ceremony or symbol is either Orthodox or Reform is not its observance or non-observance; it is rather the right to change it when necessary, to drop it when no longer meaningful, and to innovate when desirable." On the conflict between exercise of autonomy and attempts to establish standards of conduct see Dana E. Kaplan, "Reform Jewish Theology and the Sociology of Liberal Religion in America: The Platforms as Response to the Perception of Socioreligious Crisis," *Modern Judaism* 20, no. 1 (February 2000), 71–72. Cf. Simon Rocker, "Growing Through the Open Door," *The Jewish Chronicle* (London), May 24, 2002, 26.

In his autobiography, Irving Howe describes how he watched, "at first with hostility and then with bemusement," his intellectual acquaintances seeking a way back to religion. A lifelong skeptic and professed non-believer, he writes that he himself found the temples to be inauthentic and uninspiring and their formless spirituality non-compelling. To him, the American Jewish community appeared to contain "little genuine faith, little serious observance, little search- ing toward belief. The temples grew in size and there was much busywork and eloquence, but God seldom figured as a dominant presence." But surely for reli- gious belief, asserts Howe, there must be "more than fragile epiphanies;" there must be "a persuasion of strength."[257] In this Howe is, of course, correct. It is with R. Judah ben Tema's charge to be "strong as a lion" in divine service[258] that both *Tur* and *Shulhan Arukh* introduce the laws of *Orah Hayyim*.

Judaism is a demanding faith, a praxis and, *pace* Mendelssohn, a universe of belief. Judaism is not a religion without peoplehood, nor a peoplehood with- out religion, and certainly not a religion without God. Far from a fuzziness, the path to spirituality in Judaism is structured and limned with prescriptive detail. The table of contents and the orderly progression of Rabbenu Bahya's classic *Hovot ha-Levavot* and R. Moshe Hayyim Luzzatto's *Mesillat Yesharim* illustrate the regimen and discipline these authorities posit as essential in the quest for spiritual attainment.

There are no simplistic answers to the struggles of faith. To some belief comes easier than to others. R. Hirsch's perceptive comment that the *shul* is our school for adults points to the truism that, to the extent that belief can be taught, the liturgy and the synagogue are designed to instruct and to inculcate fundamentals of belief. Ideally, the *shul* becomes a crucible of faith.

Of the making of creative prayerbooks there may be no end. But whether these hundreds of works have engendered more profound or genuine prayer is open to question. Ultimately, the experience of spirituality in prayer is con- tingent upon faith. A trenchant folk explication of a difficult stanza in the *Ve-Khol Ma'aminim* prayer of the High Holy Day liturgy conveys this concept. According to that interpretation, the phrase "*Ha-vadai shemo ken tehillato*"[259] should be understood as meaning: "To the extent that one is certain of His name, to that extent can one praise Him." Such an understanding expresses the

---

257 *A Margin of Hope: An Intellectual Autobiography* (San Diego, New York and London: Harcourt Brace Jovanovich, 1982), 278–279.

258 *Avot* 5:23.

259 Lit.: "Whose name is certainty, so is His praise." The four-letter name of God transcends time and connotes necessity or "certainty" of existence.

notion that, when the reality of God is taken as a certainty, man's prayers flow; when certainty of God is absent, prayer comes haltingly at best.[260]

Over the centuries, Jews consistently manifested an unwavering, bedrock faith and welcomed prayer as a haven, a comfort and a fountain of inspiration. As Jews we have a propensity for faith; we have a legacy if we but claim it. For *ma'amanim b'nei ma'amanim* (believers and sons of believers), prayer, even if difficult, is always possible and spirituality in prayer, even if at times elusive, is attainable.

ADDENDUM

Of Women and Prayer: A Personal Reflection[261]

As the vehicle for communication between man and God, prayer is at one and the same time both the medium of supplication for human needs ("A prayer of the afflicted when he is overwhelmed, and pours out his complaint before the Lord," Psalms 102:1) and the expression of human yearning for knowledge of, and the experience of closeness to (*devekut*), the divine ("As the hart pants after the water brooks, so pants my soul after You, oh God. My soul thirsts for God, for the living God: when shall I come and appear before God?" Psalms 42:2–3). It is those dual aspects of prayer that are incorporated in the structure of the quintessential *tefillah*, that is, the *Shemoneh Esreih*, in the supplications that are preceded and followed by blessings of praise and thanksgiving respectively.

If there are aspects of human life that lose luster or vigor with the passage of years, there are counterbalancing areas in which appreciation and sensitivity become more keen. I doubt whether youngsters are as aware of the healing balm of *Shabbat* as are people of mature years. Surely, *Shabbat* is a spiritual treasure whose "light and joy" is appreciated increasingly as one grows older. So, too, with prayer. It is only with the unfolding of time that one comes to perceive more fully its focal role in our lives.

As the body ages, as one becomes more sharply aware and keenly conscious of physical frailty and of one's utter, total dependence on the *Ribbon Olamim*, one's prayers assume a more urgent and pressing form. With the

---

260 For this interpretation I am indebted to Louis I. Rabinowitz, *Sabbath Light* (Johannesburg: Fieldhill Pub. Co., 1958), 3.

261 In keeping with the theme of the conference at which this paper was originally presented the Orthodox Forum Steering Committee encouraged presenters to include personal reflections in their papers.

passage of time, for many, there also come the blessings—and the worries—of an expanding personal and familial universe. Prayers for parents and spouse are augmented by prayers for children and, as the circle of dear ones expands, for children's children, for friends and their children and grandchildren. Of the well-known Yiddish jokester Hershele Ostropoler it was related that he prayed with utmost brevity. "What do I have to pray for?" said he. "I have but a wife and a goat, so my prayer is over very quickly: Wife, goat; goat, wife. What more need I say?" With the fullness of years and the blessings of families, our prayers expand.

But, with the passage of years, the overpowering urge to reach beyond the confines of the mundane grows as well. One experiences much more intensely the need to find meaningfulness in one's existence, the need to cleave to the Ineffable, the need to find an expression for the longings of the soul. And so it is that *tefillah* in both its manifestations assumes an even greater importance.

But how approach an awesome, majestic God? We Jews have always felt an intimacy with God even in our reverence.

My sainted grandfather, of blessed memory, in his frail old age, was wont to eat his evening meal at a late hour and to fall into a doze during the Grace after Meals. Inexplicably, he would almost invariably break off his loud recitation of the Grace immediately prior to *Raḥem na* ("have mercy") and, after several moments of slumber, he would arouse himself and continue at the exact point at which the recitation was interrupted. He would then add his one interpolation in Yiddish: "*Raḥem na, heiliger Bashefer, darbarmdiger Gott!*" (Have mercy, Holy Creator, merciful God).

We approach the *Ribbono shel Olam* in prayer as the all-merciful God upon whose infinite loving kindness and boundless compassion we are dependent and to whose graciousness we appeal. In praying for the recovery of a person suffering from sickness it is customary to identify the person in prayer by means of that individual's matronym (in contrast to prayers for the repose of the soul of the deceased and other liturgical use of a person's name in which the patronym is employed). Several reasons for this practice have been advanced, some quite cogent, some arcane.[262] Perhaps yet another reason may be suggested for this age-old custom.

---

262 A primary source for the practice is a comment of the *Zohar*. The *Zohar* points to the phrase in Psalms uttered by King David, "*ve-hoshi'a le-ben amatekha*—and grant salvation to the son of your maidservant" (Psalms 86:16), as a paradigm for prayer and notes that the Psalmist invokes the maternal-filial relationship in his appeal. A petition for heavenly largesse, the *Zohar* adds, must be punctiliously accurate. When the mother's

Prayer is offered for the very life of a person afflicted with illness. In almost every situation, there is an individual whose emotional involvement with the patient is particularly intense, namely, the patient's mother, whose heart and soul is concentrated on the well-being of her child. The Psalmist tells us, "*Lev nishbar ve-nidkeh Elokim lo tivzeh*"—"A broken and contrite heart, O Lord, Thou wilt not disdain" (51:19). As the *Kotzker* long ago is said to have remarked: "There is nothing as whole as a broken heart."[263] Little wonder, then, that prayers directed to the Throne of Mercy on behalf of a sick person are offered in nomenclature that by allusion invokes the supplications of two "whole" broken hearts, of both child and mother.

The prayer that serves as the core of the liturgy, the *Amidah*, is modeled on the prayer of Hannah. Basic characteristics of the *Amidah* are ascribed to actions of Hannah. While Hannah was *medabberet al libbah* ("speaking in her heart"), only her lips moved but her voice was not heard (I Samuel 1:13) as she "poured out her soul before the Lord" (I Samuel 1:18). The words of Hannah, uttered in "great anguish and distress" (I Samuel 1:15), constitute the paradigm for prayer. The Talmud derives many attributes of prayer from her heartfelt petition: to pray with concentration, with lips moving, in a low voice, and not in a state of inebriation. The Sages further teach that the power of sincere petition may be learned from the Almighty's answer to Hannah's plea, that the appellation "Lord of Hosts" was first addressed to God by Hannah[264] and that the nine blessings recited in the *Rosh ha-Shanah* liturgy correspond to the nine times she invoked the name of God in her prayer (I Samuel 2:1–10).[265]

One may wonder why the Sages modeled the most fundamental of all prayers on that of Hannah. The most obvious reason is that the prayer of Hannah represents an instance of prayer that is demonstrably genuine, one

name is employed there can be no doubt that the individual has been correctly identified whereas paternal identity is not beyond question. See *Zohar* 84a, *Lekh Lekha*, s.v. *va-ye-lekh le-masa'av*. See also R. Yehudah Leib Zirelson, *She'elot u-Teshuvot Gevul Yehudah* (Pietrkow, 1906), *Orah Ḥayyim*, no. 2 and R. Ovadiah Yosef, *Yabi'a Omer*, II (Jerusalem, 1955), no. 11. Other authorities advance more abstruse reasons for the practice. See reasons and sources cited by Josef Lewy, *Minhag Yisra'el Torah*, vol. 1, rev. ed. (Brooklyn: Fink Graphics, 1990), no. 139, 185.

263 See R. Yitzhak Mirsky, *Hegyonei Halakhah be-Inyanei Shabbat u-Mo'adim* (Jerusalem: Mossad Harav Kook, 1989), 152.

264 *Berakhot* 31a-b; *Yoma* 73a; and *Yerushalmi, Berakhot* 4:1 and 9:1.

265 *Berakhot* 29a. Cf. the discussion of Leila L. Bronner, "Hannah's Prayer: Rabbinic Ambivalence," *Shofar* 17, no. 2 (Winter 1999), 36–48. Unfortunately, the writer's polemic against rabbinic law prompts her to view the matter through a distorted prism, erroneously to find a willful rabbinic suppression of women and to discover ambivalence where there is none.

that all would concede without cavil to be a prayer of sincerity, of intensity and of truth.

In the introduction to his commentary on the *siddur*, R. Jacob Emden discusses the characteristics of genuine prayer. One aspect of genuine prayer, he maintains, is the element of *ḥiddush*, of novelty, rather than rote mouthing of words. Another hallmark of genuine prayer is prayer that contains a petition for something greatly desired and requested of the Almighty in full recognition that the Deity has the power to respond to that request.[266] Moreover, the prayer of the afflicted arouses God's mercy[267] and prayer that is accompanied by tears assuredly evidences proper devotion. Thus, claims R. Jacob Emden, "prayer with a tearful eye is desirable and well received for it emanates from the depths of the heart and therefore unto the uppermost heavens does it reach."[268] The prayer of Hannah quite obviously fulfills those criteria.

It is self-evident that models such as Hannah's prayer or Rachel's tears ("A voice is heard in Ramah, lamentation and bitter weeping, Rachel weeping for her children ... refusing to be comforted," Jeremiah 31:14) are emblematic of a woman's deep longing for children and of a woman's depth of care and concern for children in this life—and even thereafter.[269] Such heartfelt prayer may be uttered by any person. Yet, all but the most doctrinaire advocate of absolute gender neutrality would concede that this type of openly emotional prayer is more often characteristic of women.

Dr. Haym Soloveitchik concludes his frequently cited, intriguing article, "Rupture and Reconstruction: The Transformation of Contemporary Orthodoxy,"[270] with a reflection concerning contemporary Orthodox society that he bases upon "personal experience."[271] He suggests that religious Jews who find that they have lost the ability to feel the intimacy of the divine presence now seek this presence in fulfilling the exacting demands of divine

---

266 *Siddur Amudei Shamayim*, 5a. Cf. R. Judah Loeb b. Bezalal, Maharal of Prague, *Netivot Olam, Netiv ha-Avodah*, chap. 3, who maintains that prayer is the ultimate form of adoration of the Deity because it presupposes recognition of God's absolute mastery over the universe and man's complete dependence upon, and inability to survive without, God.

267 *Siddur Amudei Shamayim*, 411a.

268 Ibid., 5a. Cf. *Berakhot* 32b, "R. Eleazar also said: From the day on which the Temple was destroyed the gates of prayer have been closed ... but though the gates of prayer are closed the gates of weeping are not closed."

269 *Bereshit Rabbah* 82:11 and *Eikhah Rabbah, petiḥah*, 24. Cf. Rashi, Genesis 48:7 and Radak, Jeremiah 31:14.

270 *Tradition* 28, no. 4 (Summer 1994), 64–130.

271 Ibid., 98ff.

commandments. Dr. Soloveitchik describes his own experiences at High Holy Day services in a variety of different venues in both *ḥaredi* and non-*ḥaredi* communities over a period of thirty-five years and how he has found those services wanting by comparison to those he attended years ago in the company of ordinary lay people in Boston. What he has found missing has been a sense of fear, the presence of courtroom tears, and an intimation of immediacy of judgment.

May I humbly offer a somewhat different conclusion based upon a somewhat different "personal experience." Apart from hypocrites and pietistic show-offs (of whom every society has its quota), I doubt if those who seek exactness in observance of mitzvot do so unless they experience the immediacy of *yirat shamayim* and *yirat ha-din*. The youngsters who are assiduous in mitzvah observance, who seek out every stringency based upon halakhah, who worry about the precise size of a *ke-zayit*, who use the largest *kiddush* cup, who investigate the pedigree of an *etrog*, who will not stray from a stricture of *Mishnah Berurah*, may or may not at times be misguided. But, excluding those engaged in holier-than-thou grandstanding, they *are* motivated by fear of Heaven and the awareness of the reality of the divine presence that hovers over their lives. It is the fear of invoking divine displeasure and the joy of fulfilling the divine will, both prompted by "the touch of His presence,"[272] that fuel their zeal.

I teach in a building located on Lexington Avenue and 30th Street. When I arrive early in the morning, I walk past groups of young women heading up Lexington Avenue toward 35th Street and the Stern College campus. Invariably, one or another of those young ladies has her face so deeply buried in a small *siddur* that I am concerned for her physical safety as she dashes to school while concentrating on the *shaḥarit* prayer. My classmates in Stern College for Women's pioneering class were fine women all, but I do not recall this type of *davening*. When I enter the Touro College Women's Division some minutes later there are always young women in a corner of the library or in the student lounge busily completing the *shaḥarit* prayer. Again, I do not recall similar devoutness from my earliest years of teaching.

For the past fifty years I have spent the High Holy Days among ordinary lay people at services probably not so very different from the Boston congregation of Dr. Soloveitchik's youth. The level of observance and knowledgeability of those congregants varies greatly. But they bring an earnestness and sincerity to prayer, keep small talk to a commendable minimum, follow the *shaliaḥ tzibbur* to the best of their ability, and become, on those Days of Awe, welded into a

---

272 Cf. ibid., 103.

community of prayer of which it is an honor to be a part. Moreover, during this period, I have been privileged to travel quite extensively throughout the United States, Canada, Israel, and many cities in Europe and to have attended worship services in a variety of different venues in *ḥaredi* and non-*ḥaredi* communities.

From Lakewood to Bobov, from Yeshivat Rabbenu Yitzchak Elchanan to Mir, including the *bet midrash* on the Bar Ilan campus, I have observed serious and devout *davening* and a distinct sense of awe in every yeshiva *bet midrash*. For the most part, with the notable exception of synagogues in Moscow and Berlin,[273] I have found worship services in synagogues as well to be both edifying and moving. To be sure, the loud crying and sighing I associate with European, Yiddish-speaking worshipers of my childhood is no longer common. But that manner of expression involved an edge of theatricality and/or hysteria that was part of the European mode whereas our own age has adopted a cooler demeanor. What has impressed me most of all is the fact that during this period the quality of *davening* at the synagogues I have attended has improved noticeably and consistently. Yes, there are still congregations in which there is more conversation during *tefillah* than there should be. Yet, if anything, I have found that, over the years, there has been a decided change for the better in halakhic observance in many of these synagogues.[274] The sense of immediacy and intimacy in prayer is quite palpable and those who come to pray do so with concentration and genuine devotion.

If I have found Dr. Soloveitchik's observation to be so different from my own, I do have a plausible explanation for the discrepancy. Perhaps it *is* different on the other side of the *meḥitzah*. On the women's side, there is so much prayer with a tearful eye that "emanates from the depths of the heart and therefore unto the uppermost heavens does it reach."

---

273 Services in Moscow in the 1970s and 1980s were noisy social occasions. The synagogue served as a social and political meeting place and religious services were but incidental in nature and a distraction. The synagogue in Berlin suffered from the transplantation there of individuals who came with the Moscow-type experience and mentality.

274 Years ago I would be somewhat nervous whenever my husband was accorded an *aliyah* at a synagogue away from home. More often than was comfortable, he would find a flaw in the script of sufficient gravity to disqualify the *Sefer Torah* and necessitate the removal of a second scroll from the Ark. In those days, synagogues were negligent in maintenance of Torah scrolls and the run-of-the-mill Torah reader was neither sufficiently learned nor sufficiently attentive to identify an error. The situation has changed dramatically. Younger rabbis tend to be more knowledgeable and conscientious, younger Torah readers are more meticulous, and synagogue officials have learned to be more sensitive to the need to assure the *kashrut* of Torah scrolls.

But there is a vast abyss between personal petition, serious and intense as it may be, and *hishtapkhut ha-nefesh*, the outpouring of the soul, of which Rav Kook writes, "Prayer actualizes and brings into light and perfect life that which is concealed in the deepest recesses of the soul."[275] And there is a vast abyss between personal petition, serious and intense as it may be, and the awareness of a responsibility for, and the interdependence of, fellow Jews that translates into the essence of communal prayer, an entreaty and beseeching for mercy on behalf of the pain and the anguish, the loss and the severedness, of each and every person in *kelal Yisra'el*. How far we are from such prayer! There goes out to all of us, men and women alike, the imperative to bestir ourselves from the trivialities and the superficialities, the partisan and the divisive, and to heed the call of the ship-master, "What meanest thou, O sleeper? Arise, call upon thy God"—"*Mah lekha nirdam? Kum kra el Elokekha!*"[276]

275 *Olat Re'iyah*, vol. I, 12.
276 Jonah 1:6.

Index

CPSIA information can be obtained
at www.ICGtesting.com
Printed in the USA
LVHW081614130521
687357LV00004B/125

9 781644 692639